MW01255981

"No area of Christian theology is more obscure, complex, confused, and convoluted than the doctrine of sin. It is therefore splendid to have such a clear, thorough, erudite, and comprehensive examination of the doctrine by Thomas McCall. Beginning with Scripture, McCall takes into account the varying approaches within the great central tradition of the church, not only on sin as action but also the knotty problems of original sin and fallenness, and helps us to wrestle with the issues in the light of the gospel. This is a tour de force."

Thomas A. Noble, Professor of Theology, Nazarene Theological Seminary; Senior Research Fellow, Nazarene Theological College, Manchester, United Kingdom

"McCall has given us a work for which to give thanks. His study of the oft-overlooked topic of sin is both intensive and extensive. Reaching from a thorough examination of sin in the Bible, through the contributions of systematics, to the implications of modern science, he has explored the dimensions of this foundational topic with great erudition, but also with sensitivity and restraint. He expounds the various positions in such thorny topics as original sin in depth and with clear insight. He treats all positions fairly and sympathetically and offers measured conclusions. All who want to become informed on this topic will need to turn to this book."

John Oswalt, author, *Called to Be Holy* and *The NIV Application Commentary: Isaiah*

"In an age when speaking of sin has become unfashionable and even evangelical churches shy away from corporate practices of confession in their liturgies, McCall offers a much-needed, comprehensive treatment of the doctrine of sin. Firmly grounded in Scripture but also drawing on the breadth and depth of the theological tradition from the Patristics to today, he weaves together a rich and varied tapestry of thought on the topic. Throughout he offers measured, fair evaluation of competing viewpoints, pointing out the biblical and theological strengths and weaknesses and defending his own position in a clear, scholarly way. This book is an excellent contribution to the literature on sin."

Mary L. Vanden Berg, Professor of Systematic Theology, Calvin Theological Seminary

"McCall boldly takes on the challenge of explicating and defending the unfashionable doctrine of sin, armed with a command of the rich resources of biblical, systematic, and historical theology, as well as the virtue of analytic clarity of argument. The result is a robust, fair, and illuminating treatment of this dark and difficult doctrine that will be a valuable resource for Christians of all traditions."

Jerry L. Walls, Scholar in Residence and Professor of Philosophy, Houston Baptist University

AGAINST GOD AND NATURE

Foundations of Evangelical Theology Series
JOHN S. FEINBERG, GENERAL EDITOR

To Know and Love God: Method for Theology
DAVID K. CLARK

Light in a Dark Place: The Doctrine of Scripture
JOHN S. FEINBERG

No One Like Him: The Doctrine of God
JOHN S. FEINBERG

God the Son Incarnate: The Doctrine of Christ
STEPHEN J. WELLUM

He Who Gives Life: The Doctrine of the Holy Spirit
GRAHAM A. COLE

Against God and Nature: The Doctrine of Sin
THOMAS H. McCALL

Against the Darkness: The Doctrine of Angels, Satan, and Demons
GRAHAM A. COLE

The Cross and Salvation: The Doctrine of Salvation
BRUCE DEMAREST

Sojourners and Strangers: The Doctrine of the Church
GREGG R. ALLISON

AGAINST GOD AND NATURE

THE DOCTRINE OF SIN

THOMAS H. MCCALL

WHEATON, ILLINOIS

Hardcover ISBN: 978-1-4335-0117-3
ePub ISBN: 978-1-4335-6522-9
PDF ISBN: 978-1-4335-6520-5
Mobipocket ISBN: 978-1-4335-6521-2

Library of Congress Cataloging-in-Publication Data

Names: McCall, Thomas H., author.
Title: Against God and nature : the doctrine of sin / Thomas H. McCall.
Description: Wheaton : Crossway, 2019. | Series: Foundations of evangelical theology series | Includes
    bibliographical references and index.
Identifiers: LCCN 2018041313 (print) | LCCN 2018051210 (ebook) | ISBN 9781433565205 (pdf) | ISBN
    9781433565212 (mobi) | ISBN 9781433565229 (epub) | ISBN 9781433501173 (hc)
Subjects: LCSH: Sin—Christianity—History of doctrines. | Sin—Biblical teaching.
Classification: LCC BT715 (ebook) | LCC BT715 .M365 2019 (print) | DDC 241/.3—dc23
LC record available at https://lccn.loc.gov/2018041313

Crossway is a publishing ministry of Good News Publishers.

SH		29	28	27	26	25	24	23	22	21	20	19
15	14	13	12	11	10	9	8	7	6	5	4	3	2	1

In Memory of Robert E. Whitaker (d. 2010)
I want a principle within.

CONTENTS

Series Introduction 13

Preface 17

Abbreviations 19

CHAPTER 1:   INTRODUCTION 21

    I. The Study of Sin

    II. Sources for the Study of Sin

    III. The Shape of This Study

    IV. Approaching the Study of Sin: The Appropriate Posture

CHAPTER 2:   SIN ACCORDING TO SCRIPTURE: A FIRST LOOK 33

    I. Introduction

    II. Biblical Vocabulary

       A. Major Old Testament Terms for Sin

       B. Important New Testament Terms for Sin

    III. A Biblical Theologogical Overview

       A. Sin in the Beginnings

       B. Sin in Israel's Continuing Story

       C. Sin in Israel's Wisdom Literature

       D. Sin According to Israel's Prophets

       E. Sin in the Synoptic Gospels and the Acts of the Apostles

       F. Pauline Hamartiology

       G. Sin in Hebrews and the General Epistles

       H. Johannine Hamartiology

    IV. Sin in Biblical Theology: A Summary of Several Key Themes

       A. The Royal-Legal Metaphor

       B. Familial Metaphors

       C. The Nuptial Metaphor

       D. Conclusion: Sin as Idolatry

CHAPTER 3:   THE ORIGIN OF SIN 113

    I. Introduction

    II. Temptation and Fall

       A. The Setting

       B. The Way of Temptation

       C. The Fall

    D. *The Immediate Consequences of the Fall*

    E. *Further Theological Reflection*

  III. The Origin of Human Sin

    A. *Ultimate Cosmic Dualism Is Ruled Out*

    B. *Divine "Authorship" or Causation of Sin Rejected*

    C. *Necessity of the Fall Is Inconsistent with Scripture*

    D. *The Story Line of Scripture*

  IV. The Origin of Angelic Sin

    A. *The Biblical Witness*

    B. *Insights from the Christian Tradition*

    C. *Conclusion*

CHAPTER 4:   **THE DOCTRINE OF ORIGINAL SIN** 149

  I. Introduction

  II. The Major Theological Options: A Brief Description

    A. *(Merely) Symbolic and Existentialist Interpretations*

    B. *Corruption-Only Doctrines*

    C. *Corruption and Guilt: Federalism*

    D. *Corruption and Guilt: Realism*

    E. *Corruption and Guilt: Mediate Views*

    F. *Conditional Imputation of Guilt*

  III. The Scriptural Basis Revisited

    A. *A Brief Overview of Romans 5:12–*

    B. *Important Phrases*

    C. *Views Excluded by the Text*

    D. *Views Consistent with the Text*

    E. *Conclusion*

  IV. The Metaphysics and Morals of Original Sin (Once Again)

    A. *Edwardsian Realism*

    B. *Modified Edwardsian Realism*

    C. *Mediate Views: With Molinism*

    D. *Federalism*

    E. *Corruption-Only Views*

  V. Conclusions

    A. *Summary*

    B. *Original Sin and Christian Witness*

CHAPTER 5:   **THE "SIN NATURE" AND THE "NATURE" OF SIN** 207

  I. Introduction

  II. Does the Believer Have "Two Natures"? Understanding Talk of the "Sin Nature"

    A. *Human Nature and Sin: Some Clarifications and an Important Methodological Reminder*

          B. *Two-Nature Hamartiology Introduced*

          C. *Two-Nature Hamartiology Considered*

     III. The "Nature" of Sin

          A. *Contrary to Nature*

          B. *Contrary to Reason*

          C. *Contrary to God*

     IV. Sin and Sins: Some Important Distinctions

          A. *Sins of Commission and Sins of Omission*

          B. *Sins against God, Sins against Neighbor, Sins against Self*

          C. *Grievous Sins and Less-Grievous Sins*

          D. *Intentional Sins and Unintentional Sins*

          E. *Mortal Sins and Venial Sins*

          F. *Remissible Sins and Irremissible Sins*

          G. *Individual or Personal Sins and Social, Structural, or Systemic Sins*

          H. *The "Seven Deadly Sins"*

CHAPTER 6:   **"THE WAGES OF SIN": THE RESULTS OF SIN** 279

     I. Enslavement and Debility

          A. *Augustine and the Battle with "Pelagianism": Learning from Historical Theology*

          B. *Enslaved and Ensnared*

     II. Depravity

     III. Guilt and Shame

     IV. Sin and Death

          A. *The "Wages of Sin": An Introduction to the Topic (That Needs No Introduction)*

          B. *Seeing through the Complications: Some Distinctions in Pursuit of Clarity*

          C. *Any and All Death?*

          D. *Moving Forward*

          E. *Summary*

     V. The Judgment and Wrath of God

          A. *The Wrath of God*

          B. *The Love of God*

          C. *Love and Wrath in Scripture: A Brief Summary*

          D. *Love and Wrath in the Hands of the Theologians*

          E. *Love, Wrath, and the Gospel*

CHAPTER 7:   **"WHERE SIN ABOUNDED": SIN AND GRACE** 339

     I. Sin and Gracious Providence

          A. *Some Central Theological Affirmations*

    B. *Some Notable—But Flawed—Attempts at Doctrinal Formulation*

    C. *The Traditional Doctrine Once More*

  II. Sin and Prevenient Grace

  III. Sin and Justifying Grace

  IV. Sin and Regenerating, Converting Grace

    A. *Repentance*

    B. *Adoption*

    C. *Regeneration*

    D. *The Familial Depiction*

  V. Sin and Sanctifying Grace

    A. *The Nuptial Context and Content of the Doctrine of Sanctification*

    B. *But Can It Actually Happen? A Closer Look at Romans*

    C. *But Does It Happen? Holiness and the Christian Life*

    D. *Conclusion*

CHAPTER 8:   CONCLUSION 379

Appendix: The Original Sinners 383

  I. Introduction

  II. The Challenge

  III. The Problem? Toward Clarification

  IV. Some Possibilities

    A. *The Refurbishment Proposal(s)*

    B. *The Hyper-Adam Proposal*

    C. *The Genealogical-Adam Proposal*

  V. Taking Stock

  VI. Conclusion

Scripture Index 405

General Index 423

Why another series of works on evangelical systematic theology? This is an especially appropriate question in light of the fact that evangelicals are fully committed to an inspired and inerrant Bible as their final authority for faith and practice. But since neither God nor the Bible change, why is there a need to redo evangelical systematic theology?

Systematic theology is not divine revelation. Theologizing of any sort is a human conceptual enterprise. Thinking that it is equal to biblical revelation misunderstands the nature of both Scripture and theology! Insofar as our theology contains propositions that accurately reflect Scripture or match the world and are consistent with the Bible (in cases where the propositions do not come per se from Scripture), our theology is biblically based and correct. But even if all the propositions of a systematic theology are true, that theology would still not be equivalent to biblical revelation! It is still a human conceptualization of God and his relation to the world.

Although this may disturb some who see theology as nothing more than doing careful exegesis over a series of passages, and others who see it as nothing more than biblical theology, those methods of doing theology do not somehow produce a theology that is equivalent to biblical revelation either. Exegesis is a human conceptual enterprise, and so is biblical theology. All the theological disciplines involve human intellectual participation. But human intellect is finite, and hence there is always room for revision of systematic theology as knowledge increases. Though God and his word do not change, human understanding of his revelation can grow, and our theologies should be reworked to reflect those advances in understanding.

Another reason for evangelicals to rework their theology is the nature of systematic theology as opposed to other theological disciplines. For example, whereas the task of biblical theology is more to describe biblical teaching on whatever topics Scripture addresses, systematics should make a special point to relate its conclusions to the issues of one's day. This does not mean that the systematician ignores the topics biblical writers address. Nor does it mean that theologians should warp Scripture to address issues it never intended to address. Rather it suggests that in addition to expounding what biblical writers teach, the theologian should attempt to take those biblical teachings (along with the biblical mind-set) and apply them to issues that are especially confronting the church in the theologian's own day. For example, 150 years ago, an evangelical theologian doing work on the doctrine of man would likely have discussed issues such as the creation of man and the constituent parts of man's being. Such a theology might even have included a discussion about human institutions such as marriage, noting in general the respective roles of husbands and wives in marriage. However, it is dubious that there would have been any lengthy discussion with various viewpoints about the respective roles of men and women in marriage, in society, and in the church. But at our point in history and in light of the feminist movement and the issues it has raised even among many conservative Christians, it would be foolish to write a theology of man (or, should we say, a "theology of humanity") without a thorough discussion of the issue of the roles of men and women in society, the home, and the church.

Because systematic theology attempts to address itself not only to the timeless issues presented in Scripture but also to the current issues of one's day and culture, each theology will to some extent need to be redone in each generation. Biblical truth does not change from generation to generation, but the issues that confront the church do. A theology that was adequate for a different era and different culture may simply not speak to key issues in a given culture at a given time. Hence, in this series we are reworking evangelical systematic theology, though we do so with the understanding that in future generations there will be room for a revision of theology again.

How, then, do the contributors to this series understand the nature of systematic theology? Systematic theology as done from an evangelical Christian perspective involves study of the person, works, and relationships of God. As evangelicals committed to the full inspiration, inerrancy, and final authority of Scripture, we demand that whatever appears in a systematic theology correspond to the way things are and must not contradict any claim taught in Scripture. Holy Writ is the touchstone of our theology, but we do not limit the source material for systematics to Scripture alone. Hence, whatever information from history, science, philosophy, and the like is relevant to our understanding of God and his relation to our world is fair game for systematics. Depending on the specific interests and expertise of the contributors to this series, their respective volumes will reflect interaction with one or more of these disciplines.

What is the rationale for appealing to other sources than Scripture and other disciplines than the biblical ones? Since God created the universe, there is revelation of God not only in Scripture but in the created order as well. There are many disciplines that study our world, just as does theology. But since the world studied by the nontheological disciplines is the world created by God, any data and conclusions in the so-called secular disciplines that accurately reflect the real world are also relevant to our understanding of the God who made that world. Hence, in a general sense, since all of creation is God's work, nothing is outside the realm of theology. The so-called secular disciplines need to be thought of in a theological context, because they are reflecting on the universe God created, just as is the theologian. And, of course, there are many claims in the nontheological disciplines that are generally accepted as true (although this does not mean that every claim in nontheological disciplines is true, or that we are in a position with respect to every proposition to know whether it is true or false). Since this is so, and since all disciplines are in one way or another reflecting on our universe, a universe made by God, any true statement in any discipline should in some way be informative for our understanding of God and his relation to our world. Hence, we have felt it appropriate to incorporate data from outside the Bible in our theological formulations.

As to the specific design of this series, our intention is to address all areas of evangelical theology with a special emphasis on key issues in each area. While other series may be more like a history of doctrine, this series purposes to incorporate insights from Scripture, historical theology, philosophy, etc., in order to produce an up-to-date work in systematic theology. Though all contributors to the series are thoroughly evangelical in their theology, embracing the historical orthodox doctrines of the church, the series as a whole is not meant to be slanted in the direction of one form of evangelical theology. Nonetheless, most of the writers come from a Reformed perspective. Alternate evangelical and nonevangelical options, however, are discussed.

As to style and intended audience, this series is meant to rest on the very best of scholarship while at the same time being understandable to the beginner in theology as well as to the academic theologian. With that in mind, contributors are writing in a clear style, taking care to define whatever technical terms they use.

Finally, we believe that systematic theology is not just for the understanding. It must apply to life, and it must be lived. As Paul wrote to Timothy, God has given divine revelation for many purposes, including ones that necessitate doing theology, but the ultimate reason for giving revelation and for theologians doing theology is that the people of God may be fitted for every good work (2 Tim. 3:16–17). In light of the need for theology to connect to life, each of the contributors not only formulates doctrines but also explains how those doctrines practically apply to everyday living.

It is our sincerest hope that the work we have done in this series will first glorify and please God, and, secondly, instruct and edify the people of God. May God be pleased to use this series to those ends, and may he richly bless you as you read the fruits of our labors.

John S. Feinberg
General Editor

The psalmist asked, "What is man, that thou art mindful of him?" (Ps. 8:4 KJV). This question is a deep cry of the human heart, one that has found eloquent expression in countless mumbled prayers and many great works of literature. Famously, Shakespeare's Hamlet exclaims: "What a piece of work is a man! how noble in reason! how infinite in faculties! in form and moving, how express and admirable! in action, how like an angel! in apprehension, how like a god! The beauty of the world! the paragon of animals! and yet to me, what is this quintessence of dust?"[1] But Hamlet soon follows this question with another (this time for Ophelia): "Get thee to a nunnery, why wouldst thou be a breeder of sinners? I am myself indifferent honest, but yet I could accuse me of such things that it were better my mother had not borne me: I am very proud, revengeful, ambitious, with more offenses at my beck than I have thoughts to put them in, imagination to give them shape, or time to act them in. What should such fellows as I do, crawling between earth and heaven? We are arrant knaves, all; believe none of us."[2] The study of sin addresses such issues. It explores some of the deepest mysteries of human existence, and it does so from the vantage point and with the resources of Christian theology. It eventually leads us from Hamlet's haunting question to Lady Macbeth's chilling wail as she is unable to escape her guilt while scrubbing at the indelible bloodstains on her hands: "Out, damned spot! Out, I say!"[3] The study of sin leads us there, but it does not leave us there. Instead, it brings us to a recognition of our desperate need of divine grace, and it points us ahead to the beauty and hope of the Christian gospel.

The study of sin has done this for me, but I have not done such study alone. I owe a debt of gratitude to many colleagues and friends. My colleague and series editor John S. Feinberg has offered much encouragement and has exhibited great patience. Bill Deckard of Crossway has been an excellent editor. Numerous student assistants have provided wonderful help; here special thanks are due to Dr. Stephen B. Smith, Dr. Ray Degenkolb, Jesse Wilson, Fellipe do Vale, and Drew Everhart. I am grateful to the Board of Regents of Trinity Evangelical Divinity School for sabbatical leaves.

I cannot adequately express my gratitude, appreciation, and love for my

---

[1] William Shakespeare, *Hamlet*, II.ii.
[2] Shakespeare, *Hamlet*, III.i.
[3] Shakespeare, *Macbeth*, V.i.

children Cole, Josiah, Madelyn, and Isaac. Life with them—and hope for them—make me want to hate sin with a holy hatred and long for the establishment of justice and righteousness in our world. And I cannot even begin to properly give thanks to my wife, Jenny, whose unfailing love for me makes me ever more hungry for holiness.

I dedicate this book in memoriam to a mentor who lived with steadfast integrity: Dr. Robert E. Whitaker (d. 2010). *I want a principle within.*

AB	Anchor Bible
CD	Karl Barth, *Church Dogmatics*, ed. G. W. Bromiley and T. F. Torrance, 14 vols. Edinburgh: T&T Clark, 1956–1975
EDBT	*Evangelical Dictionary of Biblical Theology*. Edited by Walter A. Elwell. Grand Rapids, MI: Baker, 1996
FPhilos	*Faith and Philosophy*
JournRT	*Journal of Reformed Theology*
NICNT	New International Commentary on the New Testament
NICOT	New International Commentary on the Old Testament
NIDNTTE	*New International Dictionary of New Testament Theology and Exegesis*, 2nd ed. Edited by Colin Brown. 4 vols. Grand Rapids, MI: Zondervan, 2014
NIDOTTE	*New International Dictionary of Old Testament Theology and Exegesis*. Edited by Willem A. VanGemeren. 5 vols. Grand Rapids, MI: Zondervan, 1997
NPNF[1]	*Nicene and Post-Nicene Fathers*, Series 1. Edited by Philip Schaff. 1886–1889. 14 vols. Reprint, Peabody, MA: Hendrickson, 1994
NPNF[2]	*Nicene and Post-Nicene Fathers*, Series 2. Edited by Philip Schaff. 1886–1889. 14 vols. Reprint, Peabody, MA: Hendrickson, 1994
PG	Patrologia Graeca. Edited by Jacques-Paul Migne. 162 vols. Paris, 1857–1886
PL	Patrologia Latina. Edited by Jacques-Paul Migne. 217 vols. Paris. 1844–1864
SJT	*Scottish Journal of Theology*
ST	*Summa Theologica*
ThTo	*Theology Today*
TJ	*Trinity Journal*
TOTL	The Old Testament Library
WesTJ	*Wesleyan Theological Journal*
WBC	Word Biblical Commentary

ONE

INTRODUCTION

Sin is whatever is opposed to God's will, as that will reflects God's holy character and as that will is expressed by God's commands. Sin is fundamentally opposed to nature and reason, and it is ultimately opposed to God. The results of sin are truly catastrophic—sin wreaks havoc on our relationships with God, one another, and the rest of creation. It is universal in human history and manifests itself in various cultural expressions. It wrecks human lives, and it leaves us broken and vulnerable. It also leaves us needing grace and longing for redemption.

I. The Study of Sin

And yet we commonly find ways to downplay, deny, or ignore the reality of sin. The words of Walter Rauschenbusch remain relevant and convicting: "We have been neglecting the doctrine of sin in our theology."[1] As Martin Luther King Jr. puts it, "In the modern world, we hate to hear this word 'sin'"—and this despite the sobering realization of the fact that sin is "one of the basic facts of the universe" and is "set forth on almost every page of the Bible."[2]

So how do we know sin? The answers may seem obvious, but the sober truth is that the very existence of sin (as a religious category and theological doctrine) is sometimes denied. Moreover, the Christians who do believe in the reality and gravity of sin often disagree over different understandings of the doctrine itself. So what sense can be made of it? How can we know it?

On one hand, it seems that sin can be known merely from observation of human existence.[3] Sin is sometimes said to be "the only empirically verifiable doctrine of the Christian faith"—and this statement is often accompanied

---

[1] Walter Rauschenbusch, *Christianizing the Social Order* (New York: Macmillan, 1914), 126.
[2] Martin Luther King Jr., "Man's Sin and God's Grace," in *The Papers of Martin Luther King Jr., Vol. 6: Advocate of the Social Gospel*, ed. Clayborne Carson (Berkeley: University of California Press, 2007), 382.
[3] For a version of this view that proceeds without reference to sin in relation to God, see Mary Midgley, *Wickedness: A Philosophical Essay* (New York: Routledge, 2001), esp. 6–7.

by the assumption that it clearly *is* empirically verifiable.[4] As King expresses the point, "we just need to look around a little, that's all, and we discover it everywhere."[5] Sin can be known through the study of human existence and experience; we learn of sin through social and intellectual history, through psychology and sociology—and we learn of it by introspection. There is much to be said for this approach, for it is intuitive to many people not merely that unfortunate things happen but that many things are wrong—*morally wrong*— with our world. Moreover, witness to the depravity of humanity can be found in many religious and philosophical traditions. For instance, an ancient Sumerian inscription tells us that "never has a sinless child been born to its mother."[6] The Chinese philosopher Xunzi claims that all people "are born with feelings of hate and dislike in them. . . . Thus, if people follow with their inborn dispositions and obey their nature, they are sure to come to struggle and contention, turn to disrupting social divisions and order, and end up becoming violent. . . . it is clear that people's nature is bad, and their goodness is a matter of deliberate effort."[7] The evidence is clear enough that even Karl Barth, when commenting on Romans 3, will say that "[t]he whole course of history pronounces this judgment against itself. . . . If all the great outstanding figures in history . . . were asked their opinion, would one of them assert that men were good, or even capable of good? Is the doctrine of original sin merely one doctrine among many? Is it not rather . . . THE Doctrine which emerges from all honest study of history?"[8] On this approach, much can be known about sin apart from divine revelation; "even those who do not know that Jesus Christ is Lord know sin."[9]

On the other hand, many theologians argue forcefully that we cannot really know sin apart from divine revelation.[10] As William H. Willimon says, "We have no means of being cognizant of sin without the grace of God."[11] For Christians, knowing sin *as sin* "is derivative of and dependent on what Chris-

---

[4] Reinhold Niebuhr, *Man's Nature and His Communities* (New York: Scribner, 1965), 24, cited in Ted Peters, *Sin: Radical Evil in Soul and Society* (Grand Rapids, MI: Eerdmans, 1994), 326.

[5] King, "Man's Sin and God's Grace," 383.

[6] "Sumerian Wisdom Text," trans. S. N. Kramer, in *Ancient Near Eastern Texts Related to the Old Testament*, ed. James B. Pritchard, 3rd ed. (Princeton, NJ: Princeton University Press, 1969), 590. I owe this reference to an unpublished paper by Neil Arner.

[7] Xunzi, *Xunzi: The Complete Text*, trans. Eric L. Hutton (Princeton, NJ: Princeton University Press, 2014), 248–249. I owe this reference to an unpublished paper by Neil Arner.

[8] Karl Barth, *The Epistle to the Romans*, trans. Edwyn C. Hoskyns, 6th ed. (Oxford: Oxford University Press, 1968), 87.

[9] William H. Willimon, *Sinning Like a Christian: A New Look at the Seven Deadly Sins* (Nashville: Abingdon, 2005), xiii. See also Willimon, "A Peculiarly Christian Account of Sin," *ThTo* (1993): 220–228.

[10] And many, many more theologians will argue that we do not have an *adequate* understanding of sin apart from grace. Thus Martin Luther's famous *Smalcald Articles* say that original sin has "caused such a deep, evil corruption of nature that reason does not comprehend it; rather, it must be believed on the basis of the revelation in the Scriptures" (cited in Robert Kolb, "The Lutheran Doctrine of Original Sin," in *Adam, the Fall, and Original Sin: Theological, Biblical, and Scientific Perspectives*, ed. Hans Madueme and Michael Reeves [Grand Rapids, MI: Baker Academic, 2014], 109).

[11] Willimon, *Sinning Like a Christian*, xii.

tians know about God as revealed in Christ."[12] Barth articulates a thunderous statement of this view:

> As the opposition of man to God, his neighbour, and himself, sin is more than a relative and limited conflict which works itself out only in himself and which can therefore be known in the self-consciousness and self-understanding which he can have of himself. As the one who commits sin man is himself totally and radically compromised. Where there is a true knowledge of sin, it can be only as an element in the knowledge of God, of revelation, and therefore of faith, for which he cannot in any way prepare himself. Man is corrupt even in his self-understanding, even in the knowledge of his corruption. He cannot see, therefore, beyond the inner conflict and its purely relative compass. He can never really see his sin, and himself as the man of sin. He cannot turn to a true knowledge of his corruption, but only evade it. God and His revelation and faith are all needed if he is to realise the accusation and judgment and condemnation under which he stands, and the transgression and ensuing need in which he exists.[13]

Barth is certain that accurate self-diagnosis is impossible. Willimon concurs: "The only means of understanding our sin with appropriate seriousness and without despair is our knowledge of a God who manages to be both gracious and truthful. . . . Only through the story of the cross of Christ do we see the utter depth and seriousness of our sin."[14]

There seems to be a further problem. If sin is what the Bible says it is and does what the Bible says it does, then it is "deceitful" and causes *blindness* (Jer. 17:9; cf. John 12:40; Heb. 3:13; 1 John 2:11). As Ian McFarland points out, "Because sin is something of which everyone is guilty all the time, the very capacity to know it and name it is vitiated by human beings' status as sinners. It follows that human beings can know the depth of their sin only as it is forgiven—and thus only as it is made known to us by the one who forgives. . . . the concept only has meaning from *within* the context of Christian belief."[15]

But Barth also raises another concern; this is the worry that our attempts at such self-diagnosis are not only impossible but are also idolatrous. As he puts it,

> Nor is it clear how it can be otherwise than that a doctrine of sin which precedes Christology and is independent of it should consciously or unconsciously, directly or indirectly, move in the direction of [idolatry]. To affirm evil as such it is forced to have an independent standard of good and evil and to apply that standard. But independently of Christology what standard can

---

[12] Willimon, *Sinning Like a Christian*, xiii.
[13] Karl Barth, *CD*, IV/2, 379.
[14] Willimon, *Sinning Like a Christian*, xiv.
[15] Ian McFarland, *In Adam's Fall: A Meditation on the Christian Doctrine of Original Sin* (Malden, MA: Wiley-Blackwell, 2010), 21, emphasis original.

there be other than a normative concept constructed either from philosophical or biblical materials or a combination of the two?[16]

Accordingly, when we so much as try to understand sin apart from God and
his revelation in Christ, we thereby do so with reference to a moral compass
that has some kind of independent authority. But, for Barth, there can be no
such moral authority independent of God and his revelation in Christ, and
therefore such an effort is impossible. And, so the criticism goes, since any
such supposed moral authority would be an autonomous entity standing in
judgment apart from God, it would be an idol. The upshot of this is plain: the
very effort to understand sin apart from God's revelatory and salvific action
can itself be an act of sin. Such an effort is itself doomed to failure—and it
only deepens the problem.

One interesting way of approaching the doctrine of sin is exemplified in
the evangelical theologies of Jonathan Edwards (1703–1758) and John Wesley
(1703–1791). For all their sharp disagreements over disputed matters of doctrinal importance, they held a great deal in common theologically—and nowhere
more clearly than with respect to the doctrine of sin. The work of Edwards
on the doctrine of sin is well known; what is not as well known is the parallel
work being done across the Atlantic by the evangelist and itinerant minister
John Wesley. Wesley's work, which predates that of Edwards by less than a
year, shares several fascinating features with the more famous treatise written
by his American contemporary.[17] The fact that they have theological disagreements is well known, and their reputations for debate are well deserved.[18] But
with respect to their doctrines of sin, the agreement is both considerable and
important; and where there are disagreements, they do not run along the pre-
dictable "Calvinist vs. Arminian" lines—if anything, Wesley is arguably in
closer continuity with the confessional Reformed tradition than is Edwards.
For while Wesley defends the treatment of hamartiology in the Westminster
Confession of Faith (1646)—even down to the details of the federalist account
of imputation—Edwards is more willing to diverge in creative ways.[19] Interest-

---

[16] Barth, CD, IV/1, 365.
[17] Andrew C. Russell reports that the books were published "within a three-month time period" ("Polemical Solidarity: John Wesley and Jonathan Edwards Confront John Taylor on Original Sin," WesTJ [2012]: 73).
[18] Their *positions* are opposed on various points, but often not directly. Edwards does not address Wesley directly
and scarcely shows awareness of him. He does make positive mention of Wesley along with George Whitefield
and the other "New Methodists" (Jonathan Edwards, *Sermons and Discourses*, The Works of Jonathan Edwards,
vol. 22, ed. Harry S. Stout and Nathan O. Hatch, [New Haven, CT: Yale University Press], 108; I thank Doug
Sweeney for this reference). Wesley's stance toward Edwards will vary from appreciative (he provided an abridged
version of Edwards's *Religious Affections* for the Methodist revivals) to adversarial (e.g., with respect to Edwards's
determinism). See John Wesley, "Thoughts upon Necessity," in *Works of John Wesley*, vol. 10 (Grand Rapids, MI:
Zondervan, n.d.), 463–467. But for all their disagreements, Wesley refers to Edwards as, "That great man, President
Edwards, of New England" ("A Thought on Necessity," *Works of John Wesley*, vol. 10, 475).
[19] On Edwards's doctrine of sin, see Oliver D. Crisp, *Jonathan Edwards and the Metaphysics of Sin* (Aldershot, UK:
Ashgate, 2014). This is not the only area where the assumption that Edwards is the exemplar of orthodox Reformed
theology is questionable. See Oliver D. Crisp, "Jacob Arminius and Jonathan Edwards on Creation," in *Reconsider-*

ingly, not only do they write at the same time, but both are exercised to defend the historic Christian doctrine of original sin from attacks on various fronts. Both are concerned to combat the "latitudinarian" and "deist" denials of original sin—indeed, both respond directly and extensively to John Taylor's work.[20] Both are concerned to account for the reality of sin's enslaving power *and* to account for the responsibility of the human sinner.

Wesley begins his treatise on the doctrine of original sin with what amounts to a phenomenology of religion. In "Part One" of what is a long and demanding work, he argues from observations of human history and society. This notably includes reliance on Christian Scripture, and he places special emphasis on the antediluvian verdict: "The LORD saw that the wickedness of man was great in the earth, and that every intention of the thoughts of his heart was only evil continually" (Gen. 6:5). But while Wesley's work here appeals to the Bible, it extends far beyond biblical sources to include ancient Near Eastern and Greco-Roman literature as well. Here Wesley points out how even the most "civilized" peoples tolerated and sometimes even applauded all manner of personal and social sins (including not only exploitation of various subjugated peoples but also sexual malfeasance and savagery as well as abortion and infanticide). He moves from this to an account of contemporary "paganism" and "heathenism," and here he gives a sweeping survey of social practices in Africa, Asia, and the Americas (as he understands them). He notes that across the world we see "gluttons, drunkards, thieves, dissemblers, and liars" who are "implacable" and "unmerciful."[21] Looking across contemporary Muslim cultures, he notes their "gross" and "horrible notion of God" as well as the widespread proclivity toward violence against all who might disagree with them.[22]

Turning his focus to "the Christian world," Wesley criticizes Orthodox cultures for their ignorance and superstition.[23] Meanwhile, he is convinced that many Roman Catholics are actually deists (rather than orthodox Christians),

---

ing Arminius: Beyond the Reformed and Wesleyan Divide, ed. Keith D. Stanglin, Mark G. Bilby, and Mark Mann (Nashville: Abingdon, 2014), 91–112. On "federalism," see chapter 4 in this present volume.

[20] Interestingly, while Edwards refers to Taylor's doctrine as "Arminian" theology, Wesley (who surely counts as an "Arminian" if anyone does) attacks the same doctrine and even the same book! In a letter to Augustus Toplady, Wesley says of Taylor (Edwards's "Arminian") that "I verily believe that no single person since Mahomet has given such a wound to Christianity as Dr. Taylor" (cited in Thomas C. Oden, *John Wesley's Scriptural Christianity: A Plain Exposition of His Teaching on Christian Doctrine* [Grand Rapids, MI: Zondervan, 1994], 159; and in Michael J. McClymond and Gerald R. McDermott, *The Theology of Jonathan Edwards* [Oxford: Oxford University Press, 2012], 347n26).

See John Taylor, *The Christian Doctrine of Original Sin Proposed to Free and Candid Examination* (London: 1740). Taylor engages in lengthy and detailed (even appealing to the use of Hiphil) exegesis (e.g., 46–47) of important biblical passages, and he denies that there is either guilt (e.g., 99) or "depravity of nature" (e.g., 103) communicated from Adam to his progeny. He also denies that Adam was a type or figure of Christ (e.g., 46), and he concludes that Adam's sin impacted humanity only by bringing *temporal* sorrow and *physical* death (e.g., 30, 35, 46).

[21] John Wesley, "Original Sin," in *The Bicentennial Edition of the Works of John Wesley, Volume 12: Doctrinal and Controversial Treatises I*, ed. Richard P. Heitzenrater, Frank Baker, and Randy L. Maddox (Nashville: Abingdon, 2012), 180.

[22] Wesley, "Original Sin," 186.

[23] Wesley, "Original Sin," 187.

and he points to both the prevalence of individual crimes (e.g., murder) and the potency of institutionalized corruption and violence in the Inquisition and the wars of religion against the Protestants that have plagued Europe.[24] But while he is sharply critical of "heathens," Muslims, and Roman Catholics, Wesley saves special invective for Protestant cultures. He exempts no group or class from his scathing critique: it is not merely the undereducated or economically suppressed strata of society who engage in willful and heinous sin; to the contrary, all manner of evildoing is all too evident within the highest echelons. Drawing upon recent historical work, he concludes that the "last century" is only

> a heap of conspiracies, rebellions, murders, massacres; the very worst effects that avarice, faction, hypocrisy, perfidiousness, cruelty, rage, madness, hatred, envy, lust, malice, and ambition could produce. . . . How many villains have been exalted to the highest places of trust, power, dignity, and profit! By what method have great numbers in all countries procured titles of honor and vast estates? Perjury, oppression, subordination, fraud, panderism were some of the most excusable. For many owed their greatness to sodomy or incest: others, to the prostituting of their own wives or daughters: others, to the betraying of their country or their prince; more, to the perverting of justice to destroy the innocent.[25]

And this, Wesley is convinced, is the state of "Christian" and even Protestant peoples too.

Wesley concludes that the universal misery of humanity is both the source and the result of the sin that plagues humanity. Thus "sin is the baleful source of affliction; and consequently, the flood of miseries which covers the face of the earth . . . is demonstrative proof of the overflowing of ungodliness in every nation under heaven."[26] Wesley then turns to "Part Two," his "Scriptural Method of Accounting" for this universal depravity. He works through two distinct sets of scriptural texts: those that directly prove the doctrine of original sin, and those that illustrate it. Especially important here is Matthew 15:19: "For out of the heart come evil thoughts, murder, adultery, sexual immorality, theft, false witness, slander." He also shows how the doctrine of sin is integrally related to other major points of Christian doctrine, and thus how a proper understanding of it is vital to a proper understanding of the gospel itself.

Jonathan Edwards proceeds along similar lines. Also arguing directly against John Taylor, he begins with observations about the human condition and then moves to a biblically grounded theological understanding of that condition. In "Part One," he draws upon "observation" and "experience" to

---

[24] Wesley, "Original Sin," 187–190.
[25] Wesley, "Original Sin," 191 (citing Jonathan Swift's *Gulliver's Travels*).
[26] Wesley, "Original Sin," 211.

present "Evidences from Facts and Events." These "observations" demonstrate the following: first, that "All mankind do constantly, in all Ages, without fail in any Instance, run into that moral evil which is in effect their own utter and eternal Perdition," that from this it follows that "all mankind are under the influence of a prevailing effectual tendency in their Nature to that Sin and Wickedness," and that this depravity is a "propensity to sin *immediately, continually,* and *progressively.*"[27]

After laying out these depressing lines of evidence, Edwards addresses what he takes to be common "evasions," and he argues that universal mortality proves the doctrine of original sin. He then turns to Scripture to offer a theological account of this depraved human condition, and only after this does he turn to address objections to the doctrine (and it is only here that Edwards engages in his speculative metaphysics).

While certainly not endorsing all their judgments (e.g., about other cultures and religions), and without following them in the details of their proposals (with respect to both exegesis of particular texts and metaphysical speculation), I think that there is much that is right about the general approaches of Wesley and Edwards. They are correct to point out that "general revelation" shows us that something is desperately wrong with humans in their current condition; we know that *something* is seriously wrong from common human experience.[28] And they are absolutely right to insist that we can come to an adequate understanding of just *what* has gone wrong only in light of God's "special revelation" (as this comes reliably through the truthfulness of Holy Scripture and ultimately in the Truth that is incarnate as Jesus Christ).[29] For although we find that recognition of the *reality* of sin is unavoidable, given observation of human experience, and although we can learn much *about* sin by study of that human experience, we cannot have an adequate understanding of it precisely *as sin* apart from divine revelation and the theological reflection that is made possible by that revelation.[30]

II. Sources for the Study of Sin

Evidence of sin is splashed across the pages of human history. Tendencies toward sinful behavior are embedded deep within the human psyche. The stark

---

[27] Jonathan Edwards, *The Works of Jonathan Edwards*, vol. 3, *Original Sin*, ed. Clyde A. Holbrook (New Haven, CT: Yale University Press, 1970), viii.
[28] Furthermore, as we shall see, recent work in social and moral psychology serves to reinforce these intuitions. Indeed, some of this work also offers insights into the perversity and deceptiveness of human sinfulness.
[29] Such an approach is broadly traditional, yet it still finds resonance with more recent "apocalyptic" approaches to biblical and systematic theology. For instance, Douglas Campbell admits that "insights from nature and creation are to be welcomed" in the theological task so long as any such claims made "in terms of natural theology [are] subject to christological revision" ("Douglas Campbell's Response to Warren J. Smith," in *Beyond Old and New Perspectives on Paul: Reflections on the Work of Douglas Campbell*, ed. Chris Tilling [Eugene, OR: Cascade, 2014], 95).
[30] See the similar point made by Peter J. Gentry and Stephen J. Wellum, *Kingdom through Covenant: A Biblical-Theological Understanding of the Covenants* (Wheaton, IL: Crossway, 2012), 624–625.

reality of sin's consequences is portrayed, in penetrating, vivid, and powerful ways, in the text of sacred Scripture. Sin is everywhere; the manifestations are legion, and the effects are both deep and pervasive. Sin is also both evasive and sinister, and it is not easy for us to come to grips with it. So how are we to study it?

In this volume we approach the theological task with the conviction that Scripture is finally normative and supremely authoritative in theology. We learn about sin precisely *as sin* from the biblical revelation; without the Bible we might know that something is wrong with the human condition, but we would not know it accurately *as sin*. As the inspired and authoritative witness to God's self-disclosure, as this culminates in Christ and the Holy Spirit, the Bible is properly understood as revelation (in the appropriate sense) and is the "norming norm" (*norma normans*) that is the final authority in all matters of theology. As such, it informs, guides, and corrects our theological endeavors. As Oliver D. Crisp puts it, the Bible is the "final arbiter of matters theological for Christians as the particular place in which God reveals himself to his people" and the "first-order authority in all matters of Christian doctrine."[31] Accordingly, in this study we seek to learn about sin from its depiction in the Bible. As an exercise in "canonical-theological" interpretation of Scripture, we take Scripture in its canonical form and interpret it to learn about God and all things as they relate to God.[32] More specifically, we appreciate the literary and theological unity of the Bible, and Scripture guides and norms our understanding of what sin is in relation to God.

Of course the Bible is never interpreted in a conceptual vacuum, and the broad Christian tradition is vitally important for the study of sin. While this tradition is a doctrinal source and authority that is subordinate to and ruled by Holy Scripture (the *norma normata*), nonetheless it is a functional and valued authority in theology. When we ignore the history of doctrine, we very often merely reinvent the doctrinal wheel. Indeed, sometimes we do not even succeed in getting a wheel that is round. What William J. Abraham diagnoses as "doctrinal amnesia" is an all-too-common malady in much contemporary theology and church life—too often, contemporary Christians have neglected or forgotten the insights and lessons for which previous generations paid so dearly.[33] Sometimes the neglect is unintentional and benign; at other times,

---

[31] Oliver D. Crisp, *God Incarnate: Explorations in Christology* (New York: T&T Clark, 2009), 17.

[32] This is not to discount the place of other (e.g., historical-critical) approaches to the study of the Bible.

[33] William J. Abraham, *Waking from Doctrinal Amnesia: The Healing of Doctrine in the United Methodist Church* (Nashville: Abingdon, 1995). What Abraham says about his denomination applies more broadly. Sometimes, neglect of historic Christian teaching on sin shows up in surprising places. For instance, John V. Fesko's generally well-informed and helpful work on the theology of the Westminster Standards does not include any sustained reflection on the doctrine of sin in the Westminster Confession and Catechisms—indeed, the index to the book lists sin on only one page! See John V. Fesko, *The Theology of the Westminster Standards: Historical Context and Theological Insights* (Wheaton, IL: Crossway, 2014), 222.

however, the rejection of the insights of the Christian tradition is more akin to what Thomas C. Oden refers to as "modern chauvinism."[34] This is the assumption—an assumption that is sometimes hegemonic in "liberal" or "progressive" and "conservative" circles alike—that whatever is newest is best, and whatever is older is likely mistaken or confused. In this study of the doctrine of sin, we will work hard to avoid the temptation to ignore or forget the lessons that may be learned from the Christian tradition. In an effort to draw from the rich resources of historic Christian doctrine, we will listen carefully to the important creeds and councils of the church. And we shall also listen attentively and respectfully to major theologians of the Patristic, medieval, Reformation/post-Reformation periods (as well as modern theologians).

As a work of systematic theology, this study of the doctrine of sin seeks to incorporate insights from other relevant disciplines as well. Accordingly, we learn what we can from other areas of inquiry; in particular, we benefit from both the questions raised and (at least in some cases) the answers or partial answers given by history, sociology, anthropology, and social and moral psychology. In addition, philosophy plays a minor but important role in this work. The role it plays is "ministerial" rather than "magisterial"; in other words, it works to assist rather than to dominate theology.[35] It is simply indispensable in helping us understand not only the challenges to the doctrine of sin (from the proponents of heresy and from secularists alike) but also the doctrinal formulations of the tradition's major theologians. And the conceptual tools offered to us by logic and metaphysics can help us in understanding and articulating the doctrine today.[36]

I deal with many topics in the pages that follow, and I am aware that many of these issues deserve book-length treatment in their own right, and that, while some of the topics have received such treatment, more work awaits. Where I have not treated an issue exhaustively, I only hope that I have said things that are true and helpful, and that perhaps I have pointed further research in the right direction. Moreover, I am aware that I engage with a wide range of texts and concepts, and I am further aware that I do so without the expertise of the specialists who work in the various disciplines and sub-disciplines. As D. Stephen Long notes, "many scholars work their entire vocation to make a contribution to a minute historical or theological aspect" of important texts and figures. Long is correct; scholars work for decades to

---

[34] Thomas C. Oden, *Requiem: A Lament in Three Movements* (Nashville: Abingdon, 1995), 118.
[35] See Kevin J. Vanhoozer, "Christ and Concept: Doing Theology and the 'Ministry' of Philosophy," in *Doing Theology in Today's World: Essays in Honor of Kenneth S. Kantzer*, ed. John D. Woodbridge and Thomas McComiskey (Grand Rapids, MI: Zondervan, 1991), 99–145.
[36] See further Thomas H. McCall, *An Invitation to Analytic Christian Theology* (Downers Grove, IL: IVP Academic, 2015).

gain a better understanding of, say, the worship practices of Israel as depicted in the Prophets and as compared to their ancient Near Eastern neighbors; the proper interpretation of the first chapter of Paul's letter to the Romans; the Manichaean background to Augustine's hamartiology; or the relevance of psychological studies of narcissism. Long is also right that the systematic theologian is impoverished without the work of such specialists. As he says, "[W]e need this kind of scholarship."[37] I interact with the relevant primary sources and, at least as far as I am able, with the work of the specialists in the various disciplines and sub-disciplines, and I do so gratefully. With Long, however, I do so with a keen awareness of the limitations that come with being a "generalist": these include "dangers of not understanding the nuances of a specific discipline from the inside, misrepresenting it, and thus forcing its insights into a framework that is so alien to it that those who practice it no longer discover what they practice in its representation."[38] I am aware that I may well make mistakes that the specialists to whose work I am so deeply indebted will see. If so, then I welcome correction. At the same time, however, I am confident that the main lines of the teaching offered here are both true and salutary.

III. THE SHAPE OF THIS STUDY

We will begin our study of sin with a survey of the depiction of sin and its consequences in Scripture. This overview will set us up for more extended examinations and analyses of important doctrinal issues. This initial overview is important for several reasons. First, and most importantly, work on the doctrine of sin in systematic theology should be grounded in how the Bible portrays sin and in what the Bible actually says about sin. Accordingly, this volume begins with a summary of sin as it is portrayed in the Old and New Testaments of Christian Scripture. Second, despite the flowering of biblical theology as a discipline over the past few decades, the doctrine of sin has received remarkably little attention.[39] While I am keenly aware that there is a great deal more that could be said about any of the texts mentioned or issues discussed, I am also convinced that we need to see how the doctrine of sin matters to the ca-

---

[37] D. Stephen Long, *The Perfectly Simple Triune God: Aquinas and His Legacy* (Minneapolis: Fortress, 2016), xii.

[38] Long, *Perfectly Simple Triune God*, xii.

[39] So, for instance, the doctrine of sin is not even important enough in Georg Strecker's work to warrant a single mention in the subject index of his massive tome (Georg Strecker, *Theology of the New Testament*, ed. Friedrich Wilhelm Horn, trans. M. Eugene Boring [Louisville: Westminster/John Knox, 2000], 740–748). The eight-hundred-page volume by Peter J. Gentry and Stephen J. Wellum is better, but it mentions sin on only five pages; see the index entry for "sin" in Gentry and Wellum, *Kingdom through Covenant*, 821. Thomas Schreiner's book of biblical theology mentions sin exactly one time in a volume of seven hundred pages (at least if the index is to be trusted); see Thomas R. Schreiner, *The King in His Beauty: A Biblical Theology of the Old and New Testaments* (Grand Rapids, MI: Baker Academic, 2013), 713. There are some notable exceptions, of course, perhaps chief of which is Mark J. Boda, *A Severe Mercy: Sin and Its Remedy in the Old Testament* (Winona Lake, IN: Eisenbrauns, 2009). Boda, however, focuses entirely on the OT and thus does not trace important thematic elements through the entire biblical canon.

nonical story line of Scripture. Thus we begin with an overview of the biblical depiction of sin.

This initial overview will set us up for closer analyses of several important doctrinal issues. Chapter 3 explores "The Origin of Sin," and here we look closely not only at the mystery of the origin of human sin but also at the even more perplexing mystery of the origin of angelic sin. Chapter 4 addresses "The Doctrine of Original Sin," and the problematic nature of the relation of the first humans and their primal sin to the rest of humanity is examined in detail. Chapter 5 turns attention from original sin to sins of action, from Adam and his relation to us to our own sinful behaviors and inclinations. After working to clear away some unfortunate but common misconceptions about "The Sin Nature," I argue that sin should be properly understood as against nature, against reason, and—always and ultimately—against God. I then explore several important but often overlooked distinctions (e.g., greater and lesser sins, mortal and venial sins, individual and corporate sins). In chapter 6, we take a closer look at the results of sin. Here attention is given to the debilitating impact of sin, and lessons are drawn from the perennial struggles with Pelagianism. The impact of guilt and shame, the meaning of "total depravity," and the proper understanding of death as "The Wages of Sin" are examined. Finally, the judgment and wrath of God are seen in relation to both the character of God and the reality of sin. Chapter 7 looks at the relationship between sin and grace; here attention is focused on sin and divine providence, sin and prevenient grace, and sin and saving grace (including not only justification but also regeneration and sanctification). Chapter 8 draws some conclusions from the study as a whole, and an Appendix analyzes issues and challenges related to "The Original Sinners" (the historicity of Adam and Eve).

IV. APPROACHING THE STUDY OF SIN: THE APPROPRIATE POSTURE

While the study of sin is so extensive as to be intimidating, the gravity of the subject is almost overwhelming. To study sin is not only to look across the vast landscape of human history but also to be confronted by the mirror of Scripture—and to be reminded again of the depths of human depravity. To study sin theologically is to come to a deeper understanding of oneself—to truly know sin is to know the sinner introspectively.

But it is not only that. We can begin to understand sin rightly only in relation to God—and thus to know sin better is to know God better. To better understand sin is to better understand the justice, righteousness, and holiness of God. And to better understand sin is to better understand the glorious mercy of the triune God whose nature is holy love. Perhaps, then, it is appropriate to begin with this prayer of St. Anselm:

O Lord our God,
Grant us grace to desire you with our whole heart;
that desiring you,
we may seek and find you;
and finding you we may love you;
and loving you we may hate those sins from which you have redeemed us;
for the sake of Jesus Christ. Amen.[40]

[40] Quoted in Andrew Davison, Andrew Nunn, and Toby Wright, eds., *Lift Up Your Hearts: Prayers for Anglicans* (London: SPCK, 2010).

TWO

SIN ACCORDING TO SCRIPTURE:
A FIRST LOOK

I. INTRODUCTION

For any recognizably Christian understanding of reality, the centrality of the sheer, unalterable, majestic, holy love of God is unavoidable. The holiness of the triune God is unmistakable in Scripture—and the blazing brilliance of God's holiness shines into and exposes human life for what it really is. And what human life is—more properly, what it has become, what we have made of it—is anything but a reflection of God's own spotless purity and boundless love. When seen as a properly *theological* category, sin is revealed as the perversion, the twisting, the ruin, of humanity. And however skilled we may become at denial or avoidance (as we shall see, these are some of the very results of sin), God is too good to leave us in our delusion. Instead, we get the sober truth: "All have sinned and fall short of the glory of God" (Rom. 3:23). "None is righteous" (v. 10). "The wages of sin is death" (6:23).

II. BIBLICAL VOCABULARY

The wide range of biblical terms for sin testifies both to the importance of the concept in Scripture and to the difficulty involved in tight or neat definitions or descriptions of sin. We shall begin with a brief overview of some of the most common biblical terms for sin. While these terms are sometimes used synonymously (or with significant semantic overlap), they each make an important contribution to our recognition and understanding of sin.[1] An initial overview of these basic biblical data will aid our broader study of the doctrine of sin.

---

[1] It is important to keep in mind the distinction between *words* and *concepts*, and to remember that various words can convey the same concept.

A. Major Old Testament Terms for Sin

The terms that appear with greatest frequency in the OT to refer to sin are *ḥaṭṭā't, pešaʿ, ʿāwōn, rešaʿ,* and *raʿ.*[2]

ḤĀṬĀ', ḤAṬṬĀ', ḤAṬṬĀ'T (חטא)

Ḥaṭṭā't is the most general term. Not surprisingly, it often appears in English translations simply as "sin." But more basically, it means to deviate; to "miss the mark." In some of its more than two hundred uses in the OT, it is used in a strictly literal and what we might call "horizontal" or nontheological sense. For instance, in Judges 20:16 we read of the seven hundred marksmen who could sling stones "and not miss." But *ḥaṭṭā't* is often used to speak of moral failure, and here it can refer to the whole gamut of human erring. Sometimes it is used with reference to those who fail unintentionally (e.g., Lev. 4:13–14), while at other points it is used to describe those who in arrogance *try* to miss the mark.

Primarily, though, it simply expresses the fact: the target has been missed. As such, of course, it presupposes the idea of a target. There is a goal, a target, a mark. And the most basic point is this: the target has been missed. Sin is a failure to reach what was intended. As such, sin has an undeniably objective quality to it. Biblically, it cannot be reduced to a mere psychological sense of disapproval; it is not merely subjective. To fall short, to miss the mark, is to sin. Whether or not the sinner feels bad about it is rather beside the point. The mark, the target, the goal, the expectation or standard was there—and it was missed.

But a word of caution is in order here. Frank admission of the objectivity of sin—we are guilty of transgression whether or not we recognize it or admit it, whether we feel badly about it or not—should not lead us to overlook the volitional element that is often highlighted in the use of these terms. Understanding sin as "missing the mark" might encourage a view of sin as primarily unintentional. We sometimes picture someone such as a basketball player who, despite his complete concentration and best efforts, still misses the free throw when the game is on the line. The player surely missed the mark, but not for lack of intention or effort. Accordingly, we might be tempted to think that sin is primarily to be understood as something that we intend to avoid but just cannot quite escape. In other words, despite our best and unwavering intentions to do the right thing, we nonetheless fail.

---

[2] In addition to the standard lexicons, for helpful studies see Alex Luc, "חטא," in *NIDOTTE*, 2:87–93; and Richard E. Averbeck, "חטאת," in *NIDOTTE*, 2:93–103; Elmer A. Martens, "Sin, Guilt," in *Dictionary of the Old Testament: Pentateuch*, ed. T. Desmond Alexander and David W. Baker (Downers Grove, IL: IVP Academic, 2002), 765–769; P. Jensen, "Sin," in *Dictionary of the Old Testament: Historical Books*, ed. Bill T. Arnold and H. G. M. Williamson (Downers Grove, IL: IVP Academic, 2005), 900–901; Mark J. Boda, "Sin, Sinners," in *Dictionary of the Old Testament: Prophets*, ed., Mark J. Boda and J. Gordon McConville (Downers Grove, IL: IVP Academic, 2012), 713–714.

This could encourage a rather lax attitude toward sin, but nothing could be further from the biblical truth. The terms *ḥāṭā'* and *ḥaṭṭā't* indeed do show the objective nature of sin, but the most common usages of the terms show that there is an important volitional element often involved. As Ryder Smith says, "[T]he hundreds of examples of the word's *moral* use require that the wicked man 'misses the right mark *because he chooses* to aim at a wrong one' and 'misses the right path *because he deliberately* follows a wrong one'—that is, there is no question of an innocent mistake or of the merely negative idea of 'failure.'"[3] Or as Millard Erickson puts it, the word suggests "not merely failure, but a decision to fail, a voluntary and culpable mistake."[4]

Āwōn (עָוֹן)

The volitional element is seen much more clearly and emphasized even more strongly in the biblical language that speaks of perversion. In the OT, *'āwōn* is more focused on the personal causes—and effects—of sin. Often appearing in English translations as "iniquity" or "guilt," the word connotes twistedness, and the basic idea is one of perversion.[5]

Directly in contrast to what is straight, upright, well-formed, and healthy, sin is what is morally misshapen, crippled, broken, misleading, and crooked. Again, this presupposes something that is right, well-formed, and healthy, and it paints a picture of sin as the twisting or perversion of that rightness and health. But the emphasis in this case clearly falls upon personal engagement. It is not as if the sinful person merely suffers the effects of (someone else's) sin; rather it is the sinner who willfully chooses that which ultimately will warp and twist him to the core of his being.

The sinful actions (of *ḥaṭṭā'*, *ḥaṭṭā't*) come from an inner twistedness or perversion (*'āwōn*). *'Āwōn* occurs repeatedly in Isaiah 59:2–7, and this passage illustrates vividly the nature of this perversion and its effects:

> [But] your iniquities have made a separation
> > between you and your God,
> and your sins have hidden his face from you
> > so that he does not hear.
> For your hands are defiled with blood
> > and your fingers with iniquity;
> your lips have spoken lies;
> > your tongue mutters wickedness.
> No one enters suit justly;
> > no one goes to law honestly;

---

[3] Ryder Smith, *The Biblical Doctrine of Sin and the Ways of God with Sinners* (London: Epworth, 1953), 17.
[4] Millard Erickson, *Christian Theology*, 2nd ed. (Grand Rapids, MI: Baker Academic, 1998), 586.
[5] I owe this observation to conversations with John Oswalt.

they rely on empty pleas, they speak lies,
  they conceive mischief and give birth to iniquity.
They hatch adders' eggs;
  they weave the spider's web;
he who eats their eggs dies,
  and from one that is crushed a viper is hatched.
Their webs will not serve as clothing;
  men will not cover themselves with what they make.
Their works are works of iniquity,
  and deeds of violence are in their hands.
Their feet run to evil,
  and they are swift to shed innocent blood;
their thoughts are thoughts of iniquity;
  desolation and destruction are in their highways.

This is a perversion that reaches and poisons everything.

The Hebrew term *'āwel* is similar, and it is often translated "wickedness," "injustice," or "unrighteousness." This word often expresses the idea of twistedness or perversion with great force. It is the opposite of justice and righteousness. More precisely, it is the opposite of the justice and righteousness *of God*, who is the standard of righteousness and justice. As Deuteronomy 32:4 says of God, God is to be understood as "the Rock, his work is perfect, for all his ways are justice. A God of faithfulness and without iniquity, just and upright is he." To be sinful is to pervert those standards, to twist them for our own purposes.

Pešaʿ (פשע)

More directly volitional yet is the language of rebellion. The Hebrew word *pāšaʿ* expresses this idea, and the usages of it in the OT do so poignantly. Synonyms are *mārad* (which carries political overtones) and *bāgad* (which connotes personal treachery). What we see here is a violation of trust; here we have personal rebellion against a sovereign and betrayal of a trusting parent. This rebellion is intentional; it is done directly *to* the other party and in full (or at least adequate) awareness of the nature of the act. As rebels commit treason against "the house of David" (e.g., 1 Kings 12:19), so also humans rebel against their Creator and Lord when they commit sinful actions.

So sin is rebellion, but it is not rebellion against some abstract standard or distant moral code. No, it is rebellion against God. It is treason against the good governance of the Sovereign, and it is betrayal of the trusting love of the Father. As Isaiah 1:2 puts it, "Children have I reared and brought up, but they have rebelled against me" (cf. Matt. 10:21 and Mark 13:12). Anthony Thiselton observes that "Children who rebel against their parents undertake a wilful act that *results in a broken relationship.*"[6]

Rešaʿ (רשע)

The Hebrew word *rešaʿ* (and its cognates) points to the wickedness and resulting guilt of sin.[7] To commit acts of wickedness is to do the opposite of what is right, and in the Hiphil (causative) form of *hiršîaʿ* it means "to condemn" or "to pronounce guilty."[8] What it means to be a sinner is this: it is to commit acts of wrongdoing, and it is to be recognized and pronounced guilty for those actions. It is the refusal to reverence, worship, obey, and glorify God as the one who is holy and as the one who as such is the standard of holiness. It is the rejection of God—it is the refusal to accept God's standards of holiness and his personal and transforming relational presence.

Raʿ (רע)

The term *raʿ* is a general term for evil. It encompasses both what is now sometimes referred to as "natural evil" and "moral evil" or sin. But often it is used powerfully to refer to the affections and actions—and the results of those actions—of sinful people. As Jensen observes, "[T]he refrain in Judges and 1–2 Kings, 'doing evil in the sight of the Lord,' emphasizes the ultimate reference point for the narrator's evaluation. Since the Lord's will for Israel's moral and religious behavior is revealed in the law and freshly applied by the prophets, the word often describes Israel's failure to hear and obey."[9]

B. Important New Testament Terms for Sin

Among the many words used in the NT with reference to sin, several stand out as especially important.[10] These include *hamartia, anomia, parabasis, paraptōma, asebeia,* and *adikia.*

---

[6] Anthony C. Thiselton, *The Hermeneutics of Doctrine* (Grand Rapids, MI: Eerdmans, 2007), 267, emphasis original.

[7] Forms of *rsh* are also translated in the Septuagint as *anomia* (e.g., 1 Sam. 24:13–14) and *adikia* (e.g., Ex. 2:13).

[8] See Martens, "Sin, Guilt," 767.

[9] Jensen, "Sin," 900.

[10] For helpful overviews, see E. P. Sanders, "Sin, Sinners (New Testament)," *Anchor Bible Dictionary*, ed. David Noel Freedman, 6 vols. (New York: Doubleday, 1992), 6:40–47; Leon Morris, "Sin, Guilt," in *Dictionary of Paul and His Letters*, ed. Gerald F. Hawthorne, Ralph P. Martin, and Daniel G. Reid (Downers Grove, IL: IVP Academic, 1993), 877–881; Stanley E. Porter, "Sin, Wickedness," in *Dictionary of the Later New Testament and Its Developments*, ed. Ralph P. Martin and Peter H. Davids (Downers Grove, IL: IVP Academic, 1997), 1095–1098; M. F. Bird, "Sin, Sinner," in *Dictionary of Jesus and the Gospels*, ed. Joel Green, Scot McKnight, and I. Howard Marshall (Downers Grove, IL: InterVarsity Press, 1992), 863–869.

HAMARTIA (ἁμαρτία) AND HAMARTANŌ (ἁμαρτανω)

This word (and its cognates), commonly translated simply as "sin," is often used as a rendering of *ḥaṭṭā't* (and cognates) in the Septuagint.[11] Moises Silva observes that the "NT writers never use the term with a concrete/physical meaning ("fail to hit a target") or even with the sense "error, failure in judgment."[12] Instead, the uses of the term are distinctly religious and moral in nature: "rebellion, corruption, violation, trespassing, disobedience, etc."[13]

ANOMIA (ἀνομια)

We read in 1 John 3:4 that sin (*hamartian*) is "lawlessness" (*anomian*). Sin is the "transgression of the law" (KJV); it is violation of what God has commanded. Sin is doing what God has proscribed, and it is failing to do what he has prescribed. It is opposition to the law of God, and as Smith says, "whenever *anomia* is used, the concepts of law and judgment are present, and, in the characteristic and more numerous instances, the reference is . . . to anything and everything that any man knows that God has commanded."[14] Indeed, it includes not only discrete acts of lawlessness but also "a frame of mind" that revels in its rebellion.[15]

PARABASIS (παραβασις) AND PARABAINŌ (παραβαινω)

This term denotes transgression; overstepping proper boundaries. It is used in the Septuagint to refer to the act of stepping outside of God's prescribed boundaries (e.g., Ex. 32:8), of stepping outside the vows of marriage (e.g., Num. 5:12, 19–20, 29), and other actions of culpable neglect or deliberate malfeasance.[16] Notably, it is used "especially" of breaking the covenant (e.g., Josh. 7:11; Ezek. 16:59; 17:15–19; 44:7; Hos. 6:7; 8:1).[17] In the NT, the term is used to refer to "transgression" of God's will and ways.

PARAPTŌMA (παραπτωμα)

This term is similar to the previous one in that it also refers to the crossing of God-ordained boundaries. But it is often a stronger term than *parabasis*, for it

---

[11] See the discussion in Erickson, *Christian Theology*, 587.
[12] Moises Silva, "ἁμαρτάνω," *NIDNTTE*, 1:258–259.
[13] Silva, "ἁμαρτάνω," 259.
[14] Smith, *Biblical Doctrine of Sin*, 145.
[15] Walter Bauer, William Arndt, F. Wilbur Gingrich, and Frederick W. Danker, *A Greek-English Lexicon of the New Testament and Other Early Christian Literature* (Chicago: University of Chicago Press, 1979), 71.
[16] See Silva, "παραβαίνω," *NIDNTTE*, 3:606.
[17] Silva, "παραβαίνω," 606.

is used to emphasize the willful nature of the transgression, and it can refer to a "habit of wrongdoing" that is an "offense against God."[18]

Adikia (ἀδικία)

The Septuagint often translates ʿāwōn with adikia ("unrighteousness"), and after hamartia this becomes the most common NT word for sin. The semantic domain of this word is that of the law court; it concerns judicial decisions. But it cannot be limited to merely forensic statements, for it concerns not only the legal status of the wrongdoer (as wrongdoer) but also the behavior and character of the one who commits the acts of sin. Thus it refers to injustice and wickedness. The adjective adikos "is used several times as the precise antonym of dikaios" ("righteous" or "just").[19] It is in contrast to the righteousness of God's people (e.g., 1 Cor. 6:1), and it is directly opposed to the righteousness of God. As Silva explains, "the criterion for determining what counts as adikia is the righteousness of God, which discloses human unrighteousness (Rom. 3:5, 26; 9:14)."[20]

Asebeia (ἀσέβεια)

The use of asebeia reinforces the irreducibly and profoundly theological or God-ward orientation of the concept of sin: sin is impiety and godlessness. Sin is the deliberate rejection of God and God's ways. And it unleashes all manner of evil in the world: ungodliness causes unrighteousness (Rom. 1:18), and from this follows "all manner of unrighteousness, evil, covetousness, malice" that produces "envy, murder, strife, deceit, maliciousness" (Rom. 1:29). Such people are "gossips, slanderers, haters of God, insolent, haughty, boastful, inventors of evil, disobedient to parents, foolish, faithless, heartless, ruthless" (Rom. 1:29–31).

III. A Biblical Theological Overview

A survey of the major terms takes us only so far, and indeed an overreliance on the "meanings of terms" can be misleading.[21] As Anthony Thiselton observes, the differences between these terms is "pronounced" but not "clear-cut, depending on context."[22] Mark J. Boda notes some problematic aspects of a "theology-by-word-study approach" when he says that "[t]he problem with this [method] was not only the fallacious practice of etymologizing and the unhealthy consideration of words apart from their linguistic context but,

---

[18] Thiselton, Hermeneutics of Doctrine, 269.
[19] Silva, "ἀδικέω," NIDNTTE, 1:158.
[20] Silva, "ἀδικέω," 158.
[21] See D. A. Carson, Exegetical Fallacies, 2nd ed. (Grand Rapids, MI: Baker Academic, 1996), 27–64.
[22] Thiselton, Hermeneutics of Doctrine, 266.

more importantly, the inappropriate equation of biblical word and theological theme."[23] So while a review of the terms used for sin is helpful, it serves only as a beginning point. To see the biblical portrayal of sin, we need to see it within the broad biblical story. For as Jay Sklar points out, "sin is central to the Bible's story."[24] To help us catch a glimpse of that, in this section I offer an initial overview of that story. What follows is far from exhaustive, but it serves both to provide a "big picture" and to set the stage for closer examination and more focused discussion of important issues.

A. Sin in the Beginnings

The creation account itself hints at the possibility (though *not* the necessity) of sin (Gen. 2:16–17). And we get no farther than the opening verses of the next chapter before we see the temptation of the first humans (3:1–7). Created by the hand of God, and enlivened by nothing less than God's own breath (or Spirit) (2:7), the first humans are placed within a setting of *shalom*.[25] Adam and Eve enjoy a harmonious relationship with the rest of creation, they delight in each other, and they share fellowship and trusting communion with their Creator. Things are as they should be; they are as God intended them to be. But Eve first listens to the questioning suggestions of the tempter, and Adam then listens to Eve. They reach for, and take, what God has commanded them to leave alone. The consequences are immediate and nothing short of devastating. Shame immediately settles upon Adam and Eve, and they are fearful (3:7–10). Adam and Eve immediately find themselves estranged and alienated from the rest of creation. Instead of a creation of *shalom*, they now find themselves facing hardship and suffering in their daily lives and in their future (vv. 16–19). They are alienated from each other (v. 12). Most importantly, they are estranged from their Maker.

The biblical story of "the fall" (as it has come to be called in subsequent theology) is as simple and straightforward as it is short. Yet this account is crucial for understanding the biblical drama. It portrays the situation before the fall, it assumes human responsibility for the actions that could have been avoided, and it shows us that the consequences of sin reach into every area and relationship of life. Everything—the integrity of the first human persons, their mutual relations, their relationship to their environment, and ultimately their relation to their Creator—is fundamentally wrecked by what they have done. As Sklar observes, "Genesis 3 has outlined an understanding of sin that will be

---

[23] Mark J. Boda, *A Severe Mercy: Sin and Its Remedy in the Old Testament* (Winona Lake, IN: Eisenbrauns, 2007), 6.
[24] Jay Sklar, "Pentateuch," in *T&T Clark Companion to the Doctrine of Sin*, ed. Keith L. Johnson and David Lauber (New York: Bloomsbury T&T Clark, 2016), 3.
[25] See Cornelius Plantinga Jr., *Not the Way It's Supposed to Be: A Breviary of Sin* (Grand Rapids, MI: Eerdmans, 1994).

filled in as the biblical story progresses. In its basic contours, sin is disobedience to God, destructive in its results (in our relationship with the Lord, one
another, and the world), associated with an evil power who desires humanity's
harm, and calls forth both God's justice in punishing it and his mercy in forgiving it—with the promise that he will see to its ultimate defeat."[26] Above all,
the "opening acts" of Scripture show us that sin is fundamentally *against God*,
and that these devastating consequences are the direct result of the rupture of
relationship between human creatures and the Lord who made them.

As the story unfolds in Genesis, we see illustrated both the universal spread
and the vicious character of sin. No sooner do we get outside of Eden (in
the canonical narrative) before the oldest son of Adam and Eve murders his
younger brother (Gen. 4:1–10). As Daniel Doriani observes, "In Cain's sin we
have an early hint of the virulence and intractability of sin. . . . While sin was
external to Adam and Eve, it appears to spring up spontaneously from within
Cain; it is a wild force in him, which he ought to master lest it devour him"
(v. 7).[27] Sin progresses throughout the nascent human race; not only is there
vice and violence, now there is also pride for those evil actions (vv. 23–24). As
the human race extends, so also does the reach and depth of perversion and
depravity. By the time we come to Genesis 6, the Lord sees that "the wickedness of man was great in the earth, and that every intention of the thoughts of
his heart was only evil continually" (6:5). Although Noah is "righteous" and
"blameless" (v. 9), we find that "the earth was corrupt in God's sight, and the
earth was filled with violence" (v. 11). God sends a flood to cleanse the earth
(7:1–8:14), and he again gives warnings about sin and its consequences as he
makes a covenant with Noah and his family after the flood (9:1–17). But it does
not take long (in the canonical narrative) before we see the heights of human
arrogance as the humans attempt to build a tower to heaven *for their own
honor and glory* (11:1–4). Here we see the reach and spread of sin; it encompasses "the whole earth" (11:1). We also see the depth and ridiculousness of
sin—these sinful people actually think that they can gain glory for themselves
by building such a tower, and they are too blinded to see their own foolishness.

Genesis 12 marks an important and pivotal shift in the biblical narrative.
Where ruin has come to all the world through the sin of one man (cf. Rom.
5:12–21), so also the divine plan of redemption begins a great reversal with
one man as God makes a covenant with Abram, calls him to be the father of
"a great nation," and tells him that "in you all the families of the earth shall
be blessed" (Gen. 12:1–3). Abram believes God, takes him at his word, and
follows him. As he believes God's promise, God "credits" that belief to him

[26] Sklar, "Pentateuch," 10.
[27] Daniel Doriani, "Sin," in *EDBT*, 736.

"as righteousness" (cf. 15:6 NIV). And so the progress of redemption begins to roll forward, as God chooses a man, through whom he will make a nation, and from which nation will come *the promised Savior* of all the world. Yet as the story unfolds in Genesis, we find ample evidence that sin impacts Abram and his family as well. Abram lies—twice—about his own wife (apparently he is more willing to risk losing her to the Egyptians and Abimelech than he is to stand true with her) (12:10–20; 20:1–17). His son Isaac is a gift of grace, but he apparently learns the family values well, for he too lies about his wife (Gen. 26:1–10).[28] Abram is soon estranged from Lot, who moves close to Sodom (13:10–13). Warfare ensues, and Abram is caught in a web of violence as he is forced to rescue his nephew (14:1–16). Abram and Sarai fail to trust God, and they pull their servant Hagar into sexual servitude to Abram. When Hagar has a child, she finds herself mistreated by Sarai (16:1–15). The sin of nearby Sodom and Gomorrah (which includes both sexual sin and other forms of injustice and oppression against the poor) is so extensive and grave that not even ten righteous people can be found there (18:16–33).[29] The men of Sodom try to rape their visitors, and judgment follows (19:1–28). Lot escapes, but only to commit incest with his own daughters (19:30–38).

When Isaac reaches old age, his younger son Jacob swindles his older son Esau, and estrangement follows swiftly as Esau seeks revenge upon Jacob (27:1–28:22). Jacob himself is taken advantage of by a dishonest family member (29:1–30). The conflict continues between the members of the extended family, until Jacob finally runs away from his father-in-law—with the situation being further complicated by the presence of idolatry (ch. 31). Jacob is so convinced of his own abilities and control that he even resists God's blessing to the point that he "wrestles" with God (32:22–32). The story of Jacob's family continues with the rape of his daughter, deceitfulness and intrigue, and nothing short of mass murder (ch. 34).

Jacob's son Joseph is sold by his envious brothers into slavery, and his brothers tell their father that he died an accidental death (ch. 37). The story becomes, if anything, even more sordid, as Judah becomes sexually involved with his daughter-in-law (who has disguised herself as a cultic prostitute) (ch. 38). The descendants of Abraham live among sinful, treacherous, debauched, and violent people—and they act little or no better. And when Joseph (now a highly placed official in Egypt) is finally reunited with his brothers, he calms their fears by summarizing what has been a powerful theme all throughout the sickening saga: "you meant evil against me, but God meant it for good" (50:20).

---

[28] Claus Westermann notes that Isaac's very name ("laughter") signifies the graciousness of God's gift. See Westermann, *Genesis: An Introduction*, trans. John J. Scullion, SJ (Minneapolis: Fortress, 1992), 177.
[29] For helpful discussion, see Victor P. Hamilton, *The Book of Genesis: Chapters 18–50*, NICOT (Grand Rapids, MI: Eerdmans, 1995), 20–21.

Boda notes that "the book of Genesis provides a description of the fundamental cause and universal extent of human sinfulness"; it is clear that human sin "spoils the idyllic conditions of the garden created by God for fellowship with humanity. Having broken God's command, humans experience shame, divine judgment, and estrangement as they are banished from the garden." Thus, "throughout Genesis 1–11, sin is described as violating God's command (chaps. 2–3), disobeying God's creation mandate to fill the earth (Genesis 11) and exercise dominion (Genesis 3), seeking to become like God (Genesis 3) and murdering (Genesis 4, 9:46)."[30] Boda also notes that Genesis "links the remedy of this dilemma to the emergence of Israel within the world," for "[t]hrough Israel, God will bring blessing to all nations, which includes the return to fellowship with God, enjoyment of his creational blessings, and fulfillment of his creational mandate."[31]

Exodus opens with the descendants of Israel living in Egypt. They are slaves, and this condition is seen typologically in Scripture as representative of the consequences of sin. The situation is so dire that the Egyptian ruler orders the mass murder of all young male Hebrew children (Ex. 1:15–22).[32] The violence is so pervasive that even Moses is drawn into it (2:11–15). God promises that he will deliver Israel, and as he begins to take decisive action to liberate Israel we hear echoes of the Abrahamic covenant: Israel is God's "firstborn son" (4:22). The plagues that God unleashes upon the Egyptians are meant to discredit the gods of Egypt, and thereby to warn the people of idolatry as well as rescue them from it. As God rescues his people from oppression and bondage and leads them forward, he provides them with detailed and meticulous instructions for avoiding sinful action that will place them in the peril of God's own wrath.

The Decalogue (Ex. 20:1–17; Deut. 5:1–21), and the law more generally, is a revelation of God's will and thereby a precious gift from him (Lev. 18:1–5).[33] It is a gift provided for both Israelite and foreigner (e.g., Lev. 22:17f.; 24:10f.).[34] Here it is especially important to note several features about the purpose of the law and the relationship of God's people to that law. First, we need to see that the law is given within the context of God's active deliverance of his people. More specifically, it is given within the framework of the covenant that God has made with his people. Second, we need to understand what the law

---

[30] Boda, *Severe Mercy*, 32, cf. 117.
[31] Boda, *Severe Mercy*, 32, 34.
[32] For insightful discussion of "Pharaoh's sinister logic," see William H. C. Propp, *Exodus 1–18: A New Translation with Introduction and Commentary*, AB (New York: Doubleday, 1999), 141–142.
[33] The fact that the law demands utter allegiance is underscored by Nobuyoshi Kiuchi, *Leviticus*, Apollos Old Testament Commentary 3 (Downers Grove, IL: InterVarsity Press, 2007), 332.
[34] As John E. Hartley notes, the "alien who lived in Israel had the opportunity to worship Yahweh as his God. . . . He did not have to adhere to a higher standard nor were any concessions made for him" (*Leviticus*, WBC [Dallas: Word, 1992], 361).

(understood within the covenantal framework) was intended to teach: it was intended to teach both the holiness of God and the sinfulness of the naive and overconfident sinner.[35] Third, it is vitally important to understand that the law was given to prepare sinners for the reception of grace.[36] More specifically, with the law and its condemnation comes divine provision of atonement (e.g., Lev. 22:32f.; 26:40f.).

The story of sin in the history of Israel is, in many ways, an ugly and even awful one. Israel promises that they will be faithful and loyal to Yahweh, repeatedly saying that they will "be obedient" to "all the words that the LORD has spoken" (Ex. 24:3–8). And almost immediately they are committing treason against God by making a golden calf to worship (32:1–4).[37] In doing so, they have "broken the first commandment and violated the covenant at its core."[38] When Moses confronts them, he emphasizes that they have "sinned a great sin" (v. 30), and they dare not presume upon God's forgiveness.[39] Instead, they must destroy the idol, and then drink it (as powder in their water) so that it could be removed from them as the filthy waste that it is.[40] As the story proceeds, we see that this incident is indicative of a general trend, for Israel repeats this sin again and again.

Sin takes many forms and has many manifestations. Idolatry, irreverence, disrespect (of fellow humans, and especially of parents), murder, adultery, theft, dishonesty, covetousness, and injustice—in all of their manifestations—are typical of the "vice lists" of the Pentateuch (e.g., Ex. 20:1–23:33). Sins are both individual (with provision made for atonement for that person) and social or corporate (with provision made for atonement for all) (e.g., Lev. 4:13–21). Sins may be committed unintentionally as well as intentionally or volitionally, and the person or group that sins unintentionally is also said to be guilty (e.g., Lev. 4:1–35; 5:14–19; Num. 15:22–29). Sin covers the whole scope of human activity and behavior. It covers economic and political activities. It impacts and twists social activities. It perverts and skews familial relationships—and sexual sins (of various kinds) are particularly proscribed by God's law. Sin goes far beneath our actions themselves, however, for it is portrayed in the law as something that infects our "affections" as well (e.g., "covetousness").

---

[35] John N. Oswalt, *Called to Be Holy: A Biblical Perspective* (Nappanee, IN: Evangel, 1999).
[36] Theologically, we would want to affirm as well that there are other "uses" of the law (e.g., to restrain sinfulness).
[37] Terence E. Fretheim observes that the scene in Exodus 32 is "Genesis 3 all over again" (*Exodus*, Interpretation: A Biblical Commentary for Teaching and Preaching [Louisville: John Knox, 1991], 279). On this point see also J. Gerald Janzen, *Exodus*, Westminster Bible Companion (Louisville: Westminster/John Knox, 1997), 226–227.
[38] Thus Thomas Joseph White, OP, *Exodus*, Brazos Theological Commentary on the Bible (Grand Rapids, MI: Brazos, 2016), 266.
[39] The caution against presumption is seen in Moses's use of "perhaps" (*ulay*) here. See the helpful discussion by Victor P. Hamilton, *Exodus: An Exegetical Commentary* (Grand Rapids, MI: Baker Academic, 2011), 553–555.
[40] See the discussion of Douglas K. Stuart, *The New International Commentary, Volume 2: Exodus* (Nashville: Broadman & Holman, 2006), 677–678.

Sin is not abstract; sins are said to be against other human persons. But sins are ultimately against God; even the importance of the command to keep the Sabbath holy is based on the holiness of God and his sanctification of his people (e.g., Ex. 31:13). Sin is ultimately against God, and in this light we can note that it often takes two characteristic forms that are closely related: *rebellion* and *unbelief* (e.g., Deut. 1:26–46). Unbelief is evidenced by the complaining and "grumbling" of the people of God (e.g., Num. 14:2, 26–38; 16:41; Ex. 14:11; 17:3). Rebellion is seen very vividly in the idolatry against which God's people are so often warned (e.g., Lev. 19:4; 26:1–2; Deut. 4:15–21; 6:14–15; 7:5, 25–26; 8:19–20; 11:16–17; 12:1–7; 13:12–18; 16:21–22; 17:2–7; 27:15; 29:17–28; 31:16–18). Rebellion and unbelief are portrayed as being at the root of many sins, and they are closely linked: "So I spoke to you, and you would not listen; but you rebelled against the command of the LORD . . ." (Deut. 1:43).

The consequences or results of sin are utterly devastating. Sin wreaks havoc at the "horizontal" level—it breaks families and shatters entire communities (e.g., Num. 5:1–31; 25:1–9). In particular, the poor and the oppressed suffer for the sins of the community; this is so serious that God pronounces uncompromising judgment: "Cursed be anyone who perverts the justice due to the sojourner, the fatherless, and the widow" (Deut. 27:19; cf. 15:7–11; 16:19). But it does even more devastation "vertically," for it brings those who are sinners under the judgment and wrath of God. God promises that he will use Israel's own enemies to chastise and discipline her; just as he has used Israel to punish the other nations for their iniquities (cf. Gen. 15:16; Deut. 7:17–26), so also he will use the pagan peoples to chastise Israel (Deut. 28:15–68). Again and again we are told, in no uncertain terms, that sin places us under the wrath of God (e.g., Num. 11:1–10, 33–34; 12:9; 14:26–38; 16:20–33; 20:12; Deut. 4:21–25). And just as God's wrath is not some unreasonable and uncontrolled passion, so also is it not inert. To the contrary, the wrath of God produces the most serious consequences. Sin results in nothing less than separation from God—and the inevitable death that is entailed by such separation (e.g., Num. 3:10; 4:20; 15:30–31; 21:6–9; Deut. 7:9–26; 17:2–7; 21:21; 24:16).

As deadly as sin is, however, it does not have the last word. God promises, and then he provides, atonement and reconciliation. The gravity of sin is so profound that some kind of atonement *must* be made for there to be any hope of reconciliation and life (e.g., Num. 18:21–22). Amazingly, however, *God* is the one who offers atonement. Just as in the covenant, where the stronger (in this case, the greater-than-which-cannot-be-conceived) party takes the initiative and offers himself, so also it is Yahweh who does so with respect to atonement. It is *God* who provides for the sacrificial system, it is God who lays down the conditions of the various sacrifices, and it is God who graciously accepts the sacrifices. God will not finally abandon the people with whom he has made the covenant (e.g., Lev. 26:40–45; Deut. 4:25–31). And it is none other than God himself who makes provision for the atonement that his holiness demands. God promises that he will restore those who turn to him (e.g., Lev. 22:32–33; 26:40–45; Num. 29:7–39).

Sin is deadly serious, for God is omniscient; just as no sin escapes his notice, so also no sin escapes judgment. "Be sure your sin will find you out" (Num. 32:23). For Moses as much as for Paul, "the wages of sin is death" (Rom. 6:23). And for Moses as much as for the author of Hebrews, this is true because "our God is a consuming fire" (Heb. 12:29; cf. Deut. 4:24). It is no wonder that "the people of Israel said to Moses, 'Behold, we perish, we are undone, we are all undone'" (Num. 17:12). But for Moses as well as for Paul, it is also true that "where sin increased, grace abounded all the more" (Rom. 5:20).

Boda offers a helpful summary of sin in the Torah. He notes that it is

> a dynamic force that causes impurity and threatens the presence of Yahweh among the people. The elaborate priestly system presented in Exodus–Numbers shows the constant concern to protect and preserve the tabernacle from the impurity caused by imperfection and sin within the created order. This system was concerned not just with the sacred precincts but also with the entire camp that surrounded it. This demanded the vigilance of all Israel . . . [41]

In addition,

> Sin, however, is not just a dynamic force but also a violation of basic justice that brings on the violator a response in kind. . . . These violations of basic justice are all placed in covenant frameworks, and thus sin of this sort is fundamentally a betrayal of covenant relationship, not a violation of an abstract legal code. . . . At the core of the covenant is the Decalogue, which defines sin first and foremost in terms of humanity's relationship with Yahweh, then in terms of relationships with fellow humans, and finally in terms of humans' relationships with non-humans. [42]

B. Sin in Israel's Continuing Story

Sometimes the situation portrayed in Joshua and Judges is referred to as a "vicious cycle." But Raymond Dillard has pointed out that the scene described in Judges is better viewed as a "downward spiral" rather than as a repetitious cycle. [43] Joshua leads the people of Israel into the land of Canaan, but their initial success is followed by a series of defeats and partial victories. There is "rebellion" and "breach of faith" (Josh. 22:16), enough to bring "wrath" on

---

[41] Boda, *Severe Mercy*, 119.
[42] Boda, *Severe Mercy*, 110.
[43] Raymond B. Dillard, "Theology of Judges," in *EDBT*, 735.

"all the congregation of Israel" (v. 20). Within a generation of the death of Joshua, the apostasy was so complete that they "did not know the LORD or the work that he had done for Israel" (Judg. 2:10):

> The people of Israel did what was evil in the sight of the LORD and served the Baals. And they abandoned the LORD, the God of their fathers, who had brought them out of the land of Egypt. They went after other gods, from among the gods of the peoples who were around them, and bowed down to them. And they provoked the LORD to anger. They abandoned the LORD and served the Baals and the Ashtaroth. So the anger of the LORD was kindled against Israel. . . . And they were in terrible distress. (Judg. 2:11–15)

Dillard offers a helpful summary of this sorry state:

1. The children of Israel do evil in the eyes of the Lord (2:11; 3:7, 12; 4:1; 6:1; 10:6; 13:1).
2. Although the nature of this evil is rarely spelled out, their sin prompts the anger of God and results in oppression at the hands of some foreign nation (2:14; 3:8; 4:2; 10:9). . . .
3. During their oppression, the Israelites cry out to the Lord (3:9, 15; 6:6–7; 10:10).
4. The Lord hears their cry and raises up a deliverer, one of the judges (2:16; 3:9, 15; 10:1, 12). The deliverer is chosen and empowered by the Spirit of the Lord (3:10; 6:34; 11:29; 13:25; 14:6, 19).
5. It is often reported that this deliverance was followed by the submission of the enemy and a period of peace during which the deliverer judged Israel, followed by the death and burial of the judge (3:10–11; 8:28–32; 10:2–5; 12:9–15).[44]

And then, inevitably it seems, the time of peace and prosperity brings complacence and disregard for the Lord and his ways, shortly followed by outright disobedience and rebellion. And even the gains made by the judges are themselves marred by outright sin. As Dillard notes, we do not know of Ehud's relationship to God, but we do know that he "delivers Israel by deceit and treachery."[45] The story of Deborah's victory includes "factionalism and intertribal disunity that will ultimately culminate" in the mess with which the account ends.[46] Gideon "pursues a personal vendetta (8:10–21)" and "eventually succumbs to false worship that leads Israel astray (8:22–27)."[47] Finally we read that "everyone did what was right in his own eyes" (Judg. 21:25).

Israel's history is recounted in Scripture in a way that highlights rather than downplays or diminishes its sin. Early Israel's religious leaders are often

---

[44] Dillard, "Theology of Judges," 434.
[45] Dillard, "Theology of Judges," 435.
[46] Dillard, "Theology of Judges," 435.
[47] Dillard, "Theology of Judges," 435.

portrayed as inept and spiritually weak, and very often as corrupt. Eli's sons are said to be "worthless men" who "did not know the LORD" and instead treated the sacrificial system with "contempt" and indeed were "blasphemers" (cf. 1 Sam. 2:12–17; 3:13). The religious leaders attempt to use the cultic artifacts as means of manipulating the Lord (4:1–10). Samuel's own sons turn away from the Lord and his ways as well; they "took bribes and perverted justice" (8:3).[48]

Israel's lack of trust in God is seen in her throbbing desire to have a king. Yahweh recognizes that their craving demands for a king are nothing less than their rejection of *him* as their king (1 Sam. 8:6–9; 10:17–19). Nor does Israel's situation improve (at least not much, or at least not for long) when she gets a king. Saul's reign has barely begun before his lack of trust leads to disobedience of God's command (1 Sam. 13:8–15; 15:17–23; 1 Chron. 10:13). The story of Israel's rulers during the united kingdom is filled with intrigue, deception and treachery, unreasonable rage, and stark cruelty. It is a story of false starts and halfhearted measures; it is a saga of weakness and hypocrisy (e.g., 1 Sam. 24:16–22; 26:21–25). In many places, it spares nothing in portraying the stark and ugly depravity of the situation. When Saul's reign and life come to a tragic end (1 Sam. 31:1–13), David's reign begins with a covenant and promise of a divinely constituted reign that will not end (2 Sam. 7:4–17). For a while he rules with "justice and equity" (2 Sam. 8:15; 1 Chron. 18:14) as well as kindness (2 Sam. 9:1–13; 1 Chron. 19:2), but as the story progresses we find David ensnared in sin as he commits adultery and murder (2 Sam. 11:2–25). His own confession says it with simple clarity: "I have sinned against the LORD" (2 Sam. 12:13; cf. Psalm 51). David's own home soon becomes a hall of moral horrors, a rogues' gallery of deception, rape and incest, fratricide, conspiracy, treason, and rebellion (2 Sam. 13:1–18:33). And despite the fact that David solemnly charges Solomon to "be strong, and show yourself a man, and keep the charge of the LORD your God, walking in his ways and keeping his statutes, his commandments, his rules, and his testimonies, as it is written in the Law of Moses," Solomon fairly quickly departs from the Lord's will and ways (1 Kings 2:2–3; cf. 1 Chron. 28:9–10). He first "loved the LORD" but "sacrificed and made offerings at the high places" (1 Kings 3:3). This tendency to "[tolerate] worship of the Lord at these places" soon turns into "full-blown apostasy (1 Kings 11:7–8)."[49] He even builds a place of worship for Molech, who is often associated with child sacrifice and the burning of the victim (cf. Lev. 18:21; 2 Kings 16:3; 21:6; Jer. 32:35).[50] Not surprisingly, the people follow their leader, and soon the whole nation is worshiping other gods (e.g., 1 Kings 11:31–33).

When the kingdom is divided, the situation only deteriorates further.

---

[48] This is in contrast to Samuel himself (1 Sam. 12:1–5).
[49] *The ESV Study Bible* (Wheaton, IL: Crossway, 2008), 597 (comment on 1 Kings 3:2).
[50] *ESV Study Bible*, 617–618 (comment on 1 Kings 11:7–8).

Jeroboam leads Israel into idolatry (1 Kings 12:28–31), and Rehoboam leads Judah further into sinful patterns of worship and behavior as well (1 Kings 14:23–24). Again and again we read that the kings do what is "evil in the sight of the LORD" and bring divine wrath upon themselves and their people (cf. e.g., 1 Kings 15:30; 16:7, 26; 21:22; 22:51–52; 2 Kings 10:29–31; 13:11; 14:24; 15:9, 18, 24, 28; 21:2, 20; 23:32, 36–37; 24:8–9, 19; 2 Chron. 22:4; 33:2; 36:5, 9, 12). Ahaz of Judah "even burned his son as an offering" (2 Kings 16:3). Israel is finally captured and carried into exile by the Assyrians. As they had been warned from the earliest times and in the strongest terms, the Lord used their godless enemies to chastise and punish them for their sins. The verdict is clear:

> And this occurred because the people of Israel had sinned against the LORD their God, who had brought them up out of the land of Egypt from under the hand of Pharaoh king of Egypt, and had feared other gods and walked in the customs of the nations whom the LORD drove out before the people of Israel, and in the customs that the kings of Israel had practiced. And the people of Israel did secretly against the LORD their God things that were not right. They built for themselves high places in all their towns, from watchtower to fortified city. They set up for themselves pillars and Asherim on every high hill and under every green tree, and there they made offerings on all the high places, as the nations did whom the LORD carried away before them. And they did wicked things, provoking the LORD to anger, and they served idols, of which the LORD had said to them, "You shall not do this." Yet the LORD warned Israel and Judah by every prophet and every seer, saying, "Turn from your evil ways and keep my commandments and my statutes, in accordance with all the Law that I commanded your fathers, and that I sent to you by my servants the prophets."
>
> But they would not listen. . . . They despised his statutes and his covenant that he made with their fathers and the warnings that he gave them. They went after false idols and became false. . . . They abandoned all the commandments of the LORD their God, and made for themselves metal images of two calves; and they made an Asherah and worshiped all the host of heaven and served Baal. And they burned their sons and their daughters as offerings . . . and sold themselves to do evil in the sight of the LORD, provoking him to anger. (2 Kings 17:7–17)

Despite being blessed by several good kings (especially Hezekiah, 2 Kings 18:3; 2 Chron. 29:2; and Josiah, 2 Kings 22:2; 2 Chron. 34:2), and despite the fact that God sent prophets to warn them (2 Chron. 24:19), Judah finally meets the same end as the northern kingdom (2 Kings 25:21). As Mark Chavalas notes, "Their tragedy was a product of God's judgment."[51] And this judgment comes upon them strictly for what they have done and have made of themselves. David understood well the responsibility that rests upon the people: "If you seek him,

---

[51] Mark Chavalas, "Theology of First and Second Kings," in *EDBT*, 454.

he will be found by you, but if you forsake him, he will cast you off forever" (1 Chron. 28:9).[52]

God is gracious, and he sustains the exiles (perhaps most famously seen in Esther) even as he provides opportunities for repentance and return from exile. Upon return from exile, the "remnant" immediately began to prepare the renewal of the sacrificial system and to rebuild the foundations of the temple (Ezra 3:2–7). Ezra confesses the sins of the people: "O my God, I am ashamed and blush to lift my face to you, my God, for our iniquities have risen higher than our heads, and our guilt has mounted up to the heavens. From the days of our fathers to this day we have been in great guilt. . . . And after all that has come upon us for our evil deeds and for our great guilt," still the Lord has "punished us less than our iniquities deserved and [has] given us such a remnant as this" (Ezra 9:6–7, 13). As Ezra prays, the people join him in confession (Ezra 10:2). When Nehemiah hears of the troubles encountered by the remnant, he confesses sin both corporately and individually: "confessing the sins of the people of Israel. . . . Even I and my father's house have sinned. We have acted very corruptly against you and have not kept the commandments, the statutes, and the rules that you commanded your servant Moses" (Neh. 1:6–7). The people bring their confession as well, couching it within the framework of the covenant and contrasting it with the character and actions of God. God is the one who alone is the sovereign Creator of all, and he is the one who made a covenant with Abraham. He is the one who is righteous and who keeps faith. He is the one who rescued the people of Israel from the oppression and slavery of Egypt, and it is he who led them and sustained them in the wilderness. It is he who graciously gave them the Torah, and it is he alone who provided for all their needs (Neh. 9:6–15). *This* is the God to whom the people belong, and it is this God to whom they owe their full allegiance.

But "they and our fathers acted presumptuously and stiffened their neck and did not obey your commandments. They refused to obey and were not mindful of the wonders that you performed among them, but they stiffened their neck and appointed a leader to return to their slavery in Egypt" (Neh. 9:16–17). Again God is contrasted with the sinful people: "But you are a God ready to forgive, gracious and merciful, slow to anger and abounding in steadfast love, and did not forsake them" (v. 17). They confess that God continued to give them protection by day and by night, that God instructed them about all that they needed to know, and that he blessed them with nourishment and sustenance. They recount further how God led them into the land that he had promised for them—and then how once again "they were disobedient

---

[52] See the discussion of Rodney K. Duke in "Theology of Chronicles," in *EDBT*, 93. The theme of personal responsibility is evident throughout, and it is particularly sharp in 2 Chronicles 6:36–42; 7:19–22; 12:14.

and rebelled against you and cast your law behind their back and killed your prophets, who had warned them in order to turn them back to you, and they committed great blasphemies" (v. 26). Again and again, they recall, God has had mercy upon them and has forgiven them. But again and again, they turned away from God and "acted presumptuously and did not obey your commandments, but sinned against your rules, . . . and they turned a stubborn shoulder and stiffened their neck and would not obey" (v. 29). Summarizing their own history and their own plight, the people do all that they can do. They throw themselves upon "the great, the mighty, and the awesome God, who keeps covenant and steadfast love" (v. 32). Their history of sin—and the incomparable righteousness of their God—is encapsulated in this statement: "Yet you have been righteous in all that has come upon us, for you have dealt faithfully and we have acted wickedly" (v. 33).

C. Sin in Israel's Wisdom Literature

The books of Israel's "wisdom" offer much insight into the nature of sin; in places we see reinforcement of themes that are already prevalent, while at other points we see development of other elements.

SIN IN JOB

Boda notes that "The book of Job provides an important vantage point from which to observe debate within the wisdom tradition over the theology of sin and its remedy."[53] The basic story that unfolds in the book of Job is well known: Job is introduced (by the narrator) as a man who was "blameless and upright, one who feared God and turned away from evil" (Job 1:1). The *satan* approaches the Lord and engages in conversations about God's people (1:6–12; 2:1–6). The Lord releases Job from his protection, and Job promptly suffers terrible tragedies (1:13–19; 2:7). Job's wife then tells him to "curse God and die" (2:9). When he refuses either to give up his claims to innocence or to curse God, his friends come to comfort him with their presence (2:11). After a week of silent solidarity, they then engage in extended dialogue with him. Following this, God speaks from the whirlwind—finally—and pronounces a verdict (38:1–40:2; 40:6–41:34; 42:7–8). Throughout, this "literary masterpiece" offers some important insights into the portrayal of sin in Scripture.[54]

Job's friends (Eliphaz, Bildad, and Zophar) take "retribution theology" to be obviously true: virtuous people are rewarded for the good deeds they do, and vicious people are punished for their misdeeds and acts of malfeasance. Since Job is suffering, the reason for this suffering is not hard to discern; clearly,

[53] Boda, *Severe Mercy*, 377.
[54] Boda, *Severe Mercy*, 378.

Job has committed some grievous sins and is harboring sinful affections in his refusal to admit and confess those sins (e.g., Job 8:20; 11:6, 11, 13–20; 15:2–35; 18:1–21; 20:2–29; 22:2–30). Job is unconvinced by his friends' simplistic truisms. He resists the conclusions they draw from such retribution theology (e.g., 21:2–34; 24:1–25; but cf. 27:13–23). He laments the fact of his own miserable existence (e.g., 3:1–26; 10:1–22; 14:1–12), even "[cursing] the day of his birth" (3:1). As the other characters in the story recognize (e.g., 32:1; 33:9; 34:5), Job consistently and forcefully protests that he is in fact innocent of the sin that would bring about such suffering (e.g., 9:20; 11:4; 12:4; 13:18; 23:10–11; 29:5–25; 31:1–40; but cf. 7:21). On the other hand, Job points directly to divine agency with respect to his suffering, for he is convinced that it is caused by God (e.g., 6:4; 9:17–23; 12:1–25; 16:7–22; 19:6–29; 23:15–16; 27:2–12; 30:19–31). Following Job's defense of his own innocence, Elihu rebukes both Job and his friends (and sets the stage for God's own address). Elihu insists upon the truth of God's justice and righteousness as absolutely bedrock (34:10–30; 36:5–37:23). He concludes not only that God is "great in power," but also that "justice and abundant righteousness he will not violate" (37:23).

Then God speaks "out of the whirlwind" (Job 38:1; 40:6), and he takes Job on a tour of the cosmos that is his creation (38:1–40:2; 40:6–41:34). This tour emphasizes the power and sovereignty of God, but it does more than this. Indeed, it does *much* more than this. For here Job is given powerful and vivid reminders of the delight that God takes in his creation and the care that he exercises over it. For God makes clear his joy (e.g., 38:4–7), and he uses deeply relational and familial—indeed, frankly maternal—language to depict his care for his creation (e.g., 38:28–29).[55] God shows that he does not simply decree and dictate but instead guides and cares and nourishes.[56] The book then concludes with the delivery of God's fearsome verdict to Job's friends (42:7) and his comforting verdict to Job (42:8) as well as Job's restoration (42:10–17).

Throughout the book of Job, "retribution theology" is central to the narrative. The final verdict on it, however, is never entirely clear. As Daniel Estes says, "God's rule of the world cannot be reduced to the tidy formula of rigid retribution theology."[57] At the same time, however, the book does not completely reject all elements of such theology; clearly, sin has consequences.[58] What we do know with greater clarity are these important points: sinful people indeed do suffer (and will suffer) the consequences of their deeds; it is possible

---

[55] This is a point sometimes overlooked by commentators, e.g., Marvin H. Pope, *Job: Introduction, Translation, and Notes*, AB (New York: Doubleday, 1965), 299–300).
[56] I owe these insights to Eleonore Stump's magisterial treatment of Job, *Wandering in Darkness* (Oxford: Oxford University Press, 2012), 177–226.
[57] Daniel J. Estes, *Handbook on the Wisdom Books and Psalms* (Grand Rapids, MI: Baker Academic, 2005), 42.
[58] See Boda, *Severe Mercy*, 394.

to suffer while innocent; and we should maintain our belief in both divine sovereignty and divine goodness in the face of such suffering.

SIN IN THE PSALMS

The Psalms are a rich repository of insight into the nature and effects of sin. In contrast to some earlier scholarship which has tended to see the Psalter as a mere library or collection of disparate works, recent scholarship has done much to help us see the unitive and organic nature of the Psalter as a whole. Particularly helpful here (especially with respect to the doctrine of sin) is the work of Mark Boda. He notes that the first two Psalms set up the rest of the book, and they do so by highlighting the human problem.[59] Psalm 1 begins by drawing an immediate and sharp contrast between the one who is righteous and the one who is wicked. The righteous person lives according to wisdom and is blessed (Ps. 1:1), he takes "delight . . . in the law of the LORD" (v. 2), and he faces a hopeful future with stability (v. 3). The wicked person, on the other hand, will "not stand" but will "perish" (vv. 5–6). Psalm 2 then broadens this to a global scope; here, doom is forecast for the wicked while those who take refuge in the sovereign Son will be blessed (Ps. 2:12). The remainder of the Psalter is concerned with this predicament. Throughout various poetic genres and subgenres, and in all manner of ways, the Psalms display the insidious nature of sin and its destructive power. The Psalms then culminate (in the "Hallel Psalms") in praise to God for what he has done on our behalf, and in the heart of the book we can learn much about sin and its consequences. As Boda notes, "The rhetorical shape of the Psalter then points to the key role played by the fate of the royal house for the ultimate remedy for sin laid out in Psalm 1. Though God will ultimately judge the wicked, he offers a pathway for all who suffer or sin to experience his blessing."[60]

The Psalms portray sin in various ways and as seen from various angles. Sinners are full of arrogance (e.g., Pss. 10:2–4; 12:3–4; 52:1; 73:6–9; 94:2–7; 101:5; 119:21, 70; 140:5). Sin is portrayed as rebellion and thus as intentional (e.g., 2:2–3; 36:1); on the other hand, the Psalter is also attentive to "hidden faults" (along with "presumptuous sins") (e.g., 19:12–13).[61] Sin is lack of integrity (e.g., 5:9; 12:2; 28:3; 36:2–4; 50:18; 52:1–4; 55:20–21), and it breeds violence and oppression (e.g., 7:1–17; 10:1–10; 26:4–5, 9–10; 42:9; 56:6–7; 57:6; 58:2; 59:6–7; 64:1–6; 71:4; 82:2–3; 94:20–21; 109:2–5; 140:2–3). Disturbingly, sin is universal, for "there is none who does good. . . . They all have fallen away; together they have become corrupt; there is none who does good, not even one"

---

[59] See Boda, *Severe Mercy*, 448.
[60] Boda, *Severe Mercy*, 450.
[61] See the helpful discussion in Boda, *Severe Mercy*, 406–407.

(53:1–3; cf. 12:1–2; 14:3; 58:3).[62] Sin is folly (e.g., 14:1; 39:8; 53:1; 69:5; 74:22; 92:6; 94:8; 107:17)! Idolatry (e.g., 16:4; 78:58; 96:5; 97:7; 106:19–23, 36–39; 115:4–8; 135:15–18) and violent oppression (e.g., 15:3–5; 37:12–15; 55:23) are portrayed in the Psalms as especially vile. Sin is its own punishment, for "his mischief returns upon his own head, and on his own skull his violence descends" (7:16; cf. 9:15–16; 34:21; 37:15; 54:5; 69:22; 81:12; 94:23; 106:41). Sin brings the sinner under the wrath and judgment of God (e.g., 21:8–12; 60:1–3; 64:7–9; 68:1–35; 69:24; 73:18–20; 75:2; 78:17–66; 88:7, 16; 90:7–8; 91:8; 95:11; 104:35; 110:5–7; 119:118, 155; 146:9; 147:6) and leaves him able only to hope for mercy (e.g., 6:2, 9; 25:11–22; 38:1–22; 40:11–17; 41:4; 79:8–13; 85:1–13; 86:11–13; 103:2–22; 107:28; 124:8; 130:3–4, 8).

Two psalms stand out as illustrative of this teaching and as especially important for hamartiology: Psalms 32 and 51. Psalm 32 begins,

> Blessed is the one whose transgression is forgiven,
>   whose sin is covered.
> Blessed is the man against whom the LORD counts no iniquity,
>   and in whose spirit there is no deceit.
>
> For when I kept silent, my bones wasted away
>   through my groaning all day long.
> For day and night your hand was heavy upon me;
>   my strength was dried up as by the heat of the summer.
>
> I acknowledged my sin to you,
>   and I did not cover my iniquity;
> I said, "I will confess my transgressions to the LORD,"
>   and you forgave the iniquity of my sin. (Ps. 32:1–5)

Psalm 32 thus begins with a statement of "blessedness": "Blessed is the one whose transgression is forgiven, whose sin is covered. Blessed is the man against whom the LORD counts no iniquity, and in whose spirit there is no deceit" (Ps. 32:1–2). Blessedness is, of course, an important theme in the Psalms (as elsewhere in the OT). As Boda points out, however, generally the one who is "blessed" is the one who does God's will.[63] In this psalm, to the contrary, it is the *sinner* who is blessed, for here the blessing is given to the sinner! The blessedness comes not with innate innocence but instead with divine forgiveness. Significantly, three major terms are used for wrongdoing: "transgression" (*peša'*), "sin" (*ḥaṭṭā't*), and "iniquity" (*'āwōn*). As we have seen, the first of these (*peša'*) speaks to an act of rebellion; here the psalmist admits to "inten-

---

[62] This emerges as a dominant theme—despite the occasional protestations of the psalmists (e.g., Pss. 17:2–5; 18:20–24; 26:1–7).
[63] Boda, *Severe Mercy*, 418.

tional refusal to do God's will."[64] The second (ḥaṭṭā't) is the more general term for wrongdoing, and the third ('āwōn) for the state of twistedness that is the result of human sin; this is "dispositional, speaking of an inner condition."[65] Without forgiveness from God, the psalmist says that his "bones wasted away" and his "strength was dried up" (Ps. 32:3–4). But divine blessing comes with his confession of that sin, and this is referred to in several significant ways as well. Corresponding to the three words for human sin, we find in this psalm three terms for divine response. Boda points out that the first of these terms for forgiveness (nāśā') is "commonly used for carrying away a physical object" (cf. 2 Sam. 5:21; Mic. 2:2; Song 5:7).[66] Theologically, it is used to refer to the removal of the guilt and stain of sin. The second (kipper) refers to "covering"; as Boda explains, when used in the Qal form it refers to something being concealed rather than publicly proclaimed.[67] The last term refers to counting or reckoning, and it means that something is no longer held against the other; in other words, the judgment against the offending party is no longer held but instead is vacated. Put together, what this psalm teaches is that God no longer holds the sin *against* the sinner; it no longer comes between them. Instead, it has been carried away from their relationship.[68] It is no longer accounted or held against the sinner. It has been covered by grace.

The result, then, is that the offending sinner is changed: "in whose spirit there is no deceit" (Ps. 32:2). In other words, this psalm makes it plain that while forgiveness comes from God precisely to *sinners*, the forgiving grace of God does not merely change the legal status of the sinner. To the contrary, God's intention is to change *the sinner*. Accordingly, this psalm continues to extol the transforming work of God—the work that makes sinful people truly "upright in heart" (Ps. 32:11). Boda offers an insightful summary: "The second half of the Psalm reminds the audience that the ultimate goal of Yahweh's mercy is not forgiveness but rather a transformation of one's inner disposition ("spirit," v. 2; "understanding," v. 9) and a fundamental change in behavior ("way," v. 8). God's merciful forgiveness is an invitation to submit to his loving mentorship, to avoid the "sorrows of the wicked," and to enjoy the protection and status of the 'righteous' and 'upright in heart.'"[69]

Psalm 51 is perhaps even more famous. As the prayer of David after he has been confronted by the prophet Nathan about his sin against Bathsheba and

[64] Dennis F. Kinlaw with John N. Oswalt, *Lectures in Old Testament Theology* (Anderson, IN: Warner, 2010), 254.
[65] Kinlaw, *Lectures in Old Testament Theology*, 254.
[66] Boda, *Severe Mercy*, 419.
[67] Boda, *Severe Mercy*, 419.
[68] Kinlaw notes that "to get the full implications of this you have to go to other parts of the Old Testament and ultimately to the New Testament . . . (for) when you see this in light of the whole Scripture, what you are going to see is the Cross, because this is what is described in Isaiah 53; the servant bears our griefs, our sins, and our transgressions. They are not spoken away. They are moved from the back of the person who committed them to the back of the one who did not commit them, much as was true of the scapegoat in Leviticus 16" (*Lectures in Old Testament Theology*, 255).
[69] Boda, *Severe Mercy*, 422–423.

Uriah (as well as the nation of Israel), it contains vivid and powerful insights about the nature of sin:

> Have mercy on me, O God,
>   according to your steadfast love;
> according to your abundant mercy
>   blot out my transgressions.
> Wash me thoroughly from my iniquity,
>   and cleanse me from my sin!
>
> For I know my transgressions,
>   and my sin is ever before me.
> Against you, you only, have I sinned,
>   and done what is evil in your sight,
> so that you may be justified in your words
>   and blameless in your judgment.
> Behold, I was brought forth in iniquity,
>   and in sin did my mother conceive me.
> Behold, you delight in truth in the inward being,
>   and you teach me wisdom in the secret heart.
>
> Purge me with hyssop, and I shall be clean;
>   wash me, and I shall be whiter than snow.
> Let me hear joy and gladness;
>   let the bones that you have broken rejoice.
> Hide your face from my sins,
>   and blot out all my iniquities.
> Create in me a clean heart, O God,
>   and renew a right spirit within me.
> Cast me not away from your presence,
>   and take not your Holy Spirit from me.
> Restore to me the joy of your salvation,
>   and uphold me with a willing spirit.
>
> Then I will teach transgressors your ways,
>   and sinners will return to you.
> Deliver me from bloodguiltiness, O God,
>   O God of my salvation,
>   and my tongue will sing aloud of your righteousness.
> O Lord, open my lips,
> and my mouth will declare your praise.
> For you will not delight in sacrifice, or I would give it;
>   you will not be pleased with a burnt offering.
> The sacrifices of God are a broken spirit;
>   a broken and contrite heart, O God, you will not despise.
>
> Do good to Zion in your good pleasure;
>   build up the walls of Jerusalem;

then will you delight in right sacrifices,
in burnt offerings and whole burnt offerings;
then bulls will be offered on your altar. (Ps. 51:1–19)

Several points stand out in this important psalm. First, we see that the psalmist here uses several words for his malfeasance. In this text we again see rebellion or transgression (*peša'*), and we also see the sick and twisted inner condition (*'āwōn*) as well as "sin" understood more generally (*ḥaṭṭā'*).[70] Second, and closely related, is the confession that sin is always and ultimately against God (Ps. 51:4).[71] Third, we see that sin penetrates deeply into the human condition. Indeed, it is "original" in some sense: "in sin did my mother conceive me" (v. 5). Fourth, we also see that the text offers a vivid and varied description of God's work in salvation: God not only "[hides his] face from our sins" (v. 9), he also actually cleanses us from sin (v. 7), and restores joy as he creates (*bārā'*) a "clean heart" (v. 10). The emphasis here is clearly on divine action rather than human reformation.[72] And this action is decisive, for the term used for "create" (*bārā'*, rather than *'āśâ*) is the word used in Genesis 1 for divine creative action.[73] Finally, we see that the defeat of sin has significant ramifications for the broader community (vv. 13–19).

Boda helpfully summarizes the hamartiology of the Psalms. He notes that the Psalter draws an unmistakable contrast between the righteous and the wicked; at the same time, however, he also observes that the Psalms show that "*sin is a universal reality.*"[74] In the Psalms we see admission of guilt as well as God's discipline. We also see that "not only the innocent but also the guilty can seek *Yahweh's favor through prayer.*"[75] With admission of guilt and confession of sin come restoration and blessing. As Boda puts it, "It is clear from these psalms that God disciplines through suffering in order that people might admit their sin and cry for his forgiveness and cleansing based on his merciful character," and this forgiveness is accompanied by "*renewal* beyond forgiveness and cleansing as the psalmists cry for a divine work within them in order to create in them a *new heart and spirit* and to *impact the community* as a whole through their example."[76]

---

[70] Mitchell Dahood, SJ, notes that the common translation of "transgressions" is "altogether too pallid," for the "fundamental notion" is of active rebellion and intentional revolt (*Psalms II: 51–100*, AB [New York: Doubleday, 1968], 2–3).

[71] See the helpful comments by John Calvin, *Commentary on the Book of Psalms, Volume Second*, trans. James Anderson (Grand Rapids, MI: Eerdmans, 1949), 285–286.

[72] See the helpful discussion in Kinlaw, *Lectures in Old Testament Theology*, 259–260.

[73] John Goldingay notes that this is a "rare verb, suggesting the sovereign power God exercises in doing something seemingly impossible" (*Psalms, Volume 2: Psalms 42–89*, Baker Commentary on the Old Testament Wisdom and Psalms (Grand Rapids, MI: Baker Academic, 2006), 133.

[74] Boda, *Severe Mercy*, 451, emphasis original.

[75] Boda, *Severe Mercy*, 451, emphasis original.

[76] Boda, *Severe Mercy*, 451, emphasis original.

Sin in Proverbs

Sin is portrayed in Proverbs in close relation to folly and in distinct contrast to wisdom: "the fear of the Lord is the beginning of knowledge; fools despise wisdom and instruction" (Prov. 1:7; cf. 9:10). We see sin portrayed as something that is vicious rather than virtuous (e.g., Prov. 9:1–18; 10:1–32). Pride and arrogance, along with greed, sloth, dishonesty, injustice, and oppression are highlighted as especially heinous, and we are told that

> [t]here are six things that the Lord hates,
>   seven that are an abomination to him:
> haughty eyes, a lying tongue,
>   and hands that shed innocent blood,
> a heart that devises wicked plans,
>   feet that make haste to run to evil,
> a false witness who breathes out lies,
>   and one who sows discord among brothers." (Prov. 6:16–19)

We see sin doubling back upon itself as punishment for sin, for "these men lie in wait for their own blood; they set an ambush for their own lives" (Prov. 1:18; cf. 5:22; 8:36; 10:24; 11:5–6, 29; 13:13; 14:32; 28:10; 29:5–6). Part of the folly of sin is the self-entrapment of the sinner, for "such are the ways of everyone who is greedy for unjust gain; it takes away the life of its possessors" (1:19). The fate of the wicked is sobering and tragic (e.g., 1:17–19; 2:16–19, 22; 4:19; 6:15; 7:22–27; 9:18; 11:19, 23; 13:9; 15:29; 24:20). The wise, on the other hand, seek knowledge from God (e.g., 1:1–7; 2:6–15; 3:3–10, 13–35; 4:5–18; 7:1–4; 8:10–21) and accept his discipline as a "severe mercy" (e.g., 3:11–12; 12:1; 15:5; 20:30; cf. 14:24; 15:10).[77]

Boda's helpful summary is insightful:

> [T]he vast majority of wisdom is concerned with the ethical, identifying wickedness with folly and righteousness with wisdom. Wisdom is associated with righteous actions ("righteousness, justice and equity," 1:3, 2:9) and righteous qualities ("walk in the way of righteousness, in the midst of paths of justice," 8:20). Categories of people connected to wisdom include "the good" (2:20), "the righteous" (2:20; 3:33; 4:18), "the upright," (2:21; 3:32), and "the blameless" (2:21), all terms with an ethical dimension.
>
>   Those who reject wisdom and represent folly include "the wicked" (2:12, 22; 3:25, 33; 4:14, 19; 5:22; 9:7), "the strange woman/adulteress" (2:16; 5:3, 6; 6:24; 7:5), "the treacherous" (2:22), "the violent" (3:31), "the devious" (3:32), and "the evil" (4:14). Characters such as these speak "perverse things" (2:12), "walk in the ways of darkness" (2:13), "delight in doing evil" (2:14), "rejoice in the perversity of evil" (2:14), walk on "crooked" paths (2:15), are "devious"

---

[77] I here borrow the title of Boda, *Severe Mercy*, and, earlier, Sheldon Vanauken, *A Severe Mercy* (New York: HarperCollins, 1977).

(2:15), "do evil" (4:16, 27; 5:22–23; cf. 3:7), and commit adultery (2:16; 5:3, 6, 15–20; 7:5). These sorts of people are associated with evil qualities including wickedness (4:17), violence (4:17), perversity (4:24; 8:7, 13), corruption (4:24), crookedness (8:7), pride (8:13), and arrogance (8:13).[78]

Proverbs echoes many other themes found in Scripture, but it also adds a distinctive point of emphasis: sin is *folly*; it is what is opposed to the natural order and *telos* of the universe. Sin is, thus, profoundly *against nature*. It is also, of course, always profoundly *against God* (e.g., Prov. 3:33; 6:16–19; 8:13; 12:22; 16:2; 17:15; 20:23; 21:2–3). Indeed, "the eyes of the LORD are in every place, keeping watch on the evil and the good" (15:3). As Michael V. Fox points out, "If God can see into the dark and distant recesses of the underworld, called both Sheol and Abaddon ('destruction'), how much more does his omniscience reach into the much shallower and more accessible depths of the human heart." Thus the sinner "must fear God—actually be afraid of him—for he is watching *you*, everywhere, always."[79]

Sin in Ecclesiastes and Lamentations

Ecclesiastes and Lamentations offer especially poignant expressions of the results or consequences of sin. "Vanity of vanities," says the Preacher of Ecclesiastes, speaking vividly of the utter futility and pointlessness of life that is lived without proper relationship to the Creator. Apart from being rightly related to the Source of life and meaning, nothing ultimately matters. For example, neither rank hedonism (e.g., Eccles. 2:1–11) nor brilliant accomplishments (e.g., 1:16–18; 2:12–26) can provide lasting meaning and purpose. To the contrary, they amount only to "vanity and a striving after wind" (e.g., 1:14, 17; 2:11; 4:4, 16; 6:9). The basic problem is human sin and wickedness, and the Preacher makes it clear that this is not from God or according to God's original design: "God made man upright, but they have sought out many schemes" (7:29). Sin pervades human existence, for wickedness is found even in "the place of justice" and the "place of righteousness" (3:16). The Preacher is especially exercised against oppression and injustice toward our neighbors (e.g., 4:1; 5:8–9; 7:7), and he rails against "the sacrifice of fools" who offer worship to God without due awareness of or sorrow for their sin (5:1–3). He recognizes that the wicked will be punished for their sin (e.g., 8:13), but he also shows awareness that such punishment is not always swift (e.g., 8:11). Such delay, he laments, can give rise to further evil (8:11), and he laments further that the righteous are not spared suffering and grief in this life (9:1–2). Overall, his verdict is both

---

[78] Boda, *Severe Mercy*, 364–365.
[79] Michael V. Fox, *Proverbs 10–31, A New Translation with Introduction and Commentary*, Anchor Yale Bible, vol. 18B (New Haven, CT: Yale University Press, 2009), 593.

unmistakable and grim: "the hearts of the children of man are full of evil, and madness is in their hearts" (9:3). As Christopher Ansberry puts it, "For Qohelet, humans are perverse, limited creatures."[80] Therefore the Preacher urges his listeners to "[r]emember also your Creator in the days of your youth" (12:1), and he concludes with this summary of warning and exhortation: "The end of the matter; all has been heard. Fear God and keep his commandments, for this is the whole duty of man. For God will bring every deed into judgment, with every secret thing, whether good or evil" (12:13–14).

If Ecclesiastes carries warnings about sin, Lamentations records the sorrow that comes from it. The confession of sin is open and frank; there is no thought of trying to hide or mitigate the wickedness of sin. Instead, the grievous nature of it is confessed (e.g., Lam. 1:8–9, 17–18, 20). Both the people and their leaders have been sinful (e.g., 4:13). And the results of the sin are devastating indeed. Jerusalem has become enslaved and now weeps and suffers "bitterly" (e.g., 1:1–2, 4; cf. 5:1–15). The consequences are striking in their horror: infants now starve and children beg for food (4:4), and mothers have even resorted to cannibalism (4:10)! The conclusion is both plain and poignant: "[W]oe to us, for we have sinned!" (5:16). Make no mistake, according to Lamentations, such sins have brought the sinners under the disapproval and fury of God (e.g., 2:1–6, 22; 3:1, 43; 4:11; 5:22). Indeed, Lamentations does not hesitate to attribute the sufferings of the sinners to divine agency (e.g., 1:5, 13–14; 2:1–8; 3:1–16). But Lamentations also makes it clear that the display of God's wrath is not final: "For the Lord will not cast off forever, but, though he cause grief, he will have compassion according to the abundance of his steadfast love; for he does not willingly afflict . . . or grieve the children of men" (3:31–33). For "the steadfast love of the Lord never ceases; his mercies never come to an end; they are new every morning," and God's faithfulness is "great" (3:22–23; cf. 3:32). Thus God is the hope of salvation (e.g., 3:26, 55–58).

SIN IN THE SONG OF SONGS

The Song of Songs (Song of Solomon) is often neglected in discussions of the doctrine of sin. And this neglect is understandable at some levels, for it is not as if the book is filled with explicit depictions or incisive proscriptions about sin. But the book is nonetheless important for us, for it helps to set the overall stage so that we can better understand the full depths and ramifications of sin and its destructive consequences. So while the book's importance may be more *indirect* than direct, it indeed does have a contribution to make. More specifically, it does so by using nuptial imagery to portray a right relationship with God. As we shall see in due course, this is an important contribution to a full-orbed biblical concept of sin.

---

[80] Christopher Ansberry, "Writings," in *T&T Clark Companion to the Doctrine of Sin*, 59.

D. Sin According to Israel's Prophets

Denouncements of sin, warnings about the consequences of sin, pronouncements of divine judgment for sin, calls to repent of sin, longings for restoration from sin, and other sin-related themes dominate the messages of the canonical prophets.[81]

A Case Study: The Beginning of Isaiah as a Window into the Prophetic Message

For instance, Isaiah begins with a blistering indictment of God's people:

> Hear, O heavens, and give ear, O earth;
>> for the LORD has spoken:
> "Children have I reared and brought up,
>> but they have rebelled against me.
> The ox knows its owner,
>> and the donkey its master's crib,
> but Israel does not know,
>> my people do not understand."
>
> Ah, sinful nation,
>> a people laden with iniquity,
> offspring of evildoers,
>> children who deal corruptly!
> They have forsaken the LORD,
>> they have despised the Holy One of Israel,
>> they are utterly estranged.
>
> Why will you still be struck down?
>> Why will you continue to rebel?
> The whole head is sick,
>> and the whole heart faint.
> From the sole of the foot even to the head,
>> there is no soundness in it,
> but bruises and sores
>> and raw wounds;
> they are not pressed out or bound up
>> or softened with oil.
>
> Your country lies desolate;
>> your cities are burned with fire;
> in your very presence
>> foreigners devour your land;
>> it is desolate, as overthrown by foreigners.
> And the daughter of Zion is left
>> like a booth in a vineyard,

---

[81] I here refer to the "latter prophets" (both "major" and "minor").

like a lodge in a cucumber field,
>like a besieged city.

If the LORD of hosts
>had not left us a few survivors,
we should have been like Sodom,
>and become like Gomorrah.

Hear the word of the LORD,
>you rulers of Sodom!
Give ear to the teaching of our God,
>you people of Gomorrah!
"What to me is the multitude of your sacrifices?
>says the LORD;
I have had enough of burnt offerings of rams
>and the fat of well-fed beasts;
I do not delight in the blood of bulls,
>or of lambs, or of goats.

"When you come to appear before me,
>who has required of you
>this trampling of my courts?
Bring no more vain offerings;
>incense is an abomination to me.
New moon and Sabbath and the calling of convocations—
>I cannot endure iniquity and solemn assembly.
Your new moons and your appointed feasts
>my soul hates;
they have become a burden to me;
>I am weary of bearing them.
When you spread out your hands,
>I will hide my eyes from you,
even though you make many prayers,
>I will not listen;
>your hands are full of blood.
Wash yourselves; make yourselves clean;
>remove the evil of your deeds from before my eyes;
cease to do evil,
>learn to do good;
seek justice,
>correct oppression;
bring justice to the fatherless,
>plead the widow's cause.

"Come now, let us reason together, says the LORD:
though your sins are like scarlet,
>they shall be as white as snow;
though they are red like crimson,

they shall become like wool.
If you are willing and obedient,
   you shall eat the good of the land;
but if you refuse and rebel,
   you shall be eaten by the sword;
   for the mouth of the LORD has spoken."

How the faithful city
   has become a whore,
   she who was full of justice!
Righteousness lodged in her,
   but now murderers.
Your silver has become dross,
   your best wine mixed with water.
Your princes are rebels
   and companions of thieves.
Everyone loves a bribe
   and runs after gifts.
They do not bring justice to the fatherless,
   and the widow's cause does not come to them.

Therefore the Lord declares,
   the LORD of hosts,
   the Mighty One of Israel:
"Ah, I will get relief from my enemies
   and avenge myself on my foes.
I will turn my hand against you
   and will smelt away your dross as with lye
   and remove all your alloy.
And I will restore your judges as at the first,
   and your counselors as at the beginning.
Afterward you shall be called the city of righteousness,
   the faithful city."

Zion shall be redeemed by justice,
   and those in her who repent, by righteousness.
But rebels and sinners shall be broken together,
   and those who forsake the LORD shall be consumed.
For they shall be ashamed of the oaks
   that you desired;
and you shall blush for the gardens
   that you have chosen.
For you shall be like an oak
   whose leaf withers,
   and like a garden without water.
And the strong shall become tinder,
   and his work a spark,

and both of them shall burn together,
    with none to quench them. (Isa. 1:2–31)

Here God calls his people to account in a court. The legal setting is nothing short of cosmic, for the "heavens" and "earth" are called as witnesses (Isa. 1:2).[82] While the imagery is royal and legal, the language used of God's own people is familial, for they are his "children" (v. 2). They are identified as rebels (vv. 2, 5), and their sin has resulted in lack of knowledge (v. 3). The warning is unmistakable, for their situation as rebels is dire. They are described as "sinful" and "laden with iniquity" and as "[dealing] corruptly" (v. 4). The sin is said to be intergenerational (v. 4). They have forsaken Yahweh, who has graciously made a covenant with them, and they are now separated from "the Holy One" (v. 4).

They have spurned Yahweh and turned their backs on him, and disaster is coming upon them. They are now described as people who are weakened by disease; from the tops of their heads to the soles of their feet, nothing has escaped the effects of sin (Isa. 1:5–6). Indeed, there is "no soundness" in them (v. 6). Moreover, their sin has now contaminated the entire nation (vv. 7–8). In a direct and deliberately provocative move, Isaiah even compares God's people to Sodom and Gomorrah (vv. 9–10). Their sin has infected their worship as well, and Yahweh makes his views of this very clear indeed: their sacrifices are an "abomination" (v. 13). He will not listen to the prayers of those who work iniquity and whose "hands are full of blood" (v. 15). Thus he implores his people to clean themselves up (v. 16). Instead of doing evil, he pleads, "do good," "seek justice," and confront oppression wherever it is found (v. 17).

In addition to the legal imagery and familial language, Isaiah also conceives of God's relationship with his people in frankly nuptial terms. He says that Jerusalem has "become a whore," for where she was once full of justice and righteousness, she is now filled with murder and corruption (Isa. 1:21–23). In particular, this injustice is evident in the treatment of the fatherless and widows (vv. 17, 23).

Central to Isaiah's prophecy is a ringing proclamation of the promise of salvation: "Come now, let us reason together. . . . though your sins are like scarlet, they shall be as white as snow; though they are red like crimson, they shall become like wool" (Isa. 1:18). Yet this comes conditionally rather than unconditionally—and the condition is their willing obedience (vv. 19–20, 27–28). The warnings of judgment are stern, but they are not completely opposed to the promises of restoration. For though God's people are impure, God's disci-

---

[82] This legal setting, complete with a witness gallery cosmic in scope, is commonly noted by biblical scholars, e.g., Brevard S. Childs, *Isaiah*, TOTL (Louisville: Westminster/John Knox, 2001), 17. Joseph Blenkinsopp titles this pericope, "The Great Arraignment" (*Isaiah 1–39*, AB (New York: Doubleday, 2000), 3.

plining activity is for their good as he will work to remove their "dross" (vv. 22, 25–26). The fate that awaits those who do not repent, however, is desperate indeed: they will be weak rather than strong—as an oak that withers and a garden without water—and they will burn without rescue or relief (vv. 30–31).

The thunderous messages of the prophets against sin center on several important themes: they are concerned with sin against humanity, and they are concerned ultimately with sin against God. We will look at these in turn.

Injustice and Immorality: Sins against Humanity

The prophets bring warnings and calls to repentance to the people of Israel (and Judah). But their concerns are much broader, for they also carry prophecies from God that are intended directly for other cities, nations, and people groups as well. Thus Moab is called out for its pride and arrogance (Isa. 16:6) along with corresponding sins (e.g., Isa. 15:1–16:14; Jer. 48:1–47; Ezek. 25:8–11; Zeph. 2:8; Amos 2:1–3). Similarly, the Philistines are warned (e.g., Isa. 14:28–32; Jer. 47:1–7; Ezek. 25:15–17). The Ammonites are facing divine judgment (e.g., Jer. 49:1–5; Ezek. 25:1–7; Amos 1:13–15), as is Cush (e.g., Isa. 18:1–7). Edom is called to account as well (e.g., Jer. 49:7–22; Ezek. 25:12–14; Amos 1:11–12; Obad. 1–9). The superpowers of the era do not escape either. Egypt faces utter ruin (e.g., Isa. 19:1–15; 20:1–6; Jer. 46:1–28; Ezek. 29:1–16). Similarly, Assyria is warned of impending doom (e.g., Isa. 10:5–19; 14:24–27; Jonah 3:4; Nah. 1:2–3:19). And Babylon will not escape the consequences of its sin either (e.g., Isa. 13:2–22; 14:3–23; 20:1–6; 47:1–15; Jer. 50:1–51:64). Indeed, the entire earth—Jew and Gentile alike—is under the condemnation of God (Isa. 24:1–23). For "the Lord is enraged against all the nations" (Isa. 34:2).

Throughout—and whether directed toward the "elect" or the non-elect—the prophets cry out against arrogance, violence, greed, and injustice. Thus Isaiah denounces greed when he pronounces "woe" to "those who join house to house, who add field to field, until there is no more room" (Isa. 5:8; cf. 2:7). He warns against the hedonism and debauchery of the pleasure-seekers who "run after strong drink" (Isa. 5:11; cf. 5:22) as well as against pride and haughtiness (Isa. 2:11–12, 17; 3:9; 5:15, 21). He excoriates those who would "draw iniquity with cords of falsehood" and "call evil good and good evil, who put darkness for light and light for darkness, who put bitter for sweet and sweet for bitter" (Isa. 5:18, 20). Yahweh is in court, and he is sitting in judgment over those who plunder others and take advantage of the poor (e.g., Isa. 3:13–15; 5:23). Sexual sins will not go unpunished (e.g., Isa. 3:16–17).

These themes reverberate throughout the messages of the prophets. Jeremiah says that those who take advantage of the poor have their blood upon them (Jer. 2:34). Sinners reject truth, justice, and righteousness (e.g., Jer. 4:2;

6:13; 8:10), particularly in their oppression of the fatherless and the needy (e.g., Isa. 59:1–15; Jer. 5:26–28; 7:5; 9:6; 21:12–14; 22:1–17; Amos 2:7; 5:11–13, 18, 24; 6:12; Mic. 2:1–13; 3:1–3, 9; 6:11–12; Nah. 3:1; Zech. 7:8–11; Mal. 3:5–6). God declares that he loves justice but hates "robbery and wrong" (Isa. 61:8). Common vices include theft, murder, dishonesty, all manner of sexual sins, and, of course, idolatry (e.g., Jer. 7:8–10; 9:2–8; cf. Ezek. 22:6–15; Amos 2:6–8; Zech. 8:16–17; Mal. 2:14). Where there is "no faithfulness or steadfast love, and no knowledge of God in the land," there is all manner of malfeasance: "swearing, lying, murder, stealing, and committing adultery; they break all bounds, and bloodshed follows bloodshed" (Hos. 4:1–2). Sin even goes so far as to include human sacrifice (e.g., Jer. 7:31; 19:4–5) and cannibalism (e.g., Isa. 9:20; Ezek. 5:10; Mic. 3:3). Throughout, the arrogance of sin is repulsive (e.g., Isa. 2:11; Mal. 4:1); indeed, in our pomp and our arrogance we are no better than "maggots" to God (Isa. 14:11). Sin renders us like "a rotting corpse covered with worms."[83]

The scope of sin is universal. As Isaiah puts it, "[E]veryone is godless and an evildoer, and every mouth speaks folly"; therefore "wickedness burns like a fire" (Isa. 9:17–18). All of us "have gone astray; we have turned—every one—to his own way" (Isa. 53:6).[84] Jeremiah concurs: our protests of innocence are hollow (Jer. 2:35), for "you have all transgressed against me, declares the LORD" (Jer. 2:29). A righteous person cannot be found (Jer. 5:1). Their "backsliding" is "perpetual" (Jer. 8:5), and "no man relents of his evil" (Jer. 8:6). Instead, sinners "add sin to sin" (Isa. 30:1).

These sins bring shame upon the sinners (e.g., Jer. 2:36; 3:25; 13:26; 14:4; Dan. 9:7–8; Hab. 2:15–16). They leave us filthy and polluted (Isa. 64:6). These sins also leave humans guilty before God, and they stand condemned before him (e.g., Isa. 24:4–6; Jer. 2:3). As Isaiah puts it, "[Y]our iniquities have made a separation between you and your God, and your sins have hidden his face from you" (Isa. 59:2). And such sin and guilt is so deep that sinners can do nothing to save themselves: "Though you wash yourself with lye and use much soap, the stain of your guilt is still before me, declares the Lord GOD" (Jer. 2:22). For we have "stiff necks" and stubborn hearts that refuse to turn toward God (e.g., Isa. 46:12; Jer. 7:24–26; 11:8; Ezek. 2:4, 7; Zech. 7:11–12). "Can the Ethiopian change his skin or the leopard his spots?" Of course not. "[Nor can you] do good who are accustomed to do evil" (Jer. 13:23). For "the heart is deceitful above all things, and desperately wicked" (Jer. 17:9 KJV).

---

[83] John N. Oswalt, *The Book of Isaiah, Chapters 1–39*, NICOT (Grand Rapids, MI: Eerdmans, 1986), 318.
[84] Oswalt notes that the repeated use of "all of us" here emphasizes "the extent of the problem," which invites "an extension to the whole human race" (*The Book of Isaiah, Chapters 40–66*, NICOT [Grand Rapids, MI: Eerdmans, 1998], 389).

IDOLATRY AND INFIDELITY: SIN AGAINST GOD

All sin is ultimately against God, and the prophets are at pains to emphasize the "vertical" dimension of sinfulness. And absolutely central to all this is the issue of *idolatry*.[85] As Isaiah puts it, "their land is filled with idols" (Isa. 2:8; cf. Jer. 1:16; 2:8; 5:7; 7:30; 8:19; 9:13–14; 11:10; 18:15). Despite the persistent and somber warnings, God's people have "forsaken the covenant of the LORD their God and worshiped other gods and served them" (Jer. 22:9; cf. 25:4–7). But such idols are weak and worthless, and worship of them is utterly futile (e.g., Isa. 2:18–22; 10:10–11; 41:21–29; 42:8; 44:9–20; 46:1–12; 57:1–13; Jer. 2:28; 10:1–9; 16:18; 51:17–18; Ezek. 14:1–11). According to Jeremiah and Micah, there is a sense in which idolatry is *the* sin of Judah (e.g., Jer. 17:1–9; 19:4–5; Mic. 1:5–6), and the declaration of this is at the heart of Micah's own vocation (Mic. 3:8). It is linked closely with nuptial imagery and with the corresponding sin of prostitution (e.g., Jer. 2:23–24; Mic. 1:7).

The prophets reserve invective for the false prophets and spiritual leaders who either actively lead people astray or refuse to challenge the sins of the people and political leaders. The people do not want to hear about the sinfulness of their actions or the consequences that await them; they are "unwilling to hear the instruction of the LORD" and instead tell their prophets to "speak to us smooth things" (Isa. 30:9–10). Jeremiah offers this blistering indictment of the religious leaders: "From the least to the greatest of them, everyone is greedy for unjust gain; and from prophet to priest, everyone deals falsely. They have healed the wound of my people lightly, saying, 'Peace, peace,' when there is no peace" (Jer. 6:13–14; cf. 8:11). So not only are these religious leaders guilty of the same sins as the general population, but they also knowingly deceive God's people for their own gain. The prophets and priests are "ungodly" (Jer. 23:11), and they "commit adultery and walk in lies" as they "strengthen the hands of evildoers, so that no one turns from his evil" (Jer. 23:14). They tell lies about God, and they do so for selfish purposes (e.g., Jer. 23:23–26). They have "disheartened the righteous falsely," and they have "encouraged the wicked, that he should not turn from his evil way to save his life" (Ezek. 13:22). God responds by asking, "Is not my word like fire, . . . and like a hammer that breaks the rock in pieces?," and by thundering, "Therefore, behold, I am against the prophets, declares the LORD" (Jer. 23:29–30; cf. 27:9–10, 17–18; Ezek. 34:1–10).

Insincere worship is no better than rank idolatry to God. God knows that some sinners "honor" him "with their lips" while "their hearts are far" from him (Isa. 29:13). Such "worship" is pointless and worthless. Even worse, it is repulsive to God: "What use to me is frankincense that comes from Sheba, or

---

[85] For an insightful study, see Richard Lints, *Identity and Idolatry: The Image of God and Its Inversion* (Downers Grove, IL: IVP Academic, 2015).

sweet cane from a distant land? Your burnt offerings are not acceptable, nor your sacrifices pleasing to me" (Jer. 6:20). Indeed, according to Amos, God says that

> I hate, I despise your feasts,
>> and I take no delight in your solemn assemblies.
> Even though you offer me your burnt offerings and grain offerings,
>> I will not accept them;
> and the peace offerings of your fattened animals,
>> I will not look upon them.
> Take away from me the noise of your songs;
>> to the melody of your harps I will not listen. (Amos 5:21–23)

Instead, God says, "let justice roll down like waters, and righteousness like an ever-flowing stream" (Amos 5:24). Similarly, Micah considers the question of how we can approach God: "With what shall I come before the LORD, and bow myself before God on high?" Will God "be pleased" with burnt offerings (Mic. 6:6–7)? Are our transgressions so grave as to require infant sacrifice (as practiced by Israel's pagan neighbors)? No, says the prophet, for, "He has told you, O man, what is good; and what does the LORD require of you . . . ?" (Mic. 6:8). And what is this? "To do justice, and to love kindness, and to walk humbly with your God" (Mic. 6:8).

God is portrayed as King and Judge throughout the Prophets, and sin is seen in a corresponding way: sin is treacherous rebellion against God. The King is seen in his glory (e.g., Isa. 6:1–3; 58:8; Ezek. 10:1–22)—and sin is the rebellious refusal to worship and obey the sovereign and all-glorious God. Isaiah tells us that God knew, from before the time they were born, that his people would be rebels (Isa. 48:8), and this rebellion is what plays out in human history (e.g., Jer. 2:20). This is a "rebellious house" (e.g., Ezek. 3:27; 12:1–2, 9; 17:12; 44:6). God's people rebelled against him in the wilderness (Ezek. 20:13), and they have not stopped rebelling (e.g., Isa. 58:1–5; Ezek. 24:3–14).

But while the royal and legal language are both prevalent and powerful in the Prophets, and while the depiction of sin as lawbreaking rebellion is prominent, such imagery does not begin to exhaust the descriptions of sin that are found there. While there are other metaphors in play (notably filial and even maternal, e.g., Isa. 66:13; Jer. 3:14), it is significant that nuptial language is used by the prophets to offer a graphic depiction of sin and its consequences. God sings for his "beloved" (Isa. 5:1) but then is appalled at their rejection of him (Isa. 1:21; 5:8–30; cf. Jer. 18:13; Mal. 2:13–17). This has resulted in a "certificate of divorce," for the "iniquities" and "transgressions" have taken their toll (Isa. 50:1). Jeremiah brings the word of the Lord in telling his people that he remembers her "love as a bride" (Jer. 2:2). But this is no sweet walk down memory lane, for he delivers this indictment: "[Y]ou have played the whore with many lovers" (Jer. 3:1). Indeed, he says, "By the waysides you have sat awaiting lovers" (Jer. 3:2). Closely linking idolatry with prostitution, he says that "on every high hill and under every green tree you bowed down like a whore" (Jer. 2:20; 3:6; cf. Ezek. 6:9). "Surely, as a treacherous wife leaves her husband, so have you been treacherous to me" (Jer. 3:20).

Ezekiel describes sin in very lurid terms: "[Y]ou trusted in your beauty and played the whore because of your renown and lavished your whorings on any passerby; your beauty became his" (Ezek. 16:15). He goes on to say, "you took . . . your garments" and "beautiful jewels" and "played the whore" (vv. 16–18). Even child sacrifice was part of the ritual (vv. 20–21):

> How sick is your heart, declares the Lord GOD, because you did all these things, the deeds of a brazen prostitute, building your vaulted chamber at the head of every street, and making your lofty place in every square. Yet you were not like a prostitute, because you scorned payment. Adulterous wife, who receives strangers instead of her husband! Men give gifts to all prostitutes, but you gave your gifts to all your lovers, bribing them to come to you from every side with your whorings. So you were different from other women in your whorings. No one solicited you to play the whore, and you gave payment, while no payment was given to you; therefore you were different. (Ezek. 16:30–34)

Here, as elsewhere (perhaps most famously in Hosea), we gain several insights into the biblical depiction of sin. We see the sheer irrationality of sin; what "Jerusalem" does here defies all sense. There simply is no logical case to be made for it or rational defense of it. We see the enslaving, binding, and blinding nature of sin; the sinner here is both guilty of infidelity, adultery, and prostitution *and* is trapped in a dangerous lifestyle that cannot either satisfy or sustain. We see the radical twistedness or perversion of sin, and this is displayed in stomach-churning fashion. We see the cost of sin. The sinner not only surrenders and loses the good gifts that have been lavished upon her but also forfeits the relationship with the good Giver of those gifts. And we see sin as it is in relation to God. For sin is not, and cannot be reduced to, the mere transgression of a set of laws or an abstract moral code. No—no indeed! Sin is the treacherous rejection of the Holy One for whose love we were made!

GOD AGAINST SIN: THE JUDGMENT AND MERCY OF GOD

No matter how uncomfortable it may be, the prophets will not let us avoid this terrifying conclusion: sin and sinners are under the wrath of God.[86] As Isaiah warns, "Behold, the name of the LORD comes from afar, burning with

---

[86] See the helpful discussion of divine wrath as it is depicted in Isaiah by Oswalt, *Book of Isaiah, Chapters 1–39*, 89–90.

his anger, and in thick rising smoke; his lips are full of fury, and his tongue is like a devouring fire" (Isa. 30:27). Indeed, God will "cause his majestic voice to be heard and the descending blow of his arm to be seen, in furious anger and a flame of devouring fire" (Isa. 30:30; cf. 5:25; 9:19; 51:17; 57:17; Jer. 32:30; 33:5; 36:7; 44:6; 50:13; Zeph. 2:1–2; 3:8). The extent of this wrath is nothing short of global, for "the LORD is enraged against all the nations, and furious against all their host" (Isa. 34:2; cf. 24:1–23).

The righteous wrath of God is expressed in judgment of sin. Accordingly, the prophets warn of this judgment that is coming (e.g., Mic. 1:2–16). Jeremiah warns that God has promised that "my anger and my wrath will be poured out on this place" (Jer. 7:20). As Isaiah puts it, God has "devoted them to destruction" and has "given them over for slaughter" (Isa. 34:2; cf. Amos 8:1–14). Micah concurs: God's judgment comes in the form of "disaster" (Mic. 1:12; cf. Zech. 10:3). Again, the scope is wide indeed: "I will utterly sweep away everything" (Zeph. 1:2). All peoples are guilty before God, and they will drink of the "cup of the wine of wrath" and "stagger and be crazed because of the sword that I am sending among them" (Jer. 25:15–16). The prophetic descriptions are graphic and grim: God will smear dung on faces in judgment (e.g., Mal. 2:3), and he will use Israel's sinful neighbors to chastise and discipline them.

But while the wrath of God is both real and fearsome, even the prophetic depictions of the wrath of God are not utterly barren of hope. To the contrary, the warnings about God's wrath carry within them a ray of hope, and they are accompanied by bold and beautiful declarations of that hope. Thus Jeremiah says that God's wrath "has gone forth" and "will burst upon the head of the wicked," and he says further that "the fierce anger of the LORD will not turn back until he has executed and accomplished the intentions of his mind" (Jer. 30:23–24). But just what are those "intentions of his mind"? God makes it plain that his ultimate intentions are always for *the good* of his creation (and especially for those creatures made in his image). He makes it plain that "I know the plans I have for you, declares the LORD, plans for welfare and not for evil, to give you a future and a hope" (Jer. 29:11). His stance toward sinners is unmistakable in Ezekiel's prophetic utterances: "Have I any pleasure in the death of the wicked, declares the Lord GOD, and not rather that he should turn from his way and live?" (Ezek. 18:23). To those who would give in to the apparent hopelessness of their situation as sinners and who conclude that they will simply "rot" because of their sin (Ezek. 33:10), the prophet offers this word from the Lord: "Say to them, As I live, declares the Lord GOD, I have no pleasure in the death of the wicked, but that the wicked turn from his way and live; turn back, turn back from your evil ways, for why will you die, O house of Israel?" (Ezek. 33:11). Here God reveals that his very life is tied to his good intentions for those sinners who indeed have rebelled against him: *as surely as I live, declares the Lord.* His deepest desires are for their restoration and salvation, not their destruction. His wrath, then, should not be seen as somehow opposed to his love, but rather as an expression of it.

Nor are these good intentions in any way idle. To the contrary, God's prophets promise that God will provide remedy and offer hope beyond what they can imagine in their current situation. There will be a fountain for cleansing from sin (e.g., Zech. 13:1). Thus Isaiah makes an astounding announcement about the ministry of God's suffering servant: the one whose appearance is "marred, beyond human semblance" (Isa. 52:14) will be "exalted" as he "sprinkle[s] many nations" (Isa. 52:13, 15). This suffering servant "was despised and rejected by men, a man of sorrows, and acquainted with grief" (Isa. 53:3). But he has done great things for us:

> Surely he has borne our griefs
> and carried our sorrows;
> yet we esteemed him stricken,
> smitten by God, and afflicted.
> But he was pierced for our transgressions;
> he was crushed for our iniquities;
> upon him was the chastisement that brought us peace,
> and with his wounds we are healed.
> All we like sheep have gone astray;
> we have turned—every one—to his own way;
> and the LORD has laid on him
> the iniquity of us all. (Isa. 53:4–6)

Because of God's work through his servant, sinners are invited to "come" to God to receive freely what they could never purchase: "Come, everyone who thirsts, come to the waters; and he who has no money, come, buy and eat! Come, buy wine and milk without money and without price." (Isa. 55:1). To "come" in humble reception of God's good gift of salvation means, of course, that wickedness is to be forsaken. Thus we are exhorted to

> Seek the LORD while he may be found;
> call upon him while he is near;
> let the wicked forsake his way,
> and the unrighteous man his thoughts;
> let him return to the LORD, that he may have compassion on him,
> and to our God, for he will abundantly pardon. (Isa. 55:6–7)

Jeremiah also offers hope, for he relates the calm word of God that God's people "will seek me and find me, when you seek me with all your heart" (Jer. 29:13). Jeremiah announces the promise of a new covenant:

Behold, the days are coming, declares the LORD, when I will make a new covenant with the house of Israel and the house of Judah, . . . I will put my law
within them, and I will write it on their hearts. And I will be their God, and
they shall be my people. And no longer shall each one teach his neighbor and
each his brother, saying, "Know the LORD," for they shall all know me, from
the least of them to the greatest, declares the LORD. For I will forgive their
iniquity, and I will remember their sin no more. (Jer. 31:31, 33–34)

And according to Ezekiel, when this happens—when this new life comes from
God—God's people will "not defile themselves anymore with their idols and
their detestable things, or with any of their transgressions. But I will save them
from all the backslidings in which they have sinned, and will cleanse them; and
they shall be my people, and I will be their God" (Ezek. 37:23). The new covenant will be a "covenant of peace" (v. 26), and God's presence and "dwelling
place" will be with his people (v. 27). "Then the nations will know that I am
the LORD who sanctifies Israel, when my sanctuary is in their midst forever-
more" (v. 28).

Ezekiel's vision of restoration and salvation is stunning. God promises that
idolatry will come to its bitter end, and that when this happens, "I will give
them one heart, and a new spirit will I put within them. I will remove the heart
of stone from their flesh and give them a heart of flesh, that they may walk in
my statutes and keep my rules and obey them. And they shall be my people,
and I will be their God" (Ezek. 11:19–20; cf. 14:10–11). God promises that his
Spirit will cleanse his people and give them a "new heart" (cf. Ezek. 36:25–31;
36:25–33). The breath or Spirit (*rûah*) of the Lord will bring new life to dry
bones strewn about a desert valley (Ezek. 37:1–14). Make no mistake, insists
Ezekiel, it is only God who can do such a thing, and indeed God *will* do it: "I
will do it, declares the LORD" (Ezek. 37:14). This covenant will be an "everlasting covenant," and it will restore God's people to the nuptial relationship for
which they were made (Ezek. 16:59–63).

We should not miss the sweep and scope of this prophetic vision. For it is
as broad as the reach of sin. As we have seen, the prophets warn Israel's neighbors about their sin: Moab (e.g., Isa. 15:1–16:13; Jer. 48:1–47; Ezek. 25:8–11;
Zeph. 2:8; Amos 2:1–3), Philistia (e.g., Isa. 14:28–32; Jer. 47:1–7; Ezek. 25:15–
17), Ammon (e.g., Jer. 49:1–5; Ezek. 25:1–7; Amos 1:13–15), Edom (e.g., Jer.
49:7–22; Ezek. 25:12–14; Amos 1:11–12), Egypt (e.g., Isa. 19:1–15; 20:1–6; Jer.
46:1–28; Ezek. 29:1–16), and Assyria (e.g., Isa. 10:5–19; 14:24–27; Jonah 3:4;
Nah. 1:2–3:19) are under divine indictment. But just as they are said to be guilty
for their sin, so also does God actually *lament* over their sin. For instance, even
as we learn that Moab's sins of pride and arrogance are an abomination to
God, we also learn that God *wails* in lament over Moab (e.g., Jer. 48:31). And
just as God indicts sinners everywhere and laments for sinners everywhere, so

also does he desire and provide for their salvation. Jonah offers insight that is profound (if also reluctant) when he admits his reason for running away from Nineveh (Assyria) rather than running *to* it with God's message: "I knew that you are a gracious God and merciful, slow to anger and abounding in steadfast love, and relenting from disaster" (Jonah 4:2). Accordingly, so also does God's promise extend to "the nations" as well. For even the judgments of God against the nations are given so that they might "know that I am the LORD" (e.g., Ezek. 29:6; cf. Ex. 7:5, 17; 8:22; 14:4, 18).[87] God has always been *for* the peoples of the earth (and thus has made Israel a "light for the nations"; e.g., Isa. 42:6; 49:6; cf. Jer. 4:2). And his plan is that they will all "call on the name of the LORD and serve him shoulder to shoulder" (Zeph. 3:9 NIV). Joel's vision is that the Spirit will be "pour[ed] out . . . on all flesh" (Joel 2:28). Nowhere is this more striking than in Isaiah's vision. For just as he delivers God's indictment of their sin, he also offers stunning promises for Egypt and Assyria:

> In that day there will be an altar to the LORD in the midst of the land of Egypt, and a pillar to the LORD at its border. It will be a sign and a witness to the LORD of hosts in the land of Egypt. When they cry to the LORD because of oppressors, he will send a savior and defender, and deliver them. And the LORD will make himself known to the Egyptians, and the Egyptians will know the LORD in that day and worship with sacrifice and offering, and they will make vows to the LORD and perform them. And the LORD will strike Egypt, striking and healing, and they will return to the LORD, and he will listen to their pleas for mercy and heal them.
>
> In that day there will be a highway from Egypt to Assyria, and Assyria will come into Egypt, and Egypt into Assyria, and the Egyptians will worship with the Assyrians.
>
> In that day Israel will be the third with Egypt and Assyria, a blessing in the midst of the earth, whom the LORD of hosts has blessed, saying, "Blessed be Egypt my people, and Assyria the work of my hands, and Israel my inheritance." (Isa. 19:19–25)

Reflecting on this passage, Christopher J. H. Wright concludes that

> there can be few more breath-taking passages in the Old Testament than the conclusion of Isaiah 19. Hard on the heels of the oracle of total judgment on Egypt comes a message of restoration and blessing, in which terms recalling Israel's exodus are applied to *Egypt* herself, and she turns in repentance to acknowledge God and to find pardon and healing. Before we can recover from the surprise, there is more. *Assyria too!* Assyria will join Israel in worshipping God, and on equal terms with Israel! All three will be 'a blessing on the earth,'

---

[87] Walter Kaiser Jr. argues that "the word 'know' here connotes more than a mere cognitive awareness of who God is. It expresses a desire that the Egyptians themselves might come to a personal and experiential knowledge of who Yahweh is" (*Mission in the Old Testament: Israel as a Light to the Nations* [Grand Rapids, MI: Baker Academic, 2000], 21).

God's people, God's handiwork, God's inheritance. Egypt and Assyria—the arch-enemies of Israel, crushing her on both sides, historically and geographically, as hammer and anvil![88]

These nations—Israel's very enemies—are also included in the promises of God. Just as divine judgment of sin extends to all, so also does God's gracious and merciful kindness.

So sin does not have the last word! Drawing again upon nuptial imagery, Isaiah says that "your Maker is your husband, . . . and the Holy One of Israel is your Redeemer" (Isa. 54:5). No longer will the life of God's people be a life of prostitution (Ezek. 43:8–9). Instead, atonement and sanctification await God's people (cf. Eph. 5:25–27). This will require a mediator (e.g., Isa. 52:13–53:12)—and that mediator will be our "kinsman-redeemer" (e.g., Ruth 4:13–22).[89]

E. Sin in the Synoptic Gospels and the Acts of the Apostles

As Thomas R. Schreiner points out, the Synoptic Gospels presuppose that people "need a saving work of God."[90] This is evident in several respects. The "story line of the Old Testament is assumed as a backdrop," and, as we have seen, this story is one that is filled with sin.[91] This "story line" is itself summarized in the opening genealogy of Matthew's account, for here we see a veritable rogues' gallery of sin and shame.[92] This genealogy highlights Israel's exile, and it is plain that this exile was due to Israel's sin.[93] And this "story line" picks up where the OT leaves it—with the reality of sin and the hope of salvation. Before the birth of Jesus, the priest Zechariah "was filled with the Holy Spirit and prophesied" (Luke 1:67) at the birth of his son John ("the Baptist"). He announces the ministry of his son: John will "go before the Lord to prepare his ways" and "to give knowledge of salvation to his people in the forgiveness of their sins" (Luke 1:76–77). John's ministry commences with his fulfillment of prophecy as he "prepare[s] the way of the Lord" (Matt. 3:3; cf. Isa. 40:3; Mal. 3:1). He baptizes those who come to him "confessing their sins" (Matt. 3:6), but he also refers to those who hide in hypocrisy as a "brood of vipers" who should "flee from the wrath to come" (v. 7) before they are "cut down and

---

[88] Christopher J. H. Wright, *Living as the People of God: The Relevance of Old Testament Ethics for Today* (Downers Grove, IL: InterVarsity Press, 1984), 131, emphasis original.

[89] For helpful discussion see Kinlaw, *Lectures in Old Testament Theology*, 363–377.

[90] Thomas R. Schreiner, *New Testament Theology: Magnifying God in Christ* (Grand Rapids, MI: Baker Academic, 2008), 509.

[91] Schreiner, *New Testament Theology*, 509.

[92] For helpful insight, see Christopher J. H. Wright, *Knowing Jesus from the Old Testament* (Downers Grove, IL: IVP Academic, 1992).

[93] Some NT scholars argue that Israel continued to view itself as remaining in exile (e.g., Schreiner, *New Testament Theology*, 510; and esp. N. T. Wright, *Jesus and the Victory of God*, Christian Origins and the Question of God, vol. 2 [Minneapolis: Fortress, 1996], 202–209).

thrown into the fire" (v. 10) that is "unquenchable" (v. 12). John preaches a "baptism of repentance for the forgiveness of sins" (Mark 1:4). Moving from John as the forerunner to Jesus himself, we see the evidence of sin even before we see the incarnate one. In the angelic announcement of Mary's pregnancy to Joseph, he is told that the child in Mary's womb is "from the Holy Spirit" (Matt. 1:20). Joseph then is told what to name this son: "[Y]ou shall call his name Jesus, for *he will save his people from their sins*" (v. 21). And the vicious nature of that sin is seen immediately, for Matthew's birth narrative also includes the tragic and chilling account of the slaughter of the innocents (2:16–18). When Jesus begins his ministry, it is in direct continuity with the ministry of his cousin John. As Udo Schnelle says, "Jesus begins with the message of John the Baptist. John's proclamation is a preaching of judgment and repentance (cf. 3:2)."[94] We can learn much about sin from the direct teachings of Jesus, from the sinless person of our Lord, and from the responses to Jesus that are portrayed in Scripture.[95]

The Teachings of Jesus

Jesus begins his public ministry by calling people to repentance (e.g., Matt. 4:17; Mark 1:14–15). He insists in the strongest terms that he has not come to do away with the law and the conviction of sin that it brings. Nor is he even willing to lessen its obligations or loosen its teaching on the moral life. He insists that he has "not . . . come to abolish the Law or the Prophets"; to the contrary, he has "not come to abolish them but to fulfill them" (Matt. 5:17). Against any relaxation of the Torah's conviction of sin, Jesus instead deepens the force of this conviction. For while "you have heard that it was said to those of old, 'You shall not murder, and whoever murders will be liable to judgment,'" yet, "I say to you that everyone who is angry with his brother will be liable to judgment; . . ." (Matt. 5:21–22). While "you have heard that it was said, 'You shall not commit adultery,'" Jesus says, "I say to you that everyone who looks at a woman with lustful intent has already committed adultery with her in his heart" (vv. 27–28). Again and again Jesus refuses to loosen the obligations of the moral law and the condemnation that it brings, and again and again he extends it to the affections and the depths of the human heart. And rather than lighten the law's moral obligations and accompanying punishments, he repeatedly raises the stakes. For where the punishments decreed by the Torah are frightening indeed and can even include capital punishment, Jesus takes matters even further: he makes it clear that it is the "hell of fire"

---

[94] Udo Schnelle, *The Human Condition: Anthropology in the Teachings of Jesus, Paul, and John*, trans. O. C. Dean (Edinburgh: T&T Clark, 1996), 23.

[95] As these are the subject of a forthcoming volume in this series, I do not include theological consideration of the "powers" of evil that are prominent in the Synoptics.

that awaits unrepentant and unbelieving sinners (e.g., vv. 22, 30). In his famous "Sermon on the Mount" he tells his followers that they "must be perfect, as your heavenly Father is perfect" (v. 48).

Jesus's teaching clarifies the nature of the Torah's teaching on sin both positively (through teaching on justice and righteousness) and negatively (by denouncing particular sins). For instance, Jesus insists that righteousness includes almsgiving (e.g., Matt. 6:1–4; Mark 10:17–31); without care for the poor, there is no inheritance of eternal life. His teaching includes prayer (e.g., Matt. 6:7–18), and such prayer includes petitions for deliverance from evil (Matt. 6:13; cf. Luke 11:4). Proper understanding of sin as taught by Christ as the "fulfillment" of the "Law and the Prophets" is seen to include more than outward actions, for it also involves the motivations, intentions, and affections of the human person. For while it is true that "where your treasure is, there your heart will be also" (Matt. 6:21), so also is it true that "the eye is the lamp of the body. So, if your eye is healthy, your whole body will be full of light, but if your eye is bad, your whole body will be full of darkness. If then the light in you is darkness, how great is the darkness" (Matt. 6:22–23). Thus Jesus tells the "Pharisees and scribes" that they are "hypocrites" (Matt. 15:1–2, 7). For "this people honors me with their lips, but their heart is far from me; in vain do they worship me, teaching as doctrines the commandments of men" (Matt. 15:8–9). He explains further that

> "it is not what goes into the mouth that defiles a person, but what comes out of the mouth; this defiles a person." Then the disciples came and said to him, "Do you know that the Pharisees were offended when they heard this saying?" He answered, "Every plant that my heavenly Father has not planted will be rooted up. Let them alone; they are blind guides. And if the blind lead the blind, both will fall into a pit." But Peter said to him, "Explain the parable to us." And he said, "Are you also still without understanding? Do you not see that whatever goes into the mouth passes into the stomach and is expelled? But what comes out of the mouth proceeds from the heart, and this defiles a person. For out of the heart come evil thoughts, murder, adultery, sexual immorality, theft, false witness, slander. These are what defile a person." (Matt. 15:11–20; cf. Mark 7:14–23)

Indeed, Jesus goes further. For not only is it the case that the affections of the "heart" matter along with the outward actions of keeping the Torah; Jesus teaches that it is entirely possible to keep the ceremonial law while ignoring and flaunting the "weightier matters of the law: justice and mercy and faithfulness" (Matt. 23:23). Such hypocrites are "full of greed and self-indulgence" (Matt. 23:25). So although they "outwardly appear beautiful," on the inside they are "full of dead people's bones and all uncleanness" as well as "hypocrisy and lawlessness" (Matt. 23:27–28; cf. Luke 11:44). "Out of the abundance of the heart the mouth speaks," and our words and actions betray what is really in our hearts (Matt. 12:34).

While the moral law of the Torah may seem overwhelming in its complexity (and in its relation to the civil and ceremonial law), Jesus summarizes it with stunning clarity and brilliance:

> And one of the scribes came up and heard them disputing with one another, and seeing that he answered them well, asked him, "Which commandment is the most important of all?" Jesus answered, "The most important is, 'Hear, O Israel: The Lord our God, the Lord is one. And you shall love the Lord your God with all your heart and with all your soul and with all your mind and with all your strength.' The second is this: 'You shall love your neighbor as yourself.' There is no commandment greater than these." And the scribe said to him, "You are right, Teacher. You have truly said that he is one, and there is no other besides him. And to love him with all the heart and with all the understanding and with all the strength, and to love one's neighbor as oneself, is much more than all whole burnt offerings and sacrifices." And when Jesus saw that he answered wisely, he said to him, "You are not far from the kingdom of God." (Mark 12:28–34; cf. Matt. 7:12; 19:16–30; 22:34–40)

That is it: love the Lord your God without any rival, and love your neighbor as yourself—all without any break or moral vacation.

The teachings of Jesus also reveal something of the effects or results of sin. Sin is analogous to physical ailments in various ways; thus sin is likened to illness, infirmity, and blindness (e.g., Matt. 9:1–10:1; 15:29–31; 17:14–20; Mark 2:17; Luke 5:32). In addition, the estrangement between persons that is caused by sin is vividly described (e.g., Matt. 18:15–22). In fulfillment of Isaiah's prophecy, Jesus says that

> "You will indeed hear but never understand,
>   and you will indeed see but never perceive."
> For this people's heart has grown dull,
>   and with their ears they can barely hear,
> and their eyes they have closed,
>   lest they should see with their eyes
> and hear with their ears
>   and understand with their heart . . . (Matt. 13:14–15)

Sin in Relation to the Person of Christ

Throughout the Synoptic Gospels, we learn what sin really is by the illumination of the sinless one. He brings the remedy for our sins—indeed, he himself *is* the remedy for our sinfulness and our hope of salvation. From his temptation to his triumphant resurrection and ascension, Jesus has defeated sin, death, and the devil. Although sent (*ekballō*) into the wilderness by the Holy Spirit to be tempted (Luke 4:1; cf. Matt. 4:1), Jesus conquered the tempter. He remained sinless, and even Pilate repeatedly admits that Jesus is guiltless (e.g., Luke 23:4, 22). Jesus taught that he was both the fulfillment of the Law and the Prophets and the solution to our predicament. Thus Luke's final recorded words of Jesus include these:

> "These are my words that I spoke to you while I was still with you, that everything written about me in the Law of Moses and the Prophets and the Psalms must be fulfilled." Then he opened their minds to understand the Scriptures, and said to them, "Thus it is written, that the Christ should suffer and on the third day rise from the dead, and that repentance for the forgiveness of sins should be proclaimed in his name to all nations, . . ." (Luke 24:44–47; cf. Matt. 28:16–20)

Accordingly, the proper response to Christ is of utmost significance. Rejection of Christ and his Spirit, meanwhile, leaves one in a desperate place (Mark 3:28–29).

RESPONSES TO THE PERSON AND WORK OF CHRIST

Jesus makes plain the focus of his mission: "Those who are well have no need of a physician, but those who are sick. I came not to call the righteous, but sinners" (Mark 2:17; cf. Matt. 9:13; Luke 5:31–32). He claims nothing short of authority to forgive sins (e.g., Mark 2:5–11). After healing a paralyzed person, he says, "Take heart, my son; your sins are forgiven" (Matt. 9:2). Some of the onlookers took this to be blasphemy, and to their accusations Jesus replied, "'Why do you think evil in your hearts? For which is easier, to say, "Your sins are forgiven," or to say, "Rise and walk"? But that you may know that the Son of Man has authority on earth to forgive sins'—he then said to the paralytic—'Rise, pick up your bed and go home.' And he rose and went home" (Matt. 9:4–7). And Jesus, the one with such authority to forgive sins, graciously extends the free offer of such forgiveness (e.g., Luke 7:47–50). He does so by offering himself: he gives himself as the fulfillment of the covenant, and he institutes the Eucharist with these words: "[T]his is my blood of the covenant, which is poured out for many for the forgiveness of sins" (Matt. 26:28).

But we must also be sure to see that Jesus's offer of forgiveness comes with an invitation and exhortation to discipleship. Indeed, Jesus ties the proper understanding of his own identity very closely to this invitation and demand for discipleship. Famously, he asks about common perceptions of him, and his disciples respond by observing that many people think of Jesus as John the Baptist, Elijah, Jeremiah, or another of the prophets. When he presses them about their own understanding of his identity, "Simon Peter replied, 'You are the Christ, the Son of the living God'" (Matt. 16:16). Jesus responds to this affirmation by calling Simon "Peter" and establishing the "rock" upon which his church will be built (Matt. 16:17–20). Immediately (in the text), Jesus then "began to show his disciples that he must go to Jerusalem and suffer many things from the elders and chief priests and scribes, and be killed, and on the third day be raised" (Matt. 16:21). When Peter rebukes his master for this claim, Jesus in turn chastises Peter in the strongest of terms: "Get behind me, Satan!" (Matt. 16:23). He then issues his invitation to discipleship—and he does so while making the cost of that discipleship clear: "If anyone would come after me, let him deny himself and take up his cross and follow me. For whoever would save his life will lose it, but whoever loses his life for my sake will find it" (Matt. 16:24–25; cf. Mark 8:31–38; Luke 9:22–27). Here we see that to follow Jesus is to do so wholeheartedly. It is to forsake the sins of one's own life; it is to be willing to pay whatever price is necessary. As Jesus puts it, "It is better for you to enter life crippled or lame than with two hands or two feet to be thrown into the eternal fire. . . . [and] It is better for you to enter life with one eye than with two eyes to be thrown into the hell of fire" (Matt. 18:8–9; cf. Mark 9:42–48). Indeed, to follow Jesus is to follow Jesus to *the cross*—it is to "take up our crosses" as well. As Dietrich Bonhoeffer says, "When Christ calls a man, he bids him come and die."[96] Moreover, to follow Jesus is to face the consequences of the sins of those who hate the Lord Jesus Christ and reject him. Jesus puts the warning starkly: "You will be hated by all for my name's sake" (Matt. 10:22). But "whoever does not take his cross and follow me is not worthy of me. Whoever finds his life will lose it, and whoever loses his life for my sake will find it" (Matt. 10:38–39).

Finally, we must be careful to note the consequences of wrong responses to Jesus. Jesus himself makes it undeniably clear that the threat of judgment awaits, and he makes it just as plain that this judgment is more fearsome than we dare imagine. For instance, he says that while "many will come from east and west and recline at table with Abraham, Isaac, and Jacob in the kingdom of heaven," there will be others who "will be thrown into the outer darkness," where there is "weeping and gnashing of teeth" (Matt. 8:11–12; cf. Luke 13:22–30). Thus Jesus refers to the continued sin of those who reject him in nuptial terms: this is an "evil and adulterous generation" (e.g., Matt. 12:39; 16:4).

The warnings in the Synoptic Gospels are striking both for their extent and for their intensity (e.g., Luke 16:19–31). Such statements as these are representative of those that reverberate through the Gospel accounts. To the cities that were most familiar with his ministry, Jesus says,

---

[96] Dietrich Bonhoeffer, *The Cost of Discipleship* (New York: Simon & Schuster, 1995), 89.

Woe to you, Chorazin! Woe to you, Bethsaida! For if the mighty works done in you had been done in Tyre and Sidon, they would have repented long ago in sackcloth and ashes. But I tell you, it will be more bearable on the day of judgment for Tyre and Sidon than for you. And, you, Capernaum, will you be exalted to heaven? You will be brought down to Hades. For if the mighty works done in you had been done in Sodom, it would have remained until this day. But I tell you that it will be more tolerable on the day of judgment for the land of Sodom than for you. (Matt. 11:21–24)

To clarify the meaning of the "parable of the weeds" (Matt. 13:24–30), Jesus says,

The one who sows the good seed is the Son of Man. The field is the world, and the good seed is the sons of the kingdom. The weeds are the sons of the evil one, and the enemy who sowed them is the devil. The harvest is the end of the age, and the reapers are angels. Just as the weeds are gathered and burned with fire, so will it be at the end of the age. The Son of Man will send his angels, and they will gather out of his kingdom all causes of sin and all law-breakers, and throw them into the fiery furnace. In that place there will be weeping and gnashing of teeth." (Matt. 13:37–42; cf. 13:47–50)

Jesus tells us that no one knows the day or the hour of the coming of the Son of Man (Matt. 24:36–37; Mark 13:32), but he says that it will come when it is unexpected (Matt. 24:44; cf. Luke 17:22–37). And he warns that this will be a day of reckoning, for the "worthless servant" will be faced with judgment where there will be "weeping and gnashing of teeth" (Matt. 24:51; cf. 25:30). And Jesus tells us that when he "comes in his glory" (25:31), he will judge the world from his throne:

Before him will be gathered all the nations, and he will separate people one from another as a shepherd separates the sheep from the goats. And he will place the sheep on his right, but the goats on the left. Then the King will say to those on his right, "Come, you who are blessed by my Father, inherit the kingdom prepared for you from the foundation of the world. For I was hungry and you gave me food, I was thirsty and you gave me drink, I was a stranger and you welcomed me, I was naked and you clothed me, I was sick and you visited me, I was in prison and you came to me." Then the righteous will answer him, saying, "Lord, when did we see you hungry and feed you, or thirsty and give you drink? And when did we see you a stranger and welcome you, or naked and clothe you? And when did we see you sick or in prison and visit you?" And the King will answer them, "Truly, I say to you, as you did it to one of the least of these, you did it to me."

Then he will say to those on his left, "Depart from me, you cursed, into the eternal fire prepared for the devil and his angels. For I was hungry and you gave me no food, I was thirsty and you gave me no drink, I was a stranger and you did not welcome me, naked and you did not clothe me, sick and in prison and you did not visit me." Then they also will answer, saying, "Lord, when did we see you hungry or thirsty or a stranger or naked or sick or in prison, and did not minister to you?" Then he will answer them, saying, "Truly, I say to you, as you did not do it to one of the least of these, you did not do it to me." And these will go away into eternal punishment. (Matt. 25:32–46)

The consequences of a wrong response to Jesus, and of continued rebellion against him, are uncomfortably clear.

"Unless you repent," Jesus insists, "you will all likewise perish" (Luke 13:5). Jesus pronounces "woe!" to unrepentant people (e.g., Matt. 23:13–36; Luke 6:24–28; 10:13–15; 11:46–52). But he does so as a warning to them, and his passion for their repentance and salvation is unmistakable and powerful: "O Jerusalem, Jerusalem, the city that kills the prophets and stones those who are sent to it! How often would I have gathered your children together as a hen gathers her brood under her wings, and you were not willing!" (Matt. 23:37).

SUMMARY

To summarize, we are in a position to see several things with some clarity. The Synoptic Gospels pick up and extend the story line of the OT. They also, however, signal something radically new and different: the promised Savior from sin has come! This Savior does not "abolish" the Torah or the teachings of the prophets; instead he "fulfills" them. His teachings about sin summarize the totality of the Law with beauty and power: "[L]ove the Lord your God with all your heart and with all your soul and with all your mind." And "love your neighbor as yourself" (Matt. 22:37, 39). To sin is to fail to keep those commandments. Jesus's teaching and ministry also address the effects of sin in the lives of individual persons and communities. Jesus presents himself as the Savior of the world, therefore to respond to him appropriately with repentance and belief is to embrace life, while to reject him in rebellion and unbelief is to rush headlong into death.

SIN IN THE ACTS OF THE APOSTLES

Luke's account of the beginnings of Christianity continues into Acts. Acts opens with the ascension of Christ. Jesus Christ has promised that he will send the Holy Spirit (Acts 1:5; cf. John 15:24–16:15), and he tells his disciples to wait in Jerusalem for this baptism (Acts 1:6–11). On the day of Pentecost (Acts 2:1), this promise was fulfilled in a dramatic way (vv. 2–4). Filled with the Holy Spirit, the disciples of Jesus began to proclaim the gospel. Astoundingly, people of many different languages understood what was being said (vv. 5–11). People were amazed, but some scoffed (vv. 12–13). Peter addressed this crowd, and his sermon (the first sermon of the Christian church) centered on the sin of *rejecting Christ*: "[T]his Jesus, delivered up according to the definite plan and foreknowledge of God, you crucified and killed by the hands of lawless [*anomōn*] men" (v. 23). Peter's sermon is striking in its simplicity and power: "In fulfillment of Scripture and according to God's providence, you killed the Savior, but God raised him from the dead. Now repent and believe." This sermon encapsulates much that Acts emphasizes with respect to sin and can be understood to set a pattern that is repeated throughout the book. For while various vices and sins are mentioned in Acts (e.g., 15:20, 29; 21:25), the primary focus with respect to sin is on the dangers of rejecting the crucified and risen Lord Jesus Christ or his Spirit.

The message of Acts centers on Christ and thus highlights the tragic sin of rejecting him. The pattern of gospel proclamation is consistent throughout. Peter repeats his earlier message when speaking in Solomon's Portico: "[Y]ou denied the Holy and Righteous One, and asked for a murderer to be granted to you, and you killed the Author of life, whom God raised from the dead" (Acts 3:14–15). Peter says this again to the religious leaders: "Jesus Christ of Nazareth, whom you crucified," was "rejected by you" but has now become the "cornerstone" as he was "raised from the dead" by God (4:10–11). This basic message is repeated regularly throughout the book (e.g., 5:30; 7:52; 10:39–40; 13:26–29). There is "salvation in no one else" (Acts 4:12). Therefore, Peter implores his listeners, "repent" (e.g., Acts 2:38; 3:19; 5:31; 8:22; 10:43). For "forgiveness of sins" comes through Christ (Acts 13:38)—and the sin of rejecting him brings great peril.

Similarly, the message of Acts is driven by pneumatology and thus highlights the equally frightening and tragic sin of resisting the Holy Spirit. In a particularly chilling story from the early church, Ananias and his wife Sapphira sell a piece of property and donate part of the money from the sale to the needs of the believing community (Acts 4:32–5:11). But rather than admitting that they have donated only part of the proceeds, they act as though they are so generous as to have given all of it. Peter responds with a direct question to Ananias: "[W]hy has Satan filled your heart to lie to the Holy Spirit . . .?" (5:3). Ananias hears these words and falls dead. Later his wife repeats his tragic sin and joins him in death. Later, when Stephen is arrested and brought before the council to offer an account of his teachings, actions, and beliefs (6:8–7:1), he recounts Israel's history. When he does so, he reminds them of Abraham and the covenant; of Isaac and Jacob; of Joseph and the Egyptian sojourn; of Moses, the exodus from Egypt, and the wilderness sojourn; of the gifts of Torah and tabernacle (7:2–50). And he concludes with this sobering indictment: "You stiff-necked people, uncircumcised in heart and ears, you always resist the Holy Spirit" (7:51). Beyond this, we are warned against the sin of "simony"—against the sin, that is, of trying to use or manipulate the Holy Spirit for selfish gain (8:14–25). The mission of the Holy Spirit is to cleanse our hearts by faith (15:9), and thus the sin of resisting the Holy Spirit is grave indeed.

F. Pauline Hamartiology

Paul tells the Ephesian Christians that they "were dead in the trespasses and sins in which you once walked, following the course of this world, following the prince of the power of the air, the spirit that is now at work in the sons of disobedience—among whom we all once lived in the passions of our flesh, carrying out the desires of the body and the mind, and were by nature children of wrath, like the rest of mankind" (Eph. 2:1–3). This passage encapsulates several themes that are central to Paul's hamartiology (and indeed to Pauline theology more generally). Sin is pervasive; it is related to the passions or desires of our "flesh" (sarx). It involves disobedient actions and disordered affections. Sin leaves us so utterly debilitated that we are "dead" (nekrous) in our trespasses and sins. It is universal. And, it is no longer the condition that characterizes the believers to whom Paul writes: "you were dead" when you were slaves to your passions, like the rest of humankind. As Douglas J. Moo points out, "[A]s the temporal focus of these verses suggests—'you were dead'; 'you used to live'; 'at one time'; 'we were by nature deserving of wrath'—this life under the dominion of sin is past for the believer."[97] Several important themes stand out for closer examination in Paul's understanding of sin.

ADAM AND UNGODLINESS: THE ORIGIN OF SIN

Paul teaches that "sin came into the world through one man"—Adam. As Paul explains, sin came into the world through the sin of Adam, "and death [came] through sin, and so death spread to all men because all sinned" (Rom. 5:12). It is "because of one man's trespass" that "death reigned through that one man" (v. 17). This "one trespass" has "led to condemnation for all men" (v. 18), for it is "by the one man's disobedience" that "the many were made sinners" (v. 19). Moo observes that "Paul's claim that 'sin entered the world through one man' would have been nothing new to anyone who knew his or her Old Testament or Jewish tradition."[98] He notes further that the "unbreakable connection between sin and death, made clear in Gen. 2–3, was a staple of Jewish theology."[99] While this is true, it also seems to be true that Paul recognizes the importance of this precisely because of his understanding of the person and work of Christ. So while the story of the fall is clearly present in Genesis and

[97] Douglas J. Moo, "Sin in Paul," in Fallen: A Theology of Sin, ed. Christopher W. Morgan and Robert A. Peterson (Wheaton, IL: Crossway, 2013), 107, emphasis original.
[98] Moo, "Sin in Paul," 121.
[99] Moo, "Sin in Paul," 121.

indeed is very prominent, it does not feature prominently in the OT as a whole. For Paul, however, Adam indeed is theologically important. He is not nearly so important as Christ, of course, and indeed pales in comparison (thus Paul's "much more" exclamations in Rom. 5:12–21). But Adam is important to Paul, and he is important precisely because Christ is so important. As N. T. Wright explains, "If the Messiah has been crucified, Paul reasoned, it can only be because Israel as a whole shared in the plight of all human beings."[100] So while Paul's doctrine is in a sense "innovatory," the "idea of a primal sin infecting all people, Jews included, was something found in scripture. But [Paul] went looking for it because of the revelation of the crucified Messiah."[101] The ultimate problems that Paul sees facing humanity are "Sin and Death—enemies that could be tracked . . . all the way back to Adam."[102] Accordingly, as James D. G. Dunn notes, "in these verses Paul encapsulates all human history under the two archetypal figures (note the double 'all' of 5:18)—Adam and Christ—as embodying, in effect, the only two alternatives which the gospel opens to humankind."[103]

In another sense, Paul locates the genesis of sin in a distinctly *theological* manner. Sin, that is to say, must always be understood in reference to *God*. In Romans 1, we read that

> the wrath of God is revealed from heaven against all ungodliness and unrighteousness of men, who by their unrighteousness suppress the truth. For what can be known about God is plain to them, because God has shown it to them. For his invisible attributes, namely, his eternal power and divine nature, have been clearly perceived, ever since the creation of the world, in the things that have been made. So they are without excuse. For although they knew God, they did not honor him as God or give thanks to him, but they became futile in their thinking, and their foolish hearts were darkened. Claiming to be wise, they became fools, and exchanged the glory of the immortal God for images resembling mortal man and birds and animals and creeping things. (Rom. 1:18–23)[104]

Of central importance here are the first terms used to describe sin: "ungodliness and unrighteousness of men" (*asebeian kai adikian anthrōpōn*). The first refers to the rejection of God; the second refers to the resultant state of moral evil. George Eldon Ladd argues that the "most profoundly theological word for sin" in Paul's vocabulary is *asebeia*, and he concludes that "all wickedness

---

[100] N. T. Wright, *Paul and the Faithfulness of God, Book Two, Parts III and IV* (Minneapolis: Fortress, 2013), 752.
[101] Wright, *Paul and the Faithfulness of God*, 752.
[102] Wright, *Paul and the Faithfulness of God*, 762.
[103] James D. G. Dunn, *The Theology of Paul the Apostle* (Grand Rapids, MI: Eerdmans, 1998), 94.
[104] As will be clear from what follows, I remain unconvinced (for reasons that would take us far afield) by "Apocalyptic" readings of Paul, claiming that the first chapters of Romans express the view of Paul's opponents rather than that of Paul himself. But see the impressive work of Douglas A. Campbell, *The Deliverance of God: An Apocalyptic Rereading of Justification in Paul* (Grand Rapids, MI: Eerdmans, 2009).

(*adikia*) arises from the perversion of worship."[105] Thus sin is, for Paul, ultimately the "exchange of God's value and glory for idolatry"; the replacement of a "desire or valuing of God's glory" for "the desire for idols."[106]

UNRIGHTEOUSNESS EXHIBITED: EXPRESSIONS OF SIN IN PAUL'S THEOLOGY

Such idolatry is anything but benign. It produces sins of all kinds, and these sins have horrific consequences. As Wright observes, "idolatry becomes habit-forming, character-shaping, progressively more destructive. It *enslaves* people. Ultimately, it *kills* people.[107] Paul gives eloquent witness to this reality. He uses many terms to describe this sin, and this variety suggests "the manifold forms that sin takes in human experience."[108] Various forms of *hamartia* are prevalent in Paul's work; the "word-group occurs ninety times in Paul's letters."[109] Paul also makes use of *paraptōma* (trespass) and *epithymia* ("desire" or "passion") when such desires are used wrongly, as well as various forms of *parabasis* (transgression).[110] In addition, Paul often uses terms that point to the derivative or even parasitic nature of sin. He refers to sin as *anomia* (or lawlessness). We should not think of this as the primary or ultimate way to understand sin, for as Schreiner reminds us, the "fundamental sin, according to Paul, is not the failure to keep God's law—as serious as such infractions are. The root sin is the failure to praise and worship and thank God, to glorify him as God" (Rom. 1:21)."[111] Nonetheless, *anomia* is sin.

Beyond this, Paul uses many similar terms to describe sins of various sorts. In addition to what we have seen, he will variously refer to sin as "disobedience" (*apeitheia* and *apeitheio*), as "uncleanness" (*akatharsia*), as "unbelief" (*apistia* and *apisteō*), and as "error" (*planē*), "futility" (*mataiotēs*) and other related terms.[112] Especially important are the concrete depictions he offers of activity that is sinful; we see these evidenced in the "vice lists" of Pauline theology. For instance, in Romans 1 Paul makes his indictments very specific. As we have seen, he begins with a statement that the wrath of God is revealed against all ungodliness and unrighteousness. Ungodliness or idolatry, what Dunn refers to as "misdirected religion," results in unrighteousness.[113] And this unrighteousness manifests itself in widely variant ways. When idolatry is

---

[105] George Eldon Ladd, *A Theology of the New Testament*, rev. ed., ed. Donald Hagner (Grand Rapids, MI: Eerdmans, 1993), 444–445. See also Timothy Gombis, "Paul," in *T&T Clark Companion to the Doctrine of Sin*, 97–101.
[106] Chris Tilling, *Paul's Divine Christology* (Grand Rapids, MI: Eerdmans, 2012), 121. Tilling also argues that, given Paul's divine Christology, sin is rejection *of Christ*, e.g., 92–96.
[107] Wright, *Paul and the Faithfulness of God*, 743–744, emphasis original.
[108] Moo, "Sin in Paul," 111.
[109] Moo, "Sin in Paul," 109.
[110] Moo, "Sin in Paul," 110.
[111] Schreiner, *New Testament Theology*, 522.
[112] Cf. the helpful summaries by, e.g., Moo, "Sin in Paul," 110–111; Ladd, *Theology of the New Testament*, 445; and Dunn, *Theology of Paul the Apostle*, 111–112.
[113] Dunn, *Theology of Paul the Apostle*, 114.

committed, God "gives them up" (Rom. 1:24, 26, 28) to their depravity. Paul's indictment follows:

> For this reason God gave them up to dishonorable passions. For their women exchanged natural relations for those that are contrary to nature; and the men likewise gave up natural relations with women and were consumed with passion for one another, men committing shameless acts with men and receiving in themselves the due penalty for their error.
>
> And since they did not see fit to acknowledge God, God gave them up to a debased mind to do what ought not to be done. They were filled with all manner of unrighteousness, evil, covetousness, malice. They are full of envy, murder, strife, deceit, maliciousness. They are gossips, slanderers, haters of God, insolent, haughty, boastful, inventors of evil, disobedient to parents, foolish, faithless, heartless, ruthless. Though they know God's righteous decree that those who practice such things deserve to die, they not only do them but give approval to those who practice them. (Rom. 1:26–32)

Paul echoes this in the next chapter. Addressing his Jewish brothers and sisters in particular, he warns those who "are self-seeking and do not obey the truth, but obey unrighteousness" that there "will be wrath and fury" (Rom. 2:8). Similar expressions can be found elsewhere in Romans, for we are also warned not to participate in "orgies and drunkenness, not in sexual immorality and sensuality, not in quarreling and jealousy" (13:13).

Beyond Romans, we find similar warnings from Paul that are couched in similar "vice lists." To the Corinthians he says,

> Do you not know that the unrighteous will not inherit the kingdom of God? Do not be deceived: neither the sexually immoral, nor idolaters, nor adulterers, nor men who practice homosexuality, nor thieves, nor the greedy, nor drunkards, nor revilers, nor swindlers will inherit the kingdom of God. And such were some of you. But you were washed, you were sanctified, you were justified in the name of the Lord Jesus Christ and by the Spirit of our God. (1 Cor. 6:9–11)

He warns the Galatians not to succumb to the temptation to gratify the "desires of the flesh":

> For the desires of the flesh are against the Spirit, and the desires of the Spirit are against the flesh, for these are opposed to each other, to keep you from doing the things you want to do. But if you are led by the Spirit, you are not under the law. Now the works of the flesh are evident: sexual immorality, impurity, sensuality, idolatry, sorcery, enmity, strife, jealousy, fits of anger, rivalries, dissensions, divisions, envy, drunkenness, orgies, and things like these. I warn you, as I warned you before, that those who do such things will not inherit the kingdom of God. (Gal. 5:17–21)

And he echoes this in addressing the church at Ephesus:

> But sexual immorality and all impurity or covetousness must not even be named among you, as is proper among saints. Let there be no filthiness nor foolish talk nor crude joking, which are out of place, but instead let there be thanksgiving. For you may be sure of this, that everyone who is sexually immoral or impure, or who is covetous (that is, an idolater), has no inheritance in the kingdom of Christ and God. Let no one deceive you with empty words, for because of these things the wrath of God comes upon the sons of disobedience. (Eph. 5:3–6)

We need not (and should not) take these as exhaustive lists of sins. Nor should we think that all sins are roughly equivalent for Paul.[114] He simply does not say that, nor does a sober examination of his teachings entail that conclusion. At the same time, however, we must not lose sight of the fact that Paul's understanding of sin is both wide in scope and pointed in expression. And it *matters* to God. Surely John Barclay is right when he says that, for Paul, "God will neither condone sin nor ignore its effects."[115]

THE BREADTH AND DEPTH OF SIN

For all the complexities of Paul's thought, some things are strikingly clear. One such point is this: *all* have sinned (Rom. 3:23). In much of the first chapter of Romans, Paul shows that varying manifestations of sin result from the underlying idolatrous ungodliness. The theological grounding of his indictment is in the fact that creation itself bears adequate testimony to the existence and nature of God (1:19–20). What Paul says here is as broad as all creation itself; the scope is indeed universal. But in the second chapter he focuses more directly on the sin and guilt of his Jewish brothers and sisters. Perhaps they will be tempted to agree with what Paul says in the first chapter, but think that it applies only to non-Jewish sinners who live apart from the law and without benefit of the prophets. Paul anticipates just such a response, and he warns the person who might agree with what he has said thus far but be tempted to exempt himself or herself and only judge the "others" who are "sinners." Anticipating this, Paul says that those who sit in judgment in this way also have no excuse (2:1). He warns *them* that they are "storing up wrath" for themselves (v. 5). He reminds them that all who sin will be judged—and this is true whether they have *the law* or "the law . . . written on their hearts" (vv. 14–15).

"Then what advantage has the Jew? . . . What then? Are we Jews any better off?" Paul faces these questions directly (Rom. 3:1, 9). Is there some

---

[114] Moo argues that while Paul does not "attempt any kind of systematic listing or categorization of sins," he "regularly castigates three general sins: greed or self-indulgence, inappropriate sexual relations, and harmful or negligent speech" ("Sin in Paul," 116).

[115] John M. G. Barclay, *Paul and the Gift* (Grand Rapids, MI: Eerdmans, 2015), 473.

intrinsic advantage to one's ethnic identity—does being of a particular ethnic or religious community ensure a certain road to salvation? His answer is clear indeed: "No, not at all. For we have already charged that all, both Jews and Greeks, are under sin" (3:9). As Barclay explains, Paul here makes the "surprising claim that the final judgment will take no account of the ethnic difference between Jew and Greek."[116] For "sin is counted as sin whether you have the Law or not," and, moreover, the moral law of God is available to all (in some way and to a relevant extent).[117] And if sin, guilt, and condemnation are spread across all humans—both Jew and Gentile—then Paul concludes that "None is righteous, no, not one; no one understands, no one seeks for God. All have turned aside; together they have become worthless; no one does good, not even one" (3:10–12). Both Jews and Gentiles are sinners. Both Jews and Gentiles stand guilty and condemned before God. Both Jews and Gentiles need a Savior to redeem and rescue them. Without for a moment denying or undercutting the important differences between Jews and Gentiles, Paul is absolutely clear that there is no difference at this point. "There is no distinction: for *all have sinned* and fall short of the glory of God" (3:22–23). The scope of sin is wide indeed. It encompasses all humans, both Jew and Gentile.[118] It is universal in scope.[119]

So the breadth of sin is depressingly vast. And the depth of sin is disturbingly deep. It impacts all aspects of the human person; Paul will refer to sin with respect to the "mind" (*nous*), the "heart" (*kardia*), and "the flesh" (*sarx*).[120] Sin includes, of course, our actions—*what we do* is impacted by sin. But it also infects our affections, so that what we *love and desire* is soiled by sin. Indeed, the depth of depravity is such that Paul even concludes that the human person is utterly unable to do what is good and right apart from God's action. Thus he says in Romans 7 that, when in the grip of sin, "I do not do what I want, but I do the very thing I hate" (Rom. 7:15). Even though he has "the desire to do what is right," the sinner does not have the "ability to carry it out" (v. 18). Thus the sinner will say, "I do not do the good I want, but the evil I do not want is what I keep on doing" (v. 19). The sinner is "captive to the law

---

[116] Barclay, *Paul and the Gift*, 467.

[117] Barclay, *Paul and the Gift*, 467, cf. 468.

[118] Cf. Schreiner, *New Testament Theology*, 526.

[119] Of course Jesus Christ is fully human and without sin. So, as we shall see presently, we should understand sin to be a "common" (and indeed *very common*) but not an *essential* human property.

[120] Ladd claims that "the most difficult and complicated aspect of the Pauline psychology is his doctrine of *sarx*" (*Theology of the New Testament*, 509). It can be used by Paul to denote "flesh" in a literal sense (skin and bones); it can be employed by him to refer to weakness; it can be used as a cipher for corruptibility and even corruption; it can be put to work as a synonym for sinfulness or the condition of humans as sinners. The latter usage is especially prominent and important for Pauline anthropology. But whatever usage is in view, we should not be misled into thinking that our problem is merely that we have skin or indeed that we are human. Our problem is not that we are enfleshed or that we have bodies; it is not that we are creatures. Our problem instead is that we are "carnal"—it is that we are *sinners*. For a helpful discussion of *sarx* (especially in relation to *soma*) in Paul, see Dunn, *Theology of Paul the Apostle*, 62–73.

of sin" (v. 23), and the result is that he is "wretched" (v. 24).[121] The situation of the sinner is dire indeed; the sinner is hopeless without radical change, but is also incapable of such change in his current condition. As Barclay notes, "Paul has diagnosed the human heart as senseless (1:21), hardened, and completely incapable of repentance (2:5)."[122] Accordingly, if anything is to happen that might result in the salvation of the sinner, it must be *divine action* that makes it happen: "[I]f God's righteousness is to prevail, it will be not *because of* but *despite* the condition of human beings."[123]

CONSEQUENCES OF SIN

Paul is not sanguine about the consequences of sin. He is utterly frank about what sin produces. He insists that sin produces further sin. Idolatry produces immorality; *aseibia* leads to *adikia*. Turning away from God leads to lawlessness and to all manner of disintegration and perversion. This in turn leads to "futility" and frustration (Rom. 8:20). Dunn observes that "it is no coincidence that Paul traces the outworking of human independence from God through idolatry to the 'desires of their hearts' as expressed in unclean and dishonouring sexual activity."[124] The link between idolatry and sexual misconduct is especially important for Paul (cf. 1 Cor. 5:11; 6:9–10; Gal. 5:19–21; Col. 3:5; as well as 1 Pet. 4:3; Rev. 21:8; 22:15).[125] Sin is insatiable; it is never satisfied with sin, and Paul traces out the impact of sin on individuals and on communities. Sin produces further sins.[126]

Further, sin leads to condemnation. There is "no condemnation for those who are in Christ Jesus" (Rom. 8:1)—but there indeed *is* condemnation for those who are *not* in Christ Jesus. There can be no mistaking Paul's view; for Paul, sin is under the wrath of God. Those who are "dead in the trespasses and sins" (Eph. 2:1) are said to be "by nature children of wrath" (Eph. 2:3). Paul is utterly frank: those who continue in sin have "no inheritance in the kingdom of Christ and God" (Eph. 5:5), and the "wrath of God comes upon the sons of disobedience" (Eph. 5:6). The "wrath of God is revealed from heaven against all ungodliness and unrighteousness" (Rom. 1:18). And this divine wrath is real; as I. Howard Marshall notes, "attempts to turn the wrath of God into an impersonal principle at work in human history and to see it as simply something that happens rather than also as a personal

---

[121] On the role of the law in bringing out the worst in sin and in revealing it to us, see Wright, *Paul and the Faithfulness of God*, 764–771; 895–896; 1177–1181.

[122] Barclay, *Paul and the Gift*, 463–464.

[123] Barclay, *Paul and the Gift*, 462, emphasis original.

[124] Dunn, *Theology of Paul the Apostle*, 119.

[125] Dunn, *Theology of Paul the Apostle*, 119–120.

[126] See Simon Gathercole, *Defending Substitution: An Essay on Atonement in Paul* (Grand Rapids, MI: Baker Academic, 2015), 48–54.

reaction of God have not been successful."[127] Accordingly, salvation is the reversal of condemnation. It is cast in *legal* categories. As Wright says, "the decisive statement" of Paul's soteriology in Romans 8:1–4 "is nothing if not *forensic*."[128] Salvation is, for Paul, much broader than *merely* legal in nature. But it is not less than that.

Moreover, sin brings estrangement and alienation. As Dunn points out, "the effect of sin is seen at its most serious not so much in secret vices practised in private, but in the breakdown of human relationships."[129] Put simply, "sin destroys human community."[130] Corresponding to this, it results in captivity. Promising freedom and liberation, it brings bondage.[131] Paul's familial and nuptial imagery is especially powerful here. Sin results in estrangement, and salvation is the reversal of this. Accordingly, Paul refers to adoption and other forms of union with Christ.[132] We have "received the Spirit of adoption," and now we are privileged to "cry, 'Abba! Father!' The Spirit himself bears witness with our spirit that we are children of God" (Rom. 8:15–16). And if this were not enough, we are told that if we indeed are children then we are "heirs—heirs of God and fellow heirs with Christ" (Rom. 8:17). Even more strikingly, Paul likens the church to the *bride of Christ*, and he is not afraid to describe the relationship of Christ and his people as nuptial. Accordingly, salvation is the reversal of estrangement, the overcoming of alienation, and the defeat of infidelity. It is the cleansing of the bride (Eph. 5:25–32; cf. 2 Cor. 11:2–3).[133]

Finally, sin brings death: "the wages of sin is death" (Rom. 6:23; cf. Col. 2:13; Eph. 2:1; 5:14).[134] As Wright puts it, sin is "the deadly infection of the whole human race, Israel included."[135] Paul clearly sees physical death as an enemy, but his understanding of death as a consequence of sin goes even deeper. Ultimately, it is spiritual death or final separation from God. At any rate, death, for Paul, is not at all truly natural—it is not the "way it was meant to be."[136] But it is the natural entailment of sin.[137]

[127] I. Howard Marshall, *New Testament Theology: Many Witnesses, One Gospel* (Downers Grove, IL: IVP Academic, 2004), 433.
[128] Wright, *Paul and the Faithfulness of God*, 900, emphasis original.
[129] Dunn, *Theology of Paul the Apostle*, 124.
[130] Gombis, "Paul," 102.
[131] See Schreiner, *New Testament Theology*, 534–538.
[132] For an introduction to the massive literature on the theme of union with Christ, see Constantine R. Campbell, *Paul and Union with Christ: An Exegetical and Theological Study* (Grand Rapids, MI: Zondervan, 2012).
[133] See the discussion in Tilling, *Paul's Divine Christology*, 125–136.
[134] For discussions of Paul's understanding of death (and use of the terms for it), see, e.g., Dunn, *Theology of Paul the Apostle*, 124–126; Marshall, *New Testament Theology*, 433–434; and Gathercole, *Defending Substitution*, 80–83.
[135] Wright, *Paul and the Faithfulness of God*, 754, cf. 770.
[136] Cf. Plantinga, *Not the Way It's Supposed to Be*.
[137] Wright, *Paul and the Faithfulness of God*, 755.

SUMMARY

Paul has a radically *theocentric* and indeed more precisely *Christocentric* understanding of human sin. As Wright puts it, "Sin in the human heart, darkness in the human mind, dehumanized behavior in the human life: all went together with the rule of dark forces that operated through idols, including empires and their rulers, to thwart the purposes of the one creator God."[138] Sin is, for Paul, always and ultimately *against God*. It takes a wide variety of forms as it poisons every relationship. Our intellects are "darkened" with unbelief, our affections are polluted by uncleanness, and our agency is twisted into disobedience. Sin takes various forms, and, directed toward occasional settings, Paul will highlight various expressions of sin in his "vice lists" (e.g., Rom. 1:26–32; 13:13; 1 Cor. 6:9–10; Gal. 5:17–21; Eph. 5:3–6).

Paul's account of the *solution* to the problem of sin is also radically theocentric and Christocentric. His appeal to Adam (Rom. 5:12–21) serves not to provide a theodicy but to draw the parallels to God's saving action in Christ—indeed it functions primarily to show that what has happened in Christ is far more important and more meaningful than what happened in Adam. For "where sin increased, grace abounded all the more" (Rom. 5:20). It is not sin that has the last word; rather it is *grace* that finally will "reign through righteousness" (Rom. 5:21). And, indeed, Paul is convinced that the death-grip of sin has truly been broken (1 Cor. 15:12–28, 50–58). Thus his optimism—not optimism about the innate goodness of human nature but optimism about the omnipotent grace of our triune God—led him to conclude with great clarity and confidence that "you *were* dead in the trespasses and sins" as you "lived in the passions of [your] flesh" (Eph. 2:1–3). You *were* this way—but you *are not now*. You are no longer under condemnation if you are in Christ Jesus (Rom. 8:1), and you are no longer a slave to sin. To the contrary, those who are in Christ Jesus "*were* once slaves of sin" (Rom. 6:17) but are now "set free from sin" (Rom. 6:18). Such freedom is not merely an eschatological hope—it is a real and living hopeful acceptance of a life lived *now*.[139]

G. Sin in Hebrews and the General Epistles

CHRIST AS HIGH PRIEST WHO SAVES FROM SIN IN HEBREWS

Hebrews offers a direct response to the vital question *cur Deus homo?* ("Why the God-man?"): "Since therefore the children share in flesh and blood, he himself likewise partook of the same things, that through death he might destroy the one who has the power of death, that is, the devil, and deliver all those who through fear of death were subject to lifelong slavery" (Heb. 2:14–15).

---

[138] Wright, *Paul and the Faithfulness of God*, 771.
[139] Wright refers to it as "Paul's vision of an *inaugurated* eschatology" (*Paul and the Faithfulness of God*, 760).

The book of Hebrews is centered on Christ much more than it is on sin. The person of Jesus Christ, and especially his priestly vocation, is at the heart of the book. Accordingly, sin is important to the message of Hebrews. The book presupposes much about sin, and it makes several important points with great clarity and force. Ultimately, as David Moffitt observes, we can see that "sin in Hebrews is primarily conceptualized as the refusal to obey God's voice that follows from lack of faith in God's ability to make good on his promises."[140]

Jesus Christ is the great high priest (e.g., Heb. 5:1–10; 6:20–8:13; 9:11–28; 10:19–25; 12:24; 13:8–12). He is the high priest who is both radically like and radically unlike us: while it is true that he was "made like [us] in every respect" (2:17), it is also true that "in every respect [he] has been tempted as we are, yet without sin" (4:15). He is also "holy, innocent, unstained, separated from sinners, and exalted above the heavens" (7:26). He is the priest who is both like and radically unlike the prior priests, for while he makes sacrifice for sin, he does not need to make such a sacrifice for himself (7:27). Instead, he makes such a sacrifice for others. Others make sacrifices again and again, but Christ's sacrifice is final and ultimate (e.g., 7:24). And while others make animal sacrifices, Jesus Christ offers *himself* (7:27). "Without the shedding of blood there is no forgiveness of sins" (9:22), but it is not possible "for the blood of bulls and goats to take away sins" (10:4). Thus Christ makes a single, ultimate, and final offering: himself (10:12–14). He has come to "destroy . . . the devil," and Hebrews makes it clear that Christ accomplishes this victory in his priestly and sacrificial vocation (2:14); he has come to "make propitiation for the sins of the people" (2:17). By his death and resurrection, he has defeated sin, death, and the devil.[141]

WARNINGS ABOUT SIN IN HEBREWS

Christ's death is clearly and unmistakably for "everyone" (Heb. 2:9), and Hebrews is permeated with a very urgent concern that the benefits of Christ's work might be missed or otherwise forfeited. Where the temporariness of sin's "pleasures" (11:25) is emphasized, the consequences of sin are fearsome indeed. There are immediate and stern warnings about sloth: "We must pay much closer attention to what we have heard, lest we drift away from it. . . . How shall we escape if we neglect such a great salvation?" (2:1, 3). There are warnings about hardening one's heart (e.g., 3:7–8, 13–14). Such hardening produces an "evil, unbelieving heart," and such a heart will lead one "away from the living God" (3:12). This is presented as a real and present possibility, and it is a possibility that presents a real and present danger. For it can lead one

---

[140] David Moffitt, "Hebrews and General Epistles," in *T&T Clark Companion to the Doctrine of Sin*, 114.

[141] On the importance of the resurrection in Hebrews, see David M. Moffitt, *Atonement and the Logic of Resurrection in the Epistle to the Hebrews*, Supplements to Novum Testamentum 141 (Leiden: Brill, 2011).

to "fall away from the living God" (3:12), and indeed to once again be under the "wrath" of God (3:11; 4:3). This is expressed as a concern for "brothers" (e.g., 3:12), and it is not to be taken lightly.[142] It is "a fearful thing to fall into the hands of the living God" (10:31).

We find specific warnings about particular sins. Hebrews warns against sins that are "described in the following ways: hardening of the heart (3:8), testing God (3:9), going astray (3:10), dullness of hearing (5:11; 6:12), falling away (6:6), deliberate sin (10:26), spurning God's Son, profaning the blood of the covenant, and outraging the Spirit of grace (10:29), and refusing and rejecting what God says (12:25)."[143] In particular, sexual immorality (e.g., Heb. 12:16; 13:4) and greed (13:5) are highlighted. Such failure to "obtain the grace of God" is what "defile[s]" us (12:15). And it produces deadly consequences for those who fall away from God's grace in rebellion: "For if we go on sinning deliberately after receiving the knowledge of the truth, there no longer remains a sacrifice for sins, but a fearful expectation of judgment, and a fury of fire that will consume the adversaries" (10:26–27; cf. 6:1–8). Throughout, there are concerns both that some people will miss the salvation that has been provided and that some will fall away and face God's wrath. For "our God is a consuming fire" (12:29).

PROMISE AND HOPE OF SANCTIFICATION FROM SIN IN HEBREWS

The warnings are not the final or ultimate message of Hebrews, however. To the contrary, Hebrews expresses great confidence in the sufficiency of Christ's work and hope for perseverant perfection. Hebrews is certain that the promise of a new covenant has been fulfilled in Jesus Christ, and with this covenant God says, "I will be merciful toward their iniquities, and I will remember their sins no more" (Heb. 8:12; cf. 10:16–17). There is surety that the priestly and sacrificial work of Christ will "purify" us from "dead works" so that we might "serve the living God" (9:14). The confident hope that is expressed here goes far beyond mere legal justification; it extends to cleansing, purification, and perfection. Indeed, this hope reverberates throughout the letter. Grounded upon the solid conviction that Christ is the truly perfect Son of God who has become truly human (1:1–12; 2:9), Hebrews is convinced that the holiness of the perfect one is now extended to sinners (2:11–13). Thus our sanctification becomes possible and actual through the work of Christ (10:10, 14). This offers us the "full assurance of faith" as "our hearts" are "sprinkled clean from an evil conscience" and we are made holy in body and soul (10:19–22). The eschatological vision of Hebrews is of "the righteous made perfect" (12:23). The

---

[142] Schreiner notes that the letter "warns *believers* against falling into sin and disobedience" (*New Testament Theology*, 539, emphasis original).

[143] Schreiner, *New Testament Theology*, 539.

exhortation, accordingly, is to continue in our "struggle against sin" (12:4) be-cause we understand that Christ "suffered outside the gate" precisely in order to "sanctify the people" (13:12). Thus we can do no less than "strive to enter that rest, so that no one may fall by the same sort of disobedience" (4:11).

Sin in James

James exhorts his readers to "count it all joy" when they encounter trials or temptations (*peripesēte*), for the "testing" of faith produces "steadfastness," which in turn produces nothing short of perfection (*teleioi*) when complete (James 1:2–4). But while temptation may be the occasion for moral growth, we should never regard it as something that comes from God. As James puts it, "Let no one say when he is tempted [*peirazomenos*], 'I am being tempted [*peirazomai*] by God,' for God cannot be tempted [*apeirastos*] with evil, and he himself tempts [*peirazei*] no one" (v. 13). Schreiner is correct when he says that "[n]o one can blame God for sin, as if God actually seduces people so that they sin."[144] What God gives are the gifts of goodness and perfection, and James insists that we should never think that God gives temptation or makes sin inevitable for us, and this is because God himself is necessarily good. "There is no variation or shadow due to change" in "the Father of lights" (v. 17).

So if temptations (and sin) do not come directly from God, then what are we to make of them? James tells us how temptation comes to us: "But each person is tempted when he is lured and enticed by his own desire. Then desire when it has conceived gives birth to sin, and sin when it is fully grown brings forth death" (James 1:14–15). James is saying that human desires (*epithymias*) are the occasion for temptation, that when we succumb to that temptation we sin, and that when we sin we experience death as a result. This does not, of course, mean that the desires themselves are somehow wrong or sinful. As Ladd observes, the word used here "is not of itself a word bearing any evil con-notation; in fact, Paul uses it of desire to be with Christ (Phil. 1:23)."[145] James does not give an exhaustive or detailed explanation here, and his rather terse summary of the process has invigorated many discussions within the Christian tradition of how desires which may be good in themselves become disordered in a sinful way. But although he does not say a lot, what James does say is clear indeed: temptation does not come from God, but is instead the result of disordered desire.[146]

James is aware that we all "stumble" or sin in various ways (James 3:2). He is especially exercised to combat the effects of sinful communication. What we

---

[144] Schreiner, *New Testament Theology*, 540.
[145] Ladd, *Theology of the New Testament*, 637.
[146] On the disordering of desires in James, see Moffitt, "Hebrews and the General Epistles," 119–120.

say, he insists, is reflective of our deepest affections and our spiritual condition. And it can have great destructive force:

> The tongue is a fire, a world of unrighteousness. The tongue is set among our members, staining the whole body, setting on fire the entire course of life, and set on fire by hell. . . . No human being can tame the tongue. It is a restless evil, full of deadly poison. With it we bless our Lord and Father, and with it we curse people who are made in the likeness of God. From the same mouth come blessing and cursing. (James 3:6, 8–10a)

As he goes on to say, "these things ought not to be so" (v. 10b).

James is also anxious to combat the separation of faith and works in the Christian life. This is especially evident in his condemnations of favoritism and hypocrisy. Showing deference or favoritism to the rich, he insists, is tantamount to nothing short of blasphemy (2:7)! If you "show partiality," he says, then "you are committing sin and are convicted by the law as transgressors" (v. 9). And this is serious indeed, for "whoever keeps the whole law but fails in one point has become guilty of all of it" (v. 10). Care for the widows and orphans is simply not optional (1:27). Care for the poor is absolutely nonnegotiable for God's people, for to do anything less is to have "condemned and murdered" the righteous and the needy (5:1–6). As Ladd notes, "[W]hat seems to matter most to James is showing partiality."[147]

James issues an urgent call for God's people to be active in receiving God's sanctifying grace. Human anger does not produce godly righteousness, so James exhorts his readers to rid themselves of it along with "all filthiness and rampant wickedness" (1:20–21). We are to be "doers" who are active in holy living (vv. 22–25). He commands his readers,

> [s]ubmit yourselves therefore to God. Resist the devil, and he will flee from you. Draw near to God, and he will draw near to you. Cleanse your hands, you sinners, and purify your hearts, you double-minded. Be wretched and mourn and weep. Let your laughter be turned to mourning and your joy to gloom. Humble yourselves before the Lord, and he will exalt you. (James 4:7–10)

Clearly, James is emphatic about the role of the human agent in the process of sanctification. Like other biblical authors, he sees our relationship to God in nuptial terms, and he portrays sin as adultery that makes us enemies of God (4:4). He draws upon the OT background, "where Israel's forsaking of God is nothing less than spiritual harlotry."[148] Therefore, we are to choose submission (v. 7) over selfishness (vv. 1–3).

As sober as James is about the perversity and pervasiveness of sin, however,

---

[147] Ladd, *Theology of the New Testament*, 638.
[148] Schreiner, *New Testament Theology*, 541.

he is also hopeful about the reality of deliverance from it. Thus he says that the "prayer of faith" will result in forgiveness for the one who has committed sin (5:15), and he commands his readers to "confess your sins to one another and pray for one another" (v. 16). For "if anyone among you wanders from the truth and someone brings him back, let him know that whoever brings back a sinner from his wandering will save his soul from death and will cover a multitude of sins" (vv. 19–20).

PETRINE HAMARTIOLOGY

The Petrine epistles echo many of these themes. There is a strong emphasis on the centrality and importance of sanctification, as God's people are identified as those who are "elect . . . according to the foreknowledge" of God for sanctification (1 Pet. 1:2) and as those who comprise "a chosen race, a royal priesthood, [and] a holy nation" (1 Pet. 2:9). Peter also commands his readers to be active in the rejection of sin and the pursuit of godliness: "[A]s he who called you is holy, you also be holy in all your conduct, since it is written, 'You shall be holy, for I am holy'" (1 Pet. 1:15–16). We are, then, to rid ourselves of such vices as malice, deceit, hypocrisy, envy, and slander (1 Pet. 2:1). We are to abstain from unholy expressions of the desires of "the flesh [*sarkikōn*]" (1 Pet. 2:11). Special warnings are given about various vices: repaying evil with evil, sinning by our speech (1 Pet. 3:9–10), "living in sensuality, passions, drunkenness, orgies, drinking parties, and lawless idolatry," for such "debauchery" brings fearsome consequences (1 Pet. 4:3–5). Indeed, these consequences are so serious that they can result in apostasy. For such a person is said to be enslaved (2 Pet. 2:19). Those who are said to "have escaped the defilements of the world through the knowledge of our Lord and Savior Jesus Christ" but who then are "overcome" by sin (2 Pet. 2:20) are in a fearful place. They are now in a place where "it would have been better for them never to have known the way of righteousness than after knowing it to turn back from the holy commandment delivered to them," for they are now like a dog that "returns to its own vomit" (2 Pet. 2:21–22). In addition, we are told to be on guard against false teachers who would betray us and lead us away from holiness and back into sin (2 Pet. 2:1–19; cf. Jude 4). Caution is in order, because "your adversary the devil prowls around like a roaring lion, seeking someone to devour" (1 Pet. 5:8). And continued sin "leads to final judgment."[149]

Positively, we are told not only to shun evil but also to "do good" (1 Pet. 3:11), for we now "live . . . for the will of God" (4:2). Christ's atonement has made it possible for us to "die to sin and live to righteousness" (2:24; cf. 3:18). Jesus Christ suffered for us, "leaving [us] an example, that [we] might follow

---

[149] Schreiner, *New Testament Theology*, 541.

in his steps" (2:21). When we live for righteousness, "love covers a multitude of sins" (4:8).

H. Johannine Hamartiology

The Johannine literature presents a rich and multifaceted account of sin. Sin is described in various ways and through various metaphors, the results of sin are clearly depicted, and hope for salvation from sin is vividly portrayed. Throughout, sin is very important to John's central message. As Gary M. Burge notes, "John refers to *hamartia* (sin) more than any other gospel and his first letter gives the theme thorough attention."[150]

JOHANNINE "DUALISMS"

Especially since the ground-breaking work of Rudolph Bultmann, scholars have recognized the presence and importance of what is sometimes called "dualism" in John's theology.[151] The term "dualism" is vague and potentially very misleading, but the basic lesson to be learned is that John makes powerful use of contrast in his theology.[152] For instance, we see sharp contrasts between spiritual blindness and the gift of sight (e.g., John 9:26, 39), between what is of or from this world and what is from beyond or even against this world (e.g., John 8:23; 12:31; 14:17–19, 30; 15:19; 16:20, 33; 17:6–9, 25; 18:36; 1 John 2:16; 3:2; 4:2–6), between lies and the truth (e.g., John 8:44; 14:17; 16:13; 1 John 1:6; 2:4, 21–22, 27), between unbelief and belief (e.g., John 3:18, 36; 1 John 5:10), between evil deeds and righteous deeds (e.g., 1 John 3:12), and many others. But while there are many such contrasts, three stand out as especially important: light and darkness, life and death, and love and hate.

The Gospel's prologue immediately draws a contrast between light and darkness: the Logos has life, and this life is the light of all humanity (John 1:4). While John the Baptist bore witness to the light, the incarnate Word himself *is* that light, the "true light" that "gives light to everyone" (John 1:9). This theme of light against darkness continues throughout the Gospel (e.g., 1:3–9; 3:19–21; 8:12; 9:4–5; 11:9–10; 12:35–36, 46).[153] It is continued in the first epistle. Here we are told that "God is light, and in him is no darkness at all" (1 John 1:5). To live as children who belong to God, then, is to "walk in the light" and avoid "darkness" (1 John 1:6–7; cf. 2:8–9). It is also echoed in the Revelation of John, for there we see the contrast between light and darkness in eschatological terms as well. Sin is thus the rejection of God's revelation that is the light.

---

[150] Gary M. Burge, "The Gospel and Epistles of John," in *T&T Clark Companion to the Doctrine of Sin*, 79.

[151] See especially Rudolph Bultmann, *Theology of the New Testament*, trans. Kendrick Grobel (Waco, TX: Baylor University Press, 2007); and Bultmann, *The Gospel of John*, trans. G. R. Beasley-Murray (Oxford: Blackwell, 1971).

[152] For a particularly insightful and critical engagement with Bultmann, see Richard Bauckham, *Gospel of Glory: Major Themes in Johannine Theology* (Grand Rapids, MI: Baker Academic, 2015), 109–129.

[153] See the helpful summary by Bauckham, *Gospel of Glory*, 121.

Indeed, Burge concludes that "the primary sin we witness is the rejection of God's revelation in Christ."[154]

John's prologue also begins with the affirmation that life was in the Logos (John 1:4), and this life is contrasted with the death that is produced by sin. This theme reverberates throughout Johannine theology. As Bauckham explains,

> While flesh left to itself dies, its true destiny in God's purpose is to be united with the divine life. The Son, who has eternal life in himself, becomes flesh in order to give flesh eternal life. Thus, flesh is not evil, even in its weakness and mortality, but its natural mortality means that if humans reject the Savior, who can give them eternal life, then they must die. . . . Those who choose to remain in their sins die in their sins. Death, the natural fate of creaturely life left to itself, becomes the actual fate only of sinners, because it is they who reject their Savior, who brings eternal life from God.[155]

True life, eternal life, is the life that was "made manifest" in Christ and that brings us into the filial relationship shared between Father and Son (1 John 1:2–3).

John famously tells us that "God so loved the world, that he gave his only Son, that whoever believes in him should not perish but have eternal life. For God did not send his Son into the world to condemn the world, but in order that the world might be saved through him" (John 3:16–17). Here we catch a precious glimpse into the divine motivation: God sends the Son to give life *because God loves the world*! He gives his life for those who believe and those who reject. As John says in the first epistle, "He is the propitiation for our sins, and not for ours only but also for the sins of the whole world" (1 John 2:2). This love brings eternal life for those who believe, and, as Bauckham argues, it "is a distinctive theme of John's Gospel that Jesus gave his life in love for his disciples, whom the Gospel calls 'his own' (10:3–4, 14; 13:1; cf. 15:19)."[156] Jesus tells us to "love one another as I have loved you," and he tells us further that "greater love has no one than this, that someone lay down his life for his friends" (John 15:12–13). Astoundingly, we see that this love that propels Jesus to sacrifice himself is grounded in the mutual love of the Father and Son. "As the Father has loved me," Jesus says, "so have I loved you" (John 15:9). Accordingly, the first epistle tells us not only that God loves the world but indeed that love is of the essence of God: "God *is* love" (1 John 4:8, 16). Jesus's "high priestly prayer" includes his affirmation that the Father loves Jesus's disciples "even as" he loves Jesus himself (John 17:23). The loving communion which was shared between Father and Son from "before the foundation of the world"

---

[154] Burge, "Gospel and Epistles of John," 79.
[155] Bauckham, *Gospel of Glory*, 125.
[156] Bauckham, *Gospel of Glory*, 64.

(John 17:24) is now given to the fallen but believing disciples: ". . . that the love with which you have loved me may be in them, and I in them" (John 17:26).

Sin as depicted in contrast to love is hatred. Jesus tells us that "if the world hates you, know that it has hated me before it hated you" (John 15:18). He continues by saying that "whoever hates me hates my Father also" (John 15:23). In his first letter, John draws these themes together when he warns believers not to be surprised "that the world hates you" and then goes on to say that "we know that we have passed out of death into life" by our love for fellow members of God's family (1 John 3:13–14; cf. 2:9–11). He also issues this warning: "Whoever does not love abides in death. Everyone who hates his brother is a murderer, and you know that no murderer has eternal life abiding in him" (1 John 3:14–15). For "if anyone says, 'I love God,' [but then] hates his brother, he is a liar; for he who does not love his brother whom he has seen cannot love God whom he has not seen. And this commandment we have from him: whoever loves God must also love his brother" (1 John 4:20–21).

RESULTS OF SIN

Johannine theology also makes plain just what the consequences of sin really are. Sin blinds us and leaves us weak and infirm. Burge concludes from the story of Jesus's "healing of the blind man that this story provides a metaphorical picture of the condition of Jesus's audience," and it is one that is rich in irony.[157] For while the one who is blind is now able to recognize the Savior, those who are ostensibly sight-blessed deny and reject Jesus. Thus their "guilt remains" (John 9:41). Sin clearly results in more sin. Indeed, it causes slavery to sin. In contrast to the filial picture of right relationship with God, Jesus says that "everyone who practices sin is a slave to sin. The slave does not remain in the house forever; the son remains forever" (8:34–35). With such slavery comes condemnation of sin and of the sinner: "Whoever does not believe is condemned already" (3:18). And such condemnation brings fearful consequences. For while it is true that "whoever believes in the Son has eternal life," it is also true that "whoever does not obey the Son shall not see life, but the wrath of God remains on him" (John 3:36). Revelation also speaks of those who refused to repent of their viciousness and sinfulness (e.g., Rev. 9:20–21). The fate of those who "did not repent and give [God] glory" is that they "were scorched by the fierce heat" while they "gnawed their tongues in anguish and cursed the God of heaven" (Rev. 16:9–11; cf. 12:7–17; 14:17–20). In John's apocalyptic vision, he sees them "thrown alive into the lake of fire" (Rev. 19:20; 20:11–15).

---

[157] Burge, "Gospel and Epistles of John," 81.

THE REMEDY FOR SIN

But as dour as John's theology may seem to be about the reality and consequences of sin, this is not the ultimate message. To the contrary, John's theological vision is centered on the remedy for sin that has been made by God
through the work of his Son. Once again, the themes of light, life, and love
are central to this hope. The "light that has come into the world" in the incarnate Son makes it possible for sinners to "see" and be saved. This light brings
life (cf. Rev. 21:23–25). It is driven by the holy love of the triune God who
has given the Son for salvation. This love is portrayed very powerfully in *filial*
terms in John's epistles. "Our fellowship is with the Father and with his Son
Jesus Christ" (1 John 1:3). So "see what kind of love the Father has given to
us, that we should be called children of God; and so we are" (1 John 3:1). And
it is portrayed in *nuptial* terms in John's Apocalypse, as sin is characterized
as adultery (e.g., Rev. 14:8; 17:1–18; 18:1–10) and as the canonical narrative
culminates in a wedding feast (Rev. 19:1–10).

John's theology makes some important points explicit as his teaching unfolds. John the Baptist offers his own answer to the question of *cur Deus homo*.
Why did the Son of God become incarnate? "Behold," John says, "the Lamb
of God, who takes away the sin of the world" (John 1:29). Drawing upon both
the Passover and the suffering servant (Isa. 52:13–53:12), John teaches that the
Word has become incarnate as Jesus Christ to provide atonement for the sin of
the world.[158] As Pilate recognized, Jesus Christ was not guilty for any sin of his
own at all (John 19:4, 6). "In him there is no sin" (1 John 3:5). Instead, he came
to bear away the sins of *others*. He is "Jesus Christ the righteous" (1 John 2:1).
He is our advocate (1 John 2:1), and he has come to make atonement (*hilasmos*)
for our sins (1 John 2:2; 4:10). Indeed, Christ's love is so all-encompassing that
he has come to provide atonement not only for "our" sins but also for the "sins
of the whole world" (1 John 2:2).

The work of Christ is not provided for us merely so that we can continue
in our sinfulness while hoping to escape the consequences of it. No, the work
of Christ makes it both possible and necessary to live lives of newness and holiness. God loves us, and he "has freed us from our sins" (Rev. 1:5). Thus Jesus
offers forgiveness and healing with these words: "Sin no more" (John 5:14).
The works of the world are "evil" (John 7:7), and we are to avoid the snares
of the world (e.g., 1 John 2:15–17). John places clear and strong emphasis on
sanctification: "the blood of Jesus his Son cleanses us from all sin" (1 John
1:7). This sanctification is within the context of the filial relationship; it is not
for holiness for its own sake as a kind of autonomous moral sanctity but is
instead for communion (*koinonia*) (1 John 1:3, 7). Johannine theology is clear

---

[158] See Bauckham, *Gospel of Glory*, 156–157 for helpful discussion at this point.

about the universality of sin: "If we say we have no sin, we deceive ourselves, and the truth is not in us" (1 John 1:8). And it is also clear about the reality of forgiveness and sanctification: "If we confess our sins, he is faithful and just to forgive us our sins and to cleanse us from all unrighteousness" (1 John 1:9). Thus we are not sentenced to a life of sinful bondage; instead we are set free so that we "may not sin" (1 John 2:1). The heavy emphasis of John's soteriology is on strength and victory. For though sin is strong indeed, it is no match for the power and presence of God (e.g., 1 John 2:11–14). Thus we are both enabled and commanded to "[practice] righteousness" (1 John 2:29). At the same time, however, we must understand that those who "[keep] on sinning" (1 John 3:6) and "[make] a practice of sinning" are "of the devil" (1 John 3:8). We must especially be on guard against the possibility of final apostasy. For while there are sins that do not lead to spiritual death, there indeed is also "sin that leads to death" (1 John 5:16–17).

In summary, we can see that, for John, God "is light, and in him is no darkness at all" (1 John 1:5). Therefore, we are to "walk in the light" as we enjoy communion with the Father through the Son (1 John 1:7). God is life, and to belong to him is to enjoy nothing less than eternal life. And all this is true because "God is love" (1 John 4:8, 16; cf. John 17:24). This love has been revealed supremely and finally in Jesus Christ, for while we did not even know what love truly is, God "sent his Son to be the propitiation for our sins" (1 John 4:10; cf. John 3:16–17). So while the world is filled with hatred, we are to live differently. Whoever "hates his brother is still in darkness" (1 John 2:9), but whoever lives in the light of God's holy love is set free to love accordingly. In sum, we are to live in the loving communion of the triune God, and we are to "love one another" (e.g., 1 John 3:11, 23).

IV. Sin in Biblical Theology:
A Summary of Several Key Themes

William Dyrness observes the following about sin in the OT: sin is, ultimately and always, *theological*. It is oriented toward God; it is "always related to the holy purposes of God" and always opposed to the righteous character of God.[159] Sin has an "objective" character to it, for it involves violation of divine command (whether knowingly or unwittingly). At the same time, sin is most commonly and vividly portrayed as rebellion that is both "personal" and "conscious."[160] Sin is universal "in that it has invaded all of human nature and all men everywhere" (e.g., Gen. 6:5; 1 Kings 8:46; Ps. 53:1).[161] Finally, sin

---

[159] William Dyrness, *Themes in Old Testament Theology* (Downers Grove, IL: InterVarsity Press, 1977), 107.
[160] Dyrness, *Themes in Old Testament Theology*, 108.
[161] Dyrness, *Themes in Old Testament Theology*, 109.

is portrayed as so deeply entrenched that it can be said to be "fixed" (cf., e.g., Jer. 2:24–25; 6:7; 13:23; 17:9).[162] Sin results in guilt, and it makes us liable to punishment.[163] All of this is taken up and extended in the NT, and here we find more about the depth of the perversion and the expressions of that depravity. In the NT we also find that the consequences of sin are even more dire than we might previously have thought, for here it becomes clear that the consequences of sin extend beyond this earthly existence.

Throughout the biblical canon, the relationships of humanity to God (both as creatures and as sinners) are portrayed in many illuminating ways. Three of these stand out and call for further elaboration: the royal-legal depiction, the familial analogy, and the nuptial account.

A. The Royal-Legal Metaphor

Basic and foundational to any biblical understanding of God and our relationship to him—as both creatures and sinners—is what Dennis Kinlaw helpfully refers to as the "royal-legal metaphor." He explains,

> This first metaphor has for us moderns a double meaning. While it speaks of the royal court where the sovereign reigns, it also speaks of the legal assembly where law reigns and judicial decisions are made. In our society with its separation of powers, we do not think of these two together. However, in the world of the Old Testament, the world in which Israel existed, the sovereign was the supreme judge. God was seen as both King and Judge. He was the giver of the Law and the guarantor of its execution. He was responsible for justice as well as order. He was the Protector of the weak and the inescapable Judge of those who did evil. Sovereign power and legal power were one in Yahweh. . . . Since God is one and one alone, the divine throne and the divine bench coincide. The eternal Lord and the eternal Judge are the same.[164]

This theme permeates Scripture; the OT as well as the NT consistently present God as King of kings and Lord of lords, the one who will judge the earth with righteousness. The theme of God as Sovereign Lord pervades the OT. The "kingdom of God" and the "kingdom of heaven" are prevalent themes in the preaching of Jesus. Paul proclaims the good news of the "kingdom of God" (e.g., Acts 19:8; 28:23, 31). And the biblical canon closes with a dramatic climax in which the sovereignty and justice of God is vividly portrayed. As Kinlaw reminds us, "All of creation is pictured as standing before the throne of God. In the center of that throne stands none other than Jesus, who is now

---

[162] Dyrness, *Themes in Old Testament Theology*, 109–110.
[163] Dyrness, *Themes in Old Testament Theology*, 110.
[164] Dennis F. Kinlaw, *Let's Start with Jesus: A New Way of Doing Theology* (Grand Rapids, MI: Zondervan, 2005), 47–48.

recognized as Lord and Judge. Every knee is bent to him in acknowledgment of his sovereign lordship as all creation awaits its judgment. Every creature faces its Creator Judge."[165]

Not surprisingly, the sovereignty of God is a doctrine that is treasured by Christians, as is belief in the unshakable and unimpeachable justice of God. Indeed, in several places these appear together. Psalm 93 illustrates this vividly:

> The LORD reigns; he is robed in majesty;
> > the LORD is robed; he has put on strength as his belt.
> Yes, the world is established; it shall never be moved.
> Your throne is established from of old;
> > you are from everlasting. (Ps. 93:1–2)

Psalm 96 similarly exults in the righteousness and justice of the King of the cosmos:

> Say among the nations, "The LORD reigns!
> > Yes, the world is established; it shall never be moved;
> > he will judge the peoples with equity."
>
> Let the heavens be glad, and let the earth rejoice;
> > let the sea roar, and all that fills it;
> > let the field exult, and everything in it!
> Then shall all the trees of the forest sing for joy
> > before the LORD, for he comes,
> > for he comes to judge the earth.
> He will judge the world in righteousness,
> > and the peoples in his faithfulness. (Ps. 96:10–13)

Psalm 99 echoes these themes:

> The LORD reigns; let the peoples tremble!
> He sits enthroned upon the cherubim; let the earth quake!
> The LORD is great in Zion;
> > he is exalted over all the peoples.
> Let them praise your great and awesome name!
> > Holy is he!
> The King in his might loves justice.
> > You have established equity;
> you have executed justice
> > and righteousness in Jacob.
> Exalt the LORD our God;
> > worship at his footstool!
> > Holy is he! (Ps. 99:1–5)

Clearly, God is the undisputed Sovereign over all creation. And just as surely

---

[165] Kinlaw, Let's Start with Jesus, 50.

as his sovereignty is both universal and unrivaled, it is also a just, righteous, and faithful sovereignty.

What we need to see here is the way that sin is depicted in this narrative framework. In the overarching narrative of the biblical canon, we stand before the sovereign God as subjects, as citizens. To be sure, as beings made in the *imago dei* we also are truly said to be "sovereign," for as the only creatures made in the image of the Creator and King, we are given "dominion" and the mandate to rule over the creation. More basic than that, however, is the notion that we are subjects—we are under the authority of, and accountable to, the one who is King. Accordingly, sin is depicted in this light as rebellion, as betrayal, as treason. As sinners, we break the law of the King, turn our backs on him, shake our fists in his face, and dare him to do something about it. This royal-legal depiction takes several forms in Scripture.

First we note how God's *design* for humanity (and indeed for the cosmos) has been marred. As God is sovereign as Creator, so also sin is pictured as the violation of the design: sin violates God's design plan for his creatures with respect to their relationship to their Creator, with respect to their relationships to one another, and with respect to their relationships to the rest of creation.[166] Next we see the powerful account of transgression. Sin is, as we are told directly in 1 John, *anomia*, the "transgression of the law" (KJV) or "lawlessness" (1 John 3:4). It is nothing less than—although, as we shall soon see, it is more than—the violation of a legal requirement. It is the breaking of a barrier, the crossing of a boundary. As Paul tells us, it is the violation of a normative requirement that was understood and then denied (e.g., 1 Tim. 2:14). It is the breach of covenant (e.g., Ex. 32:8; Josh. 7:11; Dan. 9:11). Accordingly, the prophets stand forth to call God's people to account for their reckless and deliberate violation; we see in Hosea's prophecy, as a vivid example, the Lord accusing his people who have "transgressed my covenant and rebelled against my law" (Hos. 8:1).

Perhaps even stronger is the language of *rebellion*. In the canonical narrative, no one other than God rightfully can make a claim to be "King of kings." In the biblical story, ultimate allegiance belongs to God—and God alone. And sin is nothing less than rebellion against the Sovereign, treason against the one to whom we are pledged. What we see here is that the refusal to obey, the transgression of the law that has been given, is portrayed as rebellion. What we see here is nothing short of high treason.

In the canonical account, such rebellion leads to *slavery* or bondage. This is played out with depressing regularity and shocking detail in the OT. God

---

[166] See Christopher J. H. Wright, *Old Testament Ethics for the People of God* (Downers Grove, IL: InterVarsity Press, 2004), 17–20.

delivers his people from the "house of slavery" in Egypt (Deut. 5:6; cf. Judg. 6:8; Jer. 34:13) and into a land where they are free to serve, obey, know, and glorify him. Then Joshua calls his people to choose: whom will you serve? (Josh. 24:14–15). He is challenging them; they must make a choice. And the choice is stark and clear: either they will serve God in faithfulness, or they will rebel against him and once again serve their enemies in "the house of slavery" (v. 17). The history of Israel stands as a sobering and tragic testament to their failure, and their example stands as a beacon to warn of the consequences of sin: rebellion against God ensures slavery to his enemies.

And as the picture of sin here is legal in orientation, so also is the accompanying portrait of salvation. Pauline theology makes this especially clear. Again, as Wright says, "the decisive statement" of soteriology in Romans 8:1–4 "is nothing if not *forensic*."[167] The NT (and Pauline theology in particular) has a developed vocabulary to help us understand salvation that comes from this metaphor: it is the language of *justification*. Salvation is pictured in legal terms; because of the work of Christ, we can be pronounced righteous and given new legal standing before the Judge.

To summarize, God is depicted throughout the biblical canon as sovereign King and righteous Judge. Humans are portrayed as creatures who are subject and also "sovereign" in the derivative but nonetheless important sense that they are the creatures made in God's image who are called to be stewards of that creation (cf. Gen. 1:26–27). Sin, accordingly, is thus lawlessness and rebellion, and it makes us guilty before God. We stand condemned as sinners before God, and the corresponding portrait of salvation is described in legal terms as well: it is *justification*.

B. Familial Metaphors

But while the royal-legal imagery is a vitally important aspect of biblical theology, it is only that—an *aspect*. For such imagery does not begin to exhaust the depth of the riches of biblical theology; indeed, many other conceptual frameworks can be found there. Central to those are the unmistakably *familial* accounts. Here God is portrayed as a parent (and particularly as *Father*). It runs throughout the canon; while it is not widespread in usage in the OT, it is not entirely absent. For instance, Israel is referred to as God's first child (Ex. 4:22), and God is explicitly compared to a father by the psalmist (e.g., Ps. 103:13). But while familial language is less prevalent in the OT, it becomes very prevalent with the advent of the Son as Jesus Christ. For Jesus teaches us to know God *as Father*. When he teaches his disciples to pray, the first words from his mouth are "Our Father . . ." (e.g., Matt. 6:9). Through his filial relationship to his Father,

---

[167] Wright, *Paul and the Faithfulness of God*, 900, emphasis original.

Jesus draws us into that fellowship and invites those who are joined in union to him also to address God as *Abba*.

The corresponding picture of what it means to be rightly related to God is also familial. As we belong to God, we know God precisely as the *children* of God. Thus to sin is to do what is wrong within the context of family. Jesus offers a penetrating account of this in the "parable of the father" (Luke 15:11–32). While this parable is sometimes referred to as the "parable of the prodigal son" (sometimes with an addendum called the "parable of the elder brother"), Jesus makes it clear who is in focus as the central character: "There was a man who had two sons . . ." (v. 11). The parable, well known and dearly beloved by many Christians (including modern Western Christians who find it easy to miss or misunderstand some of the vitally important details), puts the heinous nature of sin in bold relief. Sin, in this story, is the personal rebellion against the authority and goodness of the Father; the wayward son says, in effect, "If you won't just die already, can we at least pretend that you are dead?"[168] Sin is the arrogant and high-handed rejection of the goodness that the Father provides and offers; more fundamentally, it is the rejection of the goodness of the Father himself. Sin, in this story, is ultimately foolish and wasteful. Taking him further than he could have imagined, it lays waste to the Prodigal while making a fool of him.

The relation of the Father to the sinner is particularly intriguing here. The Father actually allows the rebellious son to leave, and to do so while not only squandering the family resources but also bringing harm upon himself and shame to the family (by the abuse of what the Father had bestowed upon him). The contrast between Aristotle's account of greatness and the portrait drawn by Jesus of the Father here is fascinating and instructive.[169] Aristotle's account of greatness includes the claim that the great or magnanimous man (for Aristotle, it must be a male) "is in no hurry" and thus *never runs*.[170] To run is inconsistent with gravitas and dignity. To run is to show need or weakness, and the great man never runs (other people run to him when he beckons; the "greater" he is, the farther and faster they will run). In sharpest and striking contrast, Jesus describes the Father as one who sees the returning wayward son at a great distance (which happens only if one is actively looking) and as the one who *runs* to his son! The Father "felt compassion, and ran and embraced

<hr/>

[168] See Kenneth E. Bailey, *The Cross and the Prodigal: Luke 15 through the Eyes of Middle Eastern Peasants* (Downers Grove, IL: IVP Academic, 2005).
[169] By "contrast" I mean a conceptual contrast; I do not mean to suggest that this contrast is present within the text of Luke's Gospel or that it was intentionally and explicitly drawn by Jesus. Nonetheless, it remains instructive. For an instructive comparison and contrast of Augustine's account with that of Aristotle, see Craig A. Boyd, "Pride and Humility," in *Virtues and Their Vices*, ed. Kevin Timpe and Craig A. Boyd (Oxford: Oxford University Press, 2014), 247–251.
[170] E.g., Aristotle, *Nichomachean Ethics* IV.3.35, trans. with introduction Terence Irwin (Indianapolis: Hackett, 1999), 59.

him and kissed him" (Luke 15:20). The Father then provides the best for him and celebrates in joy. For, as he tells his sulking older son, "it was fitting to celebrate and be glad, for this your brother was dead, and is alive; he was lost, and is found" (v. 32).

Salvation or redemption from sin is thus also to be understood in familial categories. Jesus makes this plain as well when he uses overtly familial language. Language of generation, and thus also of *regeneration*, is decidedly familial in nature. As Jesus tells Nicodemus, "unless one is born again he cannot see the kingdom of God" (John 3:3). In addition to Jesus's language of the new birth, Paul vividly describes the doctrine in familial terms (albeit somewhat different ones) when he refers to it as *adoption*. Paul here draws upon a deep background in the OT: Israel is adopted as God's child (e.g., Ex. 4:22; Deut. 32:10; Hos. 11:1), and God treats Israel as a (sometimes wayward) child (e.g., Deut. 32:10–14, 19–20; Hos. 11:3–4, 8–11; cf. Isa. 43:6; Jer. 3:12–19).[171] Paul then connects this concept to the work of the incarnate Son and the Holy Spirit (e.g., Rom. 8:15, 23; 9:4; Gal. 4:5; Eph. 1:5). We are adopted into God's family as we are joined in union with Christ, and this occurs through the work of the Holy Spirit, who is the "Spirit of adoption" (Rom. 8:15).[172] The "Spirit of God" (Rom. 8:9, 15) is the "Spirit of Christ" (v. 9), and this Spirit now "dwells" (v. 11) in those who are united to Christ. Thus Paul exclaims,

> [a]ll who are led by the Spirit of God are sons of God. For you did not receive the spirit of slavery to fall back into fear, but you have received the Spirit of adoption as sons, by whom we cry, "Abba! Father!" The Spirit himself bears witness with our spirit that we are children of God, and if children, then heirs—heirs of God and fellow heirs with Christ, provided we suffer with him in order that we may also be glorified with him. (vv. 14–17)

To summarize, sin is rightly understood not only as the transgression of a legal code but also as the fracturing of a precious and intimate familial bond. It is increasingly and intensely personal in nature. Sin is rejection and rebellion— rejection and rebellion against the Holy One who is not only the sovereign ruler of the cosmos but also the loving Father who desires the best for his children. Salvation, accordingly, is depicted in familial terms: new birth and adoption. Law is not ultimate; love is.

---

[171] For further discussion see R. E. Ciampa, "Adoption," in *New Dictionary of Biblical Theology*, ed. T. Desmond Alexander, Brian S. Rosner, D. A. Carson, and Graeme Goldsworthy (Downers Grove, IL: IVP Academic, 2000), 376–377; and William E. Brown, "Adoption," in *EDBT*, 11–12.
[172] See the in-depth discussion in Constantine R. Campbell, *Paul and Union with Christ: An Exegetical and Theological Study* (Grand Rapids, MI: Zondervan, 2012).

C. *The Nuptial Metaphor*

While the royal-legal and familial accounts of sin are commonly discussed and widely understood, the next portrait is less familiar. It is also more unsettling. This is the nuptial account.[173] As Kinlaw notes, this "metaphor is an even more intimate one than that of parent and child. It comes from the closest of all human relationships, that between a man and a woman who are bound together in the sacred covenant of matrimony."[174] Here God's relation to his people is said to be like the union of marriage in important respects. In the OT, at points this portrait is a rosy and encouraging one. For instance, Jeremiah's words from Yahweh recall "the devotion of your youth, your love as a bride" (Jer. 2:2). The Song of Songs (as traditionally interpreted as a picture of Christ's love for his church) pulsates with anticipation and excitement, and it is filled with joy and contented fulfillment in faithful love.

But while some of the portrayal is positive, much of the OT development of this metaphor is negative. Indeed, much of it is depressing and even disturbing. Worship of idols is called prostitution in the Torah (e.g., Ex. 34:15; Lev. 17:7; 20:5; Deut. 31:16). The prophets cry out in protest and warning. An entire book, Hosea, explores this in heartrending fashion (cf. Isa. 1:21–23; 5:8–30; Jer. 2:23–24; 3:1–2; 18:13; Ezek. 6:9; Mic. 1:7; Mal. 2:13–17). Perhaps nowhere is the depiction more stark than in Ezekiel's prophecy:

> But you trusted in your beauty and played the whore because of your renown and lavished your whorings on any passerby; your beauty became his. You took some of your garments and made for yourself colorful shrines, and on them played the whore. The like has never been, nor ever shall be. You also took your beautiful jewels of my gold and of my silver, which I had given you, and made for yourself images of men, and with them played the whore. And you took your embroidered garments to cover them, and set my oil and incense before them. . . . And you took your sons and your daughters, whom you had borne to me, and these you sacrificed to them to be devoured. Were your whorings so small a matter that you slaughtered my children and delivered them up as an offering by fire to them? (Ezek. 16:15–18, 20–21)

Yahweh's verdict is unmistakable: "[H]ow sick is your heart" (Ezek. 16:30). It is so sick that "you did all these things, the deeds of a brazen prostitute, building your vaulted chamber at the head of every street, and making your lofty place in every square" (vv. 30–31). Indeed, it is so perverted that "you were not like a prostitute, because you scorned payment" and instead "gave your gifts to all

---

[173] See Raymond C. Ortlund Jr., *God's Unfaithful Wife: A Biblical Theology of Spiritual Adultery* (Downers Grove, IL: IVP Academic, 1996).
[174] Kinlaw, *Let's Start with Jesus*, 57.

your lovers, bribing them to come to you from every side with your whorings" (vv. 31, 33). Their twisted perversion was so awful that even their pagan neighbors were embarrassed by it![175]

As bleak and horrific as all of this is, however, the OT also holds out a promise of hope. This is the promise of God's work to establish a new covenant and restore his bride. Thus Ezekiel looks forward in anticipation: "Yet I will remember my covenant with you in the days of your youth, and I will establish for you an everlasting covenant" (Ezek. 16:60). Similarly, God says,

> For Zion's sake I will not keep silent,
>   and for Jerusalem's sake I will not be quiet,
> until her righteousness goes forth as brightness,
>   and her salvation as a burning torch.
> The nations shall see your righteousness,
>   and all the kings your glory,
> and you shall be called by a new name
>   that the mouth of the LORD will give.
> You shall be a crown of beauty in the hand of the LORD,
>   and a royal diadem in the hand of your God.
> You shall no more be termed Forsaken,
>   and your land shall no more be termed Desolate,
> but you shall be called My Delight Is in Her,
>   and your land Married;
> for the LORD delights in you,
>   and your land shall be married.
> For as a young man marries a young woman,
>   so shall your sons marry you,
> and as the bridegroom rejoices over the bride,
>   so shall your God rejoice over you. (Isa. 62:1–5)

Sin, as horrific and terrifying as it is, still does not have the last word. Instead, the prophets look forward with hope.

This theme is picked up in the NT, and the message of hope is accentuated as anticipation builds for fulfillment. John the Baptist characterizes his own ministry with the language of marriage. When his followers question his relationship to Jesus, he responds by saying,

> [a] person cannot receive even one thing unless it is given him from heaven. You yourselves bear me witness, that I said, "I am not the Christ, but I have been sent before him." The one who has the bride is the bridegroom. The friend of the bridegroom, who stands and hears him, rejoices greatly at the bridegroom's voice. Therefore this joy of mine is now complete. He must increase, but I must decrease. (John 3:27–30)

---

[175] See the helpful discussion of Daniel I. Block, *The Book of Ezekiel 1–24*, NICOT (Grand Rapids, MI: Eerdmans, 1997), 495–497.

As Kinlaw observes,

> Jesus uses the same figure to explain himself. All three of the Synoptics give us the story of people coming to Jesus to ask him why his disciples did not fast. They noted that John's disciples and the disciples of the Pharisees made it a pattern to fast but his disciples did not. Jesus' response makes it clear that the nuptial character of Israel's election determined his understanding of his own mission: "How can the guests of *the bridegroom* fast while he is with them? They cannot, so long as they have him with them. But the time will come when *the bridegroom* will be taken from them, and on that day they will fast" (Mark 2:19–20, emphasis added).[176]

In John's Gospel the first "sign" performed by Jesus is at a wedding (John 2:1–11), and Jesus will commonly refer to his mission in terms of marriage. For "the kingdom of heaven may be compared to a king who gave a wedding feast for his son" (Matt. 22:2).

Paul's teaching employs this theme as well, and he compares the relation of Christ and the church to that between a husband and wife. The marital theme is prevalent and powerful as a metaphor for God's relationship to his people. It is also potent as a depiction of sin and its consequences, and it is beautiful with respect to the hope of salvation. And here we see the fulfillment of the promises of cleansing and renewal for God's people: "Christ loved the church and gave himself up for her, that he might sanctify her, having cleansed her by the washing of water with the word, so that he might present the church to himself in splendor, without spot or wrinkle or any such thing, that she might be holy and without blemish" (Eph. 5:25–27). Indeed, the story of the biblical canon actually climaxes with the wedding supper of the Lamb! For "'the marriage of the Lamb has come, and his Bride has made herself ready; it was granted her to clothe herself with fine linen, bright and pure'—for the fine linen is the righteous deeds of the saints" (Rev. 19:7–8; cf. 21:2, 9). And while the final depiction of the unrepentant and rebellious sinners is as "the great prostitute" that is "Babylon" (e.g., Rev. 17:1–5), the final invitation to receive the salvation provided by Christ and offered by the Spirit is this: "*The Spirit and the Bride* say, 'Come.' And let the one who hears say 'Come.' And let the one who is thirsty come; let the one who desires take the water of life without price" (Rev. 22:17).

The nuptial or marital metaphor has much to teach us. Its importance cannot be denied. As Kinlaw puts it, "If history began with a wedding in Eden and closes with one in the New Jerusalem, the biblical story runs from

[176] Kinlaw, *Let's Start with Jesus*, 61.

wedding to wedding, from temporal symbol to eternal reality."[177] Specifically, it teaches us that sin should be understood as akin to adultery and other forms of sexual infidelity and misconduct. And, importantly, it teaches us that God's salvation includes nothing less than radical renewal and cleansing—for God himself promises to make his Son's bride radiant and beautiful once again.

D. Conclusion: Sin as Idolatry

Throughout all of this, the depiction of sin as *idolatry* surfaces again and again. As Sklar notes, in addition to having obvious royal-legal connotations, idolatry is also explicitly linked to the familial and nuptial metaphors: idolatry is "a 'serving' of other gods (Exod. 23.24, 33; Deut. 7.4; 13.6), instead of faithfully serving the Lord as a son does the father he loves (Exod. 4.23); it is a 'forsaking' of the Lord for other gods (Deut. 31.16) instead of 'cleaving' to the Lord in faithful love as one might do with a spouse (Deut. 10.20; 13.4 [13.5]; 30.20; cf. Gen. 2.24). While sin is sometimes thought of today as the breaking of a rule, these metaphors emphasize that it is the breaking of a relationship, an act of treachery against the Lord, the faithful covenant king and father and husband."[178] For whom is this intended? For whom are these portraits relevant? They are relevant for all people, believers and unbelievers alike. For they portray the actual situation of believers, and they illustrate what is potentially the case for all sinners.

---

[177] Kinlaw, *Let's Start with Jesus*, 64.
[178] Sklar, "Pentateuch," 6.

CHAPTER

THREE

THE ORIGIN OF SIN

I. INTRODUCTION

Unde malum? Whence evil? Where did it all come from? Where did things begin to go downhill—and so drastically? Are sin and evil inevitable? Is sin part of the integral structure of the created order? In this chapter, we explore some perplexing issues related to the origin of sin. After a look at the primeval account of temptation and fall, we shall engage in further theological reflection on the origin of human and angelic sin.

II. TEMPTATION AND FALL

Immediately following the primeval creation accounts in Genesis, we are confronted with a fascinating and sobering narrative. Here we find the description of the "fall" of humankind into sin. Interestingly, none of the major Hebrew words for "sin" are used here. Yet the focus of this account is unmistakable; it concerns the first instance of when things went so horribly wrong. Horst Dietrich Preuss explains that although "the expression 'sin' occurs nowhere in this narrative," this is because "[i]ts content is not defined but rather narrated. 'Sin' in Genesis 2–3 consists of the desire of humans to be autonomous, to use their God-given freedom (Isa. 1:18–20) to decide against God. Sin is also understood as the failure to recognize the authority of God and as preferring to discuss the divine word rather than observe it (Gen. 3:1–3)."[1] This is consistent with the OT witness to sin generally, for as Walther Eichrodt notes, "when the Old Testament speaks of sin *the chief emphasis* unquestionably *falls on its current concrete expression.*"[2] Indeed, nowhere in Scripture is a doctrine of sin explicated or explained in any sort of abstract way. Thomas F. Torrance is right when he says that "neither in the Old Testament or the New Testament do we have a deliberate attempt to formulate a doctrine of sin first in an independent

---

[1] Horst Dietrich Preuss, *Old Testament Theology*, 2 vols., TOTL (Louisville: Westminster/John Knox, 1995), 2:171.
[2] Walther Eichrodt, *Theology of the Old Testament, Volume Two* (Philadelphia, 1961), 401, emphasis original.

or abstract way and then to show over against that background the grace and love of God in redemption."[3] Instead, we first learn about sin in the story line of the Bible; we begin to understand it as we see it in the canonical narrative. And this begins with the story of the primal sin.

A. The Setting

At the end of the creation account we find the first humans in a setting that is peaceful, safe, and beautiful—in short, a place of genuine *shalom*. *Shalom* is, as Cornelius Plantinga reminds us, what the prophets dreamed of when they longed for a day when "all nature would be fruitful, benign, and filled with wonder upon wonder; all humans would be knit together in brotherhood and sisterhood, and all humans would look to God, walk with God, lean toward God, and delight in God."[4] Plantinga describes this vision further:

> The webbing together of God, humans, and all creation in justice, fulfillment, and delight is what the Hebrew prophets call *shalom*. We call it peace, but it means far more than mere peace of mind or a cease-fire between enemies. In the Bible, shalom means *universal flourishing, wholeness, and delight*—a rich state of affairs in which natural needs are satisfied and natural gifts fruitfully employed, a state of affairs that inspires joyful wonder as its Creator and Savior opens doors and welcomes the creatures in whom he delights. Shalom, in other words, is the way things ought to be.[5]

The environment is stable and peaceful; the actions of Adam and Eve show complete and beautiful innocence.

Neither their environment nor their life together is likely best characterized as "perfect." Given the ambiguity associated with the term "perfection" and the paucity of biblical data supporting such claims, it seems best to stay close to the theologians of the Christian tradition who emphasize that Adam and Eve enjoyed total innocence. As Bonaventure says, "But man, made out of nothingness, and imperfect as he was by nature, had the capacity of acting for ends other than God; of acting for himself instead of for God, and thus not properly by the power of God, nor according to God, nor for God as an end."[6] But they indeed were innocent and blameless.

The status of Adam and Eve is, to use the traditional terms, *posse peccare et posse non peccare* rather than *non posse non peccare* or *non posse peccare*.[7]

---

[3] Thomas F. Torrance, *Incarnation: The Person and Life of Christ*, ed. Robert T. Walker (Downers Grove, IL: IVP Academic, 2008), 245.

[4] Cornelius Plantinga Jr., *Not the Way It's Supposed to Be: A Breviary of Sin* (Grand Rapids, MI: Eerdmans, 1996), 9–10.

[5] Plantinga, *Not the Way*, 10.

[6] Bonaventure, *The Breviloquium* III.1, in *The Works of Bonaventure*, vol. 2 (Paterson, NJ: St. Anthony's Guild Press, 1963), 110.

[7] Cf. Augustine, *De correptione et gratia* 33 (PL 44:956; NPNF¹ 5:485).

That is, it is possible that they either sin or not sin. It is not impossible for them to refrain from sinning, nor is it not possible for them to sin. They are, in a word, *innocent*. They are innocent of sin, but they are neither doomed to sin nor completely protected from the possibility of engaging in it.

The first humans revel in *shalom* and enjoy sweet communion. They share fellowship and communion with their Creator. Their relationship is one of complete and total trust; they are accustomed to walking with the Lord God in the garden in the cool of the day (Gen. 3:8). As John Goldingay notes, this "indicates that humanity is designed to enjoy a relaxed friendship with God."[8] Eichrodt makes a similar point, one that looks ahead and makes use of this insight to better understand the goal of redemption: "*communion with the will of God is grasped as the ultimate goal of all desire for salvation*," and thus "is not exhausted by remission of punishment, but includes as its most important content readmission to fellowship with him."[9]

The first humans also share sweet communion with each other. They are made for each other, they belong together, they are appropriate to each other. They are made to "become one flesh" (Gen. 2:24). Together bearing the image of God, they share "perfect equality as human persons" in the glorious fittingness of their irreducible differences as man and woman.[10] There is nothing in the biblical account to suggest that, prior to the fall, there was anything other than harmony, trust, and *shalom* in the relationship of Adam and Eve.

Moreover, the first humans enjoy *shalom* with respect to the rest of creation. It is clear from the creation account that they were created to "have dominion over the fish of the sea and over the birds of the heavens and over the livestock and over all the earth and over every creeping thing that creeps on the earth" (Gen. 1:26). Adam and Eve were made in the image of God, and they were to bear and reflect that image by reflecting divine sovereignty.[11] They were made to be "sovereign." As Eugene Merrill states the point, "[T]hey were created to share dominion over the earth (Gen. 1:26–27), and their essential equality in doing this is evident from the fact that it was not good for the man to be alone; he needed a partner who corresponded to him and made him complete (Gen. 2:20–23). The two in mutual forbearance were called to be the image of God in implementing the exercise of his sovereignty."[12] Their work (2:15) in Eden is

[8] John Goldingay, *Old Testament Theology, Volume One: Israel's Gospel* (Downers Grove, IL: InterVarsity Press, 2003), 136.
[9] Eichrodt, *Theology of the Old Testament*, 457, emphasis original.
[10] *Catechism of the Catholic Church*, 2nd ed., rev. in accordance with the official Latin text promulgated by Pope John Paul II (Washington, DC: United States Catholic Conference, 2000), 94.
[11] This does not exhaust the meaning of the *imago dei*.
[12] Eugene H. Merrill, *Everlasting Dominion: A Theology of the Old Testament* (Nashville: Broadman & Holman, 2006), 203. Merrill goes on to affirm a kind of "complementarian" account of gender relations (further discussion of which is beyond the scope of this work).

meaningful and rewarding; they recognize, embrace, and fulfill their calling to serve as overseers and stewards of creation.

Made in the image of God, the first humans were charged with exercising sovereignty over the rest of creation. And in the absence of sin, they did so in a state of *shalom*. They did so *together*; their work was done in the ontologically prior relationship of man and woman, vitally and beautifully distinct while essentially and fully equal. Accordingly, they did so in the joy of their innocence, in the clear purposiveness and rich meaningfulness of their life together. And all of this was in the all-important context of a right relationship with their Creator. The *Catechism of the Catholic Church* speaks for catholic (universal) historic Christianity when it says that "the first man was not only created good, but was also established in friendship with his Creator and in harmony with himself and with the creation around him, in a state that would be surpassed only by the glory of the new creation in Christ. . . . [thus] our first parents, Adam and Eve, were constituted in an original 'state of holiness and justice.' This grace of original holiness was 'to share in . . . divine life.'"[13]

B. *The Way of Temptation*

Bonaventure reflected upon the steps of the first temptation, and he offers this overview: "Then the devil, envious of man, assumed the form of a serpent and addressed the woman, first asking, 'Did God say: You shall not eat . . . ?'; then asserting, 'you shall not die'; then promising, 'you shall be like God, knowing good and evil.'"[14] The temptation begins with the serpent's beguilement of Eve, and this starts with a question: "Did God actually say, 'You shall not eat of any tree in the garden?'" (Gen. 3:1). John Calvin points out that "[a]ssuredly, when the word of God is despised, all reverence for him is gone. His majesty cannot be duly honoured among us, nor his worship maintained in its integrity, unless we hang as it were upon his lips. Hence infidelity was at the root of the revolt."[15] Bruce Waltke notes that "Satan has no advantage over Eve or us until he diverts our attention with the possibility of disobeying."[16] The serpent's question serves to plant a "seed of doubt about God's goodness,"[17] and thus raises questions about the sincerity and reliability of God. This, the first step toward sin, is to entertain the notion that God may actually be malevolent, or devious, or divided in himself.

Satan then emphasizes the divine prohibition; instead of focusing upon

---

[13] *Catechism of the Catholic Church*, 95.
[14] Bonaventure, *Breviloquium*, III.2, in *Works*, vol. 2, 112.
[15] John Calvin, *Institutes of the Christian Religion*, trans. Henry Beveridge (Grand Rapids, MI: Eerdmans, 1997), II.1 (213).
[16] Bruce K. Waltke, *An Old Testament Theology: An Exegetical, Canonical, and Thematic Approach* (Grand Rapids, MI: Zondervan, 2007), 261.
[17] William Dyrness, *Themes in Old Testament Theology* (Downers Grove, IL: InterVarsity Press, 1977), 101.

both the good gifts provided by God and the trustworthy character of her Creator, Eve allowed Satan to shift her focus to what God had prohibited.[18] This is followed by the outright denial of the word of God: "You will not surely die" (Gen. 3:4). Satan then offers the fruit as a sinful possibility.

C. The Fall

Eve then takes the forbidden fruit, eats it, and shares it with Adam. Adam, who alone appears to have received the direct prohibition (Gen. 2:16–17), takes the fruit from her and eats it with no sign of hesitation (3:6). The simplicity and seemingly inconsequential nature of these actions is stunning. Compared to what follows—and here we need look no further than the murder of Abel by his brother Cain in the next chapter—the actions themselves seem unremarkable. Eve simply takes what is offered to her, and then shares it with Adam. And all they have done is take of the fruit of a tree in the garden. Indeed, this is fruit from a tree that itself is part of a creation that has been pronounced "good" (Gen. 1:31). The action seems so benign. Is this what upsets the creation order? Is this what warps all humanity henceforth? *This?*

But the apparently benign or insignificant nature of these actions actually serves to underscore their gravity and severity. The actions of Adam and Eve were momentous, for "the heart of the temptation, symbolized by the eating of the prohibited fruit, was the desire to be like God and to be free from dependence upon him."[19] The sin itself consists not in eating fruit that elsewhere God had pronounced "good"; the sin consists in the disregard and rejection of God's will and ways. In this light, we can begin to see that it is such rejection and rebellion that is so terribly heinous—and even the things we think small or insignificant are momentous when done in opposition to the revealed will of God.

D. The Immediate Consequences of the Fall

The consequences of the fall are as far-reaching as they are serious. As Goldingay puts it, "Sin stains us, makes us disgusting, alienates us from God, leaves us unhealed. . . . [The Old Testament] has a number of ways of seeing the impact of that: blinding, exposure, shame, war, wasting, annihilation, expulsion, withering, dissolution, death."[20] The immediate consequences of the fall are also both drastic and obvious. Shame settles on Adam and Eve. In direct contrast to their unashamed nakedness (Gen. 2:25), they now realize that they are naked, and they are ashamed and afraid (3:8–11). Brevard

---

[18] As noted by Waltke, *Old Testament Theology*, 262.
[19] Brevard S. Childs, *Biblical Theology of the Old and New Testaments* (Minneapolis: Fortress, 1993), 570.
[20] John Goldingay, *Old Testament Theology, Volume Two: Israel's Faith* (Downers Grove, IL: InterVarsity Press, 2006), 278.

Childs notes that in "the age of innocence 'the man and his wife were both naked, but were not ashamed' (2.25)," and he points out that "[t]hey were unashamed because they were complete beings, sharing an uninterrupted harmony with God and the world."[21] But "suddenly" we see something very different in this narrative; there is "an entirely different terminology to depict the change. Adam said: 'I was afraid, because I was naked, and I hid myself.' (3.10). The sense of shame becomes the outward sign of inner dissolution."[22] Childs here echoes the earlier observation of Gerhard Von Rad: "Shame . . . always has to be seen as the signal of the loss of an inner unity, an insurmountable contradiction at the basis of our existence."[23] Adam and Eve now feel this shame, and it is because what is at the core of their existence—their relationship with their Creator—is now broken.

Estrangement and alienation also strike the relationships of Adam and Eve, and wreak havoc on all of these relationships. Their relationship with God is immediately altered; instead of trusting in God as their source of life and the guarantor of *shalom*, they now hide in fear and shame. As Calvin observes, "[A]s Adam's spiritual life would have consisted in being united and bound to his Maker, so estrangement from him was the death of his soul."[24] Adam and Eve's relationship with their Creator—the relationship which initiates, sustains, and nourishes life, the relationship which offers meaning and purpose to their existence, the relationship which provides rest and security, the relationship which orients and encompasses all others in their lives—is now ruptured. Torrance points out that "sin is utter separation from God, alienation from God," and this presupposes a prior and all-important relationship with God: "Sin as severance from God presupposes a life-unity with the creator given by the Holy Spirit. . . . The creature requires relation to the creator in order to be a creature. That relation is given and maintained by the Spirit of God who creates the existence of the creature, but of the creature as a reality distinct from God himself, yet wholly dependent on God for what it is."[25] But "in sin the human creature who depends on the creator for its existence and life rebels against the creator."[26] And when this rebellion occurs, when this life-giving and life-sustaining relationship is broken, everything else changes as well.

The estrangement from God produces immediate and dire consequences for the relationship of Adam and Eve. Where before they find cooperation, companionship, and delight in each other, now they distrust each other and

---

[21] Brevard Childs, *Old Testament Theology in a Canonical Context* (Minneapolis: Fortress, 1985), 224.
[22] Childs, *Old Testament Theology in a Canonical Context*, 224.
[23] Gerhard Von Rad, *Genesis: A Commentary*, rev. ed., TOTL (Louisville: Westminster/John Knox, 1973), 85.
[24] Calvin, *Institutes*, II.1 (214).
[25] Torrance, *Incarnation*, 247.
[26] Torrance, *Incarnation*, 247.

shift blame to each other. Childs offers particularly insightful commentary on this result, and it is worth quoting him at length:

> It is also not by chance that the Old Testament portrays human sexuality as the mirror of the disruption. Sex is introduced in ch. 2 as part of the gracious acts of God's good creation. God said: 'It is not good for man to be alone' (2.18). God is then pictured as escorting Eve to the astonished Adam (cf. *Genesis Rabbah*). The conclusion to ch. 2 rings with joyful enthusiasm as the man and the woman are united in one flesh.
>
> Shortly thereafter the world is filled with violence, and Lamech boasts before his several wives of his savagery (4.23f). The divine gift of human sexuality has been twisted to become a major threat to both faith and life. The rest of the Old Testament is filled with stories of sexual abuse as the once creative drive for good is unleashed with demonic power to destroy.[27]

What is exemplified in human sexuality is not limited to such expressions. Torrance's summary is apt: "The tragic situation of man revealed here is that men and women are alienated from themselves, alienated from who they were made to be, creatures and children of God."[28]

As with the relationships with God and one another, so also the relationship with creation is shattered by the fall. Adam and Eve were created and instructed to be the stewards of creation, and there is no hint in the text that their labors were anything but meaningful sources of fulfillment and joy. But with the fall, that changes as well. Because of their sin, the ground—*not Adam and Eve*—is cursed (Gen. 3:17), and Adam is told,

> in pain you shall eat of it all the days of your life;
> thorns and thistles it shall bring forth for you;
> and you shall eat the plants of the field.
> By the sweat of your face
> you shall eat bread,
> till you return to the ground,
> for out of it you were taken;
> for you are dust,
> and to dust you shall return. (Gen. 3:17–19)

Von Rad reminds us of how utterly basic was Adam's relationship with the earth; Adam had come from the soil, and he received his nourishment from it. "But this relationship has been broken, resulting in an estrangement which is

---

[27] Childs, *Old Testament Theology in a Canonical Context*, 224. Martha Nussbaum notes that "[t]he original inhabitants of the Garden were not ashamed. . . . It is when sexuality is bound up with disobedience, uncontrol, and ungovernability that a shame falls upon human beings that renders them all equally low" (*Upheavals of Thought: The Intelligence of Emotions* [Cambridge: Cambridge University Press, 2001], 554).
[28] Torrance, *Incarnation*, 242.

expressed in a silent combat between man and the soil. For man's sake a curse lies upon the soil, and it now refuses to let him win its produce easily."[29]

With the sin comes direct judgment from God. The first judgment is pronounced upon the serpent, and with it comes a curse:

> Because you have done this,
>> cursed are you above all livestock
>> and above all beasts of the field;
> on your belly you shall go,
>> and dust shall you eat
>> all the days of your life.
> I will put enmity between you and the woman,
>> and between your offspring and her offspring;
> he shall bruise your head,
>> and you shall bruise his heel. (Gen. 3:14–15)[30]

The next judgment is given to the woman:

> I will surely multiply your pain in childbearing:
>> in pain you shall bring forth children.
> Your desire shall be contrary to your husband,
>> but he shall rule over you. (Gen. 3:16)

The last judgment is given to the man.

Torrance observes that "[i]t belongs to the nature of sin to divide, to create disorder, to disrupt, to destroy fellowship." He asks, "What are the consequences of sin?" His answer is insightful, and I quote in extenso:

> Not only is the bond of communion between God and man broken, issuing in man's guilty fear of God, but the bond between man and woman is impaired: guilt and shame come in between them, and even the symbol of wearing clothes is interpreted in terms of the hiddenness of man from woman and of woman from man. The man-woman relationship is involved in the broken relation with God. With the bond between them broken, man and woman are individualised, and each is turned in upon himself or herself. But even the unity of man as male, and the unity of woman as female, within the individual heart is disrupted, in the knowledge of good and evil. Each knows that he or she is no longer what he or she ought to be.
>
> Thus the rupture in the relation between God and man, and man and woman, entails a rupture within each between what a person *is* and what the person *ought* to be. Once the constitutive bond between God and man is broken, every other relation suffers irreparable damage. And so we find the relation between man and the environment broken. . . . man now exists in

---

[29] Gerhard Von Rad, *Old Testament Theology, Volume 1* (New York: Harper & Row, 1962), 159.

[30] Goldingay points out that "although the blessing and the curse are correlative, they are not exact antonyms. God actively blesses; God does not actively curse, but declares that the snake and ground are cursed" (*Old Testament Theology, Volume One*, 139).

a state of tension with nature. Man must earn his living by the sweat of his brow, and woman has pain in childbirth. Mankind is out of gear with nature, and anxiety characterises their life.[31]

Everything—the integrity of the first humans as persons, their relations to each other, and their relationship to their environment—is broken and tragically damaged by their rebellion against God. At this point, we can see that the *Catechism of the Catholic Church* offers a helpful summary when it says that

> the harmony in which they had found themselves, thanks to original justice, is now destroyed: the control of the soul's spiritual faculties over the body is shattered; the union of man and woman becomes subject to tensions, their relations henceforth marked by lust and domination. Harmony with creation is broken: visible creation has become alien and hostile to man. Because of man, creation is now subject "to its bondage of decay." Finally, the consequences foretold for this disobedience will come true: man will "return to the ground," for out of it he was taken. *Death makes its entrance into human history.*[32]

E. Further Theological Reflection

Dietrich Bonhoeffer makes the observation that the scene of the temptation is the place of the first conversation in theology; it is "the first conversation about God, the first religious, theological conversation. It is not prayer or calling upon God together but speaking about God, going beyond him."[33] While the narrative of Genesis to this point has employed YHWH (or Yahweh, or "LORD") as what we come to know as the covenant name of God, the Serpent and Eve talk about him only as "God."[34] In other words, the Creator with whom they share relationship has now been reduced to "the deity." When we talk about God in his "absence," it becomes easy to distrust him. And when this happens, the possibility of sin is right before us. This is especially appropriate to consider when thinking about the prohibition given by God. Satan worked to get Eve to focus on the negative, and he worked further to cast suspicion on the character of God. Satan insinuated that God must be petty or somehow threatened by the possibility that the humans could "know" good and evil and thus be "like God" (Gen. 3:5). In other words, God doesn't want us to "know" good and evil, therefore he must be trying to keep something good for himself rather than share it with us. Von Rad notes that "with a father's disposition God had purposed every conceivable kindness for man; but his will was that in the realm of knowledge a limit should remain set between himself and

---

[31] Torrance, *Incarnation*, 38–39.

[32] *Catechism of the Catholic Church*, 100–101, emphasis original.

[33] Dietrich Bonhoeffer, *Creation and Fall, Temptation: Two Biblical Studies* (New York: Simon & Schuster, 1997), 76.

[34] As noted in C. John Collins, *Genesis 1–4: A Linguistic, Literary, and Theological Commentary* (Phillipsburg, NJ: P&R, 2006), 171; and Gordon J. Wenham, *Genesis 1–15*, WBC (Waco, TX: Word, 1987), 73.

mankind."[35] But Von Rad also notes that the usage of *yāda'* ("to know") here is important. Here *yāda'* is likely being used as it often is elsewhere in the OT (and indeed in Gen. 4:1, 17, 25 it is used to refer to sexual relations)—it is referring to much more than merely intellectual cognition of something; instead it refers to a personal, relational, *experiential* kind of knowledge. The use of *yāda'* is important here because it seems to indicate the divine intentions. It is not as if God was wanting to keep Adam and Eve from the knowledge of good and evil because they might benefit from it so much that they might somehow threaten God's status or reign! Far from it—God cordons off the tree of the knowledge of good and evil by the prohibition *because he desires to protect his children from it.* He knows what Adam and Eve do not know; he knows that this kind of knowledge of good and evil will be nothing other than damaging to them. Much like a father who wants to protect the innocence of his children—much like he does *not* want them to be knowledgeable about, say, abuse or rape—so God graciously prohibits Adam and Eve from what he knows will harm them. The awful irony of temptation and sin is that so often we begin to distrust God's word and doubt the sincerity or goodness of his intentions for us *at exactly the point where he is trying to protect us.* And again, as Bonhoeffer makes plain, this begins to happen whenever we think we can engage in theological discourse that is devoid of an attitude of trust or is cut off from prayer and worship.

Reflection on the fall also reminds us that life in this world is not "the way it's supposed to be."[36] Things are not as they were meant to be, nor are they gradually though steadily going in the right direction. Rather, as Goldingay states, "the Fall was a historical event that altered things in a way that human beings could not reverse. The unsatisfactory state of human life and of our world is neither its natural state nor the result of its not having (yet?) evolved to a more satisfactory one . . ."[37]

We can learn something here from the nature of temptation as well. The temptation does not come from the Creator. Temptation involves something (in this case, the fruit) that in itself and as such is *good* (and has been pronounced as such by the Creator). But it involves the illicit appropriation and use of something that God made and called good for purposes that go against God's good intentions. As James explains,

> Let no one say when he is tempted, "I am being tempted by God," for God cannot be tempted with evil, and he himself tempts no one. But each person is tempted when he is lured and enticed by his own desire. Then desire when

[35] Von Rad, *Old Testament Theology, Volume 1*, 155.
[36] Again, this is the title and theme of Plantinga, *Not the Way It's Supposed to Be.*
[37] Goldingay, *Old Testament Theology, Volume One*, 145.

it has conceived gives birth to sin, and sin when it is fully grown brings forth death. (James 1:13–15)

This is what we see played out in the scene in Eden.

Finally, we should see that divine judgment is sure and certain. What God warned about, he delivered. Divine warnings about sin can never be taken with anything less than utmost seriousness, and divine displeasure against sin is never anything to take lightly. Sin incurs nothing less than the wrath of God. Alongside this sobering realization, however, we should also remember that the judgment comes with a promise of salvation (Gen. 3:15), and we should see that the judgment itself is a statement of mercy. With the judgment and the pronouncement of a curse come the statement that the "offspring" of the woman will "bruise" the "head" of the serpent. And with these words we get the first hint or "first glimmer of the gospel. It is Christ who will destroy the works of the devil (Mt. 1:23; Col. 2:15; 1 Tim. 2:15; Gal. 4:4)."[38]

Furthermore, the pronouncement of judgment itself is important for these reasons. As Eichrodt explains, "That which makes this complex of guilt and punishment a compelling necessity is *the opposition*, revealed in sin, *between Man's conduct and God's nature*. The Holy One of Israel, whose transcendence is revealed in the fact that he carries out his personal moral will whatever the resistance, is bound to answer rebellion against himself with a punitive judgment which will reveal to the whole world how impotent sin is in fighting against him. The divine love that woos a return of love from Man must make it plain that to reject God's love is to forfeit the only salvation."[39] Judgment from God is not a matter of mere chance, nor is it "dependent upon caprice or malice," as if God were merely out to pay someone back for the insults he has suffered. No, Eichrodt is correct when he says that divine judgment of sin, in all its frightening and powerful intensity, is "rooted instead in the essential nature of God's revelation."[40]

And beyond that, it is rooted in the essential nature of God himself. With characteristic force, Torrance insists that we take with full seriousness what it means to recognize the wrath of God when he points out that

[i]t is the *wrath of the lamb*, the wrath of redeeming love. As such the very wrath of God is a sign of hope, not of utter destruction—for if God chastises us then we are sons and daughters, and not bastards, as the scripture puts it. Judgement and wrath mean that far from casting us off, God comes within the existence and relation between the creator and the creature, and negates the contradiction we have introduced into it by and in our sin. God's wrath

---

[38] Dyrness, *Themes in Old Testament Theology*, 103.
[39] Eichrodt, *Theology of the Old Testament*, 433, emphasis original.
[40] Eichrodt, *Theology of the Old Testament*, 433.

means that God declares in no uncertain terms that what he has made *he still affirms as his own good handiwork and will not cast it off into nothingness.* Wrath means that God asserts himself against us as holy and loving creator in the midst of our sin and perversity and alienation. God's wrath is God's judgement of sin, but it is a judgement in which God asserts that he is the God of the sinner and that the sinner is God's creature: it is a wrath that asserts God's ownership of the creature and that asserts the binding of the creature to the holy and loving God. . . . it must take the form of judgement over against sin, but a reaffirmation that the creature belongs to God and that he refuses to cease to be its God and therefore refuses to let it go. God's very wrath tells us that we are children of God. It is the rejection of evil, of our evil by the very love that God himself eternally is.[41]

Here, as elsewhere, it is a serious theological mistake to think of God as somehow "composed" of various and competing attributes, and then to conclude that God deals with some people according to his holiness, justice, and wrath, but others according to his mercy, grace, and love. We should not think that God is "made up of" *some love* but also *some holiness* and *some wrath*—as if he had various competing attributes that are in need of being "balanced." Not at all! Divine wrath is not the opposite of divine love. *Indifference*, not wrath, would be the opposite of love.[42] God's wrath just *is* his infinite holy love *as it is expressed against sin and wickedness.* Accordingly, as Stephen T. Davis puts it, "God's wrath is our only hope as human beings."[43]

Indeed, the biblical account itself explicitly connects the first judgment of God upon sin with the first promise of the gospel: the descendant of Eve would "bruise the head" of the serpent. In this, the famous *protoevangelium*, the promise is given: "I will put enmity between you and the woman, and between your offspring and her offspring; he shall bruise your head, and you shall bruise his heel" (Gen. 3:15). The judgment of God—because of the nature of the God who pronounces it—is reason for hope. "Where sin increased, grace abounded all the more" (Rom. 5:20).

III. The Origin of Human Sin

We now proceed to further theological reflection on the origin of human sin. Historic Christian doctrine has rejected several views outright, and it is instructive to see both what has been rejected and why these views have been rejected. But not only does historic Christian doctrine rule out certain views; it also makes some important affirmations about the origin of human sin.

---

[41] Torrance, *Incarnation*, 249–250, emphasis original.
[42] I think that I owe this point to C. S. Lewis, but I cannot locate the exact source. See C. S. Lewis, *The Problem of Pain* (New York: Macmillan, 1962), 39-48.
[43] Stephen T. Davis, *Christian Philosophical Theology* (Oxford: Oxford University Press, 2006), 213, 216.

A. Ultimate Cosmic Dualism Is Ruled Out

What must be ruled out immediately is any suggestion of any kind of cosmic dualism that would posit two (or more) equal or near-equal powers that have existed from eternity. G. C. Berkouwer summarizes dualism as the view "that proposes a primordial antithesis between two original principles (viz., light and darkness) in terms of which every form of good and evil is ultimately deduced."[44] Any view, such as the Manichaeism rejected by Augustine and the Gnosticism rejected by Irenaeus, that holds that there are two powers in heaven that are perpetually warring against one another qualifies as ultimate cosmic dualism.

Not only is there no hint of this dualism in the biblical saga of the creation and fall, such dualism actually goes directly against the grain of the text. Genesis 1–2 presents a God who is utterly and completely sovereign. He speaks the cosmos into existence; by his word alone he frames the world. He does so in the complete and—given the prevalent parallels in the ancient Near East—very striking absence of any conflict. The world does not exist as the by-product of a cosmic war between the powers of good and evil; in fact, there is no such conflict at all in Genesis 1–2. As Goldingay puts it, "[T]he First Testament does not have a concept of evil as a self-existent entity. Its first explicit references to evil (*ra'*) are illuminating. The sequence of the First Testament narrative suggests that one can understand evil only when set over against good (*ṭôb*, Gen 2:9, 17; 3:5, 22). Good preexists evil; there is good in Genesis 1, but no evil. Evil has no existence or definition in itself."[45]

David Bentley Hart rightly observes that there *is* a sort of *provisional* dualism in Scripture. He notes that many Christians have "hastened to resituate the New Testament imagery of spiritual warfare securely within the one all-determining will of God, fearing that to deny that evil and death are the 'left hand' of God's goodness in creation or the necessary 'shadow' of his righteousness would be to deny divine omnipotence as well."[46] But this will not do, says Hart, for however "disturbing . . . it may be, it is clearly the case that there is a kind of 'provisional' cosmic dualism within the New Testament."[47] To be sure, it is "not an ultimate dualism, of course, between two equal principles; but certainly a conflict between a sphere of created autonomy that strives against God on the one hand and the saving love of God in time on the other."[48] Surely Hart is right about this, but he is also correct to insist that in no way is it a dualism between equal or near-equal parties. There simply is no

---

[44] G. C. Berkouwer, *Sin*, Studies in Dogmatics (1971; repr., Grand Rapids, MI: Eerdmans, 1980), 67.
[45] Goldingay, *Old Testament Theology, Volume Two*, 254.
[46] David Bentley Hart, *The Doors of the Sea: Where Was God in the Tsunami?* (Grand Rapids, MI: Eerdmans, 2005), 62.
[47] Hart, *Doors of the Sea*, 62.
[48] Hart, *Doors of the Sea*, 62–63.

room in the creation account, or in any orthodox doctrine of God, for *that* kind of dualism. God is sovereign, and he exists *a se*. Evil has no independent existence, no ultimate status. Speaking more strictly, many theologians of the Christian tradition would say it has no "existence" at all, for it exists only as a "privation of the good." Most assuredly, evil presents no threat whatsoever to God. God alone is sovereign; beside him "there is no other" (cf. Isaiah 46:9).[49] Ultimate cosmic dualism is not a version of the Christian faith. It is not even a *perversion* of it. It is nothing less than the rejection of Christian orthodoxy.

B. Divine "Authorship" or Causation of Sin Rejected

From the other direction comes another temptation, one that is arguably more alluring to Christians who are (rightly) convinced of the truth of the doctrine of divine sovereignty. This is what Berkouwer refers to as "monism."[50] It is what may be characterized as any view that holds God to be the ultimate "author" or cause of sin, or one that entails such a conclusion (whether or not it formally affirms that God is the cause of sin). It is a view that has been affirmed in some quarters of modern theology.

F. D. E. Schleiermacher has been called the "father of modern theology."[51] His efforts to formulate the doctrine of sin are driven by his methodological commitment to understanding theology in accord with the "feeling of absolute dependence" (*Gefühl*).[52] Reflection on this consciousness leads Schleiermacher to the conclusion that "we are conscious of sin as the power and work of a time when the disposition to the God-consciousness had not yet actively emerged in us."[53] Such reflection also leads Schleiermacher to conclude that our consciousness of sin is "partly as having its source in ourselves, partly as having its source outside our own being."[54] He rejects outright the possibility that sin comes from the human agent alone. Nor is he at all friendly toward "free will defenses," and in general he shows a marked aversion to everything that might resemble Pelagianism.[55] But if sin has its source even partly outside of us, then we are faced with a perplexing question: from whence did it come?

Under the heading of "Original Sin" (*Erbsünde*) Schleiermacher says that the "sinfulness that is present in an individual prior to any action of his own, and has its ground outside his own being, is in every case a complete incapac-

[49] This theme is set forth and defended at length in John S. Feinberg, *No One Like Him: The Doctrine of God* (Wheaton, IL: Crossway, 2002).
[50] Berkouwer, *Sin*, 27–66.
[51] Stanley J. Grenz and Roger E. Olson, *Twentieth-Century Theology: God and the World in a Transitional Age* (Downers Grove, IL: IVP Academic, 1992), 39. They say that "scholars of modern Christian thought" regard him thus "almost universally."
[52] F. D. E. Schleiermacher, *The Christian Faith* (Edinburgh: T&T Clark, 1989), 271.
[53] Schleiermacher, *Christian Faith*, 273.
[54] Schleiermacher, *Christian Faith*, 279.
[55] For an extended discussion of Pelagianism, see chapter 6.

ity for good, which can be removed only by the influence of Redemption."[56] So far, this sounds much like traditional doctrines of original sin, or at least seems consistent with such doctrines: sinfulness is prior to the sinful actions themselves, somehow that sinfulness originated "outside" of us, and the effects of it are so complete and devastating that we are utterly incapable of good and in need of redemption. And Schleiermacher certainly thinks that his doctrine preserves what is really important in those older formulations. But a closer look shows just how far Schleiermacher is from the more traditional versions of the doctrine. He knows that many traditional statements of the doctrine of sin teach that the guilt for original sin comes to all of Adam's descendants, and he raises sharp criticisms of such theology: this is an "incredible turn," he says, and it is one that is "repellent and offensive."[57] He denies that the actions of some ancient people named Adam and Eve have brought sin into the human condition; instead, they serve as an "illustration of the universal process of the rise of sin as something always and everywhere the same."[58] Whereas much traditional theology has held that the actions of Adam and Eve brought corruption into human nature (not in the sense that it changes human nature into something else, but more like a drop of ink that spreads throughout and corrupts all the water in a glass), Schleiermacher denies that the human nature was changed by the actions of Adam and Eve.[59]

He explains this further: Sin has its source "partly in our own being," and this is just as it was for Adam and Eve. Sin is "original," then, in this sense: it is original in all of us. It is intrinsic to us, and it always has been. In the same way, so too was it intrinsic to Adam and Eve. But sin also has its source "partly outside" of us. Again, just what could be going on here? What does Schleiermacher mean by this claim? As we have seen, he rejects the free will defense as a possible explanation, and he also denies that sin is eternal. Nor is it ultimately outside of divine causality. The answer he offers is clear and uncompromising: sin is inherent in all of us, and for that reason it is inevitable for us. And we have this condition *because God causes us to have it*. There is, for Schleiermacher, simply no other theological possibility: God is truly said to be the "author of sin."[60] Schleiermacher shows his supralapsarian colors here; sin is "ordained by God as that which makes redemption necessary."[61] For "if we are to keep the divine omnipotence unlimited and unabridged" (as is demanded by the feeling

[56] Schleiermacher, *Christian Faith*, 282.
[57] Schleiermacher, *Christian Faith*, 286.
[58] Schleiermacher, *Christian Faith*, 303.
[59] Schleiermacher, *Christian Faith*, 295–300.
[60] Schleiermacher, *Christian Faith*, 325. See the helpful discussion of Kevin M. Vander Schel, "Friedrich Schleiermacher," in *The T&T Clark Companion to the Doctrine of Sin*, ed. Keith L. Johnson and David Lauber (New York: Bloomsbury T&T Clark, 2016), 261–263.
[61] Schleiermacher, *Christian Faith*, 335. See further the insightful work of Edwin Chr. van Driel, *Incarnation Anyway: Arguments for Supralapsarian Christology* (Oxford: Oxford University Press, 2008), 9–32.

of absolute dependence) then "we have no choice . . ."[62] As Robert M. Adams puts it, "Schleiermacher's theology of absolute dependence implies that absolutely everything, including evil, including even sin, is grounded in the divine causality."[63] Indeed, Schleiermacher's determinism is so thoroughgoing as to bring us all the way to fatalism, for what "he means is that what God actually causes exhausts all possibility, so that there is no difference for God between the actual and the possible."[64] So Schleiermacher is in direct opposition to the classical tradition (including the Reformed tradition): "In clear contrast to the language of the creeds, Schleiermacher thereby maintains that God must be acknowledged in some sense as the 'author (*Urheber*) of sin.'"[65] Schleiermacher summarizes his own position: "Our theory is that sin was ordained only in view of redemption, and that accordingly redemption shows forth as the gain bound up with sin; in comparison with which there can be no question whatsoever of the mischief due to sin, for the merely gradual and imperfect unfolding of the power of the God-consciousness is one of the necessary conditions of the human stage of existence."[66]

But there are very good theological reasons to reject such theology. Such a view, even if motivated by a proper concern to safeguard a robust doctrine of divine sovereignty, is not demanded by the biblical account of the origin of sin in the first humans. As Childs notes, it is clear from the Genesis text that "evil is not created by God, even though it erupts as a demonic force of aggressive intent."[67] Dyrness concurs: "[I]t is only clear that evil comes not from God."[68] Reflecting on the Genesis text, Waltke concludes that God "is simple goodness; there is no evil in him."[69] There is nothing in the Genesis account to make us think that God is in any way the "author" or cause of sin. To the contrary, sin is presented here, as elsewhere in Scripture, as the intruder that violates what God has created and called *good*. The consistent message of Scripture is that "God is light, and in him is no darkness at all" (1 John 1:5).

This recognition of the utter goodness of God is woven very deeply into the fabric of traditional Christian doctrines of God. The rejection of any idea that God is *a*—much less *the*—causal agent behind sin is so deep-seated in Patristic theology that the Synod of Orange (529) saves what is arguably its strongest denunciation for this view (in a statement that is primarily directed against Pelagianism and especially "Semi-Pelagianism"): "but not only do we not believe that some have been predestinated to evil by the divine power, but

[62] Schleiermacher, *Christian Faith*, 335.
[63] Robert Merrihew Adams, "Schleiermacher on Evil," *FPhilos* (1996): 563.
[64] Adams, "Schleiermacher on Evil," 565.
[65] Vander Schel, "Friedrich Schleiermacher," 262.
[66] Schleiermacher, *Christian Faith*, 338.
[67] Childs, *Old Testament Theology in a Canonical Context*, 274.
[68] Dyrness, *Themes in Old Testament Theology*, 101.
[69] Waltke, *Old Testament Theology*, 262.

also, if there be any who will believe so evil a thing, we say to them, with all detestation, anathema."[70]

Bonaventure is representative of medieval theology when he insists that the twin truths of divine sovereignty and divine goodness rule out both ultimate cosmic dualism and any suggestion that evil comes from God. "Since the First Principle, the supreme and complete Being, cannot fail either in existence or in operation, He is neither absolute evil, nor any degree of evil, nor can He in any manner be the cause of evil."[71] Bonaventure is convinced that God is "utterly good and righteous, and hence utterly kind and just. . . . It follows, then, by necessity that in the beginning He created mankind free from any sin or misery; and it also follows that, in governing mankind, he cannot permit any misery to exist in us except as a punishment of sin."[72] As perfectly and essentially *good*, it is inconceivable that God might be the cause of sin.

Aquinas is in substantial and hearty agreement with the position of Bonaventure here. But he carefully considers arguments supporting the idea that God is somehow the cause of sin. After all, doesn't the Bible simply say that God creates evil (Isa. 45:7) and brings evil upon the city (Amos 3:6)?[73] In response, Aquinas insists that "God hates sin," and "therefore God is not a cause of sin."[74] He denies that God causes sin directly; indeed, he resolutely insists that it is *impossible* for God to be a direct cause of sin. Since "sin is a departure from the order which is to God as the end," and since "God inclines and turns all things to Himself as to their last end," so it is not even possible that God "should be either to Himself or to another the cause of the departing from the order which is to Himself. Therefore he cannot be directly the cause of sin."[75] Once we understand who God is, and once we understand what sin is, we see that it is not even possible for God to be the direct cause of sin. Nor can God be the *indirect* cause of sin; God does all that he does through his wisdom and justice (which are, according to the doctrine of divine simplicity, the same as God himself). Therefore, "if someone sin it is not imputable to Him as though He were the cause of that sin."[76] What are we to make of the biblical texts which seem to say that God indeed *is* the cause of sin? Aquinas holds that these texts teach that God allows or brings punishment to evildoers but does *not* cause the evil itself. He concludes that there simply is "no comparison between fault and punishment."[77]

---

[70] See, e.g., Henry Bettenson, ed., *Documents of the Christian Church*, 2nd ed. (Oxford: Oxford University Press, 1963), 62.

[71] Bonaventure, *Breviloquium* III.1, in *Works*, vol. 2, 110.

[72] Bonaventure, *Breviloquium* III.5, in *Works*, vol. 2, 120–121.

[73] Aquinas, *ST* IaIIae, Q 79.1.

[74] Aquinas, *ST* IaIIae, Q 79.1.

[75] Aquinas, *ST* IaIIae, Q 79.1.

[76] Aquinas, *ST* IaIIae, Q 79.1.

[77] Aquinas, *ST* IaIIae, Q 79.1.

Aquinas also maintains that God is, however, in some sense the cause of the *act* of sin (though not the sin itself). The act of sin, he says, is "a movement of free will."[78] God is Pure Act and thus First Act, and he provides the primary causality for all that happens. Sin, however, is the defective use of our freedom, and this is "not reduced to God as its cause, but to human free will."[79] Aquinas offers this analogy: "even as the defect of limping is reduced to a crooked leg as its cause, but not to the motive power, which nevertheless causes whatever there is of movement in the limping," accordingly, "God is the cause of the act of sin," but "yet He is not the cause of sin, because He does not cause the act to have a defect."[80] When we turn our attention to the biblical witness to the "hardening of hearts" and spiritual blindness, Aquinas notes that this involves two things. The first is the movement of the human mind away from the divine light of grace; the second is the withdrawal of that grace. In the first sense, "God is not the cause of spiritual blindness and hardness of heart."[81] With respect to the second sense, we must remember that "God is the universal cause of the enlightening of souls" (cf. John 1:9). But he also points out that, just as a house is darkened if the windows of the house are shuttered without it being the fault of the sun that shines upon it, neither is it the fault of the Son if our souls are shuttered to his light. He also points out that God may, in such situations, also withhold his grace from those who raise obstacles against it. In such cases, there is a sense in which God can be said to be "the cause of spiritual blindness, deafness of ear, and hardness of heart."[82]

So if God is neither the direct nor the indirect cause of sin, then what does cause it? Aquinas considers the possibility that the devil is the direct cause of human sin, and he denies this outright. Agreeing with Augustine that nothing other than the human free will makes humans slaves to sin, he concludes that the devil is not the cause of sin "directly or sufficiently," but "only by persuasion."[83] The devil, that is, can tempt or "induce" us to sin, but "he cannot induce man to sin of necessity."[84] At most, he is the "occasional and indirect cause of all our sins, in so far as he induced the first man to sin, [and] by reason of whose sin human nature is so infected. . . ."[85] For "a man becomes another's slave not only by being overcome by him, but also by subjecting himself to him spontaneously: it is thus that one who sins of his own accord, becomes the slave of the devil."[86]

---

78 Aquinas, *ST* IaIIae, Q 79.2.
79 Aquinas, *ST* IaIIae, Q 79.2.
80 Aquinas, *ST* IaIIae, Q 79.2.
81 Aquinas, *ST* IaIIae, Q 79.3.
82 Aquinas, *ST* IaIIae, Q 79.3.
83 Aquinas, *ST* IaIIae, Q 80.1.
84 Aquinas, *ST* IaIIae, Q 80.3.
85 Aquinas, *ST* IaIIae, Q 80.4.
86 Aquinas, *ST* IaIIae, Q 80.4.

This view, the steady conviction that God neither is nor can be the author or cause of sin, is the view of Catholic Christianity. The Protestant theologians of the Reformation and post-Reformation periods largely concurred, and often in animated and decisive ways. As Berkouwer puts it, "the Church has confessed on the basis of [the biblical] witness: that God is not the Source, or the Cause, or the Author of man's sin. *Deus non est causa, auctor peccati*."[87] Wilfried Härle cites Martin Luther as exclaiming that to see God as the author of sin is "clearly demonic"; indeed, this is "the last step of sin, to insult God and to charge him with being the originator of sin."[88] The Lutheran confessions demonstrate this commitment both to the steadfast affirmation of the unalterable goodness of God and to the denial that God is in any way the cause or author of sin. The Lutheran *Confessio Augustana* says that the "*causa peccati*" is the free will of humans.[89] Berkouwer notes that "the Apology repeats the same idea."[90] The Formula of Concord interprets Romans 9:22 as saying that God only "endured" the vessels of wrath—but without fashioning or forming them as such.[91] Berkouwer says that "the Lutheran confessions declare that the '*praescientia Dei*' is not the *causa* of evil and that God is not the Author of hereditary sin. . . . God is not the *cause* of our sin, even in the state of our corruption." He concludes that "though Lutheran theology has contended for a certain 'relation' between God and man's sin, it has also stressed constantly the *Deus non causa peccati*."[92]

It is not only the Lutheran confessional statements that say this. The Reformed theological statements do so as well. The Reformed scholastic Johannes Heidegger says that "the cause and author of all good is God; but of evil as such the author could not be God."[93] Zacharias Ursinus agrees; he states forthrightly that "God is not the cause, effect, or author of sin," and God "neither designed nor accomplished" the fall of humankind.[94] He argues that a proper conception of the holiness of God leads us to the firm conclusion that "it is impossible, that any effect of His should be bad," and he insists likewise that the utter truthfulness of God should teach us that "there are no contradictory wills in Him."[95] Berkouwer's summary of this consensus is apt:

---

[87] Berkouwer, *Sin*, 27.

[88] Wilfried Härle, *Outline of Christian Doctrine: An Evangelical Dogmatics* (Grand Rapids, MI: Eerdmans, 2015), 398n19. Härle cites Luther from *Luther's Works* 1,179 and *Luthers Werke, Weimarer Ausgabe* 42 133, 35–36 and 134, 8–10.

[89] Cited in Berkouwer, *Sin*, 31.

[90] Berkouwer, *Sin*, 31.

[91] Cited in Berkouwer, *Sin*, 31.

[92] Berkouwer, *Sin*, 31.

[93] Cited in Heinrich Heppe, *Reformed Dogmatics* (Eugene, OR: Wipf & Stock, 2007), 323. Lucas Trelcatius Jr. likewise insists that "*Deus non est causa primi peccati*" (*Opuscula theologica omnia, duorem catalogum, prima edita*, VII [Leiden], 139).

[94] Zacharias Ursinus, *Commentary on the Heidelberg Catechism*, trans. G. W. Williard (Cincinnati: Elm Street, 1888), 34. Addressing possible objections that argue for divine causation from such texts as Isaiah 45:7 and Amos 3:6, Ursinus says that "God is the author of punishment because he is the judge of the world, but he is not the Author of sin—he merely permits it" (144–145).

[95] Cited in Heppe, *Reformed Dogmatics*, 327.

We do well to listen to the Church's voice in her scripturally-oriented confessions. The Belgic Confession, for example, states in Article 13 that 'nothing happens in this world' without God's appointment, but it also adds immediately: 'nevertheless, God neither is the Author of nor can be charged with the sins which are committed.' The Canons of Dordt (I, 15) profess that God is 'by no means . . . the Author of sin (the very thought of which is blasphemy).' In fact, 'the cause of guilt of . . . unbelief as well as of all other sins is in no wise in God, but in man himself' (I, 5).[96]

Berkouwer's conclusion of his summative overview of the Reformed confessional statements makes use of very strong language: "Opposed here is the idea of all those who insert both good and evil in one and the same schema of divine 'causality.' By doing so they can only stumble into the heresy of the *Deus auctor peccati*. This is a heresy which the confessions have constantly rejected and have refused to embrace in even the *slightest way*."[97]

Berkouwer does not shrink from using terms such as "heresy" and even "blasphemy"—but neither do the Reformed confessions. Surely this is very strong language! Why would a theologian, particularly a Reformed theologian who shares his tradition's respect for divine sovereignty, use such language? Because the very core of the Christian faith—belief in the goodness of God—is at stake here. We have rehearsed the history of this discussion at some length here to demonstrate both just how bedrock this conviction is within the Christian tradition and why it is seen as so important.

In light of what is at stake, perhaps it is no wonder that D. A. Carson summarizes the point by saying that

> God is *never* presented as an accomplice of evil, or as secretly malicious, or as standing behind evil in exactly the same way that he stands behind good. . . . "He is the Rock, his works are perfect, and all his ways are just. A faithful God who does no wrong, upright and just is he" (Deut. 32:4). "God is light; in him there is no darkness at all" (1 John 1:5). It is precisely because Habakkuk can say to God, "Your eyes are too pure to look on evil; you cannot tolerate wrongdoing" (Hab. 1:13), that he has a difficult time understanding how God can sanction the terrible devastations of the Chaldeans upon his own covenant community. Note, then, that the goodness of God is the assumption, the nonnegotiable.[98]

Or, as Berkouwer puts it, the utter, unshakable, unquestionable goodness of God is "the biblical *a priori*."[99] The origin of human sin simply cannot be traced back to the design or work of God.

---

[96] Berkouwer, *Sin*, 29.
[97] Berkouwer, *Sin*, 30, emphasis original.
[98] D. A. Carson, *How Long, O Lord? Reflections on Suffering and Evil* (Grand Rapids, MI: Baker Academic, 2006), 182, emphasis original.
[99] Berkouwer, *Sin*, 27–66.

C. Necessity of the Fall Is Inconsistent with Scripture

Perhaps someone will agree with our rejection of both the "Manichaean" and "monist" options, yet still hold that the fall is necessary. Sin and evil do not have ultimate and eternal existence in opposition to God, nor do sin and evil exist *in* God or come from him. But maybe there is yet something that makes the fall inevitable or unavoidable. Maybe there is something about human nature itself—our desires or our affections, say—that are themselves good (or at least not evil) but that will inevitably lead to human sin. In other words, humans were created as good, and nothing in them could itself be said to be evil as such, but nonetheless all humans (those originally innocent as well as those who are sinful) come with a "built-in" or "hardwired" tendency toward the fall. This view was held by some theologians in the nineteenth century (e.g., Boehme, Schelling, and Hegel),[100] and something much like it is evident in some evangelical piety (if not formal theology) today. Later I shall argue against the tendency to confuse human finitude with sin, and although much that I say there is relevant here as well, here I merely note several immediate problems with such a view.

The first such problem is that the view is not so much as suggested in Scripture. As Childs points out, there is "no canonical warrant" for the view that the depiction of sin in Genesis 1–11 should be read as "a description of the quality of existence constitutive of being human."[101] Rather, "the point of the paradisal state is to contest the ontological character of human sinfulness."[102] Let me be clear: my concern is not merely that the inevitability of the fall—the notion that the act of sin was determined for Adam and Eve—is not stated *explicitly* in the biblical account. My concern here is that it is not even *suggested* by that account. Moreover, there are reasons to wonder if such a view is even consistent with the canonical account.

This leads us to our next concern. The sheer goodness of the creation is unmistakable in the creation account. More importantly, the sheer—and necessary—goodness of the Creator is undeniable for any orthodox Christian who accepts the canonical depiction of God. But it is hard to see how God could call the creation of man and woman "good" if their fall into sin is inevitable or determined. For if it is determined, then we are left to choose between two (broad) options: either they were determined to sin because some other evil agent made it inevitable for them, or they were determined to sin because God made it inevitable for them. The first option—barring a return to the ultimate cosmic dualism just rejected as heterodox—might be understood as the view

---

[100] E.g., Georg Wilhelm Friedrich Hegel, *Lectures on the Philosophy of Religion, One-Volume Edition, The Lectures of 1827*, ed. Peter C. Hodgson (Berkeley: University of California Press, 1988), 441.
[101] Childs, *Old Testament Theology in a Canonical Context*, 226.
[102] Childs, *Old Testament Theology in a Canonical Context*, 226.

that the fallen angels determine our actions. But this is plainly wrong, and for several reasons: it cedes far too much power to Satan. As Aquinas says, the warnings of Scripture (e.g., 1 Pet. 5:8, "the devil prowls around like a roaring lion, seeking someone to devour") would be meaningless "if man were under his [Satan's] control. Therefore, the devil cannot lead man to sin of necessity."[103] Furthermore, it would destroy the moral responsibility that is so clearly and resoundingly attested to in Scripture. Surely it is wrong to say of sin that "the devil made me do it." Finally, it would again be hard to see how God could call this "good."

The second option, though, is no better. If it is wrong to say that "the devil made me do it," surely it is just as mistaken to say, "God made me do it," or, "God made the devil make me do it!" If someone renders (perhaps through the manipulation of the prior conditions and circumstances) the committing of some atrocious action unavoidable for another person, then the first person is morally responsible for that action and indeed is guilty for it. Legal systems would collapse without this basic pillar; one does not even need to *determine* an event or make it unavoidable to be guilty of it (both the hit man and the person paying the hit man are guilty of the murder). Given determinism, it is debatable indeed whether the person whose actions are determined could be morally responsible. But what seems clear is this: the agent *behind* an evil action, the one who renders the committing of it necessary, *is* guilty for the action. So if *God* makes the fall into sin unavoidable, then God would be guilty for it. But this is plainly unacceptable for any orthodox Christian, and, as we have seen, the essential goodness of God is the "nonnegotiable."[104]

But perhaps an objector would still protest by saying that it is human nature itself—not divine action or demonic action subsequent to creation—that makes the fall necessary. But if human nature itself has some sort of built-in property that makes sin somehow inevitable, then it is hard indeed to see how it is good. Beyond this, though, there is another problem, one that concerns Christology: If Jesus Christ is, as Christian orthodoxy has it, both fully divine *and fully human*, then it is indisputable that he shares all of the necessary attributes or properties of humanity. If so, then he has all of the desires or affections that are part of humanity. And yet Scripture tells us in no uncertain terms that Jesus has these human attributes *without sin* (Heb. 4:15). So it cannot be the case that these desires or affections lead humans *inevitably* to sin. On Christological grounds, therefore, we must conclude that there is nothing about human nature as such that would lead us inevitably to sin; there is nothing in

---

[103] Aquinas, *ST* IaIIae, Q 80.3, sed contra.
[104] Carson, *How Long, O Lord?*, 182.

human nature itself that makes sin necessary. The *possibility* of a fall seems necessary: the first humans were *posse non peccare et posse peccare* (able not to sin and able to sin). But Scripture does not teach that the actions of the first humans were determined or that the fall itself was inevitable.[105] The fall itself is not necessary.[106]

D. The Story Line of Scripture

So where does this leave us? We have ruled out several options; as alluring as they may be in offering comprehensive "explanations" of the fall, they cannot be sustained by a careful reading of Scripture, and they entail seriously problematic theological conclusions. But what should we *affirm* about the origin of human sin?

We do not find a definitive, explicit explanation in Scripture. We know that "sin is not part of God's design for his creation; it is an intruder into this world and human nature that is both foreign and invasive. . . . [It] is utterly destructive" and "anti-creational, seeking to undo and destroy every good blessing God intends for his world and those within it."[107] But we do not find an explicit explanation of the origin of human sin. This fact should alert us to the importance of respect for mystery, and it should lead us to admit that there is much that we do not know about the "mystery of iniquity" and its origins. Nonetheless, we can, on the basis of what Scripture *does* tell us, draw some conclusions and some further implications from those conclusions.[108]

The view of the origin of human sin that is both most in line with the canonical account and most consistent with the Christian tradition is this:[109] Adam and Eve, who were *posse peccare* as well as *posse non peccare*, sinned

---

[105] That the possibility itself is necessary is consistent with the system of modal logic known as S5, for which a core axiom is $\Diamond P => \Box\Diamond P$.

[106] For the sake of clarity, I'll state this with a bit more precision. In denying that the fall is *necessary*, we are denying that the primal sin was causally determined. Let w^* stand for the possible world that is the actual one, the one in which Adam and Eve sin by breaking the divine command. Let t stand for the time of this primal sin. In denying that the primal sin was necessary or causally determined, we are affirming that there are possible worlds that share initial world segments up to t with w^* in which Adam and Eve behave differently after t.

[107] Jay Sklar, "Pentateuch," in *T&T Clark Companion to the Doctrine of Sin*, 23, 24.

[108] Only the most stunted and deficient models of theological method would deny that we can—and should—draw theological conclusions that are not *explicitly* stated in Scripture. For example, is the doctrine of the Trinity, stated formally as such, in the Bible? Not at all; we look in vain for the passages which say that Jesus is *homoousios* with his Father. But the doctrine of the Trinity surely *is* correct, and I am convinced that it *is* biblically grounded: from the Bible we learn that there is only one God, that Jesus and the Holy Spirit are fully divine, and that Jesus and the Spirit are personally distinct from one another and from the Father.

[109] For Patristic examples of the appeal to free will in dealing with the origin of sin, see Justin Martyr, *Apologia Prima pro Christianis*, 43–44 (PG 6:391c–396c); Irenaeus, *Adversus Haereses* 4.37.1–2 (PG 7:1099b–1101a); Athanasius, *Oratio Contra Gentes* 1.2–5 (PG 25:5c–12d); Basil of Caesarea, *Homilia in Hexaemeron* 2.4–5, 6.7 (PG 29:35b–42c, 131b–134d); Gregory of Nyssa, *De Virginitate* 12 (PG 46:369–376d); Gregory of Nazianzus, *Oratio* 45.5, 45.8 (PG 36:629a–630b, 631c–634b); John Chrysostom, *Homilia de Imbellecitate Diaboli* (PG 49:241–276); John of Damascus, *De Fide Orthodoxa* 2.4, 2.11–12, 2.27, 4.18–19 (PG 94:873c–878c, 909d–930b, 959b–962b, 1181a–1194c). I owe thanks to Nathan D. Jacobs for his help on this point. It is not, of course, only Patristic theologians who hold this view. Lucas Trelcatius Jr. was a Reformed theologian (a major opponent of Jacob Arminius during the Leiden controversy) who held that Adam's sin was both contingent and free (*Opuscula theologica omnia, duorum catalogum, prima edita*, VII [Leiden], 138).

by the abuse of their God-given and God-imaging freedom.[110] Their freedom is
not complete or total; in an important sense they are not *autonomous*. Their
freedom is circumscribed and has limits, for God tells them what to do and
what to refrain from doing. This has been widely recognized and resoundingly
affirmed within the Christian tradition. For instance, Bonaventure, following
the Latin tradition that he inherited, is emphatic that the creation is *good*.
Sin does not come from the intention of God, nor is it in any sense the result
of an evil first principle that somehow stands primordially and eternally opposed to the Good. Instead, sin is a *defect*.[111] More precisely, sin is a defect
that has come about by the abuse of our God-given freedom of will.[112] As
John Goldingay puts it, Adam and Eve "are not compelled to follow God's
words, but they are not left without instructions."[113] Yet theirs is a genuine
freedom; there is no hint in the account of the fall that their actions are either
compelled by some external force or determined by some combination of
internal desires and external circumstances. Rather, what we are faced with is
the ugly reality that Adam and Eve abused the freedom with which they had
been graced. Merrill notes that this text leaves us with the conclusion that the
human person "is a creature with free will, one able to choose among various
options."[114] Consequent to the *abuse* of this freedom, "human life is lived
under the shadow of what might have been. It is not as it should be, not as
God intended, and this not because of a failure on God's part but because of
a failure on humanity's part."[115]

IV. THE ORIGIN OF ANGELIC SIN

Although there is much that is mysterious about the narrative of the fall, there
is also much that is reasonably clear: Adam and Eve sinned by their disobedi-

---

[110] Wolfhart Pannenberg points out that "from the days when the early church fathers dealt with this question, the answer of Christian theology has been that the permitting of sin and the resultant evils expresses the risk that is involved in the freedom with which God willed to endow his creatures, angels and humans" (*Systematic Theology, Volume 3*, trans. Geoffrey W. Bromiley [Grand Rapids, MI: Eerdmans, 1998], 642). He points out further that the "Christian Gnostics" were the earliest proponents of determinism against whom the early church fathers stood (439). John Frame (conflating determinism with "Calvinism") admits that "those Calvinists who place great weight on antiquity and tradition will have to concede, therefore, that the oldest extracanonical traditions do not favor their points" (John M. Frame, *The Doctrine of God: A Theology of Lordship* [Phillipsburg, NJ: P&R, 2002], 138n23).
[111] Bonaventure, *Breviloquium* III.1.3, in *Works*, vol. 2, 110.
[112] Bonaventure, *Breviloquium* III.3.2, in *Works*, vol. 2, 115.
[113] Goldingay, *Old Testament Theology, Volume One*, 133.
[114] Merrill, *Everlasting Dominion*, 200.
[115] Goldingay, *Old Testament Theology, Volume One*, 145. Various speculations have moved beyond the "story line" of Scripture" in interesting ways. For instance, Søren Kierkegaard reflects deeply on the concept of anxiety. Anxiety itself is not, for Kierkegaard, either the same thing as sin or merely the result of sin. Instead, it is a corollary of our finitude. It is the "psychological state that precedes sin," one that may be compared to a kind of dizziness. This anxiety, while not sinful itself, is instead the recognition of our finitude and creaturely responsibility, and it nonetheless exposes us to the possibility of sin. But this is not all, for anxiety may also be used for good. For anxiety may also, in God's good providence, be the instrument that drives us to find salvation. See Søren Kierkegaard, *The Concept of Anxiety: A Simple Psychologically Orienting Deliberation on the Dogmatic Issue of Hereditary Sin*, ed. and trans. with introduction and notes Reidar Thomte in collaboration with Albert B. Anderson (Princeton, NJ: Princeton University Press, 1980), 92.

ence to God; they freely chose to reject God's authority over them and gracious care for them. They had only themselves—not the devil, not their environment, certainly *not God*—to blame. This is, in brief, the biblical account of the origin of human sin.

But the fact that *someone* or *something* exists to tempt them in this pristine and primeval state of innocence raises other fascinating and important questions: who is this tempter? Where does this tempter come from? Why—indeed how—could this tempter have become evil (given the clear and outright Christian rejection of Manichaeism, Gnosticism, and other forms of cosmic dualism)? Such questions have intrigued Christian thinkers for generations.

A. *The Biblical Witness*

The direct biblical account of the identity and origin of Satan does not satisfy all of our curiosity, but it does shed some light on the subject. These elements are reasonably clear. First, both Jesus and Paul make it plain that the tempter is Satan. Jesus refers to "your father the devil" (John 8:44). Even more explicitly, Paul echoes the *protoevangelium* in saying that "the God of peace will soon crush Satan under your feet" (Rom. 16:20), and he expresses concern that the Corinthian believers might "be led astray from a sincere and pure devotion to Christ" just "as the serpent deceived Eve by his cunning" (2 Cor. 11:3).[116]

Second, Satan was part of the heavenly court; he was an angel. Waltke notes several contrasts between Satan and God: while God creates and sustains life, Satan "is malevolent and hinders life"; and where the Creator "uses speech to transform chaos into cosmos, . . . the Serpent uses speech to confuse, not order; his words are full of lies and half-truths."[117] But Waltke also points out that "the Serpent knows about divine matters that are not accessible to mortals."[118] He obviously precedes the first humans, and he knows things that Adam and Eve do not know (or at least do not *yet* know).

If Satan is—or was—an angel, then Satan is a creature. And if a creature, then surely he was created by God. Scripture tells us explicitly that not only were the heavens made by God, so also was "all their host" (Ps. 33:6); we learn in the Gospel of John that "all things were made through" the Word of God (John 1:3), and Paul tells us that by the Son "all things were created, in heaven and on earth, visible and invisible, whether thrones or dominions or rulers or authorities—all things were created through him and for him" (Col. 1:16; cf. Rom. 11:36; Eph. 3:9).[119] And once again, as we have seen in our discussion of the origin of human sin, God neither commits actions that are morally evil

---

[116] For more on this see Waltke, *Old Testament Theology*, 273.
[117] Waltke, *Old Testament Theology*, 273.
[118] Waltke, *Old Testament Theology*, 273.
[119] I rely upon Waltke here; see further his *Old Testament Theology*, 273.

(James 1:13) nor creates evil beings (Genesis 1). So we are led to conclude, as Waltke puts it, that "Satan must have rebelled against God sometime between his creation and this encounter in the garden."[120]

Several biblical passages are especially important at this point. Isaiah exclaims,

How you are fallen from heaven,
O Day Star, son of Dawn!
How you are cut down to the ground,
you who laid the nations low!
You said in your heart,
"I will ascend to heaven;
above the stars of God
I will set my throne on high;
I will sit on the mount of assembly
in the far reaches of the north;
I will ascend above the heights of the clouds;
I will make myself like the Most High."
But you are brought down to Sheol,
to the far reaches of the pit.
Those who see you will stare at you
and ponder over you:
"Is this the man who made the earth tremble,
who shook kingdoms,
who made the world like a desert
and overthrew its cities,
who did not let his prisoners go home?"
All the kings of the nations lie in glory,
each in his own tomb;
but you are cast out, away from your grave,
like a loathed branch,
clothed with the slain, those pierced by the sword,
who go down to the stones of the pit;
like a dead body trampled underfoot. (Isa. 14:12–19)

Here we learn several things: Satan wanted to be like God, as God, even above God. But he was cast down, and now he has "laid the nations low" (Isa. 14:12). He is a defeated foe, and his future is grim. But he remains both fascinating and frightening in his evil power. Ezekiel 28 contains two oracles; one is addressed to a human ruler (*nagid*) or "prince of Tyre," while the other is addressed to the angelic ruler (*melek*) or "king of Tyre." The latter is said to be, at the time of his creation, a being radiant in beauty and splendor; he was "full of wisdom and perfect in beauty" (28:12). The pronouncement says that this creature was "blameless in [his] ways" from the day of his creation (28:15).

---

[120] Waltke, *Old Testament Theology*, 273.

But then something dreadful happened, and soon he was "filled with violence" (28:16). The verdict is direct: "Your heart was proud because of your beauty; you corrupted your wisdom for the sake of your splendor" (28:17). And the sentence pronounced is unmistakable: "I cast you as a profane thing from the mountain of God, and I destroyed you" (28:16); "I cast you to the ground; I exposed you before kings, to feast their eyes on you" (28:17); "I brought fire out from your midst; it consumed you, and I turned you to ashes on the earth in the sight of all who saw you" (28:18).

Waltke notes that "Paul probably has this text in mind when he asserts that the Devil is condemned for his pride (1 Tim. 3:6)."[121] The contrast with Jesus Christ is startling and powerful: unlike the one who was very God in nature but who "did not count equality with God a thing to be grasped, but emptied himself by taking the form of a servant" and then "[humbling] himself by becoming obedient to the point of death, even death on a cross" (Phil. 2:6, 8), Satan "regards his superiority to the other creatures as being for his own exaltation and, correlatively, his advantage as an opportunity to disadvantage others. From the contrast between the serving mind of Christ versus the self-serving mind of Satan, all of history, which is still reaching for a climax, unfolds."[122]

Second Peter 2:4 tells us of the fate of Satan and the angels who rebelled with him: "God did not spare angels when they sinned, but cast them into hell and committed them to chains of gloomy darkness to be kept until the judgment." And in the Apocalypse we read of a frightful "war . . . in heaven," with "Michael and his angels" fighting against "the dragon and his angels" (Rev. 12:7). When the satanic horde was defeated, "there was no longer any place for them in heaven," and "the great dragon . . . that ancient serpent, who is called the devil and Satan, the deceiver of the whole world" was "thrown down to the earth, and his angels were thrown down with him" (Rev. 12:8–9).

B. Insights from the Christian Tradition

The broad Christian tradition has recognized and affirmed this biblical teaching. Thus the Fourth Lateran Council concludes that "the devil and the other demons were indeed created naturally good by God, but they became evil by their own doing."[123]

But these affirmations still leave us with some perplexing and intriguing questions. How did Satan—sans sin and sans even a tempter to mislead him— fall into sin? How could a being so "full of wisdom" (Ezek. 28:12), a being who resided in the splendor of heaven and the presence of God, ever fall from

---

[121] Waltke, *Old Testament Theology*, 274.
[122] Waltke, *Old Testament Theology*, 274.
[123] Quoted in the *Catechism of the Catholic Church*, 98.

that place? Christian theologians throughout the tradition have wrestled with such questions. John of Damascus is representative of much Patristic theology (especially Greek Patristic theology) when he says that Satan

> was not made wicked in nature but was good, and made for good ends and received from his Creator no trace whatsoever of evil in himself. But he did not sustain the brightness and the honor that the Creator had bestowed on him, and of his free choice he was changed from what was in harmony to what was at variance with his nature, and became roused against God who created him and determined to rise in rebellion against him, and he was the first to depart from good and become evil.[124]

The situation is similar with respect to the other fallen angels, for "being of the same nature as the angels, they became wicked, turning away at their own free choice from good to evil."[125]

Similarly, Augustine says that the nature of the good angels is the same as that of the bad angels, "since God, the good Author and Creator of all essences, created them both." The difference between the good angels and the evil ones comes, then, "from a difference in their wills and desires."[126] Indeed, for Augustine the ability of the angels to make such a choice is further evidence of the goodness of their natures: "By this very fault the nature is proved to be very noble and admirable. . . . Since every vice is an injury of the nature, that very vice of the wicked angels, their departure from God, is sufficient proof that God created their nature so good, that it is an injury to it not to be with God."[127]

Anselm of Canterbury wrestles with the difficult questions surrounding this issue in *The Fall of the Devil*. Anselm recognizes that everything that is possessed by creatures comes from God, and he is certain that whatever comes from God is good. But even brief reflection on this raises some thorny questions. Did the devil sin because God withheld from him what he needed for perseverance? Would not then God be responsible for the sin of the devil? Anselm will not countenance the notion that the devil sins because of divine intent or action, but struggles to explain just what is going on. He agrees that whatever we have comes from God (1 Cor. 4:7), yet he denies that sin is from God. Instead, he says, the ability to will is from God, and as such is good. However, what humans and angels *do* with that will, how they exercise it, is attributable to them and not to God.

Anselm addresses directly the concern that the devil lacked perseverance because God withheld it from him. There is a dilemma here: if God did not

[124] John of Damascus, *De Fide Orthodoxa* II.IV (PG 94:876; NPNF² 9:20).
[125] John of Damascus, *De Fide Orthodoxa* II.IV (PG 94:876; NPNF² 9:20).
[126] Augustine, *De civitate Dei* XII.1 (PL 41:349; NPNF¹ 2:226).
[127] Augustine, *De civitate Dei* XII.1 (PL 41:350; NPNF¹ 2:227).

give it, then it would seem that God refuses to give the good gifts that are necessary for the life and holiness of his creatures. But Anselm approaches this dilemma by saying that "God does not give it because the devil does not take it." It is not as though God refused to give what was good and necessary for the creature; it is that God gave the "will and capacity to receive perseverance" to the devil but that he refused to accept the gift of perseverance itself.[128] So the fault is with the devil, who "had the capacity to will and the capacity to receive perseverance and the will and the capacity to persevere, [but who] did not receive perseverance and did not persevere because he did not will it all the way."[129] In other words, the devil had freedom of the will, and the capacity to receive perseverance from God. But God did not, strictly speaking, give it to the devil—because the devil refused it when it was offered to him.

Anselm wants to make perfectly clear the fact that the fallen angels, as well as the good ones, had genuine freedom of the will, and that their fall from goodness was entirely their fault. Before the bad angels fell, surely the good angels could have sinned too. No angels are necessarily good, and none are necessarily evil. They are now "confirmed" in their respective states, but there are no angels that are necessarily either good or evil. God created the angels, and he sustains and empowers them to perform actions:

> So when the devil turned his will to what he should not, both his will and this turning were something real, and yet he could not have this reality except from God, since he could not will nor move his will if it had not been permitted by God, who causes all substantial and accidental natures to be, both universal and individual. Insofar as the will and its movement or turning are real they are good and come from God. But insofar as they are deprived of some justice that they ought to have, they are not absolutely bad but bad in a sense, and what is bad in them does not come from the will of God or from God insofar as he moves the will. . . . But the nature in which injustice is found is something evil, because it is something real and differs from injustice which is evil and is nothing. Therefore, what is real is made by God and comes from him; what is nothing, that is evil, is caused by the guilty and comes from him.[130]

So according to Anselm, we need take neither horn of the dilemma: it is not true that the evil of the devil is caused by God, nor is it right to think that the bad angels exist in complete independence of the "one greater than which cannot be conceived" or somehow are infected with a "prior" evil. But we are still left with the question, *why* did some of the angels, while still good, choose injustice and sin rather than righteousness? As Anselm puts the

---

[128] Anselm, *De casu diaboli* 3, *Opera omnia opscula* (Paris: 1549), 43E, cited in *Anselm of Canterbury: The Major Works*, ed. with introduction Brian Davies and G. R. Evans (Oxford: Oxford University Press, 1998), 198.
[129] Anselm, *De casu diaboli* 3, *Opera* 43G; *Major Works*, 199.
[130] Anselm, *De casu diaboli* 20, *Opera* 47F–G; *Major Works*, 223.

question, "Why does justice depart from the just angel?" His initial answer is this: strictly speaking, "it does not depart from him, but he abandons it by willing what he ought not."[131] This kind of response, of course, only invites follow-up queries, and the exchange between Anselm's "Teacher" and "Student" is intriguing:

> S: Why does he abandon it?
> T: When I say that by willing what he ought not he abandons it, I show openly why and how he abandons it. He abandons it because he wills what he ought not to will, and in this way it is by willing what he ought not that he abandons it.
> S: Why does he will what he ought not?
> T: No cause precedes this will except that he can will.
> S: And he wills because he can?
> T: No. Because the good angel could will similarly yet does not. No one wills what he can will because he can, without some other cause, although if he is unable to will he never does.
> S: Why then does he will?
> T: Only because he wills. For this will has no other cause by which it is forced or attracted, for it was its own efficient cause, so to speak, as well as its own effect.[132]

Echoing Augustine, it is obvious that Anselm is appealing to a kind of "free will defense" with respect to the problem of angelic evil. And it is equally obvious that the freedom in view is what is sometimes called "libertarian" freedom.[133] When asked if the possession of this freedom was itself the cause of the evil choice, Anselm responds by effectively saying, "[N]ot at all. Just look at the good angels; they too had this freedom, but they did not use it for evil. No, the freedom of the will itself is not evil, nor is it, strictly speaking, the cause of the sin." When pressed to give a further explanation—when asked for a sufficient cause that would be needed *in addition to* the freedom of the will and that would guarantee the action in question—Anselm resists by pointing out that there just *are* no sufficient causes beyond the free choice itself. Anselm is only echoing Augustine here.[134] And from a libertarian perspective, he is exactly right: to demand an additional sufficient cause (beyond the agent himself) is to commit the logical fallacy of begging the question against the libertarian.

Peter Lombard echoes several of these biblical affirmations and Patristic insights. He insists both that angels are *created* beings, and that whatever is created by God is created by God as *good*. Because God exists necessarily and

---

[131] Anselm, *De casu diaboli* 27, *Opera* 48M; *Major Works*, 231.
[132] Anselm, *De casu diaboli* 27, *Opera* 48M; *Major Works*, 231–232.
[133] Cf. Sandra Visser and Thomas Williams, "Anselm's Account of Freedom," in *The Cambridge Companion to Anselm*, ed. Brian Davies and Brian Leftow (Cambridge: Cambridge University Press, 2004), 179–203.
[134] Augustine, *De civitate Dei* XII.6–7 (PL 41:353–355; *NPNF*[1] 2:229–230).

as necessarily good, we cannot think that God created evil: "[T]he most excellent Creator could not be the author of evil."[135] As for the angels themselves, they do not exist necessarily, nor are they necessarily or essentially good. Much like our first parents, they are endowed with genuine freedom of the will. And again much like Adam and Eve, they first exist in a state of innocence. It is in this state of innocence that they have the possibility of conversion toward God and confirmation of their goodness on the one hand, or aversion away from God and their created goodness on the other hand. Lombard explains how this occurs:

> [O]ur consideration prompts us to inquire in what manner they were affected when they were divided by aversion and conversion. For after creation, some soon turned toward their Creator, while others turned away. Turning toward God was to cling to Him in charity; turning away, [by contrast, meant] to have hatred and be envious: for the mother of envy is pride [*superbia*], by which they wanted to make themselves equal to God. In the converted, God's Wisdom, by which they were illuminated, began to shine as though in a mirror; but those who turned away were blinded. The former were converted and illuminated by God through the aid of grace [*gratia apposita*]; the latter, however, were blinded not because they were sent anything bad, but because grace forsook them—[and] they were forsaken by grace not in such a way that grace which had previously been given was taken away, but because it was never given them so they might be converted. This, then, is the conversion and aversion by which those who were good by nature, were divided, so that some might, through justice, be good over and above that goodness, and others might be bad through transgression while that [natural goodness] was destroyed. Conversion created just [angels], and aversion created unjust ones. Both the one and the other belonged to the will, and the will in both cases was free.[136]

In this dense passage, Lombard is emphasizing several things: first, the angels (both those who are confirmed in goodness and those who turn to evil) are created by God, and are created by God as good; second, they are endowed with free will, and as such their actions are not determined; third, some of these angels used this will to turn from innocent goodness to a kind of confirmed goodness while others used this free will to turn away from God and to evil; and last, through their choice their innocent goodness was either confirmed by grace (and finally so) or destroyed through rebellion. As Philipp Rosemann explains, "[S]ome turn back to their Creator in a movement of love, with which they respond to the divine goodness (and to the intrinsic bent of their own nature created in goodness). Others, by contrast, turn away . . . ,

[135] Cited in Philipp Rosemann, *Peter Lombard*, Great Medieval Thinkers (Oxford: Oxford University Press, 2004), 98.
[136] Cited in Rosemann, *Peter Lombard*, 98–99.

unable to reconcile themselves with their finitude—with the fact that they are not God."[137] This means that "*[s]uperbia*, pride, the desire to be 'above' (*super*) that which one really is, lies at the root of all sin."[138]

Aquinas is in basic agreement with this, and he emphasizes the contribution of Isaiah 14:13 to our understanding of the fall of the devil. In agreement with the received tradition (he quotes Dionysius the Pseudo-Areopagite), he denies that the devils are evil by nature (*daemones non sunt naturaliter mali*).[139] Aquinas insists that "there is no doubt that an angel did sin by desiring to be as God."[140] He explains this further by drawing a distinction between two ways that "like God" might be understood: it might be taken as meaning either equality (*aequiparantiam*) or likeness (*similitudinem*). The second is the way that was desired by the devil (the devil would have known that the first is, strictly speaking, impossible), and this desire must be understood properly. For it is not wrong to desire to be like God "as one's nature allowed," but it is quite another to desire this "beyond the limits allowed by one's nature, for example to be the creator of heaven and earth, which only God can be." It is in this latter sense that the devil desired to be like God, and in doing so he committed the first sin: "[H]e placed his ultimate bliss in an objective to be obtained by the force of his own nature alone, rejecting the supernatural bliss which depends on the grace of God."[141]

To this point, we have seen that Anselm's account appeals to a kind of free will defense to the problem of angelic sin, and while his answer enjoys internal consistency and both removes the charge that God is the author or cause of angelic sin and avoids any suggestion of ultimate cosmic dualism, it must be admitted that Anselm's final answer leaves a great deal shrouded in mystery. Perhaps this is the right response; maybe it is best to leave matters there. Similarly, Lombard issues affirmations and denials, but without wrestling at length with the further question of why the good angels might sin. Aquinas clarifies things by pointing out that while there is an appropriate way of wanting to "be like God," the devil fell by rejecting the appropriate way for an inordinate one.

John Duns Scotus takes things a step further. He too wants to avoid the looming—and very serious—problems. Like the other theologians mentioned, he too wants to avoid any suggestion that God is the author or cause of evil. Scotus will have nothing to do with the idea that the angels sin of necessity or because of God's design. And like the other theologians canvassed, Scotus too is insistently opposed to any notion of ultimate cosmic dualism. But he is

---

[137] Rosemann, *Peter Lombard*, 99.
[138] Rosemann, *Peter Lombard*, 99.
[139] Aquinas, *ST* Ia, Q 63.4, sed contra.
[140] Aquinas, *ST* Ia, Q 63.3, responsio.
[141] Aquinas, *ST* Ia, Q 63.3, responsio.

not ready to rest content with appeals to freedom of the (angelic) will that go no further.

To gain a grasp on Scotus's account of the fall of the devil, we must understand the importance of both freedom and love for his theology. Freedom is, for Scotus, what Allan B. Wolter refers to as the "glue of the universe."[142] This refers in the first instance to divine freedom, but it extends to the freedom of creatures as well. There is, then, a "radical contingency" that is built into the structure of the created order, and it is one that stems from the freedom of the divine will. What is arguably even more important for Scotus's theology, however, is the primacy of divine love. To say that God is loving, and to say further that "God is love," is in the final analysis a Trinitarian statement for Scotus. As Marilyn McCord Adams puts it, Scotus conceives of the triune God of the Christian faith as a "maximally well-organized Lover," for the "persons of the Trinity love one another with friendship love (*amor amicitiae*), which is unselfish and so reaches out to desire other co-lovers for the Beloved."[143] God is, in the beauty and splendor of the Three-Personed life, a communion of self-giving holy love. And because divine action is in perfect accord with the divine nature (Scotus does, of course, accept a doctrine of divine simplicity), "in the act of creation God ordered all things to participation in Divine Love."[144] This means, among other things, that "all angelic and human beings are intended to be co-lovers of God."[145]

From this it should be easy to see why Scotus would reject outright any suggestion that the wicked angels fell because of God's desire or design. Because God is love, God loves the world and all that is in it, and he has ordered creation so that all angelic as well as human beings might fulfill the purpose for which they were created. It is also fairly easy to anticipate the beginning point of Scotus's account of angelic sin: it is indeed a version of a free will defense.

But it is a free will defense that he takes beyond Anselm's. He affirms—and extends—an insight that Anselm himself had offered. Anselm had drawn a distinction between what is called the "affection for justice" (*affectio iustitiae*) and the "affection for advantage" (*affectio commodi*). The "affection for justice" is a desire to see all things ordered and functioning as they *should be* ordered and functioning; it is the desire to see God properly and ultimately glorified as God should be. The "affection for advantage," on the other hand, is the desire to see things ordered so that I may benefit. Now, properly understood, and in a world rightly ordered by God, the affection for justice and the affection for

[142] Allan B. Wolter, "Preface," in *John Duns Scotus on the Will and Morality*, selected and trans. with introduction Allan B. Wolter, OFM (Washington, DC: Catholic University of America Press, 1997), xi.
[143] Marilyn McCord Adams, *What Sort of Human Nature? Medieval Philosophy and the Systematics of Christology* (Milwaukee: Marquette University Press, 1999), 69.
[144] Wolter, "Preface," xiii.
[145] Wolter, "Preface," xiii.

advantage actually converge. The proper end of all things is in God, and we should desire to see that all things actually find their end in him. And when that happens, all things are as they should be. So when I am rightly focused on God, I am most fulfilled and happy. Properly ordered, the affection for justice (the way things should be, revolving around God) and the affection for advantage (the way I want things to be) cohere. Properly ordered, neither affection nor desire is sinful. Indeed, neither the affection for advantage nor the affection for justice is inherently wrong. Instead, both of them are, in their God-ordained and God-given capacity, appropriate. But if they become wrongly ordered, *everything* becomes disordered.

And for Scotus, this is what happened at the fall of Lucifer. Scotus says that "Lucifer's very first inordinate act of will was the first benevolent love he had towards one to whom he wished well. . . . The first inordinate act, therefore, was one of benevolence towards himself."[146] But there is nothing wrong with benevolent love, so what could make this act "inordinate"? Scotus's answer is that the object of this love "was not God, for God could not have been loved inordinately."[147] Rather, the object of Lucifer's love was himself. And while love of oneself in the sense of "affection for advantage" is not wrong if placed subordinate to love for God in the sense of "affection for justice," if it is allowed to become preeminent everything is reversed. And when this happens—when our love of ourselves and our desire for our own advantage becomes paramount and supplants the love for God—our loves and lives have become disordered, and we have sinned. This is, in the case of the fall of the devil, exactly what happened: "[W]e have to say that [Lucifer] first coveted happiness immoderately."[148]

So Scotus has, in line with much of the medieval tradition, held both that creation is entirely *good* and that the sin of the devil came by the abuse of his free will. Moreover, he has gone some distance toward trying to explain just how it might be that the angels could commit sin before there was anything evil to tempt them. But why, one might yet ask, would an essentially holy and omnibenevolent God create creatures who were even capable of sinning at all? Here Scotus insists that the answer to such questions is found in a proper understanding of creation and finitude. While the creation is originally and completely good, to be a creature made *ex nihilo* is to be made from nothing and with the possibility within us of returning to that nothingness. And since evil is, for Scotus (and the Christian tradition more broadly) a privation of the good rather than anything with positive "substance" itself, to be a creature is to be liable to returning to nothingness (at least at some point). As Scotus

---

[146] Scotus, *Ordinatio* II.6.2; (Quaracchi edition); *John Duns Scotus on the Will and Morality*, 296.
[147] Scotus, *Ordinatio* II.6.2; *John Duns Scotus on the Will and Morality*, 296.
[148] Scotus, *Ordinatio* II.6.2; *John Duns Scotus on the Will and Morality*, 296.

puts it, "to be defectible in the sense of being able to return to nothingness is a consequence of every creature coming from nothing."[149] And if the created beings enjoy rationality and freedom of will (which for Scotus go together), then they will have within them the possibility of abuse of that will: "as free, the will has the option of either following the dictates of right reason and the inclination for the affection for justice or following its counterinclination, the affection for the advantageous."[150]

C. Conclusion

What are we to think of all this? How are we to weigh and evaluate the proposals of these Patristic and medieval theologians? What is clearly ruled out by Scripture? What should we say? What may we affirm (even as the kind of speculation that is consistent with Scriptural teaching)? There are several theological propositions that we *should* affirm, and several that we should recognize as speculation that is consistent with Scripture even while going beyond it.

First, we should recognize that the fallen angels are creatures; they have no independent existence, they did not bring themselves into being, nor do they sustain themselves in existence. This point should not be in doubt. Secondly, as creatures they were created as *good*. Everything that God created was recognized and pronounced good by him, and, as part of this good creation, the original state of the angels was one of goodness. Third, they have fallen by rebelling against their Creator. Fourth, they fell by the abuse of their own free will. Their fall was not a fate set by their nature, nor did God determine that they would fall. As the giant of Reformed scholastic theology Francis Turretin puts it,

> Although that fall did not happen without the intervention of divine providence, still its true cause must be sought in the angels alone and by no means in God. It must not be sought in him either with regard to prescience (which only foresees a thing as future, but does not make it so); or to his decree (which was permissive, not efficient); or to his actual permission (which is not moral, but physical, by a not hindering to which he was not bound); or to a deficiency of sustentation. . . . The sole cause, therefore, was the proper will of each devil by which individuals of their own accord turned from good to evil. They fell because they willed to fall; they could fall because they were created mutable and capable of falling.[151]

Surely there is good reason for Katherine Sonderegger to conclude that "few

---

[149] Scotus, *John Duns Scotus on the Will and Morality*, 294. Scotus here echoes Augustine, e.g., *De civitate Dei*, XII.8 (*NPNF*[1] 9:230).

[150] Wolter, "Introduction," in *John Duns Scotus on the Will and Morality*, 100.

[151] Francis Turretin, *Institutio Theologiae Elencticae, Pars Prima* (Geneva: 1688), I.IX.5 (664) (*Institutes of Elenctic Theology, Volume One: First through Tenth Topics*, trans. George Musgrave Giger, ed. James T. Dennison Jr. [Phillipsburg, NJ: Presbyterian & Reformed, 1992], 603).

matters are so settled in Christian doctrine as is the axiom that God cannot be the Author of sin."[152]

And fifth, whether this fall stems, in the first instance, from pride, an envy of humans, or a disordering of the affections is not obvious. While the first three of these affirmations follow directly from the biblical account, we should admit that the latter two are (increasingly) speculative. Still, though, we can say that they are at least consistent with what Scripture teaches, they avoid theological problems that orthodox Christianity insists should be avoided, and if they go beyond the explicit teachings of Scripture they do so in the direction in which Scripture points us.

---

[152] Katherine Sonderegger, "Finitude and Death," in *T&T Clark Companion to the Doctrine of Sin*, 388.

FOUR

The Doctrine of Original Sin

I. Introduction

Herman Bavinck is appropriately blunt: "The doctrine of original sin is one of the weightiest but also one of the most difficult subjects in the field of dogmatics."[1] His citation of Augustine seems even more pessimistic: "Nothing is so easy to denounce, nothing is so difficult to understand."[2] Thus it may be, but it is also one of the most enduring and important of theological subjects. It is a doctrine that has been affirmed by theologians of all parts of the "Vincentian Canon"; it is one that has been believed by all Christians, at all times, and in all places.[3] It has been inscribed in confessional statements of various ecclesial branches. Roman Catholic theology does not hesitate to affirm the doctrine. The children of the Reformation do not waver on the doctrine. The Lutheran Formula of Concord *begins* with an affirmation of the doctrine of original sin. Similarly, the Reformed confessions insist upon the truth of the doctrine, as do the Anglican Thirty-Nine Articles. And not only has it been affirmed, it has also been seen to be of great importance.

The doctrine of original sin enjoys an unwavering chorus of support throughout the history of the church. It does so for a reason: it has a biblical basis. Paul, in particular, connects the human condition and destiny directly to Adam. In 1 Corinthians 15:21–22 we read, "For as by a man came death, by a man has come also the resurrection of the dead. For as in Adam all die, so also in Christ shall all be made alive." And there's the *locus classicus* of the doctrine, Romans 5:12–21:

> Therefore, just as sin came into the world through one man, and death through sin, and so death spread to all men because all sinned—for sin indeed

---

[1] Herman Bavinck, *Reformed Dogmatics, Volume Three: Sin and Salvation in Christ*, trans. John Vriend, ed., John Bolt (Grand Rapids, MI: Baker Academic, 2006), 100.
[2] Augustine, cited in Bavinck, *Reformed Dogmatics: Volume Three*, 100.
[3] On the "Vincentian Canon" see, e.g., Thomas C. Oden, *The Rebirth of Orthodoxy: Signs of New Life in Christianity* (New York: HarperCollins, 2003); and Thomas Guarino, *Vincent of Lerins and the Development of Christian Doctrine* (Grand Rapids, MI: Baker Academic, 2013).

was in the world before the law was given, but sin is not counted where there is no law. Yet death reigned from Adam to Moses, even over those whose sinning was not like the transgression of Adam, who was a type of the one who was to come.

But the free gift is not like the trespass. For if many died through one man's trespass, much more have the grace of God and the free gift by the grace of that one man Jesus Christ abounded for many. And the free gift is not like the result of that one man's sin. For the judgment following one trespass brought condemnation, but the free gift following many trespasses brought justification. For if, because of one man's trespass, death reigned through that one man, much more will those who receive the abundance of grace and the free gift of righteousness reign in life through the one man Jesus Christ.

Therefore, as one trespass led to condemnation for all men, so one act of righteousness leads to justification and life for all men. For as by the one man's disobedience the many were made sinners, so by the one man's obedience the many will be made righteous. Now the law came in to increase the trespass, but where sin increased, grace abounded all the more, so that, as sin reigned in death, grace also might reign through righteousness leading to eternal life through Jesus Christ our Lord.

And yet the doctrine of original sin remains widely and even wildly unpopular in many quarters. The very influential nineteenth-century theologian Albrecht Ritschl, for instance, criticizes and dismisses the doctrine. Ritschl's legacy was such that Stanley J. Grenz and Roger E. Olson conclude that "the terms 'Ritschlian' and 'classical Protestant liberal' are nearly synonymous."[4] By his own measure, Ritschl's doctrine of sin "is in the closest formal agreement with Schleiermacher."[5] He wants to "transcend" the older debates be-

---

[4] Stanley J. Grenz and Roger E. Olson, *Twentieth-Century Theology: God and the World in a Transitional Age* (Downers Grove, IL: IVP Academic, 1992), 51.

[5] Albrecht Ritschl, *The Christian Doctrine of Justification and Reconciliation*, 2nd ed. (Edinburgh: T&T Clark, 1902), 335. Remaining distance between Ritschl and Schleiermacher can be seen, e.g., 350–51. Ritschl's indebtedness to the philosopher Immanuel Kant is well known. The association of Ritschl with Kant is well-deserved (see, e.g., Ritschl's discussion of the classical theistic arguments in *Justification and Reconciliation*, 219–223). But it is worth noting that Kant's views are not so easily equated with those of Ritschl on the doctrine of original sin. Kant recognized the presence of "radical evil" in human nature, and he says that it is both "innate" and something that has been brought upon ourselves. The statement "man is evil" can, for Kant, "mean only that he is conscious of the moral law but has nevertheless adopted into his maxim the (occasional) deviation therefrom. He is evil *by nature*, means but this, that evil can be predicated of man as a species; not that such a quality can be inferred from the concept of his species . . . for then it would be necessary . . . or, that we may presuppose evil to be subjectively necessary to every man, even to the best" (*Religion within the Limits of Reason Alone* [New York: Harper & Row, 1960], 27). Kant, then, struggled mightily to account for two important affirmations: first, that evil is both "radical" (it goes to the depths of the human person) and universal, and second, that "it must be possible to overcome it, since it is found in man, a being whose actions are free" (*Religion*, 32). So even though Kant concedes that the propensity to evil remains "inscrutable" to us, he does recognize its existence and makes clear the existence of (what John Hare calls) a vast "moral gap" between what we ought to do and what we in fact do. In doing so, Kant points to both the existence of a deep problem and the need for a redeemer. For an introduction to the rather disparate interpretations of Kant's account of moral evil, see Lawrence R. Pasternack, "Kant on the Debt of Sin," *FPhilos* (2012): 30–52; Pasternack, *Routledge Philosophy Guidebook to Kant on Religion within the Boundaries of Mere Reason* (New York: Routledge, 2014), 85–130; Allen W. Wood, "The Evil in Human Nature," in *Kant's* Religion within the Boundaries of Mere Reason: A Critical Guide, ed. Gordon E. Michalson (Cambridge: Cambridge University Press, 2014), 31–57; Wood, *Kant's Moral Religion* (Ithaca, NY: Cornell University Press, 1970), 208–248; Ingolf Dalferth, "Radical Evil and Human Freedom," in *Kant's* Religion within the Boundaries of Mere Reason:

tween Augustinians and Pelagians, and he conceives of sin as "selfish action" that is "directed in any degree whatsoever towards the opposite of the good, and leads to the association of individuals in common evil."[6] Sin is "striving, desiring, and acting against God."[7] Sin for Ritschl is, according to the insightful study of Kevin Hector, "at base, mistrust (*Mißtrauen*) toward God, though he everywhere insists that such mistrust is necessarily adjoined with immorality."[8]

Notably, Ritschl offers a penetrating account of actual sin but denies the traditional doctrine of original sin. He clearly rejects any notion of original guilt. But he also rejects any notion of original sin at all (although he thinks that he protects what is really important about it with his own affirmations). A supposedly "innate" tendency in humanity to sin could be demonstrated only by empirical observation, but we cannot really suppose that this could be done. After all, none of us has access to the intentions or even the actions of people all across the world or all throughout history.[9] He argues against the doctrine of original sin on several grounds: it is inconsistent with moral responsibility; it undermines any reason for education (which "is possible only on the presupposition that existing bad habits or evil inclinations have come to exist as the products of repeated acts of will"); and it does not have the resources to account for "distinct degrees of evil in individuals."[10] His conclusion is unmistakable: "Hence inherited sin and personal guilt cannot be combined in thought without inaccuracy or a *sacrificium intellectus*."[11] And not only does Ritschl reject any idea of original guilt; he also criticizes and rejects the Reformer Huldrych Zwingli's proposal that we suffer from original sin in the sense of depravity or corruption (in other words, we suffer from the *corruption* of Adam's sin but not from its *guilt*). Ritschl concludes that "even the possibility of maintaining Zwingli's hypothesis disappears."[12] As Ritschl sees things, we do not suffer from original sin. We only suffer from a crippling *doctrine* of original sin. Instead, he proposes that we think in terms of "habitual sin" (to account for the deep-seated nature of sin) and "the kingdom of sin" (to account for the apparent universality of sin).[13]

A Critical Guide, 58–78; John E. Hare, *The Moral Gap: Kantian Ethics, Human Limits, and God's Assistance* (Oxford: Oxford University Press, 1996).

[6] Ritschl, *Justification and Reconciliation*, 335.

[7] Ritschl, *Justification and Reconciliation*, 349.

[8] Kevin Hector, *The Theological Project of Modernism: Faith and the Conditions of Mineness* (Oxford: Oxford University Press, 2015), 192.

[9] Ritschl, *Justification and Reconciliation*, 328.

[10] Ritschl, *Justification and Reconciliation*, 337.

[11] Ritschl, *Justification and Reconciliation*, 340. Interestingly, Emil Brunner agrees with Ritschl that the realist strategy for accounting for original guilt can be held only by a *sacrificium intellectus* and likewise judges federalism to be "far more valuable and relevant" but nonetheless both "insufficient and dangerous." He also labels Ritschl's doctrine "simply a form of Pelagianism, intensified by social psychology" (Brunner, *Man in Revolt: A Christian Anthropology*, trans. Olive Wyon [Philadelphia: Westminster, 1939], 122, 125).

[12] Ritschl, *Justification and Reconciliation*, 378.

[13] Ritschl, *Justification and Reconciliation*, 339, 345.

Sin is not "infinite" in nature (if it were, Ritschl argues, we would be in danger of Manichaeism).[14] Thus sin does not, strictly speaking, require a satisfaction of infinite worth (and Ritschl is happy to rethink the person and work of Christ accordingly).[15] He concludes that sin is both a "mode of action" and a "habitual propensity" which extends over all humanity, and that as such it is the polar opposite of the kingdom of God (which Christ came to usher in).[16] Sinners make themselves guilty, and in doing so they bring about risk of "forfeiture of the privilege of Divine sonship."[17] But "in so far as men, regarded as sinners both in their individual capacity and as a whole, are objects of the redemption and reconciliation made possible by the love of God, sin is estimated by God, not as the final purpose of opposition to the known will of God, but as ignorance."[18] Clearly, for Ritschl, we are sinners in actuality. But he denies the doctrine of original sin.

Much more recently, Richard Dawkins protests, "what kind of ethical philosophy is it that condemns every child, even before it is born, to inherit the sin of a remote ancestor?"[19] But while such vituperation can be expected from the "New Atheists" such as Dawkins, criticism of the doctrine can be found among Christians as well. Edward Oakes summarizes the current situation:

> No doctrine inside the precincts of the Christian Church is received with greater reserve and hesitation, even to the point of outright denial, than the doctrine of original sin. Of course in a secular culture like ours, any number of Christian doctrines will be disputed by outsiders, from the existence of God to the resurrection of Jesus. But even in those denominations that pride themselves on their adherence to the orthodox dogmas of the once-universal Church, the doctrine of original sin is met with either embarrassed silence, outright denial, or at a minimum a kind of half-hearted lip service that does not exactly deny the doctrine but has no idea how to place it inside the devout life.[20]

Gary Anderson comments on Oakes's statement, that, simply put, "the doctrine of original sin appears woefully ill-matched to modern existence."[21] Alastair MacFadyen notes that the traditional doctrine holds that sin is contingent, radical, communicable, and universal, and he states that "the traditional understanding of original sin cannot stand alongside the base assumptions

14 Ritschl, *Justification and Reconciliation*, 368–369.
15 Ritschl, *Justification and Reconciliation*, 385–484.
16 Ritschl, *Justification and Reconciliation*, 383.
17 Ritschl, *Justification and Reconciliation*, 384.
18 Ritschl, *Justification and Reconciliation*, 384.
19 Richard Dawkins, *The God Delusion* (New York: Houghton Mifflin, 2006), 285.
20 Edward Oakes, "Original Sin: A Disputation," *First Things* 87 (November 1998): 16.
21 Gary A. Anderson, "*Necessarium Adae Peccatum*: The Problem of Original Sin," in *Sin, Death, and the Devil*, ed. Carl Braaten and Robert W. Jenson (Grand Rapids, MI: Eerdmans, 2000), 32.

of modern culture."[22] Even more blunt is the post-mortem analysis of Julius Gross: "Modern science has killed original sin."[23]

There are important questions surrounding the doctrine of original sin, and these questions must be faced squarely. One set of questions concerns the historicity of Adam and Eve. Did they actually live? Or are they merely symbolic characters? Another set of questions has to do with our relation to the sin of Adam and Eve (considered traditionally): Does original sin equate to—or entail—original guilt? Just what do we suffer as a result of the first act of human sin? Do we only suffer corruption, or do we somehow bear guilt for the first human sin (as well as for our own subsequent sinful actions)? If we are guilty, then just exactly for what are we guilty? And how might this guilt even possibly be consistent with moral responsibility? After all, if ever there seems to be a case of something over which we do not have involvement or control, then surely the sin of our most remote human ancestors would be it. What are we to make of such questions? And what actually is taught in Scripture?

Accordingly, in this chapter I shall first lay out some of the major theories of original sin; here the purpose is primarily descriptive. Following this, we return to the biblical text for a closer look at the scriptural basis of the doctrine, and here we shall ask both what is demanded by the text as well as what is consistent with the text (even if under-determined by it). This will enable us to return to the major proposals on offer, and we will evaluate them accordingly. In conclusion, I will both summarize the findings of our study and briefly reflect on the role of the doctrine of original sin in pastoral care and apologetic engagement.

II. The Major Theological Options: A Brief Description

Christian theologians throughout the history of the church have wrestled with exactly how to formulate the doctrine of original sin. Questions arise: clearly, original sin involves corruption or pollution, but does original sin also entail original guilt? If guilt is included (as well as pollution or corruption), then for what exactly are we guilty: Adam's own action of sin, or our own state of corruption? And *how* do we account for the guilt of someone else's act of sin being applied or accredited to all? As Stanley Grenz asks, "For what are we guilty—our own individual sins or also the sin of Adam? Do we begin life both sinful and guilty? Are we both depraved and condemned? Does hell await the children of Adam because of the sin he committed, or only because of the sins

---

[22] Alastair MacFadyen, *Bound to Sin: Abuse, Holocaust, and the Christian Doctrine of Sin* (Cambridge: Cambridge University Press, 2000), 29.
[23] Julius Gross, quoted in Christof Gestrich, *The Return of Splendor in the World: The Christian Doctrine of Sin and Forgiveness* (Grand Rapids, MI: Eerdmans, 1997), 228.

we commit?"[24] There have been no firm statements agreed upon or endorsed by ecumenical councils, and on several important points there has never been anything approaching theological consensus (on other points, as we shall see, there indeed has been widespread agreement). Indeed, it is not hard to spot disagreement *within* ecclesial and theological traditions. Several major options have emerged.

A. (Merely) Symbolic and Existentialist Interpretations

Modern theologians have often felt the pressure of the pronouncements of modern science (assertions that this science renders impossible belief in a historical Adam and Eve), and they have sometimes responded by denying that Adam and Eve really existed or were theologically important as such.[25]

F. R. Tennant was a British clergyman and philosophical theologian of the late nineteenth and early twentieth centuries who worked hard to take with full seriousness the implications of modern evolutionary science for the doctrine of original sin. He is well aware that the broadly traditional view of a "fall" from innocence and integrity into sin and brokenness is "almost unanimous" in the "mind of the Church from an early time," and that there are "few truths of the Christian Faith that have received more general acknowledgment than this doctrine of human nature."[26] Joining many other modern theologians, he is confident that historical-critical biblical scholarship has undermined the older theological claims.[27] He is also fully convinced that modern evolutionary science demands a thoroughgoing reconsideration of the traditional doctrine, and he is certain that intellectual honesty calls for nothing short of a complete reformulation of the doctrine. For, given the facts of evolution, it is simply incredible to believe that there was an innocent or perfect first human pair who then sinned and descended into ruin and death. What we learn from the natural sciences is that humankind has *ascended* rather than *descended*, and Christian theology simply needs to accept this fact.

Tennant notes that the doctrine of original sin includes both the "recognition of this all-pervasive taint of moral evil" in humanity and a purported explanation of that moral evil and its source.[28] He does not deny the recognition. Indeed, he works hard to oppose all forms of modern optimism that would wish to deny or even downplay the fact of universal moral evil. What he rejects about the traditional doctrine is its purported explanation of that fact.

---

[24] Stanley J. Grenz, *Theology for the Community of God* (Grand Rapids, MI: Eerdmans, 2000), 199.

[25] For further discussion, see the Appendix.

[26] F. R. Tennant, *The Origin and Propagation of Sin* (Cambridge: Cambridge University Press, 1902), 4–5.

[27] N. P. Williams, for instance, is in agreement with Tennant regarding the importance of historical-critical study of the OT (especially as read in light of other ancient Near Eastern literature); for him, the point of such study is to get inside the head of the Yahwist (e.g., Williams, *The Ideas of the Fall and of Original Sin* [London: Longman, Green, 1927], 40–51).

[28] Tennant, *Origin and Propagation of Sin*, 8.

That moral evil is both universal and debilitating is a fact, and this is one that he defends. What he will not defend is the traditional explanation of this fact; what he rejects is the myth of a fall from innocence.

Contrary to common objections to his suggestions, Tennant denies that his rejection of a historical fall entails Pelagianism or similar heresies.[29] As he puts it, "[T]he existence of sin is the sufficient basis of the doctrines of grace and redemption"—we simply do not need a historical fall to account for the Christian doctrine of salvation.[30] Moreover, not only are the traditional versions of the doctrine of sin at odds with modern science, they are also problematic theologically. The very notion of inherited guilt (as is common in Reformed theology), Tennant insists, "involves a contradiction" and thus "stands self-condemned."[31] In place of the traditional doctrine, he proposes this: what we commonly call "sin" has been part of the warp and woof of the evolution of the species, and humankind has never existed without it. But it was not "sin" in the truest sense before the evolutionary development of moral sensibilities and conscience. So in place of the notion that the first humans existed in peace and harmony with God and neighbor, "the evolutionary account of the origin of sin would substitute for it the assertion that sin does not, and cannot, exist at all without the law, and that motions in man which the first recognised sanction condemned were natural and non-moral; not sinful, even in the sense of being abnormal or displeasing to God."[32] Accordingly, "[t]o the evolutionist sin is not an innovation, but is the survival or misuse of habits and tendencies that were incidental to an earlier stage of development," and whose "sinfulness lies in their anachronism."[33]

Tennant readily admits that Paul and the other authors of Scripture seem to have believed in a "historical Adam from whom the human race derives its woes," and he sees that this conflicts with the deliverances of modern science: "whereas if we are committed to the evolutionary view of man's history and of the origin of his sinfulness, . . . it is no longer possible for us to share that belief."[34] But he also insists that modern science demands truly modern theology: "We cannot always take Scripture statements, . . . as equivalent to the observed facts of the natural sciences, and make theology merely by induction or deduction from them. This was necessarily the method of theology in the past," but it cannot be the way forward.[35] The traditional doctrine is flawed,

---

[29] Cf. Williams's Schleiermacherian resistance to Pelagianism: "[I]ts vicious doctrine of unlimited indeterminism abolished the essence of true religion by abolishing man's feeling of absolute dependence upon God . . ." (*Ideas of the Fall*, xxi).

[30] Tennant, *Origin and Propagation of Sin*, 13.

[31] Tennant, *Origin*, 20.

[32] Tennant, *Origin*, 92.

[33] Tennant, *Origin*, 93.

[34] Tennant, *Origin*, 145.

[35] Tennant, *Origin*, 145.

and fatally so. The only responsible thing to do is to give it up for dead. It is mistaken, and it does not ultimately matter: "the fictitious importance assigned by Theology, in its most scholastic and artificial periods, to the doctrines of the Fall and of Original Sin is an accident of history, not the outcome of the necessary development of the Faith."[36]

Theologians such as F. D. E. Schleiermacher, Paul Tillich, and John Macquarrie interpret the sin of Adam and Eve to be purely symbolic of the passage of humans (understood either individually or collectively) from a kind of innocence to sin and alienation. Thus "original sin" refers only to the sin that originates within each of us, and not as something related to the sins of our first parents. Similarly, Karl Barth interprets the Genesis account as "saga" rather than history (with this saga telling us that "world-history began with the pride and fall of man"), announces that "there never was a golden age," but that "the first man was immediately the first sinner."[37] Barth is critical of the notion of "hereditary sin."[38] As Grenz summarizes the view, "[T]hose who argue that Adam is a symbol do not read the Genesis narrative of the fall as the account of one man in pre-history. Rather, it is a non-discursive description of the experience of humankind or of every historical person. . . . The fall, therefore, is not an event in the primordial past but a reality that we either corporately share or individually experience."[39]

B. Corruption-Only Doctrines

Turning now to more traditional conceptions of original sin, one major option is the affirmation of *corruption* in original sin *without a corresponding affirmation of guilt*. This was the view of early (pre-Augustinian) Christian theology. J. N. D. Kelly says that, although Athanasius saw a strong connection between Adam and all humanity, and indeed held that "sin has passed to all men," he "never hints that we participate in Adam's actual guilt."[40] Greek Patristic theology generally held that "man's mortality, his subjection to pain and sickness, his ignorance, his weakness of will and enslavement to desire; . . . [his] idolatry in religion, and violence, poverty and slavery in the social sphere" are all the direct results of the fall.[41] Nonetheless, "there is hardly a hint in the Greek fathers that mankind as a whole shares in Adam's guilt, i.e., his culpability."[42] As for pre-Augustinian Latin Patristic theology, Kelly takes as representative Ambrose's view that sin as a "corrupting force" is transmit-

---

[36] Tennant, *Origin*, 150.
[37] Karl Barth, *CD*, IV/1, 508.
[38] Barth, *CD*, IV/1, 500.
[39] Grenz, *Theology for the Community of God*, 195.
[40] J. N. D. Kelly, *Early Christian Doctrines*, rev. ed. (New York: HarperCollins, 1978), 347.
[41] Kelly, *Early Christian Doctrines*, 349.
[42] Kelly, *Early Christian Doctrines*, 350.

ted to all humanity, but the guilt for Adam's sin "attaches to Adam himself, not to us."[43]

This is often understood to be the view of the Orthodox Church. Timothy Ware notes that "[m]ost Orthodox theologians reject the idea of 'original guilt.' . . . Humans (Orthodox usually teach) automatically inherit Adam's corruption and mortality, but not his guilt: they are only guilty in so far as by their own free choice they imitate Adam."[44]

The corruption-only view is present in Protestantism as well. Within the Reformed tradition itself, it was defended by the important Reformer Huldrych Zwingli. Zwingli is known for his thoroughgoing and uncompromising determinism.[45] He is convinced that God is the cause of all things; indeed, read charitably, Zwingli comes close to an outright affirmation of monocausality (in addition to omnicausality). He is also well known for his reflections on the meanings of baptism and the Eucharist. He is perhaps less known for his doctrine of original sin, but it marks an important moment in the development of Protestant hamartiology. Zwingli understands that his view is recognized by some theologians as "an unusual doctrine."[46] Zwingli is convinced that sin is the transgression of the law of God. He is further convinced that all humans (with one most notable exception) are sinners, and he is sure that sin condemns sinners to eternal punishment. This much is plain, and this much is not at all unusual in Christian theology. But Zwingli also holds that original sin is not sin as such, and it does not bring guilt and condemnation with it: "For what could be said more briefly and plainly than that original sin is not sin but a disease, and that the children of Christians are not condemned to eternal punishment on account of that disease?"[47] Zwingli argues for his view directly from Scripture; after all, he reasons, Holy Writ clearly tells us that without the law there is no transgression (e.g., Rom. 3:20; 4:15), and the biblical witness to the fact that "the son shall not bear the guilt of his father" (Ezek. 18:20) seems plain enough.[48]

We can briefly summarize Zwingli's position as follows:[49] first, all humans (other than Christ) are corrupted by the original sin of Adam. No one escapes

---

[43] Kelly, *Early Christian Doctrines*, 354.

[44] Timothy (Kallistos) Ware, *The Orthodox Church* (New York: Penguin, 1993), 224.

[45] On Zwingli's theology see W. Peter Stephens, *The Theology of Huldrych Zwingli* (Oxford: Oxford University Press, 1986); and Stephens, "The Theology of Zwingli," in *The Cambridge Companion to Reformation Theology*, ed. David Bagchi and David C. Steinmetz (Cambridge: Cambridge University Press, 2004), 80–99.

[46] Huldrych Zwingli, "Declaration of Huldrych Zwingli Regarding Original Sin, Addressed to Urbanus Rhegius," in Ulrich Zwingli, *On Providence and Other Essays*, edited for Samuel Macauley Jackson by William John Hinke (Durham, NC: Labyrinth, 1983 [1922]), 2.

[47] Zwingli, "Declaration of Huldrych Zwingli Regarding Original Sin," 3. He goes on to opine that the "most probable conclusion" regarding the children of unregenerate persons is that they too are not condemned for original sin alone (18–19).

[48] See Stephens, *Theology of Huldrych Zwingli*, 149–150.

[49] Although my summary differs from his in some respects, I am indebted to Oliver D. Crisp, "Retrieving Zwingli's Doctrine of Original Sin," *JournRT* (2016): 340–360.

this original sin; all suffer from its corruption. Second, this condition of original sin is the result of self-love. Third, while this corruption brings us to utter moral ruin, we are not somehow guilty for this inherited condition. Nor are we culpable for what Adam did in Eden. Fourth, all humans are guilty—but they are guilty for what *they* do. Their corruption inevitably produces actual sins, and we are guilty for these sinful actions. We are not guilty either for what Adam did or for having the corrupting condition itself, but we are guilty and condemned.

Thus all who live are infected by original sin, and all who develop (thus barring the cases of the children of believers) inevitably commit actual sins. Since sin incurs the wrath of God and brings well-deserved condemnation from God, all who live and develop are in point of fact objectively guilty and now stand condemned before God. Zwingli thus rejects Luther's accusation that he is a Pelagian, and he insists upon the universality and totality of original sin.[50] But original sin is to be understood in terms of corruption-only rather than as corruption-plus-guilt-for-what-Adam-did.

Arminius appears to have endorsed a corruption-only view (at least tentatively).[51] Within the Wesleyan-Arminian tradition, several important theologians (though certainly not all) in the later nineteenth century endorse this view as well. John Miley, for example, says that the notion of original guilt is "openly contradictory to the deepest and most determining principle of the Arminian system."[52] He concludes that original sin is "the corruption of the nature of every man, . . . whereby man is very far gone from original righteousness, and of his own nature inclined to evil, and that continually."[53] The "true doctrine," he insists, is "native depravity without native demerit."[54]

More recently, corruption-only doctrines have been embraced by philosophical theologians such as Richard Swinburne and systematic theologians

[50] See the discussion in Stephens, *Theology of Huldrych Zwingli*, 148–153.
[51] See the discussion in Keith D. Stanglin and Thomas H. McCall, *Jacob Arminius: Theologian of Grace* (Oxford: Oxford University Press, 2012), 149–150. This despite the fact that Arminius is something of a pioneer of the covenant theology so characteristic of federalism. For further discussion, see Raymond A. Blacketer, "Arminius's Concept of Covenant in Its Historical Context," *Nederlands Archief voor Kerkeschiendis* (2000): 193–220; and Richard A. Muller, "Toward the *Pactum Salutis*: Locating the Origin of a Concept," *Mid-America Journal of Theology* (2007): 11–65.
It should also be noted that later Remonstrant theologians modify the doctrine in some very significant ways (and sometimes reject it outright). For instance, Simon Episcopius takes a notably more restrained approach and does not address many of the traditional categories. Later, Philipp von Limborch affirms that humans are in fact sinful and guilty, bound by sin to such an extent that they cannot be free to do good or be saved apart from grace, and they face damnation. But he explicitly denies the view that Adam's sin was debilitating to Adam's progeny (with respect to either guilt or corruption); they are partially corrupted by a propensity to sin but not by sin itself. He also denies that his view is Pelagian. See Philipp van Limborch, *Theologiae Christianae* (Amsterdam: 1686), III.I–VI, 173–200; cf. van Limborch, *Compleat System or Body of Divinity* (London: 1702), 183–205.
[52] John Miley, *Systematic Theology*, 2 vols. (New York: Eaton & Mains, 1892), 1:522. See also, e.g., Randolph Sinks Foster, *Sin*, vol. 6 of *Studies in Theology* (New York: Eaton & Mains, 1899), 140–182.
[53] Miley, *Systematic Theology*, 1:523.
[54] Miley, *Systematic Theology*, 1:521.

such as Stanley Grenz.[55] Grenz concludes that "[o]riginal sin does not directly entail guilt. The possession of the fallen nature alone does not bring condemnation. Rather than declaring that guilt is directly due to original sin, the biblical writers teach that God judges us according to our works (Jer. 17:9–10; Rom. 2:6). The great Judge renders his verdict not on the basis of our fallen nature, but because of our deeds, which we do as our depraved nature expresses itself in thought and overt action."[56]

Traditionally, two aspects have been recognized as central to the notion of hereditary or original corruption (*corruptio hereditaria*). The first is the loss or privation of the original righteousness that was enjoyed by Adam and Eve in their prelapsarian state, while the second, which follows from it and comes to fill the void that is left by the loss of righteousness, is the perversion of the moral nature of humanity. Heinrich Heppe summarizes the classical Reformed statement of this position by saying that "this corruption is a twofold one: (1) 'the defect of original good' and (2) 'the succession of evil to the place of original good.'"[57] So the first aspect is strictly negative, for it concerns only the loss of what was enjoyed by the first humans and then forfeited by them in the fall. The second aspect, on the other hand, refers more to a kind of filth or pollution that now pervades the human nature. With original righteousness, our primeval parents were both free from sin and able not to sin. As Oliver D. Crisp explains, "Adam and Eve were sinless and able not to sin. As the Reformed Orthodox put it, Adam was created with a *natura integra* (morally upright nature) such that it was true that he was *posse non peccare et posse peccare* (able not to sin and able to sin). But in addition to the loss of this grace at the moment of the Fall, Adam and Eve gained a morally depraved nature or *macula*."[58]

Proponents of the "corruption-only" view are often drawn to it because they find the evidence for universal and devastating corruption to be blatantly obvious—but also because they worry that any corresponding claims about original guilt are neither demanded by the biblical evidence nor congruent with true justice. So on one hand, they find the evidence for corruption everywhere; it is all too glaringly obvious from general human experience, and it is confirmed by the Bible. The Formula of Concord pulls no punches about the state of corruption: "Original sin is not a slight, but so deep a corruption of human nature that nothing healthy or uncorrupt in man's body or soul, in inner or outward powers, remains."[59] The results of it are utterly devastating,

[55] E.g., Richard Swinburne, *Responsibility and Atonement* (Oxford: Oxford University Press, 1989), esp. 73–147. See also, e.g., Keith D. Wyma, "Innocent Sinfulness, Guilty Sin: Original Sin and Divine Justice," in *Christian Faith and the Problem of Evil*, ed. Peter van Inwagen (Grand Rapids, MI: Eerdmans, 2004), 263–276.
[56] Grenz, *Theology for the Community of God*, 206.
[57] Heinrich Heppe, *Reformed Dogmatics* (Eugene, OR: Wipf & Stock, 2007), 336.
[58] Oliver D. Crisp, *An American Augustinian: Sin and Salvation in the Dogmatic Theology of William G. T. Shedd* (Waynesboro, GA: Paternoster, 2007), 38–39.
[59] The Formula of Concord (Epitome), art. I.8.

and common human experience leads us to its recognition: who can witness the callous cruelty of young children toward their peers—much less the brutality of accomplished and sophisticated adults—and doubt the fact of the corruption of human nature? But the full extent of its destructive force is hidden from the "natural" and depraved perspective; it can be seen clearly only under the spotlight of divine revelation. As Francis Pieper puts it,

> But the full understanding of the depths of the innate corruption and its origin in the fall of our first parents is gained only from the revelation of Holy Scripture. The Smalcald Articles point out this fact in the words: "This hereditary sin is so deep and horrible a corruption of nature that no reason can understand it, but it must be learned and believed from the revelation of Scripture."[60]

The effects of this corruption are as far-reaching as they are devastating. The corruption impacts the intellect, it perverts the will, and it leaves us at enmity with God in the totality of who we are as individual persons and as societies and communities.[61] It is the fountain from which flow forth all manner of actual sins. As Pieper explains, "[A]ccording to Gal. 5:19–21 'adultery, fornication, uncleanness, lasciviousness, idolatry, witchcraft, hatred, variance, emulations, wrath, strife, seditions, heresies, envyings, murders, drunkenness, revelings, and such like' are the works of the flesh, actions proceeding from the hereditary corruption."[62] Paul summarizes the terrible effects of this corruption:

> "None is righteous, no, not one;
> > no one understands,
> > no one seeks for God.
> All have turned aside; together they have become worthless;
> > no one does good,
> > not even one."
> "Their throat is an open grave;
> > they use their tongues to deceive."
> "The venom of asps is under their lips."
> > "Their mouth is full of curses and bitterness."
> "Their feet are swift to shed blood;
> > in their paths are ruin and misery,
> and the way of peace they have not known."
> > "There is no fear of God before their eyes." (Rom. 3:10–18)

Proponents of the "corruption-only" view hold to this position because they are convinced that there is ample evidence for corruption—a corruption of the human nature that is deep and vast beyond telling. But on the other

---

[60] Francis Pieper, *Christian Dogmatics*, 4 vols. (St. Louis: Concordia, 1950), 1:541.
[61] See the illuminating discussion by, e.g., Pieper, *Christian Dogmatics*, 1:543–547.
[62] Pieper, *Christian Dogmatics*, 1:557.

hand, they typically do not find such evidence for original guilt. Furthermore, they often argue that the doctrine of original guilt is utterly contrary to true justice. Sometimes they argue from a broad sense of justice (with clear reliance on intuitions about such matters), but sometimes they argue directly *from Scripture* against the view that the sin of another is imputed to us (e.g., Deut. 24:16; Jer. 31:29–30; Ezek. 18:20). So they conclude that not only do we not need to believe in original guilt (since it isn't demanded by Scripture), we should *refrain* from the affirmation of original guilt.

This position should not be misunderstood. Proponents of the "corruption-only" view insist that we are, of course, guilty for sin. But we are guilty for the sins that *we commit*; we are not guilty for something that our first parents did. We obtain a kind of hereditary corruption from them (not unlike how purely physical defects are heritable and inherited), and we are guilty for sin as a matter of fact. But the sin for which we are guilty is *our own*; we are guilty for the sins we commit, and we are guilty for only the sins that we commit. Adam is guilty for his sins. And while we suffer the results of Adam's sin, it is our own sin for which we are guilty.

It is important not to confuse the "corruption-only" view of original sin with Pelagianism. Perhaps the view *could*—depending on how the corruption is understood with respect to its intensity and extent—give safe harbor to a kind of "Semi-Pelagianism." But a theologian could also hold to the "corruption-only" view and fully embrace what the Formula of Concord says about corruption:

> In spiritual and divine things the intellect, heart, and will of the unregenerate man are utterly unable by their own natural powers to understand, believe, accept, think, will, effect, do, work, or concur in working, anything; but that they are entirely dead to what is good, and corrupt; . . . Hence the natural free will according to its perverted condition and nature is strong and active only with respect to what is *displeasing and contrary to God*.[63]

Surely this is a far cry from Pelagianism. Moreover, it should be obvious that there is nothing about the view as such that commits it to "Semi-Pelagianism," for one can hold the corruption-only view and with consistency maintain the admission of complete inability and even "total depravity." But is it adequate as an understanding of original sin? Or does a proper understanding of original sin also demand belief in original *guilt*?

C. Corruption and Guilt: Federalism

The classical liberal theologian Albrecht Ritschl exclaims that "inherited sin and personal guilt cannot be combined in thought without inaccuracy or a

---

[63] The Formula of Concord (Thorough Declaration), art. II.7.

sacrificium intellectus."[64] Despite such protests, however, many theologians
(especially from the various branches of Protestantism) insist not only on
original corruption (*corruptio hereditaria*) but also on original guilt (*culpa
hereditaria*) as well. Thus Pieper: "Original sin, which is the sin which is not
committed but which is inborn in man since Adam's fall, embraces two things:
a) hereditary guilt, . . . the guilt of the one sin of Adam which God imputes to
all men; and b) hereditary corruption."[65] Popular or not, easy to digest or not,
proponents insist, "the imputation of original guilt belongs to the stubborn
facts which Scripture teaches as undeniable truth."[66]

So according to "federalism" (or "representationalism"), we are said to be
guilty for what Adam did; we are considered guilty for something that we did
not do and over which we had no control. To say that this view is counterintuitive is to put it mildly, and theologians who hold to both original corruption
and original guilt often feel the need to posit a theory that allows us to make
(moral) sense of the matter.

Appealing to Romans 5:12–21, the proponents of this view say that Adam
functions as our "federal" or "representative" head. We are not, they say, somehow *really* present in or with Adam (this is the view known as "realism");
instead, he functions for us or on our behalf as our "public person" or representative. Michael Scott Horton says that "Adam's covenantal role entailed that
he was the representative for his whole posterity. In fact, every person is judged
guilty in Adam, and the effects of this curse extend even to the rest of creation
(Ge 3:17–18; Ro 8:20)."[67] Similarly, Millard Erickson says that, on this view,
"Adam was on probation for us all, as it were; and because Adam sinned, all
of us are treated as guilty and corrupted. Bound by the covenant between God
and Adam, we are treated as if we have actually and personally done what he
as our representative did."[68] Henri Blocher points out that many theologians
who take this line hold that corruption actually *follows from* the guilt; on
this view, it is "because of Adam's federal headship, [that] his transgression
is charged to the account of his descendants; before they are conceived, they
are condemned and sentenced to death."[69] So, according to federalism, we are
condemned because Adam stood in for us as the representative of the whole
human race; due to his relationship to us as our "federal head" or "legally
appointed representative," his guilt thus counts as our guilt. And despite the
obvious and significant dis-analogies in Roman 5:12–21, the situation with

[64] Ritschl, *Justification and Reconciliation*, 340.
[65] Pieper, *Christian Dogmatics*, 1:538.
[66] John Theodore Mueller, *Christian Dogmatics: A Handbook of Doctrinal Theology for Pastors, Teachers, and Laymen* (St. Louis: Concordia, 1955), 217.
[67] Michael Scott Horton, *The Christian Faith: A Systematic Theology for Pilgrims on the Way* (Grand Rapids, MI: Zondervan Academic, 2011), 415.
[68] Millard Erickson, *Christian Theology*, 2nd ed. (Grand Rapids, MI: Baker Academic, 1998), 652.
[69] Henri Blocher, *Original Sin: Illuminating the Riddle* (Downers Grove, IL: IVP Academic, 2000), 73.

Christ is directly similar: because Christ stands in as the federal head or legally appointed representative of humanity (or some portion thereof), his righteousness now counts legally as ours.

Federalism has a distinguished history. Francis Turretin stands as an important representative theologian from the Reformed tradition. He summarizes the view:

> For the bond between Adam and his posterity is twofold: (1) natural, as he is the father, and we are his children; (2) political and forensic, as he was the prince and representative head of the whole human race. Therefore the foundation of imputation is not only the natural connection which exists between us and Adam (since, in that case, all his sins might be imputed to us), but mainly the moral and federal (in virtue of which God entered into covenant with him as our head). Hence Adam stood in that sin not as a private person, but as a public and representative person—representing all his posterity in that action and whose demerit equally pertains to all.[70]

This view is often taken to be "*the* Reformed view." This is understandable, for surely many Reformed theologians hold such a position.

But an overly neat and tidy categorization is inaccurate and potentially misleading here, for some theologians in the Reformed tradition—including such noteworthy theologians as Jonathan Edwards and William G. T. Shedd—do not hold to such a view; some prefer "realism." At the same time, many theologians who do not wear the label of "Reformed" maintain and defend the "federalist" position. John Wesley wrote to John Newton saying that, on the doctrine of sin, his view was not even a "hair's breadth" different from that of John Calvin.[71] Wesley's longest single treatise is written on the doctrine of original sin. In it, as we have seen, he forcefully rejects the optimistic anthropology of John Taylor (among others). Wesley says of Taylor that "I verily believe no single person since Mahomet has given such a wound to Christianity as Dr. Taylor. They are his books, chiefly that upon Original Sin, which have poisoned so many of the clergy . . ."[72] In his sermon "Original Sin," Wesley insists that all who deny the doctrine of original sin "are but Heathens still, in the fundamental point which differences Heathenism from Christianity."[73] Notably, Wesley defends the Westminster Confession by detailed exegetical study.[74]

---

[70] Francis Turretin, *Institutio Theologiae Elencticae, Pars Prima* (Geneva: 1688), I.IX.9 (679) (*Institutes of Elenctic Theology, Volume One: First through Tenth Topics*, trans. George Musgrave Giger, ed. James T. Dennison Jr. [Phillipsburg, NJ: Presbyterian & Reformed, 1992], 616).

[71] See the discussion in Barry E. Bryant, "Original Sin," in *The Oxford Handbook of Methodist Studies*, ed. William J. Abraham and James E. Kirby (Oxford: Oxford University Press, 2009), 534.

[72] See Kenneth Collins, *The Scripture Way of Salvation: The Heart of John Wesley's Theology* (Nashville: Abingdon, 1997), 31.

[73] John Wesley, "Original Sin," in *Wesley's 52 Standard Sermons* (Salem, OH: Schmul, 1988), 456.

[74] See Thomas C. Oden, *John Wesley's Scriptural Christianity: A Plain Account of His Teaching on Christian Doctrine* (Grand Rapids, MI: Zondervan, 1994), 158f.

More precisely, he defends the Confession's federalism.[75] Some of the major theologians of the Wesleyan-Arminian tradition do so as well. Thomas N. Ralston, for instance, says that "the most rational and scriptural view of the subject" is the federal view: Adam "was the federal head and proper legal representative of his posterity . . . [and] the guilt of Adam [is] imputed to them."[76] So do Richard Watson (whose work was heralded by Henry C. Sheldon as the "unrivaled textbook of American Methodism"), Samuel Wakefield, and William Burt Pope.[77] So while federalism is characteristic of the Reformed tradition, it cannot be called "*the* Reformed view," for some Reformed theologians criticize and reject it, while some decidedly non-Reformed theologians accept and defend it.

Proponents of the federalist position argue from the language of "condemnation" and "justification" in Romans 5:12–21; here, they say, we see the legal language that is characteristic of representation. We are not *really* in Christ; we are represented by him. By the parallel suggested in the passage itself, then, we should conclude that we are legally or politically represented by Adam rather than *really* in him. As the righteousness of Christ is imputed to us in a legal or forensic sense, so also the sin of Adam was imputed to us in a legal or forensic sense. Our justification comes by way of the imputation of our sins to Christ and his righteousness to us; directly parallel to that is the imputation of Adam's sin to us.

Despite its popularity, however, federalist accounts of original sin have not managed to quiet all criticism. One line of criticism is especially pertinent to those proponents who also endorse a Reformed doctrine of predestination (this is most obvious with respect to supralapsarianism, but it is not restricted to it). According to federalism, we are accounted or considered guilty by God by virtue of the fact that Adam's sin is imputed to us. But combining federalism with Reformed views of predestination yields a result that is at least odd. According to the standard Reformed doctrines of predestination, the elect have been the elect (unconditionally) from before the foundation of the world. So the person who is elect—but not yet regenerate and justified—is both "in Adam" (in the federalist sense) and thus condemned, *and* in some sense simultaneously "in Christ" (in the federalist sense) and thus

<hr>

[75] E.g., John Wesley, "The Doctrine of Original Sin," in *The Works of John Wesley*, vol. 9 (Grand Rapids, MI: Zondervan, n.d.), 261–262, 332–334.
[76] Thomas N. Ralston, *Elements of Divinity: A Concise and Comprehensive View of Bible Theology, Comprising the Doctrines, Evidences, Morals, and Institutions of Christianity* (New York: Abingdon, 1847), 120.
[77] See Richard Watson, *Theological Institutes: Or, a View of the Evidences, Doctrines, Morals, and Institutions of Christianity*, 2 vols. (New York: Bangs & Emory, 1826), 2:215–218; Samuel Wakefield, *A Complete System of Christian Theology: or, A Concise, Comprehensive, and Systematic View of the Evidences, Doctrines, Morals, and Institutions of Christianity* (Cincinnati: Cranston & Stowe, 1858), 292–300; William Burt Pope, *A Compendium of Christian Theology: Being Analytical Outlines of a Course of Theological Study, Biblical, Dogmatic, Historical*, 3 vols., 2nd ed. (New York: Hunt & Eaton, 1889), 2:48–63.

legally righteous. But condemnation and justification are contradictory. So which is it?[78]

More pressing is the concern, already mentioned, that a prima facie case can be made from Scripture that the guilt of one person is not transferred to another (Deut. 24:16; Jer. 31:29–30; Ezek. 18:20). The "realist" views (to be described next) at least try to account for the presence of personal (rather than "alien") guilt in original sin (meanwhile, as we have seen, the "corruption-only" proponents think that such an effort is a lost cause and instead focus on the guilt of actual sins that have been committed by the persons in question). The worry here is that the federalist position simply cannot account for the apparently brazen miscarriage of justice that it proposes. Note that, according to federalism, every person is *judged* guilty, and we should take care not to misunderstand what this means. As Crisp explains, on this view "there is no real transference of properties from Adam to his posterity. Adam's posterity does not gain the property of Adam's sin and guilt as the deposit of original sin. Rather, God arranges things such that Adam's progeny are treated *as if* they had sinned with Adam and *as if* they had Adam's guilt."[79] As Anthony Hoekema admits, "probably the greatest difficulty with this view is that it seems to suggest that God imputes to us the guilt of a sin that we did not commit."[80] As Henri Blocher points out, "[I]mputation of alien guilt strains the sense of justice in most readers."[81] Crisp is more blunt: "The federal view means that God makes Adam's posterity morally responsible for a sin that they did not commit. Worse still, God constitutes things such that, by way of the legal fiction of representationalism in federal theology, all of Adam's posterity must suffer as if they had committed his sin, solely because he has been appointed by God as their federal head."[82] He judges that "it seems monumentally unjust that God should condemn me for the sin of another, particularly for the sin of a long dead ancestor. Why, we might ask, should I be punished for the sin of Adam?"[83] Similarly, Michael C. Rea observes that the federalist theory stands in "obvious tension" with moral responsibility.[84] And since no doctrine of sin can even begin to make (moral and biblical) sense without an adequate concept of moral responsibility, the criticisms of federalism should be taken seriously.

---

[78] The "in some sense" is no doubt very important here, but it is also vague. Surely the Reformed theologian has room to work here in response. My point is not that this is a knockdown argument against federalism, but rather that this raises some interesting worries that deserve attention.

[79] Crisp, *American Augustinian*, 41.

[80] Anthony Hoekema, *Created in God's Image* (Grand Rapids, MI: Eerdmans, 1986), 162.

[81] Blocher, *Original Sin*, 121.

[82] Crisp, *American Augustinian*, 41.

[83] Crisp, *American Augustinian*, 41–42.

[84] Michael C. Rea, "The Metaphysics of Original Sin," in *Persons, Human and Divine*, ed. Peter van Inwagen and Dean Zimmerman (Oxford: Oxford University Press, 2007), 327.

D. Corruption and Guilt: Realism

Perhaps the most prominent alternative to the federalist position is what is often termed the "realist" view. As realists see things, there is a sense in which we are one—that is, *really* one, rather than just viewed as one in a legal sense— with Adam. That is, as Crisp explains, in some way "Adam's progeny were somehow *really* present with Adam at the point of his first sin."[85] According to Augustine,

> For we were all in that one man, since we all were that one man, who fell into sin. . . . For not yet was the particular form created and distributed to us, in which we as individuals were to live, but already the seminal nature was there from which we were to be propagated; and this being vitiated by sin, and bound by the chain of death, and justly condemned, man could not be born of man in any other state.[86]

Elsewhere, Augustine claims that "by the evil will of that one man all sinned in him, since all were that one man, from whom, therefore, they individually derived original sin."[87] Note that Augustine makes the claim that "we all *were* that one man." He is not merely saying that we are represented by that one man; his claim is not that one man stands in for us. No, we just *are* that one man—*in some sense*.

Augustine is representative, but he is not alone in holding such views. Perhaps the most famous proponent of realism (after Augustine) is Jonathan Edwards. Edwards says that

> God, in every step of his proceeding with Adam, in relation to the covenant or constitution established with him, looked on his posterity as being *one with him*. And though he dealt more immediately with Adam, yet it was as the *head* of the whole body, and the *root* of the whole tree, and in his proceedings with him, he dealt with all the branches, as if they had been existing in their root. . . .
>
> [Thus] both guilt, or exposedness to punishment, and also depravity of heart, came upon Adam's posterity just as they came upon him, as much as if he and they had all co-existed, like a tree with many branches. . . . I think this will naturally follow on the supposition of there being a *constituted oneness* or *identity* of Adam and his posterity in this affair.[88]

This bold claim calls for some explanation, and Edwards continues by saying that

---

[85] Crisp, *American Augustinian*, 42.
[86] Augustine, *De civitate Dei* 13.14.2 (PL 41:386; NPNF¹ 2:251).
[87] Augustine, *De nuptiis et concupiscentia* 2.15 (PL 44:444; NPNF¹ 5:288).
[88] Jonathan Edwards, *The Works of Jonathan Edwards*, vol. 3, *Original Sin*, ed. Clyde A. Holbrook (New Haven, CT: Yale University Press, 1970), 220, emphasis original.

> [s]ome things are *entirely distinct*, and *very diverse*, which yet are so united by the established law of the Creator, that by virtue of that establishment, they are in a sense *one*. Thus a *tree*, grown great, and a hundred years old, is *one* plant with the little *sprout*, that first came out of the ground from whence it grew, and has been continued in constant succession. . . . [though] perhaps not one atom the very same: yet God, according to an established law of nature, has in constant succession communicated to it many of the same qualities, and most important properties, as if it were *one* . . . [89]

So apparently something(s) count(s) as one if—and only if—God reckons it so, and this is what makes it *really* so. According to Edwards, all of this depends in a radical sense upon divine sovereignty, for "there is no identity or oneness" that does not depend "on the *arbitrary* constitution of the Creator."[90] We shall revisit this proposal presently when we examine the views theologically, but at this point this much should be clear (or at least reasonably clear): Edwards appears to endorse a realist (rather than a strictly federalist) view of original sin, and he bases the unity of Adam and Adam's progeny upon the arbitrary decision of the sovereign will of God.

Crisp helpfully observes that there is more than one realist view on the table at this point. One version of realism is what Crisp refers to as the "common human nature version."[91] Here Adam and his descendants are distinct individuals who share a common human nature, and the nature that they share in common is corrupt and fallen. Crisp draws an analogy with the blueprint of an automobile that is tampered with, and the prototype damaged in a dangerous way. All subsequent cars coming off the production line will be damaged in the same dangerous way as the prototype. "In a similar way, if Adam's sin affects human nature for the worse, then all subsequent instances of the same human nature will be adversely affected, as the production-line models based on the prototype, Adam."[92] This is, Crisp concludes, a "moderate version of Augustinian realism."[93] As we shall see, this type of analogy works quite well to explain corruption, but it is less than obvious that it has the resources to handle the issue of guilt.

The other version of realism is much more bold. It is a view that sees the one reality as something more like a metaphysical whole made up of Adam-and-progeny, where Adam and his descendants make up some kind of larger, organic whole that extends through time and is extended across space (to include all). In Edwards's own construal, what makes this larger metaphysical

---

[89] Cited in Rea, "Metaphysics of Original Sin," 333–334, emphasis original.
[90] Edwards, *Original Sin*, 403, emphasis original.
[91] Crisp, *American Augustinian*, 43.
[92] Crisp, *American Augustinian*, 44.
[93] Crisp, *American Augustinian*, 45.

whole being just what it is—*one thing*—is nothing more nor less than God's will exercised in an arbitrary way.

Realism promises to avoid the indictment most commonly delivered to the proponents of federalism; where federalism faces the worries associated with "legal fiction"—indeed, legal fiction that brings the condemnation of eternal damnation—realism makes claims to *real* unity with Adam and his act of sin. Yet realism is not without critics. Critics of realism are often quick to point out that Augustine misunderstood the important phrase in Romans 5:12; Augustine's Latin text read *in quo* rather than *eph hō*, thus causing him to conclude that the "in whom" was literal (rather than the "because of . . ." that reflects *eph hō* in most English translations). The defenders of realism readily grant this, however, and steadfastly maintain their view. For as Hoekema admits, "The realistic understanding of our relationship to Adam's sin, however, does not stand or fall with the Vulgate translation; even when rendered 'because all sinned,' these words can still convey the realistic view."[94]

Bavinck protests that while realism offers some helpful insights (insights that he thinks are taken up by federalism), it runs into serious problems. His concerns are illustrative of the common criticisms. First, he says, clear thinking about imputation pulls us away from realism. Imputation is true with respect to justification, and it is, he insists, an important part of Paul's message in Romans 5. But Bavinck argues that the imputation of sin is parallel to the imputation of (Christ's) righteousness for Paul, and "no one talks that way about the covenant of grace." He explains,

> We can and may indeed say that God so imputes to us the righteousness of Christ as if we ourselves had accomplished the obedience that Christ accomplished for us, but we are not, by that token, the people who personally and physically satisfied God's righteousness. Christ satisfied God's righteous requirement for us and in our place. So it is also with Adam: virtually, potentially, seminally, we may have been comprehended in him; personally and actually, however, it was he who broke the probationary command, and not we. If realism were to reject this distinction and be totally consistent, all imputation, both in the case of Adam and in that of Christ, would be unnecessary.[95]

But we know realism to be false with respect to the doctrine of justification in Christ, so parity (of Paul's parallel between Christ and Adam) should cause us to hold realism about original sin at arm's length. The defenders of realism can point out that this is one of the places where Paul's parallel between Christ and Adam breaks down, and this does something to disarm the force of the

94 Hoekema, *Created in God's Image*, 158.
95 Bavinck, *Reformed Dogmatics, Volume Three*, 102.

objection.[96] Still, though, the critics of realism can maintain that this criticism drives an important wedge between Adam and Christ (one that Paul does not make explicit), and they conclude that this weakens the realist position.

Bavinck is not done. He also criticizes realism on the distinctly Reformed grounds that realism breaks the continuity between the covenant of works and the covenant of grace, and he wonders why we would not also be responsible for the sins of all of our ancestors as well as the sin of Adam.[97] Even Jesus, he suggests, would be tainted with original sin on this view; after all, is not Christ also a descendant of Adam?[98] But perhaps Bavinck's most important criticism concerns the moral responsibility of human persons as distinct agents: "[W]hile realism does represent an excellent interest, namely, the unity of the human race, in the process it loses sight of another interest that is no less weighty, the independence of the human personality. A human is a member of a race as a whole, certainly, but in that whole he or she occupies a unique place of his or her own. Individuals are more than ripples in the ocean, more than passing manifestations of human nature in general."[99] Bavinck's own colors show through as he concludes that "[f]or that reason, physical unity in their case is not enough; an ethical, federal unity is added as well."[100]

Some theologians, perhaps especially those from the Reformed tradition, see elements of both realism and federalism that they take to be both defensible and insightful. Hoekema is an example of such theologians. He finds realism to be well-motivated in many respects, and he does not think that all of the criticisms are fatal to it. He worries, however, that it is unable to do all the work needed of a doctrine of original sin. In particular, he is concerned that it is not able to account for the *guilt* of original sin. More specifically, realism helps us understand the *corruption* of original sin; much like a physical disease or defect is passed down through the generations, so also we inherit depravity from our first parents (who themselves contracted it in the fall). To borrow Crisp's analogy and press it into service for Hoekema, all subsequent vehicles on the assembly line bear the dangerous defects of their flawed prototype. But realism simply does not have the resources to help us grapple with the fact of original guilt; to return again to Crisp's analogy, surely the vehicles in the assembly line are not culpable for their defects. After all, they did nothing to acquire them.

So what does Hoekema do to remedy the deficiencies of the realist proposal? He combines "the approaches of direct imputation [federalism] and realism." As he explains it, "[B]ecause Adam was our head and representative when he sinned, the guilt of his sin is reckoned to our account (direct

---

[96] See Hoekema, *Created in God's Image*, 160.
[97] Bavinck, *Reformed Dogmatics, Volume Three*, 103.
[98] Bavinck, *Reformed Dogmatics, Volume Three*, 103.
[99] Bavinck, *Reformed Dogmatics, Volume Three*, 103.
[100] Bavinck, *Reformed Dogmatics, Volume Three*, 103.

imputation). And because we were in Adam when he sinned, we were involved in his sin, and therefore we have been born with a corrupt nature (realism)."[101]

E. Corruption and Guilt: Mediate Views

There are other options as well. Some theologians are convinced that we are both corrupted by original sin and guilty for it—but that the sin for which we are guilty is not exactly the sin of Adam. According to these views, which are sometimes called "mediate" (sitting in a conceptual space between the corruption-only views, on one hand, and realism and federalism on the other hand), we are guilty for the condition and state of corruption. This approach has many distinguished defenders, and it deserves a closer look.

Anselm of Canterbury investigated the doctrine of original sin in conjunction with the development of his Christology. In accord with the unanimous orthodox Christian tradition, he insists that the first humans were made holy and righteous as well as free and responsible. He resolutely denies that their humanity as such was sinful, and he likewise denies that sin was inevitable or necessary. He recognizes a distinction between original sin ("the sin that each man contracts with his nature at his origin") and actual sin ("the sin that he does not contract with his own nature, but commits after he has become a person").[102] In the fall, the first humans lost the original justice or righteousness that was theirs as the endowed gift of the Creator. And, "because the whole human nature was contained in Adam and Eve, and nothing of it existed outside them, the whole of human nature was weakened and corrupted" by the results of their sin.[103] Original sin, he insists, must be injustice and opposition to righteousness. Accordingly, it must exist in the rational will of the human person.[104] It is passed down from generation to generation, and it corrupts these subsequent generations. But not only does it corrupt the members of subsequent generations, it also renders them guilty before God.

What does it mean to say that original sin leaves sinners guilty before God for that original sin? Anselm does not take the overtly "realist" interpretation of this guilt that was offered by Augustine. But nor does he take the earlier view that original sin leaves us merely corrupt and liable rather than guilty. Instead, he opts for what is now called the "mediate" view of the guilt of original sin. According to the mediate view, we are guilty for original sin as well as actual or personal sins; we are not merely corrupt, we are actually guilty. However, we are not, strictly speaking, guilty for what Adam *did*; we do not bear personal

---

[101] Hoekema, *Created in God's Image*, 166–167.
[102] Anselm, *De conceptu virginali et peccato originali* I, *Opera omnia opscula* (Paris: 1549), 49D, cited in *Anselm of Canterbury: The Major Works*, ed. with introduction Brian Davies and G. R. Evans (Oxford: Oxford University Press, 1998), 359.
[103] Anselm, *Original Sin* 2, *Opera* 49F; *Major Works*, 360.
[104] Anselm, *Original Sin* 3, *Opera* 49H–K; *Major Works*, 361–362.

guilt for the personal sins of Adam and Eve. "Each man is burdened with the sin or debt of Adam, each being propagated from Adam, although he is not implicated in the sin itself."[105] Indeed, Anselm says, "I do not think that the sin of Adam descends to infants so that they ought to be punished for it, as if they had each personally acted as Adam did, although because of his sin it came about that none of them is born without sin, or the condemnation following it."[106] So we are guilty on account of original sin, but we are not, strictly speaking, guilty for what Adam did. Instead, we are guilty on account of the sin itself. In other words, we are corrupt on account of original sin, and, while we are not guilty for what Adam did in sinning, still we are guilty for the corrupt condition in which we find ourselves on account of what Adam did in sinning. So we are guilty for original sin, since "the sin of Adam is transmitted personally in all those who are by nature propagated from" Adam.[107] And at the same time, there is "clearly a wide distance" between the sin of Adam and the sin of infants who have original sin, "because he sinned through his own will, while they sin through the natural necessity which is the outcome of his own personal will."[108]

The effects of original sin and actual, personal sins are different (in that the sins are unequal), but both leave us under condemnation and without hope of salvation apart from the work of Christ.[109] Thus, Anselm concludes, "it can be said without contradiction that original sin is the same in everyone, and that 'the son will not bear the iniquity of the father,' and 'each will bear his own burden,' and will receive 'according to his deeds' in his body 'whether good or evil,' *and* that God visits the sins of parents on their children 'unto the third and fourth generation.'"[110] On Anselm's doctrine of original sin, we are guilty for original sin as well as corrupted by it. But we are not, properly understood, guilty for what Adam did. Instead, we are guilty on account of the sin itself. Accordingly, "when an infant is condemned for original sin, he is not condemned for the sin of Adam but for his own."[111]

In the era of the Protestant Reformations, John Calvin arguably holds to a mediate account. Calvin's position on the doctrine of original sin (as it pertains to our relation to our first human parents) is interesting. He defines it as "a hereditary corruption and depravity of our nature, extending to all parts of the soul, which first makes us obnoxious to the wrath of God, and then

[105] Anselm, *Original Sin* 10, *Opera* 51B; *Major Works*, 369.
[106] Anselm, *Original Sin* 22, *Opera* 52I; *Major Works*, 378.
[107] Anselm, *Original Sin* 23, *Opera* 53B; *Major Works*, 382.
[108] Anselm, *Original Sin* 23, *Opera* 53C; *Major Works*, 382.
[109] Anselm, *Original Sin* 23, *Opera* 53E; *Major Works*, 382.
[110] Anselm, *Original Sin* 25, *Opera* 53K; *Major Works*, 385, emphasis original.
[111] Anselm, *Original Sin* 26, *Opera*, 53M; *Major Works*, 386.

produces in us works which in Scripture are termed works of the flesh."[112] He quite clearly differs from Zwingli in insisting that original sin includes both corruption and guilt (rather than merely corruption). But in spite of a tendency to read Calvin through the lens of subsequent Reformed statements of federalism, it is not obvious that he held to a federalist position. He says things that sound typically realist rather than federalist; Adam is referred to as the "root" of human nature.[113] But, as Donald Macleod points out, Calvin's views do not exactly fit into either standard realist or usual federalist categories, for both Reformed realism and Reformed federalism are versions of a notion of *immediate* imputation, while Calvin appears to favor *mediate* imputation. Thus Macleod says that

> on the contrary [to the immediate view], Calvin insisted that no one suffers eternal death on the ground of imputed sin alone:
>
>> For since it is said that we become subject to God's judgment through Adam's sin, we are to understand it not as if we, guiltless and undeserving, bore the guilt of his offense but in the sense that, since we through his transgression have become entangled in the curse, he is said to have made us guilty. Yet not only has punishment fallen upon us from Adam, but a contagion imparted by him resides in us, which justly deserves punishment.[114]

Commenting on Romans 5:12 ("death spread to all men because all sinned"), Calvin says that "we have, therefore, all sinned, because we are all imbued with natural corruption, and for this reason are wicked and perverse."[115] The natural reading of Calvin thus seems to be this: corruption precedes our acts of sin. We receive corruption from Adam, this corruption both produces acts of sin and incurs guilt, and this guilt brings us under the wrath of God.[116] Calvin summarizes his doctrine of sin:

> Let it stand, therefore, as an indubitable truth, which no engines can shake, that the mind of man is so entirely alienated from the righteousness of God that he cannot conceive, desire, or design any thing but what is wicked, distorted, foul, impure, and iniquitous; that his heart is so thoroughly envenomed by sin, that it can breathe out nothing but corruption and rottenness;

---

[112] Calvin, *Institutes of the Christian Religion*, trans. Henry Beveridge (Grand Rapids, MI: Eerdmans, 1997), II.1.8 (217).
[113] Calvin, *Institutes*, II.1.6 (215).
[114] Quoted in Donald Macleod, "Original Sin in Reformed Theology," in *Adam, the Fall, and Original Sin: Theological, Biblical, and Scientific Perspectives*, ed. Hans Madueme and Michael Reeves (Grand Rapids, MI: Baker Academic, 2014), 142.
[115] Macleod, "Original Sin in Reformed Theology," 142.
[116] Perhaps "natural reading" is too quick; Randall C. Zachman, "John Calvin," in *T&T Clark Companion to the Doctrine of Sin*, eds. David Lauber and Keith L. Johnson and David Lauber (New York: Bloomsbury T&T Clark, 2016), says that "Calvin appears to give two different answers [to the question of our relation to Adam and his sin] that appear to be in considerable tension with each other" (242).

that if some men occasionally make a show of goodness, their mind is ever interwoven with hypocrisy and deceit, their soul inwardly bound with fetters of wickedness.[117]

We are indeed guilty for sin—both actual sin and original sin. But the original sin for which we are guilty is ours. It is not, strictly speaking, the sin of Adam.

Mediate accounts are held by some theologians in the nineteenth-century Wesleyan tradition. For instance, Thomas O. Summers quite clearly endorses a mediate view.[118] Similarly, Luther Lee concludes that we are guilty for the corruption we have as well as for what we do with that corruption.[119]

Much more recently, after noting the complexities and challenges facing any interpreter of Romans 5, Henri Blocher points out that the options are usually pitched *either* as guilt for the sin of Adam (and then explained either in federalist terms while trying to make "alien guilt" understandable and palatable, or with an affirmation of realism and subsequent efforts to render plausible the claim that we somehow *are* Adam or "in Adam") or as only corruption from Adam. Accordingly, *"either* we are condemned for our own sins (and Adam's role is reduced to that of a remote fountainhead, losing much of its significance) *or* we are condemned for his sin (and the equity of that transfer is hard to see). But what if this 'either/or' were misleading? What if there were a third possibility?"[120]

Blocher points out that for Paul in Romans 5, sin is "undefined" apart from the law, thus "it cannot be made the object of judgment."[121] He offers this hypothesis: "[T]he role of Adam and of his sin in Romans 5 is *to make possible the imputation, the judicial treatment, of human sins*. His role thus brings about the condemnation of all, and its sequel, death."[122] He then offers this paraphrase of Romans 5:12–21:

> Just as through one man, Adam, sin entered the world and the sin-death connection was established, and so death could be inflicted on all as the penalty of their sins. . . .
>
> For take the period from Adam to Moses: sin was in the world, yet sin was not imputed in the absence of law, when it is viewed independently; nevertheless it was imputed through the relationship of all to Adam, and so death reigned even over people who had not sinned, as Adam had done, by violating

---

[117] Calvin, *Institutes*, II.5.19 (291).

[118] Thomas O. Summers, *Systematic Theology: A Complete Body of Wesleyan Arminian Divinity Consisting of Lectures on the Twenty-five Articles of Religion*, 2 vols. (Nashville: Publishing House of the Methodist Episcopal Church, South, 1888), 2:46.

[119] Luther Lee, *Elements of Theology: Or An Exposition of the Divine Origin, Doctrines, Morals, and Institutions of Christianity* (Syracuse, NY: A. W. Hall, 1853), 117–118.

[120] Blocher, *Original Sin*, 77, emphasis original.

[121] Blocher, *Original Sin*, 77.

[122] Blocher, *Original Sin*, 77.

a precept directly given to them. Adam's role as a racial head for condemnation makes him a type of Christ, the Head for justification.

Of course, the operation of grace in Christ is infinitely more powerful.
It miraculously reverses a desperate situation marred by millions of sins,
whereas Adam's role is to secure condemnation of condemnable deeds.

Yet it can be said that through the one disobedience of Adam, of which
all human sins are offshoots, all have been constituted sinners, just as through
the one obedience of Christ all who own him as their Head are counted
righteous.[123]

So what is this "third possibility"? Blocher explains his commitments: "With
all due respect to the Reformed theology to which I am indebted, I have been
led to question the doctrine of alien guilt transferred—that is, the doctrine of
the imputation of all of Adam's own trespass, his act of transgression."[124] But
nor does he embrace realism. He insists that the contemporary *zeitgeist* is not
driving his theology, for he is willing to submit to whatever the Bible teaches.
"If Scripture definitely taught such a doctrine, however offensive to modern
taste, I should readily bow to its authority. But where does Scripture require
it? My investigation did not find it in the only passage from which it is drawn,
Romans 5. Could it be, then, a case of laying heavy burdens upon people's
shoulders, beyond the express demands of God?"[125]

Again, just what is this "third possibility"? Blocher explains: what the
Bible teaches is that "alienation from God, the condition of being deprived and
depraved, follows immediately upon the first act of sinning—for Adam himself
and for his seed after him. It affects his descendants from the very start of their
existence, because of their relationship to him."[126] So far, this sounds strangely
familiar; it sounds like the "corruption-only" view (according to which we
receive corruption from Adam and guilt from our own actions).[127] But it isn't,
Blocher explains, for the sinful condition "is voluntary inasmuch as it implies
a disposition of the will, even in its most embryonic form; it is guilty."[128] So
we are not guilty for Adam's sinful action (even though we do suffer depravity
because of it), but we are not merely guilty of what we *do*. We are guilty for
what we *are*—and what we *are* is sinful and depraved. We are born into enmity
against God, and "enmity towards God carries guilt."[129]

Blocher notes that his view differs from federalist accounts in several
ways: he sees "no necessity for the idea that alien guilt was transferred"; he
emphasizes loss or deprivation in a "relational" (rather than strictly legal)

---

[123] Blocher, *Original Sin*, 78–79.
[124] Blocher, *Original Sin*, 128.
[125] Blocher, *Original Sin*, 128.
[126] Blocher, *Original Sin*, 128.
[127] Blocher thinks that the lines between "state" and "act" are blurred (*Original Sin*, 128–129).
[128] Blocher, *Original Sin*, 128.
[129] Blocher, *Original Sin*, 129.

framework; and he widens the notion of Adam's headship beyond forensic categories.[130] So Blocher recognizes that his view differs from federalism in several important respects (nor does it align with either common-nature realism or organic-whole realism). His view does, however, come close to the "mediate view," and even appears to be a version of it. As we have seen (from the examples of Anselm and Calvin), according to the mediate view (or at least one version of it), Adam's progeny indeed do bear the guilt of original sin, but they are not guilty for Adam's own sinful actions. This can be seen by contrast with immediate theories (the realism and federalism surveyed to this point): where immediate theories say that we are guilty for what Adam did, mediate views hold that the only guilt we bear due to original sin is guilt for our corrupt state (acts of sin, of course, are another matter entirely—surely we are guilty for those as well). The mediate view should not be confused with the "corruption only" view, for it clearly insists upon the guilt of original sin. But the guilt is not exactly guilt for Adam's action—it is guilt for the corruption. Where the immediate views say that we are *directly* or *immediately* accountable for Adam's sin, mediate views say that we are indirectly—or mediately—accountable. But on both views, as Rea explains, "our own corruption is a consequence of Adam's sin and something for which we are guilty. Thus, either way we bear guilt as a result of something Adam has done."[131] But rather than being corrupt because we are guilty (as on the immediate view), according to the mediate view "original sin is imputed to us because we are born corrupt."[132] As Grenz points out, the mediate theorist "added a step in the imputation syllogism: Adam sinned; therefore, all are depraved; therefore, all are guilty."[133]

F. Conditional Imputation of Guilt

Millard Erickson offers a proposal that is similar in some respects. He finds the "Pelagian" and "Arminian" (by which he means corruption-only) views inadequate, but he is not satisfied with either the federalist or the realist views. His own proposal is different: we suffer guilt from original sin, but it is only a *conditional* guilt (until ratified by us):

> We all were involved in Adam's sin, and thus receive both the corrupted nature that was his after the fall, and the guilt and condemnation that attach to his sin. With the matter of guilt, however, just as with the imputation of Christ's righteousness, there must be some conscious or voluntary decision on our part. Until this is the case, there is only a conditional imputation

---

[130] Blocher, *Original Sin*, 130.
[131] Rea, "Metaphysics of Original Sin," 324–325.
[132] Josua Placeus (1596–1665), quoted in Bavinck, *Reformed Dogmatics, Volume Three*, 100.
[133] Grenz, *Theology for the Community of God*, 201.

of guilt. Thus, there is no condemnation before one reaches the age of responsibility . . . [134]

The view that appropriately preserves the parallelism between "our accepting the work of Christ and that of Adam, and at the same time more clearly points out our responsibility for the first sin" is this: "We become responsible and guilty when we accept or approve of our corrupt nature. There is a time in the life of each one of us when we become aware of our own tendency toward sin. At that point we may abhor the sinful nature that has been there all the time. We would in that case repent of it. . . . But if we acquiesce in that sinful nature, we are in effect saying that it is good. By placing our tacit approval upon the corruption, we are also approving or concurring in the action in the garden of Eden so long ago."[135]

III. The Scriptural Basis Revisited

While it is important to keep in mind that the general doctrine of original sin has a much broader biblical basis than merely Romans 5:12–21 (as we have seen, the biblical witness both to the universality and totality of sin as well as moral responsibility for that sin is both broad and deep), nonetheless the passage stands as the *locus classicus* of discussions of the doctrine (with respect to the issues of guilt).[136] Unfortunately, there is hardly a word or phrase in this passage that has not been the subject of intense scrutiny, disagreement, and controversy. As Ben Witherington III says, "Here we are dealing with some of the most difficult material in all of Romans in terms of grammar and interpretation."[137] N. T. Wright concurs; he says that the passage is "terse and cryptic."[138] Fortunately, however, we need not sort out nearly all of the tangled interpretive matters, nor take a definitive stand on some of the most controversial issues, to see several important points emerge from the text. So in no way do I intend what follows as anything like a full account of the passage. Instead, in this section, I shall first offer a brief sketch of the structure of the passage as I see it. This will enable us to take a closer look at several phrases that are of crucial importance. Following this, I shall make some observations about how this all relates to the doctrinal formulations, and I will argue that while several major views are decisively ruled *out* by the passage, several others are underdetermined by this text and remain live options.

---

[134] Erickson, *Christian Theology*, 656.
[135] Erickson, *Christian Theology*, 656.
[136] Blocher does a masterful job with the broader biblical basis (*Original Sin*, 42–48).
[137] Ben Witherington III, *Paul's Letter to the Romans: A Socio-Rhetorical Commentary* (Grand Rapids, MI: Eerdmans, 2004), 145.
[138] N. T. Wright, "Romans," in *New Interpreter's Bible*, vol. 10 (Nashville: Abingdon, 2002), 523.

A. A Brief Overview of Romans 5:12–21

One of the most famous biblical declarations about sin comes from Paul:

> (12) Therefore, just as sin came into the world through one man, and death through sin, and so death spread to all men because all sinned—(13) for indeed sin was in the world before the law was given, but sin is not counted where there is no law. (14) Yet death reigned from Adam to Moses, even over those whose sinning was not like the transgression of Adam, who was a type of the one who was to come.
>
> (15) But the free gift is not like the trespass. For if many died through one man's trespass, much more have the grace of God and the free gift by the grace of that one man Jesus Christ abounded for many. (16) And the free gift is not like the result of that one man's sin. For the judgment following one trespass brought condemnation, but the free gift following many trespasses brought justification. (17) For if, because of one man's trespass, death reigned through that one man, much more will those who receive the abundance of grace and the free gift of righteousness reign in life through the one man Jesus Christ.
>
> (18) Therefore, as one trespass led to condemnation for all men, so one act of righteousness leads to justification and life for all men. (19) For as by the one man's disobedience the many were made sinners, so by the one man's obedience the many will be made righteous. (20) Now the law came in to increase the trespass, but where sin increased, grace abounded all the more, (21) so that, as sin reigned in death, grace also might reign through righteousness leading to eternal life through Jesus Christ our Lord. (Rom. 5:12–21)

Paul begins this section (in v. 12) by a point that he does not pick up again until verse 18. In verse 12 Paul says that sin came into the world through one man, and that sin brought about death, and that death spread to the entire human race. Paul returns to this point in verse 18, but in between verse 12 and verse 18 he pauses to address several related concerns. These concerns are not tangential but are central to his argument. In verses 13–14 he addresses the crucial issue of the relation of "the law" to sin and death. Here he wrestles with the question of what happens to those who do not have the law. Are they guilty for sin? Or are they somehow excluded from condemnation and shielded by their ignorance? Here I take the term "transgression" (*parabaseos*; v. 14) to refer to a particular form or mode of sinning: sinning as a willful transgression of a known law of God, as "disobedience of an express commandment."[139] This has (conceptual) echoes of the OT contrast between "high-handed" sins of outright rebellion, on one hand, and "sins of ignorance" on the other hand.[140] As Thomas Schreiner points out, Paul's purpose here is "to explain that apart from the Mosaic law sin is not equivalent to transgression. . . . This is confirmed by both Rom. 4:15 and the present context, for Paul explicitly notes in 5:14 that Adam's sin was

---

[139] Douglas J. Moo, *The Epistle to the Romans*, NICNT (Grand Rapids, MI: Eerdmans, 1996), 330.
[140] Cf. James D. G. Dunn, *Romans 1–8*, WBC (Nashville: Thomas Nelson, 1988), 275.

different in kind from those who lived before the Mosaic law in that he violated a commandment disclosed by God."[141] Wright concurs: "'[S]in' is simply wrongdoing, whether or not the sinner is aware of it; 'trespass' or 'transgression' is disobedience to a known command."[142] Schreiner explains further that "the power of death is so great that it exercises its dominion over people even if no law exists. Second, violating a commandment revealed by God increases the seriousness of sin in the sense that the sin is now more defiant and rebellious in character."[143] So Paul is explaining that sin "reigns" in death even apart from the revelation of the (Mosaic) law, and he is showing that the severity of sin and its punishment is ratcheted up immensely when the sin is committed in open rebellion against a known commandment of God.

In verses 15–17 Paul is drawing the parallel—and, more importantly, the contrasts—between Adam and Christ. Paul makes the comparative parallel clear indeed. The scope of Adam's trespass and Christ's work is the same: *all* are included. But the contrasts between Adam and Christ are all the more striking for Paul; Adam's sin "is not like" (*ouch hōs*) Christ's work (vv. 15a, 16a). As Moo helpfully puts it, "[T]he first contrast is one of *degree*: the work of Christ, being a manifestation of grace, is greater in every way than that of Adam (v. 15). The second contrast is (mainly) one of *consequence*: Adam's act brought condemnation (v. 16b) and death (v. 17a); Christ's brought righteousness (v. 16b) and life (v. 17b)."[144] On the one hand, following one sin we have judgment that brings condemnation and death for all; on the other hand, following many trespasses we have the gift that brings justification and life.

In verses 18ff. Paul again returns to the opening statement of this passage. He has not digressed, for what he has said about the relation of sin and death to *all* (even those who do not have the law of God revealed to them in explicit form) and the relation between Adam and Christ is absolutely crucial for the point he returns to here. As Wright argues, where there is a "balance" between the actions of Adam and Christ with respect to the range of their work in that both are for all, Paul is "denying that there is a *balance* between them. The gift far outweighs the trespass; Christ has not merely restored that which Adam lost, but has gone far beyond."[145] Where by one act of trespass Adam effected a change that impacts all of humanity (and all of creation) in bringing condemnation and death, by one act of righteousness "the many" (*hoi polloi*) will be made righteous. The result is that many will be "made righteous," and while this is true in a legal or juridical sense, Paul's language of righteousness "reign-

---

[141] Thomas R. Schreiner, *Romans* (Grand Rapids, MI: Baker Academic, 2000), 279.
[142] Wright, "Romans," 524n196.
[143] Schreiner, *Romans*, 279.
[144] Moo, *Romans*, 334, emphasis original.
[145] Wright, "Romans," 528, emphasis original.

ing" points us to the fact that it is not, for Paul, ever *merely* legal or forensic righteousness.[146] Of course, as many commentators are quick to point out, the overarching thrust of Paul's teaching here is to point us to the supremacy of Christ and his work on our behalf; rather than focus on sin *in and of itself*, the central theme here is the victory of Christ *over* sin and death.

B. Important Phrases

So this is the general framework of Romans 5:12–21 (the *locus classicus* of the doctrine of original sin). Within this framework, several important phrases call for focused attention. The first of these is Paul's term *eph hō* (v. 12d). Does Paul's statement mean "in him," "with him," "because of him," or what? Several major options have emerged in the scholarly literature.[147]

Traditionally, this phrase has enjoyed a definitively "realist" interpretation. Taken as a "genuine relative clause,"[148] the phrase has been understood as "in whom" (with this "in whom" taken in a literal sense). It is now a commonplace to point out that Augustine (and Ambrosiaster before him) read this in Latin translation as *in quo*. It is also now common to point out that such a translation is flawed. Some commentators worry that the antecedent "man" (*anthrōpou*) is too distant to serve as the referent.[149] More directly, and more convincingly, the phrase is less than ideally suited to convey such a thought; it seems clear that *en* would have made much more sense (than *eph*) for Paul to use to express this thought. If Augustine's translation was right, then this reading would lend strong support for the realist view. But since it is not the best reading of the text, then it would be mistaken to claim that *eph hō* somehow "demands" or "proves" some version of the realist theory. This does not, however, mean that the realist theory is thereby disproven or without support; after all, absence of a particular line of evidence for a particular theory does not mean that the theory is false.

At the other extreme, the phrase is sometimes understood in what is sometimes called a "Pelagian" sense. This approach says that Paul here refers to the actions of various human persons that are completely independent of Adam's own sin. The closest thing to a "connection" or "relation" between them would be the poor example set by Adam. The problems with this view are well known and established; in addition to the broader criticisms of Pelagianism, with respect to the interpretation of this particular passage the most pertinent points

---

[146] Cf. Wright, "Romans," 528.
[147] I leave to the side several options that I take to be (and are generally considered) unlikely or even far-fetched, for which see Schreiner's discussion, *Romans*, 273; see also Robert Jewett, *Romans: A Commentary* (Minneapolis: Fortress, 2007), 375–376.
[148] Joseph Fitzmeyer, *Romans: A New Translation with Introduction and Commentary*, AB (New York: Doubleday, 1992), 415.
[149] E.g., Schreiner, *Romans*, 274.

to make are that it does not offer an adequate account either of the universality of sin depicted here or of the condemnation that is connected to the sin of "the man." It especially struggles with verses 18–19.[150]

More recently, a "consecutive" reading has been proposed (primarily by Fitzmeyer, and largely on the basis of how this construction is used in extrabiblical Greek texts). This takes the *eph hō* to be a "consecutive conjunction."[151] Fitzmeyer explains that this

> would mean that Paul is expressing a result, the sequel to Adam's baleful influence on humanity by the ratification of his sin in the sins of all individuals. He would thus be conceding to individual human sins a secondary causality or personal responsibility for death. . . . Thus Paul in v 12 is ascribing death to two causes, not unrelated: to Adam and to all human sinners. . . . The primary causality for its sinful and mortal condition is ascribed to Adam, no matter what meaning is assigned to *eph' hō*, and a secondary causality to the sins of all human beings.[152]

More specifically, as Schreiner points out, "[o]n this reading the verse would say, 'And so death spread to all people, with the result that all sinned.'"[153]

This approach is theologically attractive in some ways. Fitzmeyer is not, as Wright explains, removing "the sense of causality between Adam's sin and those of his descendants, but [his view] allows for a 'secondary causality,' and so personal responsibility, between individual sins and individual death."[154] The major problem with the view, however, is that it seems to make Paul to be saying that death spread universally due to Adam's sin, and that *this* has resulted in universal sin. But Paul actually says that sin causes death. So for the proposal to succeed, it must import something into the meaning: the sin of Adam causes (corruption and) death, which in turn causes sin (and, in turn again, death). Now this is not impossible; as various commentators note, at various points in this passage Paul does express himself "elliptically," and so expects the reader to supply the appropriate elements for the broader meaning.[155] Still, though, recognition of this point should make the proponent of the consecutive reading more tentative. As Wright concludes, "Fitzmeyer's proposal must, I think, be regarded as at best not proven."[156]

What can safely be seen as the "majority view" among interpreters of

---

[150] Cf. C. E. B. Cranfield, *The Epistle to the Romans 1–8*, International Critical Commentary (New York: T&T Clark, 1975), 277.

[151] Fitzmeyer, *Romans*, 416.

[152] Fitzmeyer, *Romans*, 416.

[153] Schreiner, *Romans*, 274.

[154] Wright, "Romans," 527.

[155] E.g., Moo, *Romans*, 340.

[156] Wright, "Romans," 527.

Romans 5 today is called the "causal meaning."[157] Moo makes a strong case that the passage as a whole—with verse 18 taking up what verse 12 began—supports the causal reading. Sin produces death, and all die *because* all sin.[158] The causal meaning of *eph hō* seems to be the way that it is used in 2 Corinthians 5:4 and Philippians 3:12, and it appears to be the most natural reading here.[159]

Just as important as *eph hō*, however, are the words that finish the clause: *pantes hēmarton* ("all sinned"). What does Paul mean when he says here that "all sinned"? Does this claim mean that Adam's sin somehow counts as our sin (thus leaning toward federalism) or that we just were involved in his sin (thus tilting toward realism)? Or is Paul saying that every person has sinned consequently to Adam's sin (thus cohering well with the consecutive reading of *eph hō*, and with hospitable space for mediate or corruption-only views)? How should we understand Paul's claim?

Some theologians take this as a reference to Adam's sin, and they point out that Paul uses the aorist tense here. The aorist, they say, points us to the primal sin. So while it is of course true that all people commit sins, what Paul refers to here is Adam's sin—the *original* sin. But the appeal to the use of the aorist here is illegitimate. For one thing, it tries to make the verb tense do too much work. We know that Greek grammar simply will not support this kind of theological weight.[160] And in point of fact, Paul uses the aorist elsewhere to talk about the actual sins committed by individual persons: "all sinned, and come short of the glory of God" (Rom. 3:23 AT). And, as Schreiner points out, when conjoined with *pantes* the verb *hamartein* "refers regularly to voluntary sin that people commit in their own persons."[161] Schreiner judges that "it is quite improbable on linguistic grounds that 'all sinned' means 'all sinned in Adam,'" and he concludes that "the most natural way to construe *pantes hēmarton* is to see a reference to the personal and individual sin of all people. . . . When Paul says, 'all sinned,' he indeed means that every human being has personally sinned."[162]

But if Paul refers only to the actual sins of distinct persons, then what is the relation of all humans to Adam that he is trying to demonstrate? Moo asks, "[H]ow can we logically relate the assertions 'each person dies because *each person* sins [in the course of history]' and '*one man's* trespass led to

---

[157] "Most . . ." according to Wright, "Romans," 526; cf. Fitzmeyer, *Romans*, 415; Schreiner, *Romans*, 274. Dunn says that the case is "more or less settled in favor" of the causal reading (*Romans*, 273).

[158] Moo, *Romans*, 321, 327.

[159] Moo notes that it is not the meaning in Philippians 4:10, and he concludes that while the causal reading is preferable, the evidence for it "is not nearly as strong as some suggest" (*Romans*, 322).

[160] E.g., Constantine R. Campbell, *Basics of Verbal Aspect in Biblical Greek* (Grand Rapids, MI: Zondervan, 2008), 83–102.

[161] Schreiner, *Romans*, 275. See also Wright, "Romans," 526.

[162] Schreiner, *Romans*, 275.

condemnation for all people' (v. 18a)?"[163] Moo recognizes that the mediate view is a possible way to account for this, and he says that "[t]his view has much in its favor: it retains the 'normal' meaning of 'sin' in v. 12 while explaining at the same time how Paul could assert that Adam's sin brings condemnation upon all (vv. 18–19). It also explains why all people act contrary to the will of God . . ."[164] Moo does not endorse this proposal, however, for while such an account is "possible" as an interpretation of Paul's statement, it requires us to fill in too many gaps in Paul's explanation.[165] Beyond this, Moo cannot decide between federalist and realist views, for "Paul has not provided us with enough data to make a definite decision."[166]

C. Views Excluded by the Text

As we have seen, the church catholic has judged all versions of Pelagianism (and "Semi-Pelagianism") to be excluded by the overall biblical depiction of sin, and Romans 5:12–21 does nothing to reopen the door to such views. Similarly, views of the fall that deny that Adam and Eve were genuine, historical persons do not cohere well with what Romans 5 says about sin. Clearly, Paul intended a reference to a historical Adam as a real person. His parallel to Christ is illuminating, for while there are marked differences between Adam and Christ, their reality as historical persons is not one of those differences. N. T. Wright is correct when he says that "Paul clearly believed that there had been a single first pair, whose male, Adam, had been given a commandment and had broken it."[167]

D. Views Consistent with the Text

So far I have argued that fidelity to the text eliminates several views. But what about the other positions? How does all this relate to the theories of original sin already canvassed? First, we should see that if we take *eph hō* in the causal sense, then any of the major views can claim coherence with the text. Realism is not demanded by the text (as it would be if the text were to read *en hō*), but it is nonetheless consistent with Romans 5:12–21. Federalism sits comfortably with the causal sense as well, for it needs only *some* kind of causal relation to Adam. If the distinctives of the federal position *were* spelled out, of course, then it would be demanded by the text—but there is no good reason to think that the federal sense is spelled out in this way. Similarly, the mediate view allows for *some* kind of causal relation between Adam's sin, on the one hand,

[163] Moo, *Romans*, 323.
[164] Moo, *Romans*, 325–326.
[165] Moo, *Romans*, 326.
[166] Moo, *Romans*, 328.
[167] Wright, "Romans," 526.

and our corruption and corresponding guilt, on the other hand. And, perhaps surprisingly, the corruption-only view is arguably consistent with the causal sense as well. For it too holds to the fact that sin has come as a result of Adam's rebellion, and it too holds that sin has come to all. Moreover, it maintains that guilt and condemnation have come upon all as well. And since, even on the causal reading, the text does not specify just *how* that condemnation comes, the corruption-only advocates can argue that their view can fit under this umbrella as well.

What about the consecutive reading of *eph hō*? If this is the correct reading of the phrase, then it seems clear that it favors either the mediate view or the corruption-only view. It does not deny just any causality to Adam's sin, but it places the blame squarely on the sinners who follow Adam. In other words, Adam's act of disobedient rebellion *alone* is not enough to bring condemnation for everyone; Adam's sinful progeny must concur and sin as well for there to be guilt. If this does not rule out the realist and federalist views, then it seems to make them much less likely and the "fit" much more awkward.

Turning our attention to Paul's claim that "all sinned," we are now in a position to see how it relates to the major theories. As I see things, if "all sinned" means that all sinned *in or with Adam*, then the text is open to several views. Realism is consistent with this reading; it just goes on to specify *how* it is that we "all sinned *in Adam*." Federalism also takes this as a corporate account of our sin, but tells a different story about *how* it is that we "all sinned" *with Adam*. The mediate view can fit here as well—again, it offers a different account of how "all" became sinners. It takes the verb "sinned" in a somewhat "looser" sense (to use Blocher's term), so it is not as natural a fit. Nonetheless, its proponents can make an argument for its viability, and at minimum it should not be ruled out of court on these grounds. When we come to the corruption-only view, on the other hand, it is much harder to see how this view might be consistent with the claim that we all "sinned" in or with Adam. The corruption-only view claims only that we suffer depravity or corruption as a result of what Adam did (and, of course, that we suffer guilt for our own malfeasance). So it is hard to see how it might be consistent with this reading of the text.

But if we take "all sinned" to mean that all persons have committed sins (or, more broadly, have been sinful), the situation is very different. Here the corruption-only view finds hospitality and warmth. This is exactly the point that the corruption-only theorists have been making: we suffer corruption as a result of what Adam did, and we commit sinful actions (for which we *are* guilty). Similarly, the mediate theory is in friendly confines. As Moo admits, the view that "Paul assumes a 'middle term' in the connection between Adam's sin and the condemnation of all human beings" is one that "has much in its favor."[168] But what does this mean for the realist and federalist theories? It does not, so far as I can see, necessarily mean that they are mistaken. It only means that their view is underdetermined by this passage, and that they should look elsewhere for support for their view.

At any rate, we should remember that the details of the doctrine of original sin are not the primary concern of Paul—his penultimate purpose is to show that we *are* related to Adam and suffer subsequent corruption and condemnation, and his *ultimate* purpose is to show that Christ and his work are much greater! I agree with Moo when he says, "Paul has not provided us with enough data to make a definite decision" from the basis of this text alone, and that on the basis of this passage alone, "we should probably be content with the conclusion that Paul affirms the reality of a solidarity of all humanity with Adam in his sin without being able to explain the exact nature of that union."[169]

E. Conclusion

In conclusion, the following points should be clear. First, Pelagianism is excluded by an adequate reading of Romans 5:12–21 (and even more clearly by the broader testimony of Scripture). Second, while we may both recognize some literary features in the Genesis account of the fall that are consonant with the "mythical" or "poetic" readings and benefit from some of the insights of the "existentialist" readings of the fall, a straightforward reading of Romans 5:12–21 (as well as elsewhere) leads us to believe in a real, historical Adam. Third, while none of the major theories of original sin can claim to be *demanded* by the text of Romans 5, it is hard to rule out any of them on the basis of this important passage. This does not mean that we are left at an utter standstill, however; it only means that the viability (or lack thereof) and strength of the various theories will have to be decided on other, and broader, theological grounds. Can they account for *both* our connection to Adam *and* our moral responsibility as individual persons? We now return to closer consideration of this question.

IV. THE METAPHYSICS AND MORALS OF ORIGINAL SIN (ONCE AGAIN)

With these considerations in mind, let us return to our consideration of the dogmatic formulation of the doctrine of original sin. Having already seen that taking seriously the teaching of Scripture will eliminate some positions, what are we to make of the other remaining views on offer?

---

[168] Moo, *Romans*, 325.
[169] Moo, *Romans*, 328.

A. Edwardsian Realism

The work of the great American theologian Jonathan Edwards on the doctrine of original sin is truly impressive. Against the many attacks made by deists and other rationalists, Edwards mounts a powerful defense of the doctrine. (His common label "Arminian" for his opponents is not entirely helpful, for John Wesley, as we have seen, also defended the doctrine of original sin against some of the same critics.) Edwards argues at great length from the biblical witness to the pervasiveness and effects of sin, and much of what he does is powerful and well done. His treatise remains a treasure trove of insight and argument, and it stands as a model of humble and powerful theological engagement with the critics of Christian orthodoxy. However, the fact that he does well with the general biblical arguments for the nature, extent, and results of sin does not mean that what he says about the metaphysics and morals of the doctrine is also biblically grounded. And surely it does not mean that it is beyond the reach of critical analysis or above reproach.

Edwards makes some statements that could lead one to take him as a federalist,[170] but I believe that on the whole he is better interpreted as a realist.[171] He says things that indicate that he is more of an "organic whole realist" than he is a "common human nature realist." Exactly how we should interpret this kind of realism is a matter to which we shall return shortly, but at this point it is important to consider some of the more peculiar features of Edwards's own view. These are, in turn, his commitment to determinism, his advocacy of a Lockean view of personal identity, and his endorsement of occasionalism.

Edwards's massive treatise on *The Freedom of the Will* is well known, and his commitment to determinism is well established. We need not review all the details here, but a brief overview will help us to see the relevance of this for his doctrine of original sin. Edwards is a determinist. According to determinism, "any event is determined, . . . just in case there are conditions (e.g., the decrees of fate, the foreordaining acts of God, antecedent physical causes plus laws of nature) whose joint occurrence is (logically) sufficient for the occurrence of the event; it *must* be the case that *if* these determining conditions jointly obtain, the determined event occurs."[172] According to determinism, "for *every* event that happens, there are conditions such that, given them, nothing else could have happened. For *every* event that happens, its happening was caused or necessitated by prior factors such that given these prior factors, the event in question

[170] E.g., Edwards, *Original Sin*, 259–260. Curiously, Edwards is taken by Bavinck to be a mediate theorist (cf. Bavinck, *Reformed Dogmatics, Volume Three*, 100).
[171] See further Oliver D. Crisp, *Jonathan Edwards and the Metaphysics of Sin* (Aldershot, UK: Ashgate, 2005).
[172] Thus Robert Kane, "Introduction," in *Oxford Handbook of Free Will*, 2nd ed., ed. Robert Kane (Oxford: Oxford University Press, 2011), 4, emphasis original.

had to occur."[173] Edwards is a "soft determinist" or "compatibilist"; he believes that determinism is compatible with human freedom and moral responsibility. So long as we act in such a way that we do what we want to do, and in the absence of external constraint or compulsion, we do what we do "freely."

Determinism (of the "soft" or "compatibilist" variety) is quite popular in some sectors of contemporary Christianity (especially given the resurgence of "Calvinism" within evangelicalism), and Edwards is often taken to be the premier defender of it. Despite its recent popularity, however, there are reasons to think that close examination of the notion shows that it is unsuited for any theology that demands moral responsibility (as does the doctrine of original sin and the entire Christian worldview). Thomas P. Flint offers an argument that demonstrates this worry:[174] It is implausible to think that we have moral responsibility for events over which we have no causal control. Nor do we bear responsibility for the fact (if indeed it is a fact) that such events over which we have no causal control add up to determine all future events and leave us with only one future that is physically possible. But if this much is true, then it is hard indeed to see how we might be morally responsible for our actions. In addition, there are biblical passages that do not seem at all easy to square with determinism.[175] Consider, by way of example, 1 Corinthians 10:12–13:

> Therefore let anyone who thinks that he stands take heed lest he fall. No temptation has overtaken you that is not common to man. God is faithful, and he will not let you be tempted beyond your ability, but with the temptation he will also provide the way of escape, that you may be able to endure it.

From this we learn that there are at least two alternative possibilities: the way of sin and the way of escape. As William Lane Craig concludes, in the case of the believer who falls into sin, "God had provided a way of escape that one could have taken but that one failed to do so. In other words, in precisely that situation, one had the power either to succumb or to take the way out—that is to say, one had libertarian freedom. It is precisely because one failed to take the divinely provided way of escape that one is held accountable."[176] The theological debates over freedom and determinism continue, and it would be premature for either side to claim a swift or easy victory. Clearly, this is not the place for

[173] J. P. Moreland and William Lane Craig, *Philosophical Foundations for a Christian Worldview* (Downers Grove, IL: IVP Academic, 2003), 268, emphasis mine. See further William Hasker, *Metaphysics: Constructing a Worldview* (Downers Grove, IL: InterVarsity Press, 1983), 32; and Michael C. Rea, *Metaphysics: The Basics* (New York: Routledge, 2014), 252.

[174] Thomas P. Flint, *Divine Providence: The Molinist Account* (Ithaca, NY: Cornell University Press, 1998), 28–29. For the (modern) *locus classicus* of such arguments, see Peter van Inwagen, *An Essay on Free Will* (Oxford: Oxford University Press, 1983), 55–105.

[175] For further discussion, see Thomas H. McCall, *An Invitation to Analytic Christian Theology* (Downers Grove, IL: IVP Academic, 2015), 46–81.

[176] William Lane Craig, "A Middle Knowledge Response," in *Divine Foreknowledge: Four Views*, ed. James K. Beilby and Paul R. Eddy (Downers Grove, IL: IVP Academic, 2001), 202.

a full treatment of such issues. Still, though, it should not be hard to see that there are important worries in the neighborhood, and these are concerns that Christians *of all people* should take seriously. It should be even easier to see that the full-blown Edwardsian theory will not be attractive to those who are convinced by (philosophical and theological) objections to determinism.

Edwards makes use of another highly contested metaphysical notion. It comes in consideration of the question of what constitutes personal identity. Reflecting on the difficult issue of personal identity through time, he follows John Locke's idea that the same consciousness is what gives personal identity. Edwards is convinced that Locke's position goes some distance (even if it does not go far enough) to help explain how it is that a forty-year-old man is the same person that he was when he was an infant. Despite the fact that the man "is now constituted of different substance, and the great part of the substance probably changed scores (if not hundreds) of times, . . . yet God, according to the course of nature, which he has been pleased to establish, has caused, that in a certain method it should communicate with that infantile body, in the same life, the same senses, the same features, and many [of] the same qualities, and in union with the same soul; and so, with regard to these purposes, 'tis dealt with by him as one body."[177]

The Lockean view of personal identity is subject to criticism on various fronts, and it is safe to say that it is less than wildly popular. The criticisms that are not particularly theological in nature need not detain us here. What is interesting for our purposes is the way that Edwards employs the notion, and the way that he moves forward when armed with it. He thinks that Locke's view captures something that is essential to personal identity, but he also says that it alone is not enough. Taken alone, it only pushes the question back one more level, for we still find ourselves asking, "Why this way?" And "this way" of accounting for personal identity depends solely upon the will of the divine sovereign. This way of accounting for personal identity, he argues, depends upon "divine establishment"—indeed, it depends upon "an arbitrary constitution of the Creator."[178]

The way that Edwards connects this account of personal identity to the doctrine of original sin is fascinating:

> From these things it will clearly follow, that identity of consciousness depends wholly on a law of nature; and so, on the sovereign will and agency of God; and therefore, that personal identity, and so the derivation of the pollution and guilt of past sins in the same person, depends on an arbitrary divine constitution: and this, even though we should allow the same consciousness not

[177] Edwards, *Original Sin*, 398.
[178] Edwards, *Original Sin*, 398–399.

to be the only thing which constitutes oneness of person, but should, besides that, suppose sameness of substance requisite. For if same consciousness be one thing necessary to personal identity, and this depends on God's sovereign constitution, it will still follow, that personal identity depends on God's sovereign constitution.[179]

So continuity or oneness of personal identity depends entirely upon the arbitrary decree of God's sovereign will, and the "derivation of guilt and pollution" come in the same way. It is no different with respect to original sin than it is with respect to personal identity more generally.

But what does Edwards mean by "arbitrary constitution"? Further consideration of this question brings us to the place where we clearly see Edwards's occasionalism. Classical Christian doctrines of creation and providence stress the reality and importance of divine preservation and concurrence. God sustains or preserves what he has created out of nothing; without his continued providential activity, anything and everything created would pass out of existence. The created order depends upon him moment by moment for its continued existence. Moreover, God's providential activity in concurrence is a necessary condition for the activity of any created beings; if God did not grant them the power to act, they simply would be unable to act. Edwards endorses such doctrines: he agrees that "God not only created all things, and gave them being at first, but continually preserves them, and upholds them in being."[180] But Edwards goes beyond such traditional affirmations, and he thinks that genuine understanding of such claims naturally pushes us beyond them. For if God upholds all things, then they are dependent upon him. And if they are dependent upon him, then they are an effect. As an effect, of course, they must have a cause. The cause of their continued existence obviously cannot be found in themselves, so it must be the case that this cause must be found in the sovereign will of the Creator.

So Edwards moves from a deeply traditional account of divine preservation and concurrence to the less traditional idea that God creates continuously. Children and acorns, along with their parents and oaks, "are truly immediately created or made by God; so must the existence of each created person and thing, at each moment of it, be from immediate *continued* creation of God." If so, then "it will certainly follow from these things, that God's *preserving* created things in being is perfectly equivalent to a *continued creation*, or to his creating those things out of nothing at *each moment* of their existence. If the continued existence of created things be wholly dependent on God's preservation, then those things would drop into nothing, upon the ceasing

---

[179] Edwards, *Original Sin*, 399.
[180] Edwards, *Original Sin*, 400.

of the present moment, without a new exertion of the divine power to cause them to exist in the following moment."[181] This signals yet another step. Where Edwards has already moved from preservation and concurrence to continuous creation, he now goes a step further: he has embraced creation *ex nihilo* moment by moment.

As Edwards explains,

> It will follow from what has been observed, that God's upholding created substance, or causing its existence in each successive moment, is altogether equivalent to an *immediate production out of nothing*, at each moment, because its existence at this moment is not merely in part from God, but wholly from him; and not in any part, or degree, from its antecedent existence. . . . Therefore the antecedent existence is nothing, as to any proper influence or assistance in the affair: and consequently God produces the effect as much from *nothing*, as if there had been nothing *before*. So that this effect differs not at all from the first creation, but only *circumstantially*; as in first creation there had been no such act and effect of God's power before; whereas, his giving existence afterwards, *follows* preceding acts and effects of the same kind, in an established order.[182]

This means that there is no identity at all other than what God establishes by his sovereign and arbitrary decree. God simply *"treats them as one"*—and in doing so God makes them so.[183] For *"divine constitution* is the thing which *makes truth."*[184]

So with respect to personal identity, what makes the infant and the forty-year-old the same person is nothing other than the mere fact that God, in his moment-by-moment work of *creatio ex nihilo*, creates "identical" replicas of the earlier creature(s) and then says that they are "one and the same" person. And as with personal identity more generally, so also with respect to original sin. Edwards here attempts to combine realism with occasionalism: all humanity is "truly to partake of the sin of the first apostasy, so as that this, in reality and propriety, shall become *their* sin; by virtue of a real union between the root and the branches of the world of mankind . . ."[185]

Following several early modern philosophers (perhaps most notably, Malebranche and Berkeley), and holding a view espoused earlier by some prominent Muslim philosophical theologians (the most prominent is al-Ghazali), Edwards is here clearly embracing the doctrine of occasionalism. Occasionalism may be summarized as the conjunction of

---

[181] Edwards, *Original Sin*, 401–402.
[182] Edwards, *Original Sin*, 402, emphasis original.
[183] Edwards, *Original Sin*, 403, emphasis original.
[184] Edwards, *Original Sin*, 404, emphasis original.
[185] Edwards, *Original Sin*, 407.

(O1) For any state of affairs *p* at time *t*, if (i) there is any substance that caus-ally contributes to *p*'s obtaining at *t*, and (ii) no created substance is a free cause of *p* at *t*, then God is the strong active cause of *p* at *t*;

and

(O2) No material substance has any active or passive causal power at all.[186]

So for exactly *all* states of affairs at *all* times, God is the only causal agent. God creates *ex nihilo* moment by moment, and in doing so *God* does all that is ever done.

Beyond the fact that it strikes most people as utterly bizarre—even a phi-losopher and theologian so careful and measured as Thomas Aquinas once called the view "stupid"—there are several problems with occasionalism.[187] Indeed, these problems are significant. At one level, occasionalism collides with what we take to be the implications of a plain reading of Scripture (not to mention common sense). One need look no further in Scripture than the cre-ation account itself to see that God created living creatures to reproduce "ac-cording to their kind"—but if occasionalism is true then no living creature has, strictly speaking, ever done so. Adam might have *thought* that he begot Seth by active causality, but in reality he did not do so. Instead, a much earlier version of Adam looked at Eve with a gleam in his eye, a slightly less earlier version of Adam "knew" Eve, and a somewhat later version of Adam held his baby boy (with untold numbers of Adams in between). But of course *Adam* did not do these things, for he would have had to have and exercise active causal powers in order to do so. What we have instead are untold millions of creatures, all bearing a strong resemblance, and all named "Adam," who exist in immediate succession. None of them actually *do* anything—none of them last long enough to do anything even if they were equipped with the requisite causal powers. Surely this is not the "plain teaching of Scripture," nor is it a "good and necessary consequence" of what is plainly taught in the Bible. Indeed, there is good reason to think that occasionalism runs directly counter to the Bible. For as C. John Collins has argued, there are exegetically grounded rea-sons to be deeply suspicious of occasionalism; for instance, the Hebrew noun *miqreh* is used to signify "chance" occurrences that sharply "distinguishes between the ordinary course of events and miraculous interventions."[188]

---

[186] This summary follows Alfred J. Freddoso, "Medieval Aristotelianism and the Case against Secondary Causation in Nature," in *Divine and Human Action: Essays in the Metaphysics of Theism*, ed. Thomas V. Morris (Ithaca, NY: Cornell University Press, 1988), 82–83.

[187] See Freddoso, "Medieval Aristotelianism," 99.

[188] C. John Collins, quoted in Lydia Jaeger, *What the Heavens Declare: Science in Light of Creation* (Eugene, OR: Cascade, 2012), 61n4. See further C. John Collins, "*Miqreh* in 1 Samuel 6:9: Chance or Event?," *The Biblical Translator* (2000), 144–147.

More crucial to our discussion of the doctrine of original sin is the elephant in the room—the problem of moral responsibility. According to occasionalism, Adam does not actually *take and eat* the forbidden fruit. Again, no creature called Adam exists long enough to do so. Instead, what we have is one creature named "Adam" (we'll call him Adam1) who looks askance at the fruit in his wife's hand and turns up his nose at the thought of it; this creature is replaced by another (we'll call him Adam2) who looks with some interest at the fruit (and perhaps with more interest at Eve's come-hither look), and then this creature is replaced by another (Adam3) who reaches for the fruit and yet another (Adam4) who bites into the fruit (there are, of course, untold battalions of Adams in between our numbered Eden-dwellers, but this need not concern us here). Even if any of these creatures *were* to last long enough to commit some action, according to occasionalism they do not have causal powers at all (at least not active causal powers, or at least no such powers that they could put to work). Recall that for occasionalism, God is the only active cause. But here is the problem: if "Adam" does not exist long enough to do these things, then surely he is not responsible for them. Even if one grants Edwards's claim—inadequately supported though it is—that God's arbitrary decision makes them count as the same person, this doesn't do enough to help. For even if we allow some metaphysical continuity between the different creatures called "Adam," the fact remains that for occasionalism God is the only active causal agent. Thus God—indeed, *only God*—is the cause of the first sin, and of all subsequent sins as well. But if Adam *isn't* the cause of any action, then surely he cannot be held morally responsible *for* such actions! Such considerations lead even someone as sympathetic as Oliver Crisp to conclude that this is nothing short of a "fatal flaw" for Edwards's view.[189]

If possible, things actually get worse for occasionalism. The problem here is not only that moral responsibility for sin is lost (if occasionalism is true). As we have seen, *Adam* wasn't the cause of the first sin. He could not have been, indeed, he did not last long enough to do anything, and he would not have had the needed causal powers even if he would have been around long enough. So just who *is* the causal agent responsible for the first sin? The answer is clear, and it is the same answer that must be given to the question of who is responsible for *every* sin. The answer should strike us as downright blasphemous, but it is unavoidable nonetheless: *God* is, and must be, the causal agent responsible for sin. He is the only causal agent, so there simply are no other possibilities. And if he is the only causal agent responsible for sin—if sin is the direct and intended result of his agency, and the direct and intended result of *only* his agency—then is not God the only real sinner? What else is there to

[189] Crisp, *Jonathan Edwards and the Metaphysics of Sin*, 130.

conclude? I conclude that full-blown Edwardsian realism—despite its boldness and rigor—is not only flawed but fatally so. For as Philip Quinn puts it, on this account "the great Christian doctrine of original sin is not defended but dissolved."[190]

B. Modified Edwardsian Realism

As we have seen, the "common human nature" version of realism seems unable to do all the work that it is called to do. For while it offers a possible and plausible account of the common human corruption that is part of original sin, it does not appear to have the resources to account for original guilt. And as I have just argued, the full-blown Edwardsian version of realism encounters various problems and is flatly inconsistent with the moral responsibility that is utterly vital to a doctrine of original sin. But what about realism more generally? In particular, are there resources within the Edwardsian approach (properly shorn of its determinism and occasionalism) that can offer help in reckoning with the problem of original guilt?

Recall Edwards's belief that "Adam's posterity are from him, as it were in him, and belonging to him, according to an *established course of nature*, as much as the branches of a tree are, according to the *course of nature*, from the tree, in the tree, and belonging to the tree . . ."[191] As he explains, "God, in each step of his proceeding with Adam, in relation to the covenant or constitution established with him, looked on his posterity as being *one with him*. . . . And though he dealt more immediately with Adam, yet it was as the *head* of the whole body, and the *root* of the whole tree; and in his proceedings with him, he dealt with all the branches, as if they had been existing in their root."[192] Such language is suggestive indeed.

As Rea points out, it is suggestive of what he calls the "organic whole theory." The organic whole interpretation of Edwards takes him to be saying that all of humanity—the sum total of Adam-and-progeny—"are all together parts of a single, spatiotemporally extended object."[193] As Rea explains, "On this view, Adam and his posterity comprise successive stages of a persisting individual which is (in some sense) a moral agent and which is such that all of its stages, or temporal parts, are personally accountable at least for the one salient crime committed by its Adamic parts."[194] To many people this sounds implausible: "What, Adam is really an earlier temporal part of a single thing called 'Adam, me, and everyone else'? I am really a part of Adam? Really?" The

---

[190] Philip Quinn, "Divine Conservation, Continuous Creation, and Human Action," in *The Existence and Nature of God*, ed. Alfred J. Freddoso (Notre Dame, IN: University of Notre Dame Press, 1983), 66.
[191] Edwards, *Original Sin*, 385.
[192] Edwards, *Original Sin*, 389.
[193] Rea, "Metaphysics of Original Sin," 334.
[194] Rea, "Metaphysics," 334.

defenders of the view, however, will say that it seems so implausible only if one assumes *endurantism* rather than *perdurantism* as an account of identity and persistence through time. Some explanation is in order: where the endurantist thinks that an object persists through time if and only if the whole thing exists at more than one time, the perdurantist thinks that objects have distinct temporal parts. The version of perdurantism that is sometimes called "worm theory" illustrates this: just as physical parts of a worm are extended through space, so also there are temporal parts that are possessed by whatever has them. As Rea explains, "On this view, . . . just as material objects have distinct *spatial* parts in every subregion of the total region of space that they fill at a time, so too they have numerically distinct *temporal* parts at every time or period of time in their careers."[195]

To return to Edwards and his defense of realism, one way of interpreting Edwards here is to take him as saying that Adam-and-progeny together make up one big "organic whole"—a giant space-time worm—that bears responsibility for the fall.[196] Where the worm-theory perdurantist more generally would argue that personal identity for an individual (say, Adam himself) should be understood in terms of Adam's temporal parts, Edwards would be extending this suggestion to say that *all humanity* is included in one spatio-temporal whole. As Rea summarizes it, "According to the Organic Whole Theory, every human being is part of Humanity, a four-dimensionally extended object composed of every individual human being, including Adam. If the worm theory were false, there would be no such thing as Humanity (or, at any rate, it would not be the sort of thing that could include Adam and us as parts). It is for this reason that the Organic Whole Theory is committed to that view. And, on this view, we all bear guilt for Adam's sin because we are all temporal parts of Humanity, which committed the sin of Adam by way of its Adamic temporal part."[197] So goes the proposal.

But how does it fare? Several distinctly theological problems loom (in addition to strictly philosophical objections to perdurantism).[198] One problem is this: there seems to be no good reason why the later temporal parts of Adam-and-progeny should be guilty only for the first sin of Adam. Indeed, why should the later parts not be responsible for sins committed by other earlier temporal parts (the temporal parts between Adam and the most recent sinner)? Why only Adam's *first* sin—indeed, why only Adam's sin(s)? The second problem is much more intense, and it goes right to the heart of any doctrine of

---

[195] Rea, "Metaphysics," 335, emphasis original.
[196] As he is interpreted by Paul Helm, *Faith and Understanding* (Edinburgh: Edinburgh University Press, 1997), 152–176.
[197] Rea, "Metaphysics," 338.
[198] I am here indebted (as in a more general sense throughout this discussion) to Rea, "Metaphysics of Original Sin," 339–341.

original sin. We can see it in the form of a question: how is the organic whole theory consistent with moral responsibility? It certainly does not look like it is consistent with moral responsibility, nor is it clear how it could be. It is hard to see how the later temporal parts of the whole (Adam-plus-progeny) could have done anything to prevent the fall from occurring. If the later temporal parts are distinct persons—and surely they are—then (by virtue of being *later* temporal parts) they were not involved with respect to consciousness and will. If the later temporal (personal) parts have no control, then it is hard to see how they might be responsible for what the first temporal (personal) parts actually did.

Finally, and very seriously, the notion that Adam-plus-progeny comprise an actual moral agent is problematic. As Rea puts it, "[I]t seems wholly inappropriate to view something like Humanity as a moral agent."[199] Just as my temporal parts are not distinct moral agents (I cannot try to escape punishment for some wrongdoing by claiming that it wasn't me but rather some earlier temporal part of me that did it), so also it is with humanity as a whole. As Rea puts it, "[L]ike my temporal parts, Humanity is not the subject of thoughts tokened in those brains, and so there is no reason to regard it as the agent of acts of will that are tokened in them."[200] More importantly, persons— individual agents—are found guilty as such in Scripture. Overall, the organic whole version of realism does not look promising, even when it is not burdened by determinism and occasionalism.

But the organic whole interpretation is not the only one available. What is sometimes called the "fission theory" is also possible as an interpretation of Edwardsian realism. Fission theory relies on four-dimensionalist metaphysics (but not, as with the organic whole theory, on worm theory).[201] Moving from four-dimensionalism to the theory itself, Hud Hudson asks us to follow a thought experiment that illustrates the theory and its appeal. As he explains,

> [I]t seems to many of us who tend to favor some sort of psychological criterion of identity over time that Hannah would survive if the right hemisphere of her brain were transplanted into a brainless body and the rest of her (old) body were destroyed. Similarly, it seems that Hannah would survive if the left hemisphere of her brain were transplanted into a brainless body and the rest of her (old) body were destroyed—presupposing, of course, the widely accepted prediction that the resulting person (at post-transplant times) would exhibit the right kind of psychological connections with Hannah (at pretransplant times). So, where (if anywhere) does our protagonist end up if Hannah undergoes brain bisection, whereupon each hemisphere of her brain

---

[199] Rea, "Metaphysics," 341.
[200] Rea, "Metaphysics," 341.
[201] For helpful explanation and defense, see Michael C. Rea, "Four-Dimensionalism," in *The Oxford Handbook of Metaphysics*, ed. Michael Loux and Dean Zimmerman (Oxford: Oxford University Press, 2005), 246–280. Summarized briefly, four-dimensionalism is the view that presentism is false (where presentism is understood as the view that only present objects exist).

is transplanted into a different brainless body and the rest of her (old) body is destroyed? Given our former admissions, we seem constrained to say that each of the resulting persons would be our Hannah—a verdict which seems absurd owing to the facts that the resulting persons are two, not one, and that identity is transitive. *Four-Dimensionalism to the rescue*: There were two overlapping people who literally shared a temporal part prior to the transplant and who went their separate ways afterwards. What we have here is simply the temporal analog of the case of conjoined twins that share some but not all of their spatial parts.[202]

With this background, we are in a position to see how the fission interpretation of realism relates to the doctrine of original sin. As Rea summarizes it,

> The Fission Theory . . . says that Adam and his posterity are distinct individuals who share a common temporal stage or set of temporal stages (namely, whatever stages of Adam were involved in Adam's sin, and perhaps all the preceding ones as well). On this view, Adam undergoes fission at the time of his first sin, splitting into billions of different people, only one of whom gets kicked out of Eden, fathers Cain and [Abel], and does the various other deeds traditionally attributed to Adam.[203]

So on the fission theory, we really are distinct individuals, but we also *really* were present in Adam. Is this not what the realist version of original sin is after? Is not realism successful?

Or is it? What are we to make of the fission theory as a resource for thinking about original sin? I first make an observation; I follow this observation with two remaining theological concerns. The observation concerns the metaphysics involved, and here the point to be made is simply that this theory relies upon four-dimensionalism (though not worm theory, as does organic whole theory).[204] To people who find four-dimensionalism plausible, the price will not seem unbearably steep. But to those who find problems with such metaphysics, the fission theory will share those problems.[205]

Hudson raises several worries about the application of fission theory to the doctrine of original sin. One is that fission theory still does not leave you and me in the "appropriate psychological or causal relations" to the "stage" or (purported) shared temporal part of me that was one with Adam in committing the primal sin so very long ago.[206] Whatever one thinks of fission theory on its own, when applied to our relation to Adam it still leaves us with a massive temporal gap (of thousands of years) between our (purported) existence and

---

[202] Hud Hudson, "Fission, Freedom, and the Fall," in *Oxford Studies in Philosophy of Religion*, vol. 2, ed. Jonathan L. Kvanvig (Oxford: Oxford University Press, 2009), 65.
[203] Rea, "Metaphysics of Original Sin," 334.
[204] See Rea, "Metaphysics," 343–344.
[205] For discussion of these, see Theodore Sider, *Four-Dimensionalism* (Oxford: Oxford University Press, 2001).
[206] Hudson, "Fission, Freedom, and the Fall," 71.

action in, with, and "as" Adam and our current existence as active sinners. This leads Hudson to conclude that the proposal is finally to be judged a "failure."[207]

But another concern with fission theory is more distinctly theological. It has to do with the parallel drawn between Adam and Christ by Paul in Romans 5. It is true that there are significant differences between Adam and Christ, and between our relation to Adam and our relation to Christ in this passage. But the differences have to do primarily with the result of their actions—again and again, the work of Christ is said to be "much more" or "greater than" the actions of Adam. And although Paul does not specify exactly *how* we are related to either Adam or Christ, it seems to go directly against the flow of the text to suggest that our relationship to Adam is somehow *stronger* or *closer* than is our relationship with Jesus. But if we were to accept fission theory, we would be forced to one of two alternatives. On the one hand, we could accept the conclusion that our relation to Adam just is closer and stronger (metaphysically) than is our relation to Christ. But, again, this seems to go against the grain of the text, which so clearly emphasizes the superiority of Christ and of our relation to him. On the other hand, we could hold that our relation to Christ just *is* as strong as or stronger than is our relation to Adam. What this means for soteriology is less than pellucid—perhaps we would have *fusion theory* as the counterpart to Adam's fission. Maybe this could be supported by an appeal to Paul's strong insistence that we are "in Christ" (read in a metaphysically heavy sense). But even this move is not shielded from criticism: short of universalism, Paul's language of "in Christ" is reserved for *some* but not all, while what Paul says about Adam and Christ in Romans 5 is nothing short of universal in scope. I do not claim that this kind of concern amounts to a fatal defeater for the fission theory, but it seems that such a concern awaits those who would promote, defend, or endorse the theory. So in addition to the distinctly philosophical criticisms (which I do not deal with here), problems still loom large.

C. Mediate Views: With Molinism

Recall that according to so-called "mediate" views of original sin, we are guilty for the corruption rather than for the actions of Adam. The challenge here, as with other options on offer, is to reconcile this claim with our moral responsibility. We are morally responsible only for what we could have avoided, and it is hard to see how we could be responsible for the corruption that we have inherited. So this view seems to be no better off than the theories that would hold us guilty for what Adam actually did. As Rea puts it, the moral responsibility thesis holds

---

[207] Hudson, "Fission, Freedom, and the Fall," 78. This despite his obvious respect for Rea's metaphysical prowess.

(MR) A person P is morally responsible for the obtaining of a state of affairs S only if S obtains (or obtained) and P could have prevented S from obtaining.[208]

And it *seems* obvious that we could have done nothing to avoid the inheritance of corruption. But is it so obvious?

Sophisticated defenders of the mediate view are not convinced that it is so obvious. Given the right metaphysical adjustments, proponents of this view hold that it is possible to square original sin (including guilt) with moral responsibility by means of the mediate position (possibly combining elements of Erickson's "conditional" view). The metaphysical background is important here, and several concepts need to be made clear. The first of these concepts is that of a "counterfactual." A counterfactual is a claim of the form "if it were the case that p, then it would be the case that q."[209] A counterfactual of freedom, in turn, is a conditional of the form "if S were in circumstances C, then S would freely do A."[210] The next concept is that of "possible worlds." Possible worlds are not alternative universes inhabited by aliens; we are not talking here of science fiction. The term's use here is strictly metaphysical, and it is familiar to anyone who is acquainted with, say, time-travel movies or romantic comedies involving alternative scenarios. A possible world is, in the words of John S. Feinberg, "the complete sequence of persons, objects, events, and actions throughout the whole history of that world from beginning to end."[211] As Alvin Plantinga puts it, a possible world is a "maximally consistent state of affairs."[212] Existence *across* possible worlds—the existence, that is, of an individual in more than one possible world (as opposed to such rivals as "counterpart theory")—is what is meant by "transworld identity." Alvin Plantinga, one of the pioneers in the recent rehabilitation of modal logic and metaphysics, has extended the notion of transworld identity into "transworld depravity," and he has employed it in his use of the free will defense. Basically, "transworld depravity" refers to the condition of anyone who sins in multiple possible worlds.[213] So from the notions of possible worlds and transworld identity we move to transworld depravity, and to this we now add some distinctly "Molinist" commitments. First, we have the Molinist commitment that there are counterfactuals (some with false antecedents) that are true of all persons. Second, for any counterfactual of freedom that is true of some person, it is (or was)

---

[208] Rea, "Metaphysics of Original Sin," 320.

[209] Michael J. Loux, *Metaphysics: A Contemporary Introduction*, 2nd ed. (New York: Routledge, 1998 and 2002), 192.

[210] Rea, "Metaphysics of Original Sin," 346.

[211] John S. Feinberg, *No One Like Him: The Doctrine of God* (Wheaton, IL: Crossway, 2002), 211.

[212] For further discussion, see Alvin Plantinga, *The Nature of Necessity* (Oxford: Oxford University Press, 1974).

[213] For more precision, see Plantinga, *Nature of Necessity*, 186.

possible that the person in question has (or had) the ability to prevent that counterfactual from being true.[214]

From this whirlwind tour of some of the important metaphysical features of Molinism, we are now in a position to see how this maps onto our consideration of the doctrine of original sin. The person who suffers from transworld depravity just *will* fall into sin (in all worlds where he suffers from it). It is not the case that it is, strictly speaking, *necessary* that the transworldly depraved person fall into actual sin. As Rea points out, "The fact that suffering from TWD (transworld depravity) guarantees that P will fall into sin is perfectly consistent with the claim that it is possible that P not fall into sin . . ."[215] Moreover, according to Molinism, "each of us has the power to prevent our suffering from TWD."[216] Thus it is "up to us" whether or not we suffer from TWD.[217] If we had refrained from sinning, then we clearly would not have suffered from it.[218] And, of course, if whether or not we suffer from transworld depravity is something that is within our power, then we can truly be morally responsible for it. As Rea summarizes it,

> One option, then, for those interested in developing a theory of original sin under Molinist assumptions is to identify TWD with the sort of corruption that DOS [the doctrine of original sin] takes to be a consequence of the Fall. After all, it seems to be the right *sort* of property. We have it from birth, and we have it contingently. Moreover, there is no in-principle obstacle to supposing that our suffering from it is, in some sense, a consequence of Adam's sin. We have already acknowledged that, though the counterfactuals that constitute us as TWD-sufferers have been true from the beginning of time, there are nevertheless things we can do (or could have done) such that, had we done them, we would not have suffered from TWD. . . . Finally, since we have the power to prevent our ever having suffered from it, if TWD *were* identified with the corruption that is brought about by the Fall, the resulting theory of original sin would be consistent with (MR) [moral responsibility].[219]

So on this view, all human persons suffer from the original corruption of transworld depravity.[220] They have this from birth: "[I]f it is ever true that P suffers from TWD, it is *always* true that P suffers from TWD."[221] This corruption itself entails guilt. But since it was within our power whether or not we suffer from TWD, then we are morally responsible for it.

It may seem initially implausible to think that we have counterfactual

214 Here I closely follow Rea, "Metaphysics of Original Sin," 345.
215 Rea, "Metaphysics," 347.
216 Rea, "Metaphysics," 347.
217 Rea, "Metaphysics," 348.
218 Rea, "Metaphysics," 350.
219 Rea, "Metaphysics," 350.
220 "All human persons" of course excludes Jesus, and it is also true that neither Adam nor Eve suffered from it *from birth*. In addition, some Christians would hold that Mary was exempt from it as well.
221 Rea, "Metaphysics," 348.

power over the past. But closer reflection shows that this sense of implausibility is misplaced. We do, after all, have *some* counterfactual power over the past. It is not, for instance, within my power to make it true that Napoleon Bonaparte abandoned his warmongering to become a priest and a pacifist, nor is it within my power to make it true that God believed such a thing about Napoleon a million years ago. As Plantinga has argued, however, it *is* (or may be) within my power to mow my lawn today—and thus to make it true that a million years ago God believed that I would do so.[222] It almost goes without saying that this way of thinking about original sin relies on the success of Molinism generally—and that Molinism remains contested among philosophers and theologians.[223] But for those who can embrace Molinism, the mediate view offers a way to hold both to the full-blown or robust doctrine of original sin (including not only original corruption but also original guilt) and to the moral responsibility without which the doctrine of sin collapses entirely.

D. Federalism

Despite its roots within historic Protestant theology (both Reformed and Wesleyan) and its widespread popularity within evangelicalism, the federalist position seems to face the stiffest challenges with respect to moral responsibility. Recall that federalism holds that Adam was our representative head in a legal or political sense, and that his decision has affected the rest of us as that of a sovereign ruler impacts the future of his nation and all descendants. As Adam's guilt comes upon him, so also it comes upon all of us. Thus his sin—both the corruption and the guilt—is imputed to all humanity. It is small wonder that this is sometimes spoken of as "alien guilt."[224]

We have seen that the biblical basis for federalism is less than solid. Perhaps the theory may be consistent with biblical teaching, but it is not demanded by it. But the theory faces bigger problems. Critics of federalism often conclude that the problems with federalism are simply overwhelming: where realist theories can offer ostensible explanations about how it is that we are "in" or "with" Adam, federalists cannot make such claims at all and are forced to fall back on purely forensic or legal categories. But how is it, the critics ask, that we can be legally guilty for something for which we are not *really* guilty? How is this not just legal fiction? And does not legal fiction simply make a mockery of justice and righteousness? The analogies with political leaders fall far short, the critics aver; while an electorate might suffer the *consequences* of the decision of their leader, they do not share in the guilt for *everything* that he has done. They may,

[222] Alvin Plantinga, "Ockham's Way Out," in *The Analytic Theist: An Alvin Plantinga Reader*, ed. James F. Sennett (Grand Rapids, MI: Eerdmans, 1998), 258–292.
[223] E.g., Ken Perszyk, ed., *Molinism: The Contemporary Debate* (Oxford: Oxford University Press, 2011).
[224] G. C. Berkouwer, *Sin*, Studies in Dogmatics (1971; repr., Grand Rapids, MI: Eerdmans, 1980), 424–435.

after all, simply vote for him thinking that he will do one thing only to see him do another. And at any rate, no one was around to vote for or approve Adam as our federal head at all. So how, once again, is this not legal fiction?

Perhaps the most common response from federalists is to say something along these lines: "[W]e would have done the same as Adam if we had been in his place, and this makes it fair for God to judge him on our behalf or in our place." But does this answer offer help to the federalist? The first thing to note is that no reason is immediately obvious as to why we should simply assume that all of us *would* have done the same thing as Adam. There is nothing in Scripture that says this, nor is it obvious that it is a "good and necessary consequence" of what Scripture does teach. But before dismissing the federalist response too quickly on such grounds, we should recall the notion of transworld depravity. Given transworld depravity, several things follow: first, those who suffer from it have a corruption that leads them to sin in various possible worlds; second, if they suffer from transworld depravity, then surely God (as omniscient) knows both that they suffer from it and that they commit actual sins. In other words, given transworld depravity, the statement "we would have done the same thing as Adam if we were in his place" is possibly true.

But is this enough to help the federalist? Assuming that it is true that all humans *would have done* the same as Adam if in his place, how does that make it right or just to judge the rest of us for what he alone actually *did*? It is far from obvious how the truth of such counterfactuals renders us legally guilty, or that it is just to judge someone for what they would have done rather than for what they *have* done. The federalist will be, I think, quick to remind us that we are not in fact being judged for what we might have done; we are being judged for the sin of Adam *because Adam was our federal head*. We are judged because Adam acted as our "federal head" and "for us," and he represents us by doing what we would have done.

Maybe there is another way for those who are attracted to elements of federalism to benefit from its helpful insights. This might be done by combining elements from various views in the following way: We are corrupted by original sin. Our corruption entails that we will inevitably (apart from the intervention of divine grace) commit discrete acts of sin. We are, strictly speaking, guilty for what we do with that corruption. But what we do with (and out of) that corruption in the committing of actual sin—and here the view draws from the insights of federalism—is affirm or ratify what Adam did in his representation of us. We know from Scripture that this committing of sin is exactly what all humans (other than Christ, of course) have done; in point of fact, all have sinned (Rom. 3:23). These sinful actions that are ratifications of Adam's sin make us guilty for the actual sins that we commit. But they also—and here the view intersects with the mediate account—render us guilty for the very corruption that we affirm by our discrete acts of sin. So, on this proposal, we are guilty for *both* actual sin and original sin. And, on this proposal, our guilt may not be inconsistent with the bedrock principles of moral responsibility.

At any rate, as we have seen, federalism—at least common or standard-issue federalism—does not enjoy the "plain" or "clear" theological foundation that its proponents sometimes claim for it. Meanwhile, it is beset with serious liabilities. But for those attracted to it, it might be possible to affirm its central claims without falling prey to the common and serious objections. Doing so will, however, require some adjustments to the theory.

E. Corruption-Only Views

As we have seen, what I am calling corruption-only views are prevalent in the early church (both "East" and "West"), adherence continues to this day in Orthodox circles, and the view has distinguished defenders in the history of Protestant theology as well. It is not a version of Pelagianism (which denies the doctrine of original sin). It does not entail commitment to "Semi-Pelagianism" (which denies that we are completely helpless apart from the intervention of grace).[225] It does not so obviously violate the deep intuitions about justice that seem to be compromised by federalism and (at least some versions of) realism. The proponents of the view can claim consistency with Paul's clearest teaching on the subject (Rom. 5:12–21 and 1 Cor. 15:21–22). Moreover, the view can stake a considerable claim with respect to overt biblical support. After all, as its defenders are quick to point out, Scripture teaches that "Fathers shall not be put to death because of their children, nor shall children be put to death because of their fathers. Each one shall be put to death for his own sin" (Deut. 24:16). Indeed, "everyone shall die for his own iniquity" (Jer. 31:30a). This seems plain: everyone who sins will bear guilt for their personal sin, but not for the sins of others.

This is stated in the Torah, and it is repeated in the Prophets. Perhaps nowhere is it made more obvious than in Ezekiel's prophecy. Ezekiel leaves no room for doubt; for the prophet as much as for the apostle, the "soul who sins shall die" (Ezek. 18:4), for the "wages of sin is death" (Rom. 6:23). Ezekiel makes it clear that the one who is "righteous" shall not perish but shall live (Ezek. 18:6–9). On the other hand, the son who is wicked—the son who commits idolatry against God or injustice against his neighbor—indeed will perish. It does not matter how holy and just his father is; the sinner will die (vv. 10–13). The point is clear: "he shall die for his [own] iniquity" (v. 18). Moreover, Ezekiel anticipates the following rejoinder: "Yet you say, 'Why should not the son suffer

---

[225] See further the discussion of "The Results of Sin" in chapter 6.

for the iniquity of the father?'" (v. 19). His response? "The soul who sins shall die. The son shall not suffer for the iniquity of the father, nor the father suffer for the iniquity of the son" (v. 20).

Beyond this, such a view is consistent with some of the most important Protestant confessions. As Crisp has argued, this proposal is consistent not only with the Anglican Thirty-Nine Articles (1563) but also with both the Belgic Confession (1561) and the Scots Confession (1560). All of these statements unambiguously affirm corruption, but none demand belief in original guilt.[226] Crisp offers what he calls a "moderate Reformed doctrine of original sin"; this includes the following commitments:

1. All human beings after the first primal sin (barring Christ) possess original sin.
2. Original sin is an inherited corruption of nature, a condition which every human being possesses from the first moment of generation.
3. Human beings are not culpable for being generated with this morally vitiated condition.
4. Fallen human beings are not culpable for primal sin either. That is, they do not bear original guilt.
5. The morally vitiated condition normally inevitably yields actual sin.
6. Fallen human beings are culpable for their actual sin and condemned for it, in the absence of atonement.
7. Possession of original sin leads to death and separation from God . . .[227]

This position has a venerable history, and it deserves to stand alongside the other positions as an important option for orthodox Christians.

V. CONCLUSIONS

A. Summary

We have covered a lot of ground in this chapter. After noting the outline and basic contours of the doctrine of original sin, as well as some of the perennial and contemporary challenges to it, I offered a guided tour of some of the most important of the historic Christian theories of original sin. Here we surveyed both realism and federalism, as well as "mediate" views and the "corruption-only" theory. This was followed by a closer look at what is often considered the *locus classicus* of the doctrine; here we looked at several of the most important features of Romans 5:12–21. This closer look at Romans 5:12–21 enabled us to return to the various theories. Ruling out both the mythopoetic and Pelagian views as being inconsistent with the plain teaching of Scripture, I argued that

---

[226] Oliver D. Crisp, "On Original Sin," *International Journal of Systematic Theology* (2015): 258–259.
[227] Crisp, "On Original Sin," 264. The claim that this *"normally* inevitably yields actual sin" allows for unusual cases such as infants who die without reaching a state of moral maturity, the severely mentally impaired, etc.).

the full-blown theory of Edwardsian realism is also fatally flawed. With respect to realism more generally, however, I made the case that the picture is more complex. For although the organic whole theory seems doomed to failure (and the "common nature" version accounts for corruption but struggles with respect to guilt), the fission theory is somewhat more promising for those able to accept the metaphysical commitments. I argued further that the mediate view comes with a (metaphysical) price but is workable for those who can accept Molinism. It is harder, on the other hand, to be optimistic about the federalist view. Meanwhile, the corruption-only view remains viable.

To summarize, some views are ruled out by the demands of divine revelation (mythopoetic or purely symbolic as well as Pelagian views). Others (e.g., Edwardsian realism, organic whole realism) can claim consistency with Romans 5 but then run into trouble when evaluated by broader theological criteria (such as moral responsibility). Other views are consistent with the demands of Christian orthodoxy and should be considered possible. Of these, some will be deemed more plausible than others—but of course what counts as "plausible" will vary (as plausibility is weighted against other factors). For those who can accept four-dimensionalist metaphysics, such views as fission theory realism might be acceptable. For Molinists, the mediate view will likely be attractive. For those who cannot accept either, the corruption-only theory awaits; it offers consistency with both explicit biblical teaching on sin and death and the broader biblical witness to moral responsibility.

B. Original Sin and Christian Witness

Original sin is, as I have argued, a doctrine that is well-established by Scripture and attested to by the broad Christian tradition. The *fact* of original sin is beyond dispute for Christians. But it still presents a stumbling-stone in some ways. The fact that we suffer from the actions of our most ancient ancestors seems *prima facie* hard to square with moral responsibility. And without moral responsibility, of course, there is no point in talking about sin at all. This is the point at which the various theories of original sin come into play. They do not "prove" the doctrine of original sin. Only divine revelation can establish it (although common human experience can give us unmistakable indications that *something* is terribly wrong). The various theories of original sin do not fully explain the doctrine, nor do they remove the mystery. What they propose to do is something more modest: they purport to show how the doctrine might be *possibly* true, and the proponents of the various views all wish to do so in ways that are consistent with the overall teachings of Scripture. To be clear, none of the versions of realism or federalism, neither immediate nor mediate theories, provide proof or full explanation of original sin. The theological proposals, and their accompanying metaphysical theories, are attempts at showing how the doctrine of original sin might be both true and consistent with moral responsibility (as Scripture demands). That the doctrine *is* true is a conclusion to be drawn from reception of divine revelation.

In all of these discussions, however, we should not lose sight of three important points. First, we should remember that sin is *against reason*. So we should not be surprised if the doctrine strikes people as counterintuitive. The second point, however, is more directly applicable to apologetics. It is this: that without the doctrine of original sin the misery and depravity of the world around us—as well as that within us—remains opaque and hopelessly mysterious. Clarifying the point that the misery and horrors of this world remain utterly opaque and impenetrable without the doctrine, Blaise Pascal says that "[c]ertainly nothing jolts us more rudely than this doctrine, and yet, but for this mystery, the most incomprehensible of all, we remain incomprehensible to ourselves."[228] Or again, "[W]ithout the Christian doctrine of sin one can understand nothing; with it one can understand everything."[229] Even an atheist such as Michael Ruse sees the importance and fecundity of the doctrine:

> I think Christianity is spot on about original sin—how could one think otherwise, when the world's most civilized and advanced people (the people of Beethoven, Goethe, Kant) embraced that slime-ball Hitler and participated in the Holocaust? I think Saint Paul and the great Christian philosophers had real insights into sin and freedom and responsibility, and I want to build on this rather than turn from it.[230]

So while the doctrine of original sin presents some challenges (again, *prima facie* it seems quite implausible), it also has such explanatory power as to be of great apologetic value. For by it we can begin to understand the depravity of the world.

The third point is related to the foregoing. It is one of pastoral relevance as well as theological and apologetic importance: the doctrine of original sin is, paradoxically, something that explains and awakens (or intensifies) within us the hope for something better. Things are *not* right, and we find within us a longing that things *will* be made right. G. K. Chesterton states this powerfully:

> The Fall is a view of life. It is not only the only enlightening, but also the only encouraging view of life. It holds, as against the only real alternative philosophies, . . . that we have misused a good world, and not merely been entrapped into a bad one. It refers evil back to the wrong use of the will, and

---

[228] Blaise Pascal, cited in Bernard Ramm, *Offense to Reason: A Theology of Sin* (New York: Harper & Row, 1985), 1.
[229] Pascal, cited in Ramm, *Offense to Reason*, 145.
[230] Michael Ruse, "Darwinism and Christianity Redux: A Response to My Critics," *Philosophia Christi* 4 (2002): 192.

thus declares that it can eventually be righted by the right use of the will. Every other creed except that one is some form of surrender to fate. A man who holds this view of life will find it giving light on a thousand things, on which mere evolutionary ethics have not a word to say.[231]

Chesterton argues that the doctrine of original sin offers the best explanation, not only of the current human condition but also of the hope that swells within the human heart. It is, he says, "only by stating the truth of original sin" that "the extremes of good and evil by which man exceeds all the animals by the measure of heaven and hell" can really be accounted for.[232] And it is only the doctrine of original sin that can allow us to make sense of the eloquent cries of the great poets, "and nowhere more than in the poetry of pagans and skeptics: 'We look before and after, and pine for what is not'; which cries against all prigs and progressives out of the very depths and abysses of the broken heart of man, that happiness is not only a hope, but also in some strange manner a memory; and that we are all kings in exile."[233]

The doctrine of original sin is, then, for all its mystery, very important in many ways. As Ramm puts it, although the Christian doctrine of sin is "offensive to reason," it remains true that without it "much of human life and history remains forever opaque," but with it "a shaft of light is cast upon personal existence, social existence, and the course of history, giving clarity that nothing else in the religions, nor the philosophies, of the world can provide."[234] Accordingly, we need to "retrieve it and bring it alive for the twenty-first century."[235]

---

[231] G. K. Chesterton, *As I Was Saying: A Chesterton Reader*, ed. Robert Knille (Grand Rapids, MI: Eerdmans, 1985), 160, as cited in C. John Collins, *Did Adam and Eve Really Exist? Who They Were and Why You Should Care* (Wheaton, IL: Crossway, 2011), 158.
[232] Chesterton, *As I Was Saying*, 160.
[233] Chesterton, *As I Was Saying*, 160.
[234] Ramm, *Offense to Reason*, 163.
[235] Denis Edwards, *How God Acts: Creation, Redemption, and Special Divine Action* (Minneapolis: Fortress, 2010), 129.

FIVE

THE "SIN NATURE" AND
THE "NATURE" OF SIN

I. INTRODUCTION

Sin takes many forms and expresses itself in widely variant ways. In this chapter I shall argue that sin should be understood as being contrary to nature, contrary to reason, and, ultimately, contrary to God. And we shall explore some important insights about sin that are grounded in Scripture and developed in the Christian tradition. First, however, it may be helpful to address one very popular but very problematic way of thinking about sin.

II. DOES THE BELIEVER HAVE "TWO NATURES"?
UNDERSTANDING TALK OF THE "SIN NATURE"

A. Human Nature and Sin: Some Clarifications and
an Important Methodological Reminder

To this point, we have seen that sin is depicted in Scripture as both universal and fixed. None of us has escaped the corruption of sin, and none of us is able to change our behavior or our inclinations so as to overcome it. The reach of sin is to all humanity, and the stain of its pollution is deeper than can be cleansed or overcome by even the "best" of us. In light of this vivid and stark testimony of Scripture, Christian theologians have rightly affirmed both *original sin* (which we have examined) and *total depravity* (which will be explored in more detail in the next chapter). Thus we are led to the unfortunate and depressing conclusion that *all* of us are sinners, and that *none* of us are able to justify or purify ourselves.

But with these affirmations come some important questions, and such questions have served to spark controversy over the proper understanding of the "nature" and character of sin. Before addressing such questions and issues directly, it is important to remind ourselves of how such questions are to be

208 □ AGAINST GOD AND NATURE

addressed. Here, as elsewhere, is where Christology is so vitally important in understanding the nature of what it means to be human. As Thomas F. Torrance points out, Jesus Christ is the "humanizing Man" and the "personalizing Person."[1] Torrance argues that what is sometimes called the "epistemological significance of the *homoousion*" is of vital importance.[2] In our efforts to understand God, he says, we should look first and last not to some kind of a priori or abstract concept but to the revelation of God in Jesus Christ; the fact that Jesus Christ is *homoousios* with the Father means, among other things, that we should look to Jesus Christ for our full and final revelation of who God is. As there is no other God somewhere behind the back of Jesus, so also it is true that we can trust God's revelation of himself to us in Jesus Christ. But what Torrance says of the "epistemological significance" of the incarnation is also important for our understanding of humanity. We indeed should learn about the identity of God through the incarnate Son—from the fact that Jesus is *homoousios with the Father*. So also should we learn about genuine and authentic human identity from the incarnate Son—from the fact that Jesus Christ is *homoousios with us*. So rather than starting with the sinful, broken, devastated remnants of the *imago dei* that we see all around us, we should start with Jesus to see the "true image." And rather than allowing the diseased specimens to dictate what our understanding of normal or "healthy" looks like, we should take our cue from the only human person who is truly healthy and whole. We should allow Jesus Christ—he who is fully and completely human—to inform us of what true humanity really is.

And when we do this, we are reminded that Jesus Christ was truly and completely human—"yet without sin" (Heb. 4:15). Minimally, from this we should learn that one need not be sinful to be human. But there is more to see here as well, and a brief introduction to some important developments in Christology (and especially the metaphysics of the incarnation) will help us at this point. In response to charges that the orthodox doctrine of the incarnation is not only false but indeed necessarily false, philosophical theologians have responded by drawing out several important distinctions.[3] Thomas V. Morris draws a distinction between an *individual-essence* and a *kind-essence*. The former is "the whole set of properties individually necessary and jointly sufficient for being numerically identical with *that individual*."[4] The properties are "individually necessary"—that is, they must all be possessed. And they are

---

[1] Thomas F. Torrance, *The Mediation of Christ* (Colorado Springs: Helmers & Howard, 1992), 69.
[2] Kang Phee Seng, "The Epistemological Significance of the Homoousion in the Theology of Thomas F. Torrance," *SJT* (1992): 341–366.
[3] Among the most (in)famous of such criticisms of the classical doctrine is that of John Hick, ed., *The Myth of God Incarnate* (London: SCM, 1977); and Hick, *The Metaphor of God Incarnate* (Louisville: Westminster/John Knox, 1993).
[4] Thomas V. Morris, *The Logic of God Incarnate* (Ithaca, NY: Cornell University Press, 1986), 38.

"jointly sufficient"—that is, if you have all of them, you surely are numerically identical with that individual. The kind-essence or kind-nature, on the
other hand, is a "shareable set of properties individually necessary and jointly
sufficient for membership in that kind."[5] Drawing upon this, Morris points
out further the crucial but easily overlooked distinction between *common* and
essential human properties. A *common* human property is any property that
is possessed by most (or, conceivably, even all) humans. An *essential* human
property, on the other hand, is a member of the set of properties individually
necessary and jointly sufficient for being a member of the kind-essence *humanity*. In his now well-known discussion, Morris observes that "a common
human property will be one which many or all human beings have," but he
says that we must take care not to confuse this with essential properties.[6] "We
need," he insists, "to be clear that a property's being common or even universal
for members of a kind does not entail that it is essential for the kind, such that
membership in the kind would be impossible without its exemplification."[7] It
is common for humans to have hair, but surely it would not be right to deny
that someone is human because she lacked it. The property *being born on earth*
is a common human property, but it would be wrong to deny that someone is
really human because he was born on, say, a lunar colony or in a space shuttle.
"The property of living at some time on the surface of the earth may now be
a universal human property, but it is not an essential one."[8] Morris employs
this distinction to defuse objections to orthodox Christology, and I judge his
use of it to be helpful in many ways. But it has obvious relevance here as well.

For the property of *being sinful* is—according to Christian orthodoxy—
a *common* human property. It is one that is possessed by the vast majority of
humans. Indeed, only one human person is exempt from it: Jesus Christ is like
us "in every respect, . . . yet without sin" (Heb. 4:15). But the fact that Jesus
Christ *is* fully and completely human yet without sin speaks volumes about a
proper understanding of what it really means to be human. He is fully human,
yet without sin. So genuine, authentic human nature does not include the properties associated with sinfulness. Compare a scenario in which all of the human
persons in an environment are ill; the physicians and the nurses as well as the
patients all suffer from a fatal disease. Some are farther along than others,
and the physicians and nurses have enough skill, training, and medicine to be
able to bring some small measure of aid and comfort to the other patients, but
together all are afflicted with the debilitating and finally fatal disease. Imagine
the situation with the arrival of a person who was not afflicted with the disease.

[5] Morris, *Logic of God Incarnate*, 39.
[6] Morris, *Logic of God Incarnate*, 63.
[7] Morris, *Logic of God Incarnate*, 63.
[8] Morris, *Logic of God Incarnate*, 63.

She alone is healthy; only she does not suffer from the awful disease. In this situation the *common* human property would be *being stricken with the disease*. But it would not follow at all that this is an *essential* human property; it simply would not be right to say that the new arrival is less than human or somehow other than human because she does not match up to the "normal" description. Surely it would be wrongheaded to say that the only person in the environment who did *not* suffer from the disease must not really be human, and it would be even more wildly perverse to say that she could not be human *because* she does not suffer from the disease.

Yet something like this seems to be at work in our understanding of human sin. Because it is so very common and thus what we readily take to be the "normal" human condition, we are tempted to think that this must be the *essential* human condition. Because we all suffer from it, we easily conclude that it must be "what it means to be human." "So we sin? Well, so what? We are, after all, 'only human.'" But reflection on the human condition in the light of orthodox Christology puts it all in a very different light. If being sinful is essential to being human, then Christ is either a sinner (and thus himself in need of salvation) or not really human (and thus not able to be our Savior). Either way leads to outright heresy. What Christ reveals to us in the incarnation, however, is that being sinful is *not* essential to human nature. He was fully and completely human—yet without sin. Sin is not essential to being human. To the contrary, as we shall see shortly, it is a *perversion* of genuine, authentic, and healthy humanity.

B. Two-Nature Hamartiology Introduced

Some Christians in the evangelical traditions believe that the Christian has "two natures." The regenerate believer, as a "new creature in Christ Jesus," has a new nature. But short of perfection and glorification, the believer also has the "old nature." This is what is often called "the sin nature." For instance, the influential dispensationalist theologian Lewis Sperry Chafer uses "the sin nature" and "original sin" synonymously, and he insists that believers have two natures.[9] Chafer wants us to remember that sin is "a perversion of God's original creation and in that sense is an abnormal thing," and he recognizes that the term "nature" works for the doctrine of sin only with a "secondary meaning" of the word.[10] Unfortunately, however, Chafer does not tell us much about the precise meaning of "nature" (secondary or otherwise), and in point

---

[9] Lewis Sperry Chafer, *Systematic Theology, Volume II: Angelology, Anthropology* (Dallas: Dallas Seminary Press, 1947), 283. Charles C. Ryrie largely follows Chafer at this point, e.g., *Basic Theology* (Wheaton, IL: Victor, 1986), 218. We should not assume, however, that "two-nature hamartiology" is essential to dispensationalism.
[10] Chafer, *Systematic Theology, Volume II*, 285, 288.

of fact he eschews "metaphysical considerations at all."[11] But this lack of clarity about what a nature is does not discourage Chafer from putting the concept to theological work. "Unregenerate people," he insists, "have but one nature, while those who are regenerate have two natures. There is but one fallen nature, which is from Adam, and one new nature, which is from God."[12] The unregenerate person has only one nature, and this is "the sin nature." The regenerate believer, on the other hand, continues to have the sin nature but also has "a new divine nature."[13] The presence of these two natures in the believer "results in conflict," for they are diametrically and violently opposed to each other.[14]

In one of the more illuminating treatments of the issue, William Combs says that "there is a sense in which the believer can properly be said to have two natures, and yet there is a sense in which the believer can properly be said to have one nature."[15] In what is clearly an advance over Chafer's reticence to define "nature," Combs moves toward a definition of nature; a nature is a "complex of attributes."[16] Using this definition, he mounts an energetic defense of this view.

But not all evangelical theologians are inclined to agree. J. I. Packer notes that this "line of teaching" is "widespread," but he resists it as "misleading."[17] What are we to make of this? Is there a strong case for either view? And does it even matter, or is it only a matter of semantics? After first looking at the case for the "two-natures" view, I shall argue that there is very good reason to reject the view.

C. Two-Nature Hamartiology Considered

In considering the arguments in support of the "two-natures" view, the first thing to recognize is that no one claims to make a direct case for the view from exegesis of the Bible. As Combs readily admits, "[I]t is important to note that the meaning of the term *nature* as it is used in the debate over one or two natures in the believer is primarily a theological issue, not one of scriptural usage."[18] Even though *physis* is used in Ephesians 2:3 to inform us that we too were "by *nature* children of wrath," there is no reason to think that this text refers to the possession of *two* natures—there is nothing here to rule out the possibility that we are at one point "children of wrath" by nature as unbelievers

---

[11] Chafer, *Systematic Theology, Volume II*, 288.
[12] Chafer, *Systematic Theology, Volume II*, 348.
[13] Chafer, *Systematic Theology, Volume II*, 347.
[14] Chafer, *Systematic Theology, Volume II*, 347.
[15] William W. Combs, "Does the Believer Have One Nature or Two?," *Detroit Baptist Seminary Journal* (1997): 81.
[16] Combs, "Does the Believer," 84.
[17] J. I. Packer, *Rediscovering Holiness* (Ann Arbor, MI: Servant, 1992), 83. Much earlier, B. B. Warfield had offered scathing criticisms of Chafer's view, e.g., "A Review of Lewis Sperry Chafer's *He That Is Spiritual*," *Princeton Theological Review* (1919): 215. See the helpful discussion of Randall Gleason, "B. B. Warfield and Lewis S. Chafer on Sanctification," *Journal of the Evangelical Theological Society* (1997): 241–258.
[18] Combs, "Does the Believer Have One Nature or Two?," 82.

and then no longer so as believers.[19] And while the NIV refers to the "sinful nature" in Romans 7:18, 25, it does so as a translation of Paul's uses of *sarx* (flesh) rather than having anything to do with *nature* as such (or in the metaphysical sense). But while there is no argument directly from the use of *physis* in Scripture, the proponents of the two-nature view maintain that it nonetheless has a proper *theological* usage. It is, they insist, the best way to account for the biblical descriptions of the struggle within the Christian life (notably, from a particular reading of Rom. 7:14–25).

Crucial to this strategy is the definition of *nature*. Combs follows J. Oliver Buswell in holding that "a nature is by definition a complex of attributes."[20] Combs applies this to Christology before employing it in defense of the view that believers have two natures:

> By defining *nature* as "a complex of attributes," we can, for instance, correctly speak of Christ as having both a human and divine nature. By a human nature we mean he possessed all those attributes or characteristics essential for true humanity and, in like manner, by a divine nature we mean he possessed all those attributes or characteristics essential for true deity. Natures are not persons and natures do not act; thus Christ was one person with two natures. Therefore, it is perfectly acceptable to use the two-nature terminology to describe Jesus Christ. Orthodox theology has traditionally used such terminology even though it is not found in the Bible. But, as Smith has wisely observed, "it is perfectly proper to speak of *the* (single) nature of Jesus as the God-Man." . . . In describing Christ as having one nature or two natures, a different *meaning* is not being given to the term *nature*—a "complex of attributes"; rather, we are simply grouping various attributes of the one person into either one or two groups emphasizing different aspects of the one person. . . . we may conclude that, theologically, two-nature terminology seems quite helpful, if not essential, for understanding the one God-man.[21]

Combs then applies this to hamartiology. By "understanding *nature* as a complex of attributes, one is perfectly justified in using the term to describe the believer as having either one or two natures."[22] The "sin nature" is the complex property of being sinful, while the "new nature" is "the capacity to serve God and righteousness acquired through regeneration";[23] thus the proponents of the two-natures view conclude that "it is perfectly valid to speak of the believer as having two natures—old and new—as long as the term *nature* is understood to refer to a complex of attributes" or "set of characteristics."[24]

---

[19] As is seen by Combs, "Does the Believer," 82–83.
[20] Combs, "Does the Believer," 84. See further J. Oliver Buswell, *A Systematic Theology of the Christian Religion, Volume One* (Grand Rapids, MI: Zondervan, 1962), 303. Interpreted charitably, this is an "abstractist" account of nature, on which see Alvin Plantinga, "On Heresy, Mind, and Truth," *FPhilos* (1999): 182–193.
[21] Combs, "Does the Believer," 84–85.
[22] Combs, "Does the Believer," 85.
[23] Combs, "Does the Believer," 85.
[24] Combs, "Does the Believer," 103.

Unfortunately, there are several problems with this view, and some of them are severe indeed. These can be seen more clearly in the light of reflection on the operative definition of *nature* that is employed in defense of the two-nature view. The notion here is that a nature is a "complex of attributes." Here we run into several difficulties. First, the two-natures view opens the door to *agnosticism* about natures. While Combs at one point characterizes the human nature as "all those attributes or characteristics essential for true humanity" and the divine nature as "all those attributes or characteristics essential for true deity,"[25] he also says that in referring to the two natures of Christ "we are simply grouping various attributes of the one person into either one or two groups emphasizing different aspects of the one person."[26] But if this—our activity of "grouping" or "clustering" attributes in various packages—is all that there is to natures, then we have no reason to predicate only one or two rather than *many* natures to a person. For on such a view of natures, we simply have no way of knowing how many such natures there are apart from our "grouping" activity.

Even worse, on a plausible interpretation, the Buswell-Combs view of natures is an *anti-realist* (or perhaps a "conventionalist") one.[27] Again, if our activity of drawing up groups or clusters is what makes a nature to be what it is, then we lose grip on a realist account of natures. If our "clustering" activity makes it true that there are two natures rather than one (or one rather than two or more), then the natures do not exist independently of our "clustering" activity—and thus we lose a realist account. But this is, so far as I can see, completely consistent with a straightforward reading of the two-natures position (as articulated by Chafer and Combs). Combs says that it would be perfectly acceptable—if unusual—to hold to a one-nature (monophysite) Christology. As he puts it, "[I]f we were to describe the God-man as having one nature, we would include all those attributes which are essential to both natures—human and divine."[28] As I understand this, his point is that because we are dividing and lumping attributes together, it is fine to do so in different ways: we can rightly and helpfully describe Christ as having two natures (humanity and divinity, respectively), and we can rightly and helpfully describe him as having one nature (humanity-divinity). Combs does not draw this conclusion, but altogether, Christ would seem to have (at least) three natures: the human nature, the divine nature, and the human-divine nature. So it seems that, strictly speaking, the number of Christ's natures is up to us, and there is no "truth" to the matter beyond what we decide. Without equivocation (because nature is

---

[25] Combs, "Does the Believer," 103.
[26] Combs, "Does the Believer," 84.
[27] By "anti-realism" about natures I mean simply the view that there are no such things apart from human opinions or decisions about them. On "conventionalism," see the discussion in E. J. Lowe, *A Survey of Metaphysics* (Oxford: Oxford University Press, 2002), 113–114.
[28] Combs, "Does the Believer," 84.

used in the same sense with respect to both one-nature claims and two-nature claims), on this proposal we can say both that Christ has one nature and that he has two—and we can also say that he has three. We can say such things because the "truth" of the matter depends on our activity of "clustering" these attributes. Does Christ have one nature or two (or perhaps as many as six)? It depends; if we are lumping all of his properties together, then he has one—but if we are dividing them into two clusters, then he has two. So the truthfulness of an answer to this question depends on *us*. What is this if not an anti-realist view of natures?

Turning back to hamartiology, does the believer have one nature or two? It depends; if we are lumping all of his properties together, then he has one—but if we are dividing them into two clusters, then he has two. Again, the truthfulness of an answer to this question depends on us. And again, what is this if not an anti-realist view of natures? The proponents of the two-natures view might want to avoid anti-realism (and its implication that there is no divine nature that is independent of our clustering work), but how they might do so is somewhere short of obvious.

An obvious way to avoid agnosticism and anti-realism is by endorsing a better view of natures. Where defining nature as "a complex of attributes" is vague and leaves open the door to agnosticism and anti-realism, a better formulation helps us avoid these problems. Suppose that we understand a nature or kind-essence as *the full set of properties, individually necessary and jointly sufficient for inclusion in that natural (or supernatural) kind.*[29] Where reference to a mere "complex of attributes" opens the door to agnosticism and anti-realism, the proffered definition does not do so at all. Not just *any* cluster of attributes, no matter how random or contrived, could really count as a nature. Instead, only the conjunction of those that are *individually necessary* and *jointly sufficient* counts as a nature. They are *individually necessary*: all of them must be possessed to qualify for kind-nature membership. Furthermore, they must be possessed in all "possible worlds" (more precisely, all possible worlds inhabited by the bearer). And they are *jointly sufficient*: if you have all of them, then you indeed are a member of the natural kind. Such a view is vastly superior to the "cluster of attributes" view; it preserves what is right about the "cluster view" but without its liabilities.

These are not trifling quibbles about abstract metaphysical subtleties. To the contrary, a misunderstanding of the meaning of "nature" produces problems in doctrinal formulation. This is evident in several places; because Combs begins with Christology as an illustrative parallel, it is appropriate to revisit

---

[29] As we have seen in Morris, *Logic of God Incarnate*, 62–70; see also Alvin Plantinga, *The Nature of Necessity* (Oxford: Oxford University Press, 1974), 44–69; and Kenneth Konyndyk, *Introductory Modal Logic* (Notre Dame, IN: University of Notre Dame Press, 1986), 88–92.

his conclusions. He seems to think that it is entirely legitimate and even quite helpful to hold to what translates as a kind of monophysitism. To be fair, he also thinks that classical two-natures Christology is acceptable: "[W]e may conclude that, theologically, two-nature terminology seems quite helpful, if not essential, for understanding the one God-man."[30] But there are several problems with his formulation, and some of them are deep indeed. First, it simply is not true historically that two-natures Christology is only "quite helpful" but somehow not central to orthodox Christology. To the contrary, two-natures Christology is resoundingly affirmed in the classical creedal formulae, and one-nature Christology has just as resoundingly been rejected: according to Chalcedon, Christ is one person of "two natures, without confusion, without change, without division, without separation, the distinction of the natures being in no way annulled by the union, but rather the characteristics of each nature being preserved and coming together to form one person . . ."[31]

An affirmation of monophysitism would be a departure from the orthodox doctrine of the incarnation. One might try to avoid such an entailment by holding that the meaning of "nature" is different in one-nature affirmations than it is in two-nature claims. But Combs has already denied that the meaning of "nature" varies at all, so this route is not open to him.[32] It seems, however, that the only other way to avoid outright rejection of orthodoxy would be to affirm the anti-realist view. Again, I doubt that such a view is intended. But if realist, the two-nature view entails both an outright contradiction and a departure from creedal orthodoxy.[33] My point here is *not* to make charges of Christological heterodoxy! Rather, my point is that such an understanding of *nature* is imprecise and insufficient; it cannot do the work intended without (minimally) opening the door to deeper problems.

Turning now back to hamartiology, Combs uses his understanding of nature (as a complex of attributes that we lump together) to argue that it is permissible to speak of the believer as one who has both "one nature" and "two natures." As he puts it, "[O]ne is perfectly justified in using the term to describe the believer as having either one or two natures."[34] The believer has the "old nature" (or "sin nature"), which is the capacity or tendency to aid Satan in his rebellion against God; the believer also has a "new nature," and this is to be understood as "a disposition toward holiness."[35] If we take all these properties together, though, "our understanding of *nature* as a complex of attributes

---

[30] Combs, "Does the Believer," 85.
[31] Edward R. Hardy, ed., *Christology of the Later Fathers* (Philadelphia: Westminster, 1954), 373.
[32] Combs, "Does the Believer," 86.
[33] Combs himself chides John F. MacArthur Jr. for having "wandered so far from the way of orthodox theology" and for being "out of step with orthodoxy" ("Does the Believer," 101, 103).
[34] Combs, "Does the Believer," 85.
[35] Combs, "Does the Believer," 85.

permits us to view the believer as having one nature."[36] But while either is permissible, the two-natures view seems clearly preferable: "it is perfectly valid to speak of the believer as having two natures—old and new—as long as the term nature is understood to refer to a complex of attributes, a set of characteristics, or disposition. . . . Two-nature terminology combined with a proper understanding of regeneration and sanctification accurately represents the believer's struggle with sin as presented in Scripture."[37]

Assuming that the proponents of the two-natures view intend a realist account, there are yet problems with the view that believers have two natures. In an earlier debate, confessional Lutherans concluded that sin should not be viewed as a *substance*. The confessional Lutherans rejected the view of Matthias Flacius and insisted that sin is not a substance or concrete-nature, but neither is it an abstract essence or kind-nature that somehow really exists. If it were, then we would be faced with several broad options, none of which should be acceptable to the orthodox Christian. Maybe it was created by Satan and his minions. But this supposition cannot be true, for it would both cede Satan far more power than is testified to in Scripture *and* radically misunderstand his work—he is the *destroyer*! What the Lutheran orthodox concluded about the notion that sin is a substance—that it is *not* a substance, and that "the work of God and the work of the devil can be set forth with the greatest clearness. For the devil cannot create any substance, but can only, by way of accident, under the permission of the Lord, deprave a substance created by God"—applies as well to the view that sin is a kind-nature or abstract essence.[38] Even worse is the notion that such a "sin nature" exists necessarily, for to endorse this view would be to return to the cosmic dualism rejected by orthodox Christians everywhere. As we have seen, this was recognized as heresy; it has been steadfastly rejected by Roman Catholic, Orthodox, and Protestant theology alike. Or perhaps "the sin nature" was created by God. But this is worse yet, for to hold that it was created—as the sin that it just *is*—by God is arguably to go beyond heresy to something even worse. As the Canons of Dordt conclude, "the very thought [that God is the creator or author of sin] is blasphemy."[39]

In light of the foregoing, it seems best to conclude that the language of "sin nature" is misleading at best and should be avoided. While there is a loose and popular sense in which we can say that sinning is "second nature," this loose

[36] Combs, "Does the Believer," 85, emphasis original.
[37] Combs, "Does the Believer," 103.
[38] "The Formula of Concord," in *The Creeds of Christendom, with a History and Critical Notes, Volume III: The Evangelical Protestant Creeds*, ed. Philip Schaff (Grand Rapids, MI: Baker Academic, 2007), 105–106.
[39] Canons of Dordt, art. 15, cited in G. C. Berkouwer, *Sin*, Studies in Dogmatics (1971; repr., Grand Rapids, MI: Eerdmans, 1980), 29. This corresponds closely to the statement of Martin Luther that it is "clearly demonic" to claim that sin originates with God: "this is the last step of sin, to insult God and to charge him with being the originator of sin" (*Luther's Works* 1:179, cited in Wilfried Härle, *Outline of Christian Doctrine: An Evangelical Dogmatics* [Grand Rapids, MI: Eerdmans, 2015], 398n19).

and popular sense should not be misunderstood to be an ontological claim about the sober truth of the matter.[40] Even its proponents admit that endorsement of a "two-natures" hamartiology is not demanded by Scripture; it is not based on the NT use of *physis* but instead is a *theologoumen* offered as a way to make sense of the biblical witness to the struggle with sin that remains in the life of the believer. Since it is not demanded by Scripture, draws upon deeply flawed metaphysics, and leads to theological problems that are quite severe, we should conclude with J. I. Packer that this "widespread but misleading line of teaching" should be rejected outright.[41]

We are—all of us—sinners. We are sinners who are corrupt to the core of our existence. If we think in terms of concrete-natures, then I should say that *my human nature* has been corrupted, sickened, and twisted, and that this perversion has gone to the core of my being. If we think in terms of abstract human nature, then I should admit that the human nature *as exemplified by me* is corrupted, sickened, and twisted, and again that this perversion of sin has gone to the core of my being. But to say this is not to say that there is some *thing* (abstract or concrete) that is called "the sin nature." To reify sin in this way is to give it an independent reality that it does not have and does not deserve. To the contrary (as we shall see in this chapter), what is sometimes called the "nature" of sin (in the loose and popular sense) leads us to the conclusion that it is only parasitic, that it has no independent reality of its own but is always and only a perversion of what is *good*. So while we confess that all of us—and all aspects or "parts" of us—are tainted by sin, we should refrain from unclear and potentially problematic talk about "the sin nature." Such talk is neither exegetically warranted, metaphysically helpful, nor theologically sustained. We readily should admit that our natures are corrupted by sin, thus we are "by nature children of wrath" (Eph. 2:3). We might even refer to "the *sinful* nature" (as does the NIV as a translation of some uses of *sarx*), so long as by this we are clear that our natures, originally created as *good* and called such by God, have become corrupted by sin. But we should, I conclude, avoid misleading and troubling talk of "the sin nature." As William Burt Pope puts it, "[I]t must be remembered that, whatever sin is, it is the accident of a nature that is not in itself changed."[42]

To this point I have argued that we should not think of sin as a substance (or primary essence or individual-essence), nor should we think of it as a nature (or secondary essence or kind-essence). How should we think and talk

[40] Kathryn Tanner refers to sin as "a second nature," but she takes a view of human nature that is much more "plastic" than traditional accounts of humanity. Nonetheless, she does insist that sin is "contrary to what God intended us to be" (*Christ the Key* [Cambridge: Cambridge University Press, 2010], 70).
[41] Packer, *Rediscovering Holiness*, 83.
[42] William Burt Pope, *A Compendium of Christian Theology: Being Analytical Outlines of a Course of Theological Study, Biblical, Dogmatic, Historical*, 3 vols., 2nd ed. (New York: Phillips & Hunt, 1881), 2:38.

about our sinfulness, if not in the language of "the sin nature"? It is to consideration of such issues that we now turn.

III. THE "NATURE" OF SIN

Sin is notoriously hard to define with clear and tight precision. It resists tidy description, and it defies neat characterization. In light of this, theologians throughout the centuries have thought of sin as having these characteristics: sin is *contra naturam, contra rationem*, and—above all—*contra Deum*. Thus Augustine says that sin is a falsehood. It is what we might call "living a lie." It is turning away from the purposes for which we were created. It is rebelling against our Creator:

> When, then, a man lives according to the truth, he lives not according to himself, but according to God; for He was God who said, "I am the truth." When, therefore, man lives according to himself—that is, according to man, not according to God—assuredly he lives according to a lie; not that man himself is a lie, for God is his author and creator, who is certainly not the author and creator of a lie, but because man was made upright, that he might not live according to himself, but according to Him who made him—in other words, that he might do His will and not his own; and not to live as he was made to live, that is a lie . . . [43]

Thus sin is, effectively, against nature, against reason, and against God, and these three concepts are closely related in classical Christian doctrines of sin.

A. Contrary to Nature

To many people, it is simply intuitive that sin is "natural." The modern philosopher Georg Wilhelm Friedrich Hegel gives a sophisticated account of sin as somehow "natural." The story of modern theology cannot be understood without reference to Hegel. As David Fergusson says, "[T]he student of modern theology cannot afford to bypass Hegel's work," for "[i]ts conceptuality has entered into the bloodstream of Christian thought."[44] One of the most creative and complex thinkers in the history of Western thought, there is much to Hegel's philosophy and theology that goes far beyond the scope of our discussion. But we need not understand everything

---

[43] Augustine, *De civitate Dei*, XIV.4 (PL 41:407; *NPNF*[1] 2:264).

[44] David Fergusson, "Hegel," in *The Blackwell Companion to Nineteenth Century Theology*, ed. David Fergusson (Oxford: Wiley-Blackwell, 2010), 73. James C. Livingston says that "Hegel was a dominant influence in Christian theology for almost a century," and he notes as well that Hegel's "rich influence is still present, though often unrecognized" (*Modern Christian Thought, Volume 1: The Enlightenment and the Nineteenth Century*, 2nd ed. [Upper Saddle River, NJ: Prentice Hall, 1997], 116–117). See also Stephen D. Crites, "The Gospel according to Hegel," *Journal of Religion* (1966): 246–263; Peter Hodgson, *Hegel and Christian Theology* (Oxford: Oxford University Press, 2005); Charles Taylor, *Hegel* (Cambridge: Cambridge University Press, 1975); William Desmond, *Hegel's God: A Counterfeit Double* (Burlington, VT: Ashgate, 2003); and Cyril O'Regan, *The Heterodox Hegel* (Albany: State University of New York Press, 1994).

about Hegel's grand system to grasp several important aspects. As Bernard Ramm explains, Hegel's "scheme of the evolution of *Geist* (Mind, Spirit)" sought to show how the development of human society (in the larger world) was moving in "the shape of an ever upward-moving spiral," with each turn of the spiral "coming to a fuller clarification" and with specific moments of crisis within this process.[45] This is true with respect to aesthetics and politics as well as religion (and in the world at large) as the common antitheses are overcome (*aufheben*, or "heaved up") to show "this process of elevating something to a higher level and thus accomplishing a new and higher synthesis."[46]

When we come to hamartiology proper, Hegel holds that there is a deep antithesis within human nature. Humanity is good *by nature*—humanity is also evil *by nature*.[47] Thus "it is false to ask whether humanity is only good by nature or only evil. . . . both of them, both good and evil, are posited, but essentially in contradiction, in such a way that each of them presupposes the other. It is not that only one of them is [there], but instead we have both of them in this relation of being opposed to each other."[48] This antithesis is itself natural, but it must be transcended or overcome, and for it to be overcome, it must be overcome in such a way that it is utterly encompassed and transcended.[49]

So for Hegel, "the fall" (which he interprets symbolically rather than as something that happened historically) is necessary. Without it, humanity would not achieve full awareness of its finitude, and thus its finitude would not be transcended or overcome.[50] Indeed, the evil is inherent within the finitude, and it can be overcome or transcended only if the finitude itself is transcended or overcome. And *that* can be done only by the Divine. Furthermore, the fall, with its finitude and evil, is also necessary for God. For by overcoming or transcending it in the incarnation, death, and resurrection of Christ, God achieves his full actuality:

> This humanity, which is itself a moment in the divine life, is now characterized as alien, not belonging to God. This finitude, however, on its own account (as against God), is evil, it is something alien to God. But he has taken it [upon himself] in order to put it to death by his death. As the monstrous unification of these absolute extremes, this shameful death is at the same time infinite love.

---

[45] Bernard Ramm, *Offense to Reason: A Theology of Sin* (New York: Harper & Row, 1985), 17.
[46] Ramm, *Offense to Reason*, 17.
[47] Georg Wilhelm Friedrich Hegel, *Lectures on the Philosophy of Religion, One-Volume Edition, The Lectures of 1827*, ed. Peter C. Hodgson (Berkeley: University of California Press, 1988), 438.
[48] Hegel, *Lectures*, 441–442.
[49] Hegel, *Lectures*, 447.
[50] Hegel, *Lectures*, 446.

It is out of infinite love that God has made himself identical with what is alien to him in order to be put to death. This is the meaning of the death of Christ.[51]

When taken into God himself, this finitude and evil then becomes part of God's own life. It is then essential to God, it is part of what makes God *God*. It is then "the eternal divine history: it is a moment in the nature of God himself; it has taken place in God himself."[52]

In summary, we can see these important elements of Hegel's system. First, evil is inherent in our finitude. Second, "the fall" is necessary for humanity. It is an essential part of our aesthetic, moral, and spiritual development; it is, to borrow Ramm's phrase, a "fall upward."[53] Finally, finitude and evil are part of God's own life; sin and its overcoming are thus necessary for God too. Just as we would not be what and who we are without coming to awareness of our own finitude and thus our sin, so also God would not be who and what God is without experiencing and overcoming finitude, estrangement, and evil. The impact of Hegel's proposal for theology is hard to overestimate. As Ramm notes, "[T]his view of sin received a good hearing among some theologians of liberal Christianity. Insofar as they too rejected the historic doctrines of the Fall, Original Sin, and Depravity, they needed a theory of human sinning to account for the blatant facts of human depravity."[54]

As we shall see, the views of Hegel and the great crowd who follow in his train (whether knowingly or unwittingly) are directly opposed to the vast majority of the Christian tradition. These views are also, as we shall see, deeply mistaken. For throughout the Christian tradition, theologians have insisted, sometimes against "common sense," that sin is contrary to nature. A brief tour of some of the controversial but important turning points in this tradition helps to illustrate this.

The family of views commonly known as "Gnosticism" presented serious challenges and persuasive alternatives to catholic Christian theology in the Patristic era. In particular, Manichaeism laid down a stiff challenge to developing Christian orthodoxy.[55] Perhaps best seen as an alternative to, and apologetic against, pagan objections to Christianity, Manichaeism

---

[51] Hegel, *Lectures*, 466.
[52] Hegel, *Lectures*, 470.
[53] Ramm, *Offense to Reason*, 17.
[54] Ramm, *Offense to Reason*, 17.
[55] For some indication of the relation between Manichaeism and Gnosticism more broadly considered, see Jacob Albert van den Berg, Annemare Kotze, Tobias Nicklas, and Madeleine Scopello, eds., *"In Search of Truth": Augustine, Manichaeism, and Other Gnosticism* (Leiden: Brill, 2011). For a concise and helpful summary of Augustine's criticisms of Manichaeism (following his conversion from it to Christianity), see Matthew Levering, *The Theology of Augustine: An Introductory Guide to His Most Important Works* (Grand Rapids, MI: Baker Academic, 2013), 19–47.

insists that the cosmos is the eternal battleground between the equally (or nearly equally) powerful forces of good and evil.[56] William Mann offers a helpful summary:

> Manichaeism taught that the world is an arena in which two opposing cosmic forces incessantly contend, one good, the other evil. If one concentrates on the attributes of incorruptibility, inviolability, and immutability, it does not seem impossible for there to be two beings having those attributes in common while occupying opposite ends of the moral spectrum. Manichaeism thus offered a straightforward solution for the problem of evil: God is doing the best he can against evil, but finds himself facing an independent opponent as formidable as he.[57]

Manichaeism held that matter is evil intrinsically. Since the body is material, it is evil. And since God is not the Creator of evil, God is the Creator of the soul but not the body.[58]

Manichaeism was stoutly resisted (along with other forms and versions of Gnosticism) by the catholic theologians of developing orthodoxy. Important theologians from Irenaeus to Augustine rejected the basic premises of these views. They resolutely insisted on the following points: First, God is perfectly, eternally, and necessarily good. There is no shadow of turning in God; there simply is not even the possibility that evil exists as an element in God's own nature or being. Second, they insisted on the omnipotence and sovereignty of God. Yes, there is an ongoing struggle between good and evil, but this struggle is temporal rather than eternal. There is no eternal force of evil that exists as the cosmic counterpart to God's goodness. Evil is not a necessary feature of the world, and it does not present an ultimate threat to God's power or goodness. Together, these convictions rule out the possibility of cosmic dualism—there is not, and there cannot be, an eternal and necessary principle of evil either "inside" of or independent of the perfectly good God. Accordingly, God has created everything that exists contingently *ex nihilo*. This creation, coming from a perfectly good God, was also utterly— though *contingently*—good. Matter itself is not evil, and we must not think that the body is inherently or intrinsically sinful. Whence evil? The consistent answer is that it comes as the result of the abuse of the free will that is itself a part of the good creation. To summarize, the catholic response has been to insist upon the necessary goodness of God and the contingent (but genuine)

---

[56] Cf. C. P. Bammel, "Pauline Exegesis, Manichaeism, and Philosophy in the Early Augustine," in *Christian Faith and Greek Philosophy in Late Antiquity: Essays in Honor of Christopher George Stead*, ed. Lionel R. Wickham and Caroline P. Bammel (Leiden: Brill, 1993), 8–9.

[57] William Mann, "Augustine on Evil and Original Sin" in *The Cambridge Companion to Augustine*, ed. David Vincent Meconi and Eleonore Stump, 2nd ed. (Cambridge: Cambridge University Press, 2014), 98.

[58] Bammel, "Pauline Exegesis," 4.

goodness of creation along with an appeal to what can loosely be called the "free will defense."[59]

In their pointed and energetic rejection of Manichaeism (and other forms of Gnosticism), the theologians of the early church were insistent that sin is neither the result of God's action nor the inevitable result of some other evil power that stands opposite to God. J. N. D. Kelly notes that the Greek theologians are sometimes lumped together with Pelagian views.[60] But he also protests that this is mistaken and misleading, for while "there is hardly a hint in the Greek fathers that mankind as a whole shares in Adam's guilt," the Greek fathers in fact do have an "outline of a real theory of original sin."[61] He says that they "take it for granted that all men were involved in Adam's rebellious act." Second, "alongside their assumption of free will, they clearly hold that the Fall affected our moral nature," and they think that all manner of evil actions then follow from that. Third, they also refer to the actual "transmission of sin itself."[62]

Kelly observes further that "Latin" theology (prior to Augustine) was similar in many important respects. The prelapsarian state is one of blessedness, and the first humans enjoy innocence and (conditional) immortality. The "root cause" of the first sin is pride, according to Ambrose, and it has resulted in ruin for the entire race.[63] Kelly notes that while there are texts that might indicate the inclusion of guilt in Ambrose's doctrine of original sin, "his more general doctrine, however, is that, while the corrupting force of sin is transmitted, the guilt attaches to Adam himself, not to us."[64] Similarly with Ambrosiaster: we are all corrupted by original sin, but "we are not punished for Adam's sin, but only for our own sins. . . . 'You perceive that men are not made guilty by the fact of their birth, but by their evil behavior.'"[65] Accordingly, "the parallel truths of man's free will and his need of God's help were maintained."[66]

John of Damascus insists that "evil is nothing else than absence of good-

---

[59] For examples of the appeal to free will in dealing with the problem of evil, see Justin Martyr, *Apologia Prima pro Christianis*, 43–44 (PG 6:391c–396c); Irenaeus, *Adversus Haereses* 4.37.1–2 (PG 7:1099b–1101a); Athanasius, *Oratio Contra Gentes* 1.2–5 (PG 25:5c–12d); Basil of Caesarea, *Homilia in Hexaemeron* 2.4–5, 6.7 (PG 29:35b–42c, 131b–134d); Gregory of Nyssa, *De Virginitate* 12 (PG 46:369–376d); Gregory of Nazianzus, *Oratio* 45.5, 45.8 (PG 36:629a–630b, 631c–634b); John Chrysostom, *Homilia de Imbellicitate Diaboli* (PG 49:241–276); John of Damascus, *De Fide Orthodoxa* 2.4, 2.11–12, 2.27, 4.18–19 (PG 94:873c–878c, 909d–930b, 959b–962b, 1181a–1194c). I am grateful to Nathan D. Jacobs for pointing me to these passages.
[60] J. N. D. Kelly, *Early Christian Doctrines*, rev. ed. (New York: HarperCollins, 1978), 350. Kelly notes that Julian himself made appeal to the Greek fathers in support of his "Pelagian" views. For further discussion of the doctrine of sin in Greek Patristic theology, see Donald Fairbairn, "Athanasius," in *T&T Clark Companion to the Doctrine of Sin*, ed. Keith L. Johnson and David Lauber (New York: Bloomsbury T&T Clark, 2016), 165–179; Khaled Anatolios, *Athanasius* (New York: Routledge, 2004); and Thomas G. Weinandy, *Athanasius: A Theological Introduction* (Burlington, VT: Ashgate, 2007).
[61] Kelly, *Early Christian Doctrines*, 350–351.
[62] Kelly, *Early Christian Doctrines*, 350–351.
[63] Kelly, *Early Christian Doctrines*, 353.
[64] Kelly, *Early Christian Doctrines*, 355.
[65] Kelly, *Early Christian Doctrines*, 355–356.
[66] Kelly, *Early Christian Doctrines*, 356.

ness and a lapsing from what is natural into what is unnatural: for nothing evil is natural. For all things, whatsoever God made, are very good, so far as they were made: if, therefore, they remain just as they were created, they are very good, but when they voluntarily depart from what is natural and turn to what is unnatural, they slip into evil. . . . [E]vil is not any essence nor a property of essence, but an accident, that is, a voluntary deviation from what is natural into what is unnatural, which is sin."[67] Similarly, Thomas Aquinas exemplifies the Latin tradition when he echoes Augustine in holding that "every vice, simply because it is a vice, is contrary to nature."[68] He explains that "the will's relationship to evil is not the same as its relationship to good. Of its very nature the will seeks the good proposed by reason as its very own. And for this reason sin is said to be contrary to nature."[69]

Protestant theology wrestled with this idea—and came down decisively in favor of the conclusion that sin is contrary to nature. The Augsburg Confession (1530) teaches that "after Adam's fall, all men begotten after the common course of nature are born with sin; that is, without fear of God (*sine metu Dei*), without trust in him (*sine fiducia erga Deum*), and with fleshly appetite (*et cum concupiscentia*); and that this disease, or original fault, is truly sin, condemning and bringing eternal death now also upon all that are not born again by baptism and the Holy Spirit."[70]

The so-called "Gnesio-Lutherans," claiming to be the true inheritors and protectors of Luther's own theology, insisted on the "bondage of the will" and tilted toward the view that God has determined all things. The "Philippists," on the other hand, were much more sympathetic to the concerns of Philipp Melanchthon that endorsement of the Gnesio-Lutheran view would commit the Christian to the impossible conclusion that God is the ultimate causal agent in evildoing. Where Luther had famously insisted that the will is always "bound"—either to God or to the devil—Melanchthon was quite concerned with the implications of such statements; and while he insisted on the innate depravity and inability of human persons to save themselves, he was also "driven by the concern to stave off the criticism that Wittenberg theology taught that God was the cause of evil and to maintain the integrity of human obedience to God."[71] During the "Synergist Controversy," Matthias Flacius locked horns with Viktorin Strigel on issues related to the contamination and effects of sin as well as freedom of the will. Flacius was convinced

---

[67] John of Damascus, *De fide orthodoxa*, IV.XX (PG 94:1196B–C; NPNF² 9:94).
[68] Aquinas, *ST* IaIIae, Q 71.2.
[69] Aquinas, *ST* IaIIae, Q 78.3.
[70] "The Augsburg Confession," in *Creeds of Christendom, with a History and Critical Notes, Volume III: The Evangelical Protestant Creeds*, 8.
[71] Robert Kolb, *Bound Choice, Election, and Wittenberg Theological Method: From Martin Luther to the Formula of Concord* (Grand Rapids, MI: Eerdmans, 2005), 107.

that Melanchthon "had betrayed Luther and Christ," and he argued that any emphasis on the responsibility of the believer to respond appropriately to the gospel would lead to a corresponding loss of recognition of God's ultimate decision regarding salvation.[72] Strigel, however, opposed Flacius on these matters, and was "determined to represent Melanchthon's concern that human responsibility be maintained and to repudiate the idea that God could be the cause of evil."[73]

In a series of public disputations on these topics, Strigel made use of Aristotelian categories (of substance and accident) in his arguments. Employing this terminology, Strigel claimed that sin was only an "accident." Flacius, on the other hand, was sure that sinners are now "in the image of Satan," and he opposed Strigel in holding that original sin is "substantial" rather than "accidental."[74]

The concerns of Flacius are very understandable, and it is easy to be sympathetic to his views. Surely he is right to insist on the primacy of divine action in salvation: if God did not first act, then exactly no one would be able to come to faith. Left to ourselves, justification and regeneration would be strictly impossible. Closely related to this concern is the one that is more germane to our discussion of the nature of sin, and again it would be easy to side with Flacius in his position that sin is so pervasive and polluting that it can properly be said to be "substantial" or essential.

But there is more than one danger here. On one hand we are faced with the perennial temptation to downplay, if not ignore altogether, the reality of sin and its effects. And when looking this way it is easy to sympathize with the concerns of Flacius. But there are dangers from the other direction as well, and while these are perhaps a good deal more subtle, they are no less threatening. While the first danger would, if left unchecked, lead to a form of Pelagianism (or at least "Semi-Pelagianism"), the second would lead us down the road toward Manichaeism. And if the temptation to downplay or ignore sin might be more prevalent in some quarters, in other circles we may be allured by the opposite danger. For, rightly persuaded of the awful and damning effects of sin, evangelical Christians (in particular) might be guilty of seeing sin as so deeply entrenched in human life that it somehow becomes the norm. It is, it seems, all too easy when faced with sin in the life of a Christian to hear, "Well, she's only *human*, after all," as if to be human is to be sinful! It is, alas, even easier to *say* such things—especially when the sinner in question is the one whom we see in the mirror!

The equation of finitude, creatureliness, or humanity with sinfulness is un-

---

[72] Kolb, *Bound Choice*, 118.
[73] Kolb, *Bound Choice*, 119.
[74] See the helpful discussion by Kolb, *Bound Choice*, 119–120.

derstandable. And the more seriously we as Christians take the biblical witness to the universality and finality (apart from God's grace) of sin, the more likely are we to make such an equation. But there is a name for the view that confuses creatureliness or finitude with sinfulness—it is at least very, very, close to the ancient heresy known as "Manichaeism."[75] To hold that to live as a human— to be an *embodied* person—is to be sinful is at least uncomfortably close to the view that thinks of matter as irretrievably and fundamentally evil. This is, when called by its proper name, the heresy of Manichaeism. This is not an unusual version of the Christian faith. It is not even a mildly aberrant version of the Christian faith. It is nothing less than a wholesale rejection of that faith.

There are at least three main kinds of theological arguments against the kind of view held by Flacius, and these are stated in the Lutheran Formula of Concord. The first argument (or perhaps it is a family of arguments) concerns the doctrine of creation. As the Lutheran settlement to this controversy itself noted, if we think that sin is a substance, then we should conclude that it is created. But if so, then it seems that we are left to choose between two options: either the sin-substance was created by God, or it was created by the devil. Neither option should be acceptable for the orthodox Christian. For to hold that sin was created by the devil is both to cede him far too much power (Scripture never refers to him as a creator) and to radically misunderstand his work: Satan is the *destroyer*. On the other hand, to opt for the view that God created this sin-substance is even worse, for it is serious indeed to mistake the work of God with the work of Satan. To demean God's goodness in this way is to border on blasphemy. Again, neither of these options should be acceptable to the orthodox Christian.

The second of the major reasons to reject a Flacian-type view comes from reflection on a proper account of theological anthropology. Surely Adam and Eve were fully and completely human, yet they were not sinful prior to the fall. Yet surely they were creatures before the fall, and as such they were finite. But neither creatureliness, finitude, or their prototypical humanity is to be equated with sinfulness, nor should we suppose that it led inevitably to sin. And if they were really human, yet without sin, then surely it is possible to be human yet without sin.[76]

Perhaps most importantly, the Formula of Concord also appeals to Christology. This Christologically oriented perspective served to inform the Lutheran dogmaticians as they sought to adjudicate the debate between

[75] Kelly notes that Manichaeism is often thought of as a "Christian" heresy, but he points out that "it was really a completely independent religion embodying Christian, but also Buddhist and Zoroastrian, elements" (*Early Christian Doctrines*, 8–9).
[76] The anthropological considerations of Concord extend as well to the resurrection. Because we believe in the resurrection *of the body* and the life everlasting, we should not conflate human finitude or creatureliness with sin. As resurrected and glorified, we will be without sin, but nonetheless fully and completely human.

Flacius and Strigel (and between the Gnesio-Lutherans and the Philippists more broadly). This is apparent in both the affirmations and the denials of the Formula of Concord (1576/1584). The question, as Concord puts it, is this: "whether Original Sin is properly and without any distinction man's corrupt nature, substance, and essence . . . or whether, even after the Fall, there is a distinction between man's substance, nature, essence, body, soul, and original sin, so that the nature [itself] is one thing, and original sin, which inheres in the corrupt nature and corrupts the nature, another."[77] To answer the question, Concord makes several important affirmations. First, "[W]e believe, teach, and confess that there is a distinction between man's nature, not only as he was originally created by God pure and holy and without sin, but also as we have it [that nature] now after the Fall, namely, between the nature [itself], which even after the Fall is and remains a creature of God, and original sin."[78] The reasoning behind this affirmation is made plain: "this distinction is as great as the distinction between a work of God and a work of the devil."[79] Secondly, Concord teaches that this distinction is not a matter of indifference, but rather "should be maintained with the greatest care," and this is so because the doctrine that sin is substantial or essential "conflicts with the chief articles of our Christian faith concerning creation, redemption, sanctification, and the resurrection of the body, and cannot coexist therewith."[80]

Concord follows this with explicitly Christological reflection:

> Moreover, the Son of God has assumed this human nature, however, without sin, and therefore not a foreign, but our own flesh, into the unity of His person, and according to it is become our true Brother. Heb. 2, 14: Forasmuch, then, as the children were partakers of flesh and blood, He also Himself likewise took part of the same. Again, v. 16; 4, 15: He took not on Him the nature of angels, but He took on Him the seed of Abraham. Wherefore in all things it behooved Him to be made like unto His brethren, yet without sin. In like manner Christ has also redeemed it as His work, sanctifies it as His work, raises it from the dead, and gloriously adorns it as His work. But original sin He has not created, assumed, redeemed, sanctified; nor will He raise it, will neither adorn nor save it in the elect, but in the [blessed] resurrection it will be entirely destroyed.[81]

But what are we to make of Luther's claim that sin is "essential" or "natural" to humanity? Simply put, sin is *not* the essence or nature of humanity.

---

[77] "The Formula of Concord," in *Creeds of Christendom, with a History and Critical Notes, Volume III: The Evangelical Protestant Creeds*, 97.
[78] "Formula of Concord," 98.
[79] "Formula of Concord," 98.
[80] "Formula of Concord," 98.
[81] "Formula of Concord," 99.

But neither should we say, without further qualification, that it is only a mere accident. Instead, it is an accident that "intimately inheres, being affixed in the very nature, substance, and essence of humanity" (*sed intime inhearet infixum ipsi naturae, substantiae et essentiae hominis*).[82] The denials issued by Concord are illuminating at this point. The framers of the Concord "reject and condemn also as a Manichaean error the doctrine that original sin is properly and without any distinction the substance, nature, and essence itself of the corrupt man."[83] Offering pastorally sensitive counsel, Concord concludes that "as to the Latin words *substantia* and *accidens*, because they are not words of Holy Scripture, and besides unknown to ordinary man, they should not be used in sermons before ordinary, uninstructed people, but simple people should be spared them."[84] But Concord also recognizes the appropriate usage of scholastic categories, and so instructs that "in the schools, among the learned, these words are rightly retained in disputations concerning original sin, because they are well known and used without any misunderstanding, to distinguish exactly between the essence of a thing and what attaches to it in an accidental way."[85] And with this in mind, the only conclusion to be drawn is this: "for the distinction between God's work and that of the devil is thereby distinguished in the clearest way, because the devil can create no substance, but can only, in an accidental way, by the providence of God [God permitting] corrupt the substance created by God."[86] The Formula leaves no room for doubt: sin is, technically speaking, an accident rather than a substance.

To be sure, in both its affirmations and its denials the Formula of Concord rightly rejects Pelagianism, and it insists that "original sin is no trivial corruption but is so profound a corruption of human nature as to leave nothing sound."[87] Clearly, the Concordists leave no room whatsoever for any kind of Pelagianism or "Semi-Pelagianism."[88] But they also reject outright any suggestion that sin is essential to humanity. The Lutheran scholastic theologians agree; as Johann Andreas Quenstadt says, "original sin is not the very substance of man" but instead is something that "inheres in it after the manner of an accident . . ."[89] According to David Hollaz, it is "a corruption of human nature, which, by the Fall of our first parents, is deprived of original righteousness,

---

[82] "Formula of Concord," 104–105.
[83] "Formula of Concord," 103.
[84] "Formula of Concord," 105.
[85] "Formula of Concord," 105.
[86] "Formula of Concord," 105–106.
[87] "Formula of Concord," 100.
[88] E.g., "Formula of Concord," 110–111.
[89] Johann Andreas Quenstadt, *Theologica II*, 62; cf. Heinrich Schmid, *The Doctrinal Theology of the Evangelical Lutheran Church, Exhibited, and Verified from the Original Sources* (Philadelphia: Lutheran Publication Society, 1876), 268.

and is prone to every evil."[90] Later generations of Reformed theologians—the "Reformed scholastics"—built upon, extended, and refined the teachings of Zwingli, Calvin, and the other major Reformed theologians.[91] Johannes Heidegger claims that "[s]in is *anomia* or discrepancy from the law of God, i.e. the failure of nature and of the actions in intelligent natures, fighting with the law of God and involving them in punishment in accordance with the order of divine righteousness."[92] The insistence here is clearly that sin is both *contra naturam* and *contra Deum*. It is the "failure of nature" that is "fighting with the law of God." As such, sinful actions do not have their own independent standing; they are only *defective* or *deformed* actions. Sin is privation of the good that God created.[93] Recalling the Flacian controversy within Lutheran circles, the Reformed clearly side with the pronouncements of Concord. As Francis Turretin puts it, "The orthodox constantly maintain that sin is to be distinguished from the substance itself, as an accident and vicious quality from its subject."[94] Sin is always, then, contrary to nature.

More recently, and from a very different perspective, Donald Bloesch points out that the helpful insight from Paul Tillich's account of sin is that sin is "estrangement or alienation from the ground of our being."[95] Dietrich Bonhoeffer gives eloquent expression to this fundamental concept of sin as "contrary to nature." In Bloesch's summary, Bonhoeffer holds that "sin is not the natural but the unnatural, not the human but the inhuman. . . . While he did not repudiate the Reformation understanding of sin as rebellion against a holy God, he expanded the idea of sin to include contempt for humanity."[96] Thus "sin is not only an affront to God but a putting down of humanity. Sin is in the last analysis inhumanity, and salvation is the realization of true humanity. Sin is what diminishes humanity and undermines the human quest for hope and happiness not only in the world to come but in this world as well."[97] Josef Pieper notes that "what is meant here by *contra naturam* is something quite general: *every* sin (and not just, for example, those sexual sins called 'unnatural' in the penal codes) is understood not just as a violation of the nature of man himself but even more of the natural order as a

---

[90] David Hollaz, *Examen Theologicum Acroamaticum Universam Theologiam Thetico-Polemicam Complectens* (1763), 518; cf. Schmid, *Doctrinal Theology*, 256.

[91] On issues of continuity-discontinuity between the Reformers and their Protestant successors, see esp. Richard A. Muller, *Calvin and the Reformed Tradition: On the Work of Christ and the Order of Salvation* (Grand Rapids, MI: Baker Academic, 2012).

[92] Cited in Heinrich Heppe, *Reformed Dogmatics* (Eugene, OR: Wipf & Stock, 2007), 320. Francis Turretin agrees wholeheartedly, e.g., *Institutio Theologiae Elencticae, Pars Prima* (Geneva: 1688), I.IX.1 (651) (*Institutes of Elenctic Theology, Volume One: First through Tenth Topics*, trans. George Musgrave Giger, ed. James T. Dennison Jr. [Phillipsburg, NJ: Presbyterian & Reformed, 1992], 591). See also Johannes Cocceius, *Summa Theologiae, Ex. Scripturis Repetitia, editio secunda* (Geneva: 1665), IX.24 (282–290).

[93] E.g., Turretin, *Institutio Theologiae Elencticae*, I.IX.5 (651) (*Institutes of Elenctic Theology*, 592).

[94] Francis Turretin, *Institutio Theologiae Elencticae*, I.IX.11 (702) (*Institutes of Elenctic Theology*, 636).

[95] Donald Bloesch, *Jesus Christ: Savior and Lord* (Downers Grove, IL: IVP Academic, 1997), 37.

[96] Bloesch, *Jesus Christ: Savior and Lord*, 39.

[97] Bloesch, *Jesus Christ: Savior and Lord*, 39.

whole."[98] Cornelius Plantinga Jr., makes the point directly when he says that sin is "not the way it's supposed to be."[99]

Seeing sin in this light illumines several aspects of sin and its progression. It is often portrayed in Scripture and tradition as a kind of *pollution*, or as something akin to *corruption* or *disease*. Scripture uses this imagery in powerful ways. As Jay Sklar points out, we get no further than the third chapter of Genesis before we see this point. For here "clearly, sin is an acid that mars and distorts all that it touches."[100] Psalm 38 vividly describes the state of sin in terms that "hover between medical descriptions and metaphors for moral sickness."[101] Here we see the psalmist describe his condition as desperate: there is "no soundness in my flesh" because of God's wrath, there is "no health in my bones because of my sin," and "my wounds stink and fester because of my foolishness" (Ps. 38:3, 5). But the situation is even worse: "my sides are filled with burning, and there is no soundness in my flesh" (38:7), and "my strength fails me" (38:10). Similarly, the prophet Isaiah describes the sins of the people as rebels (Isa. 1:2, 4–5) who are corrupt (1:4). Consequently, "your whole head is injured, your whole heart afflicted. From the sole of your foot to the top of your head there is no soundness—only wounds and welts and open sores" (1:5–6 NIV). Jesus himself conceives of his own ministry in similar terms, and he compares his work to that of a physician. Upon hearing the criticisms of the Pharisees (that he was eating with tax collectors and sinners), Jesus said, "[I]t is not the healthy who need a doctor, but the sick. But go and learn what this means: 'I desire mercy, not sacrifice.' For I have not come to call the righteous, but sinners" (Matt. 9:12–13 NIV).

Care must be taken here, however, neither to confuse sin with literal physical sickness nor to think that all physical sickness is the direct result of some sin or set of sins (of the particular person who bears the disease or suffers from the injury). Scripture makes abundantly clear the fact that not all instances of sickness or injury are directly attributable to the sins of particular persons (John 9:1–12).[102] Care must also be taken not to misunderstand the imagery in such a way as to minimize or mitigate human responsibility. Although Søren Kierkegaard overstates the case when he says that "whenever sin is spoken of as a disease, an abnormality, a poison, or disharmony, the concept is falsified," he offers an important reminder that sin is not *a* disease, nor is it *like* a disease in the sense that it is merely something we acquire or "catch" but for which we

---

[98] Josef Pieper, *The Concept of Sin* (South Bend, IN: St. Augustine's, 2001), 35.
[99] Cornelius Plantinga Jr., *Not the Way It's Supposed to Be: A Breviary of Sin* (Grand Rapids, MI: Eerdmans, 1994).
[100] Jay Sklar, "Pentateuch," in *T&T Clark Companion to the Doctrine of Sin*, 9.
[101] R. E. O. White, "Disease," in *EDBT*, 182.
[102] See our discussion of "The Results of Sin" (ch. 6) for further discussion.

are not responsible.[103] In the case of sin, the "diseased" are not *merely* victims; they are also guilty of intentional wrongdoing.

But despite these qualifications, the basic point is also clear: sin is *like* a wasting disease, a sickness, a spiritual and moral cancer. As such, it leads to total paralysis and death. As Plantinga puts it, corruption is "not so much a particular sin as the multiplying power of all sin to spoil a good creation and to breach its defenses against invaders. Corruption is spiritual AIDS—the mysterious, infectious, and progressive attack on our spiritual immune system that eventually breaks it down and opens the way for hordes of opportunistic sins."[104] The human person—all the way to the core of her existence, to the *heart*—is "desperately sick" (Jer. 17:9).

Closely akin to this is the notion of sin as *pollution* or *uncleanness*. The OT's concern (in places, it could rightly be called an *obsession*) with cleanness is telling. Purity is vitally important to a proper relationship to God and the community of faith, and uncleanness poses a grave threat to such a relationship. Thus such things as skin disease (e.g., Leviticus 13–14), emission of various kinds of bodily fluids (Lev. 15:3–24, 28–30), or being contaminated by corpses (Num. 5:2–4; 6:9–12; 19:11–20; Ezek. 44:26–27) made someone "unclean" or impure. As Joe M. Sprinkle notes,

> [T]he purity system conveys in a symbolic way that Yahweh was the God of life and was separated from death. . . . Bodily discharges (blood for women, semen for men) represented a temporary loss of strength and life and movement toward death. Because decaying corpses discharged, so natural bodily discharges were reminders of sin and death. Physical imperfections representing a movement from "life" toward "death" moved a person ritually away from God who was associated with life. Purification rituals symbolized movement from death toward life and accordingly involved blood, the color red, and spring (lit. "living") water, all symbols of life.[105]

Sin leaves a stain—one that can be washed away only by God himself.[106] Reflecting upon such concerns, Plantinga notes that the traditional Christian concept of pollution reflects the biblical concept of uncleanness. Because "holiness implies not just otherness or transcendence but also wholeness, oneness, [and] purity," various diseases, substances, and bodily discharges "suggested the loss of vitality, of life itself, and hence of personal wholeness."[107] To pollute, then,

---

[103] Søren Kierkegaard, *The Concept of Anxiety: A Simple Psychologically Orienting Deliberation on the Dogmatic Issue of Hereditary Sin*, ed. and trans. with introduction and notes Reidar Thomte (Princeton, NJ: Princeton University Press, 1980), 15. See the helpful discussion of this point by Henri Blocher, *Original Sin: Illuminating the Riddle* (Downers Grove, IL: IVP Academic, 2000), 111.
[104] Plantinga, *Not the Way*, 32–33.
[105] Joe M. Sprinkle, "Clean, Unclean," in *EDBT*, 100.
[106] See the discussion in David H. Kelsey, *Eccentric Existence: A Theological Anthropology*, 2 vols. (Louisville: Westminster/John Knox, 2009), 1:436–437.
[107] Plantinga, *Not the Way*, 44.

"is to weaken a particular whole entity, such as a sound relationship, by introducing into it a foreign element," and this is displayed vividly in the biblical treatments of adultery and idolatry:

> [T]he biblical paradigm cases of pollution are idolatry and adultery, emblems of each other. In each case, some new commitment insinuates itself into an existing relationship and compromises it. In idolatry a third party gets between God and human persons, adulterating an exclusive loyalty. Idolatry violates both negative and positive law, both the first commandment's prohibition of idolatry ("You shall have no other gods before me" [Deut. 5:7]) and also the summary love command of the Deuteronomic code ("Love the LORD your God with all your heart, and with all your soul, and with all your might" [Deut. 6:5]).
>
> But, of course, idolatry violates more than a law. . . . These unhappy attitudes do break the summary law of love to God, but more basically they threaten the vital covenant relation.[108]

Accordingly, the contrast with righteousness is stunning: righteousness is *purity*. The "pure in heart" are those who are undivided in their loyalty and devotion; the psalmist says that "apart from you I have no good thing," and that those who have "clean hands and a pure heart" are those who "[do] not trust in an idol or swear by a false god" (Ps. 16:2; 24:4 NIV). Jesus blesses those who are "pure in heart," and promises that they will "see God" (Matt. 5:8), and later in the NT sinners are exhorted to "cleanse [their] hands" and the "double-minded" are called to "purify [their] hearts" (James 4:8).[109]

Similarly, understanding sin as being fundamentally contrary to nature helps us to see that it is truly a *perversion* of something that was originally created and called good. Plantinga explains that by "perversion" we mean in the broad sense "the turning of loyalty, energy, and desire away from God and God's project in the world: it is the diversion of construction materials for the city of God to side projects of our own, often accompanied by jerry-built ideologies that seek to justify the diversion."[110] More precisely, though, "to pervert something is to twist it so that it serves an unworthy end . . . instead of a worthy one or so that it serves an entirely wrong end."[111] This is, it seems, exactly the route that sin takes in its encroaching oppression. We take what God creates and calls "good"—and we twist and pervert it until it becomes only a hollow shell that retains just enough resemblance of the original good to serve as a mocking taunt.

All of this leads to *disintegration*—of both ourselves and our communities.

---

[108] Plantinga, *Not the Way*, 44–45. The "unhappy attitudes" are "ingratitude," "perversity," "discontent," and "stubbornness."
[109] See Plantinga, *Not the Way*, 46.
[110] Plantinga, *Not the Way*, 40.
[111] Plantinga, *Not the Way*, 40.

When we reject the purposes for which we were made—when we reject our Maker—we begin to "come apart." At the level of individual persons, we often see this, and we hear it expressed in terms of "lack of wholeness" or "loss of integrity." Psalm 38 tells not only of the havoc that sin causes (again, as something akin to a physical disease); it also speaks forcefully of the effects on the wholeness of the sinner: "my heart pounds, my strength fails me; even the light has gone from my eyes" (Ps. 38:10 NIV). And then Psalm 38 goes on to show the broader effects of sin, for just when he needs them most, the sinner's iniquity repulses his friends: "My friends and companions avoid me because of my wounds, my neighbors stay far away" (Ps. 38:11 NIV). Plantinga notes that Christians have recognized this at least from the time of Augustine: "sin despoils persons, groups, whole societies. Corruption disturbs shalom—twisting, weakening, and snapping the thousands of bonds that give particular beings integrity and that tie them to others."[112] As Plantinga concludes, "Scriptural writers fear 'double-mindedness' not merely because it shows disloyalty and ingratitude but also because its perpetrator becomes its victim. Divided worship destroys worshipers. Divided love destroys lovers. To split the truly important longings and loyalties is to crack one's own foundations and to invite the crumbling and, finally, the disintegration of life itself. A divided house cannot stand."[113]

This brings us to the conclusion that sin is a *privation of the good*—a *parasite*. An overarching biblical theology shows this; sin comes into the created order only as a surprise, as an intruder, as something that does not belong there. The first humans sin by partaking of fruit that God had created and called *good* (notwithstanding the divine command to leave it alone). The progress of redemption that flows through the pages of history—and the very language that is used in the Bible for sin—speaks to the fact that it does not really belong: *un*cleanness, *un*righteousness, *un*faithfulness, law*lessness*. To be a sinner is, as Plantinga observes, to be "anti-law, anti-righteousness, anti-God, anti-Spirit, anti-life."[114] More precisely, Paul's descriptive pattern in Romans 1 illustrates this as well. Here we see a poignant description of humanity, one that emphasizes that the truth has been *exchanged* for a lie (Rom. 1:25), that the sinners have *exchanged* "the glory of the immortal God for images made to look like a mortal human being and birds and animals and reptiles" (v. 23 NIV), and that God "gave them over" to what is *unnatural* and *impure*. So the pervasive sense of sin given in Scripture is that it is *opposed to God's good purposes in creation*.

Consideration of such issues has led many theologians in the tradition

---

112 Plantinga, *Not the Way*, 32.
113 Plantinga, *Not the Way*, 46.
114 Plantinga, *Not the Way*, 87.

to conclude that sin is best understood as something parasitic on goodness, something that is a deprivation that leads to depravity. Plantinga makes the point with force, and I quote in extenso:

> Sin is always a departure from the norm and is assessed accordingly. Sin is deviant and perverse, an *in*justice or *in*iquity or *in*gratitude. Sin in the Exodus literature is *dis*order and *dis*obedience. Sin is faithlessness, lawlessness, godlessness. Sin is both the overstepping of a line and the failure to reach it— both transgression and shortcoming. Sin is a missing of the mark, a spoiling of goods, a staining of garments, a hitch in one's gait, a fragmenting of the whole. Sin is what culpably *disturbs* shalom. Sinful human life is a caricature of proper human life. . . .
>
> The reason is that sin is a parasite, an uninvited guest that keeps tapping its host for sustenance. Nothing about sin is its own; all its power, persistence, and plausibility are stolen goods. Sin is not really an entity but a spoiler of entities . . . [115]

Norman Geisler concurs when he says that "evil is like rot to a tree or rust to a car; both rot and rust corrupt the good substance (tree or car), but neither rot nor rust exists *in and of itself*." For this reason, sin is rightly said to be "*a privation or lack in a good substance*, a distortion of something pure"; it "*exists only in something good, as a corruption of its goodness*."[116] C. S. Lewis's conclusion, which can safely be said to be representative of a great deal of the Christian tradition, is apt: "Goodness is, so to speak, itself: badness is only spoiled goodness. And there must be something good first before it can be spoiled."[117]

Sin is contrary to nature—*unnatural*.[118] Sin is "a denial of reality."[119] Sin is—as classical theologians have put it—a *privation*, a *parasite*. It is the hideous perversion of what God created and pronounced "good." It is the twisting of— and departure from—the way things were "meant to be." It is the deep corruption, the devastating disease, that eats into and rots away the goodness of those creatures in the image of the Holy One. Truly, there "is no health in us."[120]

B. Contrary to Reason

Humans *know* that there is something deeply and dreadfully wrong with us. As W. H. Griffith Thomas says, "Nothing is so prevalent as this fact in all religions, for there is a universal consciousness, exemplified in history,

---

[115] Plantinga, *Not the Way*, 88–89.
[116] Norman L. Geisler, *Systematic Theology, Volume Three: Sin and Salvation* (Minneapolis: Bethany, 2004), 106, emphasis original.
[117] C. S. Lewis, *Mere Christianity* (New York: Macmillan, 1943), 35.
[118] Tanner, *Christ the Key*, 131.
[119] Kevin J. Vanhoozer, *Biblical Authority after Babel: Retrieving the* Solas *in the Spirit of Mere Protestant Christianity* (Grand Rapids, MI: Brazos, 2016), 106.
[120] As many liturgical confessions put it.

confessed in literature, and experienced in life, that man is out of harmony with the law of his nature."[121] We see this exemplified all around us. Words such as "senseless" and "pointless" are used most often—and with complete sincerity—in description of outrageous acts of violence.[122] A young father who serves as a police officer is called to a house regarding a domestic dispute, and then is ambushed by a man in a bulletproof vest and armed with automatic weapons. Thousands of mourners file past the grieving family, and many say something like, "I'm so sorry . . . this just doesn't make any sense . . . it's just all so senseless." A teenager loads his shotgun, walks around the house to the window of his sister's bedroom, and then points the weapon through the window and splatters the flesh of his sister around her bedroom. Stunned friends, grieving parents, and hardened law enforcement officers alike all shake their heads and say, "This is just so senseless." But despite this "universal consciousness"—and amazing, in light of it—we do not know the depths of our depravity or the seriousness of our condition without divine aid. This is because sin is *contra rationem*.

Theologians ancient and modern testify to this fact. Dionysius the (Pseudo-)Areopagite calls evil *alagon*.[123] Thomas Aquinas is representative of the Latin scholastics when he says that "vice is contrary to human nature only to the extent that it is contrary to the order of reason."[124] Martin Luther, in his comments on Romans 11, says that those whose eyes are "darkened" are those "who do not look to grace, which is from above," but rather "their eyes [have] become blurred, . . . they remain curved in on their own understanding (*curvi in sensum suum*)."[125] Wayne Grudem offers a helpful summary when he says that

> all sin is ultimately irrational. It really did not make sense for Satan to rebel against God in the expectation of being able to exalt himself above God. Nor did it make sense for Adam and Eve to think that there could be any gain in disobeying the words of their Creator. . . . It is not the wise man but "the fool" who "says in his heart, 'There is no God'" (Ps. 14:1). It is the "fool" in the book of Proverbs who recklessly indulges in all kinds of sins (see Prov. 10:23; 12:15; 14:7, 16; 15:5; 18:2; et al.). Though people sometimes persuade themselves that they have good reasons for sinning, when examined in the cold light of truth on the last day, it will be seen in every case that sin ultimately just does not make sense.[126]

---

[121] W. H. Griffith Thomas, *The Principles of Theology: An Introduction to the Thirty-Nine Articles* (London: Church Book Room, 1963), 157.
[122] As noted by Plantinga, *Not the Way It's Supposed to Be*, 113.
[123] Cited in Pieper, *Concept of Sin*, 43.
[124] Aquinas, *ST* IaIIae, Q 71.2.
[125] Cited in Matt Jenson, *The Gravity of Sin: Augustine, Luther, and Barth on* Homo Incurvatus in Se (New York: T&T Clark, 2006), 72.
[126] Wayne Grudem, *Systematic Theology: An Introduction to Bible Doctrine* (Grand Rapids, MI: Zondervan, 1994), 493.

As Plantinga summarizes the point, "[B]ecause it is futile, because it is vain, because it is unrealistic, because it spoils good things, sin is a prime form of folly."[127]

However, an important qualification is in order. When we say that sin is contrary to reason, we should not take that to mean that all sin is erratic, arbitrary, or utterly nonsensical. Surely some of it is. We likely all know people who engage in *obviously* self-destructive ways, people who make us shake our heads and say, "Why do they do that—it just makes no sense at all." But surely not all sin is irrational in this way. The criminal mastermind who schemes to devise and execute the "perfect crime" is in an important sense acting *according to* reason. When theologians claim that sin is contrary to reason, the proper meaning is not that the actions are performed in the utter absence of *any* reason. Nor is it the case that sin is something that "just happens." It is instead the blindness caused by turning away from the light. It is the crazy, nonsensical action that is done with awareness of the action and its consequences. As Pieper says, "[S]in goes contrary to reason by a deliberate act committed with full and clear understanding of what one is doing and with full responsibility."[128] Sin as irrational does not mean that it is done with no awareness or control. Instead, what is meant is this: sin is *contrary to reason rightly ordered*. William G. T. Shedd puts it this way when he says that sin is "not a natural, or a rational act; but unnatural and irrational. Sin is the 'mystery of iniquity'. . . . Self-determination to evil is contrary to pure reason. Sin is the divorce of will from reason."[129] Indeed, the "inexplicableness of evil is contained in the very conception of evil."[130] Sin is what is contrary to the reason that inheres in the (natural) created order, the way things were established by God, the way things "ought to be."

Karl Barth is blunt and forceful:

[A]s the basic dimension of human sloth stupidity [*Dummheit*] is sin. It is disobedience, unbelief, and ingratitude to God, who gives Himself to be known by man in order that he may be wise and live. It is thus a culpable relapse into self-contradiction; into incoherent, confused and corrupt thought and speech and action. . . . Whether great or small, every confidence or trust or self-reliance on what we can, and think we should, say to ourselves when we reason apart from the Word of God is stupid. Every attitude in which we think we can authoritatively tell ourselves what is true and good and beautiful, what is right and necessary and salutary, is stupid. All thought and speech and action which we think we can and should base on this information is

[127] Plantinga, *Not the Way*, 126.
[128] Pieper, *Concept of Sin*, 42.
[129] William G. T. Shedd, *Dogmatic Theology*, 3 vols. (Grand Rapids, MI: Zondervan, 1953), 2:156–157.
[130] Shedd, *Dogmatic Theology*, 2:157.

stupid. And this whole frame of mind is self-evidently, and even more acutely, stupid . . . [131]

Nowhere is this theme more pronounced than in the ugly reality and prominence of self-deception. We find ourselves able to deceive ourselves about other people. Often—with some people *very* often—we assume the worst case possible about others. We instinctively find ourselves believing that the most negative explanation (of their behavior) must be the correct one, and we find ourselves easily convinced that the people we dislike (or whom we suspect harbor a dislike for us) are sinister to some level and worthy of suspicion. On the other hand, with respect to other people—the "good guys" or those on "our side"—we find it difficult if not impossible to come to grips with the sober and glaring truth. Deceit is hard work, but nowhere are we willing to work harder. We tell ourselves lies about the most important things in life. We work hard to be convincing. Sometimes we convince others. And sometimes we convince ourselves.

Moreover, we often find it easy to convince ourselves of something other than the truth about *ourselves*. As is common with the diagnosis of sin, surely owing to the nature of the case, it is easier to recognize self-deception in someone else than it is in oneself. Think of the addict whose life is in tattered pieces and who is barely functional, and yet who says, "I'm alright; I may have a problem, but it isn't too big for me to handle. I'm fine. I don't need help. I can handle this thing."

We observe the folly of sin with particular clarity in the life of Israel in the OT. The ancient Israelites received clear warnings about the consequences of sin. As Christopher J. H. Wright notes, "God warned Israel that if they behaved in the same way as the Canaanites, God would treat Israel as his enemy on the same terms as the Canaanites, and inflict the same punishment on them by using other nations (Lev. 18:28; Deut. 28:25–68). The land that had vomited out the Canaanites would be perfectly capable of repeating its expurgation if Israel indulged in the same repulsive Canaanite practices. The same YHWH who acted in moral judgment on Israel's enemies would act in precisely the same way on Israel itself."[132] The prophets repeat these warnings in thunderous lament. Wright points out that "[i]f anything, the Old Testament argues that Israel's status as God's elect people exposed them all the more to God's moral judgment and historical punishment than any of the surrounding nations, including those they conquered (cf. Amos 3:2)."[133] Yet Israel refused to

---

[131] Karl Barth, *CD*, IV/2, 412–413; cf. Karl Barth, *Die Kichliche Dogmatik, Vierter Band: Die Lehre der Versöhnung* (Zurich, 1964), 464.
[132] Christopher J. H. Wright, *Old Testament Ethics for the People of God* (Downers Grove, IL: InterVarsity Press, 2004), 476.
[133] Wright, *Old Testament Ethics for the People of God*, 477.

heed these warnings; she continued to tell herself that her election was safe, that God was for her and against her enemies, and that everything would turn out well. She deceived herself about her sin and its consequences. Her sin was *contra rationem*.

It is no wonder, then, that Proverbs repeatedly portrays sin as *folly*. While "fear of the LORD is the beginning of knowledge; fools despise wisdom and instruction" (Prov. 1:7; cf. 9:10). The wise seek knowledge from God (e.g., Prov. 1:1–7; 2:6–15; 3:3–10, 13–35; 4:5–18; 7:1–4; 8:10–21) and receive discipline from God as a good thing (e.g., Prov. 3:11–12; 12:1; 15:5; 20:30). Sin is folly precisely because it is opposed to God and nature, and it results in the self-entrapment of the sinner: for sinners "lie in wait for their own blood; they set an ambush for their own lives" (Prov. 1:18; cf. 5:22; 8:36; 10:24; 11:5–6, 29; 13:13; 14:32; 28:10; 29:5–6). David H. Kelsey says that sin is "living foolishly in distorted faith"; it is "folly—that is, an inappropriate response to the triune God relating to us creatively. The opposite of living in 'the fear of the LORD' that leads to life, to sin is to live in distorted faith in God."[134] It is, then, "radically absurd."[135] Plantinga is right when he observes that "[s]inful life is a partly depressing, partly ludicrous *caricature* of genuine human life."[136] Truly, "[t]he heart is deceitful above all things, and desperately sick; who can understand it?" (Jer. 17:9).

C. Contrary to God

Recognizing that sin is both *against reason* and *against nature* drives us to the heart of any discussion of sin: sin is always, and in the first instance, *against God*. As Oliver O'Donovan puts it, "Sin is always 'against,' since it is constituted as a refusal of some aspect of good reality, and all sins are against God, the creator, sustainer, and redeemer of all good reality."[137] C. S. Lewis points out these interconnections between sin as against God and sin as against nature when he says that "the only way that I can make real to myself the seriousness of sin is to remember that every sin is the distortion of an energy breathed into us—an energy which, if not thus distorted, would have blossomed into one of those holy acts whereof 'God did it' and 'I did it' are both true descriptions. We poison the wine as He decants it into us; murder a melody He would play with us as the instrument. We caricature the self-portrait He would paint. Hence all sin, whatever else it is, is sacrilege."[138]

Recognizing that sin is always and foremost *against God* is vitally important.

---

[134] Kelsey, *Eccentric Existence*, 1:408.
[135] Kelsey, *Eccentric Existence*, 1:412.
[136] Plantinga, *Not the Way It's Supposed to Be*, 199.
[137] Oliver O'Donovan, *Finding and Seeking: Ethics as Theology, Volume 2* (Grand Rapids, MI: Eerdmans, 2014), 18.
[138] C. S. Lewis, *Letters to Malcolm*, in *The Quotable Lewis*, ed. Wayne Martindale and Jerry Root (Wheaton, IL: Tyndale, 1989), 547.

H. Ray Dunning reminds us that "it is crucial to any discussion of sin to recognize that it is a religious category . . . [for] it has meaning only in terms of one's relation to God," and he rightly warns us that "[a]ny attempt to understand the nature of sin that ignores this will pervert the truth."[139] Sin is the rupture of a rightly ordered relationship with God.[140] The fundamental fact that sin is contrary to God has been recognized throughout the Christian tradition. Put simply, sin "consists in voluntarily turning away from God."[141] As Pieper notes, "under all its numerous modifications, this statement represents the claim of the Great Tradition, unerringly maintained throughout history."[142]

Aquinas further insists that it is, strictly speaking, *impossible* for God to be the cause of sin. It is impossible because "God cannot be directly the cause of sin, either in Himself or in another, since every sin is a departure from the order which is to God as the end: whereas God inclines and turns all things to Himself as to their last end, . . . it is impossible that he should be either to Himself or to another the cause of departing from the order which is to Himself. Therefore He cannot be directly the cause of sin," and "in like manner neither can He cause sin indirectly."[143]

Ludwig Ott speaks for the broad Roman Catholic consensus when he says that sin consists (first) in turning away from God and (therefore) turning to the creature.[144] From the Anglican tradition, Griffith Thomas distinguishes between vice (wrongdoing done against ourselves), crime (wrongdoing against our neighbor), and—ultimately—sin, which is "wrongdoing against God."[145] The Lutheran theological tradition does not hesitate to agree with the conviction that sin is ultimately against God.[146] Martin Chemnitz insists that God is not the author or cause of sin (*Deum non esse causam peccati*); God "neither desires nor approves of sin, neither does he influence the will to sin" (*nec impellere voluntates ad peccandum*).[147] Johann Quenstadt adds that God is not the cause of sin "in part nor in whole"; God does "not desire sin, but hates it." Representative of the Reformed tradition is Johannes Cocceius: sin is that

[139] H. Ray Dunning, *Grace, Faith, and Holiness: A Wesleyan Systematic Theology* (Kansas City, MO: Beacon Hill, 1988), 284. See also J. Kenneth Grider, *A Wesleyan-Holiness Theology* (Kansas City, MO: Beacon Hill, 1994), 257.

[140] This point is made by James William McClendon Jr., *Doctrine: Systematic Theology, Volume II* (Nashville: Abingdon, 1994), 132.

[141] Pieper, *Concept of Sin*, 56. Søren Kierkegaard puts it like this: sin is "before God, or with the conception of God, in despair not to will to be oneself, or in despair to will to be oneself" (*The Sickness unto Death: A Christian Psychological Exposition for Upbuilding and Awakening*, ed. and trans. Howard V. Hong and Edna H. Hong, with introduction and notes [Princeton, NJ: Princeton University Press, 1980], 77). See also Kristen K. Deede, "The Infinite Qualitative Difference: Sin, the Self, and Revelation in the Thought of Søren Kierkegaard," *International Journal for Philosophy of Religion* (2003): 25–48.

[142] Pieper, *Concept of Sin*, 56.

[143] Aquinas, *ST* I–II, Q 79.1.

[144] Ludwig Ott, *Fundamentals of Catholic Dogma* (Rockford, IL: Tan, 1974), 112.

[145] Griffith Thomas, *Principles of Theology*, 158.

[146] E.g., John Theodore Mueller, *Christian Dogmatics: A Handbook of Doctrinal Theology* (St. Louis: Concordia, 1955), 230.

[147] Martin Chemnitz, *Loci Theologici* (Wittenberg: 1615), 146; cf. Schmid, *Doctrinal Theology*, 254.

"in which the creature departs from God's likeness."[148] Sin is opposed to the law of God; it is rebellion against the Creator and Judge. Moving deeper, it is whatever is opposed to the will of God. As Heidegger puts it, "[T]he cause and author of all good is God; but of evil as such the author could not be God."[149] Instead, it is mere privation (*privatio*) of the good.[150] Ursinus concurs: "God is not the cause, effect, or author of sin."[151] Because God is absolutely holy, "it is impossible that any effect of His should be bad." And because God is absolutely truthful, "there are no contradictory wills in Him." In Heinrich Heppe's summary of Ursinus, since "God hates sin, He cannot will it."[152] The Arminian and Wesleyan traditions concur wholeheartedly; indeed, Jacob Arminius insists that to affirm (or to affirm things that would entail) that God is the cause of sin is the ultimate blasphemy (*summa blasphemia*).[153]

More recently, Kelsey affirms this when he concludes that sin "is defined by direct reference to God. It is defined theocentrically; it is always 'against God.' It is not fundamentally constituted by a mis-relating to ourselves and to our neighbors but by mis-relating to God."[154]

Christians from various theological traditions agree on this basic fact, and they do so for very good reason: it is unmistakable, when the biblical text is taken seriously. It is exactly what happened when our first parents fell. It is exemplified in the first table of the Decalogue:

> "You shall have no other gods before me.
>
> "You shall not make for yourself a carved image, or any likeness of anything that is in heaven above, or that is on the earth beneath, or that is in the water under the earth. You shall not bow down to them or serve them, for I the Lord your God am a jealous God, . . .
>
> "You shall not take the name of the Lord your God in vain, . . .
>
> "Observe the Sabbath day, to keep it holy, as the Lord your God commanded you." (Deut. 5:7–12)

It is the direct violation of what the Lord Jesus referred to as "the first and greatest" commandment: "Love the Lord your God with all your heart and with all your soul and with all your strength . . ." (Mark 12:30). It was recognized by Joseph when, as a slave in the house of his master Potiphar, he was

[148] Johannes Cocceius, *Summa Theologiae*, XXIV.2 (282). I employ the translation of Heppe, *Reformed Dogmatics*, 322. Cocceius goes on to say that the creature was *intelligentia rectum est & bonum, in quo est simulitudo Dei*. I employ Heinrich Heppe's translation (in his *Reformed Dogmatics*) here and wherever possible.
[149] Johannes Heidegger, *Corpus Theologiae Christianae* (Zurich: 1700), X.viii (333).
[150] Heidegger, *Corpus Theologiae Christianae*, X.viii (333).
[151] Zacharias Ursinus, *Tractionum Theolocarum* III (1584), 218. See the discussion in Heppe, *Reformed Dogmatics*, 326.
[152] Heppe, *Reformed Dogmatics*, 327; see Ursinus, *Tractionum*, 219.
[153] Jacob Arminius, *Disputationes publicae*, XXXI.5 (in *Opera theologica* [1629]); cf. *Examen thesium D. Francisci Gomari de predestinatione* (1645), 154 (*The Works of James Arminius* [London, 1825–1875; repr. Grand Rapids, MI: Baker, 1986], 3:654).
[154] Kelsey, *Eccentric Existence*, 1:409–410.

tempted to sleep with Potiphar's wife; his response to her is telling indeed: "How then can I do this great wickedness and sin against God?" (Gen. 39:9). Similarly, David becomes keenly aware of this when he cries out after being confronted with his sins of adultery and murder: "Against you, you only, have I sinned, and done what is evil in your sight" (Ps. 51:4). Sin extends to creation as well. As Kelsey notes, it is "distorting at once sinner, fellow creatures, and the networks of relations in which they interact."[155] But ultimately, sin is *against God*. Sin is "contrary to God" in these ways: sin is contrary to the law of God, sin is contrary to the will of God, and—most fundamentally—sin is contrary to the character or nature of God.

Contrary to the Law of God

We come to know that sin is contrary to God because we learn that it goes against his moral law. Sin is *anomia*. "Everyone who makes a practice of sinning also practices lawlessness; sin is lawlessness" (1 John 3:4). "The mind that is set on the flesh is hostile to God, for it does not submit to God's law; indeed, it cannot" (Rom. 8:7). Sin is thus a violation of the direct commands of God. It is disobedience to what he has made known in his law. The Lutheran dogmatician John Mueller summarizes the point well: "According to Scripture, man should be in complete conformity with the divine will, . . . as this is revealed in the divine Law. . . . Every departure from the norm of the divine law is sin . . . , no matter whether it consists in a state or condition . . . or in actual deeds."[156] As the Lutheran Catechism puts it, "[E]very transgression of the divine Law in desires, thoughts, words, and deeds" is sin.[157] Reformed statements such as the Westminster Shorter Catechism concur: "sin is any want of conformity to, or transgression of, the law of God," and Reformed theologians give great emphasis to this point.[158]

But just *what* is meant by "the divine law"? We must take care at this juncture to see that this refers primarily to the *moral* law of God. While the civil and ceremonial law was binding in the OT—and thus disobedience to it was sin—and while it is the case that Christians may continue to learn much about the character and purposes of God from the ceremonial and civil law, Christians are no longer bound by it. What we are bound to is the moral law of God as summarized in the classic words of Jesus in his response to the question of which is the greatest commandment: "You shall love the Lord your God. . . . [and] your neighbor as yourself" (Mark 12:30–31).

[155] Kelsey, *Eccentric Existence*, 1:412; cf. 2:1040.
[156] Mueller, *Christian Dogmatics*, 210. Cf. Francis Pieper, *Christian Dogmatics*, 4 vols. (St. Louis: Concordia, 1950), 1:528.
[157] Mueller, *Christian Dogmatics*, 225.
[158] See Heppe, *Reformed Dogmatics*, 320, 321, 322, 323.

There is another perplexing issue here as well. In thinking of sin as the transgression of the law, just as it is natural to ask not only about *what* is meant by "the law of God," it is also natural to ask *who* might have access to that law. At this point we need to see that knowledge of the law comes from two primary sources: the moral law of God revealed in Scripture, and the human conscience or what Kant famously referred to as "the moral law within."[159] The first category concerns the moral law of God as it is revealed in the text of Scripture, while the second is verified by the Bible. Here the *locus classicus* is to be found in Romans 2. Here we read that the Gentiles, who "do not have the law" (the written law), "show that the work of the law is written on their hearts, while their conscience also bears witness . . ." (Rom. 2:15). The Reformed theologian W. G. T. Shedd explains that "the moral law violated by the free will of man is both written, and unwritten: the law of nature, and the decalogue. . . . The two laws are originally and essentially the same. The ethics of man's rational nature as he came from the Creator's hand, and of the decalogue, are identical. The now existing difference between the two is due to apostasy."[160] We must take care not to misunderstand the point here. I am not claiming that the consciences of all people offer the same deliverances at all times. I am not claiming that the human conscience is an inerrant or foolproof guide. Nor am I claiming that the knowledge of God that is available by what theologians sometimes refer to as "general revelation" is recognized and *received* by all people (still less would I suggest that they could do so apart from divine grace!). To the contrary, both Scripture and common human experience make it obvious that the sober truth of the matter is otherwise: rather than grateful acknowledgment and reception of the moral law given through either Scripture or general revelation, people *reject* and *deny* it. The argument is not that all people accept the moral law; it is that this moral law is, by grace, available to them.

But if we should not misunderstand it, nor should we lack appreciation for the theological point being made. God has not "left himself without witness" (cf. Acts 14:17), and his moral law is knowable through the consciences of depraved and unregenerate people. This again reminds us of the grace and goodness of God, but it also reminds us that *no one* has excuse for sin. As Shedd says, "such being the connection between the unwritten and written law, it follows that sin in the heathen is the same in kind with sin in Christendom. Free and responsible human will, in both instances, transgresses a common law and ethics. The difference between the violation of the unwritten law and the written, is one of degree only. 'As many as have sinned without law, shall also

---

[159] As Immanuel Kant put it when he exclaimed that "Two things fill the mind with ever new and increasing admiration and awe . . . : *the starry skies above me and the moral law within me*" (*Critique of Practical Reason* [New York: Longmans, Green, 1954], 170).
[160] Shedd, *Dogmatic Theology*, 2:166.

perish without law; and as many as have sinned in the law, shall be judged by the law,' Rom. 2:12."[161]

CONTRARY TO THE WILL OF GOD

In saying that sin is contrary to the law of God, we are also saying that it is contrary to the will of God. Robert Jenson is correct when he says that the "only possible definition of sin is that it is what God does not want done."[162] Barth is similarly and appropriately blunt: sin is "plainly and simply that which God did not, does not, and will not desire."[163] Ursinus states the point with force in insisting that sin comes from the abuse of human freedom and *not* by divine design: "But because the will of men has been depraved by the devil and by itself, it effects sin, a thing which God neither in creating nor in moving the will intends or thinks to effect."[164] Nothing is more basic to the definition of sin than this: it is contrary to the will of God. And, as Barth points out, "in Him there is no paradox, no antinomy, no division, no inconsistency, not even the possibility of it. He is the Father of lights with whom there is no variableness nor interplay of light and darkness. . . . What He is and does He is and does in full unity with Himself."[165] For, in the words of Horst Dietrich Preuss, God's will is "undivided, and there is *one* divine will that is active in all spheres. . . . [Sin] has to do with doing something that displeases YHWH and that does not correspond to his will."[166]

CONTRARY TO THE NATURE OF GOD

Romans 3:23 speaks of the *universality* of sin: "*all* have sinned." But Romans 3:23 also offers a valuable insight into the character of sin. It tells us that to sin is to fall short of God's *glory*. J. Rodman Williams observes that sin, which "may be defined as the personal act of turning away from God and his will," is not less than but *more* than mere transgression of divine law: "the act is ultimately not against the law but against His person. . . . Sin is against God—against His holiness, love, and truth; it is deeply and profoundly personal."[167] Grudem helpfully notes that seeing sin as *merely* contrary to the law of God does not go far enough: "Sin is directly opposite to all that is good in the character of God. . . . It contradicts his holiness, and he must hate it."[168] The

[161] Shedd, *Dogmatic Theology*, 2:167.
[162] Robert W. Jenson, *Systematic Theology, Volume 2: The Works of God* (Oxford: Oxford University Press, 1999), 133.
[163] Barth, *CD*, IV/1, 352. Here (as elsewhere) he is critical of Schleiermacher (who offers the "most complete . . . and promising achievement of the new Protestantism") and of "the great Hegel" (375–376).
[164] Ursinus, *Tractionum*, 219. See further the discussion in Heppe, *Reformed Dogmatics*, 328.
[165] Barth, *CD*, IV/1, 186.
[166] Horst Dietrich Preuss, *Old Testament Theology*, 2 vols., TOTL (Louisville: Westminster/John Knox, 1995), 2:177, emphasis original.
[167] J. Rodman Williams, *Renewal Theology* (Grand Rapids, MI: Zondervan, 1988), 222.
[168] Grudem, *Systematic Theology*, 492.

Reformed scholastic Ursinus elaborates on this point. He insists that "God is not the cause, effect, or author of sin," and he argues for this in several ways.[169] First, says Ursinus, to suggest that God wills sin is to miss the point of the vast biblical witness to the contrary. Consider, by way of example, the statement of Genesis 1:31 that God "saw everything that he had made, and behold, it was very good." Or consider the words of the psalmist:

> For you are not a God who delights in wickedness;
>   evil may not dwell with you.
> The boastful shall not stand before your eyes;
>   you hate all evildoers.
> You destroy those who speak lies;
>   the LORD abhors the bloodthirsty and deceitful man. (Ps. 5:4–6)[170]

But beyond the direct biblical teaching about God's view of sin, insists Ursinus, the vital theological affirmations about the divine nature also count for a lot. He points to the holiness, truthfulness, and righteousness of God. God's absolute holiness makes it "impossible that any effect of His should be bad," and the utter truthfulness of God means "that there are no contradictory wills in Him."[171] Divine justice is important here as well; summarizing the point made by Ursinus, Heinrich Heppe says that "since God attests that He hates sin, He cannot will it," and "whatever one effects in another he cannot rightly punish. But since God is righteous in His punishment of all sins, He can neither wish nor effect sin."[172]

Richard Watson forcefully emphasizes the fact that sin is ultimately against God. This is so because complete allegiance to—and reliance upon—God is what is both right and best for us: "Indeed, if rational beings are under a law at all, it cannot be conceived that less than this could be required by the good and holy being, their Creator. They are bound to render all love, honour, and obedience to him by a natural and absolute obligation; and, as it has been demonstrated in the experience of man, any thing less would be not only contrary to the Creator's glory, but fatal to the creature's happiness."[173] Surely such theological voices, representative of the depth and breadth of the Christian tradition, are correct: sin is contrary to God's law because the divine law reflects the divine will, and sin is ultimately contrary to the nature of God because the divine will and the divine nature cannot be separated.[174] Sin is, above all else, always and ultimately against God. As we have seen, some process theologians

---

[169] Ursinus, *Tractionum*, 218. I here employ the translation of Heppe, *Reformed Dogmatics*, 326.
[170] Ursinus, *Tractionum*, 218; cf. Heppe, *Reformed Dogmatics*, 327.
[171] Ursinus, *Tractionum*, 219; and Heppe, *Reformed Dogmatics*, 327.
[172] Heppe, *Reformed Dogmatics*, 327.
[173] Richard Watson, *Theological Institutes: Or, A View of the Evidences, Doctrines, Morals, and Institutions of Christianity*, 2 vols. (New York: Bangs & Emory, 1826), 2:163.
[174] Watson, *Theological Institutes*, 2:160.

disagree with this conclusion; Marjorie Suchocki exclaims that "sin is first and foremost a rebellion against creatures," and she works for nothing short of a complete "reversal of the tradition" in seeing "rebellion against creation as the fundamental sin."[175] From a point of view informed by Scripture, however, it must be said that Suchocki is simply wrong.

And as sin is against God, so also is God against sin. God is resolutely and implacably opposed to sin. Sin "is the enemy of God, and God is the enemy of sin."[176] "God is light, and in him is no darkness at all" (1 John 1:5). None at all. Barth puts it well when he says,

> [t]he superiority with which God confronts sin in Jesus Christ is that of His unconditional No to this element and to us as its representatives. It is a No in which there is no hidden Yes, no secret approval, no original or ultimate agreement. It is the No of the implacable wrath of God. Sin is the enemy of God, and God is the enemy of sin. Sin has no positive basis in God, no place in His being, no positive part in His life, and therefore no positive part in His will and work.[177]

Sin is whatever is against God. And God is against whatever is sin.

IV. Sin and Sins: Some Important Distinctions

Theologians within the Christian tradition have long recognized some important hamartiological distinctions. Pastoral and practical considerations have often been seen as important here. The purpose of drawing these distinctions is to better expose the variety of forms that sin takes—and all of this so that with better exposure comes increased ability to fight and defeat them. This is important partly because of the deceitful nature of sin; shining the light of divine revelation upon our sins enables us to recognize them—even in the "blind spots"—for what they really are. As Mueller points out, understanding sin in this way can have pastoral or "practical" benefits, for seeing sin in its manifold expressions and sinister forms will help us "to cleanse ourselves from all filthiness of the flesh and spirit . . . and to perfect holiness in the fear of God, 2 Cor. 7,1; Heb. 12, 1–2."[178]

A. Sins of Commission and Sins of Omission

The first such distinction to be seen is between sins of commission and sins of omission. Sins of commission (*peccata commisionis*) are those actions per-

---

[175] Marjorie Suchocki, *The Fall to Violence: Original Sin in Relational Theology* (New York: Continuum, 1994), 16, 13.
[176] Barth, *CD*, IV/1, 409.
[177] Barth, *CD*, IV/1, 409.
[178] Mueller, *Christian Dogmatics*, 228.

formed in which direct and positive commandments of God are violated. Sins of omission (*peccata omissionis*), on the other hand, are those actions which are *not* performed but which God commands.[179] As mentioned earlier, this has important pastoral implications. It is not enough for a Christian to say, "Today I have kept myself from violation of the negative commands of God; I have not done what he has told me not to do." Even if a Christian were correct in saying this, it would be insufficient, for not only are we enjoined to refrain from doing what God has forbidden, so also are we commanded to "love [our] neighbor as [ourselves]" (Mark 12:31). Genuine sinlessness must consist both in refraining from doing what God has told us to reject *and* in doing all that he has commanded us to do.

B. Sins against God, Sins against Neighbor, Sins against Self

Traditional theology has also drawn a distinction between sins that are solely against God, sins that are against our neighbors, and sins against ourselves. Sins against ourselves are those activities that bring either bodily or spiritual harm to ourselves; "the sexually immoral person sins against his own body" (1 Cor. 6:18). Sins against our neighbors are those exemplified in the second table of the Decalogue. Sins against God are such things as idolatry and blasphemy.[180] Observing such distinctions should not lead us to the conclusion that some sins are *not* against God—as we have seen, *all* sin is ultimately against God. But sins committed against God also harm us and our neighbors—and we must not allow ourselves to be blinded to the impact of our sin on ourselves and our fellow creatures.[181]

C. Grievous Sins and Less-Grievous Sins

The venerable distinction between grievous sins and less-grievous sins may appear to be somewhat less obvious and somewhat more controversial. It is, however, deeply ingrained in the tradition of Christian theology. Thomas Aquinas wrestles with the difficult issue of the comparison of sins. Are all sins equal, or are some sins objectively worse than others? He answers by noting that it was the "opinion of the Stoics" that "all sins are equal," and he continues by arguing that the Stoic view has given rise to "the error of certain heretics" who "hold all sins to be equal."[182] He juxtaposes this answer to that of our Lord Jesus Christ: why would Jesus refer to "the greater sin" (John 19:11) if all sins

---

[179] See Mueller, *Christian Dogmatics*, 230.
[180] See Heppe, *Reformed Dogmatics*, 351.
[181] On this point see Mary McClintock Fulkerson, "The Imago Dei and a Reformed Logic for Feminist/Womanist Critique," in *Feminist and Womanist Essays in Reformed Dogmatics*, ed. Amy Plantinga Pauw and Serene Jones (Louisville: Westminster/John Knox, 2006), 95–106.
[182] Aquinas, *ST* IaIIae, Q 73.2.

indeed are equal? Aquinas rejects the notion that all sins are equivalent. And he does so forcefully—he even calls the view heresy. So even though inordinate self-love (there indeed is a proper kind of self-love) is the cause of every sin, the sins themselves are not the same.

What are we to make of this? Every transgression of God's law is sin, and sin is punishable by death (Rom. 6:23). Yet Scripture also speaks of sins in terms of gradation. We all sin; as Paul puts it, "All have sinned and fall short of the glory of God" (Rom. 3:23; cf. Luke 13:3). Yet Jesus pronounces judgment upon his religious opponents that compares their sin with that of Pilate: they were committing the "greater sin" (John 19:11). Furthermore, Jesus teaches that sins committed in ignorance are not on the same level as sins committed in full recognition of God's command and rebellion against it (Luke 12:47–48).[183] Theological traditions have also noted a special designation for "crying sins" or "sins crying to heaven" (peccata clamantia).[184] This latter category refers to those sins that are especially grievous: sins committed against helpless, defenseless, or innocent people; sins of oppression or injustice more generally; or sins against "the helpless, strangers, widows, orphans, the poor, the enslaved . . . who cannot help themselves and therefore cry out to God that he would intervene."[185] These are evident in Scripture: God says to Cain that "your brother's blood is crying to me from the ground" (Gen. 4:10); the sins of Sodom are such that "the outcry against its people has become great before the LORD" (Gen. 19:13; cf. 18:20); the cries of the oppressed Israelites in Egypt reach to God (Ex. 3:7–10), as do the cries of the foreigners, widows, and orphans and the worker who suffers injustice (Deut. 24:14–15). As Martin Chemnitz puts it, these are called "peccata clamantia because Scripture says that these sins, even though men remain silent, cry out to God and call for his vengeance."[186] All sin is against nature and reason, and all sin is contrary to God's law, God's will, and God's character or nature. As such, all sin separates from God and makes the sinner liable to punishment. Yet there are, it seems, some sins that are especially grievous, and the redeemed saints of God—as they come to reflect and even share God's holiness, justice, and mercy—should also understand that some sins "cry out."

D. Intentional Sins and Unintentional Sins

The distinction between intentional sins and unintentional sins (and the closely related categories of voluntary sins and involuntary sins, or sins of ignorance and sins of knowledge) is also deeply rooted in the tradition, but it is as well

---

[183] See Mueller, Christian Dogmatics, 230; Pieper, Christian Dogmatics, 1:567.
[184] E.g., Mueller, Christian Dogmatics, 232; Pieper, Christian Dogmatics, 1:570; Heppe, Reformed Dogmatics, 352.
[185] Pieper, Christian Dogmatics, 1:570.
[186] Cited in Pieper, Christian Dogmatics, 1:570.

the occasion for disagreement among Christians. On one hand, there are Christians who deny that unintentional sins (or involuntary sins, or sins committed in ignorance) are really worthy of being called "sins" at all. On the other hand, some Christians do not see any legitimate distinction between them at all. I think that both sides are wanting to hold onto a legitimate insight, but that neither side is entirely right.

Representative of the first view is the Wesleyan-Holiness theologian Richard S. Taylor.[187] Taylor is concerned that "those who insist on rolling mistakes, 'sins of ignorance,' and human shortcomings into the same basket as a stubborn spirit and evil affections and conscious choice of evil, and labeling every act that falls below absolute standards of righteousness a true act of sin" are taking a dangerously *legalistic* view of sin.[188] To do this, he says, is to run over very important differences; surely an act of willful and intentional rebellion against God, one that is done in full awareness of what God desires and commands, is vastly different from an act that transgresses the law of God but does so out of ignorant sincerity. Taylor insists that the proper Christian attitude toward sin is one of "abhorrence," and he is convinced that seeing *all* acts of transgression as sin will inevitably result in callous consciences and careless attitudes toward sin; after all, if it all counts as sin, then why worry about some sins any more than others? His solution is to "tighten" the definition of sin: sin is not just *any* transgression of God's law, it is the *willful* transgression of a *known* law of God. Thus he says that two conditions are necessary to render an act sinful: "first, a knowledge of the evil. . . . Secondly, a consent to evil is necessary. Desire must unite with the will before sin is conceived."[189] The first condition may be met one day but not the day before; therefore, "when light on a certain matter arrives that matter instantly changes in its relationship to sin and ignorance. It may have been committed innocently yesterday, but has become an act of sin today."[190] The second condition means that sin is not sin "properly so called" unless and until it is done with a conscious decision to do it *as sin*.

At the other end of the spectrum (from Taylor) are those Christian "truisms" that reflect the popular piety of much contemporary North American evangelical life. Sin is simply sin, and it must be terribly judgmental for Christians to weigh or sift sins. Indeed, if there is one sin that is more grievous than

---

[187] In my judgment, Taylor's account is representative of only one strand of Wesleyan-holiness hamartiology (and historically not at all the dominant one). John Wesley's own views on the issue are a matter of some debate. For a helpful examination, see Mark K. Olson, "John Wesley's Doctrine of Sin Revisited," *WesTJ* (2012): 53–71. It should also be noted that Taylor is hardly offering something novel within the Christian tradition; Peter Abelard, among others, denied that unintentional "sins" are really sins at all—see the discussion in John Marenbon, *The Philosophy of Peter Abelard* (Cambridge: Cambridge University Press, 1997), 279.

[188] Richard S. Taylor, *A Right Conception of Sin: Sin in Its Relation to Right Thinking and Right Living* (Kansas City, MO: Beacon Hill, 1945), 69.

[189] Taylor, *Right Conception of Sin*, 73.

[190] Taylor, *Right Conception of Sin*, 73.

others, perhaps it is the sin of judging (someone else's) sins.[191] "Perfect people not allowed." "All sin is equal, and we are all sinners." Such slogans appear on church signs and throughout sermons, and they reflect something that is deeply ingrained.

What are we to make of such views? Must we side with either position? Is there any wisdom to be found? Thomas Aquinas is especially exercised to show the importance of the distinctions between sins of weakness or ignorance, on one hand, and sins that are committed with full awareness and malicious intent. For there "is a sin which takes us unawares on account of the weakness of human nature: and such like sins are less imputable to one who is more virtuous, because he is less negligent in checking those sins, which nevertheless human weakness does not allow us to escape altogether. But there are other sins which proceed from deliberation."[192] Sins of ignorance are sins nonetheless; indeed, the ignorance itself may be culpable. Aquinas draws a crucial distinction between "invincible ignorance," which is not voluntary and not within our power and thus not properly a sin, on the one hand, and, on the other hand, what he calls "vincible ignorance."[193] So being ignorant of what we are unable to know is not a sin, but being wilfully ignorant of what we could—and should—know indeed is sin. Some things are knowable and should be known; if we fail to know these things through our own negligence, we commit sins of omission and are responsible for those sins. In other cases, however, we cannot be at fault for our ignorance. We are, however, held accountable for our actions, and not all acts done in ignorance are non-culpable, since we may be ignorant out of voluntary and sinful negligence.[194]

In light of the foregoing, my contention is this: when we look carefully at what Scripture teaches, we shall see that Scripture does refer to both intentional (and voluntary) and unintentional (and involuntary) actions that violate the law of God as sin. We also see, however, that Scripture marks an important difference between them. On one hand, Scripture clearly tells us that "sin is the transgression of the law" (KJV) or "lawlessness" (ESV; 1 John 3:4). It is lawlessness, transgression of the law. Similarly, both Leviticus 4 and 5 and Numbers 15 teach us that sins that are committed "unintentionally" are nonetheless still considered to be sins. Indeed, this is true both of the sins of individuals and of the sins of the entire community (e.g., Lev. 4:13–35; Num. 15:22–29). It even extends to the "foreigners residing among" the Israelites (Num. 15:26 NIV). We are told explicitly that "if anyone sins and does what is forbidden in any of the LORD's commands, even though they do not know it, they are guilty and will

---

[191] I take this to be one of the many reasons that church discipline is so difficult (and often nonexistent) in contemporary North American evangelicalism.
[192] Aquinas *ST* IaIIae, Q 73.10.
[193] Aquinas, *ST* IaIIae, Q 76.2.
[194] Aquinas, *ST* IaIIae, Q 76.3.

be held responsible" (Lev. 5:17 NIV). Sin is said to be just that—*sin*—irrespective of the knowledge base or the intentions of the person(s) in question. The actions done in transgression of God's law are called what they are—sin—and they stand in need of atonement.

On the other hand, unintentional sins are clearly labeled as such; they are "unintentional." As such, they are distinguished from those sins committed with full awareness of, and in full rejection of, God's will and law. Unintentional sins are qualitatively different from those sins which are committed "defiantly" or "with a high hand" (*bəyād rāmâ*). Atonement is available for the former, while the high-handed sins are those that result in being "cut off" (Num. 15:30–31). Indeed, there may be another important category here as well; Jay Sklar argues forcefully that we should recognize three categories: there are unintentional sins; there are intentional sins that may not be committed "with a high hand"; and there are the "high-handed" sins of apostasy.[195]

This brings us to two important theological conclusions.[196] First, we should admit the truth taught by Scripture: sin of any kind is, strictly speaking, *sin*. While Taylor may be right to raise concerns about antinomianism and related problems, the proper response is not to deny the label of "sin" to what the Bible clearly portrays as exactly that. As such, all sin—sins of ignorance, "infirmity," or "weakness" as well as all others—brings us to the place where we need the atoning work of Christ. John Wesley offers wise counsel here. Even though he thinks that sin is best understood as "a voluntary transgression of a known law" (and insists that, although 1 John is of course correct in saying that "all sin is a transgression of the law," this does not entail that "all transgression of the law is sin"), he also recognizes that there is much common ground in this dispute and that there are important lessons to be learned by all.[197] As Wesley says to his opponents, "[T]his is a mere strife of words. You say that none is saved from sin in *your* sense of the word," but "you cannot deny the possibility of being saved from sin, in *my* sense of the word."[198]

The practical and pastoral importance of this fact should not be missed. No one—not even the godliest saint—is ever beyond the need of the atoning work of Christ. We all rely, moment by moment, upon the gracious work of God for us. Moreover, recognition of this fact might save conscientious and introspective Christians from narcissistic self-justification or spiritual navel-gazing. Confronted with the reality of sin in the life of the Christian, the proper

---

[195] Jay Sklar, "Pentateuch," 15–21. See also Marilyn McCord Adams, *Christ and Horrors: The Coherence of Christology* (Cambridge: Cambridge University Press, 2006), 253.
[196] Admittedly, recognition of this distinction raises other important issues that take us beyond the scope of this discussion. For insightful treatment, see Robert Merrihew Adams, "Involuntary Sins," *The Philosophical Review* (1985): 3–31.
[197] E.g., John Wesley, "On Perfection," in *Works of John Wesley*, vol. 6 (Grand Rapids, MI: Zondervan, n.d.), 417.
[198] Wesley, "On Perfection," 417–418.

Christian response should be repentance and efforts at reconciliation with anyone harmed by the sin—it should *not* be the reflexive response of, "Well, I didn't *mean* to hurt you . . . so leave me alone and get over it." Recalling Thomas Aquinas's distinction between "vincible" and "invincible" ignorance, we should be aware that the line between "sins of ignorance" and "willful transgression" is not always clear-cut.[199] At any rate, the distinction should never be used as an excuse for license. Nor should the proper response be to launch a self-guided inquisition of the inner psyche: for continually asking, "Well, did I intend this exact outcome . . . or didn't I?" is again to focus on the sinner and away from the Savior. Confronted with my own transgression, I do no good to myself or my neighbor to focus on myself by denying that my action was *really* sinful. If I sin against my neighbor and my Lord, I should confess that sin, trust God for his forgiveness in Christ and empowerment by the Holy Spirit, and seek further reconciliation while thanking God for his provision in Christ. I should not seek to do for myself what God has done for me in Christ. I should not seek to justify myself.

But the second theological conclusion is also important: "high-handed" sins are importantly different from other sins. Recognition of the fact that *all* transgression of God's law, regardless of knowledge or intent, is sin does not offer license to continue in intentional sin, nor does it make provision for any sense of nonchalance about sins committed in open rebellion and defiance of God and his law. To the contrary, Scripture gives explicit and grave warnings to those who sin "defiantly." Looking more carefully at the nature of such admonitions takes us to our next distinctions.

E. Mortal Sins and Venial Sins

At this point we come to a distinction that has been the subject of some controversy in Protestant theology. Is there a legitimate distinction between venial sins (*peccata venialia*) and mortal sins (*peccata mortalia*)? This distinction is often associated with medieval theology and with contemporary Roman Catholic theology, and for very good reason.[200] For Thomas Aquinas, for instance, "venial sins are distinguished from mortal sins because the latter destroy the bond of charity between the sinner and God while the former do not."[201] Mortal sin "consists in turning away from our last end which is God."[202] It is "high-

---

[199] Aquinas, *ST* IaIIae, Q 76.2. Suppose that one forgets a promise made and thus does not fulfill it. Is this intentional, or is it not? Forgetfulness is an infirmity (one that likely comes with our finitude), but in some cases it seems to be true that people may (genuinely) forget the promise because they simply did not *care* about it and properly attend to it.

[200] For instance, see the discussion by Richard of St. Victor, *De differentia peccati mortalis et venialis* (PL 196:1191–1194).

[201] See Frederick Christian Bauerschmidt, "Thomas Aquinas," in *T&T Clark Companion to the Doctrine of Sin*, 216.

[202] Aquinas, *ST* IaIIae, Q 77.8.

handed," deliberate, and intentional sin. It is sin that is unrepentant; it is the sin that "leads to death." It is sin that deserves and receives eternal punishment. Sin that is venial, on the other hand, may be so in three ways:

> First, through its cause, i.e. through having cause to be forgiven, which cause lessens the sin; thus a sin that is committed through weakness or ignorance is said to be venial. Secondly, through its issue; thus every sin, through repentance, becomes venial. . . . Thirdly, by its genus, e.g. an idle word. This is the only kind of venial sin that is opposed to mortal sin.[203]

Venial sin is sin that may result in "temporal punishment," and it is sometimes referred to as "wood, hay, and stubble" (cf. 1 Cor. 3:12–15).[204] "We must therefore say that the very venial sins that insinuate themselves into those who have a care for earthly things, are designated by wood, hay, and stubble. For just as these are stored in a house, without belonging to the substance of the house, and can be burnt, while the house is saved, so also venial sins are multiplied in a man, while the spiritual edifice remains, and for them, man suffers fire, either of temporal trials in this life, or of purgatory after this life, and yet he is saved for ever."[205]

The Roman Catholic Catechism distinguishes between mortal sins and venial sins as follows: mortal sin "destroys charity in the heart of man by a grave violation of God's law; it turns man away from God, who is the ultimate end and his beatitude . . . ," while a venial sin "allows charity to subsist, even though it offends and wounds it."[206] This calls for more explanation. For a sin to be mortal, it must meet three conditions. Its object must be a "grave matter," and it must be "committed with full knowledge and deliberate consent."[207] It is obvious that unintentional sins (or sins of ignorance) cannot qualify as mortal sins on this definition; they must be done with awareness of what is happening and by an act of willful transgression. But what counts as a "grave matter"? A grave matter is what is "specified by the Ten Commandments, corresponding to the answer of Jesus to the rich young man: 'Do not kill, do not commit adultery, do not steal, do not bear false witness, do not defraud, honor your father and your mother."[208] It is deliberate, rebellious, high-handed sin; it is sin by which we *intentionally* contradict the love of God (by, say, blasphemy) or love of neighbor (by, say, adultery or murder).[209]

Venial sin, on the other hand, is rightly considered sin; because it is a

---

[203] Aquinas, *ST* IaIIae, Q 77.8.

[204] Aquinas, *ST* IaIIae, Q 89.2.

[205] Aquinas, *ST* IaIIae, Q 89.2.

[206] *Catechism of the Catholic Church*, 2nd ed., rev. in accordance with the official Latin text promulgated by Pope John Paul II (Washington, DC: United States Catholic Conference, 2000), 454.

[207] *Catechism of the Catholic Church*, 455.

[208] *Catechism of the Catholic Church*, 455.

[209] *Catechism of the Catholic Church*, 455.

violation of God's law, it counts as nothing less than sin. But some sins do not violate a grave matter; as Aquinas points out, one is hard pressed to say that "thoughtless chatter or immoderate laughter" are as egregious as adultery, murder, or the torture of innocents.[210] Still other sins do violate a more serious matter, but are performed "without full knowledge or complete consent."[211] So while it *is* sin, it is not the same as other sin. Nor does it have the same consequences. What are we to make of venial sin? If it is not "mortal sin," is it a light matter? Is it to be treated with indifference, or swept under the rug? No, we should see it as serious, for it "weakens charity, it manifests a disordered affection for created goods; it impedes the soul's progress in the exercise of the virtues and the practice of the moral good; it merits temporal punishment."[212] Moreover, it puts us in an increasingly dangerous situation, for if not dealt with by repentance, it can lead us to harden our hearts and become callous or indifferent to mortal sin. So we should take it seriously, for, as sin, it is contrary to nature, contrary to reason, and contrary to God—it is opposed to God's holy law, God's perfect will, and God's righteous character. As such, it may lead to the most horrific of consequences. But we should not confuse sins committed in ignorance or weakness with those committed in open rebellion against God.

So we can see that the distinction between mortal and venial sins is rightly associated with Roman Catholic theology. But it also has a proper home in several *Protestant* traditions. In addition to (some) Anglicans, (most) Methodists (who hail from the Anglican tradition), Arminians (from the Reformed tradition), and many Restorationist, Baptist, and Holiness-Pentecostal traditions, the Lutheran tradition has reserved a rightful place for the distinction between mortal and venial sins (although in some cases the terms themselves are not used). Hollaz distinguishes between *peccatum veniale* and *peccatum mortale*, and he says that mortal sins are those which are both deliberate and voluntary.[213] According to Hollaz, venial sins are those sins which are done involuntarily by those who are regenerate, but such sins do not remove the grace of the Holy Spirit or extinguish faith. Mortal sins, on the other hand, are those sins which result in wrath and condemnation.[214] Mortal sins are those committed with knowledge and consenting volition, and they are committed either by the unregenerate or by rebellious persons who have been regenerated (but who are now in grave danger). The distinction "does not arise from the desert of sin, for every sin, of itself, and by its own nature, in a court of law is damnable;

---

[210] *Catechism of the Catholic Church*, 455.
[211] *Catechism of the Catholic Church*, 456.
[212] *Catechism of the Catholic Church*, 456.
[213] Hollaz, *Examen Theologicum*, II.4.20 (547). Barth mentions this statement but (wrongly) references it to II.4.9 (*CD*, IV/2, 493). See also the extensive treatment by Johann Gerhard, *Loci Theologici* II.9.20 (223–234).
[214] Hollaz, *Examen Theologicum*, 547, 551; cf. Schmid, *Doctrinal Theology*, 274.

but (1) from the different conditions of the subject . . . [and] (2) From the estimate which God has made in the Gospel."[215] Mueller says that "mortal sins are those which result in the death of the sinner."[216] These include all of the sins of unbelievers, but they also include those sins of believers "which force the Holy Spirit to depart from one's heart [and] which destroy faith." These are to be distinguished from venial sins; while venial sins "in themselves merit eternal death," they are "sins of weakness" or "involuntary sins" rather than sins of outright rebellion against God, and they "are daily forgiven to the believer."[217]

Even the story of Reformed theology is more complex than it is sometimes thought to be on this point. Heppe notes that "to begin with even Reformed dogmatics was inclined to recognise the distinction between venial and mortal sins as an essential one."[218] He quotes Heinrich Bullinger: "All the sins of our thought, words, and deeds are by no means equal to each other. . . . Now the godly in all ages have unanimously transmitted it from Scripture, that certain sins are venial or daily; I mean the slips and errors done out of ignorance or weakness rather than of wickedness and committed by otherwise holy men, who daily pray for the remission of their debts."[219] Bullinger makes some important statements here: there is an important difference between sins of ignorance or weakness and sins of rebellion, and the articulation of this difference via the distinction between mortal and venial sins can claim *unanimous* support from godly theologians. Zacharias Ursinus locates his discussion under the preferable heading of "reigning" versus "not reigning" sins, but he also allows for a proper usage of the distinction between mortal and venial sins. For although every sin can be said to be "mortal" in the sense that it deserves punishment (which is death), it is only sin that remains regnant that eventuates in eternal death. Venial sin, on the other hand, "does not call for eternal death" because it "does not reign in the regenerate who resist it by the grace of God."[220]

However, as Heppe notes, polemic against Roman Catholic theology eventually led some Reformed theologians down a different path, and many Reformed theologians finally decided in favor of the view that *every* sin committed by an unbeliever is mortal and no sin committed by a believer can be mortal. For instance, Barth refers to the distinction between mortal and venial sins as one held by "the Romanists and Lutherans," and he rejects it

---

[215] Hollaz, *Examen Theologicum*, 547; cf. Schmid, *Doctrinal Theology*, 274; see also the detailed discussion in Quenstadt, *Theologica II*, 147–151.
[216] Mueller, *Christian Dogmatics*, 568.
[217] Mueller, *Christian Dogmatics*, 231; cf. Pieper, *Christian Dogmatics*, 1:568.
[218] Heppe, *Reformed Dogmatics*, 349.
[219] Heinrich Bullinger, *Compendium Christianae Religionis* III.III (Tiguri: 1569), 35; see the discussion in Heppe, *Reformed Dogmatics*, 349. Bullinger contrasts venial sins with mortal sins, which he describes as "premeditated."
[220] Zacharias Ursinus, *Commentary on the Heidelberg Catechism*, trans. G. W. Williard (Cincinnati: Elm Street, 1888), 45.

forcefully.[221] For, he claims, the distinction "assumes a quantitative concept of sin which cannot be united with the decisive seriousness of the divine judgment and the human situation under this judgment."[222] But even with Calvin the language of "mortal" and "venial" does not disappear. Instead, Calvin concludes that all "the faults of the saints are venial, not by their nature but because they receive pardon by the mercy of God."[223] Note here that the difference between mortal and venial sins is not to be found in the sins themselves, nor does it have anything to do with the knowledge or motivation of the person committing the sin. As Heppe puts it, if we are thinking about the sins themselves "and according to the rigour of the law," then "all . . . we consider to be mortal, not one venial."[224] Rather than stemming from the nature of the sin itself or the motivation of the sinner, the difference between mortal and venial sins is located elsewhere: the doctrine of predestination—and only the doctrine of predestination—enables us to distinguish between mortal and venial sins. So for the Reformed, all sins of those predestined for salvation are venial, and all sins of those predestined to damnation are mortal.

What are we to make of the distinction between mortal and venial sins? Is it legitimate? Or is it misleading and potentially even harmful to the assurance of the believer? Given the disagreement among evangelical Protestants, it is natural to ask these questions. On one hand, some evangelicals view the distinction itself with suspicion. On the other hand, even Reformed theologians admit that the distinction enjoys the "unanimous" support of the Christian tradition (at least *up to* the Reformation era, and with strong support thereafter among confessional Protestants). More importantly, it is grounded upon a clear—if commonly overlooked—biblical basis. Johannine theology sharply distinguishes between the "sin that does not lead to death" and the "sin that leads to death" (1 John 5:16 NIV). Thus we read, "All wrongdoing is sin, but there is sin that does not lead to death" (1 John 5:17).[225] It is not plausible to take this merely as a reference to physical death, for as Robert W. Yarbrough observes, "this would also suggest that he was also addressing the issue of prayers for the dead, something foreign to this epistle as well as in the rest of the NT."[226] Thus we are left with an important distinction between venial and mortal sins, and, as "intentional" or "high-handed" sins, the mortal sin of apostasy is deadly (cf. Heb. 6:4–6; 10:26–31).

---

[221] Barth, *CD*, IV/2, 492.

[222] Barth, *CD*, IV/2, 493.

[223] Cited in Heppe, *Reformed Dogmatics*, 350.

[224] Heppe, *Reformed Dogmatics*, 351, quoting Heribert Rissen.

[225] A proper understanding of the Johannine development and use of the contrast between "life" and "death" makes a merely physical interpretation of this passage very implausible. John regularly uses "life" in close connection with salvation, and "death" is preeminently spiritual death in John's theology.

[226] Robert W. Yarbrough, *1–3 John*, Baker Exegetical Commentary on the New Testament (Grand Rapids, MI: Baker Academic, 2008), 308.

F. Remissible Sins and Irremissible Sins

Theologians from many traditions also draw a distinction between *remissible* and *irremissible* sins, and central to all discussions of this is the issue of the "sin against the Holy Spirit." In the Synoptic Gospels we find this statement of Jesus: "Therefore I tell you, every sin and blasphemy will be forgiven people, but the blasphemy against the Spirit will not be forgiven. And whoever speaks a word against the Son of Man will be forgiven, but whoever speaks against the Holy Spirit will not be forgiven, either in this age or in the age to come" (Matt. 12:31–32; cf. Mark 3:28–29; Luke 12:10). These are stern words indeed, but how are they to be understood? More precisely, *what* is this irremissible sin against the Holy Spirit? *Who* commits it? And *why* is it irremissible?

Some theologians in the Reformed tradition offer a clear set of answers to such questions. *What* is the sin against the Holy Spirit? According to Heidegger, it is the "complete denial of evangelical truth thoroughly recognised, as well as hatred of it and attacks against it, proceeding not from common human infirmity but from singular malice and devilish hatred of it, wholly devoid of repentance or slackening."[227] It is, by extension, also against Father and Son.[228]

Who commits it? At one level, of course, soteriological Reformed theologians hold that *all* sins committed by the reprobate are irremissible. After all, God did not elect them for salvation, and the incarnate Son did not die for their sins. So in one sense, all sins of the reprobate are irremissible, while all sins committed by the elect are remissible. But there is a lot more to the classical Reformed story here. Strictly speaking, the sin against the Holy Spirit "can never be incurred by an elect but only by a rejected person, *and only by a rejected person who has experienced the effectiveness of God's means of grace through the Church.*"[229] So while only the reprobate are liable to this sin, only some of those poor souls designated by God for damnation are eligible. More precisely, it is only those destined for damnation who are part of the covenant community and who have experienced the joy of knowing God. As Heppe explains the Reformed view, "[T]he only person guilty of this sin is the man who has known Christ through the gracious working of the Holy Spirit and experienced His blessed fellowship, yet falls away from Christ and becomes the enemy of Christ and His kingdom."[230]

Whereas earlier Protestant theologians (Heppe mentions Philipp Melanchthon) had tended to follow Augustine's teaching that the sin against the Holy Spirit is "final impenitence" or resistance to the Holy Spirit that is finalized

---

[227] Heidegger, *Corpus Theologiae Christianae*, X.lxxiii (358).
[228] Heidegger, *Corpus Theologiae Christianae*, X.lxxiii (358).
[229] Heppe, *Reformed Dogmatics*, 354, emphasis mine.
[230] Heppe, *Reformed Dogmatics*, 355–356.

at death, some Reformed theology came to see things somewhat differently.[231] Heppe notes that the Reformed tradition swung away from this Augustinian understanding, and he offers this view as representative: the sin against the Holy Spirit is what Heppe summarizes as "the voluntary sin of the man who was already really in possession of the [Holy] Spirit and had entered into the enjoyment of life eternal . . ."[232]

So according to this Reformed view, those who commit this unforgive-able sin are among those who are predestined by God to hear and receive the gospel. They are those sinners who are predestined by God to respond in faith to the gospel—at least initially. The faith is genuine; and as such it comes from the only real source of genuine faith: God. They are people who "know Christ," people who have "experienced his blessed fellowship," people who "really" possess the Holy Spirit within them and who relish and delight in "the enjoyment of life eternal." Unfortunately, however, these are also people who are predestined to reject the Lord and Savior Jesus Christ. The atoning work of Christ was never intended for them in the first place, and the work of the Holy Spirit—that work that convicts them of their sin, gives them genuine faith, and allows them to enjoy the blessed fellowship of the triune God—was never intended to sustain them in their faith. On determinist Reformed theologies, God determines that they will commit this unforgiveable sin. The God who determines all things determines that they will "taste and see that the Lord is good"—but will then be damned to an existence in hell without him.[233] So once again: who commits this unpardonable sin against the Holy Spirit? The person who does so belongs to a subset of the reprobate: he is one who for a while receives the gracious working of the Holy Spirit "in the same relation as the converted elect—only that he is not elect and therefore has only for a time and in passing entered into relationship with the [Holy] Spirit."[234] This sin can be committed only

---

[231] See Heppe, *Reformed Dogmatics*, 356.

[232] Heppe, *Reformed Dogmatics*, 356. I take Heppe to be drawing from Cocceius, *Summa Theologia*, XXIX.48 (330).

[233] The relation of historic Reformed theology to determinism is vexed and controversial. On one hand, there is the (widespread) assumption that Reformed theology is overtly committed to some form of determinism; this view is stoutly defended by Paul Helm, e.g., "*Reformed Thought on Freedom*: Some Further Thoughts," *JournRT* (2010): 185–207; Helm, "Jonathan Edwards and the Parting of the Ways," *Jonathan Edwards Studies* (2014): 42–60; Helm, "Turretin and Edwards Once More," *Jonathan Edwards Studies* (2014): 286–296. See also the insightful work of James N. Anderson and Paul Manata, "Determined to Come Most Willingly: Some Challenges for Libertarian Calvinism," *JournRT* (2017): 272–297. On the other hand, notable scholars question or deny this commitment. See, e.g., Willem J. van Asselt, J. Martin Bac, and Roelf T. te Velde, eds., *Reformed Thought on Freedom: The Concept of Free Choice in Early Modern Reformed Theology* (Grand Rapids, MI: Baker Academic, 2010); Oliver D. Crisp, "John Girardeau: Libertarian Calvinist?," *JournRT* (2014): 284–300; Crisp, *Deviant Calvinism: Broadening Reformed Theology* (Minneapolis: Fortress, 2014); Richard A. Muller, "Jonathan Edwards and the Absence of Free Choice: A Parting of the Ways in the Reformed Tradition," *Jonathan Edwards Studies* (2011): 3–22; Muller, "Jonathan Edwards and Francis Turretin on Necessity, Contingency, and Freedom of Will: In Response to Paul Helm," *Jonathan Edwards Studies* (2014): 266–285; and Muller, *Divine Will and Human Choice: Freedom, Contingency, and Necessity in Early Modern Reformed Thought* (Grand Rapids, MI: Baker Academic, 2017).

[234] Heppe, *Reformed Dogmatics*, 357.

by a reprobate person, and only by a reprobate person who is chosen for a period of temporary faith.

Why is this sin unpardonable? A common Reformed answer is exemplified by Petrus van Mastricht: "the most correct thing to say [is] that it is irremissible for the same divine cause and will by which all sins of the reprobate are irremissible, that of course it was not God's will that Christ should satisfy for them, neither did Christ will to expend his death on the remission of this sin."[235] There is nothing about the sin itself that is unforgiveable; God could forgive this one too if he so desired. Instead, it is irremissible because God caused it to be so.

It is hard to fully evaluate this view of the sin against the Holy Spirit without a complete analysis of the "system" of theology in which it finds its proper home. Still, though, it is possible to make some judgments about it. Here the first point to make is that there is no hint of this view in the texts in question; there simply is nothing to indicate that this is the proper understanding of the "unforgiveable sin" in either Matthew 12:31–32 (again, cf. Mark 3:28–29 and Luke 12:10) or 1 John 5:16–17. Moreover, it is hard to make sense of such a view in light of what *is* in the text. It appears that Jesus is offering a *warning* in these passages. He is not telling us of the fate of those chosen for this kind of reprobation. Instead, he is warning his hearers not to commit this sin. Graham Cole observes that Jesus's "appeal to reason suggests that the Pharisees had not yet fallen into the abyss. As Packer argues, 'Jesus saw that the Pharisees were getting close to committing this sin, and he spoke with them in hope of holding them back from fully lapsing into it.'"[236] But on this Reformed reading, Jesus would be issuing a warning not to commit the very action that they were predestined to do (or that, *for all anyone knows*, they were predestined to do). In other words, Jesus would be admonishing them not to do what God wills for them to do and in fact has determined that they will do.

This leads us directly to the next point: this view undermines the very basic and very important theological affirmation that sin is *contrary to the will of God*. Scripture tells us in many passages (and in many ways) that God desires the salvation of all. God is "not wishing that any should perish . . ." (2 Pet. 3:9). Yet on the view in question, *this* sin—the one that is irremissible, the one that ensures damnation—*is* committed in exact accordance with the will of God. But on a proper understanding of sin, this simply is not so much as possible.

Finally, this view undercuts belief in the goodness and trustworthiness of God—and, consequently, undercuts the assurance of the believer. On this view,

---

[235] Petrus van Mastricht, *Theoretico-Practica Theologia*, 2nd ed. (1698), IV.III (464), quoted in Heppe, *Reformed Dogmatics*, 360.
[236] Graham A. Cole, *He Who Gives Life: A Theology of the Holy Spirit* (Wheaton, IL: Crossway, 2007), 176–177. Cole quotes J. I. Packer, *Concise Theology: A Guide to Historic Christian Beliefs* (Wheaton, IL: Tyndale, 1993), 217.

God *says* that he takes no pleasure in the death of the wicked (Ezek. 33:11)—yet he predestines some to commit this sin against the Holy Spirit. Christ *warns* both the Pharisees (Matt. 12:31–32 and Mark 3:28–29) and his own disciples (Luke 12:10) not to commit this sin—yet God's all-determining decree predestines some to commit this sin. The Holy Spirit draws sinners to himself, enables them to experience the "blessed fellowship" of the triune God, gives them a real "enjoyment of life eternal"—and then abandons them to eternal damnation.

Much more accurate, and much more satisfying, is the more broadly consensual view of this sin. On this account, *what* the irremissible sin amounts to is this: It is final and settled impenitence. It is the ultimate rejection of what God has provided for sinners in Christ Jesus as this is brought to us by the Holy Spirit. It is what Mueller calls the "perverse, persistent denial and rejection of the divine truth after the latter has been sufficiently acknowledged and accepted as such, joined with voluntary and atrocious blasphemy. . . . it is the malicious and blasphemous rejection of the Gospel by a hardened sinner, who through the gracious operation of the Holy Ghost has been fully convinced of its divine truth."[237] As Cole puts it, "Blaspheming the Spirit is not an episode but a way of life. Put another way, this is the sin of persistent impenitent unbelief. John Paul II was right to describe this as 'the radical refusal to be converted.'"[238] The question "*Who* commits it?" is likewise readily answered: it is committed by those who have tasted of the fruits of the gospel but who are finally impenitent. And *why* is it irremissible? Simply because outside of Christ there is no Savior and no salvation, and without the Holy Spirit we have no access to Christ.

One final question has important pastoral implications. What are we to make of those sincere and conscientious Christian believers who worry that they may have committed the sin against the Holy Spirit? Here I am in full agreement with Packer and Cole: "Christians who fear that they may have committed it . . . show by that anxiety that they have not done so."[239]

G. Individual or Personal Sins and Social, Structural, or Systemic Sins

Recent work on the doctrine of sin has done much to alert us to the reality of the social dynamic and impacts of sin. Where many modern Christians (perhaps especially modern *Western* Christians) tend to see sin as the discrete actions of individual persons, theologians and other theorists (including social scientists) from around the world and especially from oppressed or marginalized communities protest that such individualist understandings of sin are far

---

[237] Mueller, *Christian Dogmatics*, 233.
[238] Cole, *He Who Gives Life*, 177.
[239] Packer, *Concise Theology*, 217, quoted in Cole, *He Who Gives Life*, 177.

too narrow and myopic. Accordingly, theologians from the "Majority World" (or the "Global South") as well as liberationist, feminist, and womanist theologians from "the West" argue forcefully that any adequate understanding of sin must account for more than the obvious point that individual persons commit sinful actions. As D. Stephen Long observes, the "beneficial results of this theological expansion have been profound."[240] In particular, such insights help us to see the impact of sin on social "structures." Because so much of this work is done by various types of "liberation theologians," a brief look at the context of these claims might be helpful.

Classical liberal theology was driven by the desire to understand (and, when necessary, revise) the truth claims of the Christian faith in accord with the claims of common human experience, language, and culture. As David Tracy puts it, "[T]he enterprise of liberal Christian theology will be the attempt to show how a proper reinterpretation of modernity's most basic value commitments and a proper reinterpretation of Christianity's historic claims to truth and value can be—indeed must be—reconciled."[241] This was doubtless true with respect to classical theological liberalism, but matters have changed significantly. Claims about "common human experience" are now often seen as hopelessly mistaken—there simply is no such thing (at least not one that is relevant to the important issues at stake). Moreover, such claims about "common human experience" may be dangerously misleading, for they usually serve to cloak the status of some privileged group that pretends to be common or universal. Again, there is no such (relevant) thing as "common human experience"; rather, there are many such experiences. Importantly, the experiences of oppressed persons and groups deserve a hearing. And when such a hearing is gained, the resultant doctrines of sin begin to look very different.

These different theologies are in what has come to be known as "theologies of liberation."[242] These take various forms; Latin American liberation theologies, black theologies, feminist theologies, and womanist theologies are some of the most prominent. All tend to reject important elements of traditional doctrines of sin, and many react negatively to Reinhold Niebuhr in particular.

Ramm notes that there is something paradoxical about Latin American liberation theologies of sin. On one hand, there is very little direct and focused discussion of sin. On the other hand, "almost every volume of its literature is a tractate on sin."[243] Latin American liberation theologians often argue that traditional theology has focused very heavily—indeed almost exclusively—

---

[240] D. Stephen Long, *The Perfectly Simple Triune God: Aquinas and His Legacy* (Minneapolis: Fortress, 2016), 276. Long notes the difficulties with labels (273–274).
[241] David Tracy, *Blessed Rage for Order: The New Pluralism in Theology* (San Francisco: Harper & Row, 1988), 26.
[242] D. Stephen Long rightly notes that any attempt to label such theologies is "fraught with difficulty" (*Perfectly Simple Triune God*, 273).
[243] Ramm, *Offense to Reason*, 142.

on *individual sin*. In other words, the focus (some might say the "obsession") has been on the sin of individual persons, and sometimes further on the individual sins committed by individual persons. Thus traditional hamartiology asks questions such as these: Are there distinctions between sins? Are some sins worse than others? Which sins can I "get away with" (maybe venial sins but not mortal sins)? How might I escape the consequences (either temporal or eternal) of my sins? When traditional theology does consider more corporate or social concerns, even the way it does so shows evidence of myopia, for consideration of the doctrine of original sin is most often concerned with this type of question: Am *I* responsible for the sins of my most remote ancestor? By contrast, as Ramm points out, the emphasis of Latin American liberation theologians "lies rather on those social sins causing so much grief . . . : imperialism, neocolonialism, exploitation, international cartels, dictatorial governments, landlessness of the masses, endemic unemployment, brutal dictatorships, hunger, and disease."[244]

Gustavo Gutierrez describes (or perhaps defines) sin as a "breach of friendship."[245] Jose Ignacio Gonzalez Faus insists that humans are sinners (rather than basically good people who occasionally err and blunder).[246] Sin is something for which we are culpable; it is not merely a matter of "weakness."[247] He defines sin as "oppressing the truth through injustice," and he argues that one of the characteristics of sin is its ability to blind sinners to their own wrongdoing and resultant dilemma.[248] Faus does not deny the personal responsibility of individuals, but he focuses attention on the notion of "structural sin." "*When human beings sin, they create structures of sin, which, in turn, make human beings sin.*"[249] Consequently, to fight sin is to fight political, social, and economic oppression, and salvation from sin is (or at least definitely includes) liberation from political and economic oppression. Latin American liberation theologians are well aware of the criticisms made of their proposals by such important theologians as Hans Urs von Balthasar and Joseph Ratzinger (Benedict XVI). As Faus puts it, such traditional theologians accuse the notion of "structural sin" as "denaturing what is most profound in sin—that it is the fruit of a personal and responsible freedom," and they conclude that, since personal and responsible freedom cannot be applied to impersonal forces or societal structures, "the concept

---

[244] Ramm, *Offense to Reason*, 143.
[245] Gustavo Gutierrez, *A Theology of Liberation: History, Politics, and Salvation* (Maryknoll, NY: Orbis, 1988), xxviii, 24, 85, 100–101, 102–103, 226n101.
[246] Jose Ignacio Gonzalez Faus, "Sin," in *Systematic Theology: Perspectives from Liberation Theology*, ed. Jon Sobrino and Ignacio Ellacuria (Maryknoll, NY: Orbis, 1993), 194.
[247] Faus, "Sin," 195.
[248] Faus, "Sin," 195–196.
[249] Faus, "Sin," 198, emphasis original.

of structural sin goes against Christian teaching on sin."[250] But liberation theologians press on undaunted, for "[s]in also means that which God rejects or cannot accept in any way. Therefore denying the notion of structural sin is equivalent to saying that the present situation of the world (and in particular the third-world countries) is not a situation that arouses God's rejection and anger."[251]

Black liberation theology shares much in common with Latin American liberationist theology.[252] But as its situation is different, so also are its formulations of the doctrine of sin. According to James Cone, black theology is "*a rational study of the being of God in the world in light of the existential situation of an oppressed community, relating the forces of liberation to the essence of the Gospel, which is Jesus Christ.*"[253] The theological task is "to explicate the meaning of God's liberating activity so that those who labor under [sin's] enslaving powers will see that the forces of liberation are the very activity of God."[254] Using all the sources of theology (black experience, black history, black culture, revelation, Scripture, and tradition), black theology is "normed" by "the manifestation of Jesus as the black Christ who provides the necessary soul for black liberation."[255]

For Cone, sin cannot be defined by "white theology," and only black theology can properly account for the presence and power of sin. "Black theology believes that the true nature of sin is perceived only in the moment of oppression and liberation. . . . This means that the whites, despite their self-proclaimed righteousness, are rendered incapable of making valid judgments on the character of sin."[256] Therefore, "only blacks can talk about their sin."[257] Sin, which is a "community concept," cannot be understood—much less adequately dealt with—when considered in abstraction.[258] It is "a condition of human existence in which we deny the essence of God's liberating activity as revealed in Jesus Christ. It is a way of life in which we cease to be fully human and we make choices according to our private interests, identifying the ultimate with an alien power. It is accepting slavery as a condition of human existence by denying the freedom grounded in God's activity. Sin is an alienation from the

[250] Faus, "Sin," 199.
[251] Faus, "Sin," 199.
[252] Paulo Freire says that black liberation theology and Latin American liberation theology are "unquestionably linked" ("Foreword to the 1986 Edition," in James Cone, *A Black Theology of Liberation* [New York: Orbis, 1986], ix).
[253] James Cone, *Black Theology of Liberation*, 1, emphasis original. "White theology," on the other hand, is "not Christian theology at all" (9). I am taking Cone's work as representative of much that is important in black theologies of liberation, but we should also be aware of the movement and variety within black theology. See, e.g., J. Kameron Carter, *Race: A Theological Account* (New York: Oxford University Press, 2008).
[254] Cone, *Black Theology of Liberation*, 3.
[255] Cone, *Black Theology of Liberation*, 38. He also says that "black theology refuses to accept a God who is not identified totally with the goals of the black community" (27).
[256] Cone, *Black Theology of Liberation*, 106.
[257] Cone, *Black Theology of Liberation*, 108.
[258] Cone, *Black Theology of Liberation*, 104.

source of humanity in the world, resulting in human oppression and misery."[259] This summary, however, is not sufficiently concrete for Cone's purposes, and he fleshes out further what sin means for black theology:

> Because sin represents the condition of estrangement from the source of one's being, for blacks this means a desire to be white. It is the refusal to be what we are. Sin, then, for blacks is loss of identity. It is saying yes to white absurdity— accepting the world as it is by letting whites define black existence. To be "in sin" is to be contented with white solutions for the "black problem" and not rebel against every infringement of white being on black being.[260]

Feminist and womanist theologians also raise their voices in discussions of sin.[261] They generally wish to treat sin as something that is deadly serious, but they also push back against traditional renderings of the doctrine. Diane Leclerc says that the traditional or "Augustinian" doctrine of sin is "squarely balanced upon a pessimistic anthropology and an equally fatalistic misogyny."[262] Accordingly, it misses "insights that arise when 'women's experience' is given credence as a theological source."[263] Catherine Keller summarizes well the common feminist critique of traditional approaches: for feminist theology, "the traditional definitions of sin as pride, arrogance, self-interest and other forms of exaggerated self-esteem miss the mark in the case of women, who in this culture suffer from too little self-esteem, indeed too little self."[264] Traditional views (and here it should be noted that Niebuhr's position is often taken to be "the traditional view," and he is very often the target in these discussions) are criticized as too individualistic. Theologians of the broader Christian tradition, despite any important differences among them, were united by something far more important—and far more insidious—than whatever disagreements may have separated them. What united them (even if the unity was so deep and so basic that it was unrecognized) was the assumption that the human person (the "man") is fundamentally or "essentially" an individual who may share social relations with God and with other creatures. To sin, on this way of seeing things, is fundamentally to succumb to the temptation to assert

---

[259] Cone, *Black Theology of Liberation*, 106.

[260] Cone, *Black Theology of Liberation*, 108–109.

[261] Once again, it is worth noting that feminist theologies of sin are widely variegated, and what follows here is only a brief summary of some of the most influential elements. For instance, Katie G. Cannon promotes a "black womanist" account, and Carter Heyward offers a feminist doctrine that emphasizes heterosexism as a particularly deadly sin. See Katie G. Cannon, *Black Womanist Ethics* (Atlanta: Scholars Press, 1988); and Carter Heyward, *Touching Our Strength: The Erotic as Power and the Love of God* (San Francisco: Harper & Row, 1989); as well as the overview by Christine M. Smith, "Sin and Evil in Feminist Thought," *ThTo* (1993): 208–219.

[262] Diane Leclerc, *Singleness of Heart: Gender, Sin, and Holiness in Historical Perspective* (Lanham, MD: Scarecrow, 2001), 1.

[263] Leclerc, *Singleness of Heart*, 1.

[264] Catherine Keller, *From a Broken Web: Separation, Sexism, and Self* (Boston: Beacon, 1988), 40. See further the helpful discussion by Derek R. Nelson, *What's Wrong with Sin? Sin in Individual and Social Perspective from Schleiermacher to Theologies of Liberation* (New York: T&T Clark, 2009).

THE "SIN NATURE" AND THE "NATURE" OF SIN □ 263

oneself against God and others in pride and attempted domination. Many feminist theologians, however, will say that while such an account may have some limited value for describing the quintessential sins of *men*, it clearly misses the mark when it comes to women. Indeed, the mere fact that men can so easily assume that their view is universal may itself be a reflection of the blinding force of that prideful domination. What is needed instead, some feminists argue, is a replacement of such outmoded anthropology with a "Marxist-Hegelian perspective" on human personhood, for there is no "self" apart from the social relationships, and the "external relations of the self form the understanding which a person has of him or herself."[265]

So feminist theologians will often criticize the individualism (or sometimes the "essentialism") that undergirds "the traditional view," and they follow this criticism with one that penetrates to the core of their worries about the doctrine of sin. The traditional account of sin tends to view it as the prideful assertion of the self against God and others (and with devastating consequences for others as well as for the self). Indeed, much traditional hamartiology sees pride as the root of all other sins. But while this understanding may be insightful and accurate (Daphne Hampson says that "Niebuhr's analysis contains deep insights")—it is still androcentric and does not really address the characteristic sins of women.[266] In place of the standard traditional view—or, perhaps, "augmenting" it—feminist theologians propose an alternative.[267] As Valerie Saiving says, the temptations of women *as women* "have a quality which can never be encompassed by such terms as 'pride' and 'will-to-power.' They are better suggested by such items as triviality, distractibility, and diffusiveness . . . in short, underdevelopment or negation of the Self."[268] Judith Plaskow thus concludes that sin is the "failure to take responsibility for self-actualization."[269] Sin may be the prideful assertion of the self; for men this may be the standard production. But sometimes (and especially, or perhaps even strictly, for women) it is the lack of pride and the failure to assert oneself. Sin cannot be reduced to the idolatry of the will-to-power, for any adequate doctrine of sin must also be able to account for "relational idolatry."[270] As Daphne Hampson points out, this concept has the potential to "turn Christian theology as they [women] have imbibed it upside-down."[271] Moreover, for many feminist theologians sin should be seen as "structural" (perhaps primarily as structural); sin is not,

---

[265] Daphne Hampson, *Theology and Feminism* (Oxford: Blackwell, 1991), 124.
[266] Hampson, *Theology and Feminism*, 122.
[267] E.g., Leclerc, *Singleness of Heart*, 157.
[268] Valerie Saiving, "The Human Situation: A Feminine View," in *Womanspirit Rising: A Feminist Reader in Religion*, ed. Carol P. Christ and Judith Plaskow (San Francisco: Harper & Row, 1979), 37.
[269] Judith Plaskow, quoted in Hampson, *Theology and Feminism*, 123.
[270] Leclerc, *Singleness of Heart*, 156.
[271] Hampson, *Theology and Feminism*, 123. For Hampson herself, turning Christian theology upside down shook so much out of it that there is nothing left of it. She now describes herself as "post-Christian."

in the first instance, the problem of one person in rebellion against God and estranged from others. Rather, "sin is the sin of the domination of one class by another, and indeed (and perhaps primarily) the sin of sexism—which has gone unrecognized in male theology."[272] And once again, a particular view of salvation accompanies such a doctrine of sin. For feminists who hold that the characteristic sin of women is to have too little pride or assertion of self, the liberating power of the gospel empowers women to do what needs to be done. And for feminists who focus on structural sin, any gospel that is really "good news" will announce and enact the defeat of such structures of oppression. As Hampson says, for such theologians "there must first be a social revolution, so that the conditions which lead to alienation are overcome, before individuals can come into their own. It is not simply that human pride and domination of others must needs be eliminated. There must be an empowering of those who at present are disempowered."[273]

What these theologians have in common is a deep sense that sin cannot adequately be considered in individualistic terms. They insist that sin impacts societal structures and cultural systems, and they are exercised to shine a spotlight on those areas that often lie hidden from analysis and criticism. One need not accept all their judgments (and at various points some liberationist assessments and recommendations are opposed to classical Christian orthodoxy and should be deemed out of step with Scripture),[274] but we should be open to the possibility that they may offer helpful—if sometimes uncomfortable—insights into sin and its impact. In particular, we should be open to any insights that we might gain about the structural impact of sin.

Stephen Ray illustrates how structural sin can permeate a society to the point where it seems "natural." Using as an example the ways in which issues of social and economic as well as geographical location are tied to the sin of racism, he offers this reflection on the "history of exclusion" of ethnic minorities in the United States:

> This residential and commercial exclusion of Black persons from the spaces of economic opportunity and material well-being which was frequently violent—yet always state sanctioned—is perhaps the most constant thread which runs through the racial history of the United States. Whether we are considering the physical conditions of educational institutions or the geographic location of residential communities relative to economic opportunity and cultural flourishing, the history of this nation has demarked the appropriate spaces

[272] Hampson, *Theology and Feminism*, 125.
[273] Hampson, *Theology and Feminism*, 125.
[274] Daniel L. Migliore helpfully observes that any "adequate doctrine of sin will recognize that sin against the grace of God is not only titanic, Luciferian rebellion but also the timid, obsequious refusal to dare to be fully human by God's grace" (*Faith Seeking Understanding: An Introduction to Christian Theology* [Grand Rapids, MI: Eerdmans, 1991], 131). In this light, not all differences between traditional and liberationist or revisionist accounts are as drastic as they may initially appear.

for Black persons and communities are ones of exclusion. Put another way, decrepit and underfunded schools that prepare children for an economy which no longer exists, structurally dilapidated communities distant from economic opportunity and surrounded by environmentally threatening industries or their remnants, whose physical and economic condition breeds crime and despair, are taken to be the *natural* condition of Black people, thereby leaving unquestioned the ways that fiscal policy, housing practices, and extra-legal violence have created these conditions, again and again.[275]

When this happens, several results follow: there is sin against the members of these excluded communities as they are denied justice in access to goods; there is sin within these communities as desperate people commit acts of moral evil; and this entire process both becomes "normalized" and acts as a further instrument of sinful oppression. This, Ray concludes, offers a snapshot of how sin becomes structurally embedded.

So any adequate account of sin will also recognize the reality that sin becomes "institutionalized" as it perverts and warps social structures and institutions—which then in turn become breeding grounds for further sinful activities. Frustrated by the reality that this point is all-too-easily missed, overlooked, ignored, or denied by people who benefit from such institutions while being all-too-painfully-obvious to those who suffer from the hegemony of such systems, theologians "from the margins" insist that hamartiologies must come to a reckoning with the unpleasant but undeniable fact that entire social systems have been built upon evils such as racism, colonialism, sexism, and nationalism.

Reinhold Niebuhr gives eloquent expression to some of these concerns when he says that while the "religious dimension of sin is man's rebellion against God," the accompanying "social dimension of sin is injustice."[276] At the base of all sin is "man's pride and will-to-power."[277] Such pride is expressed in many ways; we can be proud of our power and knowledge, but we can also be proud of our self-righteousness.[278] In addition to "individual egotism," Niebuhr warns that egotism can be expressed in "group pride" as well, and he worries that the "group pride" may actually be more "arrogant" and indeed "ruthless."[279] But Niebuhr is not content merely to target one social group or class. And he is aware that sin can pervade such systems as capitalism as well as other economic systems.[280] But he also cautions that "a too simple

[275] Stephen Ray, "Structural Sin," in *T&T Clark Companion to the Doctrine of Sin*, 423–424, emphasis original.
[276] Reinhold Niebuhr, *The Nature and Destiny of Man: A Christian Interpretation*, One Volume Edition (New York: Scribner, 1949), 179. Niebuhr himself is routinely castigated and used as an example of *insensitivity* to such concerns, but at various points he shows keen awareness of the issues.
[277] Niebuhr, *Nature and Destiny of Man*, 179.
[278] Niebuhr, *Nature and Destiny of Man*, 188.
[279] Niebuhr, *Nature and Destiny of Man*, 208.
[280] Niebuhr, *Nature and Destiny of Man*, 191.

radicalism does not recognize how quickly the poor, the weak, the despised of yesterday, may, on gaining a social victory over their detractors, exhibit the same arrogance and the same will-to-power which they abhorred in their opponents."[281]

The liberationist claims about social sin and structural evil are not free of criticism. In some treatments of "social sin" and "structural evil" by revisionist theologians we are left with the distinct impression that sin is only (or at least primarily) what the powerful *oppressors* do and the systems they create—as if such bifurcation is always so neat, tidy, and convenient and as if it were not also possible for the *oppressed* to be sinful too. But is it not the case that many people are both sinned against (through discrimination and oppression) and sinful in their actions toward others? Is it not possible for people who are underprivileged, marginalized, disadvantaged, and oppressed to marginalize and oppress others in turn? Does not this actually happen? Is not this what the Bible calls *sin*? And are not sinners held accountable for this sin? Does not the Bible clearly teach that *all* have sinned and fall short of the glory of God (Rom. 3:23)? Are we not told—and in no uncertain terms—that *no one* is righteous (Rom. 3:10)?

We should, then, be skeptical of any doctrine of sin that scapegoats some sinners while seeming to leave the rest untainted. At the same time, however, we should not assume that the sins of the oppressed and the sins of the oppressors take the same forms, or that they are somehow always or necessarily equally heinous. Nor, importantly, do we dare miss the valid and important points that are being made by revisionist and "Majority World" theologians. For it is unde-niable—from human history and experience as well as from Holy Writ—that the evil actions of powerful people in fact do shape social institutions. In turn, these same systems further foster and foment moral depravity and thus result in ever-increasing human suffering. As one particularly sobering example, we can see the impact of mass incarceration on the moral fiber of persons and societies. Consider these statistics about incarceration in the United States (as reported by William Placher):

> From the early twentieth century until the mid-1970s the United States impris-oned about 110 people for every 100,000 of population. The figure doubled in the late 1970s and 1980s, . . . so that today . . . about [600 out of every] 100,000 Americans are in [jail or] prisons. Comparable figures . . . would be 36 per 100,000 for Japan, from 50 to 120 for countries of Western Europe, 229 for the famous "police state" of Singapore, and 368 for South Africa at the height of the crisis before the change to majority rule.[282]

[281] Niebuhr, *Nature and Destiny of Man*, 226.
[282] William C. Placher, "Visiting Prisoners," in *The Blackwell Companion to Postmodern Theology*, ed. Graham Ward (London: Blackwell, 2001), 179. Although Placher's figures are dated, they suffice for illustration of the theological point.

Since Placher penned those words, the statistics have become even more stark. For as of 2012, the number had climbed to 750 per 100,000 (in the United States).[283]

Clearly, the United States incarcerates people at a stunningly high rate, and, just as clearly, this trend has grown across the twentieth and into the twenty-first centuries. Moreover, it is impossible to ignore how these matters are related to issues of race and ethnicity. As Placher notes, the ratio of black versus white males who are incarcerated is staggeringly lopsided, with the result that "more black men are in jail or prison than in college or university—in California, four times as many. Black males in the United States are incarcerated at four times the rate of black males under the white regime in South Africa."[284] In some cities in the United States, more than half of black males are either incarcerated, on probation or parole, or awaiting sentencing.[285]

So people—and when referring to "people" we should be aware that black males are overrepresented at an alarming rate—are incarcerated. They are punished. But all too often, this punishment itself produces deleterious effects, and these effects sadly encourage more and deeper sin. We can see this in the effects on the perpetrators themselves. Conditions in many prisons are deplorable, and the penal institutions are often unable or unwilling to provide adequate protection for the inmates.[286] Violence and aggression—including sexual violence—is commonplace, and it has disastrous effects on the inmates, who suffer mental health problems and who become ever more morally deformed (as well as more efficient in crime).[287] Moreover, these penal institutions often become what are effectively "crime schools" and fertile recruiting grounds for gangs.

We can also see the effects of this on communities.[288] When parents are taken to prison, children are left behind. Family ties are damaged, and cycles of poverty and accompanying despair are intensified. In such environments where there is little economic opportunity but ample opportunity to engage in criminal activity (some of which is enjoyable, some of which is lucrative, and some of which raises one's social standing in a community), where time behind bars is very normal and sometimes almost expected, where there is much despair and little hope, the cycle of sin and its effects is only strengthened and

---

[283] See Michelle Alexander, *The New Jim Crow: Mass Incarceration in the Age of Colorblindness* (New York: New Press, 2012), 6; and Peter K. Enns, *Incarceration Nation: How the United States Became the Most Punitive Democracy in the World* (Cambridge: Cambridge University Press, 2016).

[284] Placher, "Visiting Prisoners," 179.

[285] Placher, "Visiting Prisoners," 179.

[286] Cf. Atul Gawande, "Hell Hole," *The New Yorker*, March 30, 2009, 36–43.

[287] The threat of sexual violence is so well known and so deeply rooted that it has now become a tool in deterrence from crime. As Placher points out, the "Scared Straight" programs take teenaged boys "identified as potential troublemakers" to "prisons where inmates harangue them about how eagerly they will welcome such good looking young boys as sexual victims" ("Visiting Prisoners," 180).

[288] See Stephen Raphael and Michael A. Stroll, eds., *Do Prisons Make Us Safer? The Benefits and Costs of the Prison Boom* (New York: Russell Sage Foundation, 2009).

deepened. Meanwhile, others profit financially from the current penal system and are emboldened or encouraged to consider themselves and their communities to be morally superior.[289] So some people and communities have little incentive to work for change (and sometimes considerable incentive to oppose it), while others have little opportunity to bring about such change. Thus, again, the cycle is strengthened and deepened.[290]

Thus moral evil leads to further moral evil. It becomes institutionalized and embedded within the very fabric of the social order, and it is further supported by claims about truth and justice, good and evil. Indeed, even the concept of sin itself can be used to strengthen the hegemony that keeps oppressive evils in place. This is vividly illustrated in Harper Lee's classic *To Kill a Mockingbird*. Grace Merriweather relates to her friend Gertrude how she rightfully and successfully scolded her "help":

> Gertrude, I tell you there's nothing more distracting than a sulky darky. Their mouths go down to here. Just ruins your day to have one of 'em in the kitchen. You know what I said to my Sophy, Gertrude? I said, "Sophy," I said, "you simply are not being a Christian today. Jesus Christ never went around grumbling and complaining," and you know, it did her good. She took her eyes off that floor and said, "Nome, Miz Merriweather, Jesus never went around grumblin." I tell you, Gertrude, you never ought to let an opportunity to go by to witness for the Lord.[291]

While it indeed is true that sin is always *personal* and that *persons* sin, nonetheless it is also true that "sins give rise to social situations and institutions that are contrary to divine goodness. 'Structures of sin' are the expression and effect of personal sins. They lead their victims to do evil in their turn. In an analogous sense, they constitute a 'social sin.'"[292]

Beyond the current case study, this general malady infects sinful people more broadly.[293] Indeed, it seems that it does so *much* more broadly. Friedrich Nietzsche describes this general process very vividly in his discussion of "the will to power." He says that humans are capable of wielding anything and everything as an instrument by which to express their own self-interest and seize power. Thus claims to morality and truth are wielded as expressions of the will-to-power. Echoing Pontius Pilate's famous question, Nietzsche asks, "What is truth?" His answer: what we call "truth" is "a mobile army of metaphors, metonyms, and anthropomorphisms"; it is "that kind of error without

[289] See Eric Schlosser, "The Prison Industrial Complex," *The Atlantic* (December 1998): 51–77.
[290] Cf. Enns, *Incarceration Nation*, 7–10.
[291] Harper Lee, *To Kill a Mockingbird* (New York: HarperCollins, 1960), 265–266.
[292] *Catechism of the Catholic Church*, 457.
[293] For a brief but pointed discussion of how sin impacts relationships that involve money, race, sex, and gender, see Marguerite Shuster, *The Fall and Sin: What We Have Become as Sinners* (Grand Rapids, MI: Eerdmans, 2004), 149–158.

which a certain species of living cannot exist."[294] For "all that exists consists of interpretations," and what we call "truths" are "illusions that we have forgotten are illusions."[295] None of this is benign, for in reality it is undeniable that "knowledge" works "as an instrument of power."[296]

Although Nietzsche's rhetoric is bloated and his own anti-Christian proposals are hopeless, nonetheless he illustrates very vividly how claims to truth and goodness—and sometimes even doctrines of sin—are readily turned into mere expressions of the will-to-power that are in turn used for oppression. Taking a cue from Nietzsche, Michel Foucault works to expose the history of incarceration for what it often is: a subtle but powerful expression of the will-to-power.[297] This suspicion is expressed and expanded in Jean-Francois Lyotard's definition of "postmodernism": "simplifying to the extreme, I define postmodern as incredulity toward metanarratives."[298] Similarly, Karl Marx and Marx-inspired critical theorists offer incisive critique of how political and economic systems promote oppression and deepen injustice while claiming truth and moral authority.[299] What moderns such as Nietzsche and Marx along with "postmoderns" such as Foucault and Lyotard provide is an unwitting but uncannily penetrating phenomenology of the effects of sin. We need not take their prescriptive suggestions to be authoritative (and indeed we *should not*) to find their descriptions helpful. And at the end of the day, as Alvin Plantinga notes, we should not *need* to gain these insights from atheists.[300]

We can, however, benefit from the insights of liberation theologians (of various stripes). We need not endorse all their constructive moves to find valuable and penetrating insights in their criticisms and proposals. And at any rate, although all Christians should be grateful for the persistence of "liberation theologians" in pointing out these matters, we should not see it as merely "their" concern. After all, as we have seen, the prophets rail against such systems of injustice and oppression. And, as Christopher Ansberry observes, the Psalms offer vivid and powerful depictions of structural sin:

> This structural vision of sin contributes to the conceptual metaphor *sin is a power*. When despicable character types enjoy communal favour or occupy positions of power, . . . they oppress the weak, exploit those entrusted to their care, and breed communal corruption. This perspective on structural sin

---

[294] Cited in Anthony C. Thiselton, *Interpreting God and the Postmodern Self: On Meaning, Manipulation and Promise* (Grand Rapids, MI: Eerdmans, 1995), 5.
[295] Cited in Thiselton, *Interpreting God and the Postmodern Self*, 5.
[296] Cited in Thiselton, *Interpreting God and the Postmodern Self*, 6.
[297] See especially Michel Foucault, *Discipline and Punish: The Birth of the Prison*, trans. Alan Sheridan (New York: Vintage, 1977).
[298] Jean-Francois Lyotard, *The Postmodern Condition: A Report on Knowledge*, trans. Geoff Bennington and Brian Massumi (Minneapolis: University of Minnesota Press, 1984), xxiv.
[299] See the insightful work of Merold Westphal, *Suspicion and Faith: The Religious Uses of Modern Atheism* (New York: Fordham University Press, 1998).
[300] See Alvin Plantinga, *Warranted Christian Belief* (Oxford: Oxford University Press, 2000), 136n4.

serves as the backdrop of Psalm 73, where the wicked are depicted as a walking advertisement for pride, violence and oppression, for they are prosperous, healthy, wealthy, and at peace (Ps. 73:3–12). And this vision of structural sin is reiterated in Psalm 94, where the wicked prevail within the community, crush the people, and kill the widow, the stranger and the orphan (Ps. 94:3–6; cf. 146:7–9). As a power, sin's reach is not limited to the individual; it possesses the capacity to infiltrate the structures of the community and overpower its constituents.[301]

Scripture makes plain the sobering reality that corporate entities can be sinful (e.g., Rev. 2:1, 4; 2:12, 14–15; 2:18, 20; 3:1; 3:14–22). Moreover, it warns us that our struggle is "against principalities, against powers" (Eph. 6:12 KJV). Millard Erickson is correct to point out that Scripture portrays "the world" as sinful while holding corporate groups responsible for sinful actions.[302] There are valid and sobering insights here, and we must take them with absolute seriousness.

H. The "Seven Deadly Sins"

Christian theology has often thought about sin in terms of the "seven deadly sins." Bonaventure summarizes the basic idea. Actual sin "has one source, two roots, three incentives, and seven heads" (the capital sins).[303] The sole ultimate source of all actual sins is pride: "every sin, therefore, is born of pride, and tends to its full maturity and end in final impenitence."[304] The twin roots from which other sins stem are "fear that unduly restrains," and "love that unduly inflames."[305] The three incentives, as we see in 1 John, are "the lust of the flesh, the lust of the eyes, and the pride of life."[306] The seven capital sins are pride, envy, anger, sloth, covetousness, gluttony, and lust.[307] Thomas Aquinas adopts and defends the traditional account of the seven capital (sometimes referred to as "deadly") sins. Following Gregory the Great, he further divides these between "spiritual sins" and "carnal sins." He explains that these are called "capital" because the word is

> derived from *caput* (a head). Now the head, properly speaking, is that part of an animal's body, which is the principle and director of the whole animal. Hence, metaphorically speaking, every principle is called a head, and even men who direct and govern others are called heads. . . . In this way a capital vice is one from which other vices arise, chiefly by being their final cause. . . .

[301] Christopher Ansberry, "Writings," in *The T&T Clark Companion to the Doctrine of Sin*, 50–51.
[302] See further Millard Erickson, *Christian Theology*, 2nd ed. (Grand Rapids, MI: Baker Academic, 1998), 660–671.
[303] Bonaventure, *The Breviloquium* III.9.1, in *The Works of Bonaventure*, vol. 2 (Paterson, NJ: St. Anthony's Guild Press, 1963), 132.
[304] Bonaventure, *Breviloquium* III.11.5, in *Works*, vol. 2, 140.
[305] Bonaventure, *Breviloquium* III.9.1, in *Works*, vol. 2, 132.
[306] Bonaventure, *Breviloquium* III.9.1, in *Works*, vol. 2, 132.
[307] Bonaventure, *Breviloquium* III.9.1, in *Works*, vol. 2, 132.

Wherefore a capital vice is not only the principle of others, but is also their director, and, in a way, their leader.[308]

Like Bonaventure, Aquinas enumerates the capital sins as vainglory, envy, anger, sloth, covetousness, gluttony, and lust.[309]

The term "deadly sin" itself is not especially apt, for, as Aquinas himself recognizes, not all acts of vice amount to "mortal" sins.[310] Following Aquinas, Rebecca Konyndyk DeYoung suggests that a better label might be "capital vices" or "source vices," for such sins "serve as an ever-bubbling wellspring of many others."[311] As the *Catechism of the Catholic Church* explains, "[T]hey are called 'capital' because they engender other sins, other vices."[312] Traditionally, pride has often been seen as the ultimate source or fountain of all the other capital sins, and the others in turn give rise to all manner of actual sins. As DeYoung explains via appeal to an image common in medieval theology, "[W]e can think of pride as the root and trunk of a tree, which extends upward into seven main branches, each of which represents one capital vice. From those vices, in turn, grow many other branches, each of which bears poisonous fruit."[313] These seven "main branches," as noted, are vainglory, envy, sloth, avarice, wrath, lust, and gluttony.

Vainglory

Karl Barth speaks for much of the Christian tradition when he says that sin "in its totality is pride."[314] This pride takes expression in various ways, and chief among these is what has traditionally been called "vainglory." Vainglory is, in DeYoung's helpful summary, "the excessive and disordered desire for recognition and approval from others."[315] The desire to be recognized and appreciated as a person is not inherently or necessarily wrong; to the contrary, it is a concomitant of being made in God's image with a capacity to know and be known, to appreciate and be appreciated, to love and be loved.[316] But just as sin perverts or corrupts other good gifts from God, so also at this point it corrupts something that was given by God as a good gift. Proper and appropriate concern to be seen and known as one is—a creature made in God's image with inherent value and dignity—all too easily turns into the craven and idolatrous

---

[308] Aquinas, *ST* IaIIae, Q 84.3.

[309] Aquinas *ST* IaIIae, Q 84.4.

[310] See Rebecca Konyndyk DeYoung, *Glittering Vices: A New Look at the Seven Deadly Sins and Their Remedies* (Grand Rapids, MI: Brazos, 2009), 35.

[311] DeYoung, *Glittering Vices*, 33. Cf. Aquinas, *ST* IaIIae, Q 84.3.

[312] *Catechism of the Catholic Church*, 457.

[313] DeYoung, *Glittering Vices*, 33.

[314] Barth, *CD*, IV/1, 414.

[315] DeYoung, *Glittering Vices*, 60.

[316] Throughout this section, I am grateful for the insights of DeYoung (see *Glittering Vices*, 60–61); and DeYoung, *Vainglory: The Forgotten Vice* (Grand Rapids, MI: Eerdmans, 2014).

pursuit of flattery. All too often and all too easily, we love "the glory that comes from man more than the glory that comes from God" (John 12:43).

Vainglory is, in this sense, a profoundly *theological* vice. As human creatures, we are made to *glorify God*; we are made, that is, to receive and reflect God's glory as we know God and love God, as we delight in God and enjoy God, and also as we know and enjoy creation as *God's* creation.[317] In other words, vainglory is the exaltation of our own pursuit of glory over a proper concern for the glory of God. As John Piper and others have helpfully noted, Scripture consistently portrays God as being concerned with his own glory.[318] This is an important truth, but it must not be misunderstood.[319] For as Aquinas explains, God's concern for his own glory is not motivated by a concern for his own stature, prestige, or well-being for its own sake. Indeed, given the truth of the doctrine of divine aseity, it could not be otherwise. Thus it "is therefore evident that God seeks glory, not for His own sake, but for ours."[320]

As Kelsey points out, sin is "in contrast to the glory of God."[321] Vainglory is the corruption and perversion of this proper concern for our enjoyment of God's glory as it is made fully alive in us.[322] Instead of delighting in God first and foremost, and thus also truly delighting in our place in his creation and providence accordingly, we "[exchange] the glory of the immortal God" (Rom. 1:23) for simulacra that are pathetic and empty. More specifically, it is a theological vice that is known most fully in contrast with Christ. When seen in contrast to Jesus, as Barth notes, "pride is a very feeble word" to describe our sin; "the correct word is perhaps megalomania."[323] For in direct contrast to our arrogance, God has "condescended" by humbling himself and becoming obedient (Phil. 2:5–11).[324] In starkest contrast to our megalomania, God "is not egotistic in this revelation and defense of His own honour and glory, nor is He concerned about the satisfaction of His own needs."[325]

Sin as pride or vainglory takes expression in various ways. Niebuhr explains how this pride is to be analyzed in three "forms": pride of power, pride of knowledge, and pride of virtue or self-righteousness (which takes particularly nasty expression in spiritual pride).[326] It takes form in individuals and in

---

[317] For insightful discussion, see DeYoung, *Glittering Vices*, 65–67.
[318] John Piper, *God's Passion for His Glory* (Wheaton, IL: Crossway, 1998).
[319] On popular and important misunderstandings, see Thomas H. McCall, "I Believe in Divine Sovereignty," *TJ* (2008): 205–226; John Piper, "I Believe in God's Self-Sufficiency," *TJ* (2008): 227–234; Thomas H. McCall, "We Believe in God's Sovereign Goodness," *TJ* (2008): 235–246.
[320] Aquinas, *ST* IIaIIae, Q 132.1.
[321] Kelsey, *Eccentric Existence*, 1:309.
[322] As Irenaeus put it, *Gloria Dei vivens homo*—"the glory of God is man fully alive" (*Adversus Haereses* 4.20.7).
[323] Barth, *CD*, IV/1, 437.
[324] Barth, *CD*, IV/1, 437.
[325] Barth, *CD*, IV/1, 452.
[326] Reinhold Niebuhr, *The Nature and Destiny of Man, Volume 1: Human Nature* (New York: Scribner, 1941), 188.

groups.[327] It includes both "vertical" dimensions (as rebellion against God) and "horizontal" planes (as injustice); through all, it is an expression of the will-to-power.[328]

Vainglory never satisfies—at least not deeply, and at least not for long. We find ourselves craving the praise and approval of others, and we work hard to receive it. But it cannot really satisfy. We think that the one who praised us either knows too little or too much. We worry when we finally receive the praise and adulation, for we cannot be assured that it is sincere rather than conniving and selfish. Or we wonder why we didn't get more recognition and credit. We worry about the time that someone else will take the spotlight from us. Or we fret over the possibility that the expectations are now so high that we cannot meet them again; we get nervous that we will be "found out" and exposed as one-hit wonders or fraudulent tricksters. We never find the approval and flattery of mere mortals to be finally fulfilling. Indeed, we *cannot* be finally satisfied by it because we are made for something much greater and richer and deeper, and God loves us too much to let us be truly and finally satisfied by the praise and approval of mere mortals. But when we give ourselves over to it, we are easily sucked into the maelstrom. We crave approval and even flattery, and we will engage in all manner of deceitful and self-serving behavior to get it. Thus it presents itself in a wide range of symptoms. For some people, it fosters dishonesty. For some, it pulls them into webs of intrigue and deception. The moral theologians of the Christian tradition have often noticed that this is a vice that can be particularly tempting for *Christians* who earnestly and honestly desire to be holy. For, oddly enough, the temptation to *appear* holy and to *look* godly can come along with a genuine desire to *be* holy.[329] Or, alternatively, we want people to know how *unholy* we are—but so that they will recognize our *humility*. As DeYoung reminds us, "[I]t is difficult to escape vainglory, for what you do to rid yourself of it becomes for you a new source of vainglory."[330] Moreover, vainglory fosters all manner of other sins, especially disobedience, boastfulness, hypocrisy, contention, obstinacy, and discord.[331]

Such ridiculous vainglory also leaves us looking pathetic and silly. Pride leaves us puffed up with self-importance and bloated with self-desire. Barth recognizes that

> [m]an only wants to judge. He thinks he sits on a high throne, but in reality he sits only on a child's stool, blowing his little trumpet, cracking his little whip, pointing with frightful seriousness his little finger, while all the time nothing

---

[327] Niebuhr is especially worried about "group pride": "the group is more arrogant, hypocritical, self-centered, and ruthless in the pursuit of its ends than the individual" (*Nature and Destiny of Man, Volume 1*, 208).
[328] See further Niebuhr, *Nature and Destiny of Man, Volume 1*, 179.
[329] See DeYoung, *Glittering Vices*, 69–70.
[330] DeYoung, *Glittering Vices*, 71. DeYoung credits Evagrius Ponticus, a fourth-century monk, for this insight.
[331] Aquinas, *ST* IIaIIae, Q 133.5.

happens that really matters. He can only play the judge. He is only a dilet-
tante, a blunderer, in his attempt to distinguish between good and evil, right
and wrong, acting as though he really had the capacity to do it. He can only
pretend to himself and others . . .[332]

But while sin is strong, grace is stronger yet. By God's grace, we can find
our true glory by loving and glorifying God with all our heart, mind, soul,
and strength. When that happens, as DeYoung points out, we "radiate God's
beauty and goodness in the world, drawing others to that glory, a glory that
transcends the person and his or her act" of magnanimity.[333] "With God all
things are possible" (Matt. 19:26).

Envy

Envy has also been considered a "capital vice." Like the other deadly sins or
capital vices, it is rooted in distrust of God and prideful rebellion against our
Creator. At base, it is the rejection of divine providence. And it is manifested
in all manner of ways.

Envy takes a variety of forms, and it is closely related to other vicious
appetites and affections. Consumed by envy, we engage in all sorts of nefari-
ous and malicious actions: envy produces and encourages everything from
gossip to theft and destruction of property. It results especially in *schaden-
freude* and hatred.[334] People infected with envy often incite bad feelings
against their perceived rivals, point out the faults of others, and delight in
criticizing them.

Sloth

DeYoung explains that sloth is "apathy—comfortable indifference to duty and
neglect of other human beings' needs." It is sin "not merely because it makes us
lazy, but because of the lack of love that lies behind our laziness."[335] Ultimately,
as Thomas Aquinas puts it, it is "aversion to the divine good in us."[336] It is the
refusal to accept what we are created and called to be. Accordingly, it is not
merely "being lazy" in the stereotypical sense that is addressed in Proverbs
("Go to the ant, O sluggard"; Prov. 6:6), although of course it is that too. It is
any activity—even very energetic activity—that works for anything other than
the reception and extension of the love for which we are made. Barth adds that
sloth is the refusal to accept not only our place in the created order but also the

[332] Barth, *CD*, IV/1, 446.
[333] DeYoung, *Glittering Vices*, 65.
[334] See especially the insightful study of Timothy Perrine and Kevin Timpe, "Envy and Its Discontents," in *Virtues and Their Vices*, ed. Kevin Timpe and Craig A. Boyd (Oxford: Oxford University Press, 2014), 225–244.
[335] DeYoung, *Glittering Vices*, 81.
[336] Aquinas, cited in DeYoung, *Glittering Vices*, 85.

redemption provided in Christ. It is the "rejection of the outstretched hand of God, the refusal of His grace."[337] For Barth, sloth is disobedience stemming from unbelief, and it takes several forms: stupidity, inhumanity, dissipation, and inordinate care about trivialities.[338]

John Owen observes how sloth works to weaken and drain our spiritual vitality, and he makes this connection with reference to the nuptial depiction of our relation to the triune God in Scripture. Sin, he says, often "works by sloth and negligence," and "[s]o it was with the spouse in the Song of Solomon (5:2); Christ calls unto her (v. 1) with a marvelous loving and gracious invitation unto communion with himself. She who had formerly been ravished at the first hearing of that joyful sound, being now under the power of sloth and carnal ease, returns a sorry excusing answer to his call, which ended in her own signal loss and sorrow."[339]

AVARICE OR GREED

Greed is similar to the other vices in many respects. It stems from a prideful distrust of God's good purposes for us and his providence over us. It expresses itself in ambition for personal gain that is completely out of kilter. While there may be a proper place for godly ambition (it can be the proper acceptance of our vocation as God's creatures made in God's image with a mandate from him), when it turns vicious it craves power and the perceived benefits of that power: status, fame, recognition, influence, and possessions.

Scripture repeatedly warns against greed: the "love of money is a root of all kinds of evils" (1 Tim. 6:10). The accumulation of financial resources itself is not inherently sinful, but the inordinate desire for it clearly is. Thomas Aquinas defines greed as "an excessive love of or desire for money or any possession money can buy."[340] It is a condition of the heart, and of course it can be found in people who do have considerable financial wealth; but it can also be found in those who do not have such wealth but crave it.

Greed is no respecter of persons. DeYoung captures well the extent of its reach:

> The greedy person's attachment to wealth can wear many faces—an overflowing shopping cart or a single purchase, a stock portfolio that is aggressive or conservative, a wallet full of credit cards or a safety deposit box with a few carefully guarded treasures, a garage full of expensive cars or a closet jammed full of "great deals." It can affect the young, the old, and everyone in between.

[337] Barth, CD, IV/2, 408.
[338] Barth, CD, IV/2, 404–405, 495. More traditional accounts include malice, spite, faint-heartedness, despair, sluggishness in regard to commandments, as well as general laziness (e.g., Aquinas, ST IIaIIae, Q 35.4).
[339] John Owen, Overcoming Sin and Temptation, ed. Kelly M. Kapic and Justin Taylor (Wheaton, IL: Crossway, 2006), 376.
[340] Aquinas, cited in DeYoung, Glittering Vices, 100.

In all of its varied expressions, however, greed is a perverted love. Its profile has disordered desire written all over it.[341]

As "a root of all kinds of evils" (1 Tim. 6:10), greed is a "source sin." It funds many other disordered affections and fuels all manner of sinful actions. Acts of oppression and injustice flow from this root, and they deserve and incur fearsome consequences. It is overcome only by grace, and this grace is expressed in liberality.[342]

WRATH

Anger itself is not sinful—at least not inherently or necessarily so. Paul tells us to be angry without sin (Eph. 4:26), so we know that anger itself is not inherently sinful. Indeed, God is repeatedly said to be angry, and there are situations where human anger reflects God's own holiness and justice.[343] However, anger also gives opening to sin, and it often is expressed in sinful ways. We are, of course, all too aware that anger is often expressed in sinful ways. It seems that there are two basic concerns: anger can be sinful as it is wrongly motivated and wrongly directed, and even anger that is righteously motivated can all too easily lead to sin and exhibit itself in sinful expressions. As DeYoung says, "[A]nger can go wrong in its target and in the manner of its expression."[344] So "when anger has the wrong object, *what* we are angry about is inappropriate," while in the second case anger that may be righteously motivated issues in inappropriate ways and thus is concerned with *how* we are angry.[345] In the first instance we are often overly angered by trivialities that annoy us, all the while overlooking the rank idolatry and grave injustice that is all around us and perhaps even within us. In the second instance we may be righteously indignant against evil and injustice but fail to express that wrath in appropriate and godly ways. In such cases the wrath may be "irrationally expressed or wildly disproportionate," and, "[e]ven if we have a legitimate grievance, we can deal with it in destructive and disastrous ways."[346] Indeed, the tendency toward irrationality in moments of anger poses a special threat, and it may blind us to our own sinfulness. As DeYoung says, anger "has a wily way of duping our reasoning powers to justify itself," for "[w]rath is self-promoting—but in a dressed-up, self-righteous way. . . . With the banner of self-righteousness over us, anger can storm in and take over by force."[347] It is no wonder, then, that Paul lists anger in

---

[341] DeYoung, *Glittering Vices*, 100–101.
[342] See Andrew Pinsent, "Avarice and Liberality," in *Virtues and Their Vices*, 157–175.
[343] Zac Cogley helpfully illustrates this point with reference to the righteous wrath of Frederick Douglass and Martin Luther King Jr. ("A Study of Virtuous and Vicious Anger," in *Virtues and Their Vices*, 199–224).
[344] DeYoung, *Glittering Vices*, 123.
[345] DeYoung, *Glittering Vices*, 123.
[346] DeYoung, *Glittering Vices*, 124.
[347] DeYoung, *Glittering Vices*, 123.

his vice lists. Right alongside "sexual immorality, impurity, passion, evil desire, and covetousness, which is idolatry," anger and wrath are said to characterize the former life lived *outside* of union with Christ, and we are called to "put away" such vices (Col. 3:5–8). And he warns that "fits of anger" are opposed to the fruits of the Spirit and that "those who do such things will not inherit the kingdom of God" (Gal. 5:20–21).

GLUTTONY

Gluttony has also earned a place as a "source" or "capital" sin. Again, we see that it is a disordered affection. As C. S. Lewis put it, "badness is only spoiled goodness."[348] As DeYoung points out, gluttony has often been either ignored or oversimplified and thus misunderstood. It cannot be reduced to caloric intake or "body mass index," for it "is not first of all about overeating or being overweight."[349] Gluttony takes many forms and manifestations; while the most obvious instance of it concerns the abuse of food, it can take other forms as well.[350] Fundamentally, it is inordinate desire for the pleasures of God's good creation; it is valuing and cherishing—and *wanting*—such created goods above and beyond their proper place. "What's vicious about gluttony is that these pleasures dominate everything else that's important. This vice degrades us into being mere pleasure seekers. This is what gluttony is really all about."[351]

Gluttony is a "source" or "root" of many other sins. This disordered affection finds expression in ways that bring harm rather than good to our neighbor. These sins have in common the distrust that questions God's intentions for us, and they have in common the pride that assumes that we know better than God what is best for us. Thus Paul urges the followers of Jesus not to be "dominated" by their desires—even by their desires for what God has created and called good (e.g., 1 Cor. 6:12). Those whose "god is their belly," on the other hand, face their "end," which is "destruction" (Phil. 3:19).

LUST

Similarly, lust functions as a "source" or "root" of many other sins. As Colleen McCluskey points out, many secular ethical paradigms have completely flipped the moral script and now see chastity as a vice and lust as a virtue.[352] Considered theologically, however, once more we see lust as a disordered affection; it is the twisting and perversion of what God made and ordained as a

---

[348] Lewis, *Mere Christianity*, 44.
[349] DeYoung, *Glittering Vices*, 140.
[350] See further Robert B. Kruschwitz, "Gluttony and Abstinence," in *Virtues and Their Vices*, 137–155.
[351] DeYoung, *Glittering Vices*, 141.
[352] Colleen McCluskey, "Lust and Chastity," in *Virtues and Their Vices*, 115–135. Lisa Frank observes that "lust has come to be regarded as a desirable attribute for people of all ages and social positions" ("The Evolution of the Seven Deadly Sins: From God to the Simpsons," *Journal of Popular Culture* [2001]: 101).

creational good. It is desire run amok—more precisely, it is *sexual* desire gone bad. Lust is rightly considered a "capital" or "source" sin because it leads to so many other acts of transgression. Biblically, this is illustrated in David's encounter with Bathsheba and the aftermath of their affair (2 Samuel 11–12).[353] Ultimately, lust is wrong not because it cares or desires too much but because it desires too little. More precisely, it desires the most important things too little. It is sin as it trades grateful trust in the commands that express God's holy love for misplaced trust in our replacements—and thus violates both the command to love God with all our being and the command to love our neighbors as ourselves. As Frederick Buechner puts it, "Sex is sinful to the degree that . . . it unites bodies but leaves the lives inside them hungrier and more alone than before."[354]

---

[353] As noted by DeYoung, *Glittering Vices*, 170.
[354] Frederick Buechner, *Wishful Thinking: A Seeker's ABC* (New York: HarperOne, 1993), cited in DeYoung, *Glittering Vices*, 159.

CHAPTER

SIX

"THE WAGES OF SIN":
THE RESULTS OF SIN

To this point we have noted that sin has fearsome consequences. It is now time for a more sustained look at these consequences.

I. ENSLAVEMENT AND DEBILITY

Sin enslaves us. Drawing upon a vast OT background that likens sin to slavery or describes it as such, Paul describes the position of the unregenerate person as one who is enslaved. He draws a sharp contrast between those who belong to Christ and those who do not. Being united to Christ in his resurrection means that we are "no longer . . . enslaved to sin" (Rom. 6:6), and thus the one who has died and risen in union with Christ "has been set free from sin" (v. 7). For those who have been brought "from death to life," sin no longer has "dominion over" them (vv. 13–14). This freedom and life in Christ is juxtaposed sharply against Paul's portrayal of the unregenerate person:

> I am of the flesh, sold under sin. For I do not understand my own actions. For I do not do what I want, but I do the very thing I hate. Now if I do what I do not want, I agree with the law, that it is good. So now it is no longer I who do it, but sin that dwells within me. For I know that nothing good dwells in me, that is, in my flesh. For I have the desire to do what is right, but not the ability to carry it out. For I do not do the good I want, but the evil I do not want is what I keep on doing. Now if I do what I do not want, it is no longer I who do it, but sin that dwells within me.
>
> So I find it to be a law that when I want to do right, evil lies close at hand. For I delight in the law of God, in my inner being, but I see in my members another law waging war against the law of my mind and making me captive to the law of sin that dwells in my members. Wretched man that I am! Who will deliver me from this body of death? (Rom. 7:14–24)

A. Augustine and the Battle with "Pelagianism": Learning from Historical Theology

Augustine is justly famous for his development of the Christian doctrine of sin. Indeed, as Jesse Couenhoven puts it, "Augustine is known as *the* great theologian of sin."[1] Augustine was faced with stiff challenges from two directions: Manichaeism and Pelagianism. The early decades of the fifth century brought challenges from a very different direction than Augustine had previously faced. Where the challenge of Manichaeism denied the goodness of creation, other perspectives raised challenges from another angle; the view that has come to be known as "Pelagianism" questioned the meaning and importance of the fall and original sin. Historians argue that there is no monolithic entity called "Pelagianism," and Gerald Bonner says that "we can no longer think of the Pelagians as constituting a party with a rigidly-defined doctrinal system but rather as a mixed group, united by certain theological principles."[2] Rather than an overt attempt to concoct heresy, Pelagianism is likely better seen as a "reforming movement in the corrupt world of the later Roman empire."[3] Early in the controversy, Augustine himself refers to Pelagius as a "good and praiseworthy man" (at least by reputation).[4] Nonetheless, the theological movement carried forward by Pelagius, Coelestius, Julian of Eclanum, and others raised the ire of many theologians and resulted in important and extended controversy.

Pelagius, a British monk who arrived in Rome in the late fourth century, was repulsed when he encountered Augustine's doctrine of human sin. Augustine's (developing) doctrine of original sin included both the conviction that we are intimately related to the sin of Adam and that Adam's sin has left us utterly incapable of moral progress or salvation apart from the radical intervention of divine grace. Pelagius was disturbed by this teaching. J. N. D. Kelly notes that "the assumption that man could not help sinning seemed to him an insult to his Creator."[5] Rejecting the doctrine of original sin, Pelagius proposed an alternative. At the center of this theology is a commitment to human freedom, and the Pelagians use Augustine's own (earlier) arguments in support of their view. As Eugene TeSelle notes, "Pelagius and his followers were able to quote Augustine against Augustine, citing his early anti-Manichaean writings and charging that he had reverted to their position with his new emphasis on original sin

---

[1] Jesse Couenhoven, "Augustine," in *T&T Clark Companion to the Doctrine of Sin*, ed. Keith L. Johnson and David Lauber (New York: Bloomsbury T&T Clark, 2016), 181, emphasis original.

[2] Gerald Bonner, *God's Decree and Man's Destiny: Studies on the Thought of Augustine of Hippo* (London: Variorum, 1987), 31. Cf. Mathijs Lamberigts, "Pelagius and Pelagians," in *The Oxford Handbook of Early Christian Studies*, ed. Susan Ashbrook Harvey and David G. Hunter (Oxford: Oxford University Press, 2008), 273. There are scholarly debates about what properly constitutes the body of Pelagian writings, but see *The Letters of Pelagius and His Followers*, ed. B. R. Rees (Suffolk, UK: Boydell, 1991).

[3] Gerald Bonner, *St. Augustine of Hippo* (Norwich, UK: Canterbury, 2002), 353.

[4] Augustine, *De peccatorum meritis et remissione* III.5 (PL 44:189; NPNF¹ 5:70).

[5] J. N. D. Kelly, *Early Christian Doctrines*, rev. ed. (New York: HarperCollins, 1978), 357.

and the bondage of the will (Julian of Eclanum routinely referred to him as 'the Manichaean')."[6] B. R. Rees concurs; he observes that "the very arguments for man's responsibility, exercised by use of his free will, which Augustine had deployed against the Manichees, were now being adapted by Pelagius to suit his own case that man had the power to save himself."[7]

But what does Pelagius mean by "free will"? Kelly points out that Pelagius's view insists that there are three features of human agency: the power or ability to do things (*posse*), the will (*velle*), and "the realization" (*esse*).[8] The ability itself comes from God (so humans are not completely "autonomous"), but the will itself is firmly in the control of the human agent, and what we do with that will and power to accomplish things is completely up to the agent. Pelagius's concerns, however, were not primarily metaphysical; really they are theological and even practical. Harold O. J. Brown observes that Pelagius was "concerned to show that it was possible to lead a life of moral responsibility, pleasing to God; at the same time, he denounced the pessimistic, otherworldly dualism of the Manichaean movement to which Augustine was once attached and which he never seems entirely to have outgrown."[9]

We can see several important features of Pelagian theology. First, as Bonner observes, "the difference between Augustinian and Pelagian views of human choice was determined by their attitudes to Adam's primal sin and its effects upon his descendants. The Pelagians denied the existence of any transmission of Adam's guilt," and they went even further in denying any residual and debilitating impact.[10] Kelly notes that "Pelagius rejects the idea that man's will has any intrinsic bias in favour of wrong-doing as a result of the Fall."[11] TeSelle says that "what we know as Pelagianism" was really a commitment to the view that "punishment is only for individual sins" and to the notion that "sinful acts cannot affect human nature."[12] So while Augustine is convinced that Adam's sin leaves us both corrupt and guilty, Pelagius denies that "Adam's sin injured his descendants, or that there was any transmission of his fault in consequence of his transgression."[13] Pelagius's colleague and defender Coelestius puts it

[6] Eugene TeSelle, *Augustine* (Nashville: Abingdon, 2006), 37. See also Eugene TeSelle, "The Background: Augustine and the Pelagian Controversy," in *Grace for Grace: The Debates after Augustine and Pelagius*, ed. Alexander Y. Hwang, Brian J. Matz, and Augustine Casiday (Washington, DC: Catholic University of America Press, 2014), 1–13. See further Carol Harrison, *Rethinking Augustine's Early Theology: An Argument for Continuity* (Oxford: Oxford University Press, 2006), 280–287; and Jason David BeDuhn, *Augustine's Manichaean Dilemma*, 2 vols. (Philadelphia: University of Pennsylvania Press, 2010).

[7] B. R. Rees, *Pelagius: A Reluctant Heretic* (Suffolk, UK: Boydell, 1988), 15.

[8] Kelly, *Early Christian Doctrines*, 358. Cf. Augustine, *De gratia Christi et de peccato originali* I.4–5 (PL 44:362; NPNF[1] 5:218–219).

[9] Harold O. J. Brown, *Heresies: Heresy and Orthodoxy in the History of the Church* (Peabody, MA: Hendrickson, 1988), 201.

[10] Gerald Bonner, *Freedom and Necessity: St. Augustine's Teaching on Divine Power and Human Freedom* (Washington, DC: Catholic University of America Press, 2007), 67.

[11] Kelly, *Early Christian Doctrines*, 358.

[12] TeSelle, *Augustine*, 39.

[13] Bonner, *St. Augustine of Hippo*, 319.

this way: "Adam's sin injured only Adam himself, and not the human race; and . . . infants at their birth are in the same state that Adam was before his transgression."[14] To suggest anything else, he is sure, is to fall back into a kind of Manichaeism. Each infant comes into the world with a soul freshly made by God. Accordingly, it cannot be tainted with sin; otherwise, God would be the author of sin.

Second, Pelagius "equally resists the suggestion that there can be any special pressure on man's will to choose the good."[15] Such special pressure would remove the moral responsibility of the agent, and it would mean that he cannot truly gain merit for what he accomplishes. Accordingly, neither can there be any "special pressure" due to enslavement of that will: "the strongest Pelagian argument is that a just God will not hold individuals guilty of sins which they were powerless to avoid."[16] Thus Bonner concludes that there is a "fundamental difference" on this point: "for the Pelagians, man's nature remained fundamentally sound; for Augustine it had been corrupted to a degree which made human beings helpless of themselves to help themselves . . ."[17]

Given this emphasis on human freedom, we might then reasonably wonder what place grace might have in Pelagius's system. This consideration brings us to the third point: for Pelagius, the doctrine of grace is to be understood with respect to what God has done in making it possible for us to live sinlessly. Grace involves these elements:

> (a) free will itself, or the possibility of not sinning with which God endowed us at our creation; (b) the revelation, through reason, of God's law, instructing us what we should do and holding out eternal sanctions; and (c), since this has become obscured through evil custom, the law of Moses and the teaching and example of Christ.[18]

So to the charge that Pelagianism has no room for a doctrine of grace, Pelagius would respond by arguing that grace is not only real and present but also even necessary for salvation. But what does it mean to affirm the need for grace? For Pelagius, we are to understand grace in this way: without free will and the revelation of God's requirements (through reason) there would be no possibility of doing the right thing. Moreover, God has given even more grace by providing us with the law of Moses; here we have spelled out for us what we should have known through the revelation of reason. Finally, God has been gracious to us by offering up Jesus Christ as the full and complete revelation; by the teachings

---

14 Augustine, *De gratia Christi et de peccato originali* II.2 (PL 44:386; *NPNF*[1] 5:237).
15 Kelly, *Early Christian Doctrines*, 359.
16 Bonner, *Freedom and Necessity*, 90.
17 Bonner, *Freedom and Necessity*, 107.
18 Kelly, *Early Christian Doctrines*, 359. Cf. Lamberigts, "Pelagius and Pelagians," 265; and Robert F. Evans, *Pelagius: Inquiries and Reappraisals* (New York: Seabury, 1968), 95, 111.

of Christ we are instructed in righteousness, and by the example of Christ we see that righteousness can be lived out in fullness.

And, Pelagius insists, we really can—and *must*—live lives of true holiness and sinlessness that are truly pleasing to God. According to what Kelly calls "Pelagius's austere doctrine of *impeccantia*," the Christian both *can* and *must* fulfill the whole law.[19] He quotes Pelagius as saying that "a Christian is he who is one not in word but in deed, who imitates and follows Christ in everything, who is holy, innocent, unsoiled, blameless, in whose heart there is no malice but only piety and goodness."[20]

Augustine addressed the cluster of theological issues surrounding the controversy with Pelagianism in several treatises of various length and density.[21] Two early works (c. 412) dealt with the forgiveness of sins and the baptism of infants. The Pelagians insist both that human nature is unchanged by Adam's sin and that no one is guilty for what Adam did, for our guilt accrues only to the sins that *we* commit. Accordingly, no infant is sinful or guilty, for infants are neither guilty for what Adam did nor guilty for sins of their own when they have not yet done anything wrong. As Augustine describes their view, the Pelagians hold that "actual sin has not been transmitted from the first man to others by natural descent," and thus they "refuse to believe that in infants original sin is remitted through baptism, for they contend that no such original sin exists at all in people by their birth."[22] Augustine, on the other hand, is convinced that while sin is contrary to nature, it has corrupted human nature and wrought disastrous results on the entire human race (and indeed on all creation).[23] He insists forcefully that infants are sinners from conception and are saved only by baptism.[24] He recognizes the important distinction between original sin and actual sins; while these infants are not guilty of actual sins, they are nevertheless guilty of original sin.[25] What happens to those poor infants who die before they may be baptized? For Augustine, such a tragic occurrence is a sure sign of their reprobation; clearly, they are not among those who are predestined to life everlasting. He will allow that they are "in the mildest condemnation of all," but make no mistake: they suffer eternal damnation.[26] Those infants who do benefit from baptism, however, are cleansed and healed of the guilt of original sin.[27]

Augustine likewise insists that grace is utterly necessary. Grace, he explains,

---

[19] Kelly, *Early Christian Doctrines*, 360.
[20] Kelly, *Early Christian Doctrines*, 360.
[21] For a helpful analysis of Augustine's understanding of "Pelagianism," see Dominic Keech, *The Anti-Pelagian Christology of Augustine of Hippo, 396–430* (Oxford: Oxford University Press, 2012), 37–43.
[22] Augustine, *De peccatorum* I.9 (PL 44:114; NPNF¹ 5:18).
[23] Augustine, *De spiritu et littera* I.27 (PL 44:229; NPNF¹ 5:103).
[24] E.g., Augustine, *De peccatorum* II.43 (PL 44:177; NPNF¹ 5:62).
[25] Augustine, *De peccatorum* I.11, I.16, I.64 (PL 44:115–116, 118, 147; NPNF¹ 5:19, 21, 41).
[26] Augustine, *De peccatorum* I.21 (PL 44:120; NPNF¹ 5:23).
[27] Augustine, *De peccatorum* I.24 (PL 44:122–123; NPNF1 5:24).

is like light to the eye. Without light, we simply cannot see. But if we close our eyes, we are at fault for not being able to see.[28] Accordingly, both God's grace (which precedes and enables) and the exertion of the human will (which follows and cooperates) are necessary for salvation.[29] What can such grace accomplish in salvation? Augustine's view is remarkably optimistic; he allows that it is "possible for a man to be in this life without sin" by "the grace of God and man's own free will."[30] But we must also admit, he insists, that every person living indeed *has* sinned.[31] And the reason for this failure is plain: it is due to the abuse of our God-given free will.[32] Sin comes from pride, and we are sinners by virtue of our relation to Adam.[33] Salvation, on the other hand, comes from Christ in his humiliation.[34] And Augustine is convinced that this salvation indeed is glorious and beautiful.

Augustine is convinced that sin is contrary to nature and corrupts the human nature that God has created and called *good*. He also denies that sin has completely destroyed the *imago dei*.[35] Notable here is his insistence on the reality of free will: "Do we then by grace make void free will? God forbid! Nay, rather we establish free will."[36] What does Augustine mean by "free will" at this point? Does he continue to hold to his earlier (and sharply anti-Manichaean) views, or does he now embrace some form of "compatibilism"? Interestingly, Augustine opposes freedom to necessity here, for "when the ability is given, surely no necessity is imposed."[37] He denies that all human volition is determined by God: "nowhere, however, in Holy Scripture do we find such an assertion as 'There is no volition (*voluntas*) but comes from God.' And rightly is it not so written, because it is not true: otherwise God would be the author even of sins (which Heaven forbid!), if there is no volition except what comes from Him."[38] Augustine describes the free will which we have received from God as a "power, as can either incline towards faith, or turn towards unbelief," and he insists that when unbelievers reject the gospel they do so "contrary to the will of God," who truly does want "all to be saved."[39] When we abuse our freedom of the will and put it to evil use, we do not somehow undermine or overpower God's sovereignty, but we in fact do what is contrary to God's will and bring destruction upon ourselves. But when our wills are freed by grace and con-

---

[28] Augustine, *De peccatorum* II.5 (PL 44:153–154; *NPNF1* 5:45–46).
[29] Augustine, *De peccatorum* II.6 (PL 44:154–155; *NPNF1* 5:46).
[30] Augustine, *De peccatorum* II.7 (PL 44:155; *NPNF1* 5:46). Cf. *De Spiritu* 66 (*NPNF1* 5:113).
[31] Augustine, *De peccatorum* II.8 (PL 44:156; *NPNF1* 5:47).
[32] Augustine, *De peccatorum* II.26 (PL 44:167; *NPNF1* 5:55).
[33] Augustine, *De peccatorum* II.33 (PL 44:170; *NPNF1* 5:57).
[34] Augustine, *De peccatorum* II.38 (PL 44:174–175; *NPNF1* 5:59–60).
[35] Augustine, *De Spiritu* 48 (PL 44:230; *NPNF1* 5:103).
[36] Augustine, *De Spiritu* 52 (PL 44:233; *NPNF1* 5:106). "*Liberum ergo arbitrium evacuamus per gratiam? Absit.*"
[37] Augustine, *De Spiritu* 54 (PL 44:235; *NPNF1* 5:107). "*Sed contra potestas datur, non necessitas utique imponitur.*"
[38] Augustine, *De Spiritu* 54 (PL 44:235; *NPNF1* 5:107).
[39] Augustine, *De Spiritu* 58 (PL 44:238; *NPNF1* 5:109).

joined to God's will, it is possible to "love God with all our heart, mind, soul, and strength," and we can reach the place where sin no longer reigns and has dominion over us.

Within a few years (c. 415–418), Augustine was pressed to clarify further the proper relationship between nature, sin, and grace. Faced with charges that he was promoting Manichaeism, he insists—against the Manichaeans—that human nature "was created at first faultless [*inculpata*] and without any sin."[40] Augustine agrees with Pelagius that "sin is not a substance," and he agrees further that sin proceeds from the wrong use of free will.[41] As Augustine puts it, "Who does not know that man was made whole and faultless, and endowed with a free will and a free ability to lead a holy life?"[42] Sin is not natural, nor is it part of human nature per se. It was "not contracted from [the] blameless Creator"—instead, it came from the abuse of "free will [*libero arbitrio*]."[43] Sin has, however, infected human nature so that it impacts all humans and renders everyone, adults and infants alike, both helpless and guilty.[44]

Thus grace is absolutely necessary for salvation.[45] For "if Christ did not die in vain, then human nature cannot by any means be justified and redeemed, from God's most righteous wrath—in a word, from punishment—except by faith and the sacrament of the blood of Christ."[46] But Augustine is insistent throughout that grace is utterly *prevenient* (*praevenit*).[47] Grace does for us what we cannot do for ourselves; God saves by grace. Augustine employs a range of images for the salvation and restoration of the human nature that was created good by God but that has fallen into the grip of sin. God "spiritually heals the sick and raises the dead" as well as "justifies the ungodly."[48] This grace restores our ability to respond properly to God's overtures and to cooperate with God's good purposes.[49]

This grace restores our nature, indeed, to holiness of heart and life. God "heals us not only that He may blot out the sin which we have committed, but, furthermore, that He may enable us even to avoid sinning."[50] Does this mean that Augustine thinks that sinlessness is a possibility; is he then not a "perfectionist"? Augustine clears away the notion that sinlessness would amount to equality with God, and he further insists that "even if we cannot live here

---

[40] Augustine, *De natura et gratia ad Timasium et Jacobum contra Pelagium* 3 (PL 44:249; NPNF¹ 5:122).
[41] Augustine, *De natura* 76 (PL 44:285; NPNF¹ 5:148).
[42] Augustine, *De natura* 50 (PL 44:271; NPNF¹ 5:138).
[43] Augustine, *De natura* 3 (PL 44:249; NPNF¹ 5:122).
[44] Augustine, *De natura* 6 (PL 44:250; NPNF¹ 5:123).
[45] Augustine, *De natura* 4 (PL 44:250; NPNF¹ 5:122).
[46] Augustine, *De natura* 2 (PL 44:249; NPNF¹ 5:122).
[47] Augustine, *De natura* 35 (PL 44:264; NPNF¹ 5:133). For my discussion of "prevenient" grace, see the section "Sin and Prevenient Grace," in chapter 7.
[48] Augustine, *De natura* 29 (PL 44:261; NPNF¹ 5:131).
[49] Augustine, *De natura* 50 (PL 44:271; NPNF¹ 5:138); *De natura* 84 (PL 44:290; NPNF¹ 5:151).
[50] Augustine, *De natura* 29 (PL 44:261; NPNF¹ 5:131).

without sin, we may yet die without sin . . ."[51] By our own abilities it is impossible to live without sin, but Augustine also insists that we should not underestimate the grace of God nor discount the possibility that it may so radically change and restore us.[52] Thus "we do not deny that human nature can be without sin; nor ought we by any means to refuse to it the ability to become perfect, since we admit its capacity for progress—by God's grace, however, through our Lord Jesus Christ. By His assistance we aver that it becomes righteous and blessed (*justa et beata*)."[53] We must always remember that such a possibility is only by the grace of God, "through Jesus Christ our Lord, and not merely by our freedom of the will"—but we must also always believe that we may actually become "pure in heart."[54] For while no one "makes the slightest progress to true and godly righteousness" except by the "assisting grace of our crucified Savior Christ and the gift of His Spirit," yet with God it indeed is possible.[55]

The Pelagians push the point: on one hand, they say, if "sin" is unavoidable, then it is not actually sin; on the other hand, if it can be avoided, then sinlessness is possible.[56] Augustine's response is clear: "sin can be avoided, if our corrupted nature be healed by God's grace, through our Lord Jesus Christ."[57] Sin is not "natural," and God wishes us to be without sin as we are restored to original righteousness. This restoration takes place "day by day, until their righteousness becomes perfect, like fully restored health."[58] Sin is not natural, and it does not happen by necessity of nature. At the same time, however, we must always remember that the abuse of our freedom has now placed us in a situation where we are not free apart from God's grace; sin came by the "freedom of choice," and "out of this liberty produced necessity."[59] So grace is always necessary, and this grace is also sufficient for complete redemption as we respond to grace cooperatively and grow in true holiness. God's redemptive aim is the same as his original aim; God desires us to be "in every respect perfect, without any infirmity of sin whatever—a result which God not only wishes, but even causes and helps us to accomplish." Accordingly, God's grace works toward this end,

> . . . in co-operation with ourselves, through Jesus Christ our Lord, as well by His commandments, sacraments, and examples, as by His Holy Spirit also; through whom there is hiddenly shed abroad in our hearts that love, "which

---

[51] Augustine, *De natura* 37 (PL 44:265; NPNF[1] 5:134); *De natura* 41 (PL 44:267; NPNF[1] 5:135).

[52] Augustine, *De natura* 52 (PL 44:272; NPNF[1] 5:139).

[53] Augustine, *De natura* 68 (PL 44:281; NPNF[1] 5:145).

[54] Augustine, *De natura* 72 (PL 44:283; NPNF[1] 5:146).

[55] Augustine, *De natura* 70 (PL 44:282; NPNF[1] 5:146).

[56] Lamberigts observes that by this point Julian has become the "main Pelagian player in the controversy" ("Pelagius and Pelagians," 268).

[57] Augustine, *De perfectione justitiae hominis* 2 (PL 44:293; NPNF[1] 5:160).

[58] Augustine, *De perfectione* 3 (PL 44:295; NPNF[1] 5:161).

[59] Augustine, *De perfectione* 4 (PL 44:296; NPNF[1] 5:161).

maketh intercession for us with groanings which cannot be uttered," until wholeness and salvation be perfected in us, and God be manifested to us as He will be seen in His eternal truth.[60]

Does it ever happen? Are there Christians who have become so purified by grace that they can be said to be without sin? Augustine is not sure: "Now, whether there ever has been, or is, or ever can be, a man living so righteous a life in this world as to have no sin at all, may be an open question among true and pious Christians."[61] But while Augustine is not sure that it actually happens in this life, he is sure about these two certainties: such holiness really *is* possible, and such holiness is possible *only by grace.*

To summarize, sin is not natural but is contrary to nature. It has, however, so ensnared, infected, and enslaved human nature that the grace of Christ is absolutely necessary for salvation. Original sin—received in virtue of our relation to Adam—leaves us both corrupt and guilty. To deny the corruption of original sin is to deny nothing less than the Christian faith itself.[62] And the guilt is so closely related to our corruption that it is impossible to have one without the other.[63]

A synod at Carthage formally condemned Pelagianism in 418. A decade later (c. 426–429), however, Augustine is once again forced to wrestle with these issues. This time he writes in response to "the Massilians" of southern Gaul who were not defending Pelagian views but who were indeed concerned about what they took to be problematic aspects and implications of Augustine's theology. The bishop of Hippo continues to insist upon the reality of free will, and he makes extended arguments from Scripture to demonstrate that the Christian faith makes no sense without it.[64] He also continues to insist, of course, that

---

[60] Augustine, *De perfectione* 20 (PL 44:315–316; NPNF[1] 5:176).

[61] Augustine, *De natura* 70 (PL 44:281; NPNF[1] 5:145).

[62] Augustine, *De gratia Christi et de peccato originali contra Pelagium et Coelestinum* II.34 (PL 44:402; NPNF[1] 5:249).

[63] Augustine, *De gratia* II.44–45 (PL 44:407–408; NPNF[1] 5:253).

[64] Augustine, *De gratia et libero arbitrio ad Valentinum* 2–4 (PL 44:881–884; NPNF[1] 5:444–445). Just what Augustine means by "free will" is, of course, the subject of ongoing debates. To use the common labels anachronistically, is he a compatibilist (who believes that freedom and responsibility are compatible with causal determinism) or a libertarian (who believes that we are free and that freedom is incompatible with determinism)? If so, then what kind of libertarian or compatibilist is he? For interpretations of Augustine as a libertarian, see Eleonore Stump, "Augustine on Free Will," in *The Cambridge Companion to Augustine,* ed. Eleonore Stump and Norman Kretzmann (Cambridge: Cambridge University Press, 2001), 124–147. For a careful interpretation that sees the work of the very late Augustine as that of a determinist (though not a physical determinist), see Jesse Couenhoven, *Stricken by Sin, Cured by Christ: Agency, Necessity, and Culpability in Augustinian Theology* (Oxford: Oxford University Press, 2013). What does not seem to be debatable are these points: (a) that Augustine's earlier works are quite clearly libertarian, and (b) if Augustine renounces libertarianism for compatibilism, it is at some point in the anti-Pelagian controversies. What is debated, on the other hand, are these questions: (c) did Augustine ever really renounce libertarianism for compatibilism? and (d) if so, then *at what point* did he do so? By my judgments, if Augustine became a compatibilist (which seems plausible), he did so only very late in the controversy (c. 425 or after). Even many of his earlier anti-Pelagian writings (e.g., *De natura et gratia*) seem hard to interpret as consistent with determinism, and even harder to read as demanding it. But by the writing of *De gratia et libero arbitrio* (e.g., section 41), he says things that are plausibly read as compatibilist. Even so, however, it also seems clear that even the "very late Augustine" thinks that *Adam* enjoyed libertarian free will (e.g., *De correptione et gratia* 27–28, 32, 36 NPNF[1] 5:482–487).

grace is indispensable for salvation, and that without it our freedom is both helpless and pointless.[65] Grace is not earned or received in response to our meritorious actions; to the contrary, grace is always prevenient.[66] Sinners are justified by grace through faith—and this faith is always expressed in good works (without which no one will be saved).[67] Moreover, this faith itself is the gift of God, and it cannot be reduced to another (and easier) work.[68]

We also see, in these later writings, a sharpened insistence on a doctrine of unconditional predestination and an accompanying insistence upon the inscrutability of divine action and intention. God simply does whatever God wants to do, and this is good news for some people and absolutely horrifying news for others. Augustine exemplifies this in the case of two infants (born either of godly parents or of a prostitute). Suppose that the two infants die soon after birth, and that one died without the sacrament of baptism while the other died after having received it. What are we to make of such a situation? For Augustine the answer is clear: we are to conclude that the baptized child was among the elect and is in paradise, while the unbaptized infant is damned to perdition.[69] Or consider the case of two men who are called to repentance and belief: one responds positively to the gospel and the other does not. What are we to make of such a situation? One is moved by God's grace to respond positively and is (or may be) among the elect. The heart of the other man is hardened by God, and he is among the damned.[70] Or consider further the case of two persons who have been baptized: one perseveres in godly living while the other one commits mortal sin and "is left and forsaken in his present life."[71] What are we to make of this? We are to conclude that God condemns him, and further that this is due to the inscrutable nature of God's will.[72] For while it is not possible for anyone truly predestined to salvation not to persevere in godliness, nonetheless there are some who are called "children of God" (in a temporal sense) who are not predestined for perseverance (and thus not truly predestined for salvation).[73] Moreover, since no one is in a position to know what God has predestined in the secret counsels of his will, no one is in a position to know that they really are among the elect: "it is uncertain whether any one has received this gift so long as he is still alive."[74] For "who of the multitude

---

[65] Augustine, *De gratia et libero arbitrio ad Valentinum* 7 (PL 44:886; NPNF¹ 5:446–447).

[66] Augustine, *De gratia et libero arbitrio* 15 (PL 44:890; NPNF¹ 5:450).

[67] Augustine, *De gratia et libero arbitrio* 17–20 (PL 44:891–893; NPNF¹ 5:450–452).

[68] Augustine, *De gratia et libero arbitrio* 28–29 (PL 44:897–898; NPNF¹ 5:455–456).

[69] Augustine, *De gratia et libero arbitrio* 44 (PL 44:909–910; NPNF¹ 5:463). Augustine recognizes the shift in his own thinking from his earlier theology (*De Dono Perseverantia* 30 (NPNF¹ 5:537).

[70] Augustine, *De gratia et libero arbitrio* 42–43 (PL 44:907–909; NPNF¹ 5:462–463).

[71] Augustine, *De gratia et libero arbitrio* 45 (PL 44:910; NPNF¹ 5:464).

[72] Augustine, *De correptione et gratia* 11 (PL 44:923; NPNF¹ 5:476).

[73] Augustine, *De correptione et gratia* 16 (PL 44:925; NPNF¹ 5:478). Clearly, there is a great gulf fixed between Augustinian soteriology and the position that is sometimes called "Once Saved, Always Saved."

[74] Augustine, *De dono perseverantia* 1 (NPNF¹ 5:526).

of believers can presume, so long as he is living in this mortal state, that he is in the number of the predestinated?"[75] This very uncertainty is also part of God's plan, however, for "it is necessary that in this condition that should be kept hidden; since here we have to beware so much of pride."[76]

To recapitulate, several important points emerge from Augustine's theology of sin. These may be summarized as key points about creation and nature, about the fall and sin, and about salvation. With respect to creation, Augustine is diametrically opposed to Manichaean theology in his resolute insistence on the goodness of creation. Sin is thus contrary to nature. God's own goodness is reflected in his creation, and sin is whatever is opposed to that goodness.

With respect to the fall and sin, Augustine is opposed to both the Manichaeans and the Pelagians. Against the Manichaeans, he insists that the fall brought about a massive change for the worse. Where the Manichaeans hold that the material creation is always (and necessarily) evil and thus do not have a place of radical importance for a fall, Augustine insists that the fall indeed has radically altered the course of nature. Against the Manichaeans, Augustine employs his famous "free will defense." Adam, as created, was both *posse peccare* (able to sin) and *posse non peccare* (able not to sin). Sin came by the abuse of free will, and it resulted in drastic ruin. Augustine is also opposed to the Pelagians in his belief that sin brought death (natural as well as spiritual), but his opposition goes further. Against the Pelagians, he teaches that humans are no longer in the same state as Adam before the fall; we are no longer *posse peccare et posse non peccare*, for now we are *non posse non peccare*—it is not possible that we not sin, apart from the radical intervention of God's grace. We are somehow *really in Adam* (Augustine famously misinterprets the *eph hō* of Romans 5 as *in quo*), and thus Adam's condition is really ours. The doctrine of original sin then teaches that we are both corrupt and guilty as a result of Adam's sin. Moreover, original sin is to be understood in a strictly *realist* way; somehow, we really were "in" Adam when he sinned.

With respect to salvation, Augustine is again opposed to both the Manichaeans and the Pelagians. Against the Pelagians, he is utterly insistent that we are saved by God's grace or not at all. This grace is received by faith, and it works itself out in lives of genuine righteousness and holiness before God and neighbor. And this latter affirmation brings him into conflict once again with the Manichaeans, for Augustine is convinced that grace restores nature to its original goodness and thus truly enables genuine righteousness and holiness *in this embodied life.*

As we have seen, after the condemnation of Pelagianism at Carthage (418),

---

[75] Augustine, *De correptione et gratia* 40 (PL 44:940; NPNF[1] 5:488).
[76] Augustine, *De correptione et gratia* 40 (PL 44:940–941; NPNF[1] 5:488).

some important and influential theologians agreed with the rejection of Pelagianism but also objected to some elements of "Augustinian" theology.[77] Led by such luminaries as John Cassian and Vincent of Lerins, their theology is sometimes referred to as "Semi-Pelagianism."[78] Notwithstanding the common usage, the label "Semi-Pelagianism" is problematic for at least two reasons: first, it was not employed until much later (the late sixteenth or early seventeenth century), and then for strictly polemical reasons; and, second, it simply is not apt.[79] As Reinhold Seeberg says, "The name Semipelagians is not very appropriate; for the majority of the party might be more accurately described as Semiaugustinians."[80] Pelagianism is very clearly condemned by these theologians, and the doctrine of original sin is affirmed. As Seeberg puts it, "The sin of Adam is a hereditary disease," and "since the fall, there has been an *infirmitas liberi arbitrii*."[81] Thus "[t]he Pelagian theory is very positively rejected."[82] Justo Gonzalez concurs: "Cassian is clear in condemning Pelagius."[83] These theologians insist upon the necessity of grace, and they refuse to limit grace in the ways that the Pelagians had done (natural conscience, the teaching of the Law, the example of Jesus, etc.). To the contrary, "in Cassian grace possessed its full Augustinian meaning, an interior working of God within the soul."[84] This grace "calls, solicits, and inclines us, but it does not compel us to will."[85] In summary, it is clear that Alexander Hwang is correct when he concludes that the term "Semi-Pelagianism" is "historically and theologically incorrect"; theologians such as John Cassian and Vincent of Lerins were "not 'part' Pelagian, but in fact [were] anti-Pelagian."[86]

But if these theologians agreed with the condemnation of Pelagianism,

---

[77] Augustine Casiday has argued forcefully (and, to my mind, convincingly) that there is no such thing as a single and settled "Augustinian" theology during the fifth century (e.g., *Tradition and Theology in John Cassian* [Oxford: Oxford University Press, 2006]).

[78] An important and widely referenced study is that of Rebecca Harden Weaver, *Divine Grace and Human Agency: A Study of the Semi-Pelagian Controversy* (Macon, GA: Mercer University Press, 1996). On John Cassian, see esp. Casiday, *Tradition and Theology in John Cassian*; Casiday, "Rehabilitating John Cassian: Ascetic Pneumatology from John Cassian to Gregory the Great," *SJT* (2005): 270–284; and Columba Stewart, *Cassian the Monk* (New York: Oxford University Press, 1998). On Vincent of Lerins, see Augustine Casiday, "Grace and the Humanity of Christ according to Vincent of Lerins," *Vigiliae Christianae* (2005): 298–314; and Thomas Guarino, *Vincent of Lerins and the Development of Christian Doctrine* (Grand Rapids, MI: Baker Academic, 2013).

[79] Irena Backus and Aza Goudriaan locate the genesis of the term with Theodore Beza ("'Semipelagianism': The Origins of the Term and Its Passage into the History of Heresy," *Journal of Ecclesiastical History* [2014]: 25–46). Problems with the label were recognized by the older study of Owen Chadwick, *John Cassian*, 2nd ed. (Cambridge: Cambridge University Press, 1968), 127.

[80] Reinhold Seeberg, *Textbook of the History of Doctrines*, trans. Charles E. Hay (Grand Rapids, MI: Baker, 1952), 369.

[81] Seeberg, *Textbook of the History of Doctrines*, 370.

[82] Seeberg, *Textbook of the History of Doctrines*, 370.

[83] Justo Gonzalez, *A History of Christian Thought, Volume II: From Augustine to the Eve of the Reformation*, rev. ed. (Nashville: Abingdon, 1971), 56.

[84] Chadwick, *John Cassian*, 113.

[85] Joseph Tixeront, *History of Dogmas, Volume III: The End of the Patristic Age (430–800)* (Westminster, MD: Christian Classics, 1984), 268.

[86] Alexander Y. Hwang, *Intrepid Lover of Perfect Grace: The Life and Theology of Prosper of Aquitaine* (Washington, DC: Catholic University of America Press, 2009), 2–3. See also Augustine Casiday, "Cassian against the Pelagians," *Studia Monastica* (2004): 7–23.

they did not agree with the full spectrum of Augustine's teachings on these issues. For, as Rebecca Harden Weaver observes, "Augustine's own teaching on grace had raised questions and misgivings even among those who shared his rejection of Pelagianism."[87] Notably, they insist upon the reality of God's love for the world, God's desire that all be saved, and God's action on behalf of all in Jesus Christ. As Owen Chadwick explains, "The principal article in their creed is the belief that Christ died for all men without exception, so that they reject the idea that God has only elected some to salvation and has predestined others to eternal damnation."[88] Arguing from both Scripture and tradition, John Cassian, Vincent of Lerins, and others point out that the extremes of Augustine's position are innovations that degrade the glory of God, lead to moral failure, are opposed to Scripture and thus have no place within the treasury of Christian doctrine.[89] "To deny that God wills to save all men was regarded . . . as an awful blasphemy."[90] As Weaver concludes, they found elements of Augustinian teaching to be not only "novel" but also "dangerous."[91]

Joseph Tixeront summarizes the basic tenets of their view as follows:

(1) Man is able, without grace, to desire and will, but not to perform, supernaturally good deeds; he can begin to believe, but he can not impart to himself complete faith.

(2) God wills all men to be saved and offers to all the grace of salvation. All can cooperate with His grace and persevere in it, if they will.

(3) There is no absolute predestination; predestination and reprobation, considered in God, are consequent upon His foreknowledge . . . [92]

Tixeront further observes that "[o]f these three propositions the first alone seems at first blush reprehensible and tainted by Pelagianism; the other two, whilst calling for further explanation, on the whole fairly express the constant belief of the faithful."[93] He explains the first in more detail: on this view, "whilst man can at times have the thought and desire of good by himself, and can of himself answer the divine call, he cannot accomplish the good that he has conceived and desired, nor do that to which God calls him, without the aid of grace."[94] Seeberg agrees: "[T]he idea of Cassian is, that the human will has indeed been crippled by sin, but that a certain freedom has remained to it. By virtue of this, it is able to turn to God, and, just as though God had first turned

[87] Rebecca Harden Weaver, "Introduction," *Grace for Grace: The Debates after Augustine and Pelagius*, ed. Alexander Y. Hwang, Brian J. Matz, and Augustine Casiday (Washington, DC: Catholic University of America Press, 2014), xi.

[88] Chadwick, *John Cassian*, 128.

[89] Seeberg, *Textbook of the History of Doctrines*, 374.

[90] Tixeront, *History of Dogmas*, 268.

[91] Weaver, "Introduction," xix.

[92] Tixeront, *History of Dogmas*, 271.

[93] Tixeront, *History of Dogmas*, 271.

[94] Tixeront, *History of Dogmas*, 268.

to it, it is able, with the assistance of divine grace, setting before it the law and infusing the needed power, to will and to do that which is good."[95]

We can summarize their conviction in this way: all human persons suffer from original sin, and this condition leaves them unable to exercise complete faith or to do what is right. Notwithstanding this condition, however, we are (or may be) able to choose to have faith and to do good. When we so choose, God meets us and grants us complete faith and the ability to do good works so that we may live in charity. Accordingly, God's grace is absolutely necessary for salvation—but this grace is not, strictly speaking, always *prevenient*. Instead, it responds to the moral good that we are able to will and our desire for supernatural good, and it cooperates with our wills to bring salvation.[96]

Prosper of Aquitaine led the opposition to the theology of Cassian, Vincent, and the other "Massilians." As Chadwick notes, "Cassian is treated with respect" throughout this controversy; "he is a Catholic doctor, a man of weighty counsel, a wise doctor, [and] a teacher of truth" with a "knowledge of Holy Scripture [that] is more profound than that of all others."[97] Nonetheless, Prosper charges the Massilians with inventing "some hybrid third system" (*quid tertium*) that is at odds with both the heretical Pelagians and the mainstream catholics.[98] He defends Augustine's theology against several common and important charges: for instance, he denies that anyone is compelled by God's predestination to sin and thus denies a "fatal necessity" (*fatali necessitate*) as well,[99] that free will is negated or destroyed by predestination,[100] that Christ was "not crucified for the redemption of the entire world" (*totus mundi*),[101] that God's power causes anyone to sin,[102] that foreknowledge entails necessity,[103] and that prescience and predestination are the same thing.[104]

Prosper insists upon the utter prevenience of grace.[105] He denies that God's

---

[95] Seeberg, *Textbook of the History of Doctrines*, 371.

[96] See further Tixeront, *History of Dogmas*, 274.

[97] Chadwick, *John Cassian*, 133. Stewart states that "Prosper wrenched passages from *Conference* 13 to create a virtual parody of Cassian's teaching" (*Cassian the Monk*, 77).

[98] Prosper of Aquitaine, *Pro Defensione Augustini contra Cassiani presbyteri librum* 3 (PL 51:221C; *Prosper of Aquitaine: Defense of St. Augustine*, Ancient Christian Writers 32, trans. and annotated P. De Letter [New York: Newman, 1963], 76).

[99] Prosper of Aquitaine, *Pro Augustino responsiones ad capitula Gallorum* 1 (PL 51:157A–B; *Defense of St. Augustine*, 140).

[100] Prosper, *Pro Augustino responsiones ad capitula Gallorum* 6 (PL 51:160C–161C; *Defense of St. Augustine*, 144–145).

[101] Prosper, *Pro Augustino responsiones ad capitula Gallorum* 9 (PL 51:164C–166B; *Defense of St. Augustine*, 149).

[102] Prosper, *Pro Augustino responsiones ad capitula Gallorum* 11 (PL 51:166C–167A; *Defense of St. Augustine*, 152).

[103] Prosper, *Pro Augustino responsiones ad capitula Gallorum* 14 (PL 51:169B–170A; *Defense of St. Augustine*, 155).

[104] Prosper, *Pro Augustino responsiones ad capitula Gallorum* 15 (PL 51:170B; *Defense of St. Augustine*, 156).

[105] E.g., Prosper, *Pro Defensione Augustini contra Cassiani librum* 9, 13 (PL 51:235B–236A, 248D–250A; *Defense of St. Augustine*, 91, 106–107); *De vocatione omnium gentium* 1.7 (PL 51:653B–654A; *Prosper of Aquitaine: The Call of All Nations*, Ancient Christian Writers 14, trans. and annotated P. De Letter [New York: Paulist, 1952], 33–34); *De vocatione* 1.23 (PL 51:676A–678D; *Call of All Nations*, 71–76); *De vocatione* 2.26 (PL 51:711B–712A; *Call of All Nations*, 134–135).

will predestines anyone to evil actions.[106] When pressed to explain why God chooses some for salvation and not others, he will resort neither to the common Patristic doctrine that God's predestination is based on his foreknowledge nor to any account that would chalk up the damnation of sinners to God's inscrutable will. The traditional doctrine, both Greek and Latin, is plain: God predestines on the basis of his foreknowledge of the free actions of sinners. As Donato Ogliari puts it, "For both the Greek and Latin theologians, divine foreknowledge constituted the *Grundlage* of God's predestination, the key to interpret it, and the way to explain the scriptural evidence that speak of both life and death, salvation and damnation, in relation to God's agency as well as man's."[107] But Prosper will not quite allow this. Instead, he admits, we simply do not know.[108] What we *do* know, he resolutely insists, is that the doctrine of original sin means that we are all helpless as well as guilty.[109] We also know that God desires for all to be saved, and we know as well that Christ died for the sins of everyone in the world.[110] Because God is *good*, "we believe with complete trust in God's goodness that he wills all men to be saved and to come to a knowledge of the truth."[111] Therefore, the good news is that Christ died for all people *without distinction (indifferenter)* because Christ died for all *without exception (prorsus pro omnibus)*.[112]

In the latter part of the fifth century, Faustus (Bishop of Riez) took a strong stand against unconditional predestination.[113] Notably, he "defends the doctrine according to which the *initium fidei*—the first step of faith—depends upon human freedom. This freedom gives us the natural capacity to turn toward God and to seek him until there is a response."[114] Faustus was opposed by Fulgentius, who insisted on the prevenience and primacy of grace and who taught that predestination to both glory and damnation is entirely of God; the "number of the predestined is predetermined and unchangeable," and "no one who is predestined can be lost."[115] Fulgentius flatly denies that God wills the salvation of all people, and he denies that grace is given to all.[116]

The Synod of Orange (529) addressed many of these issues head-on, and

---

[106] Prosper, *Pro Augustino responsiones ad capitulum Vincentianarum* 10–15 (PL 51:132C–135C; *Defense of St. Augustine*, 171–174).

[107] Donato Ogliari, *Gratia et Certamen: The Relationship between Grace and Free Will in the Discussions of Augustine with the So-called Semipelagians* (Leuven: Leuven University Press, 2003), 309.

[108] E.g., Prosper, *De vocatione* 1.25 (PL 51:685B–686C; *Call of All Nations*, 86–87).

[109] E.g., Prosper, *De vocatione* 2.21 (PL 51:707C–708C; *Call of All Nations*, 127–128).

[110] E.g., Prosper, *Pro Augustino responsiones ad capitula Gallorum* 9 (PL 51:163C–166B; *Defense of St. Augustine*, 149–151, 164); *De vocatione* 2.1–2 (PL 51:685D–688C; *Call of All Nations*, 89–92); *De vocatione* 2.16 (PL 51:702D–704A; *Call of All Nations*, 118–119); *De vocatione* 2.19 (PL 51:706C–D; *Call of All Nations*, 125).

[111] Prosper, *De vocatione* 2.19 (PL 51:706C; *Call of All Nations*, 125).

[112] Prosper, *De vocatione* 2.16 (PL 51:703A, 703C; *Call of All Nations*, 118–119).

[113] Tixeront, *History of Dogmas*, 282.

[114] Gonzalez, *History of Christian Thought*, 60. Cf. Seeberg, *Textbook of the History of Doctrines*, 374–375.

[115] Quoted in Tixeront, *History of Dogmas*, 290–291.

[116] Tixeront, *History of Dogmas*, 290–291.

it made decisive proclamations. Orange unambiguously condemns such views as these:

- views that deny that the whole person (body and soul) were changed for the worse through Adam's sin;
- views that assert that Adam's sin harmed only him and not his progeny and deny the doctrine of original sin;
- views that hold that grace is acquired by human appeal rather than enabling us to appeal;
- views which hold that God waits for our decision before he bestows grace;
- views which say that the beginnings of faith are natural within us rather than the gifts of supernatural grace;
- views which hold that mercy is given to us in response to the efforts that we make prior to grace;
- views which hold that we can choose the eternal life of salvation, or even consent to the offer of salvation, apart from the grace that is the inward illumination and inspiration of the Holy Spirit;
- views which maintain that while some may need mercy, others can attain the grace of baptism merely by free choice.[117]

Orange resoundingly affirms that no merits precede grace, and it denies that anyone is saved apart from God's mercy. No one can do any good apart from God's grace, and God works within us to bring freedom to our wills and to conform them to his own.[118] All humanity has been vitiated by original sin, and human nature is in bondage to sin and unable to make even the first move toward God. Accordingly, without God's grace—prevenient, cooperative, and perfecting—there would be no hope of salvation:

> We ought to preach and believe, that the free will has been so inclined and weakened by the sin of the first man, that no one since would be able either to love God as he ought, or to believe on God, or to work what is good before God, unless the grace of the divine mercy had preceded him. We believe that, grace having been received through baptism, all the baptized are able and under obligation to perform by the assistance and co-operation of Christ the things which pertain to the salvation of the soul, if they have resolved to labor faithfully.[119]

Clearly, the "first step of faith—the *initium fidei*—is not in human nature, but in divine grace."[120]

But while it would be clearly incorrect to think that Orange is a victory for the Massilians, it would also be a mistake to think that "the synod was

---

[117] See J. Patout Burns, ed., *Theological Anthropology* (Philadelphia: Fortress, 1981), 113–116.
[118] Burns, *Theological Anthropology*, 116–118.
[119] From the Council of Orange, quoted in Seeberg, *Textbook of the History of Doctrines*, 382.
[120] Gonzalez, *History of Christian Thought*, 60.

truly Augustinian in its doctrine."[121] For Orange "did not sanction all his speculations."[122] As R. A. Markus points out, "The faith of Orange was neither Pelagius' nor Augustine's; it was the product of a century's thought, debate, preaching, and ascetic discipline, shaped and provoked by the two great innovators, and—no less!—by the Gallic churches' resistance to innovation."[123] Notably, what was not included was the Augustinian teaching of predestination and irresistible grace. Indeed, not only does Orange not canonize Augustine's teaching on predestination; it saves some of its strongest language of condemnation for anyone who would teach predestination to evil:

> But not only do we not believe that some have been predestinated to evil by the divine power, but also, if there be any who will believe so evil a thing, we say to them, with all detestation, anathema.[124]

Thus we can conclude with Seeberg that "the doctrine of 'grace alone' came off as victorious, but the Augustinian doctrine of predestination was abandoned. The irresistible grace of predestination was driven from the field" at the decisive Synod of Orange.[125] But the doctrine of original sin remained, and with it remained the absolute insistence upon the necessity and prevenience of grace.

The late medieval era witnessed further debates over these issues. The heritage of "high medieval" hamartiology is somewhat mixed. Aquinas, for example, clearly insists that sin leaves us unable to save ourselves and utterly dependent on God's grace. While insisting that we are hopeless and helpless without grace, he also teaches that human nature is "wounded" by sin. As Richard A. Muller sees it, "Aquinas insisted that no meritorious acts, whether 'half' or full merit (*meritum de congruo* or *meritum de condigno*) were possible before grace and that all meritorious acts after grace were fully such (*de condigno*) only on grounds of the work of grace itself, not on grounds of the ability of the human agent. In other words, Aquinas's *Summa* is quite Augustinian in its assumption that salvation occurs by grace alone."[126] These themes, while not obviously irreconcilable, do leave room for various interpretations and possible exploitation. Indeed, theologians of what is sometimes called the "late medieval period" did take these themes in various directions.

On one hand, theologians such as Gabriel Biel (d. 1495) endorse a doctrine of original sin which largely follows Aquinas and Bonaventure in seeing

[121] Gonzalez, *History of Christian Thought*, 61.

[122] Tixeront, *History of Dogmas*, 299.

[123] R. A. Markus, "The Legacy of Pelagius: Orthodoxy, Heresy, and Conciliation," in *The Making of Orthodoxy: Essays in Honor of Henry Chadwick*, ed. Rowan Williams (Cambridge: Cambridge University Press, 1989), 227.

[124] This translation is from Henry Bettenson, ed., *Documents of the Christian Church*, 2nd ed. (Oxford: Oxford University Press, 1963), 62.

[125] Seeberg, *Textbook of the History of Doctrines*, 382.

[126] Richard A. Muller, "Scholasticism, Reformation Orthodoxy, and the Persistence of Aristotelianism," *TJ* (1998): 84.

original sin neither as strictly concupiscence nor only as the lack of original righteousness but instead as both absence of original righteousness (as regards the form) and concupiscence (as regards the matter).[127] In Oberman's summary, Biel "goes beyond the position of Duns Scotus in teaching that Adam's sin not only deprived man of the gifts of grace but also corrupted his nature."[128] Accordingly, two things are vitally important for redemption: first, the nonimputation of sins is necessary for salvation; second, "man's wounded nature also has to be healed so that man's will, which in principle never lost its freedom of choice, can elicit the meritorious acts required for his acceptation by God."[129] Original justice has been forfeited by sin, and corruption now pervades human existence.

So Biel affirms the doctrine of original sin, but he also insists that it leaves the freedom of the human will intact and unscathed. He is aware that people are in different states with respect to knowledge of right and wrong, good and evil. Nonetheless, as Oberman explains, "everyone is by nature in a position to discharge" their duty before God; everyone is in a position to detest their previous sins and turn against them.[130] What is required is love. And not just any kind of love or love in just any degree; what is required as our duty is supreme love of God for God's own sake (rather than loving God as a means to the "greater" end of loving ourselves). Oberman notes that Biel is at least aware that such a requirement is difficult, but he also points out that Biel "feels that this absolute love is within the reach of natural man *without the assistance of grace*."[131] No prevenient grace is necessary for such movement.

For Biel and his compatriots, the doctrine of *facere quod in se est* is of decisive importance. *Do what is within you—do your very best!* And God will reward you accordingly. Every person, including those wounded and corrupted by original sin, has the ability to turn away from sin and toward God. Indeed, according to this position, we have this ability apart from any special prevenient grace. The difference between the elect and the reprobate amounts to the difference between those who fulfill the requirements of God's law and those who do not fulfill the requirements. Even though both are infected with original sin (Mary excepted) and in a state of mortal sin, the elect do their very best while the reprobate choose to do less than their very best. The difference is this: in actions that may be undertaken and accomplished apart from prevenient grace, the elect turn toward God and receive an infusion of grace

---

[127] See the discussion (to which the discussion in this section is deeply indebted) in Heiko A. Oberman, *The Harvest of Medieval Theology: Gabriel Biel and Late Medieval Augustinianism* (Grand Rapids, MI: Baker Academic, 2000), 121–123.
[128] Oberman, *Harvest*, 130.
[129] Oberman, *Harvest*, 128.
[130] Oberman, *Harvest*, 132.
[131] Oberman, *Harvest*, 133, emphasis original.

along with an element of merit (*meritum de congruo*), while the reprobate do not and instead receive demerit (*demerita*).[132]

Those who respond to God properly do not thereby save themselves, but they do put themselves in a position where they might be justified. As Oberman explains, justification consists of multiple parts. Initial justification takes place in baptism as sanctifying grace is infused (rather than imparted) into the soul and guilt and the accompanying punishment of sins are removed. But even though the guilt has been forgiven and the inclinations to sin have been weakened, yet such inclinations remain within us. Accordingly, further grace must be received through penance and the sacraments.[133] Taken together, then, Biel's doctrines of sin, human ability, and merit amount to "a remarkable doctrine of justification": it "is at once *sola gratia* and *sola operibus!*"[134] Justification is by grace alone "because if God had not decided to adorn man's good works with created and uncreated grace, man would never be saved."[135] But justification is by works alone as well, "because . . . God by the two laws of grace is committed, even obliged to add to this framework, infused grace and final acceptance. Once man has done his very best, the other two parts follow automatically."[136] But while Biel wants both *grace alone* and *works alone*, "it is clear that the emphasis falls on 'justification by works alone,'" and "the concept of 'justification by grace alone' is a rational outer structure dependent on the distinction between *potentia absoluta* and *potentia ordinata*."[137] This leads Oberman to conclude that "*It is therefore evident that Biel's doctrine of justification is essentially Pelagian.*"[138]

On the other hand, late medieval theologians such as Gregory of Rimini (d. 1358), Thomas Bradwardine (d. 1349), and Johann von Staupitz (d. 1524) stoutly oppose the *Pelagiani moderni* theology represented by Biel.[139] Oberman says that Gregory is representative of those medieval theologians who "took up the Augustinian themes of God's prevenient grace, the bondage of the human will before it is set free by grace, and predestination in order to emphasize that salvation is not a human achievement but the result of God's sovereign initiative in planning and implementation."[140] Bradwardine appeals to the Aristotelian distinction between active and passive power to explain John 1:12; the "power to become the sons of God" (KJV) is a passive power that is itself the

---

[132] Oberman, *Harvest*, 194–195.
[133] Oberman, *Harvest*, 134–136.
[134] Oberman, *Harvest*, 176, cf. 222.
[135] Oberman, *Harvest*, 176.
[136] Oberman, *Harvest*, 176.
[137] Oberman, *Harvest*, 177.
[138] Oberman, *Harvest*, 177, emphasis original.
[139] See the discussion in Gordon Leff, *Bradwardine and the Pelagians: A Study of His 'De Causa Dei' and Its Opponents* (Cambridge: Cambridge University Press, 1957).
[140] Heiko A. Oberman, *Forerunners of the Reformation: The Shape of Late Medieval Thought* (New York: Holt, Rinehart, & Winston, 1966), 125.

gift of God.[141] We are God's children by faith and prevenient grace, and when we freely work with this grace we will persevere to the end as God's family. Similarly, Staupitz rejects the statement (attributed to Augustine) that "[i]f you are not predestined, [then] make yourself predestined."[142] Election to salvation is strictly unconditional; it is all of grace, and we have absolutely nothing to do with it. Election "is the first grace which precedes nature and works. No one elicits or merits this grace, nor is this grace due to merits foreknown by God, nor to good use of reason in the future foreseen by God, nor to merits already performed."[143] Fusing legal and juridical with nuptial language, Staupitz insists not only that we are joined to Christ as his bride but even that "He makes our sins his own. Just as the Christian is just through the righteousness of Christ, so Christ is unrighteous and sinful through the guilt of the Christian."[144] Indeed, Staupitz concludes that Jesus's cry of dereliction should be understood in light of the fact that "I am righteous because of Your righteousness and a sinner because of my guilt," just as Christ is "a sinner because of my guilt."[145]

Reformation and post-Reformation Protestant theologians responded to this debate by insisting on human wretchedness and inability. The Lutheran scholastics insist that humans cannot simply choose the good. While we have liberty to choose between genuine alternatives, without God's grace we only have options, as Johann Quenstadt puts it, "between this and that spiritual evil."[146] Therefore, as Martin Chemnitz says, "the human will cannot, by its own powers, without the Holy Spirit, either begin interior and spiritual motions, or produce interior obedience of the heart, or persevere to the end in the course commenced and perfect it."[147] So while sinful humans remain free, apart from the grace of the Holy Spirit they are unable to choose good. By the grace of the Holy Spirit, however, they are truly enabled to choose righteousness and goodness in faith and obedience. As John Owen points out, "Blindness of mind, stubbornness of will, sensuality of affections, all concur to keep poor perishing souls at a distance from Christ. Men are made blind by sin, and cannot see his excellencies; obstinate, and will not lay hold of his righteousness; senseless, and take no notice of their own eternal concerns."[148] Along with Lutheran and Reformed accounts, Jacob Arminius concurs. Indeed, he says, our situation is such that

---

[141] Thomas Bradwardine, "The Cause of God against the Pelagians," in Oberman, *Forerunners*, 154.

[142] Johann von Staupitz, "Eternal Predestination and Its Execution in Time," in Oberman, *Forerunners*, 181.

[143] Staupitz, "Eternal Predestination," 179.

[144] Staupitz, "Eternal Predestination," 190.

[145] Staupitz, "Eternal Predestination," 191.

[146] Johann Andreas Quenstadt, *Theologica II*, 176, cited in Heinrich Schmid, *The Doctrinal Theology of the Evangelical Lutheran Church, Exhibited, and Verified from the Original Sources* (Philadelphia: Lutheran Publication Society, 1876), 284.

[147] Martin Chemnitz, *Loci Theologici* (Wittenberg: 1615), 190, cf. Schmid, *Doctrinal Theology*, 283.

[148] John Owen, *Overcoming Sin and Temptation*, ed. Kelly M. Kapic and Justin Taylor (Wheaton, IL: Crossway, 2006), 393.

I ascribe to God's grace the origin, the continuance, and the fulfillment (*het beghinsel, den voorgangh, ende de volbrenginghe*) of all good, even so far as the regenerate person himself, without this preventing and stimulating, following and cooperating grace, can neither think, will, or do good, nor also resist any evil temptation.[149]

Such sentiments are to be found across and throughout the Christian tradition. The basic convictions about the results of sin are expressed well by John Wesley:

Is man by nature filled with all manner of evil? Is he void of all good? Is he wholly fallen? Is his soul totally corrupted? Or, to come back to the text, is "every imagination of the thoughts of his heart evil continually?" Allow this, and you are so far a Christian. Deny it, and you are but a heathen still.[150]

We have invested this much in our sketch of the salient points of this history because it is widely misunderstood; as Robert Evans reminds us, such misunderstanding often results in "careless slogans."[151] But because such "careless slogans" can be easily weaponized in theological debate, it is also very important to have a clear understanding of what is at stake.[152] Notably, neither Pelagianism nor "Semi-Pelagianism" are ultimately about some particular view of the freedom of the will. Neither is primarily about guiltiness for the sin of our most remote ancestor. It is not that these issues are irrelevant, but they are not at the heart of the debates. Drawing from the historical background, we might summarize the salient points as:

(P1) the denial of original sin, with respect to both the guilt of original sin and any residual corrupting impact on the affections and volition of the human agent;

(P2) the denial of any grace that exerts a "special pressure" on the human will ("grace" is thus reduced to the reality of free will, the revelation of the divine law, and the example of sinlessness given to us in Christ).[153]

and

(P3) we somehow initiate and cause our own salvation by exercising our faith and performing good works.

---

[149] Jacob Arminius, *Declaratio sententiae*, 113–114. I here follow the translation of Keith D. Stanglin and Thomas H. McCall, *Jacob Arminius: Theologian of Grace* (Oxford: Oxford University Press, 2012), 155.

[150] John Wesley, "Original Sin," in *Wesley's 52 Standard Sermons* (Salem, OH: Schmul, 1988), 456. See further the discussion in Kenneth J. Collins, *The Scripture Way of Salvation: The Heart of John Wesley's Theology* (Nashville: Abingdon, 1997), 37.

[151] Evans, *Pelagius*, 1.

[152] This is, of course, only a thin sketch of some of the most important points rather than a history.

[153] To recall, the phrase "special pressure" comes from Kelly, *Early Christian Doctrines*, 359.

Meanwhile, the most important element of "Semi-Pelagianism" can be summarized as the view that

(SP) the beginning of our salvation is (or may be) from us not God.[154]

For according to "Semi-Pelagianism," while we are tainted and wounded, we are not—or at least *some of us are not*—in the place where we cannot initiate the salvation that God may then bring to completion.

B. Enslaved and Ensnared

Clearly, sin ensnares and enslaves us (John 8:34).[155] As Nicholas E. Lombardo observes, "[T]he devil leads us to sin, and by sinning we become slaves to sin."[156] But this must not be misunderstood. As sinners, we indeed are slaves to sin and utterly unable to free ourselves. We are much like poor Edmund in C. S. Lewis's famous *The Lion, the Witch, and the Wardrobe*; it as if we have been taken captive by a powerful and malicious foe who has bound us with chains and thrown us into a dungeon from which we have no hope of escape. We are enslaved, and our predicament is so dire that we have no hope of rescue apart from the intervention of a powerful liberator. But we are much like poor Edmund in another way as well, for we are not innocent victims who have been kidnaped against our wills. To the contrary, again like Edmund, we are imprisoned precisely because we have fallen to temptation and committed treason against our great King. We are enslaved by our own complicity with evil. As Kevin J. Vanhoozer puts it, "Sin is that inward curvature of one's existential spine that creates alienation between oneself and others."[157] As sinners—indeed, precisely as enslaved and hopeless sinners—we stand guilty and condemned by the only one who can offer hope.

Sin is closely related to addiction. As Cornelius Plantinga Jr. says, "[T]o look at addiction is to look at significant dynamics of sin."[158] We must be careful here, for it is easy to make faulty assumptions or draw the wrong conclusions from an initial observation of the relationship between sin and addiction. The study of addictions is itself a complicated business, as there are many factors involved (including chemical, neurological, psychological, cultural, social, and spiritual factors), and the relation to sin is less than straightforward.[159]

---

[154] See the discussion by Richard Cross, "Anti-Pelagianism and the Resistibility of Grace," *FPhilos* (2005): 199–201.
[155] For further discussion of the enslaving power of sin (especially with respect to ideologies), see David H. Kelsey, *Eccentric Existence: A Theological Anthropology*, 2 vols. (Louisville: Westminster/John Knox, 2009), 1:598–599.
[156] Nicholas E. Lombardo, OP, *The Father's Will: Christ's Crucifixion and the Goodness of God* (Oxford: Oxford University Press, 2013), 183.
[157] Kevin J. Vanhoozer, *Faith Speaking Understanding: Performing the Drama of Doctrine* (Louisville: Westminster/John Knox, 2014), 157.
[158] Cornelius Plantinga Jr., *Not the Way It's Supposed to Be: A Breviary of Sin* (Grand Rapids, MI: Eerdmans, 1995), 129.
[159] See the helpful discussion in Plantinga, *Not the Way*, 130.

We should especially be careful not to equate every instance of addiction with sin (as some addictions clearly seem to be formed non-culpably). Nonetheless, with these cautions in mind, we can see something of the progress and enslaving nature of sin by paying theological attention to addiction.

Plantinga notes that "addictions often include sin—or, putting matters the other way around, that some sin displays the addictive syndrome."[160] With this understanding, we can look at this relationship between addiction and sin from two angles: we can look at what observation of addictions teaches us about the enslaving progress of sin, and we can look at what we should make of addiction theologically. So what does our understanding of addiction reveal about the enslaving nature of sin? Plantinga observes that the "dynamics of addiction" often go along these lines:

1. Repetition of pleasurable and therefore habit-forming behavior, plus escalating tolerance and desire
2. Unpleasant aftereffects of such behavior, including withdrawal symptoms and self-reproach
3. Vows to moderate or quit, followed by relapses and attendant feelings of guilt, shame, and general distress
4. Attempts to ease this distress with new rounds of the addictive behavior (or with the first rounds of a companion addiction)
5. Deterioration of work and relationships, with accompanying cognitive disturbances, including denial, delusions, and self-deceptions, especially about the effects of the addition, and the degree to which one is enthralled by it
6. Gradually increasing preoccupation, then obsession, with the addictor
7. Compulsivity in addictive behavior: evidence that one's will has become at least partly split, enfeebled, and enslaved
8. A tendency to draw others into the web of addiction, people who support and enable the primary addiction. These "codependents" present certain addictive patterns of their own—in particular, the simultaneous need to be needed by the addict and to control him. The codependent relationship is thus one in which primary and parasitic addictions join.[161]

This pattern is repeated again and again in human history and in individual lives. It vividly illustrates the patterns and progress of sin as it enslaves and destroys human persons.

And what theological sense can be made of addiction? Here again Plantinga is helpful. He observes that "what drives addiction is longing—a longing not just of the brain, belly, or loins but finally of the heart."[162] He explains, further that

---

[160] Plantinga, *Not the Way*, 144.
[161] Plantinga, *Not the Way*, 145.
[162] Plantinga, *Not the Way*, 131.

[b]ecause they are human beings, addicts long for wholeness, for fulfillment, and for the final good that believers call God. Like all idolatries, addiction taps this vital spiritual force and draws off its energies to objects and processes that drain the addict instead of filling him. Accordingly, the addict longs not for God but for transcendence, not for joy but only for pleasure—and sometimes for mere escape from pain.[163]

Sin gains its addictive power, then, by subverting the very desires that were given to us by our Creator to turn us to God. Thus sin takes what is intended for our good and turns it into our destruction.

As it enslaves us, sin also blinds us. While we are cautioned not to make any equations between physical blindness and sin or to make assumptions about direct causality (cf. John 9:1–3), we do see Jesus drawing contrasts between spiritual blindness and the gift of sight (e.g., John 9:39, 41). Sin effectively darkens and occludes our moral vision. But not only does it do so in a general or a vague sense, it does so with a kind of double-blindness. For on the one hand it clouds and destroys our moral senses and our understanding of life *coram Deo*, but on the other hand it also blinds us to our own blindness. In other words, it destroys our moral senses—and it does so while beguiling us with the ridiculous notion that we have wonderful clarity and insight.

Social and moral psychologists study two interesting phenomena that are important for our understanding of sin at this point. The first of these is what is sometimes called "illusory superiority." Put simply, this is the assumption that one is "better and more competent than others."[164] This sort of self-deception is very widespread; whatever the issue, people tend to think of themselves as better than everyone else. Notably, this condition seems especially elevated in issues related to morality, for people generally think of themselves as more moral than others and ascribe to themselves "lower levels of hostility" and "higher levels of responsibility."[165] In other words, while everyone is sure that *other* people are morally flawed, they are also sure that they are well above average. As Christian Miller paints the picture, we think that even if we are not "saints," neither are we "morally corrupt."[166] Others are messed up, but "we

---

[163] Plantinga, *Not the Way*, 131.
[164] For illuminating discussion, see Vera Hoorens, "Self-Favoring Biases, Self-Presentation, and the Self-Other Asymmetry in Social Comparison," *Journal of Personality* (1995): 793. See further, Vera Hoorens, "Self-Enhancement and Superiority Biases in Social Comparison," *European Review of Social Psychology* (1993): 113–140; M. D. Alicke, "Global Self-Evaluation as Determined by the Desirability and Controllability of Trait Objectives," *Journal of Personality and Social Psychology* (1985): 1621–1630.
[165] Hoorens, "Self-Favoring Biases," 793. See also Barry R. Schlenker, Marisa L. Miller, and Ryan M. Johnson, "Moral Identity, Integrity, and Personal Responsibility," in *Personality, Identity, and Character: Explorations in Moral Psychology*, ed. Darcia Narvaez and Daniel K. Lapsley (Cambridge: Cambridge University Press, 2009), 316; and Steven Hitlin, *Moral Selves, Evil Selves: The Social Psychology of Conscience* (New York: Palgrave Macmillan, 2008), 129–138.
[166] Christian B. Miller, *The Character Gap: How Good Are We?* (Oxford: Oxford University Press, 2018), x. See also Miller, *Character and Moral Psychology* (Oxford: Oxford University Press, 2014); Miller, *Moral Character: An Empirical Theory* (Oxford: Oxford University Press, 2013).

are honest, kind, trustworthy, and reasonably virtuous people."[167] This under-standing of our moral character, Miller argues, has been shown by studies in moral psychology to be "badly mistaken."[168]

The second interesting phenomenon is what is sometimes referred to as "self-licensing"; this is what happens when people decide that "past good deeds can liberate individuals to engage in behaviors that are immoral, unethical, or otherwise problematic, behaviors that they would otherwise avoid for fear of feeling or appearing immoral."[169] Similarly, we give ourselves credit for not hav-ing been as bad as we might have been.[170] Putting these together (as so often is the case), we have a situation in which most people see themselves as morally superior to their neighbors—and are also willing to let themselves commit vicious actions. In other words, because they "know" that they are morally better than others, they can afford some wrongdoing. Indeed, sometimes we credit ourselves for not being as bad as we might have been—and then spend that "moral credit" in ways that are wrong.[171] Indeed, we tend to be harshest in our judgment of those we deem "hypocrites"—even as all the while we blind ourselves to our own hypocrisy.[172]

Such studies confirm the judgment of Joseph Butler when he said that "many men seem perfect strangers to their own characters," for they display "an absence of doubt or distrust, in a very great measure, as to their moral character and behaviour."[173] Of course, none of this is remotely surprising to the prophets and apostles. Surely it is true that "the heart is deceitful above all things, and desperately sick; who can understand it?" (Jer. 17:9). As Scripture warns us again and again, sin results in self-deception (e.g., Gal. 6:3; Rom. 1:18–21).[174] And as it also warns us, such self-deception is deadly (e.g., 1 John 1:8).

We must take the binding and blinding power of sin with full seriousness. Accordingly, we must constantly be vigilant against the perennial temptations of Pelagianism and what is commonly called "Semi-Pelagianism," for these

---

[167] Miller, *Character Gap*, x.

[168] Miller, *Character Gap*, x.

[169] Anna C. Merritt, Daniel A. Effron, and Benoit Monin, "Moral Self-Licensing: When Being Good Frees Us to Be Bad," *Social and Personality Psychology Compass* (2010): 344.

[170] Shahar Ayal and Francesca Gino, "Honest Rationales for Dishonest Behavior," in *The Social Psychology of Morality: Exploring the Causes of Good and Evil*, ed. Mario Mikulincer and Phillip R. Shaver (Washington, DC: American Psychological Association, 2012), 149–151.

[171] See Daniel A. Effron, Dale T. Miller, and Benoit Monin, "Inventing Racist Roads Not Taken: The Licensing Effect of Immoral Counterfactual Behaviors," *Journal of Personality and Social Psychology* (2012): 916–932.

[172] Daniel A. Effron and Benoit Monin, "Letting People Off the Hook: When Do Good Deeds Excuse Transgres-sions?," *Personality and Social Psychology Bulletin* (2010): 1618–1634; Benoit Monin and Anna Merritt, "Moral Hypocrisy, Moral Inconsistency, and the Struggle for Moral Integrity," in *The Social Psychology of Morality: Exploring the Causes of Good and Evil*, ed. Mario Mikulincer and Phillip R. Shaver (Washington, DC: American Psychological Association, 2012), 167–184.

[173] Joseph Butler, *Fifteen Sermons*, ed. T. A. Roberts (London: SPCK, 1970), 91, cited in John Webster, *Barth's Moral Theology: Human Action in Barth's Thought* (Grand Rapids, MI: Eerdmans, 1998), 65.

[174] See the penetrating work of Gregg A. Ten Elshof, *I Told Me So: Self-Deception and the Christian Life* (Grand Rapids, MI: Eerdmans, 2009).

views would beguile us into believing that we really are not so bad and that our situation is not so dire. As we have seen, the especially salient points of Pelagianism can be summarized as:

(P1) the denial of original sin, with respect to both the guilt of original sin and any residual corrupting impact on the affections and volition of the human agent;
(P2) the denial of any grace that exerts a "special pressure" on the human will ("grace" is thus reduced to the reality of free will, the revelation of the divine law, and the example of sinlessness given to us in Christ).[175]

and

(P3) we somehow initiate and cause our own salvation by exercising our faith and performing good works.

Meanwhile, the most important element of "Semi-Pelagianism" can be summarized as the view that

(SP) the beginning of our salvation is (or may be) from us not God.[176]

For according to "Semi-Pelagianism," while we are tainted and wounded, we are not—or at least *some of us are not*—in the place where we cannot initiate the salvation that God may then bring to completion.

On the basis of the biblical witness to sin and its effects, the orthodox (Latin) tradition has resolutely and forcefully rejected both Pelagianism and "Semi-Pelagianism." As we have seen, the Synod of Orange (529) unambiguously condemns the notion that the whole person (body and soul) was not changed for the worse by Adam's sin, along with any concomitant denials of original sin. Orange denies the view that God waits for our decision before he bestows grace, and it makes the affirmation that we absolutely need the mercy and grace of God to even *begin* to hunger for salvation. It says that only God can save, and it further says that it is God's grace that even enables us to appeal to him for salvation.

As we have seen, there are good reasons—biblically grounded reasons—to affirm the doctrine of original sin and to reject any notion that we might either fully save ourselves or even be able to initiate the process of salvation. The words of Joshua remain true today: "You are not able to serve the LORD, for he is a holy God" (Josh. 24:19). We are, after all, "dead in . . . trespasses and sins" (Eph. 2:1). As John Barclay concludes, "Paul has diagnosed the human

---

[175] Again, the phrase "special pressure" comes from Kelly, *Early Christian Doctrines*, 359.
[176] See the discussion by Richard Cross, "Anti-Pelagianism and the Resistibility of Grace," *FPhilos* (2005): 199–201.

heart as senseless ([Rom.] 1:21), hardened, and incapable of repentance (Rom. 2:5)."[177] There are good reasons, that is, to hold (P1), (P2), (P3), and (SP) at arm's length. But to reject these notions as mistaken—even to reject them as grievously mistaken and as formally heretical—does not of itself mean that we must embrace all the doctrines that are also (currently) held by many theologians who reject Pelagianism and "Semi-Pelagianism."

It is important to be clear here. The issue dividing Pelagians and "Semi-Pelagians," on the one hand, from their opponents, on the other hand, concerns the ability of human sinners. More accurately, it has to do with their *inability*. Those who are non-Pelagian and non–Semi-Pelagian admit that sinners have no innate or remaining ability either to save themselves or even to take the first steps toward salvation. The issue is not determinism. It is not as if the heretics are indeterminists and the orthodox are determinists (even so-called "soft determinists" or "compatibilists"). Matters are not that simple, and this simply is not the line that separates them. After all, many non-Pelagians and non–Semi-Pelagians and even fierce *anti*-Pelagians were not committed to determinism ("soft" or otherwise). Nor is the issue about guilt for Adam's sin, for, again, some non-Pelagians and non–Semi-Pelagians (and even very forceful anti-Pelagians) did not believe that we are guilty for what Adam did.[178] More precisely, the rejection of Pelagianism and "Semi-Pelagianism" does not entail Augustine's (later and mature) doctrine of predestination. Nor does it entail acceptance of a doctrine of "limited" or "definite" atonement. To the contrary, such a doctrine is actually rejected by many of the most important Patristic *opponents* of "Semi-Pelagianism."[179] Nor, further, does it entail the truth of the doctrine of irresistible grace. It is true, as Richard Cross argues, that "if grace is irresistible, then we have no causal role in the reception of grace, and Pelagianism is thus *ipso facto* false."[180] But it does not follow from this admission that the doctrine of irresistible grace is the *only* way to avoid Pelagianism and "Semi-Pelagianism." For as Cross also argues, there are other theological strategies that enable one to avoid both the heretical options *and* the doctrine of irresistible grace—indeed, by his count, there are no fewer than six such ways![181] What is needed is a doctrine of the *prevenience* of grace—whether or not that grace is resistible. Even such a redoubtable opponent of Pelagianism as Augustine (including the

[177] John M. G. Barclay, *Paul and the Gift* (Grand Rapids, MI: Eerdmans, 2015), 463–464.
[178] These would include not only corruption-only proponents such as Zwingli and Arminius but also mediate theorists such as Anselm and (at least arguably) Calvin.
[179] E.g., Prosper, *Pro Augustino responsiones ad capitula Gallorum* 9 (PL 51:163C–166B; *Defense of St. Augustine*, 149–151, 164); *De vocatione* II.1–2 (PL 51:685D-688C; *Call of All Nations*, 89–92); *De vocatione* II.16 (PL 51:702D–704A; *Call of All Nations*, 118–119); *De vocatione* II.19 (PL 51:706C–D; *Call of All Nations*, 125).
[180] Cross, "Anti-Pelagianism and the Resistibility of Grace," 200.
[181] Cross, "Anti-Pelagianism and the Resistibility of Grace," 201–210. See also Kevin Timpe, "Grace and Controlling What We Do Not Cause," *FPhilos* (2007): 284–229; and Timpe, "Cooperative Agency, Cooperative Grace," *European Journal for Philosophy of Religion* (2015): 225–247.

late Augustine of the anti-Pelagian controversies) does not seem to think that grace is irresistible. For, as he puts it, "when the ability is given, no necessity is imposed."[182]

II. DEPRAVITY

Moral psychology tells us that we are not nearly so good as we want to think we are. We are not nearly so honest, kind, courageous, self-giving, and generally *good* as we tell ourselves we are. As Christian Miller reminds us, "[T]he results of hundreds of studies in psychology" undermine this confidence in our goodness.[183] We are capable of all sorts of wrongdoing either by overt action or by passive neglect, and indeed we can do (or approve, or passively observe) all manner of horrific actions. At the same time, however, we are also capable of acts of virtue and even heroism. As Miller observes, "[O]ur hearts are not morally pure"—but nor are they as terrible as they might be.[184] Rather, "our hearts are a messy blend of good and evil."[185] The verdict of moral psychologists and sociobiologists (as well as evolutionary psychologists) is grim. They tell us that the tendencies to evil seem "hardwired" into us (so as to be memetic if not actually genetic). In other words, the more we learn from these disciplines about humanity, the more implausible Pelagianism seems (on empirical grounds). It is important not to overconclude here, and common claims about "genetic determinism" (or "chromosomal violence") are overblown.[186] Even Richard Dawkins, for instance, says that although humans are "built as gene machines and cultured as meme machines" they nonetheless "have the power to turn against" these creators.[187] For "[w]e, alone on earth, can rebel against the tyranny of the selfish replicators."[188] From the perspective of Christian theology, Dawkins seems inconsistent because, in the absence of good arguments to think otherwise—in the absence of the possibilities brought by grace—his protestations that we indeed *can* rebel against our selfishness look like mere bluster. But his work is also insightful in some ways, for it reminds us of the bleakness of the human condition.

When studies in sociobiology and moral psychology tell us that humans are

---

[182] Augustine, *De Spiritu* 54 (PL 44:235; NPNF¹ 5:107).

[183] Smith, *Character Gap*, x.

[184] Smith, *Character Gap*, xi.

[185] Smith, *Character Gap*, xi.

[186] See the helpful work of Susan Brooks Thistlethwaite, "A Gene for Violence? Genetic Determinism and Sin," in *Adam, Eve, and the Genome: The Human Genome Project and Theology*, ed. Susan Brooks Thistlethwaite (Minneapolis: Fortress, 2003), 145–160. Thistlethwaite shows how feminist critique has been helpful in exposing the flaws that have led to the determinist conclusions. See also Neil Messer, *Selfish Genes and Christian Ethics: Theological and Ethical Reflections on Evolutionary Biology* (London: SCM, 2007), 133–145. Denis Alexander, *Genes, Determinism, and God* (Cambridge: Cambridge University Press, 2017).

[187] Richard Dawkins, *The Selfish Gene* (Oxford: Oxford University Press, 1989), 201.

[188] Dawkins, *Selfish Gene*, 201.

"naturally" bent toward evil and yet still somehow capable of acts of goodness, they confirm what we seem to know in our most candid self-reflective moments, and yet such insights still manage to bother us by reminding us that these judgments apply to us as well as to others. But what sense do we make of these insights theologically?

Famously, the Protestant Reformers described our sin as *depravity*. A bit more controversially, sometimes the depravity is said to be *total*. This claim is deeply rooted in the theological (especially Protestant) tradition, and the affirmation of it extends beyond "Reformed" circles. Sin produces depravity, and the extent of this depravity is universal: all children, "without exception, are originally depraved."[189] We are sinners "by nature," but Calvin is at pains to show that this must be properly understood: "we say, then, that man is corrupted by a natural viciousness, but not by one which proceeded from nature. . . . [I]t was rather an adventitious event which befell man, than a substantial property assigned to him from the beginning. We, however, call it *natural* to prevent any one from supposing that each individual contracts it by depraved habit."[190] Sin expresses itself in all manner of sins. And even though Calvin will "confess that all these iniquities do not break out in every individual," nonetheless it "cannot be denied that the hydra lurks in every breast."[191]

Sin darkens the intellect, and it also enslaves the will. It can, then, in an important sense be considered "total" (as Calvin understands the human soul to be composed of intellect and will). So insistent is the Genevan Reformer that our wills are utterly enslaved by sin that he excoriates his theological forebears: "Moreover, although the Greek Fathers, above others, and especially Chrysostom, have exceeded due bounds in extolling the powers of the human will, yet all ancient theologians, with the exception of Augustine, are so confused, vacillating, and contradictory on this subject, that no certainty can be obtained from their writings."[192] This does not mean that we are not free, for Calvin draws an important distinction between *necessity* and *compulsion*.[193] In other words, Calvin is best understood as a "compatibilist" (or "soft determinist"): although the sinner "sins necessarily, nevertheless [he] sins voluntarily."[194] Calvin insists that "we must, therefore, repudiate the oft-repeated sentiment of Chrysostom, 'Whom he draws, he draws willingly;' insinuating that the

---

[189] John Calvin, *Institutes of the Christian Religion*, trans. Henry Beveridge (Grand Rapids, MI: Eerdmans, 1997), II.1.6 (215).
[190] Calvin, *Institutes*, II.1.10 (219).
[191] Calvin, *Institutes*, II.3.2 (251).
[192] Calvin, *Institutes*, II.2.4 (226).
[193] E.g., Calvin, *Institutes*, II.2.5 (228).
[194] Calvin, *Institutes*, II.4.1 (265); cf. II.3.5 (254). Cf. Paul Helm, *John Calvin's Ideas* (Oxford: Oxford University Press, 2004), 157–183.

Lord only stretches out his hand, and waits to see whether we will be pleased to take his aid."[195]

Calvin affirms that human depravity is completely debilitating, but this understanding is far from idiosyncratic to him. Indeed, major Wesleyan theologians affirm the doctrine of total depravity too (while not adopting Calvin's views of human freedom).[196] Wesley does not hold back at all: human sinners are "filled with all manner of evil," "void of all good," "wholly fallen," and "totally corrupted."[197] Richard Watson endorses and employs the term: "the true Arminian, as well as the Calvinist, admits the doctrine of total depravity."[198] Thomas Ralston and other Methodists concur.[199]

But what does the claim *mean*? What does it mean to say that sinners are *totally depraved*? And how could one even begin to defend such a view—is it not obvious that there are different degrees of sinfulness, and is it not obvious that not everyone (and perhaps not anyone) actually commits all possible sins or the most heinous sins possible?

It is important to be clear about what is meant by this venerable claim. And it is also important to understand what is *not* meant by this claim. Perhaps it will be helpful to clear away some conceptual brush by addressing some common misperceptions and misunderstandings. First, total depravity does not mean that every sin is equally bad. As we have seen, Jesus himself shows us that we should not fall into this confusion; there really are such things as "greater" sins (John 19:11). Second, total depravity does not mean that every person (or even every unregenerate person) is equally depraved by sin. To the contrary, the doctrine of total depravity is fully consistent with the conviction that some people are far more scarred and vitiated by sin than others. Nothing about the doctrine entails that, say, Mother Theresa was as morally flawed as Adolf Hitler or Josef Stalin. Surely the doctrine should be viewed with suspicion if it were to teach or imply such a conclusion. But it does not, and to think so is simply to misunderstand the doctrinal claim. Nor yet, as Michael Scott Horton notes, does it mean that "we are incapable of any justice or good before fellow humans."[200]

---

[195] Calvin, *Institutes*, II.3.10 (260).

[196] To clear away a couple of common confusions: total depravity does not entail determinism (either historically or conceptually), and indeterminism is not synonymous with Pelagianism or "Semi-Pelagianism" (again, either historically or conceptually). To think this is to make some rather basic category mistakes (mistakes that would likely be avoided by proper engagement with the tradition of Christian theology).

[197] Wesley, "Original Sin," 456.

[198] Richard Watson, *Theological Institutes, Or A View of the Evidences, Doctrines, Morals, and Institutions of Christianity*, 2 vols. (New York: Bangs & Emory, 1826), 2:210.

[199] Thomas N. Ralston, *Elements of Divinity: A Concise and Comprehensive View of Bible Theology; Comprising the Doctrines, Evidences, Morals, and Institutions of Christianity, with Appropriate Questions Appended to Each Chapter* (New York: Abingdon, 1847), 125. See further the discussion in Thomas H. McCall, "But a Heathen Still: Wesleyan Theology and the Doctrine of Original Sin," in *Adam, the Fall, and Original Sin: Theological, Biblical, and Scientific Perspectives*, ed. Hans Madueme and Michael Reeves (Grand Rapids, MI: Baker Academic, 2014), 147–166.

[200] Michael Scott Horton, *The Christian Faith: A Systematic Theology for Pilgrims on the Way* (Grand Rapids, MI: Zondervan Academic, 2011), 433.

So what *is* meant by the doctrinal admission that we are "totally depraved"? Horton says that "[o]ur bondage to sin in Adam is complete in its extensiveness, though not in its intensity."[201] We can be a bit more precise. Several points are included in the claim: our depravity is what can be called *broadly extensive* in the sense that we all suffer from it, and our depravity is what can be called *narrowly extensive* in the sense that all parts or aspects of every person are impacted by it. Perhaps a bit more explanation is in order.

First, depravity can be said to be "total" in the broadly extensive sense that it impacts all members of the human race. All members of the human race— other than Christ—suffer from it.[202] This aspect of the extent of depravity is summarized well by Katherine Sonderegger:

> From Adam and Eve radiate out the contamination that seeps into every heart, every deed, every death, every created thing. This is the state or condition of the Fall; it is universal and it is global. From this condition, creatures call out for salvation, a deliverance from finitude, sin and death."[203]

"There is no distinction: for all have sinned and fall short of the glory of God" (Rom. 3:22–23).

The second way that this depravity is said to be "total" is in the sense that all parts or aspects of the human person are negatively impacted by it. As Horton explains, "What is meant by 'total' is that the whole nature of humanity, not only the body and its desires but the soul, mind, heart, and will is corrupt."[204] In other words, it is not merely our "bodies" that suffer from the effects of sin. Nor is it only our "minds" or our "wills" or our "emotions." To the contrary, the claim is that we are holistic persons who suffer from the effects of sin as whole persons (although sin "disintegrates" us). Accordingly, we suffer the "noetic effects" of the fall; our cognitive faculties do not function as they were made and meant to function.[205] Our "thinking" (Rom. 1:21) has been tainted in various ways. Søren Kierkegaard observes that the "natural man" is "ignorant of what is truly horrifying, yet is not thereby liberated from shuddering and shrinking—no, he shrinks from that which is not horrifying."[206] Similarly, sin impacts us physically, and our "bodies," which are now "temple[s] of the Holy Spirit" (1 Cor. 6:19) also long for their liberation from the effects of sin. Affectively and volitionally, we are depraved; we do not want what we ought to want or will what we ought to will. As Karl Barth puts

---

[201] Michael Scott Horton, *For Calvinism* (Grand Rapids, MI: Zondervan, 2011), 15, cited in Scott R. Burson, *Brian McLaren in Focus: A New Kind of Apologetics* (Abilene, TX: Abilene Christian University Press, 2016), 138n7.
[202] Although it is also clear from Scripture that Christ suffers *for* it or *because of* it.
[203] Katherine Sonderegger, "Finitude and Death," in *T&T Clark Companion to the Doctrine of Sin*, 390.
[204] Horton, *Christian Faith*, 433.
[205] See Alvin Plantinga, *Warranted Christian Belief* (Oxford: Oxford University Press, 2000), 199–240.
[206] Søren Kierkegaard, *The Sickness unto Death: A Christian Psychological Exposition for Upbuilding and Awakening*, ed. and trans. Howard V. Hong and Edna H. Hong with introduction and notes (Princeton, NJ: Princeton University Press, 1980), 8.

it, the corruption of sin is "both radical and total. . . . It . . . takes place at the basis and centre of the being of man, in his heart; and . . . the consequent sinful perversion then extends to the whole of his being without exception."[207] This means that

> in the whole sphere of human activities there are no exceptions to the sin and corruption of man. There is no territory which has been spared and where he does not sin, where he is not perverted, where he still maintains the divine order and is therefore guiltless. At every point man is in the wrong and in arrears in relation to God. . . . Because his pride is radical and in principle, it is also total and universal and all-embracing, determining all his thoughts and words and works, his whole inner and hidden life, and his visible external movements and relationships.[208]

There is a third sense in which depravity can be said to be total: it expresses itself in all that unsanctified sinners *do*. As Kathryn Tanner explains,

> Because the means to our knowing and loving God is also the means by which we know and choose anything well, in losing the ability to know and love God, all our acts are ruined. Everything we do, even in the pursuit of penultimate created goods, is done in the wrong way, because done without the one thing necessary for every good in life, the gift of God's own goodness through Word and Spirit.[209]

This depravity further alienates us and separates us from God and from human community. Such alienation is the result of guilt, and it produces further shame.

III. GUILT AND SHAME

Sin produces both guilt and shame. Eleonore Stump observes that "no one doubts that guilt and shame are distinct, but there is considerable controversy over the nature of the distinction."[210] She offers the insightful suggestion that we think about these in terms of their relation to love. Following Thomas Aquinas, love "consists in two mutually governing desires:

> (i) a desire for the good of the beloved;
> and
> (ii) a desire for union with the beloved."[211]

How does this relate to shame and guilt? "A person who is and feels shamed and a person who is and feels guilty each anticipates a repudiation, on the part of real

---

[207] Karl Barth, *CD*, IV/1, 492.

[208] Barth, *CD*, IV/1, 496.

[209] Kathryn Tanner, *Christ the Key* (Cambridge: Cambridge University Press, 2010), 63.

[210] Eleonore Stump, "The Atonement and the Problem of Shame," *Journal of Philosophical Research*, forthcoming, 3. See also Stump, *Wandering in Darkness: Narrative and the Problem of Suffering* (Oxford: Oxford University Press, 2010), 141–149.

[211] Stump, "Atonement and the Problem of Shame," 3.

or imagined others, of both of the desires of love as regards himself. But a person in the grip of guilt will tend to focus more on the first desire, and a person suffering from shame will tend to worry more about the second."[212] So, on Stump's account, (i) relates more directly to guilt, while (ii) is concerned more directly with shame. The guilty person is aware that he has sinned against the good of the other, and he is objectively guilty. As such, he worries that the person(s) who has been sinned against now may no longer desire for his good. The shamed person, on the other hand, is concerned that the aggrieved party has no desire for union.

It is a commonplace that guilt is the consequence of sin. And for good reason: Scripture teaches us that sin brings guilt and results in condemnation but that Christ saves us from it (e.g., Rom. 8:1). But Scripture also shows us that sin produces *shame*. Indeed, as Wilfried Härle observes, "It is striking how great a significance the phenomenon of being ashamed has in primeval biblical history (particularly in Gen. 2:25–3:21). At the conclusion of the creation narrative it is explicitly noted that the first human beings were naked and were not ashamed (Gen. 2:25), and correspondingly, the first consequence of the fall proves that they were ashamed (Gen. 3:7, 10)."[213]

So in addition to the guilt that is more commonly acknowledged, we should also understand that sin results in shame.[214] Shame debilitates persons and their relationships, and consequently results in further alienation from one another and from God. Shame harms both the sinner and those who live in community with the sinner. As Stump points out, there are some important distinctions with respect to shame: there is the shame that results from one's own sin, there is the shame that is the consequence of someone else's wrongdoing,[215] there is the shame that follows from the corruption of nature, and there is the shame that comes with "being a member of the human race."[216] The latter is related to original sin, while the others are most directly related to acts of sin.

IV. Sin and Death

A. The "Wages of Sin": An Introduction to the Topic (That Needs No Introduction)

Death is our final enemy, and it awaits us all. There simply is no getting around it. But no matter how accustomed to it we might think that we are, no matter

---

[212] Stump, "Atonement and the Problem of Shame," 3.

[213] Wilfried Härle, *Outline of Christian Doctrine: An Evangelical Dogmatics* (Grand Rapids, MI: Eerdmans, 2015), 413.

[214] For interesting observations on the effects of guilt and shame on us, see Jesse J. Prinz and Shaun Nichols, "Moral Emotions," in *The Moral Psychology Handbook*, ed. John M. Doris and the Moral Psychology Research Group (Oxford: Oxford University Press, 2010), 111–146.

[215] Stump points to various examples from history (e.g., victims of violence by the Taliban and the Nazis) and from Scripture (e.g., the story of the famine in Israel as a response to their treatment of the Gibeonites) ("Atonement and the Problem of Shame," 4).

[216] Stump, "Atonement and the Problem of Shame," 6.

how "normal" we might consider it to be, still there is something in human experience that sees death as something *bad*. Sonderegger puts the point eloquently:

> We know in our bones the pain and horror of corruption and death. No century is as drenched in death as is the twentieth; and the twenty-first may well teach us a death of species and habitats and homelands that previous eras could only reserve for a nightmarish invasion, an apocalypse. But it does not require a world history lesson to teach us the anguish and limit of loss: the diminishment of a single life can do this very well indeed. A day of hunger or pain could do this; even an hour. A body riddled with cancer—an entirely natural, biological phenomenon—can sear this into our attention. . . . This is the state and destiny of human creaturehood.[217]

Scripture tells us plainly that sin results in death. In Eden, the Creator tells "the man" that failure to keep the divine command will lead to death: "but of the tree of the knowledge of good and evil you shall not eat, for in the day that you eat of it you shall surely die" (Gen. 2:17). The lie of the serpent in the temptation went directly to this warning as the tempter told the woman, "[Y]ou will not surely die" (Gen. 3:4). "The wages of sin is death" (Rom. 6:23).

B. Seeing through the Complications: Some Distinctions in Pursuit of Clarity

This much is obvious. But what, more precisely, does it mean to say that death is the result of sin? Does "death" here refer only to what some people call "spiritual death" as separation from God? Does it refer to such spiritual death and the accompanying experience of physical death *as we now know it* (tainted with fear, despair, grief, and inconsolable loss)? Does it refer to just any physical death of humans? Does it refer more broadly to the physical death of all animals—or even more broadly yet to any sort of physical decay and decomposition in the universe? Is it all of the above? Some Christians take the clear teaching of Scripture to be that the "death" that comes from sin is just any and all death whatsoever; they insist, for instance, that there would have been no animal death (and certainly no animal predation!) before the primal sin of the first humans. Sometimes they wonder what else "death" might even possibly refer to, and sometimes they object that anything else is a departure from Christian orthodoxy.[218]

But it was not always so. For instance, Thomas Aquinas notes that "in the opinion of some" there was no animal predation before the fall. Those who hold this view think that "those animals which are now fierce and kill others,

---

[217] Sonderegger, "Finitude and Death," 386.
[218] Sometimes such charges of heterodoxy are accompanied by allegations of "compromise" with naturalistic accounts of human origins.

would, in that state, have been tame, not only in regard to man, but also in regard to other animals."[219] But Aquinas disagrees with those who hold this opinion. For while without the fall it would be the case that all animals would be under the mastery of the humans (and thus posing no threats to their safety), nonetheless they would have been what they are. Thus carnivores would have been carnivores and would have sought to "devour the flesh of others," and there would have been "a natural antipathy" between them. Thus the opinion of the unnamed "some" is, in his estimation, "quite unreasonable."[220]

Similarly, the great Reformer John Calvin notes that "some" understand the prelapsarian divine warning about death "in a 'spiritual sense,' thinking that, even if Adam had not sinned, his body must still have been separated from his soul."[221] Calvin does not embrace this view, and he insists that "the whole order of nature was subverted by the sin of man." Indeed, he says that "all the disadvantages in which man, by sin, has involved himself" include "all the evils of the present life, which experience proves to be innumerable," and he is certain that these "have proceeded from the same fountain."[222] Thus the "inclemency of the air, frost, thunders, unseasonable rains, drought, hail, and whatever is disorderly in the world" are "the fruits of sin."[223] In particular, he says, there is no "primary cause of diseases" other than sin.[224]

But when Calvin turns to the divine judgment, "you are dust, and to dust you shall return" (Gen. 3:19), he insists that God is talking about what "belongs to man's nature" rather than "to his crime or fault."[225] Adam and Eve would not have existed forever in their current condition—even apart from sin. To the contrary, they would have "passed to a better life."[226] But such a passage would not have involved any "separation of the soul from the body," nor would it have included any "corruption, no kind of destruction, and, in short, no violent change."[227] In other words, the first humans would have passed on from this life to another that is better—they would clearly, for Calvin, have "passed away" in some sense—but they would have done so without any of the negative elements that we associate with death. Subsequent to their sin, of course, "we dread death, because dissolution, which is contrary to nature, cannot naturally be desired."[228]

So what are we to make of all this? Downstream of Darwin especially, many people see death as entirely natural and even, strictly speaking, as

---

[219] Aquinas, *ST* I, Q 96.1.
[220] Aquinas, *ST* I, Q 86.1.
[221] John Calvin, *Commentaries on the First Book of Moses Called Genesis* (Grand Rapids, MI: Baker, 1979), 180.
[222] Calvin, *Genesis*, 177.
[223] Calvin, *Genesis*, 177.
[224] Calvin, *Genesis*, 177.
[225] Calvin, *Genesis*, 180.
[226] Calvin, *Genesis*, 180.
[227] Calvin, *Genesis*, 180.
[228] Calvin, *Genesis*, 180.

inevitable. Accordingly, for such people, it makes little sense to see death as the result of sin. On the other hand, some Christians insist that *all* forms of death are the result of the fall, and they sometimes view anything less than such a position as compromise with naturalism and a denial of God's word. But what are we to make of this—just what is entailed theologically by commitment to the belief that "the wages of sin is death"? Perhaps it will help to distinguish between several broad senses of the meaning of "death." We might first recognize a fairly common distinction between *physical death* and *spiritual death* (where "spiritual death" refers to the state of separation and alienation from God). Granting that spiritual death (as separation from God) is the result of sin, is physical death also attributable to sin in any sense? Consider these possibilities.[229]

We could think of the "death" in question in a very expansive sense as

(D1) the death of just any living organism whatsoever.

On (D1), the "wages of sin" would be the introduction of death into the created order, and it would impact not only humans but also all other life forms. To put it colloquially and perhaps even somewhat crudely, all living things—not only fauna but also flora and any other candidates—would suffer death as the result of human sin. Or narrowing the scope somewhat, we could think of it as something more like

(D2) the death of biological organisms that are capable of some level of higher-order cognitive functions.[230]

According to (D2), the scope of devastation as a consequence of human sin would also be very wide, but it would extend only beyond humans to the "animal kingdom"; only complex carbon-based life forms would count, and only some of these. Again, to use the colloquialism, sin would impact the fauna directly but not the flora (although, presumably, this would be impacted too in less direct ways). In other words, not death *simpliciter* but the *death of animals and humans* is the result of the fall. Narrowing the scope still further, we could think of the death referred to here as

(D3) the (physical and spiritual) death of humans.

---

[229] Obviously, this sketch could be much more finely grained and will appear rather rough-and-ready by some accounts, but what we need is something that does enough for present purposes without bogging down the discussion in unnecessary minutiae.

[230] Whatever exactly that level of higher-level cognitive functions must be, it need not concern us further here. I also leave to the side the perplexing issues of just exactly what physical death is and how it is known. For more on the latter, see John S. Feinberg and Paul D. Feinberg, *Ethics for a Brave New World*, 2nd ed. (Wheaton, IL: Crossway, 2010), 225–226.

On (D3), the "wages of sin" are the deaths of humans. Other creatures would, on this account, also die, but not as the wages of sin. They would have died anyway; it is only the humans who enjoyed prelapsarian immortality—and only humans who lost it in the fall. Moving further, we might consider the "death" in question as

> (D4) the death of humans *as it is commonly experienced by humans in the world as we know it*—where human death is inevitably accompanied by some level of suffering, dread, grief, and sorrow (whether by the one who dies, the community of the one who dies, or both).

C. Any and All Death?

With these distinctions in hand, let us return to the question before us. What is the "death" referred to in the biblical claim that sin produces death? What does it mean to say that the "wages of sin is death" (Rom. 6:23)? Let us start with consideration of (D1) (the death of just any living organism whatsoever). Fortunately, we need not linger long here, for the problems are not hard to see. These problems are, however, quite severe. First, we should note that nothing in the biblical account comes anywhere close to claiming this, and one would have to seriously overread the text to come to such a conclusion. Scripture simply is not telling us about the reasons for the decay of microorganisms and vegetative life, and we risk eisegesis to assume that it is. Second, the view is impossible to square with what we know from modern science, and it is noteworthy that no one disputes this.[231] Third, such a view is theologically problematic—at least for those traditionally minded Christians who believe that the fall of Satan pre-dates the fall of the first humans (as is suggested by the presence of a tempter in Eden). For, as it stands, the claim is very expansive in scope; so expansive, in fact, that it refers to all living organisms. So we can conclude that (D1) is not worthy of any further consideration (although, as we shall see, consideration of it serves an important heuristic function).

(D2), on the other hand (the death of biological organisms that are capable of some level of higher-order cognitive functions), enjoys enthusiastic support from some theological perspectives (especially from the proponents of "young earth creationism"). According to (D2), there was no animal predation, suffering, or death before the primal sin of the first humans; the rest of creation now suffers death as the result of the fall. In other words, the animals also receive the wages of human sin. Many of the proponents of this view assume that it is *the* view of the Christian tradition (and thus make accompanying charges of "redefinition" and "compromise" for anything other than (D2)). But as we

[231] At least no one of whom I know.

have seen in the examples of such luminaries as Aquinas and Calvin, it is not, in fact, *the* traditional view. Similarly, many of the proponents of this view take the support for it to be both powerful and obvious. But it is neither obvious nor powerful. The biblical warnings and commands do not specify that the death of animals is included in the penalty of sin. To the contrary, the focus is on the humans themselves: "*you* shall surely die" (Gen. 2:17). Nor is the penalty for sin as death ever said to extend beyond humanity. Scripture makes it clear that the broader created order *suffers* in some sense as a result of human sin, and it makes it equally plain that the work of Christ has come to restore his creation (e.g., Gen. 3:17–18; Rom. 8:19–22). But Scripture does not explicitly say that death for animals is a result of the fall. What we are told is that death has "spread *to all humanity* because all sinned" (Rom. 5:12 AT), and Paul makes it clear that his focus is on the fact that condemnation and death have come to all *humanity* (Rom. 5:18–20). The "wages of sin" are said to accrue directly to human sinners, and the witness of Scripture makes it clear that while Christ indeed is the Lord of the cosmos (e.g., Col. 1:15–20), his atoning sacrifice is directly intended for humanity.

Beyond this, however, the support for (D2) is largely generated by worries related to animal theodicy. The basic concern is about the goodness of God, and the worry here is that this bedrock theological conviction seems to be called into question or undermined by the fact that, given standard evolutionary theory, the world has witnessed millions of years of blood and gore as untold numbers of species have developed and then have been eliminated. The exact nature of the objection is not entirely clear, but the upshot seems to be this: we cannot maintain belief in the goodness of God if we also accept the notion that animal suffering is not somehow the consequence of human sin. And since we must not give up the bedrock conviction in the goodness of God, we must conclude that all animal suffering and death is the result of human sin.

But such an objection assumes a great deal. For one thing, the argument assumes that animals suffer pain and loss as we do (or at least much like we do). And this, in turn, assumes that animals enjoy advanced levels of consciousness. Some proponents of the argument make such assumptions explicit. Indeed, Douglas Kennard refers to animals as "souls" and "persons."[232] But this is exactly what must not be quickly assumed, for there are good reasons to question such assumptions; it simply is not obvious that we know enough to draw such conclusions with any confidence.[233] Moreover, the advo-

[232] E.g., Douglas Kennard, "Hebrew Metaphysic: Life, Holy, Clean, Righteousness, and Sacrifice," *Answers Research Journal* (2008): 171.
[233] E.g., Michael Murray, *Nature Red in Tooth and Claw: Theism and the Problem of Animal Suffering* (Oxford: Oxford University Press, 2008), 41–72.

cates of (D2) offer no reason to think that there are no other good candidates for such animal theodicy, or even that "skeptical theism" would not work here as a response.[234] Finally, it is not clear that the preferred strategy of the advocates of (D2) really works either—even for their own purposes. For if the real problem is with holding both to belief that God is good and to belief that animals suffer innocently, then we are still left to wonder why the animals suffer for the sin of the first humans. It is not exactly obvious why animals should suffer for the sins of humans. Surely the animals are not morally responsible for the sin of the first humans, are they? But if not, then why does a good God arrange things so that they are destined to suffer in this way? So, if there indeed is a serious and insurmountable problem of theodicy here, it is not apparent that the proponents of (D2) have the resources to handle it. But nor, as I have suggested, is it obvious that there really is such a serious and insurmountable problem, so this objection hardly works as a knockdown argument for understanding death as the "wages of sin" in the sense of (D2). Scripture does not actually say this, and the other theological arguments for it simply are not strong.

D. Moving Forward

This leaves us with (D3) and (D4). To recap, (D3) allows for animal death before the fall but insists that human death (understood in the straightforward physical sense, as well, of course, as spiritual death as separation from God) is the result of the first human sin. Thus (D3) holds that, had there been no fall, the humans would not have died. The rest of the created order would have been subject to corruption and death, but humans would have been excepted from such a fate. Tracking with Aquinas, the proponent of (D3) would say that animal predation would have been part of the original "design plan." Accordingly, Adam and Eve would have had the categories to understand the warnings about "death" before the fall; they would have been able to look around them and understand that this could happen to them too. And, consequent to the fall, humans too have been subject to corruption and death and indeed are subject to it now.

(D4) goes a step further. For not only would it allow for animal death before the fall; it would also have space for some form of human physical death before the fall. How would death be in any sense the "wages of sin" if death

---

[234] "Skeptical Theism" does not refer to skepticism about the truth of theism in the face of problems of evil. Instead, it refers to skepticism about our ability to know enough to conclude that there are no good reasons for God to act (or refrain from acting) as he does. See, e.g., Michael Bergmann, "Skeptical Theism and the Problem of Evil," in *The Oxford Handbook of Philosophical Theology*, ed. Thomas P. Flint and Michael C. Rea (Oxford: Oxford University Press, 2009), 374–399; Michael C. Rea, "Skeptical Theism and the 'Too Much Skepticism' Objection," in *The Blackwell Companion to the Problem of Evil*, ed. Justin P. McBrayer and Daniel Howard-Snyder (Oxford: Wiley-Blackwell, 2013), 482–506. For a helpful general discussion of the problems of evil, see John S. Feinberg, *The Many Faces of Evil: Theological Systems and the Problems of Evil*, rev. and expanded ed. (Wheaton, IL: Crossway, 2004).

was already a reality for humans before the fall? Taking a cue from Calvin, the answer to this question would be twofold.[235] The first line of response is to say that there was no *spiritual death* before the fall, and there would have been no separation from God at death had there been no fall. Instead, death would have been a transition to a more complete and perfect state of union with our Maker and the One for whom we have been made. The second line of response follows closely from the first: while *physical death* would have been a reality even with no sin, it would have been radically different than it is on this side of Eden. For without spiritual death and all that it brings with it, we would not have experienced physical death as we now do. We would not have been forced to face it with dread and horror, and we would not be forced to endure it with sorrow, grief, and suffering.

Some Christians might protest that all these distinctions are unnecessary. They might remonstrate that such maneuvers are merely attempts to avoid the "plain meaning" of the text, and they might insist that we should simply stick with the broadest possible quantification. After all, does not the Bible just say "death" when it refers to the consequences of sin? But what might at first seem to be the "plain meaning" actually is not so plain in this case. For the broadest quantification is (D1), and we have seen that this is a reading that is deeply flawed. Furthermore, we can see that no one holds to it—so every interpreter is drawing *some* distinctions and making judgments about them. Thus the question is squarely before us: all things considered, which interpretation is to be preferred?

There is a great deal more that could be said about this, but, by my lights, we are in a position to see several things with reasonable clarity. First, as we have seen, (D1), the death of any living organism whatsoever, is simply not plausible. Second, and now turning to (D2), the death of biological organisms capable of some level of higher-order cognitive functions, we can see that we cannot simply assume that it is demanded by either Scripture or classical orthodoxy (understood either in the narrower sense of creedal coherence or in the somewhat more expansive sense of the "Vincentian canon").[236] It may not be ruled out of bounds by biblical orthodoxy, but neither is it entailed by it. On the other hand, it suffers from lack of support and faces some fairly serious objections. As C. John Collins observes, there is nothing in the text of Genesis that "says that animals were never carnivorous until man fell."[237] He notes that the psalmist actually celebrates God's provision for large carnivores (e.g., Pss. 104:21; 147:9), and he concludes that "it is a mistake to read Genesis 2:17 as

[235] By suggesting that the proponents of this view "take a cue from Calvin," I do not mean to ascribe to Calvin all elements of this position.
[236] On the Vincentian canon, see chapter 4, note 3.
[237] C. John Collins, *Genesis 1–4: A Linguistic, Literary, and Theological Commentary* (Phillipsburg, NJ: P&R, 2006), 165.

implying that *physical* death did not affect the creation before the fall."[238] For the "focus of this death is spiritual death," and it "applies to humans and says nothing about animals."[239]

At the same time, however, as Collins points out, it "does seem that Genesis 3:19 portrays physical death as a consequence of the fall."[240] This brings us to consideration of (D3). Here we can see that while it does not ignore or even downplay physical death as a result of sin, it limits the death at issue (that is, death as a result of the fall) to humans. (D3) puts emphasis on the primacy of spiritual death (and, in turn, what that means for physical death). And this seems right; as Charles H. H. Scobie says, death is most fundamentally "separation from God."[241] Moreover, it can claim consistency with what surely seems to be clear in the Genesis account. As Collins notes, even though there is "no simple *exegetical* answer to the question of Adam's mortality," it nonetheless seems to be the case that Genesis 3 "views physical death as following from the fall."[242] (D3) has the benefit of making good sense of the warnings that came to Adam with the prohibition, "of the tree of the knowledge of good and evil you shall not eat, for in the day that you eat of it you shall surely die" (Gen. 2:17). For where (D1) and (D2) would leave Adam unsure of what "death" even is and thus less able to understand the warning, on this reading Adam could have known what death is simply by looking around him. Moreover, (D3) coheres very well with what the Bible has to say about death as the consequence of sin, for death—*human death*, that is, which clearly is the focal point of biblical teaching—really is the "wages" of sin. It puts emphasis on what the NT emphasizes: sin and death came upon humanity as a result of Adam's transgression (e.g., Rom. 5:12–21; 1 Cor. 15:21–22). In addition, it does not appear to transgress any important creedal and confessional boundaries. Moreover, it is consistent with what science tells us about the realities of animal predation and death.

But while (D3) fares well on theological grounds and can claim consistency not only with such luminaries from the tradition as Thomas Aquinas and John Calvin but also with scientific accounts of animal predation and death, critics may worry that it cannot account for mainstream modern scientific teaching about human origins. Such critics would argue that humans share a long evolutionary history with other hominins, and they appeal to a range of impressive evidence drawn from paleoanthropology, evolutionary biology, and genetics

[238] Collins, *Genesis 1–4*, 165.
[239] Collins, *Genesis 1–4*, 166.
[240] Collins, *Genesis 1–4*, 161.
[241] Charles H. H. Scobie, *The Ways of Our God: An Approach to Biblical Theology* (Grand Rapids, MI: Eerdmans, 2003), 684. Cf. George Eldon Ladd, *A Theology of the New Testament*, rev. ed., ed. Donald Hagner (Grand Rapids, MI: Eerdmans, 1993), 446. For a helpful summary of "death" in biblical theology, see Reinhard Feldmeier and Hermann Spieckermann, *God of the Living: A Biblical Theology* (Waco, TX: Baylor University Press, 2011), 385–402.
[242] Collins, *Genesis 1–4*, 161.

in support of their view.[243] The relevant claims include: (i) the biological and genetic evidence shows that the initial human community shares common ancestry with other primitive hominins; (ii) the genetic evidence shows that the initial human community must have been numbered in the thousands; (iii) the history of the developments of hominins into *homo sapiens* is one that is long and violent. The upshot of this is expressed forcefully by Arthur Peacocke:

> Biological death can no longer be regarded as in any way the *consequence* of anything human beings might have been supposed to have done in the past, for evolutionary history shows it to be the very *means* whereby they appear and so, for the theist, are created by God.[244]

In response to such science-based claims, some theologians have allowed that perhaps Adam and Eve indeed do share common ancestry with other primates.[245] In response to (i), the suggestion here is that perhaps God refurbished some existing hominins and endowed them with the *imago dei* by breathing "into [their] nostrils the breath of life" (Gen. 2:7)—and thus bestowing upon them a higher degree of abilities and functions (rationality, communicative abilities, moral sensibilities, etc.). They readily admit that while such a scenario is not demanded by Scripture, nonetheless it is consonant with the teaching of Genesis—Adam postdates the rest of the creation, and he is clearly formed from preexisting material (rather than *ex nihilo* as is creation in general). In response to (ii), they have allowed that Adam and Eve may have been part of a larger community; after all, they reason, Cain was able to find a wife (Gen. 4:17). Thus one statement puts it this way:

> God took two hominids to become the first human beings, Adam and Eve (1 Tim. 2:13). In Eve's case, God provided the new genetic information needed to make her human by using some genetic material taken from "one of" Adam's "ribs," so she too would be of Adam's race. . . . Thus Eve's existence as a person was made racially dependent upon Adam; and these two *alone* are the rest of the human race's progenitors.[246]

Alternatively, Adam and Eve would have served as the first federal representatives or "chieftains" of the initial population.[247]

---

[243] For a helpful and impressive overview of some of this evidence, see Denis Alexander, *Creation or Evolution: Do We Have to Choose?* 2nd ed. (Grand Rapids, MI: Monarch, 2014).

[244] Arthur Peacocke, *Theology for a Scientific Age: Being and Becoming—Natural, Divine, and Human* (Oxford: Blackwell, 1993), 222, emphasis original.

[245] C. John Collins lists John Stott, Derek Kidner, and C. S. Lewis as biblical scholars and theologians who hold such views (or at least are very open to them); see *Did Adam and Eve Really Exist? Who They Were and Why You Should Care* (Wheaton, IL: Crossway, 2011), 123–131.

[246] Gavin McGrath, "Soteriology: Adam and the Fall," *Perspectives on Science and Christian Faith* (1997): 252–263. See further the endorsement of C. S. Lewis's suggestion by Francis Collins, *The Language of God: A Scientist Presents Evidence for Belief* (New York: Simon & Schuster, 2006), 208–209.

[247] For further discussion, see Collins, *Did Adam and Eve Really Exist?*, 130.

Whatever judgment one renders of such strategies,[248] they still leave us with (iii). If the contemporary scientific account is true, then is not the case that the process of evolution that led to the development of humans was violent and bloody, one marked by suffering and death? And if so, then is not (D3) false—and obviously so? No, (D3) is not obviously false. For if God endows the creatures with his image and thus makes them *human* (at that moment), it is entirely possible that he granted them (conditional) immortality at that moment. Accordingly, as soon as they are human they are capable of sustained life rather than death (perhaps with a future like that envisioned by Calvin, where they do not actually "die" but where they do pass on to a better form of existence). The basic point should be clear: on this account, humanity *as such* is not condemned to death. On this view, the first humans were without sin at the moment of their creation, and neither sin nor death was inevitable for them. If any of the strategies work, then they work here too. Accordingly, (D3) should not be ruled out or dismissed on grounds of this objection.

What about (D4)? Recall that (D4) allows that death is "natural" to humanity; humans die with or without the fall. Death is simply part of the created order as such; it is just what happens, it is a "part of life." But it is not "natural" as we now experience it, and it was never intended to be what it is now. Death is often brutal and violent, and the sad truth is that death as we now experience it is accompanied by suffering, dread, and grief. According to (D4), however, we need not conclude that this is the way that things had to be. For in the absence of sin, the experience of death would be entirely different. It would not be marked by suffering, dread, or grief. Instead, it would be a celebration of the life of holiness that was lived, and in turn a celebration of the life of holiness that is now enjoyed in the presence of God.[249] So on (D4) death is natural and indeed was intended by God—but not at all as we know it. Death itself is a corollary of our finitude, but *death as we now know it* is the result of sin. In other words, physical death itself is simply natural, but spiritual death along with the changes it brings to the way that we experience physical death is the result of sin.

On this account, the contemporary scientific conclusions about human origins should not worry the Christian. Physical death is natural, and when the Bible says that the "wages of sin is death" (Rom. 6:23), it simply is not

---

[248] For further discussion, see the Appendix to this book. See also Thomas H. McCall, *An Invitation to Analytic Christian Theology* (Downers Grove, IL: IVP Academic, 2015), 145–180.

[249] The proponent of (D4) might argue that we get some glimmer (however faint) of this reality when we compare and contrast the death of a recalcitrant sinner who wasted his life with the passing of a saint who loved our Lord supremely and lived for him wholeheartedly. One is utterly tragic, while the other is marked by a profound sense of joy and gladness along with an important sense of loss and longing. If we can experience this much now, try to imagine the funeral of someone whose life was never tarnished by sin and who did not suffer the consequences of living in a sinful world. Would not the experience be radically different from death as we now know it? Would it not be an occasion of unmitigated thanksgiving for her life and celebration of her homecoming? And would not any residual longing for reunion be a profoundly holy hunger rather than lament?

talking about that kind of death. But several potential problems come with this proposal. First, to tie physical death to finitude rather than sin seems to go against the teaching of Scripture. In John's Apocalypse we read of his vision that "death shall be no more" (Rev. 21:4). But we will never stop being finite, so if finitude entails death, then it is hard to see how death will come to an end. Furthermore, drawing such a sharp bifurcation (rather than merely a distinction, as we see in (D3)) between physical and spiritual death (and then maintaining that physical death just is what it is) does not seem to cohere well with the biblical emphasis on the hope for *bodily* resurrection and renewal precisely as the *reversal of sin and its effects*. Thus Paul famously ties *bodily resurrection and immortality* to *victory over sin*: "'O death, where is your victory? O death, where is your sting?' The sting of death is sin, and the power of sin is the law. But thanks be to God, who gives us the victory through our Lord Jesus Christ" (1 Cor. 15:55–57). So critics will likely continue to worry that (D4) relaxes the connection between sin and bodily corruption, on one hand, and, on the other hand, between salvation and bodily resurrection.

Proponents of (D4) face another concern as well. As we have seen, the Council of Carthage (c. 418) decisively rejected Pelagianism. As part of that rejection, the Carthaginian theologians forcefully anathematized those who hold that Adam would have died even apart from sin. Along with the condemnations of notions that we can earn or merit salvation through our unaided efforts or that God's grace pertains only to the forgiveness of past sins (leaving current and future growth in holiness strictly up to us), the Council also approved these words:

> If any man says that Adam, the first man, was created mortal, so that, whether he sinned or not, he would have died from natural causes, and not as the wages of sin, let him be anathema.[250]

It is hard indeed to avoid the conclusion that (D4) directly contravenes the pronouncements of the council that decisively rejected Pelagianism. For contemporary Christians who find association with Pelagianism odious, this will be a problem. For Christians who think that it is important to retain as much continuity as possible with the important creeds and councils of the church, this will be a problem. However, several lines of response are open to the Christian attracted to (D4). First, she could point out that Carthage is not one of the major ecumenical councils. While it is important, it does not have (and has never had) the stature of, say, the Niceno-Constantinopolitan Creed or the Chalcedonian Formula. Second, she could note that Carthage also anathematizes other positions which are neither demanded by the rejection of Pelagianism nor at all easy

---

[250] Cited in Bettenson, *Documents of the Christian Church*, 59.

to defend. Notably, it condemns the belief that unbaptized children might be in heaven or even in some "middle place" of bliss.[251] Finally, and building upon the foregoing point, she could argue that the proponent of (D4) can stand in complete agreement with the *spirit* of Carthage while admitting disagreement with the letter of the council's law. In other words, the defender of (D4) can make a case that the position can be in complete agreement with the affirmation of original sin and the corresponding denial that we can save ourselves or even do anything good whatsoever apart from grace.

(D4) offers the promise of coherence with the pronouncements of contemporary paleoanthropology. But it will continue to find it a challenge to avoid the explicit strictures of Carthage's condemnation of Pelagianism. While we should not rule out the possibility that it may yet meet this challenge, we should also admit that more work remains for the proponents of (D4) (at least those who care about fidelity to such important historical pronouncements). Meanwhile, (D3) offers a way forward.

E. Summary

As N. T. Wright observes, "[I]dolatry becomes habit-forming, character-shaping, progressively more destructive. It *enslaves* people. Ultimately, it *kills* people."[252] The venom of sin spreads across God's good creation. It warps and twists and perverts and sickens. It results in what David Kelsey calls "a living death."[253] Finally, it brings death. "The wages of sin is death" (Rom. 6:23). And as horrible as this is, it leads to something even more terrifying.

V. The Judgment and Wrath of God

Divine revelation makes it obvious—unavoidably and very uncomfortably obvious—that sinners are under the judgment of God. As such, unrepentant and unredeemed sinners stand *condemned* before God. Nothing escapes the notice of his omniscience, and nothing escapes the judgment of his righteousness. There is, then, simply no way to avoid it and no other way to say it: sinners are under the wrath of God.

A. The Wrath of God

Paul tells us that he is "not ashamed of the gospel, because it is the power of God for the salvation of everyone who believes: first for the Jew, then for the

---

[251] Bettenson, *Documents of the Christian Church*, 59. If Carthage is right on this point, then surely many Protestants (along with many children of Roman Catholics) are condemned. Interestingly, the statement also seems to rule out a doctrine of "limbo" for infants.

[252] N. T. Wright, *Paul and the Faithfulness of God*, Book Two, Parts III and IV (Minneapolis: Fortress, 2013), 743–744.

[253] Kelsey, *Eccentric Existence*, 1:567.

Gentile" (Rom. 1:16 NIV 1984). This is because the gospel reveals a "righteous-ness from God," which is "by faith" (Rom. 1:17 NIV 1984). And then Paul immediately tells us that "the wrath of God is being revealed from heaven against all the godlessness and wickedness of men who suppress the truth by their wickedness" (Rom. 1:18 NIV 1984). Paul here says that the wrath of God is *being* revealed. He says that it is being revealed "from heaven." And notably, he says that it is being revealed against both the "wickedness" (*adikia*) and the "godlessness" (*asebeia*) of humanity.

Divine wrath is directed against "wickedness"; it is opposed to the evil af-fections and behaviors of human sinners as they violate each other and pillage God's creation. It also stands in diametric opposition to "godlessness," for it is directly pointed at all creaturely rejections of the Creator. This double-pronged focus is well-attested in both the Old and New Testaments.[254] The OT has unmistakable warnings for those who deny justice to the oppressed: "This is what the Lord says: Do what is just and right. Rescue from the hand of his oppressor the one who has been robbed. Do no wrong or violence to the alien, the fatherless or the widow, and do not shed innocent blood in this place" (Jer. 22:3 NIV 1984). God's command is clear: "administer justice every morning; rescue from the hand of his oppressor the one who has been robbed." And the warning is just as clear: "or my wrath will break out and burn like fire because of the evil you have done" (Jer. 21:12 NIV 1984).

In the OT, sins against fellow human creatures, including oppression and injustice as well as all manner of social ills and sexual perversions, are closely tied to and indeed follow from sin against God (e.g., Ex. 22:16–24). Idolatry is quickly followed by debauchery, oppression, and violence (e.g., Ezek. 22:1–29). Godlessness—expressed most commonly and most openly in the practice of idolatry but also present in all those who do not follow God wholeheartedly as well as those who do not speak truthfully of him—deserves God's wrath and threatens those who either practice or condone it (e.g., Ex. 32:1–10; Num. 25:3; 32:10–14; Job 42:7). Thus we have repeated and forceful warnings not to "forget" the Lord who rescued Israel, and we have direct and unmistakable commands to

> Fear the LORD your God, serve him only and take your oaths in his name.
> Do not follow other gods, the gods of the peoples around you; for the LORD
> your God, who is among you, is a jealous God and his anger will burn
> against you, and he will destroy you from the face of the land. Do not test
> the LORD your God as you did at Massah. Be sure to keep the commands of
> the LORD your God and the stipulations and decrees he has given you. Do

---

[254] Leon Morris points out that the witness to the wrath of God in the OT uses more than twenty Hebrew words to depict it—and with almost six hundred uses of those terms (*The Apostolic Preaching of the Cross: A Study of the Significance of Some New Testament Terms*, 3rd ed. (Grand Rapids, MI: Eerdmans, 1965), 149.

what is right and good in the LORD's sight, so that it may go well with you (Deut. 6:13–18 NIV 1984).

Idolatry is nothing less than rebellion against God, and it brings nothing but wrath and judgment (e.g., Josh. 22:16–18; 23:16).

God's wrath is opposed to the sins of Israel, both before (e.g., Num. 32:14) and during the divided kingdom (e.g., 2 Chron. 28:11–13) as well as after the exile (e.g., Neh. 13:18). God's wrath is exercised against the sinful nations as well (e.g., Ezek. 25:14, 17). Accordingly, God uses Israel to chastise and discipline her pagan neighbors.[255] He also uses those same pagan neighbors to punish Israel (e.g., Ezek. 21:1–24; Isa. 10:5–19; Hab. 1:5–11).[256] Everywhere it is clear that the people who sin do so against God's intentions for his creation; they do so in direct opposition to God's desires for them. "Now your impurity is lewdness. Because I tried to cleanse you but you would not be cleansed from your impurity, you will not be clean again until my wrath against you has subsided" (Ezek. 24:13 NIV 1984).

The consequences of sin are both breathtaking and frightening. As D. A. Carson notes,

> the wrath of God manifests itself in sword, hunger, and plague (Ezek. 6:11–14), in wasting diseases "until you perish" (Deut. 28:22), devastation (Jer. 25:37–38), scattering (Lam. 4:16), and depopulation (Jer. 50:13). God treads the nations in his winepress (Isa. 63:1–6); alternatively, God gives them the cup of his fury to drink (Isa. 51:17; cf. 63:1–2; Joel 3:13). Under the wrath of God, members of the covenant community may be "cut off" from their people (e.g., Exod. 30:33, 38; Lev. 7:20; Num. 9:13; 19:20).[257]

Carson is correct when he says that the biblical witness to the wrath of God against sin is "humbling and frightening."[258]

The wrath of God is sometimes depicted in intensely personal terms in the OT. God is, as is well known, often portrayed as a King and Judge in Scripture. But he also reveals himself as a Father, and here the personal nature of our relationship with him—and of his wrath toward us as sinners—is thrown into sharper relief (e.g., Ex. 4:22; Ps. 103:13). Seen in this light, his wrath is not detached and impersonal; nor is it the polar opposite to his love and mercy. It

---

[255] The election of Israel must not be misunderstood. Israel was chosen by God, as a corporate body (cf. Gen. 25:23), for the purpose of bringing God's salvation to the world. There were, of course, individuals within this group who finally rebelled against God and were judged by God for that rebellion (e.g., Num. 16:1–35), while there were individuals who were *not* of this group who did turn to the Lord for salvation (e.g., Matt. 1:5). Provision for salvation was made for both Israel (the "elect") and the "aliens" (e.g., Num. 15:14–16, 29–30). See especially Christopher J. H. Wright, *The Mission of God: Unlocking the Bible's Grand Narrative* (Downers Grove, IL: IVP Academic, 2006).

[256] On Isaiah 10:5–19 see D. A. Carson, "The Wrath of God," in *Engaging the Doctrine of God: Contemporary Protestant Perspectives*, ed. Bruce L. McCormack (Grand Rapids, MI: Baker Academic, 2008), 43–44.

[257] Carson, "Wrath of God," 39.

[258] Carson, "Wrath of God," 40.

is not the selfish frustration or temper of someone who is self-obsessed and irate with anyone who gets in the way of his own self-actualization or self-fulfillment. Instead it is the wrath of someone who loves deeply and powerfully—it is the wrath that says, "What are you doing to yourself? How dare you do such a thing?" As Leon Morris says, the wrath of God in the OT is "the wrath of a loving father who yearns for his children to come to him."[259]

But God also gives us self-portraits in the OT that show an even more personally intense side of divine wrath, for he portrays his relationship to his people as that of a spouse who is faithful to one who is unfaithful. Such explicitly *nuptial* terms are on display when God likens his people to those who have committed adultery by prostituting themselves and sleeping with the enemy (e.g., the Egyptians, the Assyrians, and the Chaldeans in Ezekiel 23:1–49, with the Philistines and Babylonians included in Ezekiel 16:23–29). Yahweh's charge against his people is uncomfortably straightforward and direct:

> But you trusted in your beauty and used your fame to become a prostitute. You lavished your favors on anyone who passed by and your beauty became his. You took some of your garments. . . . You also took the fine jewelry I gave you, the jewelry made of my gold and silver, and you made for yourself male idols and engaged in prostitution with them. And you took your embroidered clothes to put on them. . . . Also the food I provided for you. . . .
>
> And you took your sons and daughters whom you bore to me and sacrificed them as food to the idols. Was your prostitution not enough? You slaughtered my children and sacrificed them to idols. . . . (Ezek. 16:15–21 NIV 1984)

The Lord points out that this prostitution is so twisted that "you give gifts to all your lovers, bribing them to come to you from everywhere for your illicit favors" (Ezek. 16:33 NIV 1984). God's wrath is seen here to be "jealous anger" (v. 38 NIV 1984), and it results in judgment as God says that he will "hand you over to your lovers" who will destroy you and leave you "naked and bare" (vv. 39–41). Divine wrath is portrayed in the OT as something that is both real and personal.

Carson observes that a common misconception is that the NT is less concerned with divine wrath than the OT; for while there might be a "residue of wrath" in the NT, in general "a gentleness takes over and softens the darker period: God's love is now richer than his wrath. After all, Jesus taught his disciples to love their enemies and turn the other cheek."[260] Carson rejects this misconception: "Nothing could be further from the truth than this reading of the relationship between the Testaments."[261] Carson is right to point

---

[259] Morris, *Apostolic Preaching of the Cross*, 177.
[260] Carson, *The Difficult Doctrine of the Love of God* (Wheaton, IL: Crossway, 2000), 70.
[261] Carson, *Difficult Doctrine of the Love of God*, 70.

out both that the OT testifies to the love of God and that the NT reveals the wrath of God. John the Baptist warns both the Pharisees and the Sadducees of the "wrath to come" (Matt. 3:7; Luke 3:7). Jesus displays anger (Mark 3:5), and he claims that he is the one who is able to save sinners from God's wrath: "Whoever believes in the Son has eternal life, but whoever rejects the Son will not see life, for God's wrath remains on them" (John 3:36 NIV). Paul refers to those who are "dead in . . . transgressions and sins" (Eph. 2:1) as being "by nature deserving of wrath" (Eph. 2:3 NIV). And to those who are believers he warns of the wrath of God:

> Be imitators of God, therefore, as dearly loved children and live a life of love, just as Christ loved us and gave himself up for us as a fragrant offering and sacrifice to God.
>
> But among you there must not be even a hint of sexual immorality, or of any kind of impurity, or of greed, because these are improper for God's holy people. Nor should there be obscenity, foolish talk or coarse joking, which are out of place, but rather thanksgiving. For of this you can be sure: No immoral, impure or greedy person—such a man is an idolater—has any inheritance in the kingdom of Christ and of God. Let no one deceive you with empty words, for because of such things God's wrath comes on those who are disobedient. (Eph. 5:1–6 NIV 1984)

Because of "sexual immorality, impurity, lust, evil desires and greed, which is idolatry," Paul says, "the wrath of God is coming" (Col. 3:5–6 NIV). And the book of Revelation concludes in nuptial terms as "the Spirit and the Bride say, 'Come'" to life (Rev. 22:17) while also warning of the "wrath of the Lamb" in vivid terms (e.g., Rev. 6:16; cf. 14:10; 16:19; 19:15).

B. The Love of God

The love of God is taken for granted by most contemporary Christians. And it is true that the biblical witness to the love of God is deep, broad, and rich beyond comparison. The OT writers know that God is "compassionate and gracious . . . , slow to anger, abounding in love and faithfulness" (Ex. 34:6 NIV) and that Yahweh is "gracious and compassionate, slow to anger and rich in love" (Ps. 145:8 NIV). Similarly, the authors of the NT understand that God's love has been revealed supremely and finally in Jesus Christ. John tells us that "God so loved the world that he gave his one and only Son, that whoever believes in him shall not perish but have eternal life" (John 3:16 NIV). In his first letter, John goes deeper: "God is love" (1 John 4:8, 16). Paul exults in the sovereign supremacy of divine love: "For I am sure that neither death nor life, nor angels nor rulers, nor things present nor things to come, nor powers, nor height nor depth, nor anything else in all creation, will be able to separate us from the love of God in Christ Jesus our Lord" (Rom. 8:38–39).

But in the very familiarity lies a danger. All too often the love of God is thought of in unipersonal or monistic terms, and it is very often reduced to sentimentalization. We do not easily remember that when Paul says that nothing can "separate us from the love of God," he is talking about the love that is "in Christ Jesus our Lord" (Rom. 8:39). We do not easily remember that he is talking to those who "live in accordance with the Spirit" and are "controlled by the Spirit" (Rom. 8:5–9 NIV 1984) as they are "led by the Spirit" (Rom. 8:14) and indeed have the Holy Spirit "living in" them (Rom. 8:11 NIV). We find it easy to forget that Paul is talking about those who are "in Christ Jesus"—the same Christ Jesus who died as the "sacrifice of atonement" (Rom. 3:25 NIV) or propitiation (ESV), and that this sacrifice of atonement was necessitated by our sinfulness and rebellion (cf. Rom. 3:10–18). We easily gravitate toward John's affirmation that "God is love"—but without paying so much attention to his parallel claim that "God is light, and in him is no darkness at all" (1 John 1:5). All too often modern people (who perhaps have encountered just enough of the biblical gospel to be inoculated against it) hear that "God is love" and assume that they know well enough what this means. "Hey, I've heard the songs, read the books, and seen the movies—I know what love is. Cool! So God is like that. Sure, God loves me." In light of such rampant and complacent confusion, it is important to see a couple of points very clearly.

The first point is this: the love of God is a *holy* love. We readily assume that we know what love is. But just as John tells us that "God is love," he also goes on to tell us what love really is:

> This is how God showed his love among us: He sent his one and only Son into the world that we might live through him. This is love: not that we loved God, but that he loved us and sent his Son as an atoning sacrifice for our sins. (1 John 4:9–10 NIV)

Note that John tells us that we *did not* love God. And John tells us just *how* God showed his love to us: God showed his love to us by sending his Son to die so that we might have life. God revealed his love to us not with mere words (even important ones); he revealed his love to us when the "Word became flesh and dwelt among us" (John 1:14). Our "love" is not the standard against which love is measured. Quite the opposite is true for John: it is "not that we loved God, but that he loved us" (1 John 4:10 NIV) *This* is "how we know what love is: Jesus Christ laid down his life for us" (1 John 3:16 NIV). So we dare not use our common experience or sentiments of "love" as an adequate measure by which to understand God.

And when God sent his Son into the world, he sent him as a "propitiation" (or "atoning sacrifice") for our sins (cf. 1 John 2:2). John pulls no punches but instead is unflinching in his honest diagnosis of the human condition. We did not love God but had rebelled in sin against God. God's love for us—love that we cannot even begin truly to grasp apart from the incarnation of it in Jesus Christ—is the reason that he "sent his Son." The Son, according to John (and the general plot line of Scripture), comes into the world for a specific purpose: he comes to deal with our sin and to secure our salvation. The love of God is a *holy* love. It cannot be reduced to sentimentality or indulgence; it does not ignore or brush away or indulge our sinfulness. Instead it is expressed in a way that is pointed directly at our sin problem. There is no divine holiness that can be considered in abstraction from God's love. And there is no divine love that is not pure and holy. "God is love" (1 John 4:8, 16). "God is light, and in him is no darkness at all" (1 John 1:5). None *at all*.

The second point is this: God's love is the love of the triune life. Jesus's prayer before his trial and death offers a precious glimpse into the life of the triune God. Here we see that the love between the Father and Son is so deeply rooted within their shared life that Jesus prays that it will be known and shared by those who follow him. It is of the very essence of the God who is triune. Jesus refers to the love shared between Father and Son "before the foundation of the world" (John 17:24), and he prays that those who believe in him will be brought to "complete unity" to let the world know "that you sent me and loved them even as you have loved me" (v. 23 NIV 1984). He asks that "the love with which you have loved me" will also be known and cherished by those who belong to him (v. 26).

To affirm, with Scripture, that "God is love" is to make a statement about God's essence or nature. The statement "God is love" should not be confused with "God is loving toward us" or "God performs loving actions." Where "God acts in a loving way" speaks of *what God does*, "God is love" goes much deeper and grounds his loving action within his own intra-Trinitarian life—it speaks of *who God is*. There is no deeper affirmation that we can make about God. God's love is not arbitrary or accidental. His love is not extrinsic to him—as if it were something that he could either have or lack. It is not something added to him; he does not first exist and then develop into being someone who does loving things. The triune God does not merely decide to be loving, nor does he only act in loving ways. No, when we affirm with Scripture that "God is love" we are making the most profound and penetrating of all theological statements. We are talking about *who God is*; we are referring to the intra-Trinitarian life in which the Father, Son, and Spirit share openness, trust, *shalom*, life, and love with one another in the greatest way possible. As Thomas F. Torrance puts it,

> The Father, the Son and the Holy Spirit who indwell One Another in the Love that God is constitute the Communion of Love or the movement of reciprocal Loving which is identical to the One Being of God. It is as God the Father, God the Son, and God the Holy Spirit that God is God and God is love. As one Being, three Persons, the Being of God is to be understood as an eternal movement of Love, both in himself as the Love of the Father, the Son, and the Holy Spirit for one Another, and in his loving Self-giving to others beyond himself.[262]

There is "nothing greater, nothing better" than the love of the triune God.[263]

The fact that holy love is of the essence of the fullness of the triune life informs us that God does not in any sense *need* us. Within his own life as Father, Son, and Holy Spirit, the triune God knows no lack or need. The expression of his grace toward us is, then, completely free. God does not love us out of a lack or emptiness; instead he loves us out of the fullness of the triune life of holy love.

At the same time, God's actions are fully in accord with his nature as holy love. Because God is the triune God, because the holy love shared by Father, Son, and Spirit is of the essence of God, it is quite literally unthinkable that his actions would not be in accord with his nature. "God loves us," says Torrance, "with the very same love with which he loves himself, in the reciprocal love of the three divine Persons for Each Other in the eternal Communion of the Holy Trinity."[264] The love that God is as Father, Son, and Holy Spirit is not different from the love that he extends and offers to us (e.g., John 17:26). As Torrance explains,

> In the Communion of the Holy Trinity the Father is Father in his loving of the Son and the Spirit, and the Son is Son in his loving of the Father and the Spirit, and the Spirit is the Spirit in his loving of the Father and the Son. It is as such that the Love that flows between the Father, the Son, and the Spirit, freely flows in an outward movement of his loving activity toward us with whom God creates a communion of love corresponding to the Communion of Love which he ever is in himself. . . .
>
> It is as this infinite, unlimited, transcendent self-giving Love that God is, that God the Father, the Son and the Holy Spirit, three Persons, one Being, seeks and creates fellowship with us in order to reconcile us with himself and to share with us his own eternal Life and Love.[265]

The love of God—the love that God *is*—is an irreducibly pure and holy love.

---

[262] Thomas F. Torrance, *The Christian Doctrine of God: One Being, Three Persons* (Edinburgh: T&T Clark, 1996), 165.

[263] See Kevin J. Vanhoozer (who follows Richard of St. Victor), ed., *Nothing Better, Nothing Greater: Theological Essays on the Love of God* (Grand Rapids, MI: Eerdmans, 2001).

[264] Torrance, *Christian Doctrine of God*, 165.

[265] Torrance, *Christian Doctrine of God*, 166.

It is the love of the intra-Trinitarian life. And it is a love that is brought to us by the incarnate Son and the promised Spirit.

C. Love and Wrath in Scripture: A Brief Summary

Arguably, the witness to *both* the wrath of God and the love of God is heightened or strengthened in the New Testament (when compared with the Old). The NT places emphasis on the *everlasting* consequences of divine wrath, and it grounds the love of God within the triune life of God in a way that goes beyond the OT. But in neither the OT nor the NT are the love of God and the wrath of God seen as polar opposites. Even the terrible scene of Yahweh's judgment of his unfaithful people (Ezekiel 16) is couched within the framework of God's *love*. The discussion ends with the promise that—despite the fact of the unfaithfulness of God's people—God will "remember the covenant I made with you in the days of your youth, and I will establish an everlasting covenant with you" (Ezek. 16:60 NIV). Then you will (again) "know" me, and I will "make atonement for you," says the Lord (Ezek. 16:62–63 NIV). The psalmist also shows, through the retelling of Israel's story, that both mercy and anger are displayed. Again and again, the psalmist recounts, Israel has acted in ways that showed her unfaithfulness. And again and again, the Lord has punished her so that she would return to him. It is "in spite of all this," that "they kept on sinning"; it is "in spite of his wonders" that they "did not believe" (Ps. 78:32 NIV). The verdict is clear: "their hearts were not loyal to him, [for] they were not faithful to his covenant" (Ps. 78:37 NIV). And his stance toward them is made clear as well: "Yet he was merciful; he forgave their iniquities and did not destroy them. Time after time he restrained his anger, and did not stir up his full wrath" (Ps. 78:38 NIV). Yahweh is "the compassionate and gracious God, slow to anger, abounding in love and faithfulness, maintaining love to thousands, and forgiving wickedness, rebellion and sin" but not leaving "the guilty unpunished" (Ex. 34:6–7 NIV). For "the LORD is good, and his steadfast love endures forever" (e.g., Ps. 100:5; 106:1; 107:1; 118:1).

D. Love and Wrath in the Hands of the Theologians

The biblical witness to both the wrath and the love of God is plain. Modern theologians (academic and pastoral theologians alike) tend to deal with this witness in several ways: either they ignore the biblical depictions of divine wrath, they "de-personalize" it by viewing it as the impersonal force of the natural consequences of the sins, or they try to take full account of both the wrath and the love of God by pitting one against the other.

Some theologians take little or no notice of the biblical testimony to the wrath of God (it would be much harder to find those who ignore the biblical affirmations of the love of God).[266] Other theologians render divine wrath as what D. A. Carson describes as "the impartial and inevitable *impersonal* effects of sin in a culture."[267] The proponents of this approach usually translate the words found in Romans 3:25 and 1 John 2:2 (*hilasmos, hilasterios, hilaskomai*) to refer to "expiation" rather than "propitiation." Whereas "propitiation" deals with the wrath of God, "expiation" is directed at sin. C. H. Dodd has famously argued that the very idea of propitiation is pagan and thus foreign to any biblically acceptable doctrine of God.[268] References to God's "wrath" do not really refer to his personal antagonism toward sin; instead "the wrath of God" really means the normal consequences of sinful behavior.

Meanwhile, the defenders of "propitiation" respond that while it is surely true that we ought to reject all *pagan* notions of propitiation, it is just as surely true that there is a properly biblical and Christian account of propitiation. Thus John Stott argues that while "crude concepts of anger, sacrifice and pro-pitiation are indeed to be rejected," such a rejection "does not mean, however, that there is no biblical concept of these things at all. What is revealed to us in Scripture is a pure doctrine (from which all pagan vulgarities have been expunged) of God's holy wrath, his loving self-sacrifice in Christ and his ini-tiative to avert his own anger."[269] The biblical account is nowhere close to the pagan versions, for it is only in the Christian concept of propitiation that "it is God himself in his holy wrath [who] needs to be propitiated, God himself who in holy love undertook to do the propitiating, and God himself who in the person of his Son died for the propitiation of our sins."[270]

Another way that modern theologians wrestle with the biblical depiction of both the wrath and love of God is to argue that there must be a "strife of attributes" within God. Greg Boyd and Paul Eddy describe this position as one that sees a real dilemma for God: "This sinfulness poses a dilemma for God, for he perfectly loves us, on the one hand, but he is perfectly holy and cannot have anything to do with sin, on the other hand."[271] Stott argues (against P. T. Forsyth) that there indeed is a "strife of attributes" within God. He appeals to the biblical language of both the wrath and mercy of God,

---

[266] I could find the wrath of God mentioned only twice in Daniel L. Migliore's widely used theological textbook, both of which mentions were in reference to older (and apparently outmoded) theories of atonement. See his *Faith Seeking Understanding: An Introduction to Christian Theology* (Grand Rapids, MI: Eerdmans, 1991), 154, 158. John Macquarrie, meanwhile, denies that "'wrath' indicates anger" (*Principles of Christian Theology* [New York: Scribner, 1966], 192).

[267] Carson, *Difficult Doctrine of the Love of God*, 68.

[268] E.g., C. H. Dodd, *The Bible and the Greeks* (London: Hodder & Stoughton, 1935); and *The Epistle to the Romans* (London: Hodder & Stoughton, 1932), 21–23.

[269] Stott, *The Cross of Christ* (Downers Grove, IL: InterVarsity Press, 1986), 169.

[270] Stott, *Cross of Christ*, 175.

[271] Gregory A. Boyd and Paul R. Eddy, *Across the Spectrum: Understanding Issues in Evangelical Theology* (Grand Rapids, MI: Baker Academic, 2002), 116. I owe this reference to Graham A. Cole, *God the Peacemaker*, New Studies in Biblical Theology (Downers Grove, IL: IVP Academic, 2010), 49n47.

and says that there "surely is a conflict of emotions, a strife of attributes, within God."[272] There is a "duality" within God.[273] The sin of humanity has occasioned a crisis within God, for now God's holiness and justice demand to see sinners damned while his love and mercy desire to see them saved. God now has a "problem," and "the problem is not outside God; it is within his own being."[274] Even more boldly, Helmut Thielicke insists that "it is at the heart of the Lutheran view that God does contradict himself, that he sets his grace in opposition to his judgment and his love in opposition to his holiness; indeed, the gospel itself can be traced to this fundamental contradiction within God himself."[275]

So beyond those Christians who quietly ignore (or not so quietly *deny*) the reality of the wrath of God, there are theologians who reduce it to what Dodd calls "an inevitable process of cause and effect in a moral universe."[276] On the other hand, many contemporary theologians want to insist on the reality of God's wrath as well as his love, but they do so by pitting wrath and mercy (and holiness and love) against one another within the divine nature. How should we think about such matters?

E. Love, Wrath, and the Gospel[277]

Paul is "not ashamed of the gospel, because it is the power of God for the salvation of everyone who believes" (Rom. 1:16 NIV 1984). The gospel which he is so bold to proclaim is the gospel in which "a righteousness from God [has been] revealed, a righteousness that is by faith from first to last, just as it is written: 'The righteous shall live by faith'" (Rom. 1:17 NIV 1984). Paul says this just as he begins to speak of the wrath of God as it is "being revealed from heaven against all the godlessness and wickedness of men who suppress the truth by their wickedness" (Rom. 1:18 NIV 1984). Clearly, for Paul one cannot talk about the gospel without also talking honestly about the wrath of God. We are, according to Paul, "by nature objects of wrath" (Eph. 2:3 NIV 1984). To be saved is to be saved from God's wrath through Christ (Rom. 5:9). And to be saved is to be saved by love: "But God demonstrates his own love for us in this: While we were still sinners, Christ died for us" (Rom. 5:8 NIV 1984). "Because of his great love for us, God, who is rich in mercy, made us alive in Christ even when we were dead in transgressions—it is by grace you have been

---

[272] Stott, *Cross of Christ*, 130.
[273] Stott, *Cross of Christ*, 130–131.
[274] Stott, *Cross of Christ*, 133.
[275] Helmut Thielicke, *Theological Ethics: Volume 2, Politics* (Philadelphia: Fortress, 1969), 575. I owe this reference to Cole, *God the Peacemaker*, 49. I suspect that Thielicke's "Lutheranism" owes more to Hegel than to classical Lutheran theology, but this is not the place for an argument about such matters.
[276] C. H. Dodd, *Romans* (New York: Harper & Brothers, 1932), 23.
[277] This section, to the end of the chapter, is taken from my *Forsaken* (Downers Grove, IL: InterVarsity Press, 2012). Used by permission of InterVarsity Press.

saved" (Eph. 2:4 NIV 1984). Any holistic understanding of the gospel must take both wrath and love into account.

GOD'S RIGHTEOUS WRATH IS CONTINGENT

God's righteous wrath is always portrayed in Scripture as God's antagonism toward sin. It is rightly understood as the contingent expression of what is essential or necessary to him against sin. It is the contingent expression of the holy love that is shared between Father, Son, and Holy Spirit. Contingent here should not be confused with arbitrary; given sin, it is inevitable that God's holy and righteous love is expressed as wrath against sin. Wrath is the natural expression of God's righteous and holy character toward all that stands opposed to him. But it is a contingent expression nonetheless; it is not as though wrath is necessary or essential to God; if it were essential to him, he could not exist without it. We should not conclude that God somehow *needs* wrath—and thus sin—to be God.

GOD'S RIGHTEOUS WRATH IS THE CONTINGENT
EXPRESSION OF THE HOLY LOVE OF THE TRINITY

Scripture leaves no room for doubt about the wrath of God. It also leaves no room for doubt about the love of God. It does not, however, place the love and mercy of God, on one hand, and the holiness and wrath of God, on the other hand, in opposition to one another. We may tend to see these as if they are in tension or even opposition, but the Bible itself does not do so. Wrath and love *may* be in tension, or even contradict one another, in fallen and sinful human lives (although I am not convinced that this is always or necessarily the case—must wrath cast out love?). But why think thus of God? Why suppose that love and wrath are "in tension" within him? Scripture does not demand that we do so.

Moreover, the doctrine of divine simplicity makes such supposition impossible.[278] God's holiness and love are not opposed to each other; they cohere within his own nature. Within the simplicity of God's own triune life, it is not as if one divine person is for us and another divine person against us. Notwithstanding the popularity (within some evangelical circles) of the phrase "the wrath of the Father," it is unthinkable that the Father is full of wrath and wants to see us damned while the merciful and loving Son is on "our side." How could it be? The Father and Son are, together with the Holy Spirit, exactly one God, and their operations are always undivided. Thus it is, according to classical Trinitarian doctrine, strictly impossible that they would be divided in their

---

[278] Perhaps one need not hold to a doctrine of divine simplicity to reject the "opposition" or "strife" theories with good theological warrant. Nonetheless, the doctrine of divine simplicity makes it impossible to hold such theories.

work. Furthermore, they are of one essence (*homoousios*), and they share the same undivided divine nature. The holy justice of the Father is the same holy justice of the Son. The love of the Son is the same love as the love of the Father.

Furthermore, it is not possible that there are "competing attributes" within God. In the simplicity of the divine nature, God's holiness and his love may be formally distinct; they may be genuinely distinct, that is, but not really separable.[279] They are not, and cannot be, "opposed to" one another. Nor is there "tension" that is internal to God's own life. We cannot, with any good theological grounding or support, go beyond what the Bible tells us about the love and holiness of God to posit an internal struggle within God's own life. We cannot, with good theological conscience, make such claims as "God's holiness and justice demanded to see me damned, but—thankfully—God's love and mercy wanted me to be saved, with the result being the death of Jesus so that God could get this tension resolved"; or "part of God called for my damnation, while another part wanted my salvation, so Jesus died to deal with God's problem." As if the real problem is within God! The real root of the problem that Jesus came to deal with, according to Scripture, is *our* problem—it is *sin*. God's wrath is not the product of his holiness while his mercy is the expression of his love. God's righteous wrath is the contingent expression of his holy love—for within the simplicity of the divine life, holiness and love cohere together.

God's Righteous Wrath Is the Expression of Holy Impassible Love

We need not solve all puzzles about impassibility to see the relevance of the basic point for our discussion. God is never unconcerned about sin. He is not relaxed about it on some days. His steadfast and relentless opposition to all that stands against him knows no holidays. Within the impassible life of triune holy love, God's white-hot wrath never fluctuates or varies in its opposition to sin. As the Reformed scholastics put it, "This is terrible to wicked men: God is unchangeable which hath threatened to curse them and bring destruction upon them; they must change, or else there is no repealing of the curse. . . . [The divine] threatenings and judgments" will come upon all who do not repent.[280] On the other hand, God is not given to madness or fits of rage. As Thomas Weinandy says, "[A]nger, when applied to God, was not seen as a separate passion or an intermittent emotional state within God, but constitutive of his unchanging perfect goodness and providential care, and so must be

---

[279] This is to adopt a "Scotist" account of divine simplicity. See further Thomas H. McCall, "Trinity Doctrine, Plain and Simple," in *Advancing Trinitarian Theology: Explorations in Constructive Dogmatics*, ed. Oliver D. Crisp and Fred Sanders (Grand Rapids, MI: Zondervan Academic, 2014), 42–59; Richard Cross, *Duns Scotus on God* (Aldershot, UK: Ashgate, 2005), 99–114.

[280] See the discussion in Muller, *Post-Reformation Reformed Dogmatics, Volume Three, The Divine Essence and Attributes* (Grand Rapids, MI: Baker Academic, 2003), 319.

predicated of God in a manner suitable to the divine nature."[281] Thus there is no room within a truly Christian understanding of divine wrath for pagan notions of propitiation. Scripture reveals to us the sober truth that, as sinners, we are under the wrath of God. God's wrath must be dealt with, and the Bible teaches us that it is dealt with by the death of Christ. So propitiation is central to the gospel. But it must not be confused with pagan notions of it—as if God (or "the Father") becomes so consumed by rage that he vents his pent-up anger in a fit of bloodthirsty passion, while the loving Jesus steps up between us and the force of that wrath and so gives God just enough blood to satisfy him or "buy him off." Scripture teaches that the wrath *of God* is the "wrath of the Lamb" (Rev. 6:16). The wrath of God is God's holy and righteous love expressed in steadfast antagonism toward all that is opposed to God; it is not something that is subject to fits of rage. Nor is it something that can be either satiated or exhausted—as if God no longer cares about sin or no longer has the moral energy to do anything about it because of the work of Christ. Instead, Christ's work for us (in both propitiation and expiation, which must be closely related) is intended to save us from God's wrath by saving us from our sin. John the Baptist expressed it well when he saw Jesus: "Behold, the Lamb of God, who takes away the sin of the world!" (John 1:29).

GOD'S RIGHTEOUS WRATH, WHICH IN THE SIMPLICITY OF THE DIVINE NATURE IS THE (CONTINGENT) EXPRESSION OF HIS HOLY LOVE, IS REASON FOR HOPE

Sometimes the divine attributes are said to be "in tension with" or even "opposed to" one another. As we have seen, sometimes preachers and theologians will say, "God's love and mercy want to see me saved while his holiness and justice demand to see me punished—and the God-appointed and God-approved death of Christ is God's way of sorting out the problem that my sin has caused for him." We should note that this is a speculative proposal for thinking about the death of Christ; the fact that Scripture testifies to divine love and mercy (as it does) and also to divine holiness and justice (as it does) does not mean that Scripture teaches that the divine attributes are "in tension with" or "opposed to" one another. Nor does the fact that love and justice sometimes stand in tension for us mean that they do so for God. On the contrary, there are good reasons to think that such speculation cannot be right. God's wrath—as the expression of his holy love—is reason for hope. As Torrance puts it, "It is the *wrath of the lamb*, the wrath of redeeming love. As such the very wrath of God is a sign of hope, not of utter destruction . . ."[282]

This matters for a clear grasp of the hope of the gospel; far from being

[281] Thomas G. Weinandy, *Does God Suffer?* (Notre Dame, IN: University of Notre Dame Press, 2000), 111.
[282] Thomas F. Torrance, *Incarnation: The Person and Life of Christ*, ed. Robert T. Walker (Downers Grove, IL: IVP Academic, 2008), 249, emphasis original.

foreign to the gospel, or even annoying distractions from it, the doctrines of simplicity and impassibility are important for the gospel message. As Paul L. Gavrilyuk says, "It is precisely because God is impassible . . . that repentant sinners may approach him without despair. Far from being a barrier to divine care and loving-kindness, divine impassibility is their very foundation. Unlike that of humans who are unreliable and swayed by passions, God's love is enduring and devoid of all weaknesses with which human love is tainted."[283]

For as I have argued, the doctrine of divine simplicity teaches that the essential divine attributes are (at most) only "formally" distinct. That is, they are neither separated nor even separable. The divine attributes cannot, then, be thought of as being "opposed" or "in tension." If we accept some doctrine of divine simplicity, it is unthinkable that, say, God's righteous justice demands one thing while his love and mercy demand the opposite. Nor is it possible that some divine attributes (or divine persons) work for some results while others work for other results. John McLeod Campbell surely is closer to the mark when he says that

> the justice, the righteousness, the holiness of God have an aspect according to which they, as well as his mercy, appear as intercessors for man, and crave his salvation. . . . But *justice* looking at the sinner, not simply as the fit subject of punishment, but as existing in a moral condition of unrighteousness, and so its own opposite, must desire that the sinner should cease to be in that condition; should cease to be unrighteous—should become righteousness: righteousness in God craving righteousness in man. . . . So also of holiness. In one view it repels the sinner, and would banish him to outer darkness, because of its repugnance to sin. In another it is pained by the continued existence of sin and unholiness, and must desire that the sinner should cease to be sinful.[284]

This means a lot for our hope of salvation:

> [. . . so] that the sinner, conceived of as awakening to the consciousness of his own evil state, and saying to himself, "By sin I have destroyed myself. Is there yet hope for me in God?" should hear an encouraging answer, not only from the love and mercy of God, but also from His very righteousness and holiness. . . . [the] consolation will be not only, "Surely the divine mercy desires to see me happy rather than miserable"—but also, "Surely the divine righteousness desires to see me righteous—the divine holiness desires to see me holy— my continuing unrighteous and unholy is as grieving to God's righteousness and holiness as my misery through sin is to His pity and love."[285]

---

[283] Paul L. Gavrilyuk, *The Suffering of the Impassible God: The Dialectics of Patristic Thought* (Oxford: Oxford University Press, 2004), 62.

[284] J. McLeod Campbell, *The Nature of the Atonement*, with new introduction James B. Torrance (Grand Rapids, MI: Eerdmans, 1996), 51–52.

[285] Campbell, *Nature of the Atonement*, 52.

God is, therefore, "'[a] just God and a Saviour,' not as the harmony of a seeming opposition, but 'a Savior,' *because* 'a just God.'"[286]

George Eldon Ladd observes that "whatever modern scholars may do with it, Paul clearly felt that there was neither contradiction nor incongruity between God's love and his wrath."[287] Divine wrath is not the opposite of divine love. God's wrath is not opposed to God's love. It is not even in tension with his love. Quite the contrary is true—the righteous wrath of God is the (contingent) expression of the holy love that is the essence of God. As we learned in chapter 3, *indifference,* not wrath, would be opposed to divine love. *We* are often indifferent about sin; the sins committed by ourselves or others do not usually concern us very much unless we are somehow directly damaged by them in financial, physical, or psychological ways. But the fact that God is angry at sin tells us that God is anything but indifferent toward us or the wrong that we do! The sovereign Lord who alone enjoys blessedness and aseity does not "need" us, nor can he be "damaged" by us. The fact that he is implacably, unchangingly, and personally opposed to all that is hostile to him is a testament to his sheer goodness. He cares about our sin—and the damage it does to us—more than we do. The fact that the whole world is under the wrath of God tells us—in no uncertain terms—that the triune God of holy love cares about the whole world. Thus, as Stephen T. Davis says, "God's wrath is our only hope as human beings."[288]

---

[286] Campbell, *Nature of the Atonement,* 52, emphasis original.
[287] Ladd, *Theology of the New Testament,* 466.
[288] Stephen T. Davis, *Christian Philosophical Theology* (Oxford: Oxford University Press, 2006), 213, 216.

SEVEN

"Where Sin Abounded": Sin and Grace

The doctrines of sin and grace are closely related. As Martin Luther expresses it, "[T]he more you minimize sin, the more grace declines in value."[1] On the other hand, the more one understands the depths of sin, the more one is enabled to appreciate the heights of grace. When we see God's grace—more particularly, God's grace *in Christ*—we see both our sin and our salvation more clearly. For in sharpest contrast to our sin, as we have seen (ch. 5), "God is not egotistic in this revelation and defense of His own honour and glory, nor is He concerned about the satisfaction of His own needs. As God He does not need to choose to be the Creator, to determine Himself as such."[2] But as God— as the triune God revealed ultimately and finally in Jesus Christ—he *has* created us, covenanted with us, and brought redemption and reconciliation to us through "the Judge judged in our place." Accordingly, "we indeed can say that God hates the sin but does not cease to love the sinner."[3] And just as we know that "Jesus Christ acknowledged all men as sinners," so also we know that the Judge has come in *our* place, to bear the sins of the world, and that "when he bears it, even the greatest of sins cannot damn" someone.[4] Accordingly, in this chapter we shall look more closely at issues related to sin and grace.

I. Sin and Gracious Providence[5]

John of Damascus says that divine providence is "the care that God takes over existing things."[6] God creates from his abundant and inexhaustible goodness,

---

[1] Cited in Robert Kolb, "Martin Luther," in *T&T Clark Companion to the Doctrine of Sin*, ed. Keith L. Johnson and David Lauber (New York: Bloomsbury T&T Clark, 2016), 217.
[2] Karl Barth, *CD*, IV/1, 452.
[3] Barth, *CD*, IV/1, 406.
[4] Barth, *CD*, IV/1, 405.
[5] This section ("I. Sin and Gracious Providence") is adapted from my chapter, "Divine Providence," in *T&T Clark Companion to the Doctrine of Sin*, ed. Keith L. Johnson and David Lauber. Used by permission of the editors.
[6] John of Damascus, *De Fide Orthodoxa* II:XXIX (PG 94:964A; *NPNF²* 9:41).

and he creates to share that goodness. Having created, God does not abandon that good creation or leave it to itself. Instead, God cares for it through his providential activity. The doctrine of divine providence is thus very closely related to the doctrine of creation. God is "both Creator and Provider, and His creative and preserving and providing power is simply His good-will."[7] The doctrine of divine providence is, however, also distinct from the doctrine of creation. While both God's creative and providential actions are grounded in his primordial goodness—as the Damascene says, "God alone is good and wise by nature; since He is good, He provides"[8]—divine providential action is distinct in several important ways.

What the Damascene says is broadly representative of classical Christian accounts of providence. Richard A. Muller summarizes the doctrine as it developed in scholasticism as "the continuing act of divine power, subsequent to the act of creation, by means of which God preserves all things in being, supports their actions, governs them according to his established order, and directs them toward their ordained ends."[9] The doctrine of providence has often been considered under three broad divisions: preservation or conservation (*conservatio*), concurrence (*concursus*), and government (*gubernatio*). *Conservatio*—preservation, sustenance, or conservation—"refers to the maintenance of the *esse*, or being, of contingent things."[10] Although God does not re-create the world *ex nihilo* moment by moment, contingent entities would not continue to exist from one moment to another without his sustenance. *Concursus* refers to the fact that God not only continues to sustain his creation but also grants creatures the abilities and powers to be able to perform actions and to do things. *Gubernatio* refers to God's governance over his creation; although it is ontologically distinct from him and stands in a contingent and dependent relation upon him, nonetheless God is sovereign over and responsible for the created order. Nothing in creation escapes his notice, nothing in creation falls outside the scope of his authority, and nothing in creation threatens his sovereign reign over it. These elements are central to historic accounts of the doctrine of providence; indeed, they may safely be said to be at the very core of the classical account.

What is the relation of this historic doctrine to Christian understandings of *sin*? Sin is moral evil (we are not talking here of "natural evil," although the relationship between "moral evil" and what we sometimes take to be "natural evil" may indeed be very complex). Sin is the violation of the absolute norms that are established by God in perfect concord with the divine nature. Sin re-

---

[7] John of Damascus, *De Fide* II:XXIX (PG 94:964B; NPNF[2] 9:41).
[8] John of Damascus, *De Fide* II:XXIX (PG 94:964B; NPNF[2] 9:41).
[9] Richard A. Muller, *Dictionary of Latin and Greek Theological Terms, Drawn Principally from Protestant Scholastic Theology* (Grand Rapids, MI: Baker Academic, 1985), 251.
[10] Muller, *Dictionary of Latin and Greek Theological Terms*, 252.

sults in the spoilage of God's good creation and in the destruction of God's fragile and precious creatures; it is the "vandalism of shalom."[11] As we have seen, sin is, in classical Christian terms, rightly understood as *contra naturam* and *contra rationem*—it is always "against nature" or what is truly natural as coming from the goodness of God, and it is always "against reason." Pressing further, sin is always—and ultimately—*contra Deum*. As Robert W. Jenson says, "[T]he only possible definition of sin is that it is what God does not want done."[12] Indeed, it is against reason and against nature *because* it is against God: as Thomas Aquinas puts it, "the order of nature comes from God himself, wherefore a person does an injustice to God in the act of violating nature: *fit iniuria ipsi Deo, ordinatori naturae.*"[13] Sin is against God. It violates God's law, it is opposed to God's will, and it contradicts God's nature.

Thinking of these doctrines together (as systematic theology must do) raises some interesting questions. It also prompts some troublesome worries. If all creatures—including, of course, all wicked creatures who commit vicious actions—depend on God moment by moment for their existence, why does not God simply cease to sustain or preserve them when they sin? And what of *concursus?* Does this mean that God really *concurs* with their sinful actions; does God agree with such wickedness or give his assent to it? Does this mean that God somehow cooperates with their sin? Does God make their sinful actions successful? What are we to make of God's relation to sin in light of claims about God's *gubernatio?* If we take these important affirmations of God's sovereignty to equate to or entail determinism, then how is it possible that sin is really *contra Deum?* In other words, if we understand divine governance to mean that God determines all creaturely (and indeed all mundane) actions in accordance with the divine will, then what could it possibly mean to say that sin is the violation of God's will and is opposed to God's intentions for his creation?

In what follows, I shall explore the relation between divine providence and human sin. After making some crucial theological affirmations, we will then be in a position to see what doctrinal options can be eliminated, and we will be able to see what can and should be believed about the relation of divine providence to human sin.

A. Some Central Theological Affirmations

In any discussion of divine providence and human sinfulness, several points stand out as theologically nonnegotiable.

---

[11] See Cornelius Plantinga Jr., *Not the Way It's Supposed to Be: A Breviary of Sin* (Grand Rapids, MI: Eerdmans, 1994).

[12] Robert W. Jenson, *Systematic Theology, Volume 2: The Works of God* (Oxford: Oxford University Press, 1999), 133.

[13] Aquinas, *ST* II/II, Q 154.12, cited in Josef Pieper, *The Concept of Sin* (South Bend, IN: St. Augustine's, 2001), 49.

HUMAN RESPONSIBILITY FOR SIN

The first of these affirmations is straightforward: biblically and theologically, *humans* are responsible for human sin. As C. S. Lewis reminds us, it is humans, "not God, who have produced racks, whips, prisons, slavery, guns, bayonets, and bombs."[14] Human persons are guilty for their sin. They cannot blame their sin on anyone or anything else; they cannot say, "[T]he devil made me do it," and they dare not say that "God made me do it" (or "God made the devil make me do it"). D. A. Carson has demonstrated that Scripture attests to the reality of human moral responsibility in many ways: we see it in the sincerity and urgency of divine commands and exhortations in Scripture; we see it in the historical depictions of persons who are rewarded for their choices as well as in the stories of those who rebel against God and his commands; we see it in the unpleasant but undeniable fact that rebellious sinners are under the judgment of God and face his just wrath; and we see it in the fact that humans are, again and again, held responsible to respond rightly to the divine entreaties and commands to repent, believe, and obey.[15] As Carson says, such promises, invitations, entreaties, and commands "have bite precisely because they can be obeyed or disobeyed."[16] Human responsibility for human sin is uncomfortably plain and obvious in Scripture, and there simply is no doctrine of sin without it. Accordingly, any doctrinal formulation that would ignore (or that would entail the negation of) moral responsibility must be doomed to fail.

DIVINE GOODNESS

Similarly, the goodness of God is made plain in Scripture, and it is absolutely bedrock for classical Christian theology. As Carson puts it,

> [T]he Bible insists again and again on God's unblemished goodness. God is *never* presented as an accomplice of evil, or as secretly malicious. . . . "He is the Rock, his works are perfect, and all his ways are just. A faithful God who does no wrong, upright and just is he" (Deut. 32:4). "God is light; in him there is no darkness at all (1 John 1:5). It is precisely because Habakkuk can say to God, "Your eyes are too pure to look upon evil; you cannot tolerate wrongdoing" (Hab. 1:13), that he has a difficult time understanding how God can sanction the terrible devastations of the Chaldeans upon his own covenant community. Note, then, that the goodness of God is the assumption, the nonnegotiable.[17]

---

[14] C. S. Lewis, *The Problem of Pain: How Human Suffering Raises Almost Intolerable Intellectual Problems* (New York: Macmillan, 1962), 89.
[15] D. A Carson, *Divine Sovereignty and Human Responsibility: Biblical Perspectives in Tension* (Atlanta: John Knox, 1981), 24–35.
[16] D. A. Carson, *How Long, O Lord? Reflections on Suffering and Evil* (Grand Rapids, MI: Baker Academic, 2006), 181.
[17] D. A. Carson, *How Long, O Lord?*, 182.

The goodness of God is nonnegotiable because God is *necessarily* good. "God is light, and in him is no darkness at all" (1 John 1:5). None *at all*. And "God is love" (1 John 4:16). God is not merely loving toward his creatures (although he *is* that, of course); God's loving goodness is in no way an arbitrary or capricious love. To the contrary, God is love in the richness and fullness of the triune communion between Father, Son, and Holy Spirit. Holy love is, then, of the essence of the triune God. As David Bentley Hart reminds us, "[T]he Christian metaphysical tradition, in both the Orthodox East and the Catholic West, asserts that God is not only good but goodness itself, not only true and beautiful but infinite truth and beauty . . . thus everything that comes from God must be good and true and beautiful."[18] So God's goodness is not ephemeral or fleeting, nor is it even *possibly* so. God is, within the triune life of transcendent light and holy love that is given and received between Father, Son, and Holy Spirit, simply *good*. The triune God is perfectly good, unalterably good, unfailingly good. Accordingly, any doctrinal formulation that has as an entailment the conclusion that God performs evil actions or is supportive of evil activity is simply doomed to fail.

DIVINE SOVEREIGNTY

The supreme authority or sovereignty of God is also unmistakable in Scripture, and it too has been affirmed throughout the Christian theological tradition. God is omniscient, and nothing escapes his watch or care. God is just and holy, and no sin is too petty or trivial to escape his concern and wrath. God is omnipotent, and his authority is as boundless as his power, and no sin is too challenging or overwhelming for him. God is sovereign over—he has authority over, and is responsible for—his own good but finite and now fallen creation. God is not threatened by human sin, and neither is he complacent about it or its effects. God is the sovereign Judge, and he promises to judge the world in righteousness.

Moreover, Scripture portrays God as actively working in human history to use actions of human wickedness to achieve his own good purposes. Consider the famous scene that unfolds late in the life of Joseph. At the culmination of the story, Joseph reveals his identity to the brothers who had mistreated him and sold him into slavery to the Egyptians. Although they are afraid of this abused brother who is now a powerful Egyptian official, he asks them to "come close" (Gen. 45:4 NIV). He then displays a remarkable conviction about God's presence and action through this time: "it was to save

---

[18] David Bentley Hart, *The Doors of the Sea: Where Was God in the Tsunami?* (Grand Rapids, MI: Eerdmans, 2005), 54–55.

lives that God sent me ahead of you" (v. 5 NIV). After their father dies, the brothers are once again afraid of Joseph. In a stunning reversal of fortunes, they throw themselves down before him and offer to be *his* slaves. Again, his response is telling: "You intended to harm me, but God intended it for good to accomplish what is now being done, the saving of many lives" (50:20 NIV). There is no sense in which the Genesis account presents the shameful treatment of Joseph by his brothers as anything other than wrong—even outrageously wrong. And yet the narrative also points to God's providential actions in and through this set of events. What the brothers did was wrong, and we can only judge it as sin. But God was not absent; neither was God inactive or merely reactive. To the contrary, Joseph is convinced that God intended to use his brothers' sinful actions for the greater good of God's own beneficent purposes. And, clearly, God is successful in doing so: they committed these evil deeds with shameful intentions, but God worked to turn their evil actions for a greater good.

As another example, consider what must be, for Christians, the central and most decisive turning point of all human history: the betrayal, arrest, trial, and crucifixion of Jesus Christ. The earliest apostolic preaching of the cross insists that the death of Christ was the result of the sinful actions of the very sinners Christ came to save. There is no ambiguity about it: again and again, the gospel proclamation insists that *"you* killed him" (e.g., Acts 2:23). And it draws a sharp contrast between the actions of the sinful humans who are responsible for the death of Jesus and the actions of God: "you *killed* him"—"but God *raised him from the dead*" (NIV) (Acts 2:24 NIV; cf. 3:13–15; 4:10; 5:30; 10:39–40; 13:30). The earliest Christian preachers do not say that God killed Jesus; to the contrary, the responsibility for the death of Christ clearly falls upon sinful humanity. At the same time, however, in the early apostolic preaching there is no indication that this was in any way a senseless accident or an unforeseen tragedy. To the contrary, this proclamation of the gospel includes the affirmation that this was within the providence of the omniscient God. Jesus Christ was "handed over" according to "God's deliberate plan and foreknowledge" (Acts 2:23 NIV). "Indeed Herod and Pontius Pilate met together with the Gentiles and the people of Israel in this city to conspire against your holy servant Jesus, whom you anointed. They did what your power and will had decided beforehand should happen" (Acts 4:27–28 NIV). Clearly, then, God is sovereign over these events: God is sovereign in the sense that he is supremely authoritative and will judge human sinners for their sins, and God is sovereign in the sense that not even the death of Christ is outside of God's providential and redemptive purposes.

B. Some Notable—But Flawed—Attempts at Doctrinal Formulation

These are key elements of any theologically acceptable account of human sin and divine providence. Neither commitment to the reality of human moral responsibility for sin, on one hand, or steadfast belief in either the unalterable goodness and unshakeable sovereignty of God, on the other hand, can be surrendered. However, some attempts at theological formulation run into problems in light of these theological desiderata. Here are some of the more prominent of these problems.

From Omnicausality to Monocausality

Huldrych Zwingli, the prominent sixteenth-century Reformed theologian from Zurich, insists that nothing happens by chance. Then Zwingli goes further. He is a theological determinist: God determines all events and actions. God decides what will be done in creation, and everything that happens does so in exact accordance with God's will. Beyond this, he says that God is the cause of everything that happens. Going further yet, he also says that God is the only cause of everything that happens. So for Zwingli, it is not enough to say that God is the cause of everything that happens; he also says that "other things are not truly causes any more than the representative of the potentate is truly the potentate."[19] This means that "there can be but one cause."[20] Accordingly, "secondary causes are not properly called causes," and "this is of fundamental importance for the understanding of providence."[21] Zwingli goes on to say that *God* is the "only real cause of all things, and those nearer things which we call causes, are not properly causes, but the agents and instruments with which the eternal mind works, and in which it manifests itself to be enjoyed."[22] This means—and Zwingli recognizes that this means—that God is the author of what we must call sin. As he puts it, "[T]he Deity is himself the author of that which to us is unrighteousness, though not in the least so to him."[23]

Zwingli is clearly taking leave of (a great deal of) the Christian tradition here. Compare John of Damascus (who is representative of much classical theology on this point):

> We ought to understand that while God knows all things beforehand, yet He does not predetermine all things. For He knows beforehand those things that

[19] Huldrych Zwingli, "The Providence of God," in Ulrich Zwingli, *On Providence and Other Essays*, edited for Samuel Macauley Jackson by William John Hinke (Durham, NC: Labyrinth, 1983 [1922]), 154; for the Latin text, see *Opera D. Huldrychi Zwingli* (Zurich: 1545), 358b.
[20] Zwingli, "Providence," 157; *Opera*, 359a.
[21] Zwingli, "Providence," 138; *Opera*, 354b.
[22] Zwingli, "Providence," 157–158; *Opera*, 359b.
[23] Zwingli, "Providence," 176; *Opera*, 364a.

are in our power, but He does not predetermine them. For it is not His will that there should be wickedness nor does He choose to compel virtue.[24]

Or compare Aquinas: divine providence does not impose necessity upon everything.[25] Moreover, "God cannot be directly the cause of sin, either in Himself or in another. . . . [I]t is impossible that He should be either to Himself or to another the cause of departing from the order which is to Himself. Therefore He cannot be directly the cause of sin, [and] in like manner neither can He cause sin indirectly."[26] John of Damascus and Thomas Aquinas take this view for good reason, and they have resources to avoid the problems associated with Zwingli's view.

And Zwingli's position indeed does run into several problems. Recall our critical theological desiderata: divine sovereignty, human responsibility, and divine goodness. Zwingli's account clearly and resoundingly affirms divine sovereignty. But when we come to moral responsibility, trouble looms large. A bit of reflection shows us that there is good reason to think that divine determinism might undermine a robust account of moral responsibility. For surely we do not bear moral responsibility for events over which we have no causal control. But if determinism is true and events over which we have no causal control and for which we bear no moral responsibility entail (along with the relevant natural or causal laws) the performance of all of our actions, then we have good reason to doubt that we bear moral responsibility for those actions.[27] These issues are, of course, vexing, and the debates over freedom and responsibility continue.[28] But it is obvious that there is trouble in the neighborhood.

But things get much worse when we consider divine goodness. For Zwingli's doctrine threatens to make God the author of evil. Without a distinction between primary and secondary causality (which Zwingli does not have), it is hard indeed to defuse this threat. If God is the cause of sin, then isn't God just doing sinful things? Isn't he just committing sin? As we have seen, Zwingli actually says that "the Deity is himself the author of that which to us is unrighteousness, though not in the least so to him."[29] But apart from Zwingli's sheer assertion that this isn't sin *for God* (even though he admits that it would be so for anyone else), isn't God the cooperative sinner—does not this reduce God to being a co-sinner? Worse yet, if God is the *only cause*

[24] John of Damascus, *De Fide* II:XXX (PG 94:970B–972A; *NPNF*² 9:42).
[25] Aquinas, *ST* I, Q 22.4.
[26] Aquinas, *ST* I, Q 79.1.
[27] Here I follow the helpful summary of Thomas P. Flint, *Divine Providence: The Molinist Account* (Ithaca, NY: Cornell University Press, 1998), 28–29.
[28] A fine entry point into such debates can be found in Robert Kane, ed., *The Oxford Handbook of Free Will*, 2nd ed. (Oxford: Oxford University Press, 2011).
[29] Zwingli, "Providence," 176; *Opera*, 364a.

of sinful actions, then how are we to avoid the conclusion that God is the *only sinner*?

The Zwinglian defender might protest that, like it or not, Scripture teaches both divine omnicausality and monocausality. She might point to biblical texts where God says, "I form the light and create darkness, I bring prosperity and create disaster; I, the LORD, do all these things" (Isa. 45:7 NIV) or "When disaster comes to a city, has not the LORD caused it?" (Amos 3:6 NIV). And she might make a case that such passages teach divine causation of all things, even evil. However, a closer analysis shows that such texts do no such thing. As Aquinas explains, "[T]he order of justice belongs to the order of the universe" (and as such it is a reflection of the necessary goodness of God).[30] The order of justice "requires that penalty should be dealt out to sinners."[31] This penalty may be called "evil" (in the sense that it seems awful to the recipients of it, and indeed it may be a freely chosen sinful action of other sinners that God uses for his good and just purposes). Thus God is not, Aquinas insists, "the author of evil," and "the evil which consists in defect of action, or which is caused by the defect of the agent, is not reduced to God as its cause."[32]

FROM MONOCAUSALITY TO OCCASIONALISM

Zwingli's bold and unguarded assertions (without the standard qualifications about the distinctions between primary and secondary causes) about God's universal causality create problems, and his claims about God being the *sole* causal agent only make things worse. Indeed, his position brings us to consideration of occasionalism. Occasionalism is a radical view of divine agency that was championed by such medieval theologians as al-Ghazali and Gabriel Biel as well as such major modern figures as Nicholas Malebranche, Bishop George Berkeley, and Jonathan Edwards. In general, occasionalism holds that the cosmos is being re-created *ex nihilo* moment by moment and denies secondary causality. God is thus the "strong active cause" of every event that occurs, and no material substances have any causal powers whatsoever (either active or passive).[33] For a theologian such as Edwards, then, it turns out that "God is the sole causal agent, that is, the efficient cause of all that comes to pass."[34] And, given human sin, "God is the causal and moral agent responsible for . . . sinful actions."[35]

But if the Zwinglian view has problems, this Edwardsian position only

---

[30] Aquinas, *ST* I, Q 49.2.
[31] Aquinas, *ST* I, Q 49.2.
[32] Aquinas, *ST* I, Q 49.2.
[33] Here I rely on Alfred J. Freddoso, "Medieval Aristotelianism and the Case against Secondary Causation in Nature," in *Divine and Human Action: Essays in the Metaphysics of Theism*, ed. Thomas V. Morris (Ithaca, NY: Cornell University Press, 1988), 74–118.
[34] Oliver D. Crisp, *Jonathan Edwards on God and Creation* (Oxford: Oxford University Press, 2012), 144.
[35] Oliver D. Crisp, *Jonathan Edwards and the Metaphysics of Sin* (Aldershot, UK: Ashgate, 2005), 71.

serves to deepen them. The familiar problems with moral responsibility emerge again, and this time with even more of a vengeance. If human creatures have no causal power at all (either active or passive), then it isn't so much as possible for them to freely choose to sin. But oddly enough, neither is it possible for them to resist the "sinful" actions that move through them. And, again, it turns out that God is the ultimate causal agent who is responsible for sin. Somehow, things get even worse. For now—as the only causal agent—God is the *only sinner*. These conclusions are outrageous. Indeed, they are blasphemous.

DEISM

The devout efforts of extreme theological determinists (such as Zwingli and Edwards) undermine human responsibility and implicate God in sinful actions, but there are problems from the other direction as well. For instance, deism (as broadly represented by such Enlightenment and post-Enlightenment luminaries as Herbert of Cherbury, Matthew Toland, Anthony Collins, Thomas Woolston, Matthew Tindal, Peter Annet, Thomas Paine, and Thomas Jefferson as well as their more notorious French counterparts) seriously attenuates divine action. In the summary of Alan Charles Kor, "Deism was the categorical naturalization of divine providence."[36] Deism allows that the initial act of creation was a supernatural act, but beyond that divine providential action is limited to natural law (that is, in principle, discoverable by everyone). Moreover, Kor says, "Deism also posited a categorically general providence, excluding acts of particular providence such as supernatural revelation, miracle, answered prayer, divine intervention, and particular relationship to God."[37]

Such views amount to a serious revision of the classical doctrinal affirmations about concurrence and governance. The latter gets reduced to the presence of the laws of nature, and the former seems to drop from sight altogether. Moreover, there is no room in such revisionist accounts for the kind of divine engagement (both indirect, as in the case of the events leading to Christ's passion, which were "according to the plan and foreknowledge of God," and direct, as in the case of the miracle of Christ's passion) that we see portrayed in Scripture. So while the theological desideratum of human moral responsibility is not necessarily threatened by deistic doctrine, it is not hard to see that deistic accounts of providence fall far short of the other crucial desiderata. For divine sovereignty is emptied of its biblically grounded content, and serious questions are raised about divine goodness.

[36] Alan Charles Kor, "Deism," in *The Routledge Companion to Modern Christian Thought*, ed. Chad Meister and James Beilby (New York: Routledge, 2013), 326.
[37] Kor, "Deism," 329.

PROCESS THEOLOGY

Process theology goes even further in some important ways. In contrast to deism, it affirms divine engagement—even to the point of divine entanglement. But it works to do so without recourse to supernaturalism; indeed it sharply criticizes and categorically rejects "classical theism."[38] Process theology emphasizes several key concepts; not surprisingly, the notion of process is chief among them. As John Cobb and David Ray Griffin explain, to be actual just is to be in process, and the only things that count as actual entities are "momentary events which perish immediately upon coming into being."[39] These momentary events do not "endure through time."[40] This means that "true individuals are momentary experiences," and "what we ordinarily call individuals, the sorts of things that endure through time, are not true individuals, but are 'societies' of such."[41] Everything is, then, "essentially related" and interdependent.[42] This last claim encompasses God too; God is to be understood as the "Creative-Responsive Love" that enjoys its own cosmic adventure while luring and persuading the cosmos into evolution toward greater harmony and enjoyment.

Adding hamartiology to the mix only complicates matters further. One of the most significant statements of process theology brings it into close dialogue with feminist theology.[43] Where some articulations of process theology show very little direct engagement with the doctrine of sin, Marjorie Suchocki offers a clear and bold vision of the doctrine of sin. Suchocki knows very well that sin has traditionally been understood as ultimately being rebellion against God. In fact, it is hard to think of anything more basic to the doctrine of sin than this affirmation. But Suchocki rejects nothing less than this most basic and fundamental tenet—sin is, in the first instance, *violence against creation*. More precisely, sin is "participation through intent or act in unnecessary violence that contributes to the ill-being of any aspect of earth or its inhabitants."[44] Sin is "the violence of rebellion against creation. . . . Sin is first and foremost a rebellion against creation."[45] Seeing sin as rebellion against God is criticized by Suchocki as problematic in several ways: it "tends to cast the primary function of God as the moral lawgiver" (and thus threatens to reinforce boundaries that

---

[38] E.g., David Ray Griffin, *Reenchantment without Supernaturalism: A Process Philosophy of Religion* (Ithaca, NY: Cornell University Press, 2001).

[39] John Cobb and David Ray Griffin, *Process Theology: An Introductory Exposition* (Philadelphia: Westminster, 1976), 14.

[40] Cobb and Griffin, *Process Theology*, 19.

[41] Cobb and Griffin, *Process Theology*, 15.

[42] Cobb and Griffin, *Process Theology*, 18–22.

[43] Marjorie Hewitt Suchocki, *The Fall to Violence: Original Sin in Relational Theology* (New York: Continuum, 1994). Her view is in some ways more radical than other feminist doctrines; she wants her proposal to help "overthrow" rather than merely "supplement" Reinhold Niebuhr's doctrine (43).

[44] Suchocki, *Fall to Violence*, 12.

[45] Suchocki, *Fall to Violence*, 16.

are arbitrarily or culturally defined); it "too easily translates into a social formula for keeping marginalized and oppressed peoples in places of poverty and/
or powerlessness"; it "effectively levels the distinctions between sins"; it "renders invisible the very real and often intended victims of sin"; and it contributes
to the "devaluation of creation" while overall making humans seem more important than we really are.[46] The classical understanding of sin—as whatever
is ultimately *against God*—simply must be rejected. In its place comes this
assertion: sin is whatever does (unnecessary) violence to *creation*.

This doctrine should not be taken to mean that God has nothing to do
with sin; nor should we take it to imply that sin has no impact on God or that
God is not adversely impacted by sin. After all, Suchocki's process panentheism
entails the conclusion that whatever happens to the world *must* impact God.
"I do not," she says, "thereby assume that sin has no effect on God. Quite to
the contrary; in a process-relational world, it is impossible for God *not* to be
affected by that which happens in the world, be it sin or saintliness."[47] Sin as
rebellion against creation actually "entails sin against God as well."[48] But we
should make no mistake about Suchocki's intentions. She recognizes that she
is offering nothing less than a complete "reversal of the tradition: rather than
rebellion against God being the primary sin that engenders all others, I see rebellion against creation as the fundamental sin. Since God must experience the
world, violence in creation also entails violence against God."[49]

So on Suchocki's proposal, we are ensnared—merely by being creatures—
in a vast web of violence. Creatures *are* violent to one another; "all have
sinned." Indeed, it is hard to discern either how guilt might be reckoned or how
the violence might be transcended. "Where does sin and guilt start, and where
does it stop?"[50] She wrestles with the notion of guilt, and she concludes that
"solidarity with the human race" brings guilt, as does "passive guilt through
failure to transcend boundaries that work ill-being, or active guilt through
personal participation in acts of psychic or physical violence."[51] Thus our only
hope is for forgiveness and transformation.

But where does such hope come from? When we look at her treatment of
forgiveness and transformation, we see that Suchocki's emphasis falls heavily
on the "horizontal" dimension. Finally "the world" will be "resurrected" by
and "in" God, and—apparently—all will be well.[52] So while there is a sense in
which we "stand in need of forgiveness" by God, it is both subsumed under

---

[46] Suchocki, *Fall to Violence*, 17–18.
[47] Suchocki, *Fall to Violence*, 13, emphasis original.
[48] Suchocki, *Fall to Violence*, 13.
[49] Suchocki, *Fall to Violence*, 13.
[50] Suchocki, *Fall to Violence*, 12.
[51] Suchocki, *Fall to Violence*, 142.
[52] Suchocki, *Fall to Violence*, 158–159.

the priority of forgiveness at a creaturely level and (apparently) granted to all creation. We are left, then, to conclude that salvation is something that we achieve through the practice of nonviolence (or at least non-necessary violence) and good will toward creation.

Process theology is a complex and evolving entity itself, but it is not hard to see that problems arise for process theology when we consider our primary theological desiderata. In relation to divine sovereignty, even brief reflection shows that process theology falls far short. If God is limited in knowledge and cannot know what free creatures will do in the future, then it is hard indeed to account for the scriptural claim that the death of Christ was according to God's "definite plan and foreknowledge" (Acts 2:23). To be fair, process theology thinks that the doctrine of divine omnipotence is a "mistake," and it criticizes and rejects the doctrine of *creatio ex nihilo*.[53]

But even if process theology is willing to reject the desideratum of divine sovereignty (and, in this case, the direct witness of Scripture to the divine "plan and foreknowledge"), the other criteria will be harder for it to discard. These desiderata, however, will also be hard to maintain. Consider moral responsibility as it relates to a commonly held process view of personal identity. As we have seen, process ontology holds that actual entities are momentary events that do not endure through time, and that personal human experience is merely a string or "serially ordered society" of such events.[54] Here a problem rears its head: if actual entities do not endure through time, then they do not endure long enough to commit acts of wrongdoing. Simply put, they don't last long enough to acquire the property of being guilty for sin.[55]

Perhaps surprisingly, things get worse when we think about divine goodness. Process theology insists that God, as powerful but not omnipotent, is doing his best to combat evil in the world. Accordingly, God is "responsible" for the evil but not "indictable" for it (as he presumably would be if he were not fighting against it).[56] But there are serious concerns here. According to process theology it is true that God understood that the final triumph of evil was possible but then created nonetheless. But if God did this without knowing that he would ultimately triumph, then he was gambling that he wouldn't create a monster that would defeat him and destroy the cosmos. And this means that God was operating in a dangerously reckless way. As Stephen T. Davis

---

[53] E.g., Charles Hartshorne, *Omnipotence and Other Theological Mistakes* (Albany: State University of New York Press, 1984); and Thomas Jay Oord, ed., *Theologies of Creation: Creatio Ex Nihilo and Its New Rivals* (New York: Routledge, 2015).

[54] Cobb and Griffin, *Process Theology*, 15.

[55] If we interpret process metaphysics to hold that these events in fact do endure through time and thus serve as property-bearers, then we might avoid this problem. At the same time, it is then hard to see how we have not reintroduced substance metaphysics (albeit an odd version thereof) once again. On this see Stephen T. Davis, *Disputed Issues: Contending for Christian Faith in Today's Academic Setting* (Waco, TX: Baylor University Press, 2009), 127–128.

[56] Cobb and Griffin, *Process Theology*, 69.

argues, the deity of process theology is like a "mad scientist who fashions a monster whom the scientist hopes will behave but whom he cannot control. If the monster runs amok, the scientist's decision to make the monster will turn out to have been terribly wrong."[57] Surely this sort of recklessness casts a long shadow over the goodness of God. Even worse, process theology makes sin and evil inevitable even for God. Pierre Teilhard de Chardin makes the point with candor: "evil appears inevitably with the first atom of being which creation releases into existence."[58] But as Stephen H. Webb observes, if this is correct, then "God must be the source of evil, a conclusion Teilhard did not hesitate to embrace. . . . Original sin is so original that it begins with God's creation of the first bit of matter."[59]

C. The Traditional Doctrine Once More

Having cleared away this conceptual brush, let us return to the core elements of the more traditional accounts of divine providence. There are, of course, various versions of the broadly traditional accounts, with Molinism and Thomism taking pride of place in most discussions.[60] But what they generally hold in common is a strong commitment to the primary theological desiderata along with affirmation of conservation, concurrence, and governance.

CONSERVATION

The traditional doctrine of providence holds that God conserves, sustains, or upholds his creation in existence; were it not for divine providence, creation in general and all creatures in particular would cease to exist. Eleonore Stump explains that for Aquinas, "the notion of God's providence is derived from the concept of his goodness."[61] God sustains for the same reason that God creates: to share the goodness that is essential to his nature. Stump explains further that this goodness is not something extrinsic to God, nor is it arbitrary in any way:

> Because on the doctrine of simplicity the divine nature is identical with goodness, the goodness of creatures is measured by their relationship with God. For human persons in particular, the ultimate good and the final fulfillment of their natures consists in union with God. And because God is good, he

---

[57] Davis, *Disputed Issues*, 131.

[58] Pierre Teilhard de Chardin, *Christianity and Evolution*, trans. Rene Hague (New York: Harcourt Brace, 1969), 33, 184, cited in Stephen H. Webb, *The Dome of Eden: A New Solution to the Problem of Creation and Evolution* (Eugene, OR: Cascade, 2010), 106.

[59] Webb, *Dome of Eden*, 106.

[60] For recent work on Molinism, see esp. Flint, *Divine Providence*; William Lane Craig, "God Directs All Things," in *Four Views on Divine Providence*, ed. Dennis W. Jowers (Grand Rapids, MI: Zondervan, 2011), 79–100; Ken Perszyk, ed., *Molinism: The Contemporary Debate* (Oxford: Oxford University Press, 2011). On Thomist accounts of divine providence, see, e.g., Eleonore Stump, *Aquinas* (New York: Routledge, 2003), 455–478; and Alexander R. Pruss, "Prophecy without Middle Knowledge," *FPhilos* (2007): 433–457.

[61] Stump, *Aquinas*, 456.

does what is good for his creatures. In his dealings with human beings, then, God's ultimate aim, which takes precedence over all others, is to return human beings to himself, to unite them to himself in heaven.[62]

So God's very act of continued sustenance of his creation—even in its sinful state—is demonstration of his good intentions for it. Indeed, the fact that sinful creatures continue to exist is testimony to the goodness of God's providence.

CONCURRENCE

Matters are not, however, quite so straightforward when we consider concurrence in relation to sin. Consider the range of possible understandings (and *misunderstandings*) of what it might mean for God to "concur" with sinful actions. At a quite basic level, concurrence might be taken in the sense of provision; this is very closely related to sustenance. For in the very act of sustaining creatures with causal powers, God is continuing to provide them with those causal powers and thus enabling them to perform various actions. God does not determine what they do with those powers, but he continues both to sustain them in existence and to give them the ability to do things. Let us call this the *provision sense* of concurrence. There is also what we might call the *dual agency sense* of concurrence; here "to concur" means something like "to cooperate" in working together, as in the father who is talking to the elderly widowed neighbor with his teenage son and tells the neighbor that "we will take care of the snow removal for you this winter." Here he means something like this: "My son and I will work together to shovel your snow; we will combine our powers and cooperate for this end." This is distinct from what we might call the *replacement sense* of concurrence; this sense is much closer to the speech-act of the father who tells his elderly widowed neighbor that "*we* will take care of the snow removal" but who really means that *only the son* will do the work involved in snow removal. The father clearly intends for the neighbor's snow to be cleared, but he just as clearly intends for the son to do the hard work *instead of* him. Finally, concurrence might be taken rather generally as agreement, as when someone says, "I insist that we do *X*" and another person nods gravely and says, "I concur." Accordingly, "to concur" would then mean "to agree" or "to approve." We can call this the *approval sense* of concurrence.

Taking these in reverse order, we don't have to reflect on this for long to see that the *approval sense* of concurrence cannot be correct. Without serious qualification, we should never affirm this. Given our affirmations about divine goodness (which should be nonnegotiable for orthodox Christian theology), any view according to which God nods in agreement and says "I approve" of

---

[62] Stump, *Aquinas*, 456.

rape and torture is simply a nonstarter. Returning to our biblical examples, surely it is true that God says "I approve" of the ways that he will use the perfidy of Joseph's brothers and the malfeasance of those who conspired against Jesus for his own good purposes (in these cases, to save many lives and to redeem the world), but this doesn't mean that he approves of their sinful actions. Indeed, given the necessary and simple goodness of God's own triune life of holy love, divine approval of sin is nothing short of *impossible*.

Similarly, to understand concurrence in the *replacement sense* is surely mistaken. If we take this to mean that divine action replaces the causal efficacy of the human agency, then we are right back to the doorstep of occasionalism. And, as we have seen, this threatens to render the conclusion not only that God is a sinner but even that God is the *only* real sinner. Since any doctrinal proposal that entails blasphemy can be safely dismissed, we can reject this proposal. On the other hand, to take the replacement sense in the other direction is not much better. For if all divine agency is reduced to mere directives, and to the point where human agency is the only agency that is causally efficacious, then we have returned to the doorstep of deism.

The *dual agency* sense of concurrence is more promising; indeed, Scripture will sometimes speak of both God and a human sinner as the cause of some action (e.g., God "hardens" Pharaoh's heart, and Pharaoh "hardens" his own heart). But caution is in order here, especially when we do not consider providence in abstraction but precisely in relation to sin. Worries come from several directions. Some theologians, especially those attuned to the resources of the Christian tradition, will criticize this account for placing the causal agency of the divine and the human on the same ontological plane, with the result being that God and the human(s) are simply dividing up the workload while cooperating at the same level. In other words, they might say, to think of dual agency in this way is to underplay or ignore the important distinctions between primary and secondary causality. Moreover, this sense may open the door to other misunderstandings. Some might adopt the dual agency sense and then go on to explain it in a determinist sense; on this view, perhaps God would be doing everything through his creatures by making it impossible to do anything other than what they do. But then we would again invite the familiar criticisms of determinism. For we would once again be faced with arguments that the moral responsibility of the human agents is mitigated or negated—and at the same time we would encounter the arguments that dual agency in sinful actions would make God a co-sinner. So however we take claims about dual agency, the claim cannot plausibly be taken to mean *that*.

The *provision sense* of concurrence seems to be on more solid ground. We might wonder why God sustains sinful creatures at all, or we might at least question why he continues to grant causal powers to them when he knows that they will misuse those powers. This worry could be taken in either of two ways: we might wonder why he doesn't remove *all* ability of sinners to do things, or we might question why God doesn't remove *more* of them than he in fact does (because, for Christians who believe in miracles, it seems clear enough that *sometimes* God does just this). If we take it the first way and want to know why *anything* bad ever happens, we should remember that the overall Christian account gives us reason to believe that the world that God wanted was a good world with creatures who would freely relate to the Trinity in a relationship of holy and loving communion. As Lewis puts it,

> We can, perhaps, conceive of a world in which God corrected the results of this abuse of free will by his creatures at every moment: so that a wooden beam became soft as grass when it was used as a weapon, and the air refused to obey me if I attempted to set up in it the sound waves that carry lies or insults. But such a world would be one in which wrong actions were impossible, and in which, therefore, freedom of the will would be void. . . . That God can and does, on occasions, modify the behaviour of matter and produce what we call miracles, is part of the Christian faith; but the very conception of a common, and therefore stable, world, demands that these occasions should be extremely rare.[63]

If, on the other hand, we take the complaint in the second sense, we have recourse to "skeptical theism": just because we cannot, from our limited vantage point, *see* why God might have good and holy and just reasons to allow particular horrors and evils does not give us a good reason to conclude that there are no such good and holy and just reasons.[64]

However, the traditional accounts of concurrence are rather more complicated. The *provision sense* of concurrence is generally seen as deficient; for many theologians, it just does not go far enough. As Alfred J. Freddoso puts it, "[T]raditional philosophical theologians almost unanimously regarded as too *weak* even the strong-sounding (to modern ears) claim that God's causal contribution to non-miraculous natural effects consists precisely in His creating and conserving material substances and their causal powers."[65] The scholastics disagreed among themselves over the precise nature of the way that divine action made causal contributions (whether God contributes to the secondary cause or to the effect, etc.), but they agreed that God is sovereign over

---

[63] Lewis, *Problem of Pain*, 33–34.
[64] For defenses of "skeptical theism," see Michael Bergmann, "Skeptical Theism and the Problem of Evil," in *The Oxford Handbook of Philosophical Theology*, ed. Thomas P. Flint and Michael C. Rea (Oxford: Oxford University Press, 2009), 374–399; and Michael C. Rea, "Skeptical Theism and the 'Too Much Skepticism' Objection," in *The Blackwell Companion to the Problem of Evil*, ed. Justin P. McBrayer and Daniel Howard-Snyder (Oxford: Wiley-Blackwell, 2013), 482–506.
[65] Freddoso, "Medieval Aristotelianism," 117–118, emphasis original.

the causes that come together to produce an effect. Moreover, they generally insisted on the important distinction between primary and secondary causality; thus they would have insisted that any notion of *dual agency* must take this distinction into account. So it seems safe to conclude that they would have insisted upon bolstering the *provision sense* and providing important nuance to the *dual agency sense*. It seems just as safe to conclude that (the vast majority of) classical Christian theologians would also have rejected the *replacement* and *approval* senses of concurrence.

GOVERNANCE

Turning our attention to governance, we can see that caution is in order here as well. As Hart points out, "certainly all Christians must affirm God's transcendent governance of everything, even fallen history and fallen nature, and must believe that by that governance he will defeat evil and bring the final good of all things out of the darkness of 'this age.'"[66] Hart is correct; this much is basic to Christian theology. But Hart is also right to observe,

> It makes a considerable difference, however—nothing short of our understanding of the nature of God is at stake—whether one says that God has eternally willed the history of sin and death, and all that comes to pass therein, as the proper or necessary means of achieving his ends, or whether one says instead that God has willed his good in creatures from eternity and will bring it to pass, despite their rebellion, by so ordering all things toward his goodness that even evil (which he does not cause) becomes an occasion of the operations of grace.[67]

Hart concludes that it is only the latter view that "can accurately be called a doctrine of 'providence' in the properly theological sense; the former view is mere determinism."[68] Keeping our theological desiderata in mind, there is good reason to think that Hart is correct.

CONCLUSION: THE MYSTERIES OF PROVIDENCE AND THE HOPE OF THE GOSPEL

How does God "so order" everything so that even sinful actions "become an occasion for the operations of grace"? John of Damascus observes that God works in ways that are both mysterious and varied: for instance, sometimes God allows us to encounter misfortune for the sake of our own sanctification and his glory, sometimes it is permitted for the sake of other persons, and at other points God allows evil actions to occur "in order that something great and marvelous might be accomplished"—such as the salvation of humanity

---

[66] Hart, *Doors of the Sea*, 82.
[67] Hart, *Doors of the Sea*, 82.
[68] Hart, *Doors of the Sea*, 82.

as it was brought about through the cross.[69] More elaborate theories of *how* this happens have been proposed, and these hold promise (Molinism is especially fecund). But even if we cannot fully explain the mysterious workings of providence—even if our best attempts at detailed explanation fall somewhat short—this does not entail that there are no good explanations. It means only that we don't currently have such explanations at hand (and, I think, it may give us reason to wonder if such explanations are even accessible on this side of the eschaton). We are, however, in a good position to avoid mistaken, wrongheaded, and pastorally damaging conclusions. And theologically, we are in a position to joyfully affirm that God's providence flows from his goodness, and, far from being overwhelmed by badness, it is at work to restore sinful and broken creatures to himself.

II. SIN AND PREVENIENT GRACE

As we have seen, God's gracious providence continues to sustain rebellious sinners; it upholds morally perverted creatures in existence and brings good gifts to them. As we shall see in the next sections, God's grace justifies, regenerates, and sanctifies sinners who are guilty and filthy. But "in between" providence and salvation we find God's *prevenient* grace. According to Richard A. Muller's helpful summary, prevenient grace (*gratia praeveniens*) is "the grace that 'comes before' all human response to God. A special term is given to the grace that necessarily precedes *conversio* (q.v.), since humanity is universally sinful and incapable of salvation or of any truly good work without the help of God."[70] As Thomas C. Oden explains, prevenient grace is closely arrayed with cooperating, subsequent grace: "Prevenient grace first operates before the will can cooperate. Prevenient grace is therefore the grace that *works without us because it works before us* (*gratia operans*), but cooperating grace is the grace that *works with us as it works through us* (*gratia cooperans*). . . . God first establishes in us the disposition toward the reception of grace."[71]

The category of prevenient grace, although sometimes associated almost exclusively with Wesleyan-Arminian theology, has a long and luminous theological history (indeed, it is "Arminian" only in the sense that Arminius affirmed and employed it—and *not* in the sense that it originated with him). Augustine, for instance, repeatedly makes use of the concept.[72] Grace is both *praevenit* (goes before) and *subsequetur* (follows after); it is prevenient "so that we may be called," and it is subsequent so that "we may be glorified."[73]

---

[69] John of Damascus, *De Fide* II: XXIX (PG 94:965A–968B; *NPNF*² 9:41–42).
[70] Muller, *Dictionary of Latin and Greek Theological Terms*, 132.
[71] Thomas C. Oden, *The Transforming Power of Grace* (Nashville: Abingdon, 1993), 51–52, emphasis original.
[72] E.g., Augustine, *Sermones ad populum omnes* CLXXIV.iv.4 (PL 38:942–943); Augustine, *Contra duas epistolas Pelagianorum* IV.vi.14 (PL 44:620).
[73] Augustine, *De natura et gratia ad Timasium et Jacobum contra Pelagium* XXXI.35 (PL 44:264).

Consistent with the tradition that he has inherited, the influential medieval theologian Peter Lombard is insistent that the first humans were created *good* but then fell. Just why they fell remains a mystery, but, as Philipp Rosemann explains, Lombard's view is that "God preferred his creatures to be what they decided to be rather than creating them incapable of choice."[74] The results of this fall extend to the entire human race, and they are devastating. For while some good can be done by sinners, nonetheless "we hold steadfastly and unhesitatingly, that without prevenient and assisting grace the free will does not suffice to obtain justification and salvation."[75] With respect to original sin, Lombard recognizes that there has been a variety of views in the tradition, and he admits that there is some obscurity in the discussions. He distinguishes between concupiscence, which refers to the fleshly desires that may be the breeding ground for sin, and the sin itself. He insists on the reality of original sin, he takes a fairly straightforward "realist" (even physical) understanding of it, and he is convinced that it includes guilt as well as corruption.[76]

Linking the Augustinian emphases closely with the distinction between *operating* and *cooperating* grace, Thomas Aquinas affirms both the necessity and the reality of prevenient grace. He lists "five effects of grace in us": these are to heal the soul, to enable us to desire good, to successfully carry out our graciously enabled desire to do what is good, to persevere in doing that good, and to reach glory. Grace, "inasmuch as it causes the first effect in us, is called prevenient with respect to the second, and inasmuch as it causes the second, it is called subsequent with respect to the first effect."[77] Augustine and Aquinas are far from idiosyncratic in their affirmation and employment of the doctrine of prevenient grace; indeed, it enjoys conciliar endorsement from no less an authority than the Second Synod of Orange (529)—the very ecclesial meeting that officially rejected "Semi-Pelagianism."[78] During the Protestant Reformation, the Regensburg Agreement (1541), where important agreement on doctrines such as justification was reached by such Protestant theologians as the Reformed divine Martin Bucer and the Lutheran theologian Philipp Melanchthon as well as the Roman Catholic theologians Gasparo Contarini and Johann Gropper, insists upon the prevenience of grace.[79] Such important

---

[74] Philipp Rosemann, *Peter Lombard*, Great Medieval Thinkers (Oxford: Oxford University Press, 2004), 110. Rosemann states that there are over 1,400 commentaries on Lombard's *Sentences*. Some of the most famous of these would include the works of Alexander of Hales, Bonaventure, Thomas Aquinas, John Duns Scotus, William of Ockham, Gabriel Biel, and Martin Luther (*Peter Lombard*, 3).

[75] Peter Lombard, *Sentences* II.28.1.i; Rosemann, *Peter Lombard*, 112.

[76] Rosemann, *Peter Lombard*, 114–115.

[77] Aquinas, *ST* I–II, Q 111.3.

[78] *Canons of the Council of Orange*, canon 18, in *Creeds and Confessions in the Christian Tradition*, ed. Jaroslav Pelikan and Valerie R. Hotchkiss (New Haven, CT: Yale University Press, 2003), 695.

[79] See Anthony N. S. Lane, "A Tale of Two Imperial Cities: Justification at Regensburg (1541) and Trent (1546–1547)" in *Justification in Perspective: Historical Developments and Contemporary Challenges*, ed. Bruce L. McCormack (Grand Rapids, MI: Baker Academic, 2006), 143.

Lutheran theologians as Johann Wilhelm Baier and Johann Andreas Quenstadt hold to the doctrine as well.[80] And, as is well known, Arminian and Wesleyan theologies make use of the doctrine as well: the grace of God is "the beginning, continuance, and accomplishment of all good (*principium progressus et complimentum omnis boni*), even to this extent, that the regenerate man himself, without prevenient (*praeveniente*), or assisting, awakening, following, and co-operative (*cooperante*) grace, can neither think, will, nor do good, nor withstand any temptations to evil; so that all good deeds or movements, that can be conceived, must be ascribed to the grace of God."[81]

The doctrine enjoys such deep and broad historical support for good reason: it is well-grounded with respect to Scripture; not only is it indicated in such passages as John 1:9 and Titus 2:11, it also may be built upon a biblical theology that recognizes the depravity and inability of sinners along with the responsibility of sinners and God's genuinely good intentions for all humanity.[82] And it is vitally important. For it teaches that God *must* take the initiative to reach sinners—and it teaches that God indeed *has done so*.

III. SIN AND JUSTIFYING GRACE

As we have seen, sin is depicted in biblical terms that are unmistakably and undeniably *legal*—sin is the transgression of the law (1 John 3:4 KJV). God is portrayed throughout Scripture as King and Judge; he is the sovereign ruler over all creation who exercises his reign in justice and righteousness. Humans were created as subjects and citizens of his kingdom, and they were also created and called to be "sovereign" in a subordinate and derivative sense (e.g., Gen. 1:26–27). Sin is lawlessness (*anomia* in the NT), and the committing of sin results in objective guilt. So the sinner, precisely as a sinner, stands guilty and condemned before the sovereign and omniscient Judge and ruler of the cosmos.

Sinners who hope for rescue, therefore, need salvation that addresses the problems of lawlessness and guilt. The doctrine of justification is precisely the divinely prescribed and divinely provided remedy for sin. On Oden's summary, "[T]he nature of justification is pardon, its sole condition is faith, its sole ground is the righteousness of God, and its fruits and evidences are good works."[83] Grounded in the holy love of the triune God and made possible and

---

[80] E.g., Johann Wilhelm Baier, *Compendium Theologiae Positivae, Pars Tertia* (1695; repr., St. Louis, Officiana Synodi Missouriensis Lutheranae, 1879), 220–221. See Heinrich Schmid, ed., *The Doctrinal Theology of the Evangelical Lutheran Church* (Philadelphia: Lutheran Publication Society, 1876), 486–487.

[81] "Articuli Arminiani III," in *The Creeds of Christendom, with a History and Critical Notes, Volume III: The Evangelical Protestant Creeds*, ed. Philip Schaff (Grand Rapids, MI: Baker Academic, 2007), 547.

[82] Objections to the doctrine of prevenient grace are not uncommon in contemporary evangelicalism, e.g., Thomas R. Schreiner, "Does Scripture Teach Prevenient Grace in the Wesleyan Sense?," in *Still Sovereign: Contemporary Perspectives on Election, Foreknowledge, and Grace*, ed. Bruce A. Ware and Thomas R. Schreiner (Grand Rapids, MI: Baker Academic, 2000), 229–246; and William Combs, "Does the Bible Teach Prevenient Grace?," *Detroit Baptist Seminary Journal* (2005): 3–18.

[83] Thomas C. Oden, *The Justification Reader* (Grand Rapids, MI: Eerdmans, 2002), 3.

actual as sinful creatures are brought into union with Christ, justification is the divine action that does away with our guilt and declares us righteous before God. Building upon the vast and deep treasury of royal-legal imagery in Scripture, the language of the doctrine is heavily legal. It is "an act of God's free grace unto sinners, in which he pardons all their sin, and accepts and accounts their persons righteous in his sight, not for anything wrought in them, or done by them, but only for the perfect obedience and full satisfaction of Christ, by God imputed to them, and received by faith alone."[84] Accordingly, Christians believe that "we most wretched sinners are justified before God and saved alone by faith in Christ, so that Christ alone is our righteousness."[85] This means that "we are accounted righteous before God, only for the merit of our Lord and Savior Jesus Christ by faith, and not for our own works. Therefore, that we are justified by faith is a most wholesome doctrine, and very full of comfort."[86]

Salvation, then, is undeniably *legal* in nature. As sinners, we are lawbreakers who stand guilty before the righteous Judge of the cosmos. We need salvation from the consequences of that transgression; we need rescue from our guilt and its legal ramifications. By grace, God saves us from that guilt and its consequences. For by grace, sinners are *justified*.

IV. SIN AND REGENERATING, CONVERTING GRACE

Just as sin is depicted as legal in Scripture, so also is salvation. As we have just seen, this is the beautiful and "wholesome" doctrine of justification. But just as sin is never *merely* legal in Scripture, so also is salvation from that sin and its consequences much broader than the legal aspect. Here several elements are important: repentance, conversion, adoption, and regeneration. All these elements flow from the familial imagery of Scripture. As we have seen, humans were made to relate to God as children to a loving parent. But as we have also seen, sin has despoiled this relationship. Sin is portrayed in Scripture as the rebellious rupture of this relationship (e.g., Luke 15:11–32), and it results in estrangement and "death" (e.g., Luke 15:32). Salvation, accordingly, is depicted as reconciliation (e.g., 2 Cor. 5:11–21), adoption (e.g., Rom. 8:12–17), and even rebirth (e.g., John 3:3).

A. Repentance

As Paul Hinlicky points out, "[T]he confession of sinfulness is a necessary but not a sufficient condition (Luke 5:8). . . . Forgiveness cannot be received apart from the acknowledgment of sin, nor justification apart from the knowledge

---

[84] Westminster Longer Catechism, Q/A 70, quoted in Oden, *Justification Reader*, 39.
[85] The Formula of Concord (Epitome), quoted in Oden, *Justification Reader*, 40.
[86] "Anglican Thirty-Nine Articles," art. 11, in *Creeds of Christendom, with a History and Critical Notes, Volume III: The Evangelical Protestant Creeds*, 494.

of ungodliness, nor resurrection apart from the knowledge of death to God."[87] Thus "confession of sinfulness is part of the gospel, a true self-knowledge that corresponds to the knowledge of God who gives life to the dead and justice to the ungodly—only the dead, only the ungodly."[88] Hinlicky is right, but he is also right to sound a word of warning: "if the sinner thinks that by her work of self-hatred she makes herself acceptable," the result is nothing short of "lethal."[89]

What we see in Scripture is the command to *repent*. As Peter says, "Repent and be baptized every one of you in the name of Jesus Christ for the forgiveness of your sins, and you will receive the gift of the Holy Spirit" (Acts 2:38). But this repentance should not in any sense be understood as somehow preparatory for grace—as if somehow we make ourselves acceptable candidates for God's grace by groveling. No, we are to repent—but we are to do so with the understanding that we are led and enabled by the prevenience of God's grace. Repentance is a vital aspect of the process of change that we call "conversion," and without the genuine and authentic change that comes with conversion there is no salvation.

B. Adoption

As Oden says, "Adoption is that work of the Spirit by which we are received into the family of God and readied for eternal inheritance"; it "suggests legal means by which a child who is not of the family can be taken into the family with full rights and privileges of that relationship."[90] Those who are adopted "are no longer strangers and aliens" but instead are "fellow citizens with the saints and members of the household of God" (Eph. 2:19). As such, the adopted are now "heirs" (Titus 3:7).

C. Regeneration

Jesus tells Nicodemus that he must be "born again" (John 3:3). Without such new birth, it is impossible to "see the kingdom of God" (John 3:3). Nicodemus wonders at this teaching (e.g., John 3:4, 9), but the basic meaning is not hard to ascertain. As Oden summarizes the expression of the Formula of Concord, regeneration is "the work of the Spirit by which new life in Christ is initially imparted to one dead in sin. It implies a change in the inward person by which a disposition to the holy life is originated, and in which that life begins. It is the act of God by which the governing disposition of the person begins to be

---

[87] Paul R. Hinlicky, *Beloved Community: Critical Dogmatics after Christendom* (Grand Rapids, MI: Eerdmans, 2015), 206.
[88] Hinlicky, *Beloved Community*, 206.
[89] Hinlicky, *Beloved Community*, 206.
[90] Thomas C. Oden, *Life in the Spirit: Systematic Theology: Volume Three* (New York: HarperCollins, 1994), 195.

responsive to the reconciling God."[91] It is a new beginning, but it cannot be reduced to the kind of "new" start of self-improvement. To the contrary, it is a radically new beginning: it is the "new beginning offered by the Spirit by which one is rescued from the dominion of sin and enabled with right affections to love God and keep God's commandments . . . the radical reversal of the direction of the will by which the selfless love of God begins to take the place of the godless love of self and of idolatrized creaturely goods."[92] Based on a broad sweep of biblical teaching (e.g., John 1:13; 3:7; Titus 3:5; Phil. 3:10; Eph. 2:1–10; 4:24; Gal. 6:15; Col. 3:10; 1 Pet. 3:18), the doctrine of regeneration complements the legal language of justification.

D. The Familial Depiction

Just as sin is depicted in familial terms in the Bible, so also is salvation. Indeed, this is done in a variety of ways. These are closely related with one another and with the legal language of justification. Far from being mutually exclusive, they work together to provide a fulsome account of our relationship to God. The royal-legal and familial come together. As Samuel Wakefield puts it, "Justification consists in the pardon of the guilty, regeneration in the moral renovation of the unholy, and adoption in the gracious reception of those who are alienated from God and disinherited."[93] Michael Scott Horton concurs:

> Adoption, like justification, is simultaneously legal and relational. . . . Adoption is not a goal held out to children who successfully imitate their parents; nor is it the result of an infusion of familial characteristics or genes. Rather, it is a change in legal status that issues in a relationship that is gradually reflected in the child's identity, characteristics and actions. From the courtroom, with the legal status and inheritance unalterably established, the child moves into the security of a growing and thriving future.[94]

V. SIN AND SANCTIFYING GRACE

While many Christians (and especially many evangelical Protestants) share common and significant agreement with respect to the doctrines related to the royal-legal and familial depictions, deeper discussions of salvation are often more controverted. One such area of controversy has to do with the importance of sanctification. Properly understood, sanctification is not the destruction or marring of human nature but its restoration and renewal. As Kathryn Tanner puts

---

[91] Oden, *Life in the Spirit*, 156.
[92] Oden, *Life in the Spirit*, 156.
[93] Samuel Wakefield, *A Complete System of Christian Theology: or, A Concise, Comprehensive, and Systematic View of the Evidences, Doctrines, Morals, and Institutions of Christianity* (Cincinnati: Cranston & Stowe, 1858), 434, cited in Oden, *Life in the Spirit*, 194.
[94] Michael Scott Horton, *The Christian Faith: A Systematic Theology for Pilgrims On the Way* (Grand Rapids, MI: Zondervan Academic, 2011), 645.

it, "[R]emoval of sin simply means the elevation, strengthening, purification, and improvement" of human operations "and not the discarding of their finite human character."[95] Nonetheless, questions arise: is sanctification essential to the gospel, or is it only tangential? Hinlicky asks some important questions:

> Is the sinner's justification only and purely the divine favor of the forgiveness of sins, the nonimputation of guilt, the cancellation of punishment, an alien and imputed righteousness. . . . ? Or is it not also the healing of the soul's disordered loves, a real if inchoate rectification of the heart's desire so that it eagerly longs for the "hope of righteousness" (Gal. 5:5)? Is justification in Christ a remedy for the guilt of sins and liability to punishment or deeper still for the sinfulness that makes one guilty and worthy of rejection? Does it merely cancel the Law that accuses or does it root out the evil desire that the Law accuses? Is the enemy of God the Law or the sinfulness that the Law condemns? Is the gift of the Spirit subsequent to justification—sort of an option for those interested—or is the gift of the Spirit already the very faith, active in love for God and all His creatures, that justifies?[96]

So is sanctification essential to salvation; is it part of the gospel itself? And, however one answers that question, how "successful" is it? For what can one hope in this life? Seeing sanctification within its proper theological and biblical setting will help us arrive at answers to such questions.

A. The Nuptial Context and Content of the Doctrine of Sanctification

The doctrine of sanctification belongs within the distinctly nuptial context of the biblical canon. As we have seen, sin is depicted in Scripture in terms that are frankly sexual and nuptial: sin is spiritual adultery and prostitution (e.g., Isa. 1:21–23; 5:8–30; Jer. 2:20–24; 3:1–6, 20; 18:13; Ezek. 16:16–34; Mic. 1:7; Mal. 2:13–17). As we have also seen, both John the Baptist (e.g., John 3:27–30) and Jesus himself (e.g., Mark 2:19–20) point to the nuptial dimension of the Savior's work. Further, as we have seen, nuptial imagery is important in Pauline soteriology (e.g., Eph. 5:25).

So if our sin results in the kind of moral filth that can be likened to prostitution, then what is the answer of the gospel of grace to such sin? In a word, the gospel remedy is sanctification. Sanctification is God's work in the renovation of the justified and regenerated sinner. Both justification and sanctification are grounded in union with Christ, but they are distinct. Where justification addresses our legal status, sanctification addresses our actual lives. In sanctification, God renovates our "hearts" and transforms our "affections," and the transforming power of God's grace thus produces a changed lifestyle that

---

[95] Kathryn Tanner, *Christ the Key* (Cambridge: Cambridge University Press, 2010), 281.
[96] Hinlicky, *Beloved Community*, 210.

becomes ever more like Christ as the believer is filled with and cleansed by the Holy Spirit.[97] And sanctification is for *nuptial* purposes: "Husbands, love your wives, as Christ loved the church and gave himself up for her, that he might sanctify her, having cleansed her by the washing of water with the word, so that he might present the church to himself in splendor, without spot or wrinkle or any such thing, that she might be holy and without blemish" (Eph. 5:25–27). Dennis Kinlaw makes this point with force:

> The purpose of the Spirit in the life of the new believer is to bring that person as a part of the bride of Christ to a devotion to Christ that fulfills the demands implicit within the nuptial metaphor, demands better expressed through that figure than through either the royal/legal or familial metaphor. The relationship sought is one of total self-giving love whereby the two belong to each other in a union so complete that to touch one is to touch the other. What the Spirit seeks is a relationship of love in which Christ reigns supreme without rival or competitor as Lord and Lover within the believer. It is the relationship longed for in the ancient collect used to prepare the believer for the reception of Holy Communion: "Almighty God, unto whom all hearts are open, all desires known, and from whom no secrets are hid; cleanse the thoughts of our hearts by the inspiration of thy Holy Spirit, that we may perfectly love thee and worthily magnify thy holy name; through Christ our Lord. Amen"[98]

B. But Can It Actually Happen? A Closer Look at Romans 7

Some Christians will say that this all *sounds* good, but they will protest that the reality of the Christian life, both as experienced by themselves and as depicted in the Bible, is very different. While such sanctification may be a lofty goal, it is simply not something that is realized in this life. Consider, they will remonstrate, the words of Paul himself:

> We know that the law is spiritual; but I am unspiritual, sold as a slave to sin. I do not understand what I do. For what I want to do I do not do, but what I hate I do. And if I do what I do not want to do, I agree that the law is good. As it is, it is no longer I myself who do it, but it is sin living in me. I know that nothing good lives in me, that is, in my sinful nature. For I have the desire to do what is good, but I cannot carry it out. For what I do is not the good I want to do; no, the evil I do not want to do—this I keep on doing. Now if I do what I do not want to do, it is no longer I who do it, but it is sin living in me that does it.
> So I find this law at work: When I want to do good, evil is right there with me. For in my inner being I delight in God's law, but I see another law at

[97] For more on the relation between justification and sanctification (and the Trinitarian nature of salvation), see Thomas H. McCall, *Forsaken: The Trinity and the Cross, and Why It Matters* (Downers Grove, IL: IVP Academic, 2012), 133–144.
[98] Dennis F. Kinlaw, *Let's Start with Jesus: A New Way of Doing Theology* (Grand Rapids, MI: Zondervan, 2005), 140.

work in the members of my body, waging war against the law of my mind and making me a prisoner of the law of sin at work within my members. What a wretched man I am! Who will rescue me from this body of death? Thanks be to God—through Jesus Christ our Lord! (Rom. 7:14–25 NIV 1984)

Some Christians read this text as a description of the normal Christian life; they take it to be the definitive statement of genuine Christian life. Does not even Paul say that although he has the desire to do what is good and right, he simply does not—and indeed cannot—carry through with his desires? Doesn't even Paul say that "nothing good lives in me"? Isn't it clear that Paul's sinful nature is at war with his desire to do what is right? And is it not plain and obvious, on Paul's own confession, that the sinful nature is the one that wins?

The view that this is Paul's own Christian experience—and thus is definitive for our own expectations of the Christian life—is very common among contemporary Christians. Indeed, they are prone to ask, what else *could* be going on in this text? Such people are sometimes very surprised to learn that classical Christian exegesis has largely veered away from such an interpretation (Irenaeus, Origen, Tertullian, Basil, Theodoret, Chrysostom, Jerome, Ambrose, Cyril of Jerusalem, Macarius, among many others, have not understood Paul to be referring to his own Christian experience).[99] It seems obvious enough, they will protest: Paul actually speaks in the first person ("I"), and he speaks in the present tense. The lesson to be drawn is plain enough: if this was Paul's own experience (and if Paul was the "greatest Christian ever"), then surely the ordinary Christian life will be one that is much like it. So while it might be nice to hope and dream of a life lived in enjoyment of the holy love of the triune God, this simply is not intended or available for us at all.

But on closer examination, this interpretation is not so obvious. Indeed, a closer look shows that the evidence points *away* from what many people take to be the commonsense or straightforward reading of the text. Several considerations are important here. First, the use of the present tense does not of itself demonstrate that this is Paul's own present or current experience. He may well be using the "historical" or "dramatic" present (much like someone who is retelling the story of something dramatic that happened earlier that day might move from "then he said" to "so I say to him . . ."). Second, Paul's use of "I" here is not definitive either, at least not when read within the context of Paul's broader discussion. In the discussion immediately preceding this section, Paul uses the "I" to refer to someone who has been "put . . . to death" (Rom. 7:11 NIV) by sin—hardly reflective of Paul's view of the Christian life (e.g., Rom. 5:21; 6:23). In 7:14–25, Paul seems to be using the "I" in a way that is reflective of someone who is not yet a Christian. Ben Witherington points out

---

[99] See Oden, *Life in the Spirit*, 245–246.

that "it would be rhetorically inept for Paul to use a fictive 'I' in vv. 7–13 and then with no signal change to a non-fictive use of 'I.' Unless there is compelling evidence to the contrary, the 'I' in vv. 14–25 must also be seen as fictive because Paul is continuing another part of the same argument found in vv. 7–13."[100] As Gerald Bray admits, "Most of the Fathers believed that here Paul was adopting the persona of an unregenerate man, not describing his own struggles as a Christian. As far as they were concerned, becoming a Christian would deliver a person from the kind of dilemma that the apostle is outlining here."[101] So the main support for the common contemporary reading, which seems so straightforward and obvious, evaporates on closer consideration. Third, to understand this text to refer to Paul's own Christian life would be to introduce something that would contradict many other clear and decisive elements of Paul's testimony. He says, for instance, that the Thessalonian Christians join with God as his witnesses that he is "holy, righteous and blameless" (1 Thess. 2:10 [NIV]; see also 2 Tim. 1:12; Col. 1:12–13; Phil. 4:12–13), and that he has "kept the faith" (2 Tim. 4:6–8) even as one of those who "have not yet obtained" but are "pressing on toward the goal" (see Phil. 3:12–14).[102]

On the other hand, there are several decisive factors that weigh *against* any such reading of Romans 7:14–25.[103] First, the person described here is one who has been "sold as a slave to sin" (Rom. 7:14 NIV). But Paul has just described—in terms that no one finds uncertain—regenerate persons as those who were *formerly* slaves to sin. Christians are those who "used to be slaves to sin" (Rom. 6:17 NIV); they *were* slaves to sin (v. 20). Second, the person is here described as "unspiritual" (*sarkinos*) (7:14 NIV). But Paul follows this with a clear description of such a person as one in a state of spiritual *death* (8:6). The person described in 7:14–25 is said to be mastered by indwelling sin, and to such an extent that "it is no longer I myself who do it, but it is sin living in me" (7:17, 20 NIV). But Paul's clear description of the privileges of those who are no longer under condemnation but who are "in Christ" is very different: "You, however, are controlled not by the sinful nature but by the Spirit, if the Spirit of God lives in you" (8:9 NIV 1984). You are no longer dead and powerless, for "if the Spirit of him who raised Jesus from the dead is living in you, he who raised Christ from the dead will also give life to your mortal bodies through his Spirit, who lives in you" (8:11 NIV 1984). The person in 7:14–25 testifies that he is enslaved by sin, for it has made him "a prisoner of the law of sin at work within my members" (7:23 NIV 1984).

---

[100] Ben Witherington III, *Paul's Letter to the Romans: A Socio-Rhetorical Commentary* (Grand Rapids, MI: Eerdmans, 2004), 193.
[101] Gerald Bray, ed., *Ancient Christian Commentary on Scripture: New Testament, VI: Romans* (Downers Grove, IL: InterVarsity Press, 1998), 189–190.
[102] See Oden, *Life in the Spirit*, 244–245.
[103] For an especially helpful discussion of these issues (one to which I am indebted), see Douglas J. Moo, *The Epistle to the Romans*, NICNT (Grand Rapids, MI: Eerdmans, 1996), 445–448.

But when Paul talks about those who are "in Christ," he says that "the law of the Spirit of life set me free from the law of sin and death" (8:2 NIV 1984). Third, "we died to sin" (6:2 NIV 1984) and are freed from sin (6:7 NIV 1984) rather than being held "captive to the law of sin" (7:23).

We are now in a position to see how the life described in Romans 7:14–25 is actually *in contrast to* the life that is "in Christ" and "in accordance with the Spirit" (8:5 NIV). One (the person described in Romans 7) refers to the life of a slave. The other (the person described in Romans 6 and 8) refers to the life of a *former* slave. It is the life of one who has been emancipated and is now free. One refers to death. The other rejoices in life. One is controlled by sin and cannot escape from it. The other is controlled by the Spirit. Paul himself makes this contrast explicit:

> Those who live according to the sinful nature have their minds set on what that nature desires; but those who live in accordance with the Spirit have their minds set on what the Spirit desires. The mind of sinful man is death, but the mind controlled by the Spirit is life and peace; the sinful mind is hostile to God. It does not submit to God's law, nor can it do so. Those controlled by the sinful nature cannot please God.
> You, however, are controlled not by the sinful nature but by the Spirit, if the Spirit of God lives in you. (Rom. 8:5–9 NIV 1984)

In conclusion,[104] it seems highly unlikely that Paul is referring to his own Christian experience in Romans 7:14–25.[105] Gordon Fee says that the evidence "overwhelmingly" favors "the view that Paul is here describing life before and outside of Christ, but from the perspective of one who is himself now in Christ."[106] It is, then, both mistaken and potentially very harmful for Christians to read this as the diary or journal of their own Christian life. There are no good reasons to take this text in support of the view that the normal Christian life is one of customary defeat and failure. Of course his description of an ongoing struggle with sin resonates very deeply with Christians. And Paul *does* address the ongoing battle with sin in his letter to the Galatians. He is utterly realistic about the struggle: "the sinful nature desires what is contrary to the Spirit, and the Spirit what is contrary to the sinful nature" (Gal. 5:17 NIV 1984), and he is aware of the possibility that followers of Christ may be "caught in a sin" (Gal. 6:1 NIV). He draws the sharpest of contrasts between the "acts of the flesh" and the "fruit of the Spirit." The former "are obvious: sexual immorality, impurity and debauchery; idolatry and witchcraft; hatred,

---

[104] The following two paragraphs are adapted from my *Forsaken* (Downers Grove, IL: InterVarsity Press, 2012). Used by permission of InterVarsity Press.
[105] For a helpful summary of the interpretive options, see Witherington, *Romans*, 187.
[106] Gordon D. Fee, *God's Empowering Presence: The Holy Spirit in the Letters of Paul* (Peabody, MA: Hendrickson, 1994), 511.

discord, jealousy, fits of rage, selfish ambition, dissensions, factions and envy; drunkenness, orgies, and the like" (Gal. 5:19–21 NIV). The consequences of such a sinful lifestyle are as unmistakable as they are grim: "I warn you, as I did before, that those who live like this will not inherit the kingdom of God" (Gal. 5:21 NIV). The "fruit of the Spirit," on the other hand, is "love, joy, peace, patience, kindness, goodness, faithfulness, gentleness and self-control" (Gal. 5:22–23 NIV 1984).

A life controlled by the sin-corrupted nature is one that produces these sinful actions. Paul is clear that a return to the life dominated by sin is a possibility for the followers of Jesus (otherwise there would be no point in warning them about it). But he is equally clear that such a life is not necessary for the Christian but in fact is incompatible with inheriting the kingdom of God. The Christian is under no compulsion to live this way. Indeed, "those who belong to Christ Jesus have crucified the flesh with its passions and desires" (Gal. 5:24 NIV). Paul thus issues a command and a promise: "walk by the Spirit, and you will not gratify the desires of the flesh" (Gal. 5:16). The command is to "walk," to live each moment of life, in the presence and power of the Holy Spirit. The promise is distinct from the command and follows upon it: walking in continual surrender to and communion with the Spirit yields a lifestyle that is not hostage to the sinful nature. As Oden explains, "The Galatian audience was imperfectly formed, while growing in grace. The conflict between Spirit and flesh raged in them. They were neither wholly unjustified nor unsanctified, but believing recipients of justifying grace in whom sanctifying grace was beginning to work to bring them to full maturity in Christian freedom, wherein they might refract the image of God exquisitely."[107] Paul's words are, then, an encouragement to them: do not be surprised by the struggle with temptation or the possibility of sin, but do not despair either, for the Spirit has provided for a life of victory rather than defeat. So while Galatians 5:16–25 also speaks of the struggle with temptation experienced by Christians, it does so in ways that are markedly different from the testimony of the unregenerate person in Romans 7:14–25. For while the unregenerate person of Romans 7:14–25 struggles with sin but is defeated and enslaved, Paul's expectation and emphasis in Galatians 5:16–25 is on the ability of the Holy Spirit to bring victory over the sin that ensnares and enslaves.

C. But Does It Happen? Holiness and the Christian Life

The teaching of the NT is both clear and emphatic: "[T]his is the will of God, your sanctification" (1 Thess. 4:3).[108] This will of God is not to be understood

---

[107] Oden, *Life in the Spirit*, 246.
[108] The immediate context concerns the sexual implications of holiness, but the theological point is much broader.

in an abstract sense, and it is not in any sense an empty expression of wish or sentiment. To the contrary, it is the very reason that Jesus Christ, "our great God and Savior" (Titus 2:13), became incarnate. For "he who sanctifies and those who are sanctified all have one source," and this "is why he is not ashamed to call them brothers" and sisters (Heb. 2:11). It is the reason that the incarnate Son made atonement: he "gave himself for us to redeem us from all lawlessness and to purify for himself a people for his own possession who are zealous for good works" (Titus 2:14). In light of what God has done in Christ and the sanctifying work of the Holy Spirit who brings to fulfillment all that Christ accomplished, believers are called to live lives of holiness and righteousness before God. "For God has not called us for impurity, but in holiness" (1 Thess. 4:7). Peter thus quotes the OT in his exhortation to holiness: "As obedient children, do not be conformed to the passions of your former ignorance, but as he who called you is holy, you also be holy in all your conduct, since it is written, 'You shall be holy, for I am holy'" (1 Pet. 1:14–16; cf. Lev. 11:44–45; 19:2; 20:7). We are to understand that this holiness is all-encompassing; that it penetrates deeply into the affections and extends to all areas of life and human conduct (1 Thess. 5:23). We are to actively pursue it, for without it "no one will see the Lord" (Heb. 12:14). And we are to understand that this sanctification is accomplished by the same God who desires it for us and has made provision for it. Thus we are to be both challenged and comforted by the realization that "our God is a consuming fire" (Heb. 12:29).

Drawing on this biblical teaching, major theologians of the Christian tradition have reflected on the beauty and necessity of holiness for the Christian life.[109] Although perhaps less optimistic about the possibilities of holiness than some of his predecessors and contemporaries, Augustine is representative of some Patristic theology.[110] And, despite the fact that this is seldom noticed (at least by many contemporary scholars), Augustine takes a very positive and hopeful view of the reality of holiness in the Christian life.[111] He remains agnostic about the actuality of Christian perfection in this life while remaining adamant about the possibility; he does not testify to it himself or point to

---

[109] See the helpful work of Christopher T. Bounds, "The Doctrine of Christian Perfection in the Apostolic Fathers," WesTJ (2007): 7–27; Bounds, "Irenaeus and the Doctrine of Christian Perfection," WesTJ (2010): 161–176; Bounds, "Competing Doctrines of Perfection: The Primary Issue in Irenaeus's Refutation of Gnosticism," Studia Patristica (2010): 403–408.

[110] Although not in all respects. Augustine is at first consistent with his predecessors (and contemporaries) with respect to the interpretation of Romans 7:14–25, but he later changes his view of this text. First it is Paul pre-conversion; later he takes it to be the story of Paul's own Christian experience. Augustine does not, however, lose his optimism about grace. On these changes and developments within Augustine's theology, see Christopher T. Bounds, "Augustine's Interpretation of Romans 7:14–25, His Ordo Salutis, and His Consistent Belief in a Christian's Victory over Sin," Asbury Journal (2009): 20–35.

[111] See the work of Christopher T. Bounds as a notable exception to this trend: "Augustine's Interpretation of Romans 7:14–25," 20–35. Bounds notes that even the massive Augustine through the Ages: An Encyclopedia, ed. Allan D. Fitzgerald (Grand Rapids, MI: Eerdmans, 1999), does not include any articles on "sanctification" or "holiness."

others as exemplars but instead focuses attention on the goodness and greatness of God's grace; God is both willing and able to make us holy.[112] And, while
insisting that whatever happens that is good happens by grace, Augustine also
insists that this grace really does restore our nature to holiness of heart and life.
God "heals us not only that he may blot out the sin which we have committed,
but, furthermore, that he may enable us even to avoid sinning."[113] While on
our own strength this is impossible, we should never underestimate the power
of divine grace nor refuse to believe that it can radically transform us.[114] We
cannot purify ourselves by our own freedom of the will, but by God's grace
we actually can become "pure in heart."[115] This means that sin really "can be
avoided, if our corrupted nature is healed by God's grace, through our Lord
Jesus Christ."[116]

We should be careful to note just where and how Augustine differed from
the Pelagians. He did not differ from them with respect to the possibility of
Christian perfection in this life. They held out hope for full or complete purification from sins in this life; so did Augustine. The possibility of perfection
or complete sanctification is *not* the point of debate. The differences between
them—important as they were—lay elsewhere, for the Pelagians believed that
mere human effort could bring about perfection. *This* is exactly what Augustine denied, and he resolutely insisted that salvation—from the prevenient beginning to the perfect ending—is all of grace. Augustine did not, however,
disagree with the Pelagians on the very fundamental point about the reality of
sanctification. He did not deny that sanctification could be complete or entire
in this life. And he clearly expected a robustly triumphant Christian life marked
by freedom from willful sin. Such emphases on the possibility of Christian
perfection—and at any rate the insistence on the importance of a Christian life
that is above intentional and habitual sin—are part and parcel of the Christian
tradition throughout much medieval theology as well. For instance, Thomas
Aquinas considers the command of Jesus (Matt. 5:48) and concludes that it
must be possible "to be *in some sense* 'perfect' in this life."[117] And what is this
"sense" of "perfection"? It is a kind of perfection in love (*caritas*), loving God
with all one's being. As Thomas Noble explains, for Aquinas those who are
growing in grace may come to the point "where everything contrary to being
wholly in love with God is excluded: they love God with all their hearts."[118]

---

[112] Augustine, *De natura et gratia* 70 (PL 44:280–281; NPNF[1] 5:145).
[113] Augustine, *De natura* 29 (PL 44:261; NPNF[1] 5:131).
[114] Augustine, *De natura* 52 (PL 44:272; NPNF[1] 5:139).
[115] Augustine, *De natura* 72 (PL 44:281–282; NPNF[1] 5:146).
[116] Augustine, *De perfectione justitiae hominis* 2 (PL 44:293; NPNF[1] 5:160).
[117] Thomas A. Noble, *Holy Trinity, Holy People: The Historic Doctrine of Christian Perfecting* (Eugene, OR: Cascade, 2013), 66, emphasis original.
[118] Noble, *Holy Trinity*, 66. See also D. Stephen Long, *John Wesley's Moral Theology: The Quest for God and Goodness* (Nashville: Abingdon, 2005), 199–201; and especially Edgardo Colon-Emeric, *Wesley, Aquinas, and Christian Perfection: An Ecumenical Dialogue* (Waco, TX: Baylor University Press, 2009).

The major Protestant traditions are in agreement on this issue in many respects; indeed, emphatically so. Consider these examples from the Lutheran and Reformed theological traditions.[119] We begin with the Lutheran tradition; and, indeed, with Martin Luther. We do so not only because this is a natural place to begin, but also because the Lutheran doctrine of sanctification has been the subject of no little confusion and misunderstanding.[120] There is a fairly popular understanding of "the Lutheran view" that goes along these lines: Martin Luther's great theological discoveries taught us that we need not be overly concerned with sanctification; indeed, if we take his insights seriously, we will understand that we *must* not worry about sanctification. Did not Luther teach us that we are always sinful, but that even our most grievous sins are no match for the justifying grace of God as it is given to the elect? Did not he teach us the all-important truth of *simul justus et peccator*? And is not a focus on sanctification at best a distraction from our celebration of the great and beautiful doctrine of justification? Isn't the Reformation—and particularly Lutheranism—all about *sola gratia* and *sola fide*? And isn't it wrong—wrong not only in the sense of being mistaken but also wrong in the sense of being wrongheaded or dangerous—to turn our attention away from the celebration of the truth that God justifies *sinners* to a morbid focus on holiness?

A well-known and forceful proponent of this popular view is the Lutheran theologian Gerhard Forde. Seizing the Lutheran banner and waving it proudly, Forde asserts that sanctification is merely the "art of getting used to justification."[121] Justification is the central truth of the gospel, and sanctification is what happens to us spontaneously—as "God's secret"—when we relax and accept our justification. In Forde's words, justification by faith alone "is, after all, *the* dogma of the Protestant Reformation," and anything that might distract us from that is a cause for concern.[122] Talk about sanctification is thus "dangerous."[123] It is dangerous, and sometimes even a "disaster," for it tempts us to think that we can add something to the salvation gained for us by Christ.[124] Forde insists that to allow *any* room for "cooperation" means that "*everything* eventually depends on the human contribution," and to allow this

[119] The rest of subsection C is adapted from Thomas H. McCall, "The Sainthood of All Believers: The Bible and Sanctification," in *The Reformation and the Irrepressible Word of God*, ed. Scott M. Manetsch (Downers Grove, IL: InterVarsity Press, 2019). Used by permission of InterVarsity Press.
[120] See further Carl R. Trueman, *Luther on the Christian Life: Cross and Freedom* (Wheaton, IL: Crossway, 2015); Trueman, "Martin Luther," in *Christian Theologies of Salvation: A Comparative Introduction*, ed. Justin S. Holcomb (New York: New York University Press, 2017), 191–207; Bernhard Lohse, *Martin Luther's Theology: Its Historical and Systematic Development*, trans. Roy A. Harrisville (Minneapolis: Fortress, 2006); and Oswald Bayer, *Martin Luther's Theology: A Contemporary Interpretation*, trans. Thomas H. Trapp (Grand Rapids, MI: Eerdmans, 2008).
[121] Gerhard Forde, "The Lutheran View," in *Christian Spirituality: Five Views*, ed. Donald L. Alexander (Downers Grove, IL: InterVarsity Press, 1988), 13.
[122] Gerhard Forde, "The Christian Life," in *Christian Dogmatics, Volume 2*, ed. Carl E. Braaten and Robert W. Jenson (Minneapolis: Fortress, 1984), 397.
[123] Forde, "Lutheran View," 15; and Forde, "Christian Life," 396.
[124] Forde, "Lutheran View," 15.

is to undercut the truth of justification.[125] To allow that good works accompany and demonstrate justification is to lose the battle.[126] Instead, Forde insists that Luther was right in his teaching that we are *simul iustus et peccator*, and he calls us to appreciate Luther's advice to Philipp Melanchthon to "be a sinner and sin boldly, but believe even more boldly and rejoice in Christ."[127]

As widespread and popular as this view may be, however, it simply isn't the case that it is *the* Lutheran view. For it does not cohere with the classical Lutheran theology that is exemplified in the Lutheran scholastics.[128] And it does not come close to representing the depth and complexity of Luther's own thought. Consider this statement from Luther's Smalcald Articles:

> . . . that by faith (as St. Peter says) we get a new and clean heart and that God will and does account us altogether righteous and holy for the sake of Christ, our mediator. Although the sin in our flesh has not yet been completely removed or eradicated, he will not count or consider it.[129]

Here we see familiar Lutheran themes; the notions of forensic righteousness and imputation are at work here. But we should also note that Luther insists that we in fact *do* acquire a "new and clean heart." And there is more. Luther continues by saying that

> [g]ood works follow such faith, renewal, and forgiveness. Whatever is still sinful or imperfect in these works will not be reckoned as sin or defect for the sake of the same Christ. The whole man, in respect both of his person and of his works, shall be accounted and shall be righteous and holy through the pure grace and mercy. . . . If good works do not follow, then faith is false and not true.[130]

Note here that when Luther refers to what is sinful or imperfect, he is not talking about sinful acts *simpliciter*. Instead, he is talking about what is sinful or imperfect in our *good works*. He is aware that our best efforts to follow Christ will fall short, and he insists that these are not accounted as sin against us and do not incur God's wrath. But he also insists that the "whole man"—both person and works—are both called to be righteous and holy and indeed are changed by God's "pure grace and mercy" so that we indeed *are* righteous and holy. And he makes it plain that if this does not happen, then "faith is false and

---

[125] Forde, "Christian Life," 406–407.
[126] Forde, "Christian Life," 427.
[127] Forde, "Christian Life," 438–439; cf. Forde, "Lutheran View," 23–27.
[128] Forde surely knows that his view differs quite radically from the Lutheran scholastics. He consistently polemicizes against those who do theology "after the manner of Aristotle," and he explicitly rejects the *tertius usus* (the "third use," which is to instruct Christians in righteousness) of the law (e.g., "Christian Life," 449).
[129] "The Smalcald Articles III.XIII," in *Martin Luther's Basic Theological Writings*, ed. Timothy Lull (Minneapolis: Fortress, 1989), 534.
[130] "Smalcald Articles III.XIII," 534.

not true." For "the Holy Spirit does not permit sin to rule" in the life of the Christian; if sin does have dominion and does "what it wishes," then we can conclude nothing else than that "the Holy Spirit and faith are not present, for St. John says, 'No one born of God commits sin . . .' (1 John 1:9)."[131]

Luther excoriates those "Antinomians" who "speak beautifully and (as I cannot but think) with real sincerity" about the forgiveness of sins and justification but then "ignore the third article" of sanctification.[132] Such people, he says,

> think one should not frighten or trouble the people, but rather always preach comfortingly about the grace and forgiveness of sins in Christ, and under no circumstances use these or similar words: "Listen! You want to be a Christian and at the same time remain an adulterer, a whoremonger, a drunken swine, arrogant, covetous, a usurer, envious, vindictive, malicious!" Instead they say, "Listen! Though you are an adulterer, a whoremonger, a miser, or other kind of sinner, if you but believe, you are saved and you need not fear the law. Christ has fulfilled it all!"[133]

Such preachers, Luther thunders, "may be fine Easter preachers, but they are very poor Pentecost preachers, for they do not preach *de sanctificatione et vivicatione Spiritus sancti . . .*"[134] There "is no such Christ that died for sinners who do not, after the forgiveness of sins, desist from sins and lead a new life."[135] For a proper understanding of Christ and his benefits is much more full-orbed, much more robust, and indeed much more beautiful than the counterfeit offered by such sincere preachers. A proper understanding of Christ knows that he

> did not only earn *gratia* for us, but also *donum*, "the gift of the Holy Spirit," so that we might have not only forgiveness of, but also cessation of, sin. Now he who does not abstain from sin, but persists in his evil life, must have a different Christ.[136]

This so-called Christ is a fake, a fraud, and the person who relies upon this Christ "must be damned with this, his new Christ."[137]

To truly know Christ is to know that the incarnate Son has sent his Holy Spirit, and it is to know further that the ministry of the Holy Spirit is to truly make people holy as they are transformed into the image of the Son. Those who are filled with the Holy Spirit are those who are rightly called the *"sancta*

[131] "Smalcald Articles III.III," 527.
[132] Martin Luther, "On the Councils and the Church," in *Luther's Works*, vol. 41, ed. Helmut T. Lehmann (Philadelphia: Fortress, 1969), 113.
[133] Luther, "On the Councils," 113–114.
[134] Luther, "On the Councils," 114.
[135] Luther, "On the Councils," 114.
[136] Luther, "On the Councils," 114.
[137] Luther, "On the Councils," 114.

catholica Christiana, that is, 'a Christian holy people.'"[138] Those who are rightly called "Christians" are those who "have the Holy Spirit" who "sanctifies them daily, not only through the forgiveness of sins acquired for them by Christ, but also through the abolition, the purging, the mortification of sins, on the basis of which they are called a holy people."[139] Thus true "Christian holiness . . . is found where the Holy Spirit gives people faith in Christ and sanctifies them."[140]

It should be clear that Luther's own doctrine of sanctification is very far removed from the pervasive—and pernicious—misunderstanding. Of course Luther resolutely believes in justification by grace alone through faith alone; Christ's righteousness is imputed to us, and we are to be comforted by that reality. But he also believes—just as resolutely—in the sanctifying work of the Holy Spirit who renews us, radically transforms us, and makes us actually righteous and holy. And we are to be both challenged and comforted by that reality as well.[141]

This isn't merely Luther. The Lutheran confessional statements also proclaim the truth of sanctification. For instance, the Formula of Concord insists that

> it is not less necessary that men should be admonished to a right and pious manner of living and to good works, and reminded how necessary it is that they should exercise themselves to declare and set forth their faith and gratitude towards God by good works, than it is necessary to beware lest good works be mingled in the matter of justification.[142]

In other words, while it is true that we must always be watchful to avoid thinking that our good works contribute to our justification, so also must we beware of thinking that they do not matter. For while we are justified *sola fide* (in the instrumental sense), nonetheless we should also remember that "true faith is never alone, but hath always charity and hope in its train."[143] Important theologians of Lutheran scholasticism agree; they carefully distinguish sanctification from justification (and sometimes from regeneration), for justification deals with the legal status of sinners (through the imputation of Christ's righteous-

---

[138] Luther, "On the Councils," 143.
[139] Luther, "On the Councils," 143–144.
[140] Luther, "On the Councils," 145.
[141] See further David Yeago, "Martin Luther on Renewal and Sanctification: *Simul Iustus et Peccator* Revisited," in *Sapere teologico e unita della fede: studi in onore del Prof. Jared Wicks*, ed. Carmen Aparicio Valls, Carmelo Dotolo, Gianluigi Pasquale (Rome: Gregorian University Press, 2004): 655–674. See also Yeago, "Gnosticism, Antinomianism, and Reformation Theology: Reflections on the Costs of a Construal," *Pro Ecclesia* (1993): 37–49; Yeago, "A Christian, Holy People: Martin Luther on Salvation and the Church," in *Spirituality and Social Embodiment*, ed. L. Gregory Jones and James J. Buckley (Oxford: Wiley-Blackwell, 1997), 101–120.
[142] "The Formula of Concord," art. IV, in *Creeds of Christendom, with a History and Critical Notes, Volume III: The Evangelical Protestant Creeds*, 125.
[143] "Formula of Concord," art. III, in *Creeds of Christendom, with a History and Critical Notes, Volume III: The Evangelical Protestant Creeds*, 118.

ness) and regeneration refers to the beginning of the life of inherent holiness or righteousness that is continued in the process of sanctification.[144] For instance, Johann Baier uses the language of new creation (*nova creatio*), vivification (*vivificatio*), and spiritual resuscitation (*spiritualis resuscitio*) to refer to God's work in sanctification.[145] The principal efficient cause of our sanctification is the triune God,[146] and the ultimate goal of God's work in sanctification is the salvation of humanity to the glory of God.[147] In no sense can sanctification be considered a soteriological "option" for the Lutheran dogmaticians; those whom God declares righteous through the imputed righteousness of Christ are also truly *made* holy by the sanctifying work of the Holy Spirit.

The legacy of Reformed theology is similar in many important respects. John Calvin is perhaps the best-known proponent of Reformed theology.[148] The entire point of regeneration is to bring the heart and life of the believer into line with God's righteousness, and such a life of holy concord with God's will is the confirmation of our adoption as God's children.[149] In the work of sanctification, an authentic "love of righteousness" is "instilled and implanted" within God's people.[150] This holiness, which is the gift of God to us (and never something that we can either achieve or use as merit), is the "bond" of our union with God.[151] We are made holy by virtue of our union with Christ, and this same union truly makes us temples of the Holy Spirit.[152] It changes our affections at the deepest and innermost levels, and, as it moves from "breast" to "conduct," it results in lifestyles that are radically transformed in love of God and neighbor.[153] This sanctification, which is always and only by God's Holy Spirit, brings with it "integrity and purity of life."[154] This transformation "of the soul itself" is "afterwards manifested by the fruits produced by it."[155]

Although the holiness of redeemed persons is not yet perfect, nonetheless it is real.[156] It is also vitally important; indeed, there is a sense in which it

---

[144] See the discussion in Heinrich Schmid, *The Doctrinal Theology of the Evangelical Lutheran Church* (Minneapolis: Augsburg, 1899), 502–507.

[145] Baier, *Compendium Theologiae Positivae*, 587.

[146] Baier, *Compendium*, 592.

[147] Baier, *Compendium*, 597.

[148] On Calvin's relation to the broader Reformed tradition, see Richard A. Muller, "John Calvin and Late Calvinism: The Identity of the Reformed Tradition," in *The Cambridge Companion to Reformation Theology*, ed. David Bagchi and David C. Steinmetz (Cambridge: Cambridge University Press, 2004), 130–149; Muller, *Calvin and the Reformed Tradition: On the Work of Christ and the Order of Salvation* (Grand Rapids, MI: Baker Academic, 2012); Muller, *After Calvin: Studies in the Development of a Theological Tradition* (Oxford: Oxford University Press, 2003).

[149] John Calvin, *Institutes of the Christian Religion*, trans. Henry Beveridge (Grand Rapids, MI: Eerdmans, 1997), III.6 (2).

[150] Calvin, *Institutes*, III.6 (2).

[151] Calvin, *Institutes*, III.6 (3).

[152] Calvin, *Institutes*, III.3 (517). On the theme of union with Christ, see J. Todd Billings, *Calvin, Participation, and the Gift: The Activity of Believers in Union with Christ* (Oxford: Oxford University Press, 2007).

[153] Calvin, *Institutes*, III.6 (4).

[154] Calvin, *Institutes*, III.11 (37).

[155] Calvin, *Institutes*, III.3 (513, 515).

[156] Calvin, *Institutes*, III.3 (517).

is necessary. It can, and surely must, be distinguished from justification, but it cannot be *separated* from justification. For while we are "justified freely by faith alone, . . . yet that holiness of life, real holiness, as it is called, is inseparable from the free imputation of righteousness."[157] "Do we not see," Calvin asks, "that the Lord justifies his people freely, and at the same time renews them to true holiness by the sanctification of his Spirit?"[158] How dare we ignore the Lord's promise to "purge us from all iniquity and defilement?"[159] Those who are saved *cannot* "wallow" in the "iniquity and pollution" from which they have been rescued.[160] Those who live otherwise are guilty of nothing less than insulting God.[161] It should be clear that Calvin takes an optimistic view of what God's saving grace can do in the life of a Christian. Indeed, some interpreters go so far as to say that Calvin even thinks that "there is a state of achieved victory over sin and whole-hearted surrender which by the grace of God may be called 'perfection.'"[162]

Subsequent generations of Reformed theologians largely agree (although, in comparison to Lutheran theology and the views of Martin Luther, without the direct dependence upon, and degree of deference toward, the theology of John Calvin).[163] For instance, Johannes Wollebius recognizes the distinction between justification and sanctification as vitally important. He insists that justification deals with issues of "legal" righteousness and sanctification with "evangelical" righteousness.[164] But while they are distinct, they are also inseparable, for sanctification accompanies justification as light follows the sun.[165] Where justification declares us righteous, sanctification actually transforms us so that we are righteous. The efficient cause is the entire Trinity, the internal impulsive cause is God's free and bountiful grace, the external impulse is Christ, the external instrumental cause is the Word (the Law and the Gospel), and the internal instrumental cause is faith.[166] Notably, sanctification demands our cooperation; the Holy Spirit is the "chief agent," and nothing happens without the prior work of the Spirit, but it is also true that sanctification does not take place apart from our cooperation with the Spirit. The subject of sanctification is the entire or whole human person: *intellectus*, *voluntas*, and *affectus*.[167]

---

[157] Calvin, *Institutes*, III.3 (509).
[158] Calvin, *Institutes*, III.3 (525).
[159] Calvin, *Institutes*, III.3 (520).
[160] Calvin, *Institutes*, III.6 (3).
[161] Calvin, *Institutes*, III.6 (4).
[162] Noble, *Holy Trinity*, 70, cf. R. S. Wallace, *Calvin's Doctrine of the Christian Life* (Edinburgh: Oliver & Boyd, 1959), 321–326.
[163] See the discussion by Michael Allen, "Sanctification, Perseverance, and Assurance," in *Reformation Theology: A Systematic Summary*, ed. Matthew Barrett (Wheaton, IL: Crossway, 2017), 558.
[164] Johannes Wollebius, *Christianae Theologiae Compendium* (Basel: 1634), I.XXX.I (245). An older English translation is *An Abridgement of Christian Divinity*, trans. Alexander Ross (London: 1660), 256.
[165] Wollebius, *Abridgement of Christian Divinity*, 269.
[166] Wollebius, *Christianae Theologiae Compendium* I.XXXI.III–VI (258–259).
[167] Wollebius, *Compendium* I.XXXI.IX (259).

Through sanctification, the Holy Spirit produces righteousness that is rightly said to be *inherent* (*inherens nobis infunditer*).[168] Wollebius is far from idiosyncratic on these points; Amandus Polanus, for instance, agrees on virtually all points.[169] He celebrates the work of the Spirit, for the work of sanctification renews humanity (*novus homo*) through mortification and vivification.[170] Notably, Polanus insists that sanctification happens only by grace, and he distinguishes between different aspects of grace: grace is rightly understood as prevenient, preparing, operating, cooperating, and perfecting—and all are vital to the process of sanctification. Notably, *gratia operans* initiates the renovation of our *mentes, voluntate,* and *affectu*—and this produces obedience that is acceptable to God.[171] But while *gratia praeveniens* and *gratia operans* are necessary, so also is *gratia cooperans*, for God not only enables our cooperation but also demands it. Other witnesses could be called: Zacharias Ursinus insists that we can never have justification without also being sanctified.[172] Johannes Heidegger goes so far as to say that sanctification is our greatest need (*sanctificationis summa necessitas est*).[173] Peter van Mastricht holds that sanctification is a gift—it is a gift that is now inherent within God's children. It is never their possession or something of which they can boast; it is always and ultimately a gift. But it is not a gift that is an entity somehow exterior to them; it is an "infusion" into them, and it truly changes them.[174] Sanctification is rightly said to be *necessary*—not necessary for gaining or earning salvation (which we cannot do), but necessary for the reception of it.[175] These theologians are representative in many respects, and, by my judgment, their views are right in the mainstream of historic Reformed theology.[176]

Seen in this light, it is not at all surprising that the major Reformed confessional statements are decisive about the reality and necessity of sanctification. As the Second Helvetic Confession puts it, "Wherefore, in this matter we are not speaking of a fictitious, empty, lazy, and dead faith, but of a living,

---

[168] Wollebius, *Compendium* I.XXXI.XIII (261).

[169] E.g., Amandus Polanus, *De Partibus Gratuitae Iustificationis Nostrae Coram Deo: Theses Theologicae* (Basel: 1598); and Polanus, *Syntagma Theologiae Christianae*, vol. 2 (Basel: 1609), 2933–3030. On the importance of Polanus, see Robert Letham, "Amandus Polanus: A Neglected Theologian?," *Sixteenth Century Studies* (1990): 463–476.

[170] Polanus, *Syntagma*, 3015–3016.

[171] Polanus, *Syntagma*, 3019.

[172] See the discussion in Heinrich Heppe, *Reformed Dogmatics: Set Out and Illustrated from the Sources* (London: George Allen & Unwin, 1950), 566.

[173] Johannes Heidegger, *Corpus Theologiae Christianae* (Zurich: 1700), XXIII.vii (314).

[174] Petrus van Mastricht, *Theoretico-Practica Theologica*, (1698), VI.viii.vii (735).

[175] Van Mastricht, *Theoretico-Practica Theologica*, VI.viii.xxvii (745–746).

[176] See further, e.g., Lucas Trelcatius Jr. (one of the colleagues and opponents of Jacobus Arminius in the theological controversy at Leiden), *Disputatio theologica de justificatione hominis coram Deo*, XX (Leiden, 1604); and Trelcatius, *Opuscula theologica omnia, duorum catalogum, prima edita*, XIII (Leiden), 348–378. Trelcatius insists that sanctification is *necessary* for salvation (e.g., *Opuscula theologica omnia*, XIV, 386). See also Francis Turretin, *Institutio Theologiae Elencticae*, XVII, in *Opera Tomus I* (Edinburgh: 1847). Turretin clearly distinguishes sanctification from justification (e.g., 609–612) but also insists that sanctification and the good works that flow from it are necessary for salvation (620–623).

quickening faith. It is and is called a living faith because it apprehends Christ who is life and makes alive, and shows that it is alive by living works."[177]

Other major Protestant accounts are even more optimistic about grace and its possibilities.[178] And beyond Protestant doctrines, Roman Catholic and Orthodox doctrines of *theosis* are also confident in the aims and strength of God's purifying grace. Important differences notwithstanding, there is significant concord across ecclesial traditions: the triune God whose nature is holy love created us to share that love, and now draws us into that life of holy love while cleansing us so that we can truly belong there.

D. Conclusion

With Luther, all Christians can exult,

> Mr. Devil, do not rage so. . . . For there is One who is called Christ. In him I believe. He has abrogated the law, damned sin, abolished death, and destroyed hell. And he is your devil, you devil, because he has captured and conquered you, so that you cannot harm me any longer nor anyone else who believes in him.[179]

For while it is true that we must pursue holiness, for "no one will see the Lord" without it (Heb. 12:14), so also it is true that God *will* purify and make us holy. For "our God is a consuming fire" (Heb. 12:29).[180]

---

[177] Cited in Horton, *Christian Faith*, 655.

[178] E.g., John Wesley, *A Plain Account of Christian Perfection* (Peabody, MA: Hendrickson, 2007).

[179] Cited in L'ubomir Batka, "Luther's Teaching on Sin and Evil," in *The Oxford Handbook of Martin Luther's Theology*, ed. Robert Kolb, Irene Dingel, and L'ubomir Batka (Oxford: Oxford University Press, 214), 250.

[180] Thanks to A. Philip Brown II for helpful comments on this section.

CHAPTER

EIGHT

CONCLUSION

Sin is whatever is opposed to God's will as that will reflects God's holy character and as that will is expressed by God's commands. Sin is fundamentally opposed to nature and reason, and it is ultimately opposed to God. The results of sin are truly catastrophic. Sin wreaks havoc on our relationships with God, one another, and the rest of creation. It is universal in human history and manifests itself in various cultural expressions. Sin is rebellion against our Lord and treason against our Creator—and it is our fault. It wrecks human lives and leaves us vulnerable; apart from the grace that we so readily reject, it utterly destroys us.

As David Kelsey summarizes the doctrine, the Christian understanding of sin teaches that

> [f]irst, it is universal. All human creatures are born into it. Second, it is, in Calvin's phrase, "adventitious." It is not a change in what human creatures are. To use a classical distinction between essential and accidental properties of a substance, the condition of original sin does not involve any change in the essence or nature of human creatures; it is an accidental property. Third, in it death has a certain power it would not otherwise have. There is disagreement whether human creatures would not die at all were it not for this predicament of original sin, or whether it is only that death, which would happen in any case, now has a certain power over human creatures that it would not otherwise have. Fourth, all persons born into the condition of original sin are born into guilt. There has been disagreement whether to understand this as a share in Adam and Eve's guilt for the original act of sin, or whether to understand it as guilt that subsequent human persons properly incur for themselves. Fifth, in the condition of original sin, human creatures are in bondage.[1]

This is a helpful summary. In this work, we have seen that sin is opposed to both nature and the God of grace. After first looking at the vivid, penetrating, and powerful portrayals of sin in Scripture and seeing how the Bible develops

---

[1] David H. Kelsey, *Eccentric Existence: A Theological Anthropology*, 2 vols. (Louisville: Westminster/John Knox, 2009), 1:432–433.

a canonical account of sin, I then turned attention to the origin of sin ("originating original sin"), and there we saw that sin is not a necessary part of the furniture of the cosmos but instead is opposed to God's good creation. Following this we looked at the doctrine of original sin ("originated original sin") to explore both what is and what isn't taught or entailed by Scripture and how we might think about the corruption of human nature that has come upon humanity subsequent to the sin of our first parents. In turn, we explored the notion of the so-called "sin nature"; here I argued that we should not think of sin as either a substance or an essence of its own. Instead, we should understand it as a corruption that has no independent existence of its own but is instead parasitic on the goodness of the human nature created in God's own image and likeness (Gen. 1:26–28). Focusing upon the characteristics of sin, in the heart of the work I argued that we should think of sin as being fundamentally against nature, against reason, and, ultimately, against God. I then turned to an exposition of some traditional distinctions that are helpful in the development of a robust understanding of sin. Following this, we saw that the results of sin are dire indeed. We also saw that, while we are no match for sin, sin is no match for grace.

So where does this leave us? It leaves us with a profound awareness that something has gone badly wrong, and with a deep and desperate ache for things to be made right. The doctrine of sin reminds us of the deep goodness of creation and of the beauty of those creatures made in God's own image, and beyond this it reminds us of the beautiful and necessary goodness of the Creator. It leaves us longing for something better, and it points us beyond itself to the Holy One who promises and provides salvation. The famous French mathematician, philosopher, and polymath Blaise Pascal points out that

> [i]t is dangerous to explain too clearly to man how like he is to animals without pointing out his greatness. It is also dangerous to make too much of his greatness without his vileness. It is still more dangerous to leave him in ignorance of both, but it is most valuable to represent both to him. Man must not be allowed to believe that he is equal either to animals or to angels, nor to be unaware of either, but he must know both.[2]

And further,

> Man's greatness and wretchedness are so evident that the true religion must necessarily teach us that there is in man some great principle of greatness and some great principle of wretchedness. It must also account for such amazing contradictions.[3]

---

[2] Blaise Pascal, "Pensee 121," *Pensees* (London: Penguin, 1966), 60.
[3] Pascal, "Pensee 149," 76.

Thus "Christianity is strange; it bids man to recognize that he is vile, and even abominable, and bids him want to be like God."[4]

There is much wisdom in Pascal's observations. Martin Luther King Jr. makes the point with his characteristically great power and eloquence:

> I know you say, "Now you stand there on a somber note. You've said to us that we are sinners; we are caught in the clutches of sin in our personal lives and in our social lives." And, yes, if we stop there, I assure you we would be in a pretty tragic predicament, that man's life would be a life of nothingness, a life of endless pessimism. So that we can't stop there. And that's something of the beauty of the Christian faith, that it says that in the midst of man's tragic predicament, in the midst of his awful inclination toward sin, God has come into the picture and has done something about it. That's the beauty of our faith. It says that standing over against the tragic dimensions of man's sin is the glorious dimensions of God's grace. Where sin abounded, grace abounded even more exceedingly. That's the Christian faith. On the one hand it is the most pessimistic religion in the world, for it recognizes the tragic and awful dimensions of man's sin. But on the other hand it is the most optimistic religion in the world, for it recognizes the heightening dimensions of God's grace and how God's grace can come in and pick up. So that over against man's sin stands God's grace. Christianity, therefore, becomes the greatest pessimistic optimistic religion in the world. It's a combination of a pessimistic optimism; it sees over against man's sinfulness, man's tragic state, the graciousness of God's mercy, and His love and His forgiving power.[5]

Sin—*all sin*—is ultimately against God. It contradicts the holiness of God, it violates the justice and righteousness of God, and it stands under the wrath of God. Sinners are opposed to God and deserve God's just condemnation. But as sin is opposed to God, so also is God opposed to sin. And this fact—grounded as it is in the utter goodness of God—is our hope.

Cornelius Plantinga Jr. gets it right: "Human sin is stubborn, but not as stubborn as the grace of God and not half so persistent, not half so ready to suffer to win its way."[6] Sin does not have the last word. For in the cross and resurrection of Jesus we learn that holiness and love are stronger than sin and death. As Gerard Manley Hopkins put it,

> . . . Enough! The Resurrection,
> A heart's clarion! Away grief's gasping, joyless days, dejection.
> 　　Across my foundering deck shone
> A beacon, an eternal beam. Flesh fade, and mortal trash

[4] Pascal, "Pensee 351," 133.
[5] Martin Luther King Jr., "Man's Sin and God's Grace," in *The Papers of Martin Luther King Jr., Vol. 6: Advocate of the Social Gospel*, ed. Clayborne Carson (Berkeley: University of California Press, 2007), 387.
[6] Cornelius Plantinga Jr., *Not the Way It's Supposed to Be: A Breviary of Sin* (Grand Rapids, MI: Eerdmans, 1994), 199.

Fall to the residuary worm: world's wildfire, leave but ash:
    In a flash, at a trumpet crash,
I am all at once what Christ is, since he was what I am, and
This Jack, joke, poor potsherd, patch, matchwood, immortal diamond,
    Is immortal diamond.[7]

"Thanks be to God, who gives us the victory through our Lord Jesus Christ" (1 Cor. 15:57). Amen.

---

[7] Gerard Manley Hopkins, "That Nature Is a Heraclitean Fire and of the Comfort of the Resurrection," in *The Poems of Gerard Manley Hopkins*, ed. W. H. Gardner and N. H. MacKenzie (Oxford: Oxford University Press, 1967), 105–106, cited in David A. S. Fergusson, *The Cosmos and the Creator: An Introduction to the Theology of Creation* (London: SPCK, 1998), 86–87.

THE ORIGINAL SINNERS

I. INTRODUCTION

For much of the Christian tradition, death for humans has been understood to be the direct (though not immediate) result of the sin of the first humans. There was an original human pair or couple—"Adam and Eve"—and all humans trace their ancestry back to them. These original humans sinned—*the* "original sin"—and death for humans is a direct consequence of that primal sin. Today, however, these beliefs are widely disputed and dismissed, and those who reject the traditional beliefs often do so with appeals to contemporary science. What is the Christian who respects science and who values the advances made in paleoanthropology and genetics, but who also is committed to traditional Christian doctrine, to think? In what follows, I shall argue that there is no obvious inconsistency between these accounts, and that claims to the contrary are overblown.

For some Christians, there is nothing here that so much as gives cause for concern. They see that the science-based challenges to the historicity of Adam come from mainstream evolutionary science, and they reject such science as flawed in approach and mistaken in conclusions.[1] Other Christians, however, feel immense pressure from the science-based challenges. In this Appendix, I address such science-based challenges, and I conclude that there is no reason to believe that the historic doctrinal claim and the findings of mainstream contemporary genetic science are incompatible. This is obviously relevant for those Christians who feel pressure from the science-based challenges, for, as we shall see, the findings of contemporary genetic science do not rule out the possibility of a "historical Adam." But this may also be relevant for those Christians who do not feel such pressure, for belief in a "historical Adam" does not rule out the findings of contemporary genetic science. In other words, one need not reject historic Christian belief in a historical Adam on the grounds that "science disproves a historical Adam" or that "science tells us something

---

[1] As in many of the essays in *Theistic Evolution: A Scientific, Philosophical, and Theological Critique*, ed. J. P. Moreland, Stephen C. Meyer, Christopher Shaw, Ann K. Gauger, and Wayne Grudem (Wheaton, IL: Crossway, 2017).

that is incompatible with belief in a historical Adam," and one need not reject mainstream scientific views about human origins on the grounds that "the Bible teaches a historical Adam."[2]

II. The Challenge

The belief that death for humans is the result of the primal sin is very widespread indeed within the Christian tradition. As we have seen, Christian theologians take differing views of the exact nature of our relation to our first parents: there are "federalist" views (especially within the Reformed tradition); there are various versions of "realist" views; and there are "mediate" views as well as what could be called "corruption-only" accounts of the doctrine of original sin. But with respect to the basic convictions that there *was* a "historical Adam and Eve" and that their sin has impacted us all by exposing us to death and divine judgment, to say that the belief is "widespread" within the Christian theological traditions is a massive understatement. It is expressed in major Protestant catechisms and confessions. As an example, consider the affirmations of the Reformed tradition's Heidelberg Catechism. In response to the question "Did God create people wicked and perverse?" the answer is clear and emphatic: "No. God created them good and in his own image, that is, in true righteousness and holiness."[3] When addressing the question of the origin of our corruption, the Catechism says that this came from "the Fall and disobedience of our first parents, Adam and Eve . . ."[4] Similarly, the Belgic Confession affirms that "God created man from the dust of the earth" in the divine image and thus as "good, righteous, and holy; capable in all things to will agreeably to the will of God" but that they then became subject to death as a result of their sin.[5] Lutheranism agrees: the original humans were created "pure, and holy, and free from sin."[6] This view is also promulgated by traditional Roman Catholic teaching. For instance, the *Catechism of the Catholic Church* cautions against any flat-footed reading of Genesis, and it recognizes the "symbol-

---

[2] Unfortunately, conclusions about human origins drawn from mainstream science are often confused with distinctly *metaphysical* and even *theological* commitments that are sometimes added on to the science. On these common confusions, see Alvin Plantinga, *Where the Conflict Really Lies: Science, Religion, and Naturalism* (Oxford: Oxford University Press, 2011). On the use of distinctly theological considerations in explanations of evolution and arguments against special creation, see Stephen Dilley, "Evolution and Theology," *Dictionary of Christianity and Science*, ed. Paul Copan, Tremper Longman III, Christopher L. Reese, and Michael G. Strauss (Grand Rapids, MI: Zondervan Academic, 2017), 246–247; Dilley, "Charles Darwin's Use of Theology in the *Origin of Species*," *British Journal for the History of Science* (2011): 29–46; and Paul A. Nelson, "The Role of Theology in Current Evolutionary Reasoning," *Biology and Philosophy* (1996): 493–517.
[3] "The Heidelberg Catechism," question 6, in *The Creeds of Christendom, with a History and Critical Notes, Volume III: The Evangelical Protestant Creeds*, ed. Philip Schaff (Grand Rapids, MI: Baker Academic, 2007), 309.
[4] "Heidelberg Catechism," Question 7, 309–310.
[5] "The Belgic Confession," art. XIV, in *Creeds of Christendom, with a History and Critical Notes, Volume III: The Evangelical Protestant Creeds*, 398. The "death" spoken of here is both physical and spiritual.
[6] "The Formula of Concord," art. I, in *Creeds of Christendom, with a History and Critical Notes, Volume III: The Evangelical Protestant Creeds*, 98.

ism of biblical language."[7] But it also teaches that "our first parents, Adam and Eve, were constituted in an original state of holiness and justice."[8] And it says further that Genesis 3 "affirms a primeval event, a deed that took place at the beginning of the history of man. Revelation gives us the certainty of faith that the whole of human history is marked by the original fault freely committed by our first parents."[9]

Not only is the doctrine of original sin widely held, it is also deeply rooted. Thus the anti-Pelagian Council of Carthage (417/418) goes so far as to anathematize anyone who holds that "Adam, the first man, was created mortal, so that, whether he sinned or not, he would have died from natural causes, and not as the wages of sin."[10] And nearly ubiquitous in these discussions is Paul's teaching from the fifth chapter of Romans: "Therefore, just as sin entered the world through one man, and death through sin, and in this way death came to all people, because all sinned . . ." (Rom. 5:12 NIV).

But if it is an understatement to say that such convictions are widely held and deeply rooted within and across the various ecclesial traditions of Christian theology, it is also an understatement to say that such convictions are widely criticized and dismissed as being inconsistent with the assured conclusions of modern science. The theologian Aaron Riches expresses the worry: "the best scientific evidence would seem to contradict outright the traditional teaching of the church."[11] The famous priest and physicist John Polkinghorne observes that the doctrine of the fall is "the major Christian doctrine that I find most difficult to reconcile with scientific thought."[12] The noted philosopher of science Michael Ruse says this of the traditional Christian account (what he calls the "Augustinian" view): "According to modern science, there was no unique Adam and Eve. . . . The Augustinian solution fails in the face of modern science. It just doesn't work."[13] Similarly, the theologian and biologist Denis O. Lamoureux says that his "central conclusion" is this: "Adam never existed, and this fact has no impact whatsoever on the foundational beliefs of Christianity."[14] And the physicist Karl Giberson leaves no room for doubt: "Adam and Eve, as described in Genesis, cannot have been historical figures.

[7] The Catechism of the Catholic Church (New York: Doubleday, 1995), 106.
[8] Catechism of the Catholic Church (Doubleday, 1995), 107.
[9] Catechism of the Catholic Church (Doubleday, 1995), 110.
[10] Henry Bettenson, ed., Documents of the Christian Church, 2nd ed. (Oxford: Oxford University Press, 1963), 59.
[11] Aaron Riches, "The Mystery of Adam: A Poetic Apology for the Traditional Doctrine," in Evolution and the Fall, ed. William T. Cavanaugh and James K. A. Smith (Grand Rapids, MI: Eerdmans, 2017), 120.
[12] John Polkinghorne, Reason and Reality: The Relationship between Science and Theology (London: SPCK, 1991), 99.
[13] Michael Ruse, "Human Evolution: Some Tough Questions for the Christian," in Human Origins and the Image of God: Essays in Honor of J. Wentzel van Huyssteen, ed. Christopher Lilley and Daniel J. Pedersen (Grand Rapids, MI: Eerdmans, 2017), 158.
[14] Denis O. Lamoureux, "No Historical Adam: Evolutionary Creation View," in Four Views on the Historical Adam, ed. Matthew Barrett and Ardel B. Caneday (Grand Rapids, MI: Zondervan Academic, 2013), 37–38.

Recent work in genetics has established this unsettling conclusion beyond any reasonable doubt."[15]

Such challenges should be taken seriously. Here is what we seem to know:[16] that evolutionary history shows a great deal of predation, death, and extinction throughout the process;[17] that morphological evidence as well as genomic sequence data show that humans and other primates share a common ancestry; and that the initial human population would have had to evolve as a group and would have had to be several thousand in number.[18]

The first of these we can call the "red tooth thesis," and it affirms death before the "fall."[19] The second we can term the "common ancestry thesis." Mammals have been around for about sixty-five million years, and primates for around fifty million years.[20] Various forms of nonhuman hominins began to appear, with *Homo habilus* emerging about one-and-a-half million years ago, *Homo erectus* about a million years ago, and *Homo sapiens* perhaps a half-million years ago.[21] Various subspecies of *Homo sapiens* developed, among them Neanderthals (*Homo neanderthalensis*) and "modern humans" (as well as other hominins such as *Homo floresiensis* or "hobbits" and the "Denisovans," who may share a remote ancestor with Neanderthals).[22] Morphological

---

[15] Karl Giberson, *Saving the Original Sinner: How Christians Have Used the Bible's First Man to Oppress, Inspire, and Make Sense of the World* (Boston: Beacon, 2015), 173.

[16] In saying "seem to know," I do not here mean to indicate disagreement on either scientific or theological grounds. I do, however, intend to acknowledge the fact that the "assured conclusions" of one scientific generation are sometimes quickly revised or outright rejected by the equally assured conclusions of the next. As Hud Hudson says, "[G]iven the frequent reversals of fortune for a substantial number of once-popular claims in [biology and paleontology], one wonders why the confidence isn't a little more tempered from time to time," for sometimes the claims can be "oversold as near certainties" ("Science, Skepticism, and Supertasks: Replies to Torrance, Deng, Madueme, Goldschmidt and Lebens," *Journal of Analytic Theology* [2017]: 637). Moreover, the confidence of many scientists in their pronouncements on matters theological and metaphysical is "staggering." However, this is where we are at currently; if the situation does not change, these points generate the challenges.

[17] This may not mean (as is often thought) that suffering, death, and extinction are necessary to the process; they may not be essential to the theory of evolution itself. As S. Joshua Swamidass puts it (in personal conversation), "Evolution does not proceed by death and suffering, but by differences in reproductive success." Widespread death and extinction is, however, part of the evolutionary *history*.

[18] For a helpful overview, see Francisco J. Ayala, "Human Evolution: The Three Grand Challenges of Human Biology," in *The Cambridge Companion to the Philosophy of Biology*, ed. David L. Hull and Michael Ruse (Cambridge: Cambridge University Press, 2007), 233–254.

[19] Following Matthew Levering, I take it that there is an important distinction to be made between human death and death per se (e.g., *Engaging the Doctrine of Creation: Cosmos, Creatures, and the Wise and Good Creator* [Grand Rapids, MI: Baker Academic, 2017], 234n22). My concern here is with *human* death, as I do not find biblical or confessional support for the idea that no creatures had died apart from the sin of humans. With Basil of Caesarea, Thomas Aquinas, and many others, I find no insuperable theological objection to the view that predators were predators apart from the fall.

This is not to deny that there are interesting theological issues associated with the suffering and death of the nonhuman creation. For insightful discussion, see Michael Murray, *Nature Red in Tooth and Claw: Theism and the Problem of Animal Suffering* (Oxford: Oxford University Press, 2008).

[20] See Michael Ruse, *Darwinism and Its Discontents* (Cambridge: Cambridge University Press, 2006), 167.

[21] See Ruse, *Darwinism and Its Discontents*, 169. I note that paleoanthropologists cannot seem to find agreement with respect to these dates; for a different time line, see Richard Fortey, *Life: A Natural History of the First Four Billion Years of Life on Earth* (New York: Knopf, 1998), 304–305.

[22] See Dennis R. Venema and Scot McKnight, *Adam and the Genome: Reading Scripture after Genetic Science* (Grand Rapids, MI: Baker Academic, 2017), 61. There is some divergence of opinion regarding the relation of Neanderthals to humans (including their relation species-wise). Ruse takes Neanderthals to be a subspecies of *Homo sapiens* ("Human Evolution," 156), but others deny this. Venema and McKnight say that there was "a limited amount of interbreeding" (60). Just a decade earlier, Ayala said that the genetic evidence "indicates that interbreeding between *H. sapiens* and *H. neanderthalensis* never occurred" ("Human Evolution," 238).

evidence has been taken to suggest or demonstrate common ancestry for some time. But with the rise of genetic science and the work of the Human Genome Project, the case for common ancestry is now considered conclusive: the evidence is in, and the analysis of DNA shows that we share our remote ancestors in common with other hominins (now extinct) and indeed other primates (both extinct and surviving).[23]

We can refer to the third as the "large initial population thesis." The same genetic evidence that shows common ancestry also reveals that the initial population of humans must have evolved as a large group; indeed, the group must have emerged as at least a couple thousand interbreeding pairs. As Venema and McKnight explain, "Put most simply, DNA evidence indicates that humans descend from a large population because we, as a species, are so genetically diverse in the present day that a large ancestral population is needed to transmit that diversity to us."[24] They conclude that "every genetic analysis estimating ancestral population sizes has agreed that we descend from a population of thousands, not a single ancestral couple."[25]

III. The Problem? Toward Clarification

Taken either individually or collectively, these theses may seem to present challenges for traditional Christian belief. The statement just quoted from Venema and McKnight indicates this: as they say, the evidence suggests that there was "not a single ancestral couple." Giberson is even more emphatic: Adam and Eve "cannot have been historical figures," and this is "beyond reasonable doubt."[26] Peter Enns makes similar assertions; as he puts it, "scientific and biblical models of human origins are, strictly speaking, incompatible. . . . They cannot be reconciled."[27] But do these theses really present such challenges? Is it obvious that a historical first couple—and thus a historical fall that unleashed sin and death upon humanity—is somehow ruled out by the scientific evidence? If so, are the only options then for Christians to either reject contemporary science or abandon traditional Christian doctrine? These are important questions. For many Christians, things seem just this stark; the options are simple and binary: either a historical Adam, or contemporary genetic science. But before we address the issue directly, it might be helpful to make sure we are working with a clear sense of the alleged problem.

Note the force of the claims made by Ruse, Giberson, and Enns. They are not merely observing that there is some element of mystery here; they

[23] See Venema and McKnight, *Adam and the Genome*, 53–62.
[24] Venema and McKnight, *Adam and the Genome*, 55.
[25] Venema and McKnight, *Adam and the Genome*, 55.
[26] Giberson, *Saving the Original Sinner*, 173.
[27] Peter Enns, *The Evolution of Adam: What the Bible Does and Doesn't Say about Human Origins* (Grand Rapids, MI: Baker Academic, 2012), 138.

are not simply admitting that there is a lot that we do not know. Nor are they pointing to areas of "tension" or possible conflict. No, their confident assertions are much stronger. They are claiming that it is *impossible* to believe both the deliverances of modern science and classical Christian doctrine: these claims "*cannot* be reconciled." It is not so much as possible that both are true. Accordingly, I take it, these beliefs must be either contrary or contradictory.

If some proposition *P* is *contrary* to some proposition *Q*, then it is not possible that both *P* and *Q* are true. If *P* is true, then *Q* cannot be true; it is not so much as logically possible for *Q* to be true if *P* is true. And if *Q* is true, then *P* cannot be true. *P* and *Q* are mutually exclusive but not mutually exhaustive. It is not possible that both *P* and *Q* are true. But it is not necessary that either *P* or *Q* is true; that is, both *P* and *Q* could be false.

On the other hand, if some proposition *P* is *contradictory* to some proposition *Q*, then it is possible that either *P* or *Q* is true but not possible for both *P* and *Q* to be true, and it is not possible that both *P* and *Q* are false. If *P* and *Q* are contradictory, then they are mutually exclusive and mutually exhaustive.[28]

The upshot is this: if it is so much as possible that both *P* and *Q* are true, then they are neither contrary nor contradictory. If it is *possible* that both are true, then affirmation of *Q* cannot be taken to rule out *P*, and affirmation of *P* cannot be taken to eliminate the possibility of *Q*. Affirmation of *P* cannot be taken as reason to reject *Q*, and affirmation of *Q* cannot be taken as reason to reject *P*.

Perhaps surprisingly—at least considering how common and vehement are the assertions to the contrary—it turns out that there is good reason to doubt that the contemporary scientific consensus is inconsistent with the core of the traditional Christian belief. In other words, neither contrariness nor contradictoriness follows from the conjunction of the scientific consensus and traditional Christian belief. For indeed it is possible that both are true.

IV. Some Possibilities

In point of fact, there is more than one possible way to maintain consistency between science and Christian belief on the issue we are considering. Here are three such possibilities. I do not here endorse any of these (as the sober truth), nor do I mean to suggest that these are the only (or even the most promising) possibilities. But since possibility is all that is needed to meet the common objections, I offer possibility. Here are three such possibilities.

---

[28] See "Contradiction," in *The Stanford Encyclopedia of Philosophy*, https://plato.stanford.edu/, accessed June 12, 2018.

A. *The Refurbishment Proposal(s)*

One way to maintain consistency is to accept the standard evolutionary account of human origins but then suggest that God took two existing hominins and "refurbished" them. On this proposal, one accepts (or at least *can* accept) the "orthodox" evolutionary story; one need not quibble with the standard claims about the age of the universe, the development of life on this planet, and the emergence of mammals and other primates and then hominins that finally developed into *Homo sapiens* and then into "modern humans." On this account, prehuman hominins develop physically, mentally, and (presumably) perhaps to some degree spiritually in the long and bloody process basic to the evolutionary model. And then, at the right moment (if not the "fullness of time" then at least the set-up for that "fullness"), God acts to radically change the state, status, and future of a certain species. As the nineteenth-century Methodist theologian William Burt Pope puts it, "Created out of the dust, he [Adam] is a development of older physical types, a final development on which evolution has spent itself, found worthy at last to be the receptacle of an immortal spirit."[29] God "refurbishes" a pair of these existing creatures; God "elects" them for relationship and service.[30] These humans—and their progeny—are gifted with the divine image and the mental, relational, and spiritual gifts and responsibilities that come along with that image.

A representative statement of this comes from Peter van Inwagen, and I quote in extenso:

> For millions of years, perhaps for thousands of millions of years, God guided the course of evolution so as eventually to produce certain very clever primates, the immediate predecessors of *Homo sapiens*. At some time in the last few hundred thousand years, the whole population of our pre-human ancestors formed a small breeding community—a few thousand or a few hundred or even a few score. That is to say, there was a time when every ancestor of modern human beings who was then alive was a member of this . . . group of primates. In the fullness of time, God took the members of this breeding group and miraculously raised them to rationality. That is, he gave them the gifts of language, abstract thought, and disinterested love—and, of course, the gift of free will. Perhaps we cannot understand *all* his reasons for giving human beings free will, but here is one important one we can understand: He gave them the gift of free will because free will is necessary for love. . . .

---

[29] William Burt Pope, *A Compendium of Christian Theology: Being Analytical Outlines of a Course of Theological Study, Biblical, Dogmatic, Historical*, 3 vols., 2nd ed. (London: Wesleyan Conference Office, 1880), 1:405, as cited in David N. Livingstone, *Darwin's Forgotten Defenders: The Encounter between Evangelical Theology and Evolutionary Thought* (Grand Rapids, MI: Eerdmans, 1987), 135–136.

In many respects, Pope's Reformed contemporary B. B. Warfield takes similar views. See Bradley J. Gundlach, *Process and Providence: The Evolution Question at Princeton, 1845–1929* (Grand Rapids, MI: Eerdmans, 2013).

[30] Different versions of the refurbishment proposal may vary here; some (mind-body dualists) may take this to be or include the "ensoulment" of these hominins, others may associate this directly with the *imago dei*, etc.

God not only raised these primates to rationality—not only made of them what we call human beings—but also took them into a kind of mystical union with himself, the sort of union Christians hope for in heaven and call the Beatific Vision. Being in union with God, these new human beings, these primates who had become human beings at a certain point in their lives, lived together in the harmony of perfect love and also possessed what theologians used to call preternatural powers. . . . Because they lived in the harmony of perfect love, none of them did any harm to the others. Because of their preternatural powers, they were able somehow to protect themselves from wild beasts . . . , from disease . . . and from random, destructive natural events (like earthquakes), which they knew about in advance and were able to escape. There was thus no evil in their world. And it was God's intention that they should never become decrepit with age or die, as their primate forebears had. But. . . . They abused the gift of free will and separated themselves from their union with God.[31]

From there, we know the rest of the story. The fall brought sin and suffering, death and destruction.

The version offered by van Inwagen is only one option. Various biblical scholars and theologians have suggested some version or other of this proposal, and indeed there are different versions of it. Denis Alexander, John R. W. Stott, C. S. Lewis, Gavin McGrath, and others have posited something like this.[32] Recently, James K. A. Smith has offered something along these lines (albeit as a "provisional model as a kind of thought experiment").[33] Some people take this "refurbishment" to have happened a very long time ago, while others take it to be much more recent.[34] Some versions of this proposal would include the bestowal of a "soul"; others (such as van Inwagen's) might not. A variation might hold that God so refurbished more than the initial couple; on this twist, Adam and Eve are the "top two" (the "chieftains") but not the only two. This variant would, of course, also help to explain how the children of the first couple found spouses (without resorting to sexual relations with other non-human but biologically compatible hominins and thus raising worries about bestiality) and encountered others (as in Genesis 4).

The interesting variations notwithstanding, the basic idea held in common is not hard to grasp. Nor is it hard to see that it is not inconsistent—at least not obviously so—with the main lines of the contemporary scientific consensus. Consider first the "common ancestry thesis" in relation to this proposal. It does not take a lot of reflection to see that this proposal is neither contrary nor

[31] Peter van Inwagen, *The Problem of Evil* (Oxford: Oxford University Press, 2006), 84, 86.
[32] See the discussion in C. John Collins, *Did Adam and Eve Really Exist? Who They Were and Why You Should Care* (Wheaton, IL: Crossway, 2011).
[33] James K. A. Smith, "What Stands on the Fall? A Philosophical Exploration," in *Evolution and the Fall*, 61.
[34] Denis Alexander's model takes it to be recent; see his *Creation or Evolution: Do We Have to Choose?* (Oxford: Monarch, 2008).

contradictory to common ancestry. It accepts the standard evolutionary story as it stands: the first humans have a genetic history, and this history is one that shares much in common with the other hominins. Simply put, the first humans share ancestry in common with other creatures, so it does not violate the common ancestry thesis. Consider next the "large initial population thesis." This does not present a problem either, for the (genetic) evidence that demands a "common ancestry" is the same evidence that calls for an initial population that is large. But if the fact that the first humans share a common ancestry and genetic background with other hominins can handle the "common ancestry thesis," it can also account for the fact that a larger genetic background is demanded. What about the "red tooth thesis"? Again, the refurbishment proposal does not run afoul of this thesis. Nothing about the refurbishment proposal denies that the actual history of the evolutionary process is rough and bloody. Nothing demands that the history of the evolution of other creatures is not full of violence and horror. Indeed, nothing about it denies that the standard evolutionary history of other hominins is violent and gory. It only holds (or at least *can hold*) that the death of *humans* (now understood in distinctly theological terms, perhaps as those members of the species *Homo sapiens* who are in the *imago dei*) is the consequence of sin. Nothing about this is contrary or contradictory to the "red tooth thesis."

Recall Ruse's claim that the traditional theological account (the "Augustinian solution") "fails in the face of modern science. It just doesn't work . . ."[35] Why does he make such a claim? Why won't it "work"? It fails because "it just won't work to say that one day God put immortal souls in a pair of hominins and that did the job."[36] Passing over the caricature drawn here, we might wonder why Ruse would say such a thing. Sans argument, this would be mere bluster. So what is the argument? Ruse says this: "Either every member of the species was made in the image of God, or none was. Shared characteristics is what it means to say you have a species."[37] The actual argument remains less than pellucid, but several observations are appropriate. First, as Ruse himself surely knows, philosophers of biology cannot come to agreement on a science-based answer to the question, "What is a species?"[38] So it seems odd for Ruse

---

[35] Ruse, "Human Evolution," 158.

[36] Ruse, "Human Evolution," 158.

[37] Ruse, "Human Evolution," 158.

[38] Ernst Mayer observes that "[i]t is often said that there is no other problem in biology that is as refractory to solution as is the species problem" (*Toward a New Philosophy of Biology: Observations of an Evolutionist* [Cambridge, MA: Harvard University Press, 1988], 308). Maureen Kearney notes that the "concept of species is one of the core concepts of systematics and evolutionary biology," but she goes on to ask, "[w]hat exactly is the nature of these entities that systematists are trying to identify, compare, and classify?" Different proposals have emerged, with debates ensuing between "biological species concepts" that are "rooted in the processes thought to create species" (e.g., reproductive and/or geographic isolation), "phenetic species concepts" (roughly, physical similarities taken to be relevant), and "phylogenetic species concepts." Overall, the "topic has engendered a great deal of conceptual discussion and debate" ("Philosophy and Phylogenetics," in *The Cambridge Companion to the Philosophy of Biology*, ed. David L. Hull and Michael Ruse [Cambridge: Cambridge University Press, 2007], 222). David L. Hull

to appeal to "shared characteristics" as somehow definitive, and even stranger that he does so without benefit of explanation or argument. Second, there is good reason to think that such a purported definition would be doomed to failure. Surely not just *any* shared characteristics count as either necessary or sufficient for species-membership. I have the property *being bi-pedal*, but so do orcs and elves. I have the property *being hairy-eared*, but so do mustangs and mountain goats. Yet it is not plausible to think that we are members of the same species. Third, if we allow for a properly metaphysical account and think of species-membership in terms of kind-essences,[39] we see the importance of a distinction between *common* and *essential* properties, where "common" properties are those possessed by many or most (or perhaps even all) members of the natural kind and "essential" properties are those that are individually necessary (thus one must have all of them to qualify for kind-membership) and jointly sufficient (thus if one has them all, then one is in).[40] But once we allow for such distinctions, we can see that not all common properties are essential properties. And so there is no obvious reason to think that Ruse has a good argument in the neighborhood. Fourth, the assertion that "either every member of the species was made in the image of God, or none was" is just that—an assertion. Note that it is a distinctly *theological* assertion (and none the worse off for that). But it is one that is not supported—by either theology or science. Nor is it obvious how an argument for it might even go. Ruse himself says that Neanderthals were members of the species *Homo sapiens* (albeit as a subspecies).[41] Does he think that they must have had the image of God as well? An argument to that end would be interesting indeed, but it is far from obvious either how such an argument might go or that it would be demanded by consistency with Christian theology. Fifth, even if we were to accept Ruse's stipulation, it is less than obvious that the refurbishment proposal cannot account for it. Suppose that we think of "humanity" as a distinctly theological category (or, more modestly, as a category that has an irreducibly theological element); suppose we think of "humans" not as *Homo sapiens simpliciter* or as *Homo sapiens* who exhibit various physical abilities, characteristics, and behaviors (so-called "anatomically modern" or "behaviorally modern" humans)

offers helpful discussion of why these "tensions arise" in consideration of species ("Introduction to Part V," in *The Philosophy of Biology*, Oxford Readings in Philosophy, ed. David L. Hull and Michael Ruse [Oxford: Oxford University Press, 1998], 295).

[39] To be sure, some will resist this move; Kearney notes that some biologists and philosophers of biology argue "that evolutionary theory precludes viewing species as classes or natural kinds because classes and kinds are tied to an essentialism that is inconsistent with an evolutionary worldview" ("Philosophy and Phylogenetics," 224). She refers to David Hull, "The Effect of Essentialism on Taxonomy: Two Thousand Years of Stasis," *British Journal for the Philosophy of Science* (1965): 314–326; and to M. T. Ghiselin, "A Radical Solution to the Species Problem," *Systematic Zoology* (1974): 536–544.

[40] This distinction has been put to work in Christology in Thomas V. Morris, *The Logic of God Incarnate* (Ithaca, NY: Cornell University Press, 1986), 63.

[41] Ruse, "Human Evolution," 156.

but as *Homo sapiens* who have the *imago dei*. In other words, "humans" are those creatures who have all the properties needed to qualify as *Homo sapiens and* all the properties that are part of the *imago dei*. Put together, these are individually necessary and jointly sufficient for inclusion in the natural kind *human*. Well, in this case the relevant stipulation would be met, for all critters who are *Homo sapiens* in the divine image in fact would be humans. At any rate, as it stands, Ruse's objection is obscure. It is also less than compelling. He gives us no good reason to think that the refurbishment proposal cannot work.

B. *The Hyper-Adam Proposal*

If the foregoing proposal is one that is very closely in touch with contemporary genetic science, this next proposal sits at a much further distance from it. Indeed, it sits so far away as to be insusceptible to challenges by that science. Interestingly, it also offers possibilities for those who might worry that the refurbishment proposal sits too loose with respect to the Genesis account.[42]

Hud Hudson, a metaphysician and philosopher of religion, takes the standard, "orthodox" evolutionary account of the development of life as it stands (excepting the "gratuitous, metaphysical rider that God does not ever participate in the process").[43] He does not challenge the standard story, but he also accepts "a historical fall involving some individual or community of historical persons," and he accepts that "their rebellion had among its consequences a kind of ruin from which you and I also now suffer."[44] He also thinks that these beliefs can be held together, and that, if one makes the right moves in metaphysics, there is no inconsistency between science and theology.

These moves in metaphysics have to do with philosophy of time; more specifically, they involve commitment to the hypertime hypothesis. The details of this are very complex indeed, and are not susceptible to easy summary.[45] Nor are they uncontroversial (which should not be surprising; this is, after all, a metaphysical thesis!). The hypothesis relies on four-dimensionalist

---

[42] Further discussion of these matters will be found in the volume in this series on theological anthropology. Such worriers should, however, be mindful of these points: (a) commitment to a traditionally "high" view of biblical truthfulness and authority (including belief in biblical inerrancy) does not commit one to any particular interpretation (i.e., a "young earth" position or the view that the "days" of creation had to be twenty-four hour periods—views which at the very least are debatable on exegetical and hermeneutical grounds); (b) the Genesis account clearly presents some element of creation of the first humans *de novo* and by a special act of God—but just as clearly *not* as *ex nihilo*; (c) the first humans came *after* other creatures (and, unless we beg the question with respect to the antiquity question, we cannot assume that Scripture is telling us exactly *how long after*); (d) to say that the first humans were formed from "dust" does not necessitate the conclusion that they were made from inanimate particles (cf. Gen. 3:19; Ps. 103:14); and (e) the progeny of Adam and Eve found mates, and while it may be *possible* that they took their siblings as sexual partners, it must be admitted this assumption goes beyond anything explicitly taught in the Bible and surely would contravene the sexual ethics that are spelled out in the Bible. So perhaps such worriers should relax and consider the possibility that they should worry less. Nonetheless, the hyper-Adam proposal awaits them as another option.

[43] Hud Hudson, *The Fall and Hypertime* (Oxford: Oxford University Press, 2014), 47.

[44] Hudson, *Fall and Hypertime*, 41.

[45] See further Hud Hudson, *The Metaphysics of Hyperspace* (Oxford: Oxford University Press, 2005).

metaphysics (according to which presentism, the view that everything that exists is present, is false), and more precisely on a growing-block theory of time (according to which past objects exist along with present objects, but future objects don't [yet] exist), which Hudson then adapts as "morphing block" theory (according to which space-time blocks can gain or lose units that are "slices" of the block).[46] The hypertime hypothesis also embraces a version of multiverse theory. With these commitments, Hudson argues that the hypertime hypothesis is relevant for our discussion:

> [W]e would do well repeatedly to insist on distinguishing two different sets of claims, those reporting history and those reporting hyperhistory. History, for example, indeed reveals that "modern humans emerged as a splinter population from pre-existing hominid groups within the last quarter of a million years," and perhaps our pair appeared at a unique threshold in this development as the very first creatures also to be persons. To be sure, they never lived carefree lives of safety in a garden, immune from the dangers of a world red in tooth and claw. On the contrary, their existence was one of constant peril and entirely given over to toil for food, shelter, and the basic necessities of life. But hyperhistory has a different story to tell. This numerically same pair, *once upon a hypertime*, lived in just such a garden and in just such an innocent state, armed with preternatural gifts, blessed and protected by a special grace.[47]

Given the metaphysics of hypertime, we may have something like the following:

> In the beginning, . . . God created a spacetime and its contents whose earliest stages of growth witnessed the forming of a man from the dust of the ground, the planting of a garden into which he was placed, the adorning of that garden with trees and rivers, the imposition of a restriction on his diet, the presentation and naming of the animals, the extraction of a rib from and a companion for him, the fateful discourse of a snake . . . and a rebellion that took the form of eating forbidden fruit. And, as the block grew, this once naked and innocent pair fashioned clothing, hid themselves and were found, confessed their disobedience, and received the heavy news of its consequences. Finally, driven out of the garden, they and their world underwent a spectacular change.[48]

For, explains Hudson,

> At the hypermoment the pair exited the garden, . . . God annihilated every piece of that block save that region on its outermost edge thus occupied by these ancestors of ours and then embedded that very region and its contents

[46] For helpful discussion of the metaphysics, see Michael C. Rea, "Four-Dimensionalism," in *The Oxford Handbook of Metaphysics*, ed. Michael Loux and Dean Zimmerman (Oxford: Oxford University Press, 2003), 246–280; and Sally Haslanger, "Persistence through Time," in *Oxford Handbook of Metaphysics*, 315–354.
[47] Hudson, *Fall and Hypertime*, 191.
[48] Hudson, *Fall and Hypertime*, 190.

in a new block—a block sporting a several-billion-year history, replete with ice ages, long-dead hominids, dinosaurs, primordial soups, condensing matter, even a big bang.[49]

Thus it is possible, given the metaphysics of hypertime, to have one's Edenic cake and eat it too.

Hudson knows that this is a metaphysical account; he knows that he is defending a very traditional or "conservative" doctrine (more traditional or conservative than he actually holds) by appeal to abstract metaphysics. In fact, this is precisely his point. He is exercised to show that rejection of the traditional doctrine is not properly motivated by something called "pure science." Instead, it is motivated by science-plus-metaphysics. Even—or perhaps especially—when those metaphysical commitments are unacknowledged or even unnoticed, they are operative. Thus, as Hudson puts it, "the argument from our modern worldview" for the rejection of historic Christian doctrine is "inadequate: it misrepresents itself as a contest between religion and empirical science (a contest we are all too often to regard as akin to a match between a toddler and an 800-pound gorilla), when in fact it requires supplementation by a piece of metaphysics that has not been adequately defended or even acknowledged."[50] After all the fascinating thought experiments and speculative metaphysics, we are left with this conclusion: it is impossible to hold with consistency to both traditional doctrine and contemporary science only if we know that the hypertime hypothesis is false, but since we do not know that the hypertime hypothesis is false, then it is not impossible to hold with consistency to both traditional doctrine and contemporary science.

C. The Genealogical-Adam Proposal

In addition to the various versions of the refurbishment and the hyper-Adam proposals, another option has recently emerged, one that is well-informed by the contemporary science. S. Joshua Swamidass offers an interesting proposal. He argues that genealogical science is relevant and important in this discussion. Though often overlooked, genealogical science has much to offer for our understanding of these matters. He argues that

> [m]ost are convinced that genetic and archeological science answer [the question "Do we all descend from a single couple?"] with an unequivocal "no," [for] it appears that [we] share common ancestors with the great apes and arise as a large population, never dipping in size to a single couple. Without contradicting the findings of genetic science, genealogical science gives a different answer to the question. There are many couples, pairs of universal

---

[49] Hudson, *Fall and Hypertime*, 190–191.
[50] Hud Hudson, "An Essay on Eden," *FPhilos* (2010): 277.

genealogical ancestors, each individually from whom we all descend. These ancestors stretch from our distant past to very recently in our history. Consistent with the genetic and archeological evidence, therefore, it is possible that God could have chosen, or specially created, one of these couples for a special role. . . . such a couple could be among the ancestors of all those alive today.[51]

As we can see, Swamidass is fully aware that, when faced with the question, "Do all humans descend from a single couple?" the immediate and standard answer is "no, of course not." As he puts it, "[F]rom genetic data, the population size of our ancestors at different times is estimated. It appears that population sizes never dipped down to a single couple in the last several hundred thousand years" (which includes the rise of our species). He knows that "the conclusion is robust, based on several independent signals."[52]

But Swamidass also argues that it is an error—an error both "subtle and consequential"—to draw the conclusion that there was no individual couple from whom all humans descend. For the common and sometimes emphatic "no" to be correct, "we must have inserted into the original question a genetic notion of ancestry." But "this insertion of 'genetic' into the question neglects a key scientific fact: genealogical ancestry is *not* genetic ancestry. Genealogical ancestry traces the reproductive origins of individuals, but genetic ancestry traces the origin of stretches of DNA. A question about 'descent' can be a question about genealogies, and genealogical questions should be answered with genealogical science."[53]

And what does this genealogical science tell us? Perhaps surprisingly, it tells us that we—and by "we" is meant all living human persons as well as those alive in the past (including at the time that Paul wrote Romans)—could all share a single ancestral couple. The genealogical answer to the question, "Could all humans descend from a single couple?" is "a definitive yes."[54] What this science tells us is that such ancestors actually appear to be numerous, they are recent, and they are robust (if also unobservable). They are numerous; it appears that we share not one but many universal ancestors in common. They—at least some of them—are relatively recent. Indeed, some appear to have lived only a few thousand years ago. And although we cannot observe them directly, we expect they will robustly arise under several different scenarios.[55]

This raises the possibility that there could be a historical Adam and Eve—and a historical "fall" that brought death for humans—without any rejection of the genetic (and archeological) evidence for the large initial population the-

---

[51] S. Joshua Swamidass, "The Overlooked Science of Genealogical Ancestry," *Perspectives on Science and the Christian Faith* 70/1 (2018): 1.
[52] Swamidass, "Overlooked," 2.
[53] Swamidass, "Overlooked," 2.
[54] Swamidass, "Overlooked," 2.
[55] Thanks to Swamidass for discussion at this point.

sis and the common ancestry thesis. On this proposal, one could believe in the standard evolutionary history as it is commonly told. Life develops, that is, through the common means of descent with modification, and this includes the emergence of hominins and their primate cousins. But then, at the appropriate moment, God either selects a preexisting couple (thus perhaps intersecting with the "refurbishment proposal" but now with more scientific sophistication and plausibility) or creates one *de novo*—first the male from "the dust of the ground" and then the female from the male. This couple is in the image of God, and their lives are decisive for those who follow. They are, in the relevant sense, the first real humans. They are, then, at the "headwaters" of the human race. As Swamidass argues, nothing in this proposal forces one to reject either the common ancestry thesis or the large initial population thesis. As he puts it, "Nothing in genealogical science undermines these two conclusions."[56] Moreover, if Adam and Eve are historical persons, then "the notorious problem of intermarriage . . . [of] his descendants is avoided; their descendants mixed with a larger population of biologically-compatible beings."[57]

So it appears that the "genealogical-Adam proposal" can handle the common ancestry thesis and the large initial population thesis. But what about the red tooth thesis? Well, nothing about the genealogical-Adam proposal denies the evolutionary history prior to human history. The theory is consistent with predation and death before the fall, but it can also hold that *human* death comes as the result of the primal sin. It is worth noting that this move requires a distinctly philosophical and *theological* account of humanity (or at least an understanding that is informed by theology as well as biology and other relevant disciplines). Swamidass notes that there is much confusion associated with the term "humans" in the relevant sciences. He points out that the term is often used by scientists in public conversations for "anatomically modern humans" but is also sometimes used with reference to the entire *Homo* genus. At any rate, there is no consensus among scientists on the proper referent and usage of the term. There is, however, a need for a more philosophically precise and theologically informed use of the term. Independently, Kenneth Kemp argues that we need just such a distinction between biological, philosophical, and theological senses of humankind. He suggests that we think of "the biological species" as "the population of interbreeding individuals."[58] The philosophical account, meanwhile, is "the rational animal, i.e., a natural kind characterized by the capacity for conceptual thought, judgment, reasoning, and free choice."[59] Kemp further adopts a distinctly Thomistic account: "St. Thomas

[56] Swamidass, "Overlooked," 10.
[57] Swamidass, "Overlooked," 3, 10.
[58] Kenneth Kemp, "Science, Theology, and Monogenesis," *American Catholic Philosophical Quarterly* (2011): 230.
[59] Kemp, "Science," 230.

Aquinas argues that a certain kind of rational body is necessary for rational activity, but is not sufficient for it. Rational activity requires, in addition to the presence of a rational soul, something that is more than the power of any bodily organ, and that therefore can come into being, in each individual case, through a creative act of God."[60] The theological account is also important, and cannot be reduced to either the biological or even the philosophical. It is "the collection of individuals that have an eternal destiny"; it is those creatures who are made for friendship with God.[61] With or without the distinctly Thomist elements, such distinctions can come to the aid of Swamidass's proposal. As Kemp explains, such a proposal can handle both the genetic evidence and the traditional theological commitments. For it both "distinguishes between true (i.e., intellectual) human beings and their genetically human-like, but nonintellectual, relatives" and "recognizes that the theological doctrine of monogenesis requires only that all human beings have the original couple among their ancestors, not that every ancestral line in each individual's family tree leads back to a single original couple."[62]

V. Taking Stock

So where does this leave us? There seem to be multiple ways to hold to both the assured results of contemporary science *and* traditional Christian doctrine. Despite the overinflated claims of those who say it can't be so, a closer look shows that this simply isn't right. We have no good reason to think that it isn't possible to hold to both. Consider how Todd S. Beall summarizes what he (as a "young-earth creationist") takes to be the crucial theological desiderata: "the best interpretation [of Scripture] is that Adam and Eve are real, historical persons, created uniquely by God as the first human pair and the universal ancestors of the rest of humanity."[63] Perhaps surprisingly, it turns out that there is more than one way to meet these desiderata without rejecting contemporary genetic science and paleoanthropology.[64] There is nothing about the red tooth thesis, the common descent thesis, or the large initial population thesis that is inconsistent with Adam and Eve being real historical individuals. Nor are those theses inconsistent with the belief that Adam and Eve were created uniquely by God. Nor yet are they inconsistent with the notion that they are the universal ancestors of the rest of humanity. Nor, further, are they inconsistent with the view that human death is the result of human sin.

[60] Kemp, "Science," 230.
[61] Kemp, "Science," 230.
[62] Kemp, "Science," 232.
[63] Todd S. Beall, "Adam and Eve (First-Couple View)," in *Dictionary of Christianity and Science*, ed. Paul Copan, Tremper Longman III, Christopher L. Reese, and Michael G. Strauss (Grand Rapids, MI: Zondervan, 2017), 20.
[64] Mainstream contemporary science is, of course, inconsistent with Beall's belief that the universe is only a few thousand years old. But it need not be inconsistent with the theological desiderata outlined by Beall.

But some might shrug and say that possibility comes cheap. They may complain that what I've done here is just so much what-iffery, and they may protest that we should not be content with mere possibility. Here it seems to me that several observations are in order. First, let us revisit the nature of the claims made by those who criticize or reject traditional doctrine. Note the force of the common claims: it isn't *possible* to hold to both consistently. When encountering a claim that it is not possible to hold both some *P* and some *Q* with consistency, all one needs to do to find a defeater to that claim is to show that in fact it *is* possible. One need not show definitively *how* both *P* and *Q* are true; nor does one need to detail the exact nature of the relationship between *P* and *Q*. To defeat the claim that it is *not possible* for both *P* and *Q* to be true, one needs only to show that it *is possible* or even that it has not been shown to be *impossible*. Since the claims here are that it is not possible, this is all that is needed.

Now, to make this less abstract and to bring this home to our issue, let *P* stand for the conjunction of the red tooth thesis, the large initial population thesis, and the common ancestry thesis. Let *Q* stand for the conjunction of traditional Christian beliefs in the historicity of Adam and Eve and their primal sin that impacted us all. It is important to realize that one need not have theological evidence for *P* to conclude that *P* is true. If one has any good evidence for *P*—scientific or otherwise—then one presumably has good reason for belief that *P*. Similarly, if one has good evidence (or, more generally, good epistemic justification or warrant) for belief in *Q*, then belief in *Q* may be warranted.[65] That evidence need not be evidence drawn from the natural sciences. Lack of *scientific* evidence for *Q* does not entail that there is lack of evidence for *Q* or lack of reason for belief that *Q*. Nor is lack of scientific evidence for *Q* somehow to be counted as scientific evidence *against* *Q* (unless, of course, we have reason to expect scientific evidence for *Q*). Unless it is not possible to hold to both *P* and *Q*, evidence for *P* does not so much as count against *Q*. And, as we have seen, there is no good reason to think that it is not possible to hold to both *P* and *Q*.

Now consider the Christian who has reason to think that *P* is true: she knows that the evidence from astronomy and physics shows that our universe is very old; she knows that the evidence from geology shows that our earth is also very old (although, at about 4.5 billion years old, still something of a young whipper-snapper in comparison to the universe's 13.7 or so billion years!); she knows that the evidence from paleoanthropology and genetics shows that we share common ancestry and must have developed species-wise with a large

[65] On some epistemological accounts, one might have warrant for belief without "evidence." See, e.g., Alvin Plantinga, *Warrant: The Current Debate* (Oxford: Oxford University Press, 1993); and Plantinga, *Warrant and Proper Function* (Oxford: Oxford University Press, 1993).

group of ancestors; and she knows that the evidence from biology shows that this development happened, at least partly, via a combination of natural selection and random genetic mutations. Maybe our Christian has done advanced study in these fields and is an accomplished scientist in some one (or more) of these disciplines. Or maybe she is someone who knows enough to know what the specialists say and why they say it, who does not find herself with good reason to disagree with them, and who thinks that the intellectual virtues should incline her to accept their claims. In other words, she concludes that she has grounds for belief that P. But she also takes it that she has good grounds for belief that Q. What is she to do? If P and Q are either contrary or contradictory, then she has a real problem. But if they are not either contrary or contradictory, then it is possible that both are true and thus it should be possible to believe in both. As we have seen, it *is* possible that both are true; it is possible to believe in both consistently. Indeed, there are multiple scenarios according to which it is possible that both are true.

Suppose someone points out that it does not appear that there is any *scientific* evidence for the specifics of either the refurbishment proposal, the genealogical-Adam proposal, or the hyper-Adam proposal.[66] Nor does it appear that there is any *theological* evidence in their favor. Fair enough, but so what? This lack of support for any of these proposals does not count against either P or Q. Lack of scientific evidence in favor of, say, the hyper-Adam proposal does not count as scientific evidence against belief in a historical Adam. For that matter, lack of scientific evidence in favor of the hyper-Adam proposal does not even count as evidence against the hyper-Adam proposal, and we could only be tempted to think that it does if we are either deeply confused or under the spell of scientism. Similarly, lack of theological or exegetical support for, say, the genealogical-Adam proposal does not count as an argument against either that proposal or mainstream contemporary science. Lack of evidence for these proposals is just that—lack of evidence in their favor. Such lack of evidence counts as a salutary caution about being too enthusiastic or dogmatic in support of any of these proposals. But it does nothing to undercut grounds for belief in the deliverances of modern science or traditional Christian doctrine.

Second, it might be helpful to recognize that something similar seems to happen when scientists find reasons to hold to some proposition R that seems to be demanded by scientific evidence and some other proposition S that also seems to be called for by scientific evidence but that seems to be of questionable consistency with R. If we know that R and S are mutually exclusive (e.g., the "Einsteinian" and "Heisenberg/Copenhagen" interpretations of quantum

---

[66] Actually, such an objector would be mistaken, as there in fact is scientific evidence that renders the genealogical-Adam proposal plausible. But for the sake of discussion, let us grant the point.

theory), then we know that it is not possible that both are true. But rather than assuming this, I suggest that first we try to sort matters out—that we look for the possibility that both are true. For instance, consider what Darrell Falk does when discussing the evolution of old world and new world monkeys. After noting the proliferation and diversity of new world monkeys (currently 124 species), he compares them with old world monkeys (which tend to have narrower snouts, nostrils that face down rather than up, and very little in the way of tails rather than the long prehensile tails common in South America).[67] He notes that fossils found from about 35 million years ago show close relationships between monkeys of the old and new worlds and lead us to the conclusion that they stem from the same ancestral species. This raises a question: how, then, did they get separated? The easy answer would seem to be that the continents of Africa and South America were formerly contiguous and that the separation of the continents (which had to do with tectonic plate shifts and continental realignment) resulted in the changes that we now see in the various species of monkeys. Alas, this explanation is too easy and will not work. It will not work because the continental shift took place about 100 million years ago, and the strikingly close similarities in the fossil record are about 60–70 million years later than that. So how did they get separated? How did these monkeys get from Africa to South America? Falk tells us that "there is almost unanimous consensus" that something close to the following happened: "a small number (perhaps even a single pregnant female) was trapped on a huge tropical tree as it floated down river (possibly in a massive flood) and then, having been transported in an ocean current, the tree with its clinging cargo" made it to South America.[68] We might call this the "Pregnant Hitch-hiking Monkey Thesis." Note that Falk presents no scientific evidence—morphological, genetic, or otherwise—for the Pregnant Hitch-hiking Monkey Thesis; he gives us no evidence that this actually happened. I suspect that he fails to offer evidence because there is no such evidence for the Pregnant Hitch-hiking Monkey Thesis. Nor is it even easy to see how such evidence could be available. Sans evidence, Falk's postulation is also liable to the charge of what-iffery. To be clear, I am not saying that his claim is in fact false. It surely seems possible, and may indeed be the most plausible suggestion. It looks to me like a possible way of reconciling the belief that these monkeys share common ancestry with the belief that the continents separated tens of millions of years before the changes emerged. So far as I can see, it is no worse for being the postulate of a possibility. But so far as I can see, that is all that it is. Michael Ruse makes a similar move. As a response to problems with evolution, he raises the possibility of a multiverse

---

[67] Darrell Falk, "Human Origins: The Evolutionary Story," in *Evolution and the Fall*, 18.
[68] Falk, "Human Origins," 18–19.

as a way out of the alleged dilemma. He does so knowing that a multiverse is only a possibility (and this awareness distinguishes his use of it from that of Falk). But note carefully what he says: "I am not myself saying that multiverses do exist, but simply that serious scientists think these a possibility *and so it is legitimate to make use of them.*"[69]

We might wonder why Falk and Ruse would make such moves. Why do they appeal to mere possibilities to save their theories? Is not this just a bunch of speculative what-iffery tacked on to interesting scientific findings in order to make some pet theory workable or perhaps even a stubborn, last-ditch effort to salvage a flawed theory? Probably not, or at least not obviously. More charitably, I think that these appeals to possibility most likely are made because the scholars who make such appeals feel evidential pressure from *both* sides. In other words, they feel the strength of the arguments for both R and S, and they think that it would be a mistake to let the evidence for R force them to abandon S (or vice versa) unless it could be shown that the propositions are logically inconsistent. I do not fault them for this; I see no problem with the appeals to possibility per se—at least so long as it is admitted that these are mere possibilities rather than presented as if they are part and parcel of the science.

Returning to our topic, the issues are similar here. For Christians who feel the weight of the scientific evidence for, say, the large initial population thesis and the common ancestry thesis, and who *also* feel the strength of the theological case for traditional Christian doctrine, it is not inappropriate to show how affirmation of both might be possible. It is important to make clear where these are only possibilities, but it may also be important to demonstrate these possibilities in the face of the common and forceful objections.

VI. Conclusion

To this point I have argued that it is possible to hold to traditional Christian belief without being forced to reject contemporary science. This is a modest project, but it may be an important conclusion: those Christians who respect contemporary science and who also find compelling the theological reasons to retain traditional doctrine do not need to reject the one to retain the other. I have tried to show the possibility of coherence. I have argued that such Christians need not reject modern science in order to find the possibility of such coherence. If it were not possible that both traditional doctrine and contemporary science are true, then there would be a real problem with respect to belief in both science and traditional doctrine. But there is no such contradiction—or, more modestly, no such contradiction has been demonstrated by those who claim it. Surely modesty is appropriate. Theological questions and concerns

---

[69] Ruse, "Human Evolution," 170–171, emphasis mine.

are likely to be raised about the various proposals we have considered, and those will deserve discussion and analysis. Perhaps other and better proposals will emerge. And, at any rate, there is much that we do not know. Nonetheless, however, it is possible to believe consistently in both traditional Christian doctrine and contemporary science—at least we have no reason to think that it is impossible.

As Ruse observes, the science on human origins is "fast-moving."[70] In light of this, it would seem risky to base the defense of traditional Christian belief on some particular scientific theory. In other words, a theological anthropology and hamartiology built on, for example, an "Adam of the gaps" would be a risky venture. But in light of this, it also seems very hasty to reject traditional doctrine on the basis of appeals to "science"—especially when arguments based on "science" can be shown to be faulty as well as shot through with questionable metaphysical assumptions (whether or not those assumptions are recognized). I have shown that in fact there are *multiple* ways to consistently maintain belief in the venerable doctrine while also respecting contemporary science. For those convinced that this doctrine is true and important, contemporary science gives us no reason not to affirm it.

---

[70] Michael Ruse, *The Philosophy of Human Evolution* (Cambridge: Cambridge University Press, 2012), 62.

Genesis

1	138
1–2	125
1–11	43, 133
1:26	115
1:26–27	105, 115, 359
1:26–28	380
1:31	117, 243
2	119
2–3	43, 83, 113
2:7	40, 320
2:9, 17	125
2:15	115
2:16–17	40, 117
2:17	312, 316, 318
2:18	119
2:20–23	115
2:24	111, 115
2:25	117, 118, 311
2:25–3:21	311
3	40–41, 43, 44n37, 385
3:1	116
3:1–3	113
3:1–7	40
3:4	117, 312
3:5	121
3:5, 22	125
3:6	117
3:7, 10	311
3:7–10	40
3:8	115
3:8–11	117
3:10	118
3:12	40
3:14–15	120
3:15	124
3:16	120
3:16–19	40
3:17	119
3:17–18	162, 316
3:17–19	119
3:19	319, 393n42
4	43, 390
4:1, 17, 25	122
4:1–10	41
4:7	41
4:10	246
4:17	320
4:23–24	41
4:23f.	119
6	41
6:5	25, 41, 101
6:9	41
6:11	41
7:1–8:14	41
9:1–17	41
9:46	43
11	43
11:1	41
11:1–4	41
12	41
12:1–3	41
12:10–20	42
13:10–13	42
14:1–16	42
15:6	42
15:16	45
16:1–15	42
18:16–33	42
18:20	246
19:1–28	42
19:13	246
19:30–38	42
20:1–17	42
26:1–10	42
27:1–28:22	42
29:1–30	42
32:22–32	42

34	42		15:3–24, 28–30	230
37	42		17:7	108
39:9	240		18:1–5	43
45:4	343		18:21	48
45:5	344		18:28	236
50:20	42, 344		19:2	369
			19:4	45
Exodus			20:5	108
1:15–22	43		20:7	369
2:11–15	43		22:17f.	43
3:7–10	246		22:32–33	46
4:22	43, 105, 107, 325		22:32f.	44
4:23	111		24:10f.	43
7:5, 17	73		26:1–2	45
8:22	73		26:40–45	46
14:4, 18	73		26:40f.	44
14:11	45			
17:3	45		*Numbers*	
20:1–17	43		3:10	45
20:1–23:33	44		4:20	45
22:16–24	324		5:1–31	45
23:24, 33	111		5:2–4	230
24:3–8	44		5:12, 19–20, 29	38
30:33, 38	325		6:9–12	230
31:13	45		9:13	325
32:1–4	44		11:1–10, 33–34	45
32:1–10	324		12:9	45
32:8	38, 104		14:2, 26–38	45
32	44n37		14:26–38	45
34:6–7	331		15	248
34:15	108		15:14–16, 29–30	325n255
			15:22–29	44, 248
Leviticus			15:26	248
4	248		15:30–31	45, 249
4:1–35	44		16:1–35	325n255
4:13–14	34		16:20–33	45
4:13–21	44		16:41	45
4:13–35	248		17:12	46
5	248		18:21–22	45
5:14–19	44		19:11–20	230
5:17	249		19:20	325
7:20	325		20:12	45
11:44–45	369		21:6–9	45
13–14	230		25:1–9	45

25:3	324
29:7–39	46
32:10–14	324
32:14	325
32:23	46

Deuteronomy

1:26–46	45
4:15–21	45
4:21–25	45
4:24	46
4:25–31	46
5:1–21	43
5:6	105
5:7–12	239
6:13–18	325
6:14–15	45
7:4	111
7:5, 25–26	45
7:9–26	45
7:17–26	45
8:19–20	45
10:20	111
11:16–17	45
12:1–7	45
13:4	111
13:5	111
13:6	111
13:12–18	45
15:7–11	45
16:19	45
16:21–22	45
17:2–7	45
21:21	45
24:14–15	246
24:16	45, 161, 165, 201
27:15	45
27:19	45
28:15–68	45
28:22	325
28:25–68	236
29:17–28	45
30:20	111
31:16	108, 111

31:16–18	45
32:4	36, 132, 342
32:10	107
32:10–14, 19–20	107

Joshua

7:11	38, 104
22:16	46
22:16–18	325
22:20	47
23:16	325
24:14–15	105
24:17	105
24:19	304

Judges

Book	37
2:10	47
2:11	47
2:11–15	47
2:14	47
2:16	47
3:7, 12	47
3:8	47
3:9, 15	47
3:10	47
3:10–11	47
4:1	47
4:2	47
6:1	47
6:6–7	47
6:8	105
6:34	47
8:10–21	47
8:22–27	47
8:28–32	47
10:1, 12	47
10:2–5	47
10:6	47
10:9	47
10:10	47
11:29	47
12:9–15	47
13:1	47

13:25	47	21:22	49
14:6, 19	47	22:51–52	49
20:16	34		
21:25	47	*2 Kings*	
		Book	37
Ruth		10:29–31	49
4:13–22	74	13:11	49
		14:24	49
1 Samuel		15:9, 18, 24, 28	49
2:12–17	48	16:3	48, 49
3:13	48	17:7–17	49
4:1–10	48	18:3	49
8:3	48	21:2, 20	49
8:6–9	48	21:6	48
10:17–19	48	22:2	49
12:1–5	48n48	23:32, 36–37	49
13:8–15	48	24:8–9, 19	49
15:17–23	48	25:21	49
24:16–22	48		
26:21–25	48	*1 Chronicles*	
31:1–13	48	10:13	48
		18:14	48
2 Samuel		19:2	48
5:21	55	28:9	50
7:4–17	48	28:9–10	48
8:15	48		
9:1–13	48	*2 Chronicles*	
11–12	278	6:36–46	50n52
11:2–25	48	7:19–22	50n52
12:13	48	12:14	50n52
13:1–18:33	48	22:4	49
		24:19	49
1 Kings		28:11–13	325
Book	37	29:2	49
2:2–3	48	33:2	49
3:3	48	34:2	49
8:46	101	36:5, 9, 12	49
11:7–8	48		
11:31–33	48	*Ezra*	
12:19	36	3:2–7	50
12:28–31	49	9:6–7, 13	50
14:23–24	49	10:2	50
15:30	49		
16:7, 26	49	*Nehemiah*	
		9:6–15	50
		9:16–17	50

9:17	50
9:26	51
9:29	51
9:32	51
9:33	51
13:18	325

Job

1:1	51
1:6–12	51
1:13–19	51
2:1–6	51
2:7	51
2:9	51
2:11	51
3:1–26	52
6:4	52
7:21	52
8:20	52
9:17–23	52
9:20	52
10:1–22	52
11:4	52
11:6, 11, 13–20	52
12:1–25	52
12:4	52
13:18	52
14:1–12	52
15:2–35	52
16:7–22	52
18:1–21	52
19:6–29	52
20:2–29	52
21:2–34	52
22:2–30	52
23:10–11	52
23:15–16	52
24:1–25	52
27:2–12	52
27:13–23	52
29:5–25	52
30:19–31	52
31:1–40	52
32:1	52
33:9	52

34:5	52
34:10–30	52
36:5–37:23	52
37:23	52
38:1	52
38:1–40:2	51, 52
38:4–7	52
38:28–29	52
40:6	52
40:6–41:34	51, 52
42:7	324
42:7–8	51
42:8	52
42:10–17	52

Psalms

1:1	53
1:2	53
1:3	53
1:5–6	53
2:12	53
5:4–6	243
5:9	53
6:2, 9	54
7:1–17	53
7:16	54
9:15–16	54
10:1–10	53
10:2–4	53
12:1–2	54
12:2	53
12:3–4	53
14:1	54, 234
14:3	54
15:3–5	54
16:2	231
16:4	54
19:12–13	53
21:8–12	54
24:4	231
25:11–22	54
26:4–5, 9–10	53
28:3	53
32	54
32:1–2	54

32:1–5	54	69:5	54
32:2	55	69:22	54
32:3–4	55	69:24	54
32:8	55	71:4	53
32:9	55	73	270
32:11	55	73:3–12	270
33:6	137	73:6–9	53
34:21	54	73:18–20	54
36:2–4	53	74:22	54
37:12–15	54	75:2	54
37:15	54	78:17–66	54
38	232	78:32	331
38:1–22	54	78:37	331
38:3, 5	229	78:38	331
38:10	229, 232	78:58	54
38:11	232	79:8–13	54
39:8	54	81:12	54
40:11–17	54	82:2–3	53
41:4	54	85:1–13	54
42:9	53	86:11–13	54
50:18	53	88:7, 16	54
51	48, 54, 55–56	90:7–8	54
51:1–19	56–57	91:8	54
51:4	57, 240	92:6	54
51:5	57	93	103
51:7	57	93:1–2	103
51:9	57	94	270
51:10	57	94:2–7	53
51:13–19	57	94:3–6	270
52:1	53	94:8	54
52:1–4	53	94:20–21	53
53:1	54, 101	94:23	54
53:1–3	54	95:11	54
54:5	54	96:5	54
55:20–21	53	96:10–13	103
55:23	54	97:7	54
56:6–7	53	99	103
57:6	53	99:1–5	103
58:2	53	100:5	331
58:3	54	101:5	53
59:6–7	53	103:2–22	54
60:1–3	54	103:13	105, 325
64:1–6	53	103:14	393n42
64:7–9	54	104:21	318
68:1–39	54	104:35	54

106:1	331
106:19–23, 36–39	54
106:41	54
107:1	331
107:17	54
107:28	54
109:2–5	53
110:5–7	54
115:4–8	54
118:1	331
119:21, 70	53
119:118, 155	54
124:8	54
130:3–4, 8	54
135:15–18	54
140:2–3	53
140:5	53
145:8	327
146:7–9	270
146:9	54
147:6	54
147:9	318

Proverbs

1:1–7	58, 237
1:7	58, 237
1:17–19	58
1:18	58, 237
1:19	58
2:6–15	58, 237
2:16–19, 22	58
3:3–10, 13–35	58, 237
3:11–12	58
3:33	59
4:5–18	58, 237
4:19	58
5:22	58, 237
6:6	274
6:15	58
6:16–19	58, 59
7:1–4	58, 237
7:22–27	58
8:10–21	58, 237
8:13	59
8:36	58, 237

9:1–18	58
9:10	58, 237
9:18	58
10:1–32	58
10:23	234
10:24	58, 237
11:5–6, 29	58, 237
11:19, 23	58
12:1	58
12:15	234
12:22	59
13:9	58
13:13	58, 237
14:7, 16	234
14:24	58
14:32	58, 237
15:3	59
15:5	58, 234
15:10	58
15:29	58
16:2	59
17:15	59
18:2	234
20:23	59
20:30	58
21:2–3	59
24:20	58
28:10	58, 237
29:5–6	58, 237

Ecclesiastes

1:14, 17	59
1:16–18	59
2:1–11	59
2:11	59
2:12–26	59
3:16	59
4:1	59
5:1–3	59
5:8–9	59
7:7	59
7:29	59
8:11	59
8:13	59
9:1–2	59

9:3	60
12:1	60
12:13–14	60

Song of Solomon

5:1	275
5:2	275
5:7	55

Isaiah

1:2	36, 64
1:2, 4–5	229
1:2–31	61–64
1:3	64
1:4	64, 229
1:5–6	64, 229
1:7–8	64
1:9–10	64
1:13	64
1:15	64
1:16	64
1:17	64
1:17, 23	64
1:18	64
1:18–20	113
1:19–20, 27–28	64
1:21	68
1:21–23	64, 108, 363
1:22, 25–26	65
2:7	65
2:8	67
2:11	66
2:11–12, 17	65
2:18–22	67
3:9	65
3:13–15	65
3:16–17	65
5:1	68
5:8	65
5:8–30	68, 108, 363
5:11	65
5:15, 21	65
5:18, 20	65
5:22	65
5:23	65

5:25	70
6:1–3	68
9:17–18	66
9:19	70
9:20	66
10:5–19	65, 72, 325, 325n256
10:10–11	67
13:2–22	65
14:3–23	65
14:11	66
14:12	138
14:12–19	138
14:24–27	65, 72
14:28–32	65, 72
15:1–16:13	72
15:1–16:14	65
18:1–7	65
19:1–15	65, 72
19:19–25	73
20:1–6	65, 72
24:1–23	65, 70
24:4–6	66
29:13	67
30:1	66
30:9–10	67
30:27	70
30:30	70
34:2	65, 70
40:3	74
41:21–29	67
42:6	73
42:8	67
43:6	107
44:9–20	67
45:7	129, 131n94, 347
46:1–12	67
46:12	66
47:1–15	65
48:8	68
49:6	73
51:17	70, 325
52:13, 15	71
52:13–53:12	74, 100
52:14	71
53	55n68

53:3	71	5:26–28	66
53:4–6	71	6:7	102
53:6	66	6:13	66
54:5	74	6:13–14	67
55:1	71	6:20	68
55:6–7	71	7:5	66
57:1–13	67	7:8–10	66
57:17	70	7:20	70
58:1–5	68	7:24–26	66
58:8	68	7:30	67
59:1–15	66	7:31	66
59:2	66	8:5	66
59:2–7	35–36	8:6	66
62:1–5	109	8:10	66
63:1–2	325	8:11	67
63:1–6	325	8:19	67
64:6	66	9:2–8	66
66:13	68	9:6	66
		9:13–14	67
Jeremiah		10:1–9	67
1:16	67	11:8	66
2:2	68, 108	11:10	67
2:3	66	13:23	66, 102
2:8	67	13:26	66
2:20	68, 69	14:4	66
2:20–24	363	16:18	67
2:22	66	17:1–9	67
2:23–24	67, 108	17:9	23, 66, 102, 230, 237,
2:24–25	102		303
2:28	67	17:9–10	159
2:34	65	18:13	68, 108
2:35	66	18:15	67
2:36	66	19:4–5	66, 67
3:1	69	21:12	324
3:1–2	108	21:12–14	66
3:1–6, 20	363	22:1–17	66
3:2	69	22:3	324
3:6	69	22:9	67
3:12–19	107	23:11	67
3:14	68	23:14	67
3:20	69	23:23–26	67
3:25	66	23:29–30	67
4:2	65, 73	25:4–7	67
5:1	66	25:37–38	325
5:7	67	27:9–10, 17–18	67

30:23–24	70
31:29–30	161, 165
31:30a	201
31:31, 33–34	72
32:30	70
32:35	48
33:5	70
34:13	105
36:7	70
44:6	70
46:1–28	65, 72
47:1–7	65, 72
48:1–47	65, 72
48:31	72
49:1–5	65, 72
49:7–22	65, 72
50:1–51:64	65
50:13	70, 325
51:17–18	67

Lamentations

1:1–2, 4	60
1:5, 13–14	60
1:8–9, 17–18, 20	60
2:1–6, 22	60
2:1–8	60
3:1–16	60
3:1, 43	60
3:22–23	60
3:26, 55–58	60
3:31–33	60
3:32	60
4:4	60
4:10	60
4:11	60
4:13	60
4:16	325
5:1–15	60
5:16	60
5:22	60

Ezekiel

2:4, 7	66
3:27	68
5:10	66

6:9	108
6:11–14	325
10:1–22	68
11:19–20	72
12:1–2, 9	68
14:1–11	67
14:10–11	72
16	331
16:15	69
16:15–18, 20–21	108
16:15–21	326
16:16–18	69
16:16–34	363
16:20–21	69
16:30	108
16:30–31	108
16:30–34	69
16:31, 33	109
16:33	326
16:38	326
16:39–41	326
16:59	38
16:59–63	72
16:60	109, 331
16:62–63	331
17:12	68
17:15–19	38
18:4	201
18:6–9	201
18:10–13	201
18:18	201
18:19	202
18:20	157, 161, 165, 202
18:23	70
21:1–24	325
22:1–29	324
22:6–15	66
23:1–49	326
24:13	325
25:1–7	65, 72
25:8–11	65, 72
25:12–14	65, 72
25:14, 17	325
25:15–17	65, 72
28	138

28:12	138, 139	3:6	129, 131n94, 347
28:15	138	5:11–13, 18, 24	66
28:16	139	5:21–23	68
28:17	139	5:24	68
28:18	139	6:12	66
29:1–16	65, 72	8:1–14	70
29:6	73		
33:10	70	*Obadiah*	
33:11	70, 258	1–9	65
34:1–10	67		
36:25–31	72	*Jonah*	
36:25–33	72	3:4	65, 72
37:1–14	72		
37:14	72	*Micah*	
37:23	72	1:2–16	70
37:26	72	1:5–6	67
37:27	72	1:7	67, 108, 363
37:28	72	1:12	70
43:8–9	74	2:1–13	66
44:6	68	2:2	55
44:7	38	3:1–3, 9	66
44:26–27	230	3:3	66
		3:8	67
Daniel		6:6–7	68
9:7–8	66	6:8	68
9:11	104	6:11–12	66
Hosea		*Nahum*	
4:1–2	66	1:2–3:19	65, 72
6:7	38	3:1	66
8:1	38, 104		
11:1	107	*Habakkuk*	
11:3–4, 8–11	107	1:5–11	325
		1:13	132, 342
Joel		2:15–16	66
2:28	73		
3:13	325	*Zephaniah*	
		1:2	70
Amos		2:1–2	70
1:11–12	65, 72	2:8	65, 72
1:13–15	65, 72	3:8	70
2:1–3	65, 72	3:9	73
2:6–8	66		
2:7	66	*Zechariah*	
3:2	236	7:8–11	66

7:11–12	66
8:16–17	66
10:3	70
13:1	71

Malachi

2:13–17	68, 108, 363
2:14	66
3:1	74
3:5–6	66
4:1	66

Matthew

1:5	325n255
1:20	75
1:21	75
1:23	123
2:16–18	75
3:2	75
3:3	74
3:6	74
3:7	74, 327
3:10	75
3:12	75
4:1	78
4:17	75
5:8	231
5:17	75
5:21–22	75
5:22, 30	76
5:27–28	75
5:48	76, 370
6:1–4	76
6:7–18	76
6:9	105
6:13	76
6:21	76
6:22–23	76
7:12	77
9:1–10:1	77
9:2	78
9:4–7	78
9:12–13	229
9:13	78
10:21	36
10:22	79
10:38–39	79
11:21–24	80
12:31–32	255, 257, 258
12:34	77
12:39	79
13:14–15	77
13:24–30	80
13:37–42	80
13:47–50	80
15:1–2, 7	76
15:8–9	76
15:11–20	76
15:19	26
15:29–31	77
16:4	79
16:16	78
16:17–20	79
16:21	79
16:23	79
16:24–25	79
17:14–20	77
18:8–9	79
18:15–22	77
19:16–30	77
19:26	274
22:2	110
22:34–40	77
22:37, 39	81
23:13–36	81
23:23	76
23:25	76
23:27–28	76
23:37	81
24:36–37	80
24:44	80
24:51	80
25:30	80
25:31	80
25:32–46	81
26:28	78
28:16–20	78

Mark

1:4	75
1:14–15	75
2:5–11	78
2:17	77, 78
2:19–20	110, 363
3:5	327
3:28–29	78, 255, 257, 258
7:14–23	76
8:31–38	79
9:42–48	79
10:17–31	76
12:28–34	77
12:30	239
12:30–31	240
12:31	245
13:12	36
13:32	80

Luke

1:67	74
1:76–77	74
3:7	327
4:1	78
5:8	360
5:31–32	78
5:32	77
6:24–28	81
7:47–50	78
9:22–27	79
10:13–15	81
11:44	76
11:46–52	81
12:10	255, 257, 258
12:47–48	246
13:3	246
13:5	81
13:22–30	79
15:11	106
15:11–32	106, 360
15:32	360
16:19–31	79
17:22–37	80
23:4, 22	78

John

1:3	137
1:3–9	97
1:4	97, 98
1:9	97, 130, 359
1:12	297
1:13	362
1:14	328
1:29	100, 336
2:1–11	110
3:3	107, 360, 361
3:4, 9	361
3:7	362
3:16	327
3:16–17	98, 101
3:18	99
3:18, 36	97
3:19–21	97
3:27–30	109, 363
3:36	99, 327
5:14	100
7:7	100
8:12	97
8:23	97
8:34	300
8:34–35	99
8:44	97, 137
9:1–3	302
9:1–12	229
9:4–5	97
9:26, 39	97
9:39, 41	302
9:41	99
10:3–4, 14	98
11:9–10	97
12:31	97
12:35–36, 46	97
12:40	23
12:43	272
13:1	98
14:17	97
14:17–19, 30	97
15:9	98
15:12–13	98

15:18	99
15:19	97, 98
15:23	99
15:24–16:15	81
16:13	97
16:20, 33	97
17:6–9, 25	97
17:23	98, 329
17:24	99, 101, 329
17:26	99, 329, 330
18:36	97
19:4, 6	100
19:11	245, 246, 308

Acts
1:5	81
1:6–11	81
2:1	81
2:2–4	81
2:5–11	81
2:12–13	81
2:23	82, 344, 351
2:24	344
2:38	82, 361
3:13–15	344
3:14–15	82
3:19	82
4:10	344
4:10–11	82
4:12	82
4:27–28	344
4:32–5:11	82
5:3	82
5:30	82, 344
5:31	82
6:8–7:1	82
7:2–50	82
7:51	82
7:52	82
8:14–25	83
8:22	82
10:39–40	82, 344
10:43	82
13:30	344
13:38	82
14:17	241

15:9	83
15:20, 29	82
19:8	102
21:25	82
28:23, 31	102

Romans
1	84, 85, 232
1:5	87
1:14–15	87
1:16	324, 333
1:17	324, 333
1:18	39, 89, 324, 333
1:18–21	303
1:18–23	84
1:19–20	87
1:21	85, 89, 305
1:23	232, 272
1:24, 26, 28	86
1:25	232
1:26–32	86, 91
1:29	39
1:29–31	39
2	241
2:5	89, 305
2:6	159
2:8	86
2:15	241
3	22
3:1, 9	87
3:5, 26	39
3:9	88
3:10	33, 266
3:10–12	88
3:10–18	160, 328
3:22–23	88, 309
3:23	33, 87, 181, 200, 242, 246, 266
3:25	328, 332
4:15	177
5	173, 174, 181, 196, 203, 289
5:8	333
5:9	333
5:12	83, 168, 172, 177, 180, 181, 182, 316, 385

5:12d	179	8:7	240
5:12–21	41, 84, 91, 149–150, 162, 164, 173, 176, 177, 179, 182, 184, 201, 202, 319	8:9	107, 366
		8:11	107, 328, 366
		8:12–17	360
5:13–14	177	8:14–17	107
5:14	177	8:15	107
5:15	178	8:15–16	90
5:15a, 16a	178	8:15, 23	107
5:15–17	178	8:17	90
5:16b	178	8:19–22	316
5:17	83	8:20	89, 162
5:17a	178	8:38–39	328
5:17b	178	8:39	328
5:18	83, 84, 177, 181	9:4	107
5:18–19	180, 182	9:14	39
5:18ff.	178	9:22	131
5:19	83	11	234
5:20	46, 91, 124	11:36	137
5:21	91, 365	13:13	86, 91
6	367	16:20	137
6:2	367		
6:17	91, 366	*1 Corinthians*	
6:18	91	3:12–15	251
6:23	33, 46, 90, 201, 246, 312, 315, 321, 323, 365	4:7	140
		5:11	89
7	88, 367	6:1	39
7:7–13	366	6:9–10	89, 91
7:11	365	6:9–11	86
7:14	366	6:12	277
7:14–24	279	6:18	245
7:14–25	212, 365, 366, 367, 368, 369n110	10:12–13	186
		15:12–28, 50–58	91
7:15	88	15:21–22	149, 201, 319
7:17, 20	366	15:55–57	322
7:18	88	15:57	382
7:18, 25	212		
7:19	88	*2 Corinthians*	
7:23	89, 366	5:4	181
7:24	89	5:11–21	360
8	367	7:1	244
8:1	89, 91, 311	11:2–3	90
8:2	367	11:3	137
8:1–4	90		
8:5	367	*Galatians*	
8:5–9	328, 367	4:4	123
8:6	366		

4:5	107	*Colossians*		
5:5	363	1:12–13	366	
5:16	368	1:15–20	316	
5:16–25	368	1:16	137	
5:17	367	2:13	90	
5:17–21	86, 91	2:15	123	
5:19–21	89, 160, 368	3:5	89	
5:20–21	277	3:5–6	327	
5:21	368	3:5–8	277	
5:22–23	368	3:10	362	
5:24	368			
6:1	367	*1 Thessalonians*		
6:3	303	2:10	366	
6:15	362	4:3	368	
		4:7	369	
Ephesians		5:23	369	
1:5	107			
2:1	89, 90, 304, 327	*1 Timothy*		
2:1–3	83, 91	2:14	104	
2:1–10	362	2:15	123	
2:3	89, 211, 217, 327, 333	3:6	139	
2:4	333	6:10	275, 276	
2:19	361			
3:9	137	*2 Timothy*		
4:24	362	1:12	366	
4:26	276	4:6–8	366	
5:3–6	87, 91			
5:5	89	*Titus*		
5:6	89	2:11	359	
5:14	90	2:13	369	
5:25	363	2:14	369	
5:25–27	74, 110, 364	3:5	362	
5:25–32	90	3:7	361	
6:12	270			
		Hebrews		
Philippians		1:1–12	93	
1:23	94	2:9	92, 93	
2:5–11	272	2:11	369	
2:6, 8	139	2:11–13	93	
3:10	362	2:14	92, 226	
3:12	181	2:14–15	91	
3:12–14	366	2:16	226	
3:19	277	2:17	92	
4:10	181n159	3:7–8, 13–14	92	
4:12–13	366	3:8	93	

3:9	93	1:14–15	94
3:10	93	1:17	94
3:11	93	1:20–21	95
3:12	92, 93	1:22–25	95
3:13	23	1:27	95
4:3	93	2:7	95
4:11	94	2:9	95
4:15	92, 134, 208, 209	2:10	95
5:1–10	92	3:2	94
5:11	93	3:6, 8–10a	95
6:1–8	93	3:10b	95
6:4–6	254	4:1–3	95
6:6	93	4:4	95
6:12	93	4:7	95
6:20–8:13	92	4:7–10	95
7:24	92	4:8	231
7:26	92	5:1–6	95
7:27	92	5:15	96
8:12	93	5:16	96
9:11–28	92	5:19–20	96
9:14	93		
9:22	92	*1 Peter*	
10:4	92	1:2	96
10:10, 14	93	1:14–16	369
10:12–14	92	1:15–16	96
10:16–17	93	2:1	96
10:19–25	92	2:9	96
10:26–27	93	2:11	96
10:26–31	254	2:21	97
10:29	93	2:24	96
10:31	93	3:9–10	96
11:25	92	3:11	96
12:1–2	244	3:18	96, 362
12:4	94	4:2	96
12:14	369	4:3	89
12:23	93	4:3–5	96
12:24	92	4:8	97
12:25	93	5:8	96, 134
12:29	46, 93, 369, 378		
13:8–12	92	*2 Peter*	
13:12	94	2:1–19	96
		2:4	139
James		2:19	96
1:2–4	94	2:20	96
1:13	94, 138	2:21–22	96
1:13–15	123	3:9	257

1 John

Book	249
1:2–3	98
1:3	100
1:3, 7	100
1:5	97, 101, 128, 132, 244, 328, 329, 342, 343
1:6	97
1:6–7	97
1:7	100, 101
1:8	101, 303
1:9	101, 373
2:1	100, 101
2:2	98, 100, 332
2:4, 21–22, 27	97
2:8–9	97
2:9	101
2:9–11	99
2:11	23
2:11–14	101
2:15–17	100
2:16	97
2:29	101
3:1	100
3:2	97
3:4	38, 104, 240, 248, 359
3:5	100
3:6	101
3:8	101
3:11, 23	101
3:12	97
3:13–14	99
3:14–15	99
3:16	328
4:2–6	97
4:8, 16	98, 101, 327, 329
4:9–10	328
4:10	100, 101, 328
4:16	343
4:20–21	99

5:10	97
5:16	254
5:16–17	101, 257
5:17	254

Jude

4	96

Revelation

1:5	100
2:1, 4	270
2:12, 14–15	270
2:18, 20	270
3:1	270
3:14–22	270
6:16	327, 336
9:20–21	99
12:7	139
12:7–17	99
12:8–9	139
14:8	100
14:10	327
14:17–20	99
16:9–11	99
16:19	327
17:1–5	110
17:1–18	100
18:1–10	100
19:1–10	100
19:7–8	110
19:15	327
19:20	99
20:11–15	99
21:2, 9	110
21:4	322
21:8	89
21:23–25	100
22:15	89
22:17	110, 327

Abimelech, 42
Abraham, 42, 50, 79, 82, 226
Abraham, William J., 28, 28n33
Abram, 41–42
Acts of the Apostles, description of sin in, 81–83
Adam, 40, 41, 83–84, 122, 136–137, 158n51, 175–176, 190–191, 280; Christian belief in the "historical Adam" and challenges concerning, 383–385, 386n16, 387–388, 396–397, 398; common ancestry with other primates, 320; contrasts between Adam and Christ, 178; created with a *natura integra* (morally upright nature), 159; and Eve as the first federal representatives ("chieftains") of the initial human population, 320, 390; impact of his sin on humanity as a whole, 25n20, 223; initial innocence/ righteousness of, 114–115, 159; original state of, 385; as *posse peccare* (able to sin) and *posse non peccare* (not able to sin), 114, 135–136, 159, 289; progeny of, 158, 165–166, 167, 175, 183, 192–194; questions regarding the historicity of, 153, 154, 155, 182; relationship with the earth, 119–120. *See also* Augustine, and the battle with Pelagianism; federalism; human origins; original sin, doctrine of; realism; sin, origin of
Adams, Marilyn McCord, 145, 249n195
Adams, Robert M., 128, 249n196
agnosticism, 213, 214
Ahaz, 49
Alexander, Denis, 306n186, 320n243, 390
Alexander, Michelle, 267n283
Alexander of Hales, 358n74

al-Ghazali, 189, 347
Alicke, M. D., 302n164
Ambrose, 222, 365; view of sin as a "corrupting force," 156–157
Ambrosiaster, 179, 222
Ammonites, 65, 72
Ananias, 82
Anatolios, Khaled, 222n60
Anderson, Gary A., 152
Anderson, James N., 256n233
angelic sin, origin of, 136–137; biblical witness concerning, 137–139; conclusions concerning, 147–148; fallen angels as God's creatures, 136, 136n110, 147; insights from the Christian tradition concerning, 139–147. *See also* Satan, fall of
Anglican Thirty-Nine Articles (1563), 149, 202
Anglicans, theological tradition of concerning sin, 238
animals, 386–387; animal predation/death before the fall, 312–313, 318–319; animal theodicy, 316–317; as carnivores, 318–319; the evolution of old and new world monkeys (the "Pregnant Hitch-hiking Monkey Thesis"), 401; as "souls" or "persons," 316
Annet, Peter, 348
Ansberry, Christopher, 60, 269–270
Anselm of Canterbury, 31–32, 305n178; on the doctrine of original sin, 170–171, 175; on fallen angels and the devil, 140–142, 144; on the "free will defense" with respect to angelic evil, 142
anthropology, 29; theological anthropology, 393n42
anxiety, 136n115

Aquinas, Thomas, 134, 190, 234, 245–246, 316–317, 319, 346–347, 370, 386n19, 398; on animal predation before the fall, 312–313; on the distinction between "invincible ignorance" and "vincible ignorance," 248, 250; on the fall of the devil, 144; on forgetfulness, 250n199; on God and the cause of sin, 129–130, 237–238; on grace, 295; on love, 310; on mortal and venial sins, 250–251, 253; on the order of nature, 341; on prevenient grace, 358; on providence, 352; on the seven deadly sins, 270–275; on vice as contrary to nature, 223

Aristotle, 372; contrast between his portrait of greatness and Jesus's portrait of God the Father, 106, 106n169; distinction between active and passive power, 297

Arminius, Jacob, 135n109, 158, 158n51, 239, 305n178, 357, 377n176; on grace, 298–299

Asherah, 49

Assyria, 65, 72, 73–74

Athanasius, 135n109, 156, 222n59, 60

atonement, 44, 45–46, 202, 249, 331; divine provision of through Christ, 44, 96, 100, 328, 369; doctrine of "limited" or "definite" atonement, 305

Augsburg Confession (1530), 223

Augustine, 30, 106n169, 114n7, 125, 130, 149, 168, 170, 179, 220–223, 220n55, 232, 255, 298, 307, 357–358; on Christian holiness, 369–370, 369n110; on the doctrine of original sin, 166, 262; on the nature of angels, 140, 142; objections to "Augustinian" theology, 290; on sin as contrary to nature, 283; on sin as falsehood, 218. *See also* Augustine, and the battle with Pelagianism

Augustine, and the battle with Pelagianism, 280–300 passim, 287n64; Augustine's position on creation, 289; Augustine's position on grace, 283–284, 285–288, 291; Augustine's position on salvation, 289; Augustine's position on sin, 289; and the basic features of Pelagian theology, 281–283; charges against Augustine for promoting Manichaeism, 285; criticisms of Augustine's extreme positions, 291–292; and the issue of infant baptism, 283, 288–289; and the Pelagian view of sin, 286; and the question of free will, 281–282, 284–285, 287; and the question of grace in the Pelagian system, 282–283; use of Augustine's own arguments against him by the Pelagians, 280–281

Ayal, Shahar, 303n170

Ayala, Francisco J., 386n18

Baal, 49

Babylon, 65, 110

Babylonians, 326

Bac, J. Martin, 256n233

Backus, Irena, 290n79

Baier, Johann Wilhelm, 359; on sanctification, 375

Bailey, Kenneth E., 106n168

Bammel, C. P., 221n56

baptism, 75, 157, 223, 294, 297; infant, 283, 288–289

Barclay, John M. G., 87, 88; on Paul's diagnosis of the human heart as "senseless," 89, 304–305

Barth, Karl, 22, 156, 242, 252n213, 253, 309–310; criticism of "hereditary sin," 156; on God confronting sin through Jesus Christ, 244; on self-diagnosis, 23–24; on sin, 23; on sin as pride, 271, 272, 273–274; on sin as stupidity, 235–236; on sloth as disobedience, 275

Basil of Caesarea, 135n109, 222n59, 365, 386n19

Bauckham, Richard, 97–98, 100

Bauerschmidt, Frederick Christian, 250n201

Bavinck, Herman, 149, 185n170; criticism of realism, 168–169

Beall, Todd S., 398; on the historical Adam and Eve, 398

Beethoven, Ludwig van, 204

Belgic Confession (1561), 132, 202, 384

Bergmann, Michael, 317n234, 355n64

Berkeley, George, 189, 347

Berkouwer, G. C., 125, 126, 199n224; on the truthfulness of God, 131–132

Bettenson, Henry, 129n70, 295n124, 322n250, 323n251, 385n10

Beza, Theodore, 290n79

Bible, the: as the final authority (the "norming norm" [*norma normans*]) in matters of theology, 28–29

Biel, Gabriel, 295–296, 297, 347, 358n74; opposition to his *Pelagiani moderni* theology, 297–298

Bildad, 51

biology, 386n16, 391–392n38, 392, 397, 400; evolutionary biology, 319, 391–392n38, 392n39; sociobiology, 386

Blacketer, Raymond A., 158n51

Blenkinsopp, Joseph, 64n82

blessedness, 54–55, 222, 338

Blocher, Henri, 162, 165, 183, 230n103; on the imputation of sin, 173–176

Block, Daniel I., 109n175

Bloesch, Donald, 228

Boda, Mark J., 30n39, 39–40, 43, 46, 51, 53, 54–55; summary of hamartiology in Psalms, 57; summary of wisdom theme in Proverbs, 58–59

Bonaventure, 114, 295, 358n74; on the divine goodness and sovereignty of God, 129; on the first temptation, 116; on the goodness of creation, 136; on the seven deadly sins, 270, 271

Bonhoeffer, Dietrich, 79, 121–122, 228

Bonner, Gerald, 280–282

Bounds, Christopher T., 369nn109–111

Boyd, Craig A., 106n169

Boyd, Gregory A., 332

Bradwardine, Thomas, 297

Bray, Gerald, 366

Brown, A. Philip II, 378n180

Brown, Harold O. J., 281

Brown, William E., 107n171

Bucer, Martin, 358

Buechner, Frederick, 278

Bullinger, Heinrich, 253

Bultmann, Rudolph, 97

Burge, Gary M., 97, 98, 99

Burns, J. Patout, 294n117

Buswell, J. Oliver, 212; the Buswell-Combs view of natures as anti-realist, 213

Butler, Joseph, 303

Cain, 41

Calvin, John, 57n71, 116, 118, 163, 228, 305n178, 316, 318–319, 321, 375–376, 379; on divine judgment, 313; on the doctrine of original sin, 171–173, 175; on the prelapsarian divine warning concerning death, 313; on sin as total depravity, 307–308; on venial sin, 254

Calvinism, 24, 136n110, 186

Campbell, Constantine R., 90n132, 107n172, 181n160

Campbell, Douglas, 27n29, 84n104

Campbell, John McLeod, 337

Cannon, Katie G., 262n261

Canons of Dordt, 132, 216

Carson, D. A., 132; on the consequences of sin, 325, 326–327; on divine goodness, 342; on human responsibility for sin, 342; on the impersonal effects of sin, 332

Carter, J. Kameron, 261n253

Carthage, Synod of, 287, 289–290, 322–323, 385

Casiday, Augustine, 290nn77, 78, 86

Cassian, John, 290, 291; opposition to the theology of, 292–293

Catechism of the Catholic Church, The, 116, 121, 271, 384

Catholics. *See* Roman Catholics/ Catholicism

Chadwick, Owen, 290n79, 291, 292

Chafer, Lewis Sperry, 210–211, 213

Chalcedonian Formula, 215, 322

Chavalas, Mark, 49–50

Chemnitz, Martin, 238, 246, 298

Chesterton, G. K., 204–205

Childs, Brevard S., 64n82, 117–119, 128, 133

Christian life: holiness and the Christian life, 368–378; Paul on sanctification and the Christian life, 364–368; those filled with the Holy Spirit rightly called "*sancta catholica Christiana*" ("a Christian holy people"), 373–374

Christianity, 81, 163, 186, 204, 381, 385; Catholic, 131; contemporary, 186; historic, 116; liberal, 220; orthodox, 148; pagan objections to, 220

Christians, 21, 106, 239, 240, 247, 269, 287, 312, 322, 356, 362, 402; belief of in the "historical Adam," 383–385, 387; belief of in miracles, 355; Christian Gnostics, 136n110; and the knowledge of sin, 22–23, 225; modern/Western Christians' view of sin, 258–259; Pelagius's view of, 283; view of death, 314. *See also* Christian life

Christology, 23–24, 214–215; developments in, 208; of human nature and sin, 134–135; and the metaphysics of the incarnation, 208; orthodox Christology, 210. *See also* Formula of Concord, Christologically oriented perspective of

Chrysostom, John, 135n109, 222n59, 307–308, 365

Ciampa, R. E., 107n171

Cobb, John, 349

Cocceius, Johannes, 228n92, 256n232; on the Reformed tradition concerning sin, 238–239

Coelestius, 280, 281–282

Cogley, Zac, 276n343

Cole, Graham A., 257, 258, 332n271, 333n275

Collins, Anthony, 348

Collins, C. John, 121n34, 190, 205n231, 318–319, 320n245, 390n32; on physical death as a consequence of the fall, 319

Collins, Francis, 320n246

Collins, Kenneth J., 163n72, 299n150

Combs, William W., 215n33; the Buswell-Combs view of natures as anti-realist, 213; defense of belief that Christians have two natures, 212–214, 215; on the definition of nature, 211, 212, 213

Cone, James, 261–262, 261n253

Confessio Augustana, 131

Contarini, Gasparo, 358

corruption and guilt, 197, 200; and the conditional imputation of guilt, 175–176; corruption and guilt— federalism, 161–166; corruption and guilt—mediate views on, 170–175; corruption and guilt—realism, 162, 163, 166–170, 181, 183; corruption-only doctrines concerning original sin, 156–161, 201–202

Couenhoven, Jesse, 280, 287n64

covenants, of God with Israel. *See* new covenant; old covenant

Craig, William Lane, 186, 352n60

creatures (humans and angels), 88n120, 102, 104, 105, 136n110, 140–141, 190, 225, 356, 358; fallen angels as God's creatures, 136, 136n110, 147; goodness of God to his creatures, 352–354, 356; human creatures, 41, 272, 324, 348, 379; violence of toward each other, 350

Crisp, Oliver D., 24n19, 28, 157n49, 159, 165, 166, 185n171, 191, 256, 347nn34, 35; on the "moderate Reformed doctrine of original sin," 202; on various versions of realism, 167–169

Crites, Stephen D., 218n44
Cross, Richard, 304n176
cur Deus homo ("Why the God-man?")
   question, 91, 100
Cyril of Jerusalem, 365

Dahood, Mitchell, 57n70
David: adultery of, 48; prayer of remorse
   for his sins, 55–56, 240; on the responsibility of Israel to God, 49–50
Davis, Stephen T., 124, 338; on process
   theology, 351–352
Dawkins, Richard, 152, 306
death: on the connection between sin and
   death, 83, 180; human death, 386n19;
   physical death as a reality even before
   sin, 318; as a result of sin, 383–385;
   as separation from God, 319; slavery
   to the fear of death, 91. *See also* sin,
   and death
Deborah, 47
Deede, Kristen K., 238n141
deism, 348, 349, 354
Desmond, William, 218n44
determinism, 134, 185–187, 192, 194,
   287n64, 305, 308n196, 341, 348,
   354, 356; and Calvinism, 136n110;
   divine determinism, 346; of Edwards,
   24n18, 185, 187; "genetic determinism," 306; relation of to Reformed
   theology, 256n233; of Schleiermacher, 128; "soft" or "compatibilist"
   version of, 186, 307; of Zwingli, 157
DeYoung, Rebecca Konyndyk, 271,
   272n317; on anger, 276; on gluttony,
   277; on greed, 275–276; on sloth,
   274; on vainglory, 273
Dillard, Raymond, 46–47
Dilley, Stephen, 384n2
Dionysius the (Pseudo)-Areopagite, 144,
   234
disciples, the, 326; baptism of by the Holy
   Spirit, 81–82
"doctrinal amnesia," 28
Doriani, Daniel, 41

dualism: Johannine "dualisms," 97–99;
   provisional dualism, 125; ultimate
   cosmic dualism, 125–126, 129, 144,
   216, 221
Duke, Rodney K., 50n52
Dunn, James D. G., 84, 89, 90, 177n140,
   181n157; on "misdirected religion,"
   85
Dunning, H. Ray, 238
Duns Scotus, John, 296, 358; on the fall of
   the devil and the "free will defense,"
   144–147
Dyrness, William, 101, 128

Ecclesiastes, description of sin in, 59–60
Eddy, Paul, 332
Edom, 65, 72
Edwards, Denis, 205n235
Edwards, Jonathan, 163, 256n233, 347,
   348; on Adam's posterity, 166–167;
   arguments of against John Taylor, 26–27; determinism of, 24n18,
   185–186, 348; on the doctrine of sin,
   24; realism of, 185–192; on Taylor's
   doctrine as "Arminian," 25n20;
   theology of and disagreements with
   John Wesley, 24–25, 24n18
Effron, Daniel A., 303nn169, 171, 172
Egypt, 42, 43, 47, 49, 50, 65, 72–74,
   73n87, 82, 105, 246
Ehud, 47
Eichrodt, Walther: on communion with
   the will of God, 115; on the OT's
   emphasis on the current concrete
   expression of sin, 113; on the opposition between Man's conduct and
   God's nature, 123
Elihu, 52
Eliphaz, 51
endurantism, 193
Enns, Peter, 267n283, 387
Episcopius, Simon, 158n51
Erickson, Millard, 35, 162, 175, 197, 270
Esau, 42
essentialism, 263, 392

Estes, Daniel, 52

evangelicalism, 186, 199, 254, 359n82, 362

Evans, Robert, 282n18, 299–300

Eve, 40, 41, 122, 136–137, 190–191; and Adam as the first federal representatives ("chieftains") of the initial human population, 320, 390; common ancestry with other primates, 320; initial innocence/righteousness of, 114–115, 159; original state of, 385; as *posse peccare* (able to sin) and *posse non peccare* (not able to sin), 114, 135–136, 159, 289; questions regarding the historicity of, 153, 154, 155, 182. *See also* original sin, doctrine of; sin, origin of

"Evidences from Facts and Events" (Edwards), 27

evolution, 319–320, 386n17; evolution of old and new world monkeys (the "Pregnant Hitch-hiking Monkey Thesis"), 401; evolutionary biology, 319, 391–392n38, 392n39; on the "orthodox" evolutionary account of the development of life, 393–395; problems concerning, 401–402

Fairbairn, Donald, 222n60

faith, 360, 372; certainty of, 385; Christian faith, 21, 126, 132, 145, 225, 226, 259, 287, 355, 381; first step of (*initium fedei*), 294–295; justification by, 359, 371, 374–375, 376; living faith as opposed to dead faith, 377–378; true faith, 374

Falk, Darrell, on the evolution of old and new world monkeys (the "Pregnant Hitch-hiking Monkey Thesis"), 401–402

Fall of the Devil, The (Anselm of Canterbury), 140

false prophets, 67

Faus, Jose Ignacio Gonzalez, 260

Faustus (Bishop of Riez), 293

federalism, 161–165, 165n78, 181, 182, 183; and the concept of imputation, 24; covenant theology as characteristic of, 158n51; criticism of, 164–165, 199–200; history of in the Reformed tradition, 163–164; and moral responsibility, 199–201; popularity of, 164

Fee, Gordon D., 367

Feinberg, John S., 126n49, 197, 314n230, 317n234

Feinberg, Paul D., 314n230

Fergusson, David, 218

Fesko, John V., 28n33

"fission theory," 194–196

Fitzmeyer, Joseph, 179n148, 180

Flacius, Matthias, 216, 223–226

Flint, Thomas P., 186, 346n27, 352n60

Forde, Gerhard, on sanctification, 371–372, 372n128

forgiveness, 44, 55, 57, 74, 75, 96, 100–101, 250, 283, 322, 360, 363, 373–374; and discipleship, 78; divine forgiveness, 54; and transformation, 350

Formula of Concord (1576/1584), 131, 149, 159, 374; anthropological considerations of, 225n76; Christologically oriented perspective of, 225–227; statement on corruption, 161

Forsyth, P. T., 332

Fortey, Richard, 386n21

Foucault, Michel, 269

Fourth Lateran Council, 139

Fox, Michael V., 59

Frame, John, 136n110

Frank, Lisa, 277n352

Freddoso, Alfred J., 190n186, 347n33, 355

free will, 131, 136n110, 197, 241, 281; abuse of, 355; the fall of the devil and the "free will defense," 144–147; the "free will defense" with respect to angelic evil, 142, 145–146. *See also* Augustine, and the battle with Pelagianism, and the question of free will

Freire, Paulo, 261n252
Fretheim, Terence, 44n37

Gathercole, Simon, 89n126, 90n134
Gavrilyuk, Paul L., 337
Gawande, Atul, 267n286
genetics, 319, 383, 386, 387, 396, 399–400
Gentry, Peter J., 27n30, 30n39
Gestrich, Christof, 153n23
Giberson, Karl, 385–387
Gino, Francesca, 303n170
Gleason, Randall, 211n17
Gnesio-Lutherans, 223–224, 226
Gnosticism, 125, 220–221, 222; Christian Gnostics, 136n110. *See also* Manichaeism
God: actuality of, 219–220; agency of (including dual agency), 293, 347, 353, 354, 355–356; atonement and reconciliation for sin promised by, 45–46; as blameless for causing sin or temptation, 94, 122–123, 126–132, 216, 216n39, 238, 239; design of for humanity, 104; faithfulness of, 36, 60, 103, 105, 327, 331; as Father, 105–107, 106n169; glory of, 33, 85, 88, 181, 242, 266, 272, 272n322, 291, 309, 375; goodness of, 128–129, 132, 221–222, 293, 339, 342–343, 346–347, 352–353; goodness of reflected in creation, 133–134; as the guarantor of *shalom*, 118; holiness of, 43–44, 45, 334, 335, 337, 381; justice of, 103, 243, 335, 337; knowledge of, 23; love of believers for God, 296; love of God for humanity, 98, 291, 326, 327–331, 359; revelation of in Christ, 24, 97–98, 339; righteousness of, 89, 103, 228, 243, 252, 337; simplicity of, 334–335, 334n278, 335n279; sorrow of because of human sinfulness, 72–73; sovereignty of, 103–104, 105, 126, 129, 167, 340, 343–344, 346, 351, 355; "special revelation" of, 27; will of, 115, 252, 257, 343, 368–369;

truthfulness of, 131–132. *See also* God, as Creator; God, judgment and wrath of; God, law of given to Israel; grace
God, as Creator, 272, 339–340; conservation of creation by God, 352–353; continuous creation of, 188–189; creation of everything that exists contingently *ex nihilo*, 221–222; creation of humans within a setting of *shalom*, 40; governance of God (*gubernatio*) over his creation, 340, 341, 356
God, judgment and wrath of, 45, 70–71, 85, 89–90, 123–124, 313, 323–327, 332–333, 332n266, 372; on the final judgment taking no account of ethnic differences between Jew and Greek, 88, 323–324; God's wrath as the contingent expression of the holy love of the Trinity, 334–335; God's wrath as contingent on holy love, 344; God's wrath as the expression of holy impassible love, 335–336; God's wrath and holy love as reason for hope, 336–338; gospel accounts of, 333–334; warnings of concerning the coming judgment, 64–65, 79–81
God, law of given to Israel: as given to prepare sinners for the reception of grace, 44; intention of to teach the holiness of God and the sinfulness of the overconfident sinner, 43–44; within the framework of God's covenant with Israel, 43
Goethe, Johann Wolfgang von, 204
Goldingay, John, 57n73, 115, 120n30, 122, 125, 136; on the stain of sin, 117
Gonzalez, Justo, 290
Goudriaan, Aza, 290n79
grace, 44, 234, 274, 290, 294, 370, 372, 376, 379, 381; Aquinas's position on, 295; Arminius's position on, 298–299; Augustine's position on, 283–284, 285–287; denial of, 299; difference

between operating and cooperating grace, 358; of the Holy Spirit, 298; justifying grace, 359–360; as necessary for salvation, 285; Pelagius's view of, 282–283; prevenient grace, 297, 298, 357–359, 359n82; sin against the grace of God, 264–265; supernatural grace, 294. *See also* sin, grace, and divine providence; sin, and regenerating grace; sin, and sanctifying grace

Gregory of Nazianzus, 135n109, 222n59

Gregory of Nyssa, 135n109, 222n59

Gregory of Rimini, 297

Gregory the Great, 270

Grenz, Stanley J., 126n51, 150, 153–154, 175; on the doctrine of original sin, 159; on the fall, 156

Griffin, David Ray, 349

Griffith Thomas, W. H., 233–234, 238

Gropper, Johann, 358

Gross, Julius, 153

Grudem, Wayne, 242; on sin as irrational, 234

guilt, 151, 151n11, 159; as a consequence of sin, 310–311; inherited sin and personal guilt, 161–162; mankind's sharing in Adam's guilt, 156–157; original guilt, 158. *See also* corruption and guilt

Gutierrez, Gustavo, 260–261

Hagar, 42

hamartiology, 24; of Augustine, 30; of Hegel, 219–220; "high medieval" hamartiology, 295–296; Lutheran hamartiology, 216; Petrine hamartiology, 96–97. *See also* Johannine hamartiology; Pauline hamartiology; two-nature hamartiology

Hamilton, Victor P., 42n29, 44n39

Hampson, Daphne, 263–264, 263n271

Hardy, Edward R., 215n31

Hare, John E., 150–151n5

Härle, Wilfried, 131, 216n39, 311

Harrison, Carol, 281n6

Hart, David Bentley: on the Christian metaphysical tradition, 343; on God's governance, 356; on provisional dualism, 125

Hartley, John E., 43n34

Hartshorne, Charles, 351n53

"heathens/heathenism," 25, 26

Hebrews, description of sin in: on Christ's priestly vocation of providing salvation from sin, 91–92; promise of hope and sanctification from sin, 93–94; warnings against sin, 92–93, 93n142

Hector, Kevin, 151

Hegel, G. W. F., 133, 242n163, 333n275; on the "evolution of *Geist* (Mind, Spirit), 219; hamartiology of, 218–220

Heidegger, Johannes, 131, 228, 239, 255, 377

Heidelberg Catechism, 384

Helm, Paul, 193n196, 256n233

Heppe, Heinrich, 131n93, 159, 228n92, 239, 242n164, 243, 255; on mortal and venial sins, 253, 254, 256, 377n172

Herbert of Cherbury, 348

Heyward, Carter, 262n261

Hick, John, 208n3

Hinlicky, Paul: on justification, 363; on repentance, 360–361

Hitler, Adolf, 204, 308

Hodgson, Peter, 218n44

Hoekema, Anthony, 165; on our relationship to Adam's sin, 168; on remedies for the deficiencies of the realist position, 169–170

holiness. *See* Christian life, holiness and the Christian life; God, holiness of

Hollaz, David, 227–228, 252–253

Holy Spirit, 28, 74, 75, 107, 118, 252, 286, 294, 309, 334, 369, 376; ability of to bring victory over sin, 368; baptism of the disciples by, 81–82; empowerment given by, 250; fruits of, 368; ministry of, 373–374; resistance to by sinners, 82–83, 255–258; grace of, 298; production of righteousness by through sanctification, 377; purpose of in the life of a new believer, 364

Hoorens, Vera, 302n164

hope, 356–357; God's wrath and holy love as reason for hope, 336–338; hope for salvation, 337; hope for sinners despite God's wrath, 70–71, 71–72, 109

Hopkins, Gerard Manley, 381–382

Horton, Michael Scott, 162, 308–309, 362

Hudson, Hud, 194–196, 386n15; on the "orthodox" evolutionary account of the development of life, 393–395

human origins, 384–385, 384n2, 393n42, 398–402; conclusions concerning, 402–403; Ruse's critique of the Augustinian view (the "Augustinian solution") of human origins, 385, 391–392. See also human origins, possibilities for maintaining consistency between science and Christian belief concerning

human origins, possibilities for maintaining consistency between science and Christian belief concerning, 389; genealogical-Adam proposal, 395–398; hyper-Adam (hypertime) proposal, 393–395; refurbishment proposals, 389–393, 389n30

humanity: its common ancestry with animals (the "red tooth" theory and the "common ancestry thesis"), 386–387, 391; depravity of, 22; distinction between *common* and *essential* human properties, 209–210; distinction between *individual-essence* and *kind-essence*, 208–209; as God's creatures, 41, 272, 324, 348, 379; total depravity of, 207

Hwang, Alexander, 290

identity, personal: connection to the doctrine of original sin, 187–188, 189; Lockean view of, 187

idolatry, sin of, 44, 67–69, 85–86, 111, 156; habitual nature of, 85, 323; in Israel, 47, 49; its link with prostitution, 69; as rebellion against God, 45

imputation, 24; of Christ's righteousness, 164, 168; the conditional imputation of guilt, 175–176

incarceration, 269; disproportionate number of incarcerated blacks, 267; effects of on the family and community, 267–268; in the United States, 266–267

Irenaeus, 125, 135n109, 221, 222n59, 272n322, 365

Isaac, 42, 79, 82

Israel, OT nation of, 105; aliens living in, 43, 43n34; descendants of living in Egypt, 43; disobedience of, 50–51; division of into Israel and Judah, 48–49; election of by God, 325n255; as God's adopted child, 107; as "God's firstborn son," 43; lack of trust in God, 48; refusal to heed God's warnings, 236–237; restoration of God's people from sin, 72–74; worship practices of, 30. See also Israel, prophets of, on sin-related themes; old covenant

Israel, prophets of, on sin-related themes, 61; case study of at the beginning of Isaiah, 61–65; on the response of God (judgment and mercy) to sin, 69–74; on sins against God (idolatry and infidelity), 67–69; on sins against humanity, 65–66; warnings of judgment against sinners, 64–65

Jacob, 42, 79, 82

Jacobs, Nathan D., 222n59

James, description of sin in, 94–96; on the effects of sinful communication, 94–95

Janzen, J. Gerald, 44n37

Jefferson, Thomas, 348

Jenson, Matt, 234n125

Jenson, Robert W., 242, 341
Jeroboam, 49
Jerome, 365
Jesus Christ, 27, 28, 360, 370, 373;
  ascension of, 77, 81; on the balance between Adam and Christ,
  178; baptism of, 81; contrasts with
  Adam, 178; crucifixion/death of,
  219, 293, 344; on the effects of sin,
  77; as God's suffering servant, 71,
  100; guiltlessness of, 78; as homoousios with the Father, 208; identity
  of, 78–79; incarnation of, 208, 210,
  215, 219, 329; on the kingdom of
  God, 77, 102, 107, 361; love of God
  reflected in, 328; love of for humanity, 100; and Nicodemus, 107, 361; as
  a "propitiation" ("atoning sacrifice") for sins, 329; relation of to the
  church as a marriage between husband and wife, 108–111; relation of
  to humanity, 196; revelation of God
  through, 24, 97–98, 339; resurrection
  of, 219, 225n76, 279, 381; righteousness of, 164, 178–179; sacrifice of, 92,
  329; Sermon on the Mount teachings of, 76; teachings of clarifying
  the Torah's teaching concerning sin,
  75–77, 246, 251; teachings of on
  righteousness, 282–283; as truly and
  completely human, 208; union with,
  90, 279; warnings of concerning the
  judgment to come, 79–81; warnings
  of concerning rejection of the Holy
  Spirit, 258. See also Jesus Christ,
  parables of; Synoptic Gospels, description of sin in
Jesus Christ, parables of: of the blind
  leading the blind, 76; of the father,
  106; of the prodigal son, 106; of the
  weeds, 80
Jewett, Robert, 179n147
Job, description of sin in, 51–53
Johannine hamartiology, 97; and Johannine "dualisms," 97–99; on the

rejection of God's revelation in
  Christ, 97–98; on the remedy for sin,
  100–101; on the results of sin, 99; on
  the theme of light versus darkness,
  97–98; on the universality of sin,
  100–101
John of Damascus, 135n109, 140, 345–
  346, 356–357; on divine providence,
  339–340; on evil, 222–223
John the Baptist, 74–75, 97, 100, 109
Johnson, Ryan M., 302n165
Joseph (OT), 82, 343–344; selling of into
  slavery by his brothers, 42, 343, 354
Joshua, 46–47
Judah (country), 49, 65, 67, 72
Judah (person), 42
Julian, 222n60, 280–281, 286n56
justice, 161, 296, 336, 337, 385; sin as a
  violation of basic justice, 46, 296. See
  also God, justice of
justification, 31, 150, 164, 168, 174, 177,
  178, 224, 358, 359–363, 371–373,
  379; condemnation and justification
  as contradictory, 165; distinction
  between justification and sanctification, 376–377, 377n176; epistemic,
  399; by faith, 359, 371, 374–375, 376;
  by grace alone, 374; initial, 297; language of, 105; legal justification, 93;
  self-justification, 249; by works, 297
Justin Martyr, 135n109, 222n59

Kaiser, Walter Jr., 73n87
Kane, Robert, 185n172, 346n28
Kang, Phee Seng, 208n2
Kant, Immanuel, 204, 241; on "radical
  evil," 150–151n5
Kearney, Maureen, 391–392n38, 392n39
Keller, Catherine, 262
Kelly, J. N. D., 156–157; on Latin theology
  prior to Augustine, 222, 225n75; on
  Pelagius, 280–283
Kelsey, David H., 230n106, 237, 239, 323;
  on the Christian understanding of
  sin, 379; sin as always in contrast

to the glory of God, 272; on sin as distortion, 240

Kemp, Kenneth, 397–398

Kennard, Douglas, 316–317

Kierkegaard, Søren, 136n115, 229, 309; on sin, 238n141

King, Martin Luther Jr., 21–22, 381

kingdom of God, 152; Jesus's view of, 77, 102, 107, 361; Paul's view of, 86–87, 89, 102, 277, 327, 368

Kinlaw, Dennis, 55n68, 57n72, 74n89, 102, 108, 364; on Christ and the church as bride and groom, 110–111

Kiuchi, Nobuyoshi, 43n33

Kolb, Robert, 22n10, 223n71, 339n1

Kor, Alan Charles, 348

Ladd, George Eldon, 84–85, 88n120, 94–95, 319n241, 338

Lamberigts, Mathijs, 280n2, 286n56

Lamentations, description of sin in, 59–60

Lamoureux, Denis O., 385

law of Moses. See Mosaic law

lawlessness (anomia), 38, 76, 85, 89, 104, 105, 232, 240, 248, 359

Leclerc, Diane, 262

Lee, Harper, 268

Lee, Luther, 173

Levering, Matthew, 220n55, 386n19

Lewis, C. S., 124n42, 233, 237, 277, 300, 320nn245, 246; 342, 390; on miracles, 355

liberation theology: benefits gleaned from the insights of, 269; black, 261–262; Latin American, 259–261

Lints, Richard, 67n85

Livingston, James C., 218n44, 389n29

Lombard, Peter: on angels as created beings of God and thus good, 142–144; on prevenient grace, 358

Lombardo, Nicholas E., 300

Long, D. Stephen, 29–30, 259, 370n118

Lot, 42

Loux, Michael J., 197n209

Lowe, E. J., 213n27

"Lucifer," 146

Luther, Martin, 22n10, 131, 158, 216n39, 223, 234, 378; on justification by faith, 374; on sanctification, 371–373; on sin as "essential" or "natural" to humanity, 226–227; on sin and grace, 339

Lutheran Catechism, 240

Lutherans, theological tradition of concerning sin, 238

Lyotard, Jean-Francois, 269

Macarius, 365

MacArthur, John F. Jr., 215n33

MacFadyen, Alastair, 152–153

Macleod, Donald, 172

Macquarrie, John, 156, 332n266

Malebranche, Nicholas, 189, 347

Manata, Paul, 256n233

Manichaeism, 125, 152, 220–221, 280, 285; Augustine's opposition to, 289; resistance to, 221–222

Mann, William, 221

Markus, R. A., 295

Marshall, I. Howard, 89–90

Marx, Karl, 269

Mary, 75, 198n220, 296

Massilians, 287, 292, 294

Mayer, Ernst, 391n38

McCall, Thomas H., 29n36, 158n51, 186n175, 272n319, 299n149, 308n199, 321n248, 335n279, 364n97, 371n119

McClendon, James William Jr., 238n140

McCluskey, Coleen, 277, 277n352

McClymond, Michael J., 25n20

McDermott, Gerald R., 25n20

McFarland, Ian, 23

McGrath, Gavin, 320n246, 390

McKnight, Scot, 386n22, 387

Melanchthon, Philipp, 223, 224, 255, 358, 372

Merrill, Eugene, 115, 115n12, 136

Merritt, Anna C., 303nn169, 172

Migliore, Daniel L., 264n274, 332n266

Miley, John, 158

Miller, Christian B., 302–303, 306

Miller, Dale T., 303n171

Miller, Marisa L., 302n165

miracles, 355

Moab, 65, 72

"modern chauvinism," 29

Moffitt, David, 92

Molinism, 196–199, 203, 352, 357

Monin, Benoit, 303nn169, 171, 172

Moo, Douglas J., 83, 87n114, 178, 181–184

moral law. *See* sin, nature of, as contrary to the law of God

Moreland, J. P., 186n173

Morris, Leon, 37n10, 324n254, 326

Morris, Thomas V., 208–209, 392n40

Mosaic law, 78, 177, 178, 282

Moses, 43, 44, 46, 48, 50, 82, 150, 173

Mother Teresa, 308

Mueller, John Theodore, 162n66, 238n146, 240, 244, 253, 258

Muller, Richard A., 158n51, 228n91, 295, 335n280, 340, 375n148; on prevenient grace, 357

Murray, Michael, 316n233, 386n19

Muslims/Muslim culture, 25, 26, 189

nature, 340–341; Buswell-Combs view of as anti-realist, 213; as a complex of attributes, 212–213; definition of, 211, 212, 213; misunderstanding of the meaning of, 214–215; "sin nature," 216–217. *See also* two-nature hamartiology

Neanderthals, 386, 386n22

Nelson, Derek R., 262n264

Nelson, Paul A., 384n2

"New Atheists," 152

new covenant, promise of, 71–72

Newton, John, 163

Niceno-Constantinopolitan Creed, 322

Nicodemus, 107, 361

Niebuhr, Reinhold, 22n4, 259, 262, 263, 265, 265n276, 272, 273n327, 349n43; on the religious and social dimensions of sin, 265–266

Nietzsche, Friedrich, on the definition of truth, 268–269

Noah, 41

Noble, Thomas, 370, 376n162

Nussbaum, Martha, 119n27

Oakes, Edward, 152

Oberman, Heiko A., 296; on justification, 297

occasionalism, 192, 194, 347–348, 354; of Jonathan Edwards, 185, 188, 189; problems concerning, 190–191; teaching of concerning Adam, 191

Oden, Thomas C., 29, 357, 359–368

O'Donovan, Oliver, 237

Ogliari, Donato, 293

old covenant, 43, 50, 82, 109, 331

Olson, Mark K., 247n187

Olson, Roger E., 126n51, 150

Oord, Thomas Jay, 351n53

Orange, Synod of, 128, 293–295, 304, 358

O'Regan, Cyril, 218n44

Organic Whole Theory, 192, 193

Origen, 365

original sin, doctrine of, 22, 25, 26, 27, 113–114, 149–153, 202–203, 222, 227–228, 260, 293, 352, 385; aspects central to the notion of hereditary corruption or original corruption (*corruption hereditaria*), 159; "Augustinian" conception of, 262; and Christian witness, 203–205; connection of personal identity to, 187–188, 189; denial of, 299; "moderate Reformed doctrine" of, 202; Orthodox view of, 157; symbolic and existential interpretations of, 154–156; unpopularity of, 150–153. *See also* corruption and guilt; original sin, doctrine of, scriptural basis of; original sin, metaphysics and morals of; sin, nature of

original sin, doctrine of, scriptural basis of, 176; important phrases (*eph hō*;

pantes hēmarton) in Scripture concerning, 179–182, 183; overview of Romans 5:12–21 as the most famous declaration of, 177–179; views of consistent with Romans 5:12–21, 182–183; views of excluded by Romans 5:12–21, 182

original sin, metaphysics and moral responsibility/morals of, 184, 346; and corruption-only views concerning, 201–202; and federalism, 199–201; mediate views of moral responsibility including Molinism, 196–199; and the problem of moral responsibility, 191–192. *See also* occasionalism; realism

Ortlund, Raymond C. Jr., 108n173

Oswalt, John, 35n5, 44n35, 55n64, 66nn83, 84, 69n86

Ott, Ludwig, 238

Owen, John, 275, 298

Packer, J. I., 211, 217, 257, 258

paganism, 25; objections of to Christianity, 220

Paine, Thomas, 348

paleoanthropology, 319, 323, 383, 386n16, 398, 399

panentheism, 350

Pannenberg, Wolfhart, 136n110

Pascal, Blaise, 204, 380–381

Passover, 100

Pasternack, Lawrence R., 150n5

Paul, 46, 139, 184, 196; on adoption, 107; on anger, 276–277; "apocalyptic" interpretations of, 84n104; on bodily resurrection, 322; on the contrasts between Adam and Christ, 178; on the devil's pride, 139; and the doctrine of *sarx* in Pauline psychology, 88, 88n120, 212; on the final judgment taking no account of ethnic differences between Jew and Greek, 88; on the imputation of Christ's righteousness, 168, 178–179; on the "kingdom of God," 86–87, 89, 102, 277, 327, 368; on original sin including language and phrasing used in describing, 177–179, 179–182; on salvation for both Jew and Gentile, 323–324; on sanctification and the Christian life, 364–368; on the terrible effects of corruption, 160; on the unregenerate person as enslaved by sin, 279. *See also* Pauline hamartiology

Pauline hamartiology, 83, 87n114; on Adam's sin, 173–174; on the breadth and depth of sin, 87–89; on the connection between sin and death, 83, 180; on the consequences of sin, 89–91; on the exchange of God's value and glory for idolatry, 85; expressions of sin in Paul's theology, 85–87; on the origin of sin through Adam and ungodliness, 83–85; Paul's diagnosis of the human heart as "senseless," 89, 304–305; on the root of sin, 85; similar terms used by Paul to describe a variety of sins, 85–86; summary of, 91; theological manner of Paul in locating the genesis of sin, 84–85; warnings concerning sin couched in "vice lists," 86–87

Peacocke, Arthur, 320

Pelagianism, 128, 151n11, 161, 182, 184, 201, 227, 299, 303, 305, 308n196; condemnation of by the Synod of Carthage, 287, 289–290, 322–323; criticism/rejection of, 179–180, 322–323; denial of the transmission of Adam's guilt by, 281–282; salient points of, 304. *See also* Augustine, and the battle with Pelagianism

Pelagius, 280–283, 285, 290, 295. *See also* Pelagianism

Pentecost, 81, 373

perdurantism, 193

Perrine, Timothy, 274n334

Perszyk, Ken, 199n223, 352n60

Peter (Simon Peter), 78–79, 81–82

"Philippists," 223, 226

Philistines, 65, 326

philosophy, 29

Pieper, Francis, 160, 162, 240n156; on the doctrine of original sin, 162

Pieper, Josef, 228, 235, 238

Piper, John, 272

Placeus, Josua, 175n132

Placher, William C., 266–267

Plantinga, Alvin, 199, 212n20, 214n29, 269n300, 309n205, 384n2, 399n65; on "transworld depravity," 197–198

Plantinga, Cornelius, 40n25, 114, 229–237; on sin as addiction, 300–302; on sin as folly, 235; on sin as a parasite, 233; on sin as stubborn, 381

Plaskow, Judith, 263

Polanus, Amandus, 377

Polkinghorne, John, 385

Pope, Marvin H., 52n55

Pope, William Burt, 164, 217, 389

Porter, Stanley E., 37n10

postmodernism, 269

predestination, 164, 254, 291, 292, 297, 305; basis of, 293; irresistible grace of, 295; unconditional predestination, 288, 293

Preuss, Horst Dietrich, 113, 242

prophets. See false prophets; Israel, prophets of, on sin-related themes

Prosper of Aquitaine, 292–293

prostitution, 67, 74, 363; its link with idolatry, 69, 108, 326

Protestants/Protestant culture, 26

Proverbs, description of sin in, 58–59

providence. See sin, grace, and divine providence

Psalms, description of sin in, 53–57

psychology: moral, 27n28, 29, 306; social, 27n28, 29

quantum theory, 400–401

Quenstadt, Johann Andreas, 227, 238, 298, 359

Quinn, Philip, 192

Ralston, Thomas N., 164, 308

Ramm, Bernard, 205, 219, 220, 259, 260

Raphael, Stephen, 267n288

Ratzinger, Joseph (Benedict XVI), 260

Rauschenbusch, Walter, 21

Ray, Stephen, 264–265

Rea, Michael C., 165, 175, 394n46; on Humanity as a moral agent, 194; on moral responsibility, 196–197; on "organic whole theory," 192–198; on "transworld depravity," 198

realism: anti-realism, 214; criticism of, 168–169; Edwardsian realism, 185–192, 203; mediate views of, including Molinism, 196–199; modified Edwardsian realism, 192–196; various versions of, 167–168. See also corruption and guilt—realism

rebellion, 46; idolatry as rebellion, 45; as leading to slavery, 104–105

reconciliation, 45, 152, 250, 339, 360

redemption, 21, 41–42, 107, 115, 128, 152, 155, 226, 275, 286, 292, 296, 339; from lawlessness, 369; necessity of, 127; progress of, 232

Rees, B. R., 281

Reformation, the, 29, 131, 149, 228, 254, 298, 358; dogma of, 371

Regensburg Agreement (1541), 358

Rehoboam, 49

repentance, 50, 65, 78, 81, 89, 250, 252, 255, 288, 305, 360–361; baptism of, 75

representationalism. See federalism

Riches, Aaron, 385

righteousness, 178–179; corruption of original righteousness, 159, 227; imputation of Christ's righteousness, 164, 168, 178–179; production of through sanctification, 377; teachings of Jesus concerning, 282–283. See also God, righteousness of

Ritschl, Albrecht: criticism of the doctrine of original sin, 150–152, 150–151n5; on inherited sin and personal guilt, 161–162

Roman Catholics/Catholicism, 131; consensus of concerning what sin is, 238; as deists, 25–26; and the doctrine of original sin, 149; on the historical Adam, 384–385

Rosemann, Philipp, 143, 358

Ruse, Michael, 387–388; on the Augustinian view (the "Augustinian solution") of human origins, 385, 391–392; on the importance of the doctrine of sin, 204; on Neanderthals, 386n22, 392; response of to the problems concerning evolution, 401–403

Russell, Andrew C., 24

Saiving, Valerie, 263

salvation, 107, 299, 300, 358, 359, 377; for both Jew and Gentile, 323–324; God's promise of, 72–73; grace as necessary for, 285, 294; hope for, 337; human desire for by communion with the will of God, 115; sanctification as essential to, 363

sanctification, 31, 45, 74, 93–94, 95, 96, 371–373, 372n128; distinction between justification and sanctification, 376–377, 377n176; as essential to salvation, 363; and the filial relationship between God and Jesus, 100; Paul on sanctification and the Christian life, 364–368. See also sin, and sanctifying grace

Sapphira, 82

Sarai, 42

Satan, 134; attributes of, 137–138; contrasts between Satan and God, 137–138, 139; desire of to be like God, 138–139; fall of, 139–141; self-regard of as being superior to other creatures, 139; and the tempting of Adam and Eve, 116–117

Schleiermacher, F. D. E., 126, 150, 150–151n5; determinism of, 128; on original sin (Erbsünde), 126–128, 156

Schlenker, Barry R., 302n165

Schlosser, Eric, 268n289

Schmid, Heinrich, 227n89, 298n146, 359n80, 375n144

Schnelle, Udo, 75

Schreiner, Thomas R., 30n39, 74, 85, 93n142, 94, 180–181, 359n82; on Paul's contention that sin is not equivalent to transgression, 177–178

science, modern: effects of on theology, 154, 155, 385–387, 386n15; genealogical science, 395–398. See also evolution; human origins, possibilities for maintaining consistency between science and Christian belief concerning

scientism, 400

Scobie, Charles H. H., 319

Scots Confession (1560), 202

"Scriptural Method of Accounting" (Wesley), 26

Second Helvetic Confession, 377–378

Seeberg, Reinhold, 290–295

self-deception, 236

"self-licensing," 303

Semi-Pelagianism, 128, 161, 182, 201, 227, 290, 299, 300, 303, 305, 308n196; rejection of, 358; salient points of, 304

seven deadly sins, the, 270–271; avarice/greed, 275–276, 327; envy, 274; gluttony, 277; lust, 277–278, 277n352, 327; sloth, 274–275; vainglory, 271–274; wrath, 276–277

sexual sins, 42, 44, 65, 66, 86, 87, 89, 93, 228; and lust, 277–278, 327; sexual immorality, 327; sexual violence, 267n287

sexuality, 119n27; portrayal of in the OT, 119

shalom (peace): creation of humans within a setting of, 40; effect of corruption on, 232; enjoyment of among the first humans, 115–116; God as the guarantor of, 118; the OT prophets' longing for the return of, 114; in the relationship between Adam and Eve, 115 shame, 118; as a consequence of sin, 310–311

Shedd, William G. T., 163, 235, 241

Sheldon, Henry C., 164

Shuster, Marguerite, 268n293

Silva, Moises, 38–39

simony, 82–83

sin: as addiction, 300–302; against the grace of God, 264–265; as causing blindness, 23; Christian understanding of, 379–382; as deceitful, 23; definition of as whatever is opposed to God's will, 21; as destroying human community, 90; as a dilemma for God, 332–333; as a disease/sickness, 230; as estrangement from our being, 228–229; evidence of and sources for the study of, 27–30, 30n39; as folly, 235, 237; gravity of, 45; habitual nature of, 85, 323; knowledge of, 22; as lawlessness (*anomia*), 38, 76, 85, 89, 104, 105, 228, 232, 240, 248, 359; as leading to death, 101; as leading to disintegration of self and community, 231–232; as moral evil, 340–341; neglect of historic Christian teaching on, 28n33, 29, 30, 30n39; "objective" character of, 34, 35, 101; as "the only empirically verifiable doctrine of the Christian faith," 21–22; as parasitic, 232–233; as a perversion of God's original creation, 210; as pollution/uncleanness, 230–231; reality of, 27; social sin, 266, 268; stain of, 117, 230; structural sin, 260–261, 264–265, 268, 269–270; as a substance, 216, 217–218; as a theological category, 33; understanding of, 22n10; universality and finality (apart from God's grace) of, 225; various forms of, 44. *See also* hamartiology; original sin, doctrine of; sin, biblical theology of; sin, consequences/wages of; sin, and death; sin, grace, and divine providence; sin, nature of; sin, NT

terms for; sin, OT terms for; sin/sins, distinctions between; Synoptic Gospels, description of sin in

sin, biblical theology of, 39–40; in the biblical story of creation and the fall, 40–46; and the progression of sin, 41; sin as a dynamic force, 46; sin as fundamentally against God, 41, 45, 91, 237–240, 244, 381; sin in Israel's continuing story, 46–51; sin in Israel's wisdom literature, 51–60; sin as a violation of basic justice, 46. *See also* sin, biblical theology of, key themes

sin, biblical theology of, key themes, 101–102; familial metaphors, 105–107; nuptial metaphor, 108–111; royal-legal metaphor, 102–195

sin, consequences/wages of, 45, 77, 117–121; depravity, 306–310, 308n196; enslavement and debility as a result of, 105, 107, 261–262, 279, 300–306; guilt and shame, 310–311; impersonal effects of sin on culture, 332. *See also* God, judgment and wrath of; sin, and death

sin, and death: clarifications concerning, 312–315; determining the "death" referred to in the biblical claim, 315–317; distinctions concerning, 312–315; interpretations of by theologians, 331–333; introduction to the topic of, 311–312; issues concerning while moving forward, 317–323, 321n249; summary of, 323, 331

sin, grace, and divine providence, 339, 352; concurrence concept concerning, 353–355; conservation concept concerning, 352–353; and gracious providence, 339–341; the mysteries of providence and the hope of the Gospel, 356–357. *See also* sin, grace, and divine providence, attempts at doctrinal formulation concerning; sin, grace, and divine providence, theological affirmations of; sin, and justifying grace; sin, and regenerating grace

sin, grace, and divine providence, attempts at doctrinal formulation concerning, 345; deism, 348, 349, 354; from monocausality to occasionalism, 347–348; from omnicausality to monocausality, 345–347; process theology, 349–352, 351n55

sin, grace, and divine providence, theological affirmations of, 341; divine goodness, 342–343; divine sovereignty, 343–344; human responsibility for sin, 342

sin, nature of, 218; clarifications concerning human nature and sin, 207–210; as contrary to God, 237–240; as contrary to the law of God, 240–242; as contrary to nature, 218–233 passim, 283, 284, 287; as contrary to the nature of God, 242–244; as contrary to reason, 233–237; as contrary to the will of God, 242, 257

sin, NT terms for, 38; adikia, 39; asebeia, 39; hamartia, 38; hamartanō, 38; parabainō, 38; parabasis, 38; paraptōma, 38–39

sin, OT terms for, 34; ʻāwel, 36; ʻāwōn, 35–36, 54, 55, 57; ḥaṭṭāʼt, 34–35, 38, 54, 55; pešaʻ, 36–37, 54, 57; raʻ, 37; rešaʻ, 37

sin, origin of, 113; setting of, 114–116; existentialist readings of the fall, 184; and the fall itself, 117, 204–205; the first temptation, 116–117; immediate consequences of the fall, 117–121; literary features of the fall in the Genesis account, 184; temptation and the fall, 113–114. See also angelic sin, origin of; sin, origin of, theological reflection on

sin, origin of, theological reflection on, 121–124, 125, 135n108; divine "authorship" or causation ruled out as cause of sin, 126–132; Lutheran confessional statements concerning, 131; necessity of the fall as inconsistent with Scripture, 133–135, 135n106; Reformed theological statements concerning, 131–132; ultimate cosmic dualism ruled out as cause of sin, 125–126, 129

sin, and regenerating grace, 360; and adoption, 361; and the familial deception, 362; and regeneration, 361–362; and repentance, 360–361

sin, and sanctifying grace, 95, 297, 362–363; nuptial context of, 363–364; nuptial context and the Christian life, 364–368

sin/sins, distinctions between, 244; grievous sins and less-grievous sins, 245–246; individual and systemic sins, 258–270 passim; intentional sins and unintentional sins, 246–250; mortal sins and venial sins, 250–254; remissible sins and irremissible sins, 255–258; sins against God, neighbors, and self, 245; sins of commission and sins of omission, 244–245. See also seven deadly sins, the

"skeptical theism," 317, 317n234, 355

Sklar, Jay, 40–41, 111, 135n107, 229; on different categories of sin, 249

slavery, 342; to the fear of death, 91; the "house of slavery," 105; rebellion leading to slavery, 104–105. See also sin, enslavement and debility as a result of

Smith, Christine M., 262n261

Smith, James K. A., 390

Smith, Ryder, 35, 38

sociobiology, 306

sociology, 29

Sodom and Gomorrah, 42

Solomon, 48

Sonderegger, Katherine, 147–148, 309, 312

Song of Songs, description of sin in, 60

sovereignty, of humans over creation that reflects God's sovereignty over all things, 115–116. See also God, sovereignty of

Sprinkle, Joe M., 230n105
Stalin, Josef, 308
Stanglin, Keith D., 158n51, 299n149
Stott, John, 320n245, 332–333, 390
Strigel, Viktorin, 223–224, 226
Stroll, Michael A., 267n288
Stuart, Douglas K., 44n40
Stump, Eleonore, 287n64, 310–311, 352–353
Suchocki, Marjorie, 244; on sin as violence against creation, 349–351, 349n43
Summers, Thomas O., 173
supralapsarianism, 164
Swamidass, S. Joshua, 386n17, 395–397
Swinburne, Richard, 158–159
"Synergist Controversy," 223–224
Synoptic Gospels, description of sin in, 74–75; responses to the person and work of Jesus in, 78–81; sin in relation to the person of Jesus, 77–78; summary of, 81; teachings of Jesus concerning sin in, 75–77

Tanner, Kathryn, 217n40, 310, 362–363
Taylor, Charles, 218n44
Taylor, John, 25, 26, 163; denial of that Adam was a type of Christ, 25n20
Taylor, Richard S., 247, 249
Teilhard de Chardin, Pierre, 352
Ten Commandments, the, 251
Ten Elshof, Gregg A., 303n174
Tennant, F. R., on the doctrine of original sin, 154–156, 154n27
Tertullian, 365
TeSelle, Eugene, 280–281
te Velde, Roelf T., 256n233
Theodoret, 365
theologians: Carthaginian, 322; Catholic, 221, 358; Christian, 140, 153, 207, 356, 384; classical liberal theology, 259; feminist/womanist, 259, 262–264; Greek, 222; interpretations of God's love and wrath by, 331–333; liberation, 259–261, 269; Lutheran,

298, 359; medieval, 147, 297, 347; modern/contemporary, 29, 154, 331, 332, 333; Orthodox, 157; Patristic, 135n109; philosophical, 355; post-Reformation, 298; process, 243–244; Protestant, 131, 255, 298, 358; Reformation, 298–299; Reformed, 163, 164, 228, 240, 253–254, 255, 376–377; Reformed Scholastics, 228, 335; Remonstrant, 158n51; systematic, 158–159; Wesleyan, 247, 308
theology: "apocalyptic" approaches to biblical and systematic theology, 27n29; Augustinian, 290, 290n77; Calvinist, 376; Christian, 306, 353, 385; effects of modern science on, 154, 155, 385–387, 386n15; feminist/womanist, 259, 262–264, 262n261, 306n186; of the Greek fathers, 222, 222n60, 307; Johannine, 254; Lutheran, 376; Orthodox, 212; Patristic, 128, 135n109, 220; pre-Augustinian Latin Patristic, 156–157, 222; process, 243–244, 349–352, 351n55; Protestant theology on sin as contrary to nature, 223; Reformed, 253, 256, 256n233, 375; "retribution theology," 51–52; Roman Catholic theology concerning mortal and venial sins, 250–252; of Wesley, 24–25, 24n18; Wesleyan-Arminian theological tradition, 158, 164, 357, 359; "white theology," 261, 261n253. See also federalism, covenant theology as characteristic of; liberation theology
theosis, doctrines of, 378
Thielicke, Helmut, 333; "Lutheranism" of, 333n275
Thiselton, Anthony, 36–37, 39, 269n294
Thistlethwaite, Susan Brooks, 306n186
Tillich, Paul, 156, 228
Tilling, Chris, 85n106, 90n133
Timpe, Kevin, 274n334, 305n181
Tindal, Matthew, 348

Tixeront, Joseph, 291–293

Toland, Matthew, 348

Torah, the, 50, 82; Jesus's clarification of the Torah's teaching concerning sin, 76–77; punishments for sin decreed in, 75–76

Torrance, Thomas F., 113–114, 118–120, 329–330, 336; on the consequences of sin, 120–121; on the "epistemological significance of the *homoousion*," 208; on the wrath of God, 123–124

Tracy, David, 259

transworld depravity, 197–198

transworld identity, 197

Trelcatius, Lucas Jr., 131n93, 135n109, 377n176

Trinity, the, 355; doctrine of, 135n108; God's wrath as the contingent expression of the holy love of, 334–335

Trueman, Carl R., 371n120

Turretin, Francis, 147, 163, 228, 377n176

two-nature hamartiology: introduction to, 210–211; overview of the arguments concerning, 211–218

universalism, 196

Ursinus, Zacharias, 131, 239, 242, 243; on justification and sanctification, 377; on "reigning" versus "not reigning" sins, 253

van Asselt, Willem J., 256n233

Vanauken, Sheldon, 58n77

van den Berg, Jacob Albert, et al., 220n55

van Driel, Edwin Chr., 127n61

van Inwagen, Peter, 389–390

van Mastricht, Petrus, 257; on sanctification, 377

Vander Schel, Kevin M., 127n60

Vanhoozer, Kevin J., 233n119, 300, 330n263

Venema, Dennis R., 386n22, 387

Vincent of Lerins, 290, 291

"Vincentian Canon," 149

Visser, Sandra, 142n133

von Balthasar, Hans Urs, 260

von Limborch, Philipp, 158n51

Von Rad, Gerhard, 121–122; on Adam's relationship with the earth, 119–120; on shame, 118; on the usage of *yāda'* ("to know"), 122

von Staupitz, Johann, 297, 298

Wakefield, Samuel, 164, 362

Waltke, Bruce, 116; on the contrasts between Satan and God, 137–138, 139; on the goodness of God, 128

Ware, Timothy (Kallistos), 157

Watson, Richard, 164, 243, 308

Weaver, Rebecca Harden, 290n78, 291

Webster, John, 303n173

Weinandy, Thomas, 222n60, 335–336

Wellum, Stephen J., 27n30, 30n39

Wesley, John, 27, 185, 249, 299; belief that Roman Catholics are deists, 25–26; criticism of Orthodox cultures, 25–26; defense of hamartiology, 24; on the doctrine of original sin, 25–26, 163–164; on the misery of humanity due to the result of sin, 26; on the phenomenology of religion, 25; theology of and disagreements with Jonathan Edwards, 24–25, 24n18

Wesleyan/Wesleyan-Arminian tradition, 158, 173, 199, 239, 247, 308, 357, 359

Westermann, Claus, 42n28

Westminster Confession of Faith (1646), 24, 28, 163–164

Westminster Longer Catechism, 360n84

Westminster Shorter Catechism, 240

Westminster Standards, 28n33

White, Thomas Joseph, 44n38

White, R. E. O., 229n101

Whitefield, George, 24n18

William of Ockham, 358n74

Williams, J. Rodman, 242

Williams, N. P., 154n27

Williams, Thomas, 142n133

Willimon, William H., 22, 23

Witherington, Ben III, 176, 365, 366n100

Wollebius, Johannes, on the distinction between justification and sanctification, 376–377

Wolter, Allan B., 145

Woolston, Thomas, 348

Wright, Christopher J. H., 73, 104n166, 236–237, 325n255

Wright, N. T., 84, 85, 89n121, 90, 105, 176, 182; on the balance between Adam and Christ, 178; on the definition of sin, 178; on idolatry, 323

Xunzi, 22

Yarbrough, Robert W., 254

Zophar, 51

Zwingli, Huldrych, 151, 172, 228, 305n178, 345–347; determinism of, 157, 348; position of concerning the doctrine of original sin, 157–158, 157n47

the

FOUNDATIONS
OF EVANGELICAL
THEOLOGY

series

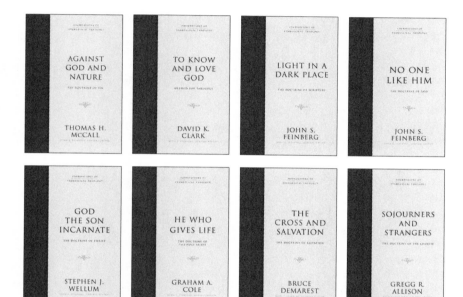

EDITED BY JOHN S. FEINBERG

The Foundations of Evangelical Theology series incorporates the
best exegetical research, historical theology, and philosophy to
produce an up-to-date systematic theology with contemporary
application—ideal for both students and teachers of theology.

For more information, visit **crossway.org**.